Social Psychology
Across Cultures

Social Psychology Across Cultures

Second edition

PETER B. SMITH

UNIVERSITY OF SUSSEX

MICHAEL HARRIS BOND

CHINESE UNIVERSITY OF HONG KONG

PEARSON

Prentice
Hall

London • New York • Toronto • Sydney • Tokyo • Singapore
Hong Kong • Cape Town • Madrid • Paris • Amsterdam • Munich • Milan

Pearson Education Limited
Edinburgh Gate
Harlow
Essex CM20 2JE
England

and Associated Companies throughout the world

Visit us on the World Wide Web at:
http://www.pearsoneduc.com

Typeset in 9.75/12pt Galliard by
Hands Fotoset, Ratby, Leicester

Printed and bound in Great Britain by Biddles Ltd,
www.biddles.co.uk

Library of Congress Cataloging-in-Publication Data

Available from the publisher

British Library Cataloguing in Publication Data

A catalogue record for this book is available from
the British Library

ISBN: 0-13-466343-8

---

9 8 7 6 5
07 06 05 04 03

Contents

Preface to the
second edition

**The intense conviction of the existence of the self apart
from culture is, as culture well knows, its robust and most
generous achievement.**

Lionel Trilling

This book is a child of its time. It is April 1997, and the writing of this guide to culture's influence on social behaviour has been facilitated by e-mail transmission, electronic searches of the psychological literature, and the internationalization of our network of colleagues. Increasing contact across cultural lines has driven the demand for the study of culture to be integrated into academic curricula. This contact stimulates an interest in one's own cultural roots, encouraging social scientists in less studied parts of the planet to contribute to the burgeoning database and development of theory in psychology.

The outpouring has been huge. It is only five years since the first edition of this text was written, but we found that this revision demanded a complete overhaul of most chapters. New sections have been written in each chapter and the number of references has increased by at least 50 per cent, with most of these additions being published after the 1993 date of the first edition. Two new chapters have been added on organizational behaviour and indigenous psychologies. As with many of the additions, these were written in response to feedback from colleagues who believed that the usefulness of the book would be enhanced by their inclusion.

We have taken suggestions from our colleagues seriously, especially those whose cultural, linguistic, educational and generational backgrounds differ from our own. We are committed to a belief in the synergy that can arise out of exploiting such diversity. We are all partial mirrors of our cultural heritages, but we believe that innocent ethnocentrism can be forged into vital internationalism through dialogue. We are very much aware that this process is far from complete: some regions of the world are much more adequately represented in what follows than are others. So, we encourage all you readers of this revision to share your reactions and suggestions with us. This input will become part of our disciplinary conversation, shaping our future, and perhaps even a third edition!

This second edition has benefited from the further tolerance of our wives, Anne and Sharon, from the support of our institutions, Sussex University and the Chinese University of Hong Kong, and from the critical comments on early drafts of various chapters by Tom Farsides, Yoshi Kashima, Yueh-Ting Lee, Kwok Leung, Mark Peterson, Felicia Pratto, Paul Redford, Jim Tedeschi and Colleen Ward. As our Persian friends often say, 'We stand in your shadow'.

We have attempted to write an engaging, insightful and comprehensive introduction to the scientific study of culture's influence on social behaviour. We have not sidestepped the difficult concepts and issues, either intellectual or political, in presenting this overview of the field. We believe that a careful reading of this book will reward you with a knowledge of the discipline and the ability to contribute towards its development. Your work, as ours, will be the judge.

Peter B. Smith
Department of Psychology
Sussex University
Falmer, Brighton
UK

Michael Harris Bond
Department of Psychology
The Chinese University of Hong Kong
Shatin, NT
Hong Kong

p.smith@sussex.ac.uk

mhb@cuhk.edu.hk

Acknowledgements

We are grateful to the following publishers and authors for permission to reproduce the tables and figures listed: Figure 3.2 by permission of Academic Press and Shalom Schwartz; Figure 3.3 by permission of Shalom Schwartz; Table 4.1 by permission of the authors; Figure 4.1 by permission of Ype Poortinga; Box 5.3 by permission of Bill Gudykunst; Table 5.1 by permission of David Trafimow; Figures 5.2, 8.1, 9.1 and 9.2 by permission of Larry Feign; Figure 5.1, CALVIN AND HOBBES copyright Watterson; reprinted with permission of UNIVERSAL PRESS SYNDICATE; all rights reserved; Figure 8.2, CALVIN AND HOBBES copyright Watterson; reprinted with permission of UNIVERSAL PRESS SYNDICATE; all rights reserved; Figure 6.1 by permission of Robert Helmreich; Box 7.1 by permission of Pergamon Press; Box 8.1 by permission of International Survey Research; the table in Box 8.4 by permission of Miriam Erez; Box 9.1 by permission of Stephen Bochner; Boxes 3.1, 10.6, 10.7 and 10.8 by permission of Sage Publications Inc.

Introduction

Psychology has had a long past, but only a recent history
Ebbinghaus, 1908

The task of this book is simply stated. We wish to advance the case for a social and organizational psychology whose findings are known to be valid in all parts of the world. Research into most aspects of psychology has through most of its history been a predominantly North American enterprise. Within the United States and Canada there exists a great diversity of cultural groups, so it is entirely possible that research undertaken there can reflect the cultural variability to be found in other parts of the world. However we can only be sure that this is so if we make thorough tests in which the different cultural groups involved in particular studies are clearly and separately identified.

Our own experiences as researchers and teachers have repeatedly taught us that a satisfying psychology can only be achieved through venturing into territory that is not clearly delineated and where we do not fully understand the behaviours taking place around us. We invite you to join us in picking our way across some of these less charted terrains, looking out in particular for what is unfamiliar or overlooked. By doing so, we hope to make some progress in addressing the types of questions listed in Table 1.1. We would argue that we can only hope to answer these questions adequately when a range of data is available that represents the full extent of variation in human behaviour. Indeed, many of them can only be answered adequately with the help of those working in academic disciplines outside the domain of psychology. As a more modest step toward answers, we shall explore what can be achieved by sampling similarities and differences in social and organizational behaviours more widely than has typically been the case.

An example of how this is a strategy that pays off is given by recent work on gender differences. In many early studies, researchers either did not note the gender balance among their subjects, or else used all male samples. Their data were then assumed to provide tests of their hypotheses with general validity. Only when researchers started to make systematic comparisons of men's and women's responses to situations did a picture start to emerge as to how gender roles are

Table 1.1 ● Some questions worth pondering

- What is universal about human nature?
- Is there one best way to run an organization?
- What has happened in countries where large-scale immigration into a nation has occurred?
- How can one understand a person who has been socialized into another culture?
- How can a native speaker of English communicate effectively to a non-native speaker of English?
- Are gender differences the same across cultural groups?
- Will increasing contact between cultures improve intercultural relations?
- Will human societies eventually merge into one global mega-society?

socialized and what are the cultural factors acting in society to sustain and to change them. However, before we can start to address specific issues such as gender, we need first to lay out some brief illustrations of the history and geographical dispersion of social and organizational psychology. In Chapter 3 we shall then focus directly upon what we mean by the concept of culture. By the time we reach Chapter 12 we shall be better able to return to the issue of how the conclusions we shall draw about culture relate to the differences found *within* a culture between subgroups such as those based upon gender and ethnic identity.

There are a number of reasons why attending to culture is a particularly timely task. Firstly, increasing travel and communication links among countries and continents are making more obvious the limitations of studies of social behaviour which are found only to hold true in one or another country. Secondly, the populations of many nations, and of communities within nations, are asserting their distinctiveness more energetically and we need to be able to understand what processes come into play when they meet and interact with one another. Finally, we must consider the possibility that the way in which people relate to each other in different cultural groups differs sufficiently that the same study will yield different results, depending on where that study is done. If this is so, psychology can only claim validity to the extent that its theories have been tested at multiple locations.

The worldview of social and organizational psychology

We shall start with a brief survey of the current situation. Research into social and organizational psychology is undertaken in all the continents of the world and the results published in numerous technical journals. The results of these studies are then transmitted to a wider non-professional audience through the medium of student textbooks. Let us consider recent North American introductory textbooks. Baron and Byrne (1994) is the best-selling US social psychology text. Its most recent edition contains around 1,700 citations, of which just over 100 refer to studies done outside North America. Greenberg and Baron's (1995) text on organizations has 1,327 citations and of these only 78 report studies done outside North America. The social psychology text by Myers (1996) gives more attention to cross-cultural issues than most other North American texts. Myers has about 2,700 citations, of which, however, only 228 are to studies done outside North America.

Recent English language social psychology texts whose authors are not themselves North American also exist. Hewstone, Stroebe and Stephenson (1996) are the editors of the best known European text, whereas Hogg and Vaughan (1995) are from Australia and New Zealand. Both of these texts contain more than 500 citations from outside North America, out of a total of nearly 2,000. However, the great majority of the 500-plus citations in both of these texts refer to studies conducted in Western Europe, Australia and New Zealand. In none of the texts mentioned above do citations to studies done in other parts of the world amount to more than 2 or 3 per cent of the total. Thus among these English-language texts, the universe of social and organizational behaviours that is being sampled is almost entirely restricted to studies done within less than a dozen of the more than 200 nations in the world, constituting little more than 10 per cent of the world's population. This unrepresentative sampling of the world's cultural groups need not be a problem if culture were not known to influence social behaviour. However, as we shall see in Chapter 2, there is strong evidence that it does.

By surveying textbooks written in other countries and other languages we can determine whether this sampling of the type of studies put before students also takes place in other parts of the world. Looking further afield, Pandey's (1981a) Indian survey of social psychology, Furuhata's (1980) Japanese text, and the social psychology volume of the Spanish language *Handbook of General Psychology* (Rodriguez and Seoane, 1989) all also show a strong preponderance of citations derived from North American studies. A volume of papers by Soviet social psychologists edited by Strickland (1984) shows a lesser preponderance, but these were papers written while the Cold War was still in progress, and we cannot be sure whether Russian psychology will continue to maintain its separate identity, following the collapse of the Soviet bloc. So, for the most part, even students in those countries that lie outside the mainstream of social and organizational psychological research read about studies done in North America.

Textbook authors will of course tend to select material for inclusion that is likely to interest their readership, by referring to issues and situations with which they are familiar. Furthermore, frequent citation of US studies is no doubt also partly attributable to the fact that there are a great many researchers into different aspects of social and organizational psychology practising in North America. Just how many there are in relation to other parts of the world is very hard to estimate. Rosenzweig (1992) reports that of the 56,000 researchers in the entire field of psychology world wide, 64 per cent are Americans, and the per centage is probably at least that high among social and organizational psychologists. Thus even those 25–30 per cent of the world's social and organizational psychologists outside

North America are exposed to a preponderance of North American studies and themselves emphasize these same studies in their own writings.

This brief examination of a variety of texts makes it clear that the selection of studies cited in each textbook is strongly influenced by the authors' nationality. Substantial numbers of well-conducted studies published in Europe, Australia, India, Japan and elsewhere are discussed only in texts that are published in those countries. Another point of view only emerges when one returns to the texts and scans those studies that are referenced from outside of the authors' own region. In some cases the reader is not told that the study being reported was in fact done in another country. Of the non-American studies reviewed in Baron and Byrne's text for example, the locations of the studies are not mentioned in 46 of the 100 cases. The 54 studies explicitly identified as non-American are of particular interest to the theme of this book. In 44 of them, Baron and Byrne directly address the question of whether the findings obtained are similar to or different from those which had been obtained in the United States. In 25 cases they report that the results did show various kinds of difference, whereas in the remaining 19 the results were found to be similar to US results. This sampling thus suggests that more than half the cited studies do yield different findings when done outside North America. We cannot yet place much emphasis upon this potentially worrisome conclusion, as results showing differences may have been selected for inclusion precisely because they are exceptional and thought to be more interesting. Furthermore, many of these studies were conducted within a single nation. We shall propose in the next chapter that if we wish to determine whether the same social process is in operation at different locations, a great deal of care will be needed to ensure that similar

---

Box 1.1   Where is psychology done?

Below, you will find three questions that we too found difficult to answer until we became involved in cross-cultural research. We pose them to you, the reader, to suggest to you that the practice of psychology is far more widely dispersed around the world than many are aware. There may be many reasons for this ignorance. Language barriers are the most immediate and obvious; others will be explored throughout the following chapters.

1. Can you identify a country with a population of around 160 million, within which there are 85,000 registered psychologists?

2. Can you identify a country, which has a population of around 125 million, in which there are two associations for social psychologists, with a combined membership of over 4,000?

3. Can you identify a country with a population of around 92 million, within which there are 90,000 psychologists? Hint: the leading university in this country has more than 600 teachers of psychology.

The answers to these questions are given at the bottom of Box 1.2 on page 6.

measures and samples are studied at each of the different locations. Studies that are explicitly designed for comparative purposes hold most promise of yielding valid conclusions.

Let us return for the moment to the predominance of North American studies in the texts that we have examined. Lonner (1989) has surveyed thirty-three US textbooks in general psychology and found a similar predominance of North American citations. The question we must now address is how problematic is this focus upon North American studies? If we were discussing textbooks on physics from different parts of the world, it is possible that we would find a similar distribution of researchers' locations. After all, as with physics, many of the best known and most able researchers in social and organizational psychology are located in North America, and it need be no surprise that textbooks give their work deservedly substantial coverage. However, what data there are suggest that North American natural scientists cite much larger numbers of researchers from other parts of the world. In 1980, 44 per cent of all citations by US natural scientists referred to foreign publications (Gielen, 1994).

It is not, however, likely that studies in physics would give different results simply because they are conducted at different locations. When we are concerned with social behaviour, there is a much stronger possibility that different results will be obtained, either because of problems inherent in translating research materials, or more simply because people in different parts of the world behave in different ways. Of course, among a nation as large and varied as the United States, we might also expect to find variations in research results depending upon which regions or which ethnic communities were sampled. Whether such variations are as large as, or much smaller than, the variations to be found when studies are compared on a world-wide basis is crucially important.

Researchers in the United States have been as alert as those in other countries to the problem of replicability, and some of them have been in the vanguard of social scientists who examine whether or not studies done in one country are replicable elsewhere. Our purpose here is thus not to make some kind of ethnocentric criticism of North American social and organizational psychologists, but rather to explore the work of those researchers from all countries who have sought to broaden the database upon which our subject rests.

We cannot hope in a work of this length to give a full account of contemporary social and organizational psychology. This book is therefore written on the basis that we assume that you, the reader, have already read or do now have access to introductory textbooks in these areas available in your country. In the next chapter we shall start to look in more detail at some of the evidence stemming from studies that have been repeated in more than one country. In later chapters we shall continue so far as possible to focus upon studies that have been conducted in two or more countries.

Before we start on our main task, let us look at what happens when two people from different parts of the world interact with one another. By looking at failures in their attempts to communicate, we can gain some further ideas as to the issues

> ### Box 1.2) What is a considerate supervisor?
>
> Leadership behaviours in electronics assembly plants in four countries were surveyed by Smith et al. (1989). The plants were in the United States, Hong Kong, Japan and the United Kingdom. In all the plants studied, supervisors who were seen as considerate towards members of the work team were positively evaluated by those whom they supervised. The focus of the study, however, was on what the supervisor actually has to do in order that he or she is perceived as considerate. Workers in the plant were asked to indicate how often their supervisors performed a variety of different behaviours. It was found that 'considerate' supervisors have to do rather different things in order to earn that label in each of the different countries. For example, one question asked about what the supervisor might do if a member of the work team is experiencing personal difficulties. Workers in Japan and Hong Kong responded that to discuss the matter with other members of the work team in the person's absence would be a considerate behaviour. In contrast, workers in the United States and the United Kingdom evaluated such public discussion as an inconsiderate thing to do. Thus the study illustrates how a specific action may have quite different meanings attributed to it depending upon the cultural context within which it is performed. In Japan and Hong Kong greater consideration is perceived to arise from third-party communication as a form of tactfulness, whereas in the United Kingdom and the United States consideration is accorded to face-to-face communication. We explore more fully why this difference exists in Chapter 6.
>
> (Answers to the questions in Box 1.1: the countries referred to are Brazil, Japan and Mexico.)

that might lead research studies done in different parts of the world to have different outcomes.

An instructive cross-cultural episode

Chan Chi Lok, a Chinese freshman at a Hong Kong university, has taken a course in Business English from Mrs Jean Robertson, a divorced British teacher recently arrived from Scotland. Mr Chan has failed his final exam and Mrs Robertson has made an appointment to meet him at 12 o'clock to discuss his poor performance. She has a 12.30 p.m. lunch date with the department chairman, George Davis.

Chan arrives with a friend at 12.20, knocks on Mrs Robertson's door, and they both enter without waiting for a response. Mrs Robertson looks up in surprise. Chan and his friend approach her chair and stand right beside her.

Chan smiles and asks, 'Have you had your lunch yet, teacher?'
Mrs Robertson replies sternly, 'Chan, sit yourself down over there,' pointing

to a chair positioned about two metres from her desk. 'I doubt you are 20 minutes late', she complains, 'and we had best speak alone.' She points at Chan's friend. 'You can wait in the hall.'

'Huh?' Chan asks, his mouth remaining open.

Mrs Robertson repeats herself slowly and Chan's friend leaves.

'We all feel you very good . . . teacher.' Mrs Robertson's mouth drops. 'Now we like to invite you to class party tomorrow. You contribute your precious time, yes?'

Mrs Robertson stares at Chan in astonishment. 'That's not possible; I book well ahead,' she retorts with furrowed eyebrows.

'Don't you like books, teacher?', asks Chan, smiling and gazing attentively.

'Chan, you must realize that we have serious matters to discuss. You have yet to explain your lateness.' Chan looks at his teacher blankly and waits. 'Chan, why were you late?'

Chan laughs and then pauses. 'Well, ah, the train was delayed', he lies, looking down, 'and the school bus was crowded, so I walk all the way to your office', he explains, telling the truth.

'Did anyone ever tell you that you are a wee bit slippery, Mr Chan?'

'Huh?'

'Mr Chan, it's impolite to say "Huh?" You should say, "I beg your pardon".'

'Sorry, teacher', mutters Chan, eyes downcast.

'Never bother', she continues, 'Your final exam mark was none too good. What way have you done so poorly?' Chan sneezes twice.

'Do you have a cold?' asks Mrs Robertson.

'No, teacher – you stink', Chan explains, referring to her perfume.

Mrs Robertson's eyes widen.

Chan responds to her apparent distress by switching back to her earlier question and explains, 'It's very difficult. But I tried very hard and re-read the b-b-b-book f-f-four times before the exam.' Chan stammers. 'All we found your test very difficult and . . .', Chan continues, referring to his classmates, 'and . . .'

'It's no good hiding behind the others; you must stand on your own two feet', Mrs Robertson interrupts Chan to challenge. 'And effort is not enough for a pass.'

'But my English has improved so much from you. Your teachings are so good. I have to pass out from this course for being promoted.'

'I'm not caring about any of that, Mr Chan. What is at issue is your ability at English. And it wasn't helped by your frequent absence from class.'

'My mother was in the hospital during this term times. I had to . . .' (Chan pauses lengthily while he searches for the word) '. . . visited her every day.'

'Your first responsibility is to your studies, Mr Chan. You could well have visited your mother fine in the evenings.'

'But who watches after my sister?' Chan retorts.

'You don't get it, do you?' Mrs Robertson sighs.

'Yes', answers Chan, puzzling his teacher further.

'Mr Chan, I'm away now, as I have a previous appointment.'

'Couldn't you just give me a compassionate pass, teacher? I really need to pass out of your course.'

'What?! A *compassionate* pass? I've never heard of the like! Anyway, I've got to run. Phone me for an appointment if you want to have a wee word about retaking the exam.'

Mrs Robertson then goes to the door and holds it open, as Mr Chan walks out to find his friend, his eyes downcast.

'Don't be late next time, Chan. If you can't get here on time, you'll never get anywhere.'

Aftermath

This encounter between Mr Chan and Mrs Robertson was the culmination of a term's interaction as student and teacher in a small class. It had been Chan's first opportunity to interact with a foreigner and Robertson's first term of teaching Chinese students. Unfortunately, little light was shed by the sparks that they generated from their encounters with one another, and their time together merely served to strengthen the negative stereotype Chan has about Western women and Robertson has about Chinese persons.

When Mrs Robertson meets her departmental chairman for lunch, she responds to his 'How are your classes going?' by complaining that she is very angry with impolite, irresponsible and illogical students. For his part, Chan later responds to his sister's concern about his depressed mood by stating that his teacher is 'a little bit unsympathetic'. Furthermore, she is 'slightly aggressive' when problems arise and legalistic about grades. His sister is not surprised to hear this criticism about a divorced woman who lunches alone with a male colleague! She is, however, surprised at the strength of her brother's criticism, because he has frequently told her that he does not understand half of what his teacher says anyway.

A typical result?

We do not intend our case study to disparage either Mrs Robertson or Mr Chan. Nor do we underestimate the real difficulties of teaching and learning English. The manner in which each of us approaches others is strongly influenced by our specific gender, age and cultural background. This may not be a problem so long as we spend time with others similar to ourselves. But unfortunately, unhappy outcomes such as occurred in this case are the norm rather than the exception in many cross-cultural encounters. Interactions across cultural lines will continue because both parties to the encounter provide the other with important services – Mrs Robertson with a well-paid job in an exotic setting, Mr Chan with access to a native speaker of English, the language 'of wider communication'. Nonetheless, they do not enjoy the process, and are often puzzled, frustrated and angry with one

Box 1.3 What's in a name?

A central component of the message of this book is that no behaviour and no spoken word has an irreducible objective meaning. Members of different groups or nations place meanings on what goes on around them, and the nuances of these meanings often serve to define identity and to separate one grouping from another. An instance of this variability is provided by the question of what to call the subject area with which this book is concerned. Among English-language researchers, there is a division between those who favour 'cross-cultural psychology' and those who favour 'cultural psychology'. French-language researchers mostly favour 'psychologie interculturelle' (Krewer and Jahoda, 1993).

Cross-cultural psychologists typically use questionnaires or structured observation schedules to test theories about differences between samples drawn from relevant ethnic groups or nations. Their orientation is closest to the empiricist content of mainstream psychology, though they would reject the criticism that they neglect theory. They typically belong to the *International Association for Cross-Cultural Psychology*, and publish in its journal, the *Journal of Cross-Cultural Psychology*.

Cultural psychologists are more concerned with the universal processes whereby cultures are transmitted or transformed by culture members (Shweder and Sullivan, 1993). They often study what occurs within a single cultural group and sometimes characterize their approach as 'indigenous psychology'. The research methods favoured by cultural psychologists are more varied, but they include discourse analysis and other more qualitative types of approach. They reject procedures that are 'merely empirical', instead requiring 'explicit . . . theory of the systemic functioning of culture' (Valsiner, 1995). They have recently established a journal, *Culture and Psychology*.

Intercultural psychologists focus primarily upon the social processes occurring when members of different cultural groups interact with one another. They reject static comparisons between groups, which they see as often having implicitly racist overtones. They are organized as *L'Association pour la Recherche Interculturelle*. They mostly publish in French, frequently in books rather than journals (e.g. Retschitzsky, Bossel-Lagos and Dasen, 1989).

Contributions from each of these perspectives are to be found in this book.

another. The delights and possible synergy to be derived from bridging the cultural divide escape them.

As we will discover, a little cultural knowledge would go a long way towards improving the outcome of such cross-cultural encounters. We would like this book to serve that end. For the twenty-first century will bring more, not fewer, such exchanges across cultural lines, as our planet continues to shrink into a 'global village'. Our increasing interdependencies will require us to 'hang together, or else we shall surely hang separately', to quote Patrick Henry. While there are numerous historical, political and economic factors that impede this process, modest progress toward 'hanging together' could be achieved with more enthusiasm and appreciation if parties to the exchanges anticipated and understood the likely problems.

We will refer to this exchange between Mr Chan and Mrs Robertson throughout this book, to give concrete illustration to the issues that we shall be discussing. We shall pay attention in particular to the way in which their cultural backgrounds led each of them to adopt different values, different styles of communication, different ways of showing emotion, and different ways of negotiating. If you, the reader, wish to satisfy your curiosity quickly as to how we perceive what went on between the two of them, you will find our fullest analysis at the end of Chapter 9. However, our original cultural backgrounds, English male and Canadian male respectively, have most probably led us to miss other problematic aspects of their exchange that are apparent to you. If so, we should be happy for you to let us know. We too are working to broaden our cultural sensitivities!

Summary

Textbooks in social and organizational psychology implicitly assume that the subject matter of psychology is concerned with universals which may be understood by sampling behaviour at any geographical location. This is a convenient myth. The interchange between Chan and Mrs Robertson gives us a first sighting of the many processes that differ both in extent and in kind around the world.

Some first steps in extending the database

If a man does not keep pace with his companions, perhaps it is because he hears a different drummer. Let him step to the music he hears, however measured or far away.

Henry Thoreau, *Walden*, 1854

Before we look in detail at the concepts that cross-cultural psychologists find most useful in guiding their studies, we need to place social psychology as a whole into some kind of social and historical context. This will be the task of the present chapter. First we shall look at the way the subject has developed over the past century. Having documented the manner in which social psychology became most firmly rooted in North America by the middle of the century, we next take eight of the best known US studies and review what has happened when they were repeated in other countries. Finally, we shall need to think through more carefully the issues that emerge from this survey, especially how best to interpret variations in findings from different cultural groups around the world.

The where and when of social psychology

The issues of importance to social psychologists have been debated throughout recorded history. To a surprising degree, we find that the points of greatest disagreement at the present time were already sketched out by the ancient Greeks. For instance, is it more fruitful to study social behaviour by focusing on individuals and their motivations and cognitions? Or, do we learn more by examining social structures and the way in which they mould our behaviours and thoughts? Aristotle would most probably have a preference for the first strategy, while Plato's thought fits the second option more closely.

Beginnings

The origins of contemporary social psychology are usually traced to Germany, although the establishment of Wundt's chair at Leipzig in 1879 was in fact preceded by the foundation of Lazarus' chair in Berne, Switzerland in 1860 (Jahoda, 1993). Wilhelm Wundt is best known for his work in psychophysics, but between 1900 and 1920 he also published 10 volumes on what he termed *Völkerpsychologie*. This term does not translate readily from the German, but his approach included material which would these days be classified as social anthropology or sociology as well as social psychology. He stressed the role of society in defining our cultural and social context and the experience of individuals within it (Jahoda and Krewer, 1997). In terms that later became widespread, he was writing as a sociological social psychologist. Other writers in Germany at around the same time laid more stress on the individual, but their work was and still is much less well known.

By the early twentieth century, both the sociological and the more individual-centred or psychological approaches were well-established in North America and in Europe. Of the first two English language textbooks published, one fell into each camp. McDougall (1908) stressed the individual's instincts, while Ross (1908) stressed uniformities in behaviour resulting from the social influences of others. During the next few years, the development of behaviourism encouraged the view that if social psychology were to become a science, it must develop precise ways of measuring behaviour and experimental methods for testing its determinants. This trend was particularly strong in the United States, as exemplified by Floyd Allport's (1924) experimentally oriented text and the great attention given subsequently to the development of valid measures of attitudes and leadership qualities, both of which were conceptualized as the individual's predispositions to behave in particular ways. However, the stress on experimentation did not occur solely in the United States, and in fact the first text on experimental social psychology was that of Moede (1920) from Germany. In other European countries such as France and the United Kingdom, sociology and social anthropology developed more strongly than social psychology at that time.

Probably the most important figure in the development of contemporary social psychology was Kurt Lewin, who worked initially in Germany. He was influential in the group that developed what was known as Gestalt psychology, which emphasized the way in which our perceptions of a stimulus are influenced by its context. Lewin's interest in the study of perception moved during the 1930s to the area of social behaviour. His emphasis upon the inter-relatedness of different elements in what he called the individual's life-space meant that he was sympathetic to those who thought we should study social systems as well as individual processes. He saw less value in abstracting one or another fragment of social behaviour and studying it in isolation. Additionally, he encouraged the use of the experimental method. He thus provided a potential bridge across the widening gap between sociological social psychologists and psychological social psychologists. He also promoted cultural integration. For instance, during the early 1930s he developed links with social psychologists not only in Europe and the United States, but also in Japan (Marrow, 1969). A Gestalt Psychology Institute was established at the University of Kyushu and a number of empirical studies reflecting Lewin's approach to leadership were completed (e.g. Toki, 1935).

The move to America

With Hitler's rise to power in 1933, Lewin and many other prominent Jewish social scientists fled from Germany, most of them going to the United States. Working first at Iowa, then at MIT, Lewin undertook classic studies in the fields of leadership and group decision, studies that we will discuss shortly. More important in the long run, he trained a succession of researchers, many of whom became key figures in the post-war flowering of American social psychology. Festinger, Kelley, Cartwright, Deutsch, Schachter, French and Thibaut were among his students. Each of these researchers developed distinctive programmes of experimental work, but it is notable that after Lewin's death in 1947, the emphasis on social systems as a whole was increasingly reduced. Gaining adequate control of the experimental environment was made the first priority, and if that meant the use of increasingly simplified settings, the gain in precision was thought worth the sacrifice in realism.

The subsequent explosive growth of North American social psychology is well known. It should be noted, however, that while psychological social psychology has become dominant, there continues a rather separate tradition of sociologically-oriented social psychology within the United States, a tradition that works more within the non-experimental methods established by, for example, Mead, Goffman and Bales (for example, Secord and Backman, 1974; Hewitt, 1994).

Spreading the word

After World War 2, social psychology outside North America had sunk to a low point. It was estimated that in the late 1950s, there were more social psychologists at the University of Michigan than in the whole of Western Europe! A substantial number of these became increasingly interested in organizational behaviour, rather than in the small groups upon which Lewin had focused most of his attention. Naturally, when social psychology was gradually re-established in universities and research institutes around the world, it was done so within the controlled, experimental spirit now firmly rooted in North America. Psychology laboratories were established and experiments conducted, as though there were no differences of importance arising from where in the world a laboratory was located.

The impact of social psychological theories originating in North America around the world continues to be strong to the present day, as we can deduce from the survey of textbooks in Chapter 1. The most notable exception to this trend has been in the former Soviet Union. There, the implicit individualism of US theories was for a long time considered unacceptable, and distinctive theories were developed instead around the concept of the collective (Strickland, 1984). Such theories should not be seen simply as something imposed by the former Soviet political system. They belong within the tradition of a more sociological approach to psychology, as exemplified by the early Russian work of Vygotsky with children, and are compatible with the collectivist values most probably endorsed at that time by Soviet scientists and people. As we shall discover in the next chapter, they are also compatible with concepts developed recently by cross-cultural psychologists.

A range of different concerns arose as social psychologists attempted to use methods developed by North Americans in their own countries. Within developing countries, an increasingly frequent complaint has been that the available theories do not address the issues that are most urgent. Psychologists in these countries have found themselves pressed to contribute directly to national development and to create theories and methods that are necessary to nation-building issues (Blackler, 1983; Sloan and Montero, 1990). Misra (1981) describes how, as a US-trained social psychologist, he began work in India on attribution theory, but ten years later was engaged in studies of effective salesmanship. Sinha (1986) likewise abandoned his commitment to experimental method and became a leading exponent of the 'indigenous psychology' movement, which proposes that distinctive theories will be required for each cultural context that is studied. Marin (1983) reports a similar trend in Latin America, with social psychologists active in community development programmes. A recent issue of the journal *Applied Psychology* (Wilpert, 1991) surveys the uses of social psychology in community development projects in Brazil, Chile, Colombia, Mexico, Puerto Rico and Venezuela. The common thread in all these third-world projects has been a move from what Moghaddam (1990) calls a 'modulative' orientation toward a 'generative' orientation. In other words, social psychologists in these countries have become less concerned with describing and analyzing the status quo, and more concerned with generating positive social changes.

A different problem, more frequently voiced by psychologists in Western Europe and other industrialized countries, is that when they attempt to replicate North American studies, they quite often obtain different results. Sometimes also they find it difficult to set up experiments in a way that their subjects consider plausible. Although North American researchers sometimes also report difficulty in replicating findings, the problem appears greater in other locations. These difficulties provide the principal starting point for the rest of this book, and we shall look at examples shortly.

The worries of the West Europeans have not, however, been solely empirical. They are concerned also that the strongly individualist manner in which many US theorists conceptualized social behaviour ignores the context within which that behaviour took place. Their view that it is the context that gives behaviour its meaning is of course connected to the preoccupations of earlier European theorists from Wundt onwards. The flavour of their critique is suggested by the pointed title of Tajfel's (1972) watershed paper, 'Experiments in a vacuum'. In the field of organizational behaviour, a similar divergence became apparent, with Americans laying emphasis upon the development of leadership skills and Europeans focusing more upon the interplay of technology and people in determining how organizations functioned.

This quick overview of the history of social and organizational psychology gives us a generalized view of the state of the subject in different regions of the world, passing over many important variations. We do this in the manner of an artist, who lays down a broad-brush outline for more detailed work later. It is now time to consider what happened when some well-known studies were transported to foreign shores. If these studies are unfamiliar to you, you may well find it useful to read fuller descriptions of them in any introductory text to social or organizational psychology.

How well do the classic studies replicate?

Conformity and independence

The most widely replicated social psychology experiment of all time is Asch's (1951) study of conformity. This is the study in which a naive subject is repeatedly asked to judge which of three lines matches another line, in the presence of several other people who frequently all give the same *wrong* answer. R. A. Bond and Smith (1996) compared the results obtained in ninety-seven different replications reported from within the United States and a further thirty-six published replications, derived from sixteen other countries. As is usual in the procedure known as meta-analysis, they computed 'effect sizes' for each study (see Box 2.1). Table 2.1 shows the averaged effect sizes obtained in the studies done in different parts of the world.

Box 2.1 Meta-analysis

Meta-analysis is a statistical technique increasingly used by psychologists to prepare a summary of the overall conclusions to be drawn from a wide range of studies addressing a similar research question. Some of the difficulties previously encountered in arriving at a valid summary are that researchers have frequently used different measurement techniques and different samples of respondents and collected their data under different circumstances. Meta-analysis rests on the assumption that one can compute 'effect sizes' which are independent of the nature of the actual measure used by a particular researcher. The effect size within a single study is computed as the difference between the scores obtained by the experimental subjects and the control subjects, divided by the standard deviation of the control subject scores. Effect sizes are then averaged across different studies, to determine whether or not whatever experimental effect is being investigated is consistently found. If the sample of studies is large enough, the influence of variations in experimental design, geographical location, date of study, etc. on effect size can then be estimated. A number of published meta-analyses are discussed in this book, with emphasis upon differences in effect size by nation.

Table 2.1 ● Asch conformity studies by national culture

Nation	Number of studies	Averaged effect size
Asch's own US studies	18	1.16
Other US studies	79	0.90
Canada	1	1.37
UK	10	0.81
Belgium	4	0.94
France	2	0.56
Netherlands	1	0.74
Germany	1	0.92
Portugal	1	0.58
Japan	5	1.42
Brazil	3	1.60
Fiji	2	2.48
Hong Kong	1	1.93
Arab samples (Kuwait, Lebanon)	2	1.31
Africa (Zimbabwe, Republic of the Congo (Zaïre), Ghana)	3	1.84

The table shows clearly that effect sizes were smaller in the studies done in North America and Western Europe than they were in the rest of the world. The sheer number of studies included in this comparison makes it tempting to draw conclusions that may be misleading. When one speaks of replications, it is easy to imagine studies having been repeated in exactly the same manner at each location. In practice, many details of the original study are not exactly reproduced, and any one of these can influence the size of effect achieved in a particular study. Bond and Smith estimated the degree to which several of these extraneous factors influenced effect sizes, by examining variations across the US studies. They found for instance that effect sizes had decreased over the years since Asch's study was first done. Effect sizes were also influenced by the size of the majority giving erroneous judgements, the gender of the subjects and several other variables. These types of factor may explain why the effect size obtained in the single Canadian study (see Table 2.1) were so much higher than in most of the US studies. However, even after Bond and Smith had taken account of these sources of variation between the different studies, the difference in effect sizes from different parts of the world was still present.

After looking at Table 2.1, we might conclude provisionally that conformity effects are stronger outside Western Europe and North America. Before we do so, we need to reflect upon the difficulty of interpreting social behaviours in different societal contexts. The concept of conformity has a negative overtone in Western societies. Independence of judgement is valued highly, and conformity is thought of as weak or supine. This connotation was confirmed in a US study by Kane and Tedeschi (1973), who found that within the format of the Asch experiment, subjects who acted independently were rated more positively by judges than those who conformed. Consider how the Asch experiment might be interpreted in one of the nations where higher effect sizes were found. The naive subject finds him or herself in a situation where fellow subjects in the experiment are evidently making a lot of incorrect judgements. Anticipating that the experimenter will later reveal who has made errors, they may choose also to give incorrect judgements in order to save later embarrassment of their peers. In one culture, the giving of correct answers may be most highly valued, while in another it may be more important to avoid embarrassment. Thus, a behaviour that we choose to think of as conformity may have a different meaning when it is located within a different context. Looked at in this way, the naive subject's behaviour might be considered not so much as conformity but more as tact or sensitivity. Further studies would be needed to test whether this is so. We should settle then for a less judgemental conclusion: social influence within the Asch experimental paradigm is stronger in non-Western societies. We defer until later chapters what may be the best explanation for this cross-national variation in effect sizes.

The negative value put upon conformity in Western societies is illustrated in another way. The Asch experiment is almost invariably described as a study of conformity, even though the original study showed that two-thirds of the judgements made by subjects were independent of the pressure upon them to give the wrong judgement. Friend, Rafferty and Bramel (1990) examined reports of the Asch studies in ninety-nine US social psychology texts. They found an increasing trend over time to concentrate upon the fact that one-third of the judgements were erroneous, and to use this as evidence of how widespread is the process of conformity in society. Friend *et al.* point out that this interpretation is precisely the opposite of what Asch was trying to show, and indeed succeeded in showing, namely that his subjects were not entirely conformist and that most judgements were entirely correct.

This type of reinterpretation of results is not an isolated instance. The findings of other classic studies, such as Milgram's work on obedience, to be discussed shortly, are often also reported as though all subjects succumbed to social pressures. One possibility is that writers of texts – including us, the writers of this one – are seeking to persuade you, the reader, that social behaviour is understandable and predictable. To assert that people sometimes, even often, act independently of those around them might seem to weaken the case for a social psychology, and encourage instead the study of personality. However, this is to set up a false dichotomy between personality and social processes. Social influence is best understood as an interaction between personality, social context and environmental factors.

But we are straying a little from our main theme. The value of Friend, Rafferty and Bramel's critique for our purposes is that it alerts us to the fact that we cannot judge whether 37 per cent of conforming responses and 63 per cent of independent ones are *high* or *low* figures until we can compare them with figures from other cultures. In a society whose members value independence and initiative as highly as do many Americans, we might expect that any evidence of conformity would be interpreted negatively. In a cross-cultural context, we now have evidence to confirm that the effect sizes obtained by Asch in his original studies are relatively low, as Asch himself believed, and not high, as many of the textbook writers assert.

What happens to social deviates?

Another classic study concerning conformity was the one reported by Schachter (1951). Schachter set up group discussions, in which accomplices were briefed to take up particular positions. In different conditions of the experiment he was either to assume and keep to a deviant position ('Deviate'), or to assume a deviant position but gradually be won over by the group ('Slider'); or to agree with the average of group opinions from the start ('Mode'). In the United States, Schachter found that the deviates quickly attracted a lot of attention, which tailed off as their opinions were found inflexible and they were rejected. Sliders received continuing attention as they moved toward a more conforming position.

Schachter modified and extended his 1951 study to examine social deviance in seven different European countries (Schachter *et al.*, 1954). In this case, the subjects were 11-year-old boys invited to join a model aeroplane club. Asked to select which of several model aeroplanes to build, the experimenter's accomplice consistently assumed the deviant position, by choosing a rather boring glider in preference to a choice from several other more attractive possibilities. The results proved much more complex than the experimenters had expected, making it difficult for them to test the complex set of Lewinian hypotheses that they had formulated. The basic problems were three. Firstly, not all groups reached agreement in the time allotted. Secondly, some groups reached agreement by agreeing with the supposedly deviant accomplice and did not reject him, as had occurred in the rather different US study. Thirdly, where there was a deviate, he was more strongly rejected in some countries than in others. Each of these effects occurred to a different extent in the various countries, as can be seen in Table 2.2. The table also includes the ranking assigned to the deviate in Schachter's preceding US study. Although the procedures in that study were different and the ranks are therefore not directly comparable, it appears that the US deviate was rejected as strongly as the French one.

In the United Kingdom, Germany and Belgium, the groups were less likely to oppose the deviate, were less critical of him even when they did oppose him, and were more likely to be persuaded by him. De Monchaux and Shimmin (1955), who conducted the British part of the experiment, suggested that by expressing their preference consistently, the supposed deviates may in fact have become leaders in some groups. It could be that, in ways unintended by the experimenters, the deviates in some countries behaved in ways that were perceived as more

	Percentage of groups agreeing against the deviate	Percentage of groups agreeing with the deviate	Percentage of groups not agreeing at all	Rank for attractiveness of deviate
Table 2.2 ● Deviance and rejection in seven European countries				
France	95	0	5	6.00
Norway	80	3	17	5.09
Holland	75	12	13	3.47
Sweden	66	9	25	4.50
Belgium	63	3	34	3.88
West Germany	50	18	32	2.01
UK	37	20	43	3.04
USA (Schachter, 1951)	–	–	–	6.11

The ranks at the right of the table indicate how much priority was given to having the deviate stay in the group: 1= top priority.

attractive than in other countries. We cannot test such speculations, but we shall see in Chapter 6 that research into influence by assertive minorities has become a favoured topic among quite a few European social psychologists, and this study appears to have stumbled upon an early experimental instance of its occurrence.

Even if this analysis is correct, we still do not have a satisfactory explanation of why there was more minority influence in some countries than in others. The countries in which there was some minority influence also appear to have been the ones where there was more argument, since a larger proportion of their groups failed to agree. It could be that in some countries the group members deferred more to authority than in others, but there is no way of knowing whether this is because of some type of cultural difference, or simply because the experimenters or their accomplices in each country behaved in slightly different ways. At the very least, we must conclude that an experimental procedure designed to study social deviance in one country can elicit behaviours more usually thought of as examples of leadership or minority influence when used elsewhere. As we noted in discussing the Asch (1951) conformity study, the same manipulation by the experimenter may take on a different meaning in a different cultural context. This type of functional inequivalence is a major hazard in comparing the results of studies conducted in different nations. Later in this chapter we discuss ways of setting up studies in ways that guard against it.

Social facilitation

An alternative and longstanding approach to the study of social influence has been focused not upon conformity or deviance but upon how much the presence of others enhances or inhibits the way that we work at tasks. Numerous studies of this effect have been conducted in Western countries, but they have yielded results that vary depending upon the task and upon who are the person or persons present (Guerin, 1993). We can speculate that this variability may arise because subjects infer different reasons for the presence of the other person, depending upon the task that they are asked to perform. In some circumstances they may feel spurred on to greater effort, while in others their performance is inhibited.

Where a whole group of co-workers are present and working upon the same task, it becomes a little easier to discern the social processes that occur. One series of experiments of this type concerns what has become known as 'social loafing'. This phrase describes a behaviour pattern based upon the fact that when several people are performing a task together, any one person may feel that he or she does not need to exert maximal effort. Indeed, in what was effectively the first recorded social psychology experiment, conducted in the 1880s, a French engineering professor named Ringelmann showed that three men did not pull on a rope three times as strongly as did one man (Kravitz and Martin, 1986). This study occurred well before what is usually said to be the earliest social psychology experiment, the US study on a similar topic by Triplett (1898).

The more recent work of Latané, Williams and Harkins (1979) concerned how loudly people shouted or clapped in groups of differing sizes, compared with when they are alone, and demonstrated similar reductions in average output. Latané's shouting experiment has been repeated using schoolchildren in India, Thailand, Taiwan and Japan, university students in Malaysia and Japan and junior managers in Japan (Gabrenya, Wang and Latané, 1985). In all these cases, some evidence of social loafing was found. However, Shirakashi (1984–5), who also used Latané's procedures, found no evidence of social loafing among Japanese students.

Karau and Williams (1993) undertook a meta-analysis of studies of social loafing effects. They contrasted 147 effects obtained in studies within the United States with 15 effects derived from studies done in Pacific Asia countries. The results of their meta-analysis are a little less clear than those of the meta-analysis of Asch conformity studies, because they included a wide variety of social loafing tasks, and the type of task also influences whether social loafing is found or not.

Karau and Williams (1993) classified tasks as simple, complex or unclear. When complex tasks were used in US studies, the social loafing effect is reduced. As Table 2.3 shows, where complex and 'unclear' tasks are combined, the mean loafing effect is undiminished, but this average conceals wide variations found for different tasks. For the five effects from Pacific Asian countries, social loafing was not merely reduced, it was reversed. Gabrenya, Wang and Latané (1985) provided the first illustration of this effect. They compared US and Taiwanese schoolchildren on a task involving the counting of tones heard over headphones. Subjects worked either individually or in pairs. They found that in this situation, social loafing was present among the US children, but the Taiwanese children actually performed *better* when working in pairs. The effect was particularly strong among ninth-grade boys.

Region	Task structure simple		Task structure unclear or complex	
	Number of effects	**Effect size**	**Number of effects**	**Effect size**
North America	121	0.55	26	0.50
Pacific Asia	10	0.45	5	−1.18

Table 2.3 ● Social loafing and culture

These means are derived from Karau and Williams (1993). Their sample did not include Earley's (1993) study, which also showed a strong cultural effect.

In a similar vein, Earley (1989) compared the performance of ninety-six managers from the United States and China on an 'in-basket' simulation of work. During a one-hour period, they had to attend to a set of work items including prioritizing interviews, filling out requisition forms, and rating job applications. They were told either that they were working alone or in groups of ten. Those working alone were advised that they should complete at least twenty items. Those in groups were advised that 200 items would be needed and that only the total number of items completed by members of the group would count. The results showed clear evidence of social loafing among the US managers, whereas the Chinese managers worked harder in the group condition than when alone. More recently, Earley (1993) has reported a similar difference between US and Chinese managers based upon ratings made of their actual performance at work, under individual and group working conditions. It is plausible that the effects found in the Gabrenya and Earley studies are due to culture rather than to variations in task structure, since each study used the same tasks with both their Chinese and their US subjects.

The likelihood that the difference in findings between the United States and China is due to cultural factors is further raised by three additional studies. Earley's (1993) study also included a sample of Israeli managers. Just as was found in China, the social loafing effect was reversed: the Israelis worked harder when they believed that they were working with a group of their peers rather than on their own. In a similar way, Matsui, Kakuyama and Onglatco (1987) found that in Japan each person in two-person student groups worked harder on average than did individuals on a number-counting task.

Yamagishi (1988) made a comparative study between Japan and the United States, which did not measure social loafing directly. Subjects in his study were informed that they were working in groups of three, but that they would not be able to monitor how much work the other members of the group were putting in. Rewards were based upon the group's productivity on a letter-matching task, but on each trial members were given the chance to opt for an individually based reward instead. Yamagishi found that the Americans were inclined to opt for the individual reward when the penalties for doing so were low, but not when they were high. However, the Japanese frequently chose the individual reward even when the penalties for doing so were high. Yamagishi concluded that the Japanese may have chosen the individual rewards because they wished to avoid the situation where they had no information on how hard the others in the group were working. By opting for the individual reward they could be certain that they would not be penalized by any social loafing that was occurring.

The range of countries from which studies have been reported is not wide, but it appears that social loafing can only be considered a universal phenomenon when detected through the simplest types of experimental tasks, such as shouting and handclapping. Where the task becomes more important and meaningful, the effect reduces, even in North America. However, Veiga's (1991) survey found self-reported loafing in work teams to be widespread among a sample of 571 managers working in US business organizations. This contrasts strongly with the reversal of the effect in non-Western nations. In later chapters we shall advance theories that attempt to show why these differences occur.

Obedience to authority

Among the most controversial and widely discussed studies reported by social psychologists is Milgram's (1974) study of obedience to authority. In this study, Milgram found that around 65 per cent of his American subjects accepted orders to give very strong electric shocks to other people in the course of a 'learning' experiment. This result occurred despite the fact that information was clearly visible to subjects that each shock was stronger than the last and that dangerously high levels of shock were being administered by the subject before the experiment terminated. Although the experiment was of course based upon deception and no shocks were actually administered, it was realistically staged, with convincing tape recordings being played of the protests and screams of the supposed victim.

Milgram's goal was to determine whether or not we are predisposed to obey an authority figure, even when that figure makes unreasonable demands and provides no reasons for doing so. A number of critics within the United States (e.g. Baumrind, 1964) suggested that such experiments are unethical, insofar as they stress and potentially humiliate the experimental subject. Despite this ethical outcry, researchers in at least eight other countries have attempted to repeat Milgram's procedures, and these studies provide us with an opportunity to review whether the findings are replicable within other cultural settings.

The results obtained are shown in Table 2.4. Several researchers included different variations in their experimental designs, as indeed did Milgram in his original series of studies. The figures given in the table show the per centage of subjects who continued to administer shocks right up to the maximum level of 450 volts under what Milgram called his 'baseline' experimental condition. In the Italian study the maximum shock level was only 330 volts, at which level Milgram found 73 per cent obedience.

Table 2.4 ● Studies of destructive obedience to authority

Study	Country	Subjects	Percentage obedient
Milgram (1963)	USA	Male general population	65
		Female general population	65
Rosenhan (in Milgram, 1974)	USA	Students	85
Ancona and Pareyson (1968)	Italy	Students	85
Mantell (1971)	Germany	Male general population	85
Kilham and Mann (1974)	Australia	Male students	40
		Female students	16
Burley and McGuiness (1977)	UK	Male students	50
Shanab and Yahya (1978)	Jordan	Students	62
Miranda et al. (1981)	Spain	Students	over 90
Schurz (1985)	Austria	General population	80
Meeus and Raaijmakers (1986)	The Netherlands	General population	92

It can be seen that the Australians and the British were rather less obedient than the Americans, the Jordanians were close to the US level and the Spaniards, Austrians, Germans, Dutch and Italians were somewhat higher. However, we cannot be very confident that the differences found tell us much about cultural differences unless we can first rule out all other differences among the ways in which the experiments were staged. In the case of experiments on shock, this comparison is particularly difficult, since in each one a particular experimental accomplice is used, and some of these confederates may have been perceived as more vulnerable, or more deserving of shocks than others. For instance, one of the 'victims' in Milgram's study was a smartly dressed businessman, whereas in the Australian study a 'long-haired' student was used.

Many other differences among the studies are also likely to have contributed to the variations in results obtained. For instance, the Dutch experiment was not actually concerned with giving shocks, but used instead a similar task where the subject was instructed to harass and criticize someone filling out an important job application form. Another difference may explain why Australian women were much less willing to give shocks than Australian men, even though Milgram found no gender difference in the United States. This difference could have arisen because the Australian women were asked to give shocks to a female victim, whereas the victims in Milgram's studies were all men.

A more useful way to learn from this batch of studies is to examine what factors caused changes in levels of obedience *within* each country and then compare these results *across* countries. Milgram found that levels of obedience in his studies varied from 0 per cent to 92 per cent. Some of the largest variations occurred when additional accomplices were introduced into the experiment. In one version of the study, this extra accomplice was the person who actually administered the shocks, when instructed to do so by the naive subject. As in the standard study, the naive subject had already been instructed by Milgram that shocks should be given whenever the 'learner' made mistakes. Thus the only difference from the 'baseline' conditions is in who actually presses the shock button. Under the 'instruct another' condition, obedience rose to 92 per cent. In the Australian study, obedience also increased when the subject was transmitting to someone else the instructions to give shocks. In this case obedience rose to 68 per cent among men and 40 per cent among women.

In another of Milgram's variations, when two extra accomplices refused to carry out their part in administering shocks, the proportion of obedient subjects fell to just 10 per cent. In the Netherlands, it fell to 16 per cent, and in the German study, when subjects saw another subject refusing, their obedience level showed a more modest decline to 52 per cent. These studies thus show that in these four countries, the actions of additional people within the experimental setting can raise or lower obedience levels considerably. In deciding whether or not to obey, learners evidently take account of the social context around them, not just the demands of the authority figure. However, this particular series of studies does not give us enough data to know whether this happens more in some countries than in others.

A different type of variation in experimental procedure was also included in the same four countries. In each of these studies, the experimenter reminded the experimental subjects that they were responsible for their own actions. In the United States, Australia and Germany this was done by telling subjects that they could choose what level of shock to administer. In the Netherlands they could choose how much to harass the job applicant. In all four countries, this reminder reduced the number of subjects inflicting maximum harm to virtually nil.

The obedience experiments tell us two things. Firstly, they make clear that substantial numbers of people in a variety of countries will carry out orders from authority, even when this compliance appears to be harming others, despite assurances from the experimenter that it is not. The countries in which these studies have been reported are, with the exception of Jordan, all advanced industrial countries, so we should hesitate before concluding that we have identified a universal aspect of social behaviour. We shall return in Chapter 5 to the question of whether similar results would be expected from other less economically developed countries.

Secondly, these studies suggest that in none of the countries studied is obedience to authority the kind of blind process that some interpreters of Milgram's work have implied. Levels of obedience can and do vary greatly, depending on the social contexts that define the meaning of the orders given. The importance of changes in this social context may also vary from country to country.

Leadership style

One of the earliest experiments reported by Lewin's research group in Iowa was a series of studies of the effectiveness of different styles of leadership in youth clubs

---

Box 2.2 **Mrs Robertson and Mr Chan – teacher and learner**

The obedience studies supposedly concern a teacher and a learner, though the teacher is required to use methods that are, to say the least, unorthodox. Our case study of Mrs Robertson and Chan Chi Lok also focused on the teacher–learner relationship. The misunderstandings between them illustrate some of the ways in which, although both accepted that it was Mrs Robertson's job to instruct, they had different ideas as to what exactly was the nature of Chan's expected performance. Mrs Robertson, for example, stressed time-keeping, grades and regular attendance, while Chan assumed that evidence of effort despite his difficult situation and (Chinese) politeness were more important.

(Lewin, Lippitt and White, 1939). As with some of the other studies reviewed in this chapter, the results are sometimes inaccurately quoted in texts. Lewin *et al.* had the youth club leaders adopt an autocratic, a democratic or a *laissez-faire* role in each club. Each of these roles and the leaders playing the roles were rotated among the clubs. The researchers concluded that the democratic leaders were the most popular with club members and that morale was highest in the democratic condition. However, when they measured how many aircraft models the clubs had made – a task in which the clubs had been engaged – the autocratically run groups were more productive. The researchers also noted that when an autocratically run club was left unattended by the leader for a while, members broke up some of the models, while in the democratic clubs, they continued their work. The *laissez-faire* clubs were both dissatisfied and unproductive.

The Lewin, Lippitt and White studies were carried through at the time of World War 2, when feelings about autocratic and democratic leadership were running particularly high. Lewin felt that it would be good to replicate the project in nations seen at that time as highly autocratic. After the war, he therefore contacted Japanese social psychologists whom he had known in the 1930s. The resulting studies (Misumi and Nakano, 1960) showed that Japanese children's preferences and level of performance varied, depending upon how complex the task was. With more difficult tasks they preferred autocratic leaders and did more work for them, but with easier tasks they preferred democratic leaders and were also more productive with them.

Meanwhile in Germany (actually, the former East Germany), the principal other defeated nation of World War 2, Birth and Prillwitz (1959) reported results essentially similar to those of Lewin, Lippitt and White. However, Meade's (1967) study in India found that the boys in his clubs preferred autocratic leadership, were less often absent and worked more productively under it. Meade (1985) extended this study, using samples of 12–14-year-old boys in India, Hong Kong, Washington, DC, and Chinese Americans in Hawaii. Only in the Washington sample was there a clear preference for democratic leadership. The Chinese Americans in

Hawaii were equally balanced in their preferences, while both in Hong Kong and in India the autocratic leader was strongly preferred. Leader styles do thus show different effects in differing countries, but the results did not match up with Lewin's expectation that the World War 2 enemies of the United States (Germany and Japan) would favour authoritarian leadership. We shall consider why there were advantages for the authoritarian style in India and Hong Kong when we have established a conceptual framework for the study of culture in Chapter 3. We shall then return to a broader range of studies of leadership in Chapter 8.

Group decision

Another well-known series of experiments involving Lewin were those in which he compared different ways of encouraging people to change their dietary habits during World War 2. These showed that American housewives were much more willing to change their behaviours after group discussion than after receiving a lecture (Lewin, 1947). The behaviours changed included serving unusual cuts of meat; having children drink more milk, cod liver oil, orange juice; and so forth. Similar studies were conducted in the United States involving actual work groups in factories deciding how new changes might be accomplished. Lewin argued that group discussion methods were effective because they provided a way in which group norms about what behaviours are desirable or undesirable might be 'unfrozen' and then 'refrozen' into a new pattern. For instance, Coch and French (1948) found that the introduction of new work procedures in a pyjama factory was more successful when employees were involved in group discussion as to how the changes should be implemented.

There is clearly a good deal in common between the enthusiasm of the Lewin group for democratic leadership and their subsequent work on group decision. However, studies of group decision in other countries have given results equally as mixed as did those of democratic leadership. Numerous studies have been reported from Japan (e.g. Makita, 1952; Misumi and Haraoka, 1958, 1960), all of which have shown that change following group discussion and decision was much greater than after lectures, as in the United States. This outcome is consistent with the group-oriented nature of Japanese society. We saw above that, under some circumstances, Japanese children preferred autocratic leaders, but this apparent inconsistency can be explained through closer analysis of how hierarchy and participation are linked in Japanese society. We shall look at this relationship in Chapter 8. In more recent times, introduction of changes in Japanese factories, through the use of discussion groups called 'quality circles' has become very widespread indeed.

Attempts to introduce changes through group discussion in factories in some other countries have been much less successful. An experiment by French, Israel and Ås (1960) used group discussion to introduce changes in a Norwegian shoe factory. Many of the workers did not perceive group discussion as a legitimate way to introduce change and they responded no more positively than did those in the control condition. This negative result may have arisen because they believed the groups to be bypassing their commitment to trade unions, or because they thought it was the role of management to propose changes.

Still less successful was an attempt to introduce group participation in a Puerto Rican garment factory (Marrow, 1964). The use of groups was seen by workers as evidence that management did not know how to manage, leading them to think the firm would soon be out of business. A number of workers left their jobs and joined other firms as a result! Juralewicz (1974) also reported an experiment on group decision in a Puerto Rican garment factory. He found no benefit from having the whole group participate in decisions, but when the group put forward representatives to discuss the changes, the group's subsequent response was significantly better.

These findings suggest that the meaning of group participation, like that of leader style, varies substantially in different countries. Indeed, research has also suggested that response to group participation varies substantially, even within the United States (Locke and Schweiger, 1979). Furthermore, many of the studies of group participation have been undertaken under 'field' conditions, in real work organizations. Research in these circumstances is much less tightly controlled than within a laboratory study, and we may expect many variables to stand in the way of exact replicability of results. We turn next to a further series of studies concerning group decision, which have been conducted in a rather more tightly structured format.

Group polarization

One particular type of group decision-making has been very frequently studied, namely the making of choices involving risk. This enthusiasm followed Stoner's (1961) initial discovery that the groups that he assembled tended to make decisions that were more risky than the average of the views of the group members. Further research both in the United States and in France (Moscovici and Zavalloni, 1969) revealed that such 'risky shifts' are not universally found, but that group decisions do tend to polarize toward one or the other extreme on scales measuring members' opinions. On some decision items, a shift toward caution is found, usually referred to as a conservative shift.

Several factors were at first thought to contribute to this process of polarization. First, it was proposed that where risk-taking is highly valued, individuals may be persuaded toward greater risk-taking by comparing their preferences with those of others and discovering that some people favour greater risks. Conversely, where caution is valued, the discovery that some group members are more cautious than oneself could be influential. On this view, the average group member over-estimates the degree to which others in the group favour risk (or caution) and moves into line with the perceived group norm. Secondly, it was thought that group decision provides opportunities for more persuasive arguments to be brought forward, at least some of which any one individual might not have considered. Finally, these studies have usually been conducted with groups of people who are initially strangers, so that the shift could be a consequence of their getting to know one another and defining their collective identity by contrasting their views with that which might be taken up by other groups.

In theory, studies of polarization from other parts of the world have considerable potential in helping to clarify which of these explanations has greatest generality. In practice, there are some difficulties in realizing this outcome. Table 2.5 shows studies of group polarization that used a format that was at least similar to the original procedures devised by Stoner. Significant average shifts towards risk after group discussion have been reported from six countries other than the United States, whereas no overall effect occurred in the studies with subjects from Germany, Taiwan, Uganda and Liberia. However, as was also found in the United States, the average shift is misleading, because certain discussion items regularly produced a shift towards caution rather than risk. The table shows that in those studies where separate means for each individual item are given, some significant shifts towards caution were also found in the results from other countries.

Table 2.5 ● Studies of group polarization

Study	Country	Subjects	Mean shift per item	Shift to risk	Shift to caution	Total items
Original Stoner items						
Rim (1964)	Israel	General	+0.6	4	2	6
Bateson (1966)	UK	Students	+0.4	–	–	5
Kogan and Doise (1969)	France	Students	+0.5	–	–	5
Lamm and Kogan (1970)	Germany	Students	+0.2	–	–	6
Jamieson (1968)	New Zealand	Workers	+0.6	8	3	12
Bell and Jamieson (1970)	New Zealand	Students	+0.5	–	–	12
Vidmar (1970)	Canada	Students	+1.4*	–	–	10
Carlson and Davis (1971)	Uganda	Students	–0.2	0	2	11
	USA	Students	+0.6	3	1	11
Semin (1975)	UK	Students	+0.9	6	0	11
Jesuino (1986)	Portugal	Students	+0.4	9	2	11
Hong (1978)	Taiwan	Students	–1.0	1	9	12
	USA	Students	+0.7	9	1	12
New items						
Fraser et al. (1971)	UK	Students	0.5	3	1	8
Gouge and Fraser (1972)	UK	Students	0.3	1	2	8
Gologor (1977)	Liberia	Students	0.0	3	3	6

* Vidmar omitted both the items that usually move toward caution.

It is notable that with the exception of three studies, all of these findings were obtained in some of the more industrialized countries of the world. Researchers in these countries have proceeded more recently to debate further explanations of why polarization occurs in groups. For instance Turner, Wetherell and Hogg (1989) and Abrams *et al.* (1990) present evidence in support of self-categorization theory (Turner *et al.*, 1987), from studies using British schoolchildren and New Zealand students. Polarization was much stronger in groups whose members were led to believe that they belonged to groups for a particular reason rather than in groups that were told that they had been randomly composed.

For our present purpose it is important to reflect upon the circumstances in which these findings were obtained. Almost all of these studies were based on *ad hoc* groups of college students, working without appointed leaders. Even the workers in Jamieson's (1968) study were strangers to one another attending evening classes. Many of the risky situations portrayed in Stoner's questionnaire are characteristic of American culture, and less likely to have meaning the further one moves from populations who are familiar with aspects of US life. Even within the studies of students, researchers frequently chose to drop some of the questionnaire items since they would not be meaningful locally.

This problem is most acute within the two African studies. These were both conducted with schoolchildren. In Liberia there was some definite evidence of polarization, whereas in Uganda there appears to have been little movement in either direction. This difference could have arisen because in the Liberian study locally meaningful items were specially constructed, whereas the imported American items employed in Uganda may well have been of lesser meaning or interest. The study by Hong (1978) is of particular interest. He used the full set of Stoner items, with samples of regular US students and with students from Taiwan who were in the United States. The shift to risk was completely reversed within the Taiwanese sample. Hong suggests that Taiwanese culture favours caution more than that of any of the other nations sampled by polarization researchers.

We have very little knowledge of the extent to which polarization occurs within groups that have a more established structure. In parts of the world where social groupings are more fixed, and hierarchies more firmly established, we might expect quite other processes to come into play, as may have been the case in the African studies, and in some of the studies of group decision reviewed earlier. Studies from within the United States (Wehmann, Goldstein and Williams, 1977) and from Portugal (Jesuino, 1986) suggest that where a leadership structure is provided, polarisation is much reduced. Semin and Glendon (1973) made a field study of a committee within a British business organization, whose task was to arrive at job evaluations. Members were required to record their preliminary judgements on a series of criteria related to each case before group discussion. No evidence of polarization after group discussion was found. Polarization may thus be an outcome that occurs in groups when they first form, or when they are developing attitudes toward new events. As such, it may be more frequent and relevant in cultural settings where group memberships are more fluid or transient.

Group conflict and cooperation

In a series of field studies, Sherif and co-workers (1953, 1961) explored the dynamics of conflict and cooperation between groups. They did so by assembling summer camps of young boys in remote settings, implementing an elaborate experimental design over several weeks. Basically this design required the creation of randomly composed groups, which were then set in competition with one another. When a situation of some hostility had been engineered between the groups, Sherif *et al.* were able to test their hypothesis that by providing shared 'superordinate' goals on which the whole camp needed to work together, the conflict and mutual prejudice that had built up could be resolved. The Sherifs and others have used this model to suggest that similar principles could be used to understand and work on a variety of real world social conflicts. Critics have doubted whether such a model is valuable in analyzing larger-scale or longer-term conflicts (e.g. Billig, 1976), but we can still learn something by considering the prior question of whether boys' camps in other countries behave in similar ways to those that the Sherifs studied.

The complexity of these impressive experiments has ensured that not many researchers have been able to replicate them. However, Tyerman and Spencer (1983) in the United Kingdom, Diab (1970) in Lebanon and Andreeva (1984) in the Soviet Union have done so. Tyerman and Spencer argue that many of the Sherifs' findings were a consequence of the temporary nature of the groupings they created. They therefore conducted a study of a boy scout troop on their regular summer camp. The four patrols in the camp initially showed the same level of in-group favouritism as was reported in the Sherif studies. However, even though the patrols had segregated quarters and engaged in a programme of competitive activities, just as occurred in the Sherif camps, no increase was found in inter-patrol hostility or stereotyping. Late in the camp it was found possible to increase intergroup cooperation by a lecture from the camp leader, a procedure Sherif had reported to be ineffective. Tyerman and Spencer conclude that behaviour within their camp was regulated by a long-established set of social norms, which were largely unchanged by the experimental manipulations introduced during the two-week camp.

Diab's camp in Lebanon mirrored Sherif's procedures more precisely. He recruited ten Christian and eight Muslim 11-year-old boys and reported that initial friendship patterns were *not* wholly along religious lines. After two random groups had been composed, they developed very different cultures. One group named themselves 'The Friends' and established a warm and cooperative climate. The other group named themselves 'Red Genie' and were highly aggressive and competitive. They stole things both from one another and from members of The Friends. During competitions, Red Genie were mostly ahead, but in the final stage The Friends passed them and took the overall prize. It proved impossible to continue the camp into the 'cooperation' phase, since the reaction of Red Genie to its defeat included stealing knives, threatening others with them, and attempting forcibly to leave the camp.

The sample of subjects in this study is small, so one should probably resist the temptation to see parallels between it and the tragic exacerbation of inter-communal conflicts that has occurred for prolonged recent periods in Lebanon. However it does illustrate a point also made by Tyerman and Spencer, that the culture of each specific group will depend not just upon externally imposed incentives of competition or cooperation, but also upon established traditions and local cultures that form a background to specific events within each group. We could only be confident of the validity of Sherif's conclusions if much larger samples had been used in the UK and Lebanon studies, so as to permit us to estimate the effect of these factors in relation to those in which Sherif was interested.

Of the replications of the Sherif studies, the only one that offers unambiguous support is Andreeva's (1984) Russian study. As Sherif would have predicted, Andreeva found that, while Pioneer youth camps were engaged in competitive sports, in-group favouritism increased, but when they switched to helping on agricultural collectives, in-group favouritism declined again. From the studies available, it appears that Sherif's findings are most clearly upheld in temporary settings, where other longer-term preoccupations are less troublesome. We shall see at later points in this book that time perspective is much longer in some parts of the world than others. Even within the United States, there is of course substantial attention to longer-term time perspectives. If we are to understand longer-term conflicts between groups, we shall need to take account of the processes that come into play as the time perspective of the relations between groups is extended.

Some second thoughts on replication

This completes our survey of attempts to replicate some of the best-known US studies in different countries. The results may at first appear rather discouraging. The only topic on which there is much evidence for consistently successful replication is the studies of obedience. There is some suggestion that social loafing and group polarization are general phenomena, but in both cases, where the experimental procedures that are used are more similar to everyday life experiences, the results from different countries start to diverge. In the areas of leadership, conformity, group decision and intergroup relations there are rather more marked differences in results.

We find ourselves in a situation a bit like that of Chan and Mrs Robertson. Our anticipations about how people will behave do not seem to be very accurate, but it is difficult to be sure why. Faced with this difficulty, we may well, like them, fall back on our existing preconceptions. Depending upon where we come from, we may account for the non-replicability of studies in different ways. A US social psychologist might point to the methodological rigour of modern US studies and the demanding standards of major US journals, and suggest that studies elsewhere may not have been conducted with quite such equal care. This line of reasoning can be pursued through further use of techniques such as meta-analysis, which enable the pooling of the results of a series of similar studies, yielding estimates of whether variations in experimental design or the location of the study can better account for the differing results obtained. We have seen that this strategy has proved fruitful in understanding the variability in results of the Asch conformity and social loafing studies. We shall note further instances in later chapters.

A European might lay more stress upon the traditions of sociological social psychology and suggest that tight experimental designs often wholly or partially distort the phenomena that we ought to be studying, by ignoring or discounting the importance of their social context. A social psychologist from a more hierarchical culture might conclude that Westerners know best how to do social psychology and feel that locally done work was unworthy of comparison and so could be ignored. Finally, a social psychologist from a developing country could argue that it was more important to focus on themes relevant to local problems and practices rather than to follow the precedents of established social psychology anyway!

Such differing perspectives may to some extent also reflect the differing values and priorities of psychologists in different parts of the world as to what psychology is for. Is it a search for scientific truth or is its prime purpose to find ways of improving the lot of humankind? We would argue that if psychologists attend more closely to cross-cultural variability in the phenomena that we study, we can contribute more adequately to both of these goals. Failures to replicate do not place limits on social psychology. Rather, they give us clues as to additional variables which can strengthen the validity of our future studies.

Identifying the way forward

If we are to avoid ethnocentric evaluations of the studies that we have reviewed in this chapter, we need to establish ways of judging what is a good cross-cultural study. Such criteria are likely to include prescriptions about method and formulations of relevant theories. Let us first consider methods. Many of the studies touched upon so far in this chapter were run in a single country, by different investigators. They were done because a particular US study had become well known, and others wished to see whether they could get similar results. However, it is very difficult for different experimenters working in different countries at different times to design and carry through studies that are closely similar. For this reason, one can never be sure whether a successful replication (or a failure to replicate) is actually due to similarities or differences between the two countries in which the studies were done. Often it could just as probably be due to differences in the samples of subjects studied, or differences in questionnaire translations, or other experimental variations unrelated to the original experimenter's concerns. Such issues are important within countries too, but they become more acute in cross-cultural work.

Method requirements

There are ways in which these methodological problems can be reduced and some of the studies already considered did employ them. For instance, it is beneficial for the same group of researchers to conduct a concurrent study in two, and preferably more than two, countries using closely similar methods and subjects, as was the case in the Schachter *et al.* (1954) study of social deviance reviewed earlier. The larger the number of countries involved, the better is the chance of understanding why the results come out as they do. Where only two countries are involved there are invariably several possible alternative explanations of differences obtained, and no clear basis for choosing between them. Also the group of experimenters will discuss the procedures to be used beforehand, thereby reducing the chances of introducing procedures that will yield peculiar effects in one or other of the locations sampled (Triandis, 1976).

Scientific logic requires that cross-cultural comparisons be made across groups that are equivalent in all respects *except* for their cultural backgrounds. If these groups are different in any other ways, then alternative explanations, called 'plausible rival hypotheses', may be advanced to explain the resulting difference. Of the many potential sources of inequivalence in cross-cultural research (Brislin, Lonner and Thorndike, 1973), we can identify the major ones:

Translation. Subjects are instructed by spoken or written word and often their spoken or written responses constitute the measures of interest in the research. These instructions and responses must be faithfully rendered into the language of comparison used in the research. The method of back-translation is most often used to establish linguistic equivalence. This is a procedure whereby the questionnaires or other measures are first translated into a form that is locally understandable, and then translated back into the first language by someone independent of the study, to check that there have been no mistranslations (Brislin, Lonner and Thorndike, 1973). Some 'decentring' of the concepts in the measure may be necessary, since a literal translation may not capture differences in the nuances of meaning that are found in different cultures. Both abstract concepts such as 'freedom' and more specific behaviours such as 'friendliness' may not translate directly. Bilingual informants are needed to ensure the closest possible equivalence.

Manipulating variables. Experiments in social psychology often involve the operational manipulation of some construct, such as loss of face, through various procedures, such as insulting the subject. This manipulation must, however, have the same meaning or impact in the cultural groups involved, For example, a collective insult such as 'All you Sicilians (Canadians) are prejudiced' would probably be perceived as stronger in a collectivist than in an individualist culture (Semin and Rubini, 1990) and hence not constitute an equal loss of face. The solution to this source of inequivalence is to consult carefully with culturally knowledgeable collaborators to establish functional similarity in the manipulations used. Once established, these manipulations must then, of course, be delivered by local experimenters speaking the native language of the subjects, or differences may result.

Subjects. The respondents in our research may play identical social roles in their cultures, e.g. as university students, political party members or participants in a training course, but despite this role similarity, they may have come from very different backgrounds within each cultural group. For example, in different cultures university students may be carefully selected on the basis of highly competitive exams, religious orthodoxy, family position, tribal affiliation or other criteria. It is difficult to compare them with university students in the West, where access to education is less restrictive and generally determined by a broader range of academic achievement.

The solution to this problem is to look beyond socially equivalent labels to the actual background of the subjects and equate for key variables other than culture. Where strict comparability is impossible, one should choose measures and examine variables less likely to be affected by the non-cultural differences. For instance, more basic psychological processes such as perception, cognition and emotion may vary less within cultures than do social and organizational processes. Alternatively, one can take responses in each culture from samples that are not precisely matched and then use statistical procedures to estimate and partial out the influence of the differences between the samples. For instance, if one sample's mean age is somewhat higher than the other, the effect of this difference can be to some extent discounted by seeing how age is related to the variable being studied within each sample. Obviously, the characteristics of cross-cultural samples must be carefully described and the use of imprecise ethnic labels (e.g. Asian-American) avoided (Trimble, 1990).

Scale usage. Verbal measures of the Likert or 'yes–no' format are often used to collect data in cross-cultural research. The interpretability of scores may be confounded, however, by culturally different ways of responding to such scales. Response sets (e.g. Hui and Triandis, 1989), such as generalized acquiescence or moderation tendencies, may interact with scale content to render outcomes non-comparable. The procedure of within-subject standardization (Bond, 1988b) can overcome this difficulty. Using this procedure, each subject's score on a particular rating scale is expressed relative to that person's ratings on all the other scales. Thus, data from someone from a nation where most people tend to answer 'yes' or 'agree' to most items can be made more directly comparable to data from someone from a nation where people more typically respond at the midpoint of rating scales. Other ways of handling these problems of response bias include elimination of scale midpoints, and reduction of the number of points on rating scales.

The research tradition. Many people grow up in cultures where political polls, consumer surveys, Kinsey-type interviews and subject-pool requirements are taken for granted, along with the assurance that response confidentiality will be honoured. Neither this research tradition nor the guarantee of anonymity can be presumed to obtain in most cultures. Social science may not be practised at all, or it may be highly politicized. There may be differences in what research procedures are regarded as ethically acceptable. These differences will probably require much more extensive consultations and explanation of research procedures if valid data are to be obtained in cultures where psychological research has been less widespread.

Is functional equivalence possible?

Even where these sound practices are followed, demographic differences between subject populations in the various countries and different nuances of language meaning will ensure that the matching of neither subjects nor measures will be exact. Doing cross-cultural social or organizational psychology can never be like reading a thermometer in different countries.

As Jahoda (1979) reminds us, these facts of cultural difference bring the 'normal' enterprise of social psychology into question. As a result, innovative methodologies must often be used to replace laboratory experiments and questionnaires, relationships with cultural informants must be discretely nurtured, and careful training of subjects must precede data collection. In all cases, the cultural context of 'doing social science' must be thoughtfully assessed, to ensure that the outcome of the resulting research has any claim to validity. Useful guidance in accomplishing these goals may be had from books exploring cross-cultural research methods in greater detail than is possible here (Brislin *et al.*, 1973; van de Vijver and Leung, 1997).

In order to take account of this inevitable variability, cross-cultural social psychology needs theories. These theories should not just be consistent with existing social psychology; they should also propose explanations as to why social processes might operate differently in different parts of the world. If we have available a theory that can account for the different effects found in the differing samples, we shall have a much more secure basis both for cross-cultural study and for psychological theory more generally (Triandis, 1988). We shall begin the search for such theories in the next chapter. But first we should look at two programmes of research that help to define more precisely the extent of the problems to be solved.

Systematic programmes of replication

Two Israelis, Amir and Sharon (1987), attempted to define how large was the problem of cross-cultural replicability. They point out that studies such as those discussed in this chapter are selectively sampled, in this case because they happen to be well-known studies. To avoid this selection bias, Amir and Sharon therefore reviewed studies published in four major US social psychology journals over a two year period, and selected six where they saw a good possibility that the variables which had been investigated in the United States would have a similar meaning in Israeli society. They then replicated each of these studies twice in Israel, firstly with a population similar to that used in the US study and secondly with a different population. Five of the original studies had used university students and one had used high-school students. Their replications used both university students and high-school students in all six cases.

The original six US studies reported a total of sixty-four significant main effects and interactions. Amir and Sharon's twelve replications generated thirty significant effects. Twenty-four of these replicated the US findings either in the comparable Israeli sample or in both samples. While this result may sound like substantial evidence of replicability, the more important figure is that none of the remaining forty significant US findings was found in the Israeli studies, and six significant Israeli findings were not found in the US originals! Amir and Sharon note that almost all of the findings which did show some replicability were main effects rather than interactions.

Amir and Sharon's findings suggest that the replicability problem is substantial. We shall review studies in Chapter 3 that suggest that the United States and Israel are in some respects culturally quite similar. The differences in replicability found would probably be even greater between more dissimilar pairs of countries. One weak link in the chain of reasoning of Amir and Sharon is that their studies were conducted about ten years after the US studies that they were replicating. However, if one believes that the processes studied by social psychologists are basic to social interaction, one should not expect major changes to occur over such a time period. Another minor irony is that they failed to notice that one of the six 'US' studies which they chose to replicate was in fact an Australian study.

The only other replication project of comparable scope is that carried through by Rodrigues (1982) in Brazil. Rodrigues provides brief details of attempts by himself and colleagues to replicate fifteen published US studies during the preceding decade. Rodrigues concludes that in only about half of them were the US findings upheld.

A theory-driven programme of research

If we accept that the replication problem is quite severe, then this conclusion accentuates our need to find theories to account for why the difficulty arises. An early example of this approach is provided by the work of Berry (1967). He studied the degree to which individuals differentiated themselves from their context in subsistence societies. The particular aspect of his ambitious project which is of interest here is how open to influence from other people these individuals were. His reasoning was that the degree of influence found would depend upon the culture of the different societies he studied. In particular, members of societies based upon hunting do not have great need to coordinate their actions with one another. On the other hand, societies that practise farming require that all members cooperate in planting and harvesting at certain times of year, and that agreement is maintained over the safe storage of food through lean times, since these matters are crucial to survival. Openness to influence should therefore be greater in agricultural than in hunting societies.

To test his hypothesis, Berry devised a procedure reminiscent of the Asch conformity studies. He asked his subjects to match a line against any one of eight other lines of varying length. However, he went on to point out to his subjects that most people say that the sixth line is the closest in length (which it was not). Berry found that over a series of trials, members of food-accumulating societies accepted the experimenter's 'help' much more than did members of hunting societies. These findings were replicated among cultures ranging from the Inuit in Canada to various societies in Africa, New Guinea and elsewhere.

However, Berry and Annis (1974) did not find the predicted differences in response to experimenter 'help' among various North-West American Indian groups. All these groups scored as high as had those from the same region in the earlier study, although they did vary on other measures that the researchers also included. Since these groups were less diverse than those studied earlier, the later study was a more severe test for Berry's theory. Acknowledging the failure to confirm their hypothesis, Berry and Annis warn that no one theory can be expected to account for all variations in social processes. In a similar way, we shall find in this book that researchers who have predicted differences in social behaviours between sharply contrasted cultures such as the United States and Japan, or the United States and China have often found support for their hypotheses. However, different and more finely grained theories will be required to detect differences between cultural groups that are closer to one another, such as Hong Kong and Singapore, or Spain and Italy. What we must search for initially are theories having a relatively broad range of validity. Berry's series of studies provides one step in that direction, but a more focused search will be needed later.

Summary

The classic North American studies frequently yield different results when repeated elsewhere. Precise cross-cultural replications of studies in psychology are difficult if not impossible to achieve. The way forward lies in designing and conducting studies in which key variations in social context are validly assessed and are used to predict differences or similarities in the effects obtained. Close consultation among researchers from the cultures involved in setting up these studies will improve their probable yield.

Culture: the neglected concept

**Every man is in certain respects
a) like all other men, b) like some other man,
c) like no other man.**

Kluckhohn and Murray (1948)

The whole of psychology can be said to be concerned with the consistency and the variability of behaviour. All that divides cross-cultural psychologists from other psychologists is their interest in understanding the reasons for variability in behaviour across the various cultural groups to be found around the world. While an interest in such issues has long been central to the practice of social anthropology, most psychologists have assumed that the processes they study are in some way more fundamental and impervious to cultural modification. Fundamental processes are not necessarily invariant, but psychologists have most typically sought to explain variations in behaviour by reference to more accepted influences, such as the individual's genetic make-up, specific life experiences or current social situations. Even if certain processes are culturally invariant, the intensity at which a given process operates may vary from culture to culture; so, in predicting behavioural differences across cultures, we will need to know the baseline from which people from a given culture begin that process.

What is culture?

In order to understand how the concept of culture may prove helpful to social and organizational psychology, we need a clear definition. Herskovits (1948) presented the view that culture comprises 'the man-made part of the environment'. Thus culture entails not only material man-made objects, such as houses, methods of transport and implements, but also social institutions, such as marriage, employment, education and retirement, each of them regulated by a host of laws, norms and rules. Such a definition provides a useful first approximation, but it does not help us to decide, for example, what conceptual units we can best use in making cross-cultural comparisons. How much difference must there be between two cultural groups before we say that they are different?

There are no agreed answers to this question. Rohner (1984) sees culture as an organized system of meanings which members of that culture attribute to the persons and objects which make up the culture. This definition implies that the concept of culture should be restricted to *what things mean* to a group of people. Most anthropologists have argued, however, that the physical objects found within a culture are also elements to be included within its definition. Jahoda (1984), for example, asserts that while the meanings that we ascribe to, for instance, the houses that we live in are important, the very existence of houses in a culture also contributes to the way in which members of that culture behave and think about other aspects of their lives. Those who are nomadic or homeless will behave differently and put a particular set of meanings upon events in their daily life, just as will those who live in apartments, hogans, farmhouses, family compounds or whatever.

The debate as to whether human artefacts generate meanings that are salient in a culture, or whether a culture creates artefacts that represent the types of meanings it gives to events is reminiscent of other long-running controversies in psychology. For instance, the relative potency of environment and heredity in determining behaviour has been fiercely and endlessly debated. Ultimately such controversies cannot be resolved, since they present as opposing causes factors that are in practice interwoven. For our purposes the more important aspect of a definition of culture is that a culture is a *relatively organized* system of shared meanings.

Rohner (1984) also proposes that we should distinguish between the concepts of culture and of social system. He defines a social system in terms of 'the behaviour of multiple individuals within a culturally-organised population, including their patterns of social interaction and networks of social relationships' (p. 127). This is in contrast to his emphasis upon defining culture in terms of the shared meanings that are given to events. Social psychologists have repeatedly found that the behaviours of individuals are not always consistent with their espoused attitudes, and Rohner's distinction parallels these findings. However, it is not easy in practice to draw a sharp line between culture and social system thus defined. Theorists such as Ajzen (1988) have shown that apparent inconsistency between attitudes and behaviour will often be explicable because several different attitudes held by the individual concurrently are all relevant to a particular behaviour. Apparent inconsistencies between a social system and the culture in which it is embedded may prove explicable in similar ways. For instance, the celebration of Christmas festivities that currently occurs in some non-Christian countries is most likely explicable in terms of the attractiveness of 'modern' commercialized systems of gift exchange, rather than in terms of the religious significance given to them by Christians. In practice, then, culture and social system as defined by Rohner will shade into one another, as the meanings of some behaviours are widely shared while others are not.

Rohner also discusses the concept of society, as widely used by sociologists. He defines a society as 'the largest unit of a territorially bounded, multigenerational population, recruited largely through sexual reproduction, and organised around a common culture and a common social system' (p. 131). This concept of society thus acknowledges the degree to which culture and social system are interwoven. Rohner notes that in many parts of the world the concept of society has become synonymous with that of nation. The power of modern governments to legislate combined with increased speed of communication and of travel suggest that it is likely that more nations will become societies. Such tendencies should not be overemphasized. The concept of nation is a Western one, and from the nineteenth century onwards national boundaries were quite often drawn on the basis of political expediency rather than to separate neighbouring societies. Within many nations today there persist clearly separable subcultures. These may be demarcated for instance primarily by religion as in Northern Ireland, by language as in Belgium, by race as in Malaysia, Singapore and the United States, and by class or by education as in many countries, for instance France and the United Kingdom. Furthermore, the recent disintegrations of the Soviet Union and Yugoslavia illustrate the fact that some nations may survive for extended periods of time despite the fact that they comprise a congeries of societies that are only loosely linked. India is perhaps the most striking example of a nation within which societies bounded by variations in religion, language and location continue to coexist. One way of reading the future is to foresee this type of intra-national diversity as likely to increase rather than decrease, owing to the large-scale movements of population currently occurring in many parts of the world. In consequence, we will have nations defining societies by a common legal and economic framework, but circumscribing ethnic, racial and linguistic distinctions whose divisive logics must be balanced within a common polity.

National cultures

It was suggested above that no definitive agreement is possible as to how to distinguish one culture from another. Our further discussion has brought us to the point of acknowledging that the history of the world over the past century has created increasingly powerful nation-states, many of which are certainly societies within Rohner's definition, and which may for some purposes be considered as cultures. After all, the cultural groups within a nation are bound by the same sets of laws and governmental policies with respect to trade, taxation, immigration, the media, religion, education and language. Much of the research to be discussed in this book reports little more detail about the cultural affiliations of the samples of respondents studied than the names of the countries in which studies were done. This lack of detail is not due to incompetence or laziness on the part of researchers. It is intimately connected to the issues to be discussed in this chapter: one cannot describe the cultural profile of a sample of respondents until an agreed set of concepts and measures is available for the purpose. As we shall see, some progress has occurred in this direction recently, but past publications cannot be expected to benefit from present progress. For practical purposes we are therefore largely restricted to using distinctions based on what we shall call national cultures.

In doing so, we need to bear in mind two major penalties that we incur on the way. Firstly, when we compare national cultures, we risk losing track of the enormous diversity found within many of the major nations of the world. We should bear in mind that differences found between any two countries might well also be found between carefully selected sub-cultures within each of those countries. Members of a nation are often more aware of its diversity than are those who live outside that nation. Even in ethnically homogeneous Japan, distinctions are perceived between those from the different islands, between *burukamin* (a traditional underclass of workers with animal products) and the others, between Japanese of Korean and Japanese descent, and between *Kanto* and *Kansai*, the two principal urban regions of Honshu, the main island. Even in geographically small nations such as the United Kingdom and the Netherlands, differences are perceived between those from the north and the south. Whether these differences are larger or smaller than differences across national boundaries is in the end an empirical question. If diversity within nations is great and representative samples are taken, we should expect cross-national comparisons to show no differences. If diversity is great and unrepresentative samples are taken, we should expect frequent failures to

---

Box 3.1) The world on the move

It is difficult to grasp the degree to which modern transportation has enhanced the degree of intermingling of populations that were previously much more separate. The figures given below for a sampling of different nations are the most recent available, but they date from the late 1980s. They will certainly have increased since that time. The great majority of these figures are contributed by tourists. We discuss interactions between tourists and locals in Chapter 10. Figures are per year.

Nation	Total foreign persons granted entry	Long-term immigrants
USA	352 million	525,000
Germany	136 million	903,000
Canada	93 million	162,000
UK	91 million	216,000
Spain	54 million	23,000
Hong Kong	30 million	9,000
Australia	3.6 million	222,000
Japan	2 million	81,000
Brazil	1.9 million	4,000
Venezuela	416,000	43,000

Source: United Nations (1990).

replicate the findings of earlier studies. Thus, we can be most confident of the validity of the findings we are to discuss where replicable, predicted differences are found.

Secondly, by focusing upon nations we risk implying that national cultures are unitary systems free from variation, conflict and dissent. Within any national culture there will be all manner of divergences in the experiences of the individuals constituting that culture. We will need to be very careful to avoid implying homogeneity in the life experiences of any two individuals within a given culture. The most fruitful way to avoid this difficulty will be to focus upon studies that rely upon characterization of the values and behaviours of the specific individuals that they study, rather than drawing upon global culture-level characterizations. This point will be explored more fully after we have presented some of the key studies.

Nations and cultures

As we saw in Chapter 2, numerous studies have been completed around the world that attempt to repeat studies originally conducted in the United States. As the results of these studies accumulate, it becomes increasingly urgent for us to have some conceptual framework that will help us to understand why one replication might 'succeed' where another 'fails'. In other words, of all the existing differences between national cultures, which are the ones upon which we as psychologists could most usefully focus in attempting to explain the different results of comparable, similar studies? Some researchers have preferred to address this question by looking at the physical environments in which we live, while others have developed a line of research that uses variations in persons' values as a basis for classification. We consider each approach in turn.

Eco-cultural approaches

We noted in the previous chapter that Berry (1967) had achieved some success in predicting conformity levels on the basis of the type of environment within which societies were located. Several attempts have been made to apply a similar approach to modern nations, focusing upon all available indices that characterize nations. In order to develop a taxonomy of such measures, researchers have isolated a host of macro-level variables, such as humidity, percentage of trade based on agriculture, gross national product per person, degree of urbanization, extent of political pluralization, proportion of the population employed in the service industries, life expectancy at birth and so forth. These have then been factor-analyzed in just the same way as personality theorists have often factor-analyzed personality trait measures in order to discern dimensions of personality.

One of the best examples of such a study was the 'Dimensionality of Nations' project, initiated by Harold Guetzkow, and reported by Rummel (1972). Some 236 macro-level variables from eighty-two nations were considered. Using factor

analysis, this set of variables was simplified and grouped into seven major dimensions, viz. economic development, size, political orientation, foreign conflict, density, Catholic culture and internal conflict. The items that mostly clearly defined
the economic development factor, for example, were (per unit of population):

number of telephones
non-agricultural population
number of radio receivers
gross national product
energy consumption
newsprint consumption
number of hospital beds
number employed in manufacturing

Using each country's score on each of these seven dimensions, Rummel was able to
present a map of national 'character'.

Two important conclusions may be drawn from this and similar studies. First, a
factor of economic development invariably emerges, usually commanding the
largest number of variables (e.g. Adelman and Morris, 1967; Marsh, 1967).
Secondly, there are always *other* factors of variation in addition to economic
development that emerge from such analyses. However, these early studies were
essentially inductive and the factors that emerged varied and were not always easy
to interpret. The researchers had no underlying guidelines as to what types of
dimension they might expect to be meaningful or significant.

Georgas and Berry (1995) attempt to remedy this deficiency. They propose that
nations may be classified ecologically and sociopolitically. Ecological indicators
include temperature, terrain, water supply and soil conditions. Sociopolitical
indicators are subdivided into those based in the economic system, the political
and judicial system, religion, the educational system and means of mass communication. Cluster analysis was then used to group together nations that resembled
one another on each of these criteria from among the total sample of 121 nations.
As one would expect, the clusters that emerged were different depending on which
set of indicators was used as the criterion for clustering. The ecological criteria, for
instance yielded four clusters of nations: fifty-three that are hot and wet, thirty-
three that are moderate, fourteen that are cold and twenty that are hot and dry.
Georgas and Berry argue that this and their other cluster analyses can be used in
deciding how to sample nations representatively. Studies that sample large numbers of similar nations may tell us less than studies that sample a smaller number of
nations that are drawn from different clusters. For instance twenty of the thirty-
three ecologically 'moderate' nations are European, so a comparative study that
was wholly European might be less representative than was at first apparent.

Georgas and Berry regard ecological and sociopolitical factors as the bedrock
upon which national cultures rest. These factors are, if you will, the independent
variables in a global experiment concerning the evolution of human cultures.
However, their model has yet to be fully developed, or widely taken up. It lacks a

---

Box 3.2 | **Sources of hypotheses about cultural effects**

The intellectual culture of psychology, like that of the biological and physical sciences, has traditionally favoured explanations that can account for the phenomena under study at a simpler, more 'basic' or reductionist level. Thus, many psychologists favour explanations derived from physiology, from genetics and from cognitive science. Cross-cultural psychologists face an equally broad array of possible sources of explanation. In the chart below, the simplest or most basic sources of hypotheses are at the left, while those at the right are more immediately and directly linked to the phenomena under study. The backgrounds of researchers who favour each approach are indicated in each column.

Source of hypotheses	Ecology	Institutions and social structure	Socialization processes	Psychological constructs
Example of explanatory variable	Temperature Subsistence mode	Kinship Social class	Family culture Organization culture	Values, beliefs norms
Background of researcher	Eco-cultural psychology	Sociology Social anthropology	Developmental and organizational psychology	Social and organizational psychology

Each of these sources of hypotheses can aid the process of unpacking the effects of culture. The present chapter focuses largely upon researchers within the first and last of these traditions, since these are most strongly represented within psychology.

---

detailed explication of the ways in which climatic or sociopolitical factors may affect day-to-day social or organizational behaviours. Furthermore, many of the sociopolitical factors could as well be read as consequences rather than causes of cultural evolution. Some researchers are exploring more detailed associations between climate and social behaviours (van de Vliert and van Yperen, 1996; van de Vliert *et al.*, 1997), and we will examine these studies in later chapters. Nonetheless, for most researchers, a more promising approach is provided by studies that seek to map cultures on the basis of variables that may be more directly linked to social and organizational processes. Almost all of this work has concerned variations in human values.

Hofstede's classic study of work-related values

A major step forward on this front was accomplished by the publication of Geert Hofstede's (1980) book, *Culture's Consequences*. Hofstede had access to morale surveys conducted by a large, American-owned multinational firm, to which he gave the pseudonym Hermes, subsequently revealed to be IBM. Comparable samples of employees in all the countries where Hermes was represented were asked to complete the survey, which was administered twice, in 1967 and from 1971 to 1973. This procedure yielded no fewer than 117,000 respondents! The items contained in the questionnaire concerned various aspects of employees' work experience, and were not formulated originally with any intention of contributing to psychological theory. From within this overall sample he selected respondents who all worked in servicing and marketing, thus maximizing comparability across nations.

Hofstede's approach was to analyze data from this data bank in such a way that he was able to make comparisons across *countries*. The size of his sample was therefore no longer 117,000 but 40, since the criteria that he developed revealed that he had adequately large samples from each of forty countries. However, the mean scores on each questionnaire item that he had for each country were of course based on a substantial number of respondents from within that country.

After he had factor-analyzed the mean scores for these forty countries, Hofstede decided that he could classify the countries along four dimensions. These dimensions were named as 'power distance', 'uncertainty avoidance', 'individualism–collectivism' and 'masculinity–femininity'. Table 3.1 shows which questionnaire responses were most useful in defining the meanings of each of these dimensions, including examples from both ends of the masculinity–femininity dimension. Hofstede discusses power distance in terms of the amount of respect and deference between those in superior and subordinate positions. Uncertainty avoidance is defined as a focus on planning and the creation of stability as a way of dealing with life's uncertainties. Individualism–collectivism has to do with whether one's identity is defined by personal choices and achievements or by the character of the collective groups to which one is more or less permanently attached. The masculinity–femininity dimension refers to the relative emphasis on achievement or on interpersonal harmony, a distinction that characterizes gender differences in values across many national cultures. Each of the forty countries was then given a score on each of the four dimensions by averaging the items defining that dimension.

Hofstede's study thus provides us with one possible way of classifying the differences found among the forty national cultures represented in his sample. Subsequently, he further enlarged his sample to cover a total of fifty national cultures and three 'regions', for each of which he pooled the data from adjacent countries that he deemed to be culturally similar (Hofstede, 1983). The rank orders of the scores received by each of the countries in his sample are shown in Table 3.2. The range of countries included is impressive indeed. The most striking omissions are the former Communist bloc and most of Africa. Hofstede's study has been criticized in a number of ways that will be considered shortly, but it is clear that in terms of global coverage it was, and until very recently has been, unrivalled.

Table 3.1 ● Hofstede's four dimensions of culture-related values

Value	Questionnaire item	Response
Power distance	How frequently, in your experience, does the following problem occur: employees being afraid to express their disagreement with their managers?	(Frequently)
Uncertainty avoidance	Company rules should not be broken, even if the employee thinks it is in the company's best interest.	(Strongly agree)
	How long do you think you will continue working for this company?	(Until I retire)
Individualism	How important is it to you to have a job that leaves you sufficient time for your personal or family life?	(Very)
	How important is it to you to have considerable freedom to adapt your own approach to the job?	(Very)
Femininity	How important is it to you to have a good working relationship with your manager?	(Very)
	How important is it to you to work with people who cooperate well with one another?	(Very)
Masculinity	How important is it to you to have an opportunity for high earnings?	(Very)
	How important is it to you to get the recognition you deserve when you do a good job?	(Very)

Hofstede also notes, as can be seen from Table 3.2, that although the dimensions of individualism–collectivism and power distance were treated by him as conceptually separate factors, they are strongly and negatively correlated with one another. One group of mostly European and North American countries emerged as high on individualism and low on power distance, whereas another group of mostly Latin American and Asian countries emerged as low on individualism and high on power distance. Distinguishing national cultures on the basis of their scores on the individualism–collectivism dimension has attracted many cross-cultural researchers in recent years and we shall refer to it frequently throughout the remaining chapters of this book. In doing so, however, we shall also need to remember its close linkage with the power distance dimension. The remaining two dimensions of uncertainty avoidance and masculinity–femininity group countries in ways that may well be important, but that are less consistent with

Table 3.2 ● Rankings of national cultures using Hofstede's classification

Country	Power distance	Uncertainty avoidance	Individualism	Masculinity
Africa (East) region	22	36	34	39
Africa (West) region	10	34	40	30
Arab region	7	27	26	23
Argentina	35	12	22	20
Australia	41	37	2	16
Austria	53	24	18	2
Belgium	20	5	8	22
Brazil	14	21	26	27
Canada	39	41	4	24
Chile	24	12	38	46
Colombia	17	20	49	11
Costa Rica	43	12	46	48
Denmark	51	51	9	50
El Salvador	18	5	42	40
Ecuador	8	28	52	13
Finland	46	31	17	47
France	15	12	10	35
Germany (West)	43	29	15	9
Great Britain	43	47	3	9
Greece	27	1	30	18
Guatemala	3	3	53	43
Hong Kong	15	49	37	18
India	10	45	21	20
Indonesia	8	41	47	30
Iran	29	31	24	35
Ireland	49	47	12	7
Israel	52	19	19	29
Italy	34	23	7	4
Jamaica	37	52	25	7
Japan	33	7	22	1
Korea (South)	27	16	44	41
Malaysia	1	46	36	25
Mexico	6	18	32	6
Netherlands	40	35	4	51
Norway	47	38	13	52
New Zealand	50	40	6	17
Pakistan	32	24	47	25
Panama	2	12	51	34
Peru	22	9	45	37
Philippines	3	44	31	11
Portugal	24	2	34	45

Table 3.2 (continued)

Country	Power distance	Uncertainty avoidance	Individualism	Masculinity
Singapore	13	53	40	28
South Africa	35	39	16	13
Spain	31	12	20	37
Sweden	47	49	10	53
Switzerland	45	33	14	4
Taiwan	29	26	43	32
Thailand	22	30	40	44
Turkey	18	16	28	32
United States	38	43	1	15
Uruguay	26	4	29	42
Venezuela	5	21	50	3
Yugoslavia	12	8	34	48

These rankings are derived from the scores given by Hofstede (1983). Rank 1 is high.

subsequent results and theorizing. Perhaps for that reason, other researchers have made less use of them to date.

Evaluating Hofstede

How should we evaluate Hofstede's contribution? His definition of culture is quite compatible with that of Rohner (1984). He defines culture as 'the collective programming of the mind which distinguishes the members of one group from another' (Hofstede, 1980, p. 21). In other words, cultures are conceptualized in terms of meanings, and it is quite appropriate to study them by assessing the values of representative samples of members from each culture. However, Hofstede is particularly careful to emphasize that his core values apply to national cultures and not to individuals. If two nations differ on a given value dimension, it would not be logical to infer that because two cultures differ, then any two members of those cultures must necessarily also differ in the same manner. For instance, someone might expect that because the United States scores higher than Guatemala on individualism, then a particular US citizen is bound to be more individualistic or lower on power distance than a particular Guatemalan. This is not so, as the frequency curves in Figure 3.1 indicate. The mean score for a national culture within Hofstede's study will be the *average* of the scores of those who responded to the questionnaire. Within each national sample there may be wide variations, so that it is perfectly possible to come across a Guatemalan who is more individualistic (further to the right in Figure 3.1) than a particular US citizen.

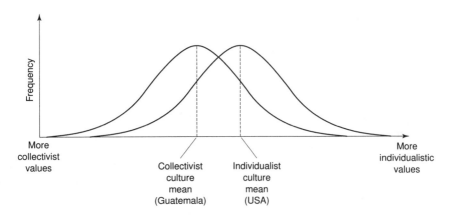

Figure 3.1 Hypothetical distributions of value scores in an individualist and a collectivist national culture. (Source: adapted from Hofstede, 1980.)

In fact, the values that are found to go together to define individualism for nations, do not go together to define individualism for individuals (see e.g. Bond, 1988b). To shift a scoring procedure developed at one level and to apply it at a lower level of analysis is labelled the ecological fallacy by Hofstede (1980, p. 29). This error is widely committed, since it is technically difficult to identify universal groupings of values into dimensions at the individual level of analysis. We discuss this difficult issue more fully later in this chapter.

One might argue that the task of social and organizational psychology is to predict how individuals behave in their social context. If Hofstede's mean scores for countries cannot be used to generate such predictions, of what use are they? The implicit flaw in this line of questioning is that social psychologists rarely attempt to predict the behaviour of a *specific* individual. What they do is attempt predictions about how populations of individuals will behave, either as individuals or in the groups and organizations to which they belong. Thus, provided that a study done in a particular country is based upon an adequately representative sample, knowledge of the Hofstede scores for that country may be helpful in interpreting the *average* results from persons in those countries.

This statement assumes that Hofstede was entirely successful in the representativeness of his own sampling within the countries he studied. There are several obvious limitations to his sampling, however. Firstly, all respondents were employees of IBM. IBM is a very well-known US corporation, which is frequently said to have a distinctive culture of its own. The fact that Hofstede found national culture differences *despite* this unifying influence could be counted as a strength of his project. It remains undeniable, however, that his sample was predominantly male, that it was drawn only from the marketing and servicing divisions and that the data were all collected at least twenty-five years ago. The only way to test whether these sampling limitations are important is to compare the results with those obtained by subsequent researchers, as we shall do shortly.

The title of Hofstede's book is *Culture's Consequences*, thereby implying that culture can act as a causal factor. When he reports, as he does, that the individualism scores of the countries in his sample correlate +0.82 with their gross national product (GNP) per head of population, it is very tempting to infer that rich countries are rich because they have individualist cultures. To do so would be hazardous indeed, as with all correlational data. An equally plausible hypothesis is that Western national cultures are mostly individualist *because* they are relatively rich. The recent rapid economic growth of Japan, Hong Kong and other non-individualist Pacific Asian countries provides further reason for doubting that individualism by itself provides the path to riches. What we should be watching for is whether rising affluence in some collectivist countries is followed by rising individualism. We shall examine the evidence on this point in Chapter 12.

We have discussed Hofstede's study at some length, since it holds a pivotal place in the contemporary development of all areas in cross-cultural psychology. The dimension of individualism–collectivism in particular has attracted a good deal of subsequent interest. Triandis (1990, 1995a) has summarized a great variety of ways in which social behaviours differ between people in individualist and collectivist national cultures, and we shall be considering these in many of the chapters that follow. Box 3.3 and our earlier description of the meeting between Mr Chan and Mrs Robertson give examples of what may have happened when members of nations varying on this dimension interact. However, before we can

Box 3.3 A taste of collectivist decision-making

Chuck and Mary Hooley from Toronto had recently arrived in Brazil, where they were to spend a holiday. After a few days relaxing at the beach and in their hotel they were delighted to be invited for an authentic local meal in a restaurant with some Brazilian acquaintances. When they were seated, the waitress soon came to the table and gave a single menu to one of their Brazilian friends, who proceeded to study it. Chuck and Mary both felt it important to take care as to what they ate, so they signalled to the waitress that they would like more menus to look at. They could see that the one their host had was in English as well as Portugese. However, she responded only by saying that the menus were all the same. Soon, the Brazilian with the menu began to make some suggestions as to what he was sure they would like to try. Chuck and Mary began to feel frustrated. They did not want to offend their host, but they did need to know what the choices were.

Meanwhile, their Brazilian colleague was puzzling as to why Chuck and Mary seemed so reluctant to accept his carefully selected recommendations. After all, in this situation the cultural norm would be for him to point out the best choices for the members of his group, and the waitress had correctly inferred that as the senior member of the group it would only be he who needed to see the menu.

Source: freely adapted from an original episode described by Brislin *et al.* (1986).

be sure that the Hofstede dimensions are indeed the most useful concepts for our purpose, we need to review some more recent studies.

Further studies of values

Discounting cultural bias. A group of researchers called the Chinese Culture Connection (1987) investigated the possibility that Hofstede's study might be biased toward Western values, simply because it derives from a questionnaire designed by various Westerners. Hofstede himself, who is Dutch, freely acknowledges that no study can hope to be entirely value-free, and disarmingly includes in his book two pages describing his own personal values, so that the reader may form a view of the author's own possible biases. The Chinese Culture Connection started its work by asking Chinese informants to list Chinese values of fundamental importance in their cultural tradition. These were then used to construct a value survey that was ultimately administered to fifty male and fifty female university students in each of twenty-three national cultures. Analysis of these data in the same manner employed by Hofstede again yielded four factors. The scores of countries along these dimensions were then compared with the scores that had been obtained by Hofstede from the same countries.

As Table 3.3 shows, three of the four factors showed substantial overlap. The importance of this finding is considerable. The two studies used measures with quite different cultural origins, were done at different times, had a different gender ratio and were directed towards quite different samples within each national culture. Yet, they supported the view that power distance, individualism–collectivism and masculinity–femininity describe dimensions of variation in values that are relatively robust. They also suggest that uncertainty avoidance and Confucian work dynamism (CWD) are less universally accessible values, though they may well still be important. Putting the results of the two studies together, we might conclude that we should add CWD to Hofstede's four dimensions if we wish to classify cultures in the most valid way possible. In a more recent book, Hofstede (1991) himself accepts this conclusion, but prefers a different name for the fifth

---

Table 3.3 ● Empirical equivalence of factors obtained by Chinese Culture Connection and by Hofstede

Chinese Culture Connection	Hofstede
Integration	Collectivism
Human-heartedness	Masculinity
Confucian work dynamism	–
Moral discipline	High power distance
–	Uncertainty avoidance

dimension. He points out that all the Confucian values clustered together in the CWD factor emphasize the virtue of taking a long-term perspective, while respondents who are low on this dimension focus more on the present and the past.

A theory-driven perspective on values. A further large-scale series of studies of values has been undertaken by an Israeli psychologist, Shalom Schwartz, and his collaborators (Schwartz and Bilsky, 1987, 1990; Schwartz, 1992, 1994). Schwartz made a detailed review of earlier theory and studies of values from both Western and non-Western sources. He proposed that only when the fundamental issues facing mankind had been identified could one judge whether value studies had sampled all the value dimensions likely to be found. Three needs were proposed as fundamental: biological needs, social coordination needs, and the survival and welfare needs of groups. From this basis, Schwartz identified fifty-six values and constructed a questionnaire in which respondents were asked to indicate how much each of these values was 'a guiding principle in my life'. To date, responses have been obtained from more than fifty countries, from most of which there were two samples, students and secondary school teachers. The countries sampled have included all the regions of the world.

Schwartz proposed that before we can be confident in establishing the dimensions of values that can best classify national cultures, we need to test whether the measures that we use mean the same thing to respondents from each different nation. If someone asserts that 'freedom' is a very important value to them, does that freedom mean the same thing in, say, Poland or Argentina as it does in the United States or Nigeria? In order to determine which values do have reasonably similar meanings at all locations, Schwartz decided first to analyze the inter-relationship of values with one another in each country separately.

Schwartz's data were analyzed by the statistical procedure known as smallest space analysis. This locates the means for each item in a multidimensional space, where the statistical distance between any two values is a measure of their psychological closeness. This procedure tells us which questionnaire items cluster together, but it does not tell us which values are most important within each national culture. Schwartz (1992) reports on separate analyses of this type for each of thirty-two samples from twenty countries. The results showed remarkable consistency, with possible minor exceptions from China and Zimbabwe. It was found that the spatial relationships of the means within two dimensions could be summarized as falling within ten domains, which he calls value-types. Each of these value-types was given a name that summarizes the values that typically fall within it. Sagiv and Schwartz (1995) extended this kind of analysis to eighty-eight samples from forty countries, and continued to find the same structural relationships among the values sampled. We may conclude that the *structure* of values is consistent across cultures. This finding does not mean that the same values are endorsed to the same degree in each nation, nor does it mean that value endorsements are necessarily constant over time. It means that there is a consistent *relationship* among all the values sampled. Figure 3.2 summarizes the ten value-types and their inter-relations.

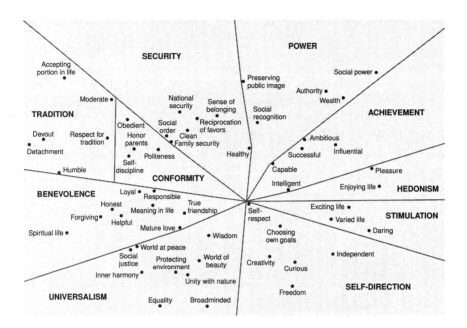

Figure 3.2 Value configuration typically obtained in Schwartz's analyses of individual-level data. (Source: Schwartz, 1992)

The strength of this project derives from its very thorough sampling of the values that might be important in various national cultures. It therefore provides checks on whether the earlier studies had significant omissions and on whether each value has a well-agreed meaning. The resultant ten value-types are clearly more numerous than those identified by Hofstede (1980) and the Chinese Culture Connection (1987). However, an examination of these value-types indicates that they represent a refinement rather than a contradiction of earlier work. On one side of Figure 3.2 lie values that would fall within Hofstede's concept of individualism, such as self-direction, stimulation and hedonism, and which Schwartz summarises as openness to change. On the opposite side lie central components of collectivism, such as security, tradition and conformity, which Schwartz summarizes as conservation. Masculinity–femininity reappears as achievement opposed to universalism, and power distance as power opposed to benevolence. Schwartz prefers to define these clusters of value-types as self-enhancement versus self-transcendence.

Despite this apparent overlap, we must not lose sight of the differences between the data analyses by Schwartz and those discussed earlier. He has completed a series of studies focused upon individuals *within* each country separately. By doing so, he is able to conclude that forty-five of his original fifty-six values do have meanings that are consistent across samples. His measure of consistency of meaning is whether or not each value consistently appears in the same value-type in all of his analyses. For instance, it was found that the values falling consistently into the 'power' value-type were social power, authority and wealth, whereas preserving my public image, and social recognition, showed less consistency. Box 3.4 shows how some of the values that did *not* show consistency can be used to aid our understanding of specific cultures.

By relying upon those values that *do* show consistent meanings across cultures, Schwartz (1994) was able to take his analysis one stage further. Averaging value scores across individuals, he undertook a further smallest space analysis comparing the structure and distribution of these country averages. Figure 3.3 shows that when this culture-level analysis was done, the structure of values was better summarized in terms of seven value-types, although the overall distribution of values is quite similar to those found earlier. To underline the importance of distinguishing between individual- and culture-level analyses, Schwartz gives these value-types different names from those used at the individual level. We shall consider why this distinction is so important shortly. For the moment, we can note that when Schwartz conducted his culture-level analysis, the polarities that emerged

---

Box 3.4) Japanese friendship and Australian loyalty

In comparing the structure of values in samples drawn from different nations, Sagiv and Schwartz (1995) discovered that certain values were interpreted in distinctive ways within particular nations. For instance, 'true friendship' is typically found to be located within the Benevolence value-type (see Figure 3.2). However, within the data provided by 542 Japanese students, 'true friendship' was located within the security value type. This pattern of value relationships indicates that for these Japanese respondents, friendship as a concept has a meaning that is mostly closely approximated by the other values comprising the security value type. These were 'sense of belonging' and 'healthy'. The values more typically associated with friendship in samples from other national cultures are 'mature love' and 'meaning in life'. Thus, Japanese students see friendship more in terms of inclusion and health, whereas elsewhere friendship has more intimate associations, being seen as akin to love and maturity, and giving meaning to life.

Sagiv and Schwartz also found a distinctive understanding of 'forgiveness' within the Japanese data. In Japan it was associated with broadmindedness and equality, whereas elsewhere it was more typically seen as linked to honesty and helpfulness. There is no suggestion, however, that distinctive interpretations of values are any more frequent in Japan than elsewhere. Sagiv and Schwartz take their analysis further by reporting that within their Australian student data, loyalty and responsibility were seen as distinctively close to obedience and politeness, compared with the more typical linkage with honesty and helpfulness in other countries. This pattern suggests that Australians see loyalty and reponsibility more in terms of external obligation and less in terms of internalized standards than do others.

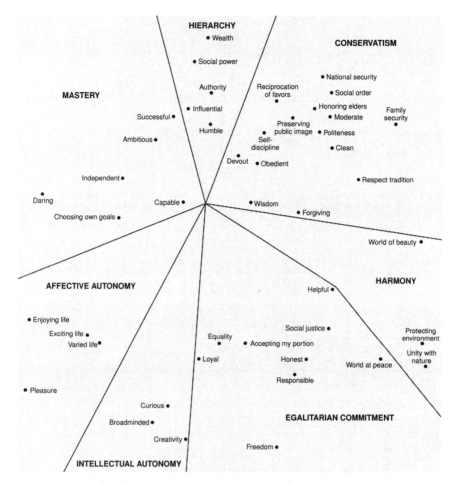

Figure 3.3 Configuration of values obtained in Schwartz's country-level analysis. (Source: Schwartz, 1994.)

(conservatism versus autonomy; mastery and hierarchy versus egalitarian commitment) are strongly reminiscent of Hofstede's dimensions of individualism–collectivism and power distance respectively.

An alternative source of value measures. One other recent study has surveyed value dilemmas across large numbers of nations. Trompenaars (1993) designed a questionnaire based upon conceptions of value dimensions mostly stemming from North American sociologists and social anthropologists (Parsons and Shils, 1951; Kluckhohn and Strodtbeck, 1961). Some of the seven proposed dimensions were similar to those advanced by other researchers (for instance, individualism–collectivism), while others (for instance, time perspective) were not. The questionnaire was completed by samples of business employees in nearly fifty countries, in the late 1980s and early 1990s.

Smith, Dugan and Trompenaars (1996) analyzed the data bank assembled by Trompenaars. Using a multidimensional scaling procedure, they concluded that the two major dimensions of culture-level variation in the responses were best described as conservatism versus egalitarian commitment, and loyal involvement versus utilitarian involvement. The first of these pairs of names was taken from Schwartz, since the content of the items defining the dimension paralleled Schwartz's results closely. The second refers to the basis on which respondents described their obligations to groups, and therefore has some conceptual and empirical similarity to Hofstede's individualism–collectivism. However, the Trompenaars survey included data from nine former communist bloc nations, none of which had been included within Hofstede's sample. Smith *et al.* argue that the inclusion of data from these nations permits a clearer separation between the dimensions which Hofstede defined as individualism–collectivism and power distance.

The three major surveys of values published since the time of Hofstede's project have thus sustained and amplified his conclusions rather than contradicted them. It is time to consider how best to use them in developing a cross-culturally valid social and organizational psychology.

Culture as a theoretical cure-all

Having discussed what we mean by national culture, and shown that there is some defensible evidence that one can classify national cultures in terms of the importance attached to different values, we are now in a position to confront some of the central dilemmas of cross-cultural research. We shall examine three. Firstly, should we be looking for universal aspects of social behaviour, in other words those that transcend national cultures? Or is it more valuable to try to understand the variations that, as we have already seen in Chapter 2, do occur? Secondly, how can we think clearly about causation? In what sense could we say that a national culture causes the social behaviour of its members? Thirdly, out of the confusing array of concepts now being advanced, what is the most useful conceptual framework to adopt? Do values provide us with the most useful basis by which to classify national cultures?

The search for universals

Whether one sees it as important to establish the universals of human social behaviour may depend partly upon the academic discipline in which one was trained. As Lonner (1980) points out, social anthropologists have spent a good deal of time attempting to identify universals. This no doubt stems from the daunting diversity of the societies which they have studied. For them, the identification of universals is a prerequisite to any type of comparative theorizing.

In contrast, most psychologists have presumed that the processes that they study are universal. About 95 per cent of our work has been centred in relatively few and somewhat similar national cultures, in fact in the high-individualist, low power distance cultures identified by Hofstede. This cultural similarity of those countries doing most psychology has made easier our unquestioned acceptance of the assumption that what is true locally must be true everywhere.

Given this assumption, the logical extension to social psychological studies first done in the United States has been to repeat them elsewhere. As we saw in Chapter 2, this procedure has given mixed results. One type of response to this confusion is to sort the studies that do replicate from those that do not, and to infer that the successful ones will contribute to developing generalizations about universals. The alternative, which we favour, is to focus on the ones that do not, and to develop theories as to the ways in which their variability in outcome may point toward universals that are not immediately apparent. In doing so, we are opting for a particular characterization of what is meant by a universal. Lonner (1980) distinguishes between simple universals (e.g. the fact of human sexuality), variform universals (e.g. the occurrence of aggression, but in forms that vary across cultures) and functional universals (e.g. theories that can explain why phenomena vary across cultures in the way that they do). It is this last type of universal that is our primary focus of attention. The road toward the establishment of such universals is a long and hard one. However, we can take note of one or two signposts along the way.

The etic-emic distinction. Berry (1969, 1989) makes use of a distinction first made by linguists, between phonetics and phonemics. While phonetics has to do with the universal properties of spoken sound, phonemics concerns the ways in which such sounds are given meaning within the context of particular words and languages. In a similar way, Berry argues that 'etic' analyses of human behaviour are those that focus on universals, principally those that in Lonner's terms are either simple or variform. For example, we all eat, we (almost) all have intimate relations with certain others, and we all have ways of attacking enemies. An 'emic' analysis of these behaviours, on the other hand, would focus on the different, varied ways in which each of these activities was carried out in any specific cultural setting. Successful emic analyses could be expected to establish generalizations that were only valid locally.

Berry argues that many of the attempts to replicate US studies in other parts of the world can be classified as 'imposed etic'. In other words, the procedures, experimental situations and measures used assume that the response being studied has the same meaning to the new participants as it did to those in the setting where the study was originally devised and that therefore responses will have an equivalent meaning in the new culture. Consider, for instance, the California F scale, a measure of deference to authority and intolerance toward minority groups developed by Adorno *et al.* (1950) in the United States, and widely used subsequently elsewhere. Kagitçibasi (1970) reported that when the scale was used in Turkey, responses to the items did not correlate with one another at all well, as they had done with the original American subjects. In Turkey, the same scale items tapped several different concepts. In another study, Pettigrew (1958) used the same scale among South African whites. He found that scores on the F scale there reflected deference to authority but did not correlate with anti-black prejudice, as it had done with American subjects. Amongst White South Africans at the time of Pettigrew's study, prejudice against Blacks was widespread and was not restricted to those who were deferential to authority. The use of such imposed etic measures could thus be a major contributor to replication failures.

Berry (1989) acknowledges that cross-cultural psychologists mostly wish to finish up by being able to discuss generalizations that are etically valid. In place of the use of imposed-etic measures, he outlines a strategy for reaching a more valid set of 'derived-etic' generalizations. These are to be arrived at by conducting parallel emic studies within a series of national cultures. By allowing measures to be constructed separately in each national culture studied, we do not force them into metric equivalence. If we nonetheless do find some convergence between the results obtained within each culture, we can be more confident that we have identified processes that are equivalent, and we would be in a position to make derived-etic generalizations both about the process and about variations in its occurrence, at least about the range of cultures we had sampled. A less elaborate procedure which some researchers have followed is to assemble a multinational group of researchers and develop measures with etic validity by repeated consultation and pilot testing of measures.

While only a few of the studies discussed in this book have followed these procedures in full, rather more have moved some way toward a derived-etic approach, compared with the procedures used by earlier researchers. Schwartz's work on values provides an excellent example. His list of fifty-six values was not originally constructed for use within any particular specific culture, and drew upon non-Western sources such as the Chinese Culture Connection (1987) survey as well as Western ones, in order to ensure comprehensiveness. Although the value list was not constructed separately in each country, researchers at each site were able to insert additional values if they sensed the need. Furthermore, as we have seen, Schwartz's data analysis was initially conducted separately for each country-sample. The results therefore provide independent tests of the way in which the meanings given to values within each sample cluster together. What Schwartz has accomplished is thus a parallel series of emic studies within different cultures. The remarkable convergence of his results from almost all samples provides a result which is not imposed-etic, but which gives an increasingly firm base for general theorizing about the structure of human values at the etic level.

We can also test the probability that the studies of values that we have reviewed have identified a validly etic set of concepts by comparing them with classifications derived from separate sources. Fiske (1991a, 1992) reviews a broad range of sociological and anthropological studies, and draws from them the proposition that there are just four elementary forms of social relations. He names these as 'communal sharing', 'authority ranking', 'equality matching' and 'market pricing'. The first two of these are defined in ways that are very close to Hofstede's conceptions of collectivism and of power distance, respectively. The remaining two dimensions are less obviously related to Hofstede's other concepts, but we need to exercise care in determining whether or not concepts identified by different researchers overlap simply on the basis of the names and definitions assigned to them.

Fiske's definition of equality matching is in terms of a relationship within which the parties are separate but relate on the basis of equal contribution. Market pricing on the other hand refers to relations where people seek to achieve a profit over one another through exploiting competitive advantage. Table 3.4 suggests ways in which Fiske's dimensions and the classifications of values by Schwartz and by Hofstede may be reconciled. In seeing possible parallels, we should bear in mind that the goals of these authors are not the same. Schwartz and Hofstede have been trying to develop etically valid classifications of the salient values of different cultural groups. Fiske is trying to classify different types of social behaviour, all of which may well occur within any particular cultural group. For instance a member of culture X might relate to blood relatives on the basis of communal sharing, to a boss at work on the basis of authority ranking, to a friend on the basis of equality matching, and to a shopkeeper on the basis of market pricing. Equally of course a member of culture X might espouse individualist values at work and collectivist values at home. If the concepts in Table 3.4 do show some convergence, that adds strength to the argument that they are encompassing a good deal of what is important about social behaviour both within and between cultures. Of course, to be scientifically sure, we must derive some measure of Fiske's orientations as practised in each culture and compare results with those from other studies.

Cultural causation of behaviour

This brings us to the second of the dilemmas listed at the beginning of this section. The issue of whether culture can ever legitimately be considered a cause of social

Table 3.4 ● Possible relations between the concepts of Hofstede, Fiske and Schwartz

Hofstede	Fiske	Schwartz
Individualism	Low communal sharing	Affective autonomy
Collectivism	High communal sharing	Conservatism
High power distance	High authority ranking	Hierarchy
Low power distance	Low authority ranking	Egalitarian commitment
Low uncertainty avoidance	–	Intellectual autonomy
Masculinity	Market pricing	Mastery
Femininity	Equality matching	Harmony

behaviour is debated by Rohner (1984). The definitions that we have discussed for culture, social system and society rest upon analyses of the beliefs and actions of their members. Consequently, if we claim that culture can explain behaviour and then use variations in behaviours to define cultural differences, we are formulating a tautology, i.e. we are saying that something may be explained by itself. However, if we claim that Individualism or some other specific value can explain some aspect of social behaviour, we are then on rather firmer ground. We have then extracted what we regard as a key element of culture and proposed that it can explain behavioural aspects of culture.

Levels of analysis. Unfortunately this still does not completely solve the problem, as we must also address the question of levels of analysis. Many of the studies to be discussed in this book will compare characterizations of particular national cultures with the average behaviour of a small sample of subjects drawn from within those cultures. In other words, we may find ourselves asserting that the collectivism of, say, Indonesian national culture *causes* a particular group of Indonesian students to make certain attributions on a questionnaire about reasons for the success or failure of their work. When expressed in this way, it is easy to see that the implication of causality is too strong to be plausible. We may in a general sense expect Indonesian national culture to be expressed in the educational system of that country, the type of students recruited, the type of teaching, and the type of assessment. But if we want to make a firmer test of causal links to individual behaviour, we should be better off knowing how collectivistic this specific group of Indonesian students in the study actually was. In other words we should use characterizations of whole cultures (e.g. collectivist values) to explain specific attributes of that culture as a whole (e.g. the type of political system that is found there, rates of disease, military expenditure and so forth). But we should use characterizations of the values of particular individuals or groups of individuals if we want to predict how those particular individuals will behave.

Culture-level measures can best be used to explain culture-level variation; individual-level measures can best be used to explain individual-level variations. Since most social psychological research is conducted with individuals, there is a pressing need for more researchers to use such individual-level measures, rather than relying on cultural-level characterisations such as those provided by Hofstede (Bond, 1996b).

The alternative strategy of analyzing the properties of cultures as a whole, using culture-level concepts and measures is, of course, also possible (Leung, 1989). For example, Sagie and Schwartz (1996) studied the correlates of value consensus in nations. They predicted that modernity would be associated with high value consensus within a nation, while democratization would be associated with greater diversity of values within a nation. Using the Schwartz data bank for the values of schoolteachers within thirty-six nations, they found support for both hypotheses. The fact that so few studies have been conducted with culture-level concepts is probably itself a reflection of the dominance of individualistic (i.e. person-centred) values in the countries where most social psychology has been undertaken (Hogan and Emler, 1978).

Confusion about levels of analysis is probably the greatest single problem in the current development of cross-cultural psychology. The difficulty is that many researchers fall victim to what Hofstede (1980) and others refer to as the *ecological fallacy*. Suppose it is shown that the nations that spend most money on medicine have the most healthy populations. Does it follow that the individuals who spend most money on medicine are also the most healthy? Most probably not; indeed it is quite likely at the individual level that the relationship would be reversed: those who were most ill would be spending most. Consider now an instance that derives more directly from the concepts we have been discussing. Nations whose values favour low power distance include most of the richest nations in the world. Does it follow that individuals who are opposed to hierarchy are likely to be rich? Certainly not: many of the most successful entrepreneurs have achieved success through taking a strongly hierarchical view of management. Exceptions to this pattern such as Steve Jobs at Apple Computer in the United States, Richard Branson at Virgin in the United Kingdom and Ricardo Semler in Brazil may achieve folk-hero status as exceptions to the rule, but their fame should not blind us to the much greater frequency of success among less-talked about figures who espouse less egalitarian values.

Smith and Schwartz (1997) outline criteria that can be used to determine whether a research question in social psychology is to be posed and answered at the individual-level or at the culture-level. Klein, Dansereau and Hall (1994) explore similar issues in relation to organization studies. If we are interested in explaining the differences across national cultures, then we must treat each culture as a single unit, and rely only on indices that characterize each nation as a whole, such as measures reflecting average values, wealth, health, climate or demographic profile. It follows that we can only successfully do studies of this type if we have available data from several dozen nations, as did the studies that we have discussed earlier in this chapter.

If we are interested in explaining similarities and differences in the behaviour of individuals, whether those individuals are all in one cultural group or spread over many groups, then an individual-level analysis is called for. However, it will be impossible to do individual-level analyses *across* national cultures, unless one takes into account culture-level differences. So, for instance, if we wish to study the relationship between employee values and absence from work across national cultures, we could first take account of the fact that absence from work is more frequent in some nations than others. Each individual's absence score must therefore be expressed in relation to the average score *for their nation* before the hypothesis could be tested. Alternatively, we could test the values–absence link across the entire sample, and then examine whether the strength of this linkage varies by nation. If the relationship does vary, it will then be necessary to determine whether or not this is due to measurement artefact (Bond, 1996b).

Triandis *et al.* (1985) proposed that in order to avoid confusion between analyses conducted at the level of cultures and analyses based at the level of individuals, we should use different but related pairs of concepts. Their suggestion was that we use the term 'allocentric' to describe a culture member who endorses collectivist values. Statistically, it is likely that such a person would be found in a collectivist culture, but the point of making the distinction is that there will also be a minority of such persons in individualist cultures. Similarly Triandis *et al.* suggest the use of 'idiocentric' to describe a culture member who endorses individualist values. The proposal is a good one, but level-appropriate terms have not yet been adopted by other researchers. Nonetheless, we shall use them in this book, even where the original authors of the studies that we cite referred to individuals as having values that were individualist or collectivist.

Unfortunately, many published studies do not provide us with the necessary data to make such distinctions, but we can be more confident of the conclusions of those which do. Leung and Bond (1989) provide fuller detail of statistical procedures that enable individual-level scores to be computed in ways that are not confounded by differences in means between different country samples. When this method was used upon the data assembled by the Chinese Culture Connection (1987), the conclusions relating to the main first factor found in that study were relatively unchanged (Bond, 1988b). This provides some assurance that the content of the culture-level factor for collectivism and the content of the individual-level idiocentrism factor do have some consistency with one another.

However, there will certainly also be divergences between the two levels of analysis. We can illustrate this by looking again at the results obtained by Schwartz (1994), in moving from his series of single-nation individual-level analyses to a characterization of nations' value profiles. Compare Figures 3.2 and 3.3: in Figure 3.2, the values 'wisdom' and 'broadmindedness' both fall within the universalism value type, indicating that there are many individuals who endorse both wisdom and broadmindness. However, in Figure 3.3, 'wisdom' forms part of the conservatism value-type, whereas 'broadmindedness' falls into the opposed value-type of intellectual autonomy. This alignment indicates that nations within which wisdom is widely esteemed are those with predominantly conservative values, whereas nations in which broadmindedness is favoured are those where intellectual autonomy is widely endorsed. There are many other examples of changing patterns of relationship as we move from the individual to the cultural level (Hofstede, 1980, Chapter 1; Leung, 1989; Shweder, 1973), so careful attention must be exercised before drawing conclusions at any one level.

A culture-level conceptual framework. This discussion of levels of analysis leaves us, the authors, and you, the reader, with a dilemma that will remain with us throughout the remainder of this book. Most of the studies we are to discuss are individual-level studies. However, the researchers who conducted them did not for the most part obtain measures of the values, beliefs, expectancies, personality types, etc. of the persons whom they studied. Most often they inferred what would be the subjects' values on the basis of country-level scores derived from Hofstede's dimensions. In discussing these studies we shall only partially be able to escape from the difficulty that this omission poses. There are two ways in which we can attempt to do so. Firstly, we can draw upon the country-level scores now available from the more recent work of Schwartz and others. Table 3.5 shows which of Schwartz's samples scored highest on each of his seven dimensions of cultural values. It is particularly interesting to note that in contrast to Hofstede's results, the strongest individualists (i.e. those highest on intellectual and affective autonomy) were Europeans rather than North Americans. The US student samples scored higher than the Europeans on the dimensions of mastery and hierarchy.

Secondly, we can rely on the probability that the best estimate of country-level dimensions of values is provided not by any one study, but by the dimensions that emerge *consistently* from all of the studies we have reviewed in this chapter, despite all the variations in subjects, measurement and timing among them. Smith and Schwartz (1997) conclude that there are two such dimensions:

1. The preferred cultural view of individual-group relations (autonomous versus embedded).
2. The preferred cultural mode of motivating responsible social behaviour and allocating resources (negotiation among equals versus acceptance of unequal hierarchical roles) (p. 103).

The autonomy versus embeddedness dimension is reminiscent of individualism–collectivism, whereas equality versus hierarchy is more reminiscent of power distance. However, whereas Hofstede's study found these two dimensions strongly intercorrelated, the differentiated view provided by more recent studies

Table 3.5 ● Samples scoring highest on each of the Schwartz country-level value domains

Value	Highest scoring samples
Conservatism	Estonians and Malays Teachers from Taiwan, Turkey and Poland
Harmony	Teachers from Italy and Finland
Egalitarian commitment	Teachers from Germany and Spain
Intellectual autonomy	Students from the Netherlands and Italy
Affective autonomy	Students from England, New Zealand and Australia
Mastery	Students from the United States Teachers from China
Hierarchy	Teachers and students from China and Zimbabwe Students from the United States

suggests that they are separate. Holding them separate enables us to broaden the conceptual framework, as shown in Table 3.6. The table introduces two new pairs of concepts, which we shall be using in discussing culture-level comparisons throughout the rest of this book. Firstly, a division is made between horizontal collectivism and vertical collectivism. While much has been written about the contrast between individualist and collectivist cultures, it is not plausible that the concept of collectivism can encompass all that we need to know about the variety of Asian, African and Latin American cultures that have been characterized as collectivist. Since the dimension of hierarchy versus equality has emerged consistently from culture-level studies, it makes sense to divide cultures in which collectivism occurs in the context of hierarchy from those in which collectivism occurs within a more egalitarian context. The Schwartz data suggest that Pacific Asian nations typically provide instances of vertical collectivist cultures, while Southern European nations are more typically horizontally collectivist. Hofstede's data suggests that Costa Rica is distinctive among Latin American nations in being horizontally collectivist.

The second paring of concepts, universalism and particularism, has not previously been much used by cross-cultural psychologists in describing the varieties of individualism. Individualism has usually been thought of as occurring within the cultural context of flat hierarchies. However, even where a society is organized on the basis of hierarchy, individuals may nonetheless devote their energies to the preservation of their interests and those with whom they choose to associate. This pattern of favouring one's immediate associates was described by Parsons and Shils (1951) as particularism. Particularism is not to be confused with collectivism. Particularists choose whom they associate with, collectivists are embedded in a network of continuing obligation. Parsons and Shils contrast particularism with universalism, a value position that asserts that all are entitled to an equal share of resources or justice. Universalism is thus similar to Schwartz's egalitarian commitment value-type and to individualism occurring within the context of low power distance.

Results of the forty-three nation analysis conducted by Smith, Dugan and Trompenaars (1996) are shown in Figure 3.4. They suggest that particularism is most distinctively endorsed in a number of Central and Eastern European states. All studies agree that what we are calling universalism and most authors call individualism is most characteristic of Northern and Western Europe, the United States, Australia and New Zealand.

Table 3.6 ● A possible classification of culture types		
Dominant value	**Embeddedness**	**Autonomy**
Hierarchy	Vertical collectivists	Particularists
Equality	Horizontal collectivists	Universalists

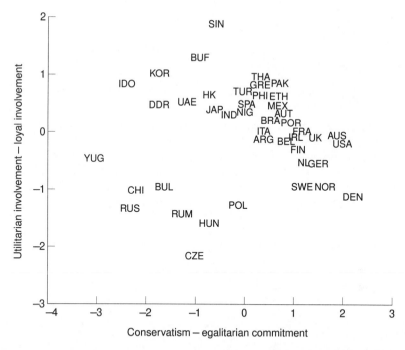

Figure 3.4 Country plot derived from the Trompenaars databank. ARG, Argentina; AUS, Australia; AUT, Austria; BEL, Belgium; BRA, Brazil; BUF, Burkina Faso; BUL, Bulgaria; CHI, China; CZE, former Czechoslovakia; DDR, former East Germany; DEN, Denmark; ETH, Ethiopia; FIN, Finland; FRA, France; GER, former West Germany; GRE, Greece; HK, Hong Kong; HUN, Hungary; IDO, Indonesia; IND, India; IRL, Ireland; ITA, Italy; JAP, Japan; KOR, South Korea; MEX, Mexico; NIG, Nigeria; NL, Netherlands; NOR, Norway; PAK, Pakistan; PHI, Philippines; POL, Poland; POR, Portugal; RUM, Rumania; RUS, former USSR; SIN, Singapore; SPA, Spain; SWE, Sweden; THA, Thailand; TUR, Turkey; UAE, United Arab Emirates; UK, United Kingdom; USA, United States of America; YUG, former Yugoslavia. *(Source: Smith et al. 1996.)*

Values and behaviour

The final question posed at the beginning of this section was whether classifications based on people's values actually provide us with the firmest basis upon which to rest cross-cultural comparisons. Many psychologists choose behaviour as the bed-rock upon which their discipline rests, but there are plenty of examples of people behaving in ways that appear at odds with their values. In order to resolve this impasse, we need to reflect upon what we mean by values and what we mean by behaviour. Values are universalistic statements about what we think is desirable or attractive. Values do not ordinarily contain statements about *how* they are to be realized. Behaviours are specific actions, which occur in a particular setting at a particular time. Box 3.5 illustrates some of the differences that emerge in the area

Box 3.5 **Universal human rights**

Doise, Clemence and Spini (1996) asked students in eighteen nations to answer eight questions about each of the thirty statements in the Universal Declaration of Human Rights. Using multidimensional scaling and cluster analysis, they found that the declaration fell into the same four segments among respondents from all nations, even though their sample included such diverse nations as Albania, Ivory Coast, Japan and the United States. Individual and culture-level analyses showed broad endorsement of the statements in the declaration. However, a more detailed study (Clemence *et al.*, 1995) conducted in France, Italy, Switzerland and Costa Rica showed wide divergences in which specific personal and governmental behaviours were seen as unacceptable. The examples below show the per centage of respondents in each country reporting that particular behaviours are unacceptable.

	France	Italy	Switzerland	Costa Rica
Government behaviours:				
War against another country	56	69	76	68
Death penalty	40	72	52	51
Expulsion of foreigners	54	30	62	41
Individual behaviours:				
Hiding an escaped convict	48	70	45	79
Denouncing a culprit	34	9	33	16
Stealing to feed someone	6	20	11	33

The differences reported cannot be explained as differences in tendency to respond to questions affirmatively, since there is no consistent trend showing any country to be more permissive of violations of human rights than the others. They most probably thus reflect real rather than artefactual differences between the cultures that were sampled in the ways that human rights are conceptualized.

of human rights, depending upon whether one focuses upon generalized statements of values or on specific behaviours.

When we think about definitions of values and of behaviour, it is apparent that the contrast has something in common with the etic–emic distinction. Schwartz and others have found that there is some etic validity to his generalizations about the range of values that humans espouse. It is hard to imagine how a similar project could be successful if it were focused upon behaviours, because the meaning of a behaviour is the meaning of the behaviour *in its context*. The wave of a hand or the giving of a kiss has no clear meaning until we specify a context. The expression of specific behaviours can perhaps best be thought of as an emic reflection of the participants' various values.

There are *some* behaviours whose meaning is relatively invariant. Bond (1991a) for instance has conducted a culture-level analysis of death rates from various types of illness and compared these with value classifications derived from the Chinese Culture Connection study. His analysis controlled statistically for level of economic development, which does of course also strongly affect the incidence of illness and death. He found for instance that deaths from myocardial infarctions were very much higher in cultural groups where people valued reputation more highly than righteousness.

However, it is not essential that we should base cross-cultural psychology on either a classification of values or on direct study of behaviour. There are further options that bridge the gap between values and behaviour. One possibility is to look at people's beliefs. Smith, Trompenaars and Dugan (1995) analyzed further data from Trompenaars' (1993) sample of forty-three nations. They examined 9,140 responses of business employees to Rotter's (1966) locus of control scale, which was designed to measure generalized expectancies as to whether events were under one's personal control or whether external factors were more potent. Smith *et al.* found that the country scores for the Rotter items defined three dimensions. Scores on the first of these differentiated nations where respondents saw themselves as having control over personal events in their lives from those where there was more emphasis on control over political events. The second dimension was defined by different beliefs about how to handle social relationships, while the third dimension was defined by beliefs about luck. These variations in what people in different nations believe are likely to affect their behaviour in ways that add additional explanatory power to the effects arising from their espoused values.

Much more specific beliefs were considered in a series of studies by Bond, Leung and Schwartz (1992) and Leung, Bond and Schwartz (1995). They proposed that differences in subjects' behaviour would be better accounted for by their *expectancies* about the outcomes of their behaviour, rather than by subjects' own values. The prediction was strongly upheld, using data from Hong Kong and Israel. One's embeddedness in national culture is thus not likely just to be a matter of having a particular set of values, but equally (or even more) a matter of knowing what outcomes are likely to arise from various actions. These action–outcome expectancies will be strongly shaped by culture.

Towards a psychological theory of culture. Teasing apart the interrelation of values, expectancies and behaviour will become an increasingly important task for the future. As Whiting (1976) pointed out, the traditional concept of culture is too broad and imprecise for scientific use; it must be 'unpacked'. For psychologists, this unpackaging takes the form of identifying constructs that relate to behaviour, such as values, motivations, beliefs, expectancies for reinforce-ment, personality traits and so forth. These constructs must be quantifiable and measured in ways that are sensitive to the various cultural backgrounds of each respondent.

The outcome of such unpackaging would be that individuals from *different* cultural groups could be located *vis-à-vis* one another in the same way as could individuals from within the *same* cultural group. So a person's cultural background would be 'unpacked' by locating that person at some point on a universally useful dimension that relates to behaviour. Different positionings on this dimension could then be used to explain differences in behaviour among typical people from different cultures, just as the positions could be used to explain differences in behaviour among people from the same cultural group (Bond, 1996b).

A case in point. An example may help here. Bond, Leung and Schwartz (1992) wanted to understand differences between Israeli and Hong Kong students in how they prefer to resolve conflicts. It was found that Israelis were more likely than the Chinese to endorse the use of arbitration, for example. In and of itself this categorical difference is not particularly illuminating. However, processes mediating the preferences for resolving conflicts had also been measured. It was found that the respondent's choice of arbitration was related to the belief that arbitration would lead to animosity reduction between the contending parties. This relationship obtained for both Israeli and Chinese respondents, indicating a culturally common process. The cultural difference that was detected in endorsing arbitration could then be explained by the finding that Israelis in general believed that arbitration was more likely to reduce animosity than did the Chinese in general. So, the same theoretical mechanism that explained variation in arbitration preferences among respondents within a culture could be shown to explain average differences between typical respondents from different cultures.

This procedure of measuring both behaviours *and* mediating processes can be extended to other domains of social behaviour. The mediating processes that are of interest will of course vary from domain to domain. Because the influence of these processes has been assessed in more than one cultural group, however, one's confidence in the potential universality of the processes will increase dramatically. The benefits of this procedure will grow stronger the more dissimilar are the cultural groups involved.

Results obtained through this approach will begin to legitimize *empirically* the attempts made by social psychologists to extend their ideas and findings beyond their traditional cultural borders of North America and Europe. The mystique of culture could then 'wither away', as it becomes replaceable by specific, defined, operationalized variables of psychological interest. Only then will the field move closer towards developing general theories of social and organizational behaviour (Triandis, 1978, 1988).

For the present, we must continue to rely on the characterizations of culture that have provided the backbone of this chapter. We shall look next at the outcomes of a variety of studies where researchers have investigated whether or not they can identify relatively universal aspects of social behaviour. If it proves to be the case that they cannot, the case is strengthened for either concentrating upon emic analyses, or else for analyzing the differences found, using the frameworks that the values researchers have provided.

Summary

Cultures are systems of shared meanings. Nations are not necessarily mono-cultural, but many modern nation-states manage their internal diversity in ways that encourage the creation of national cultures. The best conceptual frameworks currently available to guide cross-cultural research are those provided by studies of value differences. The structure of individual values shows good consistency across cultures. While preferred values vary both within and across nations, value differences across nations are sufficiently substantial that they can help us to interpret reported cultural differences. In conducting cross-cultural studies, it is essential to understand the difference between culture-level comparisons and individual-level comparisons. Culture-level classifications of values have yielded four principal culture-types: vertical collectivists, horizontal collectivists, universalists and particularists. At the individual level, the distinction between allocentrics and idiocentrics has been most influential. While value preferences have been most frequently studied, analysis of differences in beliefs and in expectancies may also be helpful.

The search for universals of social behaviour

In principle . . . there is a generalized framework that underlies the more apparent and striking facts of cultural relativity. All cultures constitute so many somewhat distinct answers to essentially the same questions posed by human biology and by the generalities of the human situation . . .

Kluckhohn, 1962

We noted in the previous chapter that psychologists have often seen their task as the identification of processes that are fundamental and universal. In this chapter we shall examine some aspects of personality and social behaviour that have been rather thoroughly examined from this etic perspective, and then draw some conclusions as to how successful this approach has been.

Some gender differences

The question as to whether there are any universal differences in the social behaviour of men and women has excited controversy, at least since the time of the classic anthropological studies of Margaret Mead (1935). Her studies showed marked variations between the three primitive societies that she studied in New Guinea in the roles attributed to men and to women. Among the Arapesh, both men and women were expected to be warm and nurturant. Among the Mundugumor, both men and women were expected to be vigorous and assertive. Among the Tchambuli, the women took care of economic activities, whereas the men were concerned with decorating themselves, dancing and gossiping.

However, more recent studies, sampling a wider range of cultures, suggest a more consistent set of gender differences. For instance, the equally famous Six Cultures Study (Whiting, 1963) found a consistent tendency to socialize girls more towards nurturance, responsibility and obedience; boys towards independence, self-reliance and achievement. This distinction between socialization for male agency and female communion (Bakan, 1966) is consistent with greater male endorsement of internal locus of control (Smith, Dugan and Trompenaars, 1997) and female endorsement of a caring morality (Stimpson, Jensen and Neff, 1992) and emotional relatedness (Kashima *et al.*, 1995) across many different cultural groups. These instrumental and expressive dimensions of socialization are separate (Hendrix and Johnson, 1985), and result in numerous consequences for adult social behaviour, as we shall discover.

Mate preferences

A great many relevant studies have been completed since these early studies, so that we now have a very substantial database against which to test propositions. Buss and his collaborators (1990), for example, conducted a study of mate preferences in thirty-seven national cultures, with a total sample of almost 9,500. Each respondent was asked to rate how important or desirable was each of eighteen qualities and to rank order a further thirteen criteria that could be used in choosing a mate. Examples of the qualities included were a dependable character, chastity and good health. The results are reported by gender (Buss, 1989) and by culture (Buss *et al.*, 1990).

The paths by which these two sets of findings were published provide an interesting example of the way in which psychology is often much more interested in universality than in variability. The variation in mate preferences accounted for by gender amounted to 2.4 per cent of the total variance. The variation accounted for by culture averaged 14 per cent. The analysis by gender was published in the widely read journal *Behavioural and Brain Sciences*, in which a sociobiological theory is advanced to account for the way in which gender differences may arise through natural selection. The theory advanced was commented upon by twenty-seven well-known discussants. It is also one of the studies featured by Baron and Byrne (1994), in fulfilment of their intention to increase coverage of cross-cultural issues. The analysis by culture, accounting for *seven times* as much variance, was published in the *Journal of Cross-Cultural Psychology*, which is read by many fewer readers.

The gender differences found were that men tended to evaluate potential mates more on the basis of youth, health and beauty, while women tended to pay more attention to earning capacity, ambition and industriousness. Buss *et al.* (1990) propose an evolutionary explanation (Kenrick, 1994) for these differences in preference. In evolutionary approaches, 'the core idea is that human psychological functioning is built upon a common genetic platform whose design is adapted to our origins. These origins are those of the "ancestral environments" of hunter-gatherers' (Wright, 1994). 'The life we live now is adapted (or maladapted) to these origins' (Nicholson, 1996, pp. 2–3). This general orientation is compatible with consistent, universal gender difference in any behavioural outcome. So, the authors propose that these differences in desired qualities exist because men seek women who are best able to produce healthy offspring, while women seek men who will be best able to care long term for them and their children (see also Sprecher, Sullivan and Hatfield, 1994). While these findings do certainly account for a small but significant proportion of the variance, focusing upon them takes attention away from the fact that in the sample as a whole men and women placed exactly the same four attributes highest on their preference list–mutual attraction, dependable character, emotional stability and maturity, and pleasing disposition. Their rankings of qualities also placed the same four items at the top–kind and understanding, intelligent, exciting and healthy.

In contrast to these uniformities between genders, there was much more substantial variance in the preferences across different national cultures. The greatest variation was found in the emphasis given to premarital chastity. Some 37 per cent of the variance on this measure was accounted for by culture. Buss *et al.* (1990) used multidimensional scaling techniques to clarify which national cultures had similar patterns of preferences. The clearest dimension to emerge was labelled by them as traditional versus modern. They suggest that it overlaps substantially with the Hofstede (1980) dimension of individualism–collectivism.

Gender stereotypes

A series of studies complementary to those of Buss has been made by Williams and Best (1982, 1990), who explored gender stereotypes in thirty different national cultures. One hundred male and female students in each country were asked to indicate whether each one of a series of adjectives on a check-list was considered in their culture to be associated with men, with women or with both equally. They found a substantial world-wide consensus about different gender roles. Men were believed to be higher on dominance, autonomy, aggression, exhibition, achievement and endurance. Women were believed to be higher on abasement, affiliation, deference, succourance and nurturance.

Best and Williams (1994) summarized these universal differences by using Osgood, Suci and Tannenbaum's (1957) three factors of affective meaning, viz. favourability, strength and activity. Using culturally specific measures of the male/female stereotypes, they found that across their twenty-five countries, the male stereotype was consistently more active and stronger, but not more favourable.

However, they were able to associate the size of these activity and strength differences with cultural variables. To quote from Best and Williams,

> the magnitude of both the strength and activity differences between the male and female stereotypes was greater in socio-economically less developed countries than in more developed countries. Strength and activity differences also tended to be greater in countries where literacy was low and the per centage of women attending the university was low. These findings suggest that economic and educational advancement may be accompanied by a reduction in the tendency to view men as stronger and more active than women. We note however that the effect was merely reduced – not eliminated. (1994, pp. 299–300)

These results for the gender stereotype may be compared to actual-self and ideal-self ratings with respect to their degree of stereotypical masculinity or femininity. Across fourteen countries, Best and Williams (1994) note that in no country were these self-concepts highly differentiated with regard to masculinity/femininity. Males' self-concepts were, of course, more masculine than were those of females, but to a much smaller degree than the stereotype differences in each country would have suggested. Also, the ideal-self was more masculine than the actual-self for *both* sexes. The size of this gender difference in ideal selves was, however, smaller than was that for actual selves. Finally, the authors note that where men's self and ideal-self ratings were relatively masculine, so were those of the women, indicating a matching principle to be operating, not a complementary principle.

As in their earlier study, Best and Williams (1994) examined the size of the masculine/feminine differences in actual- and ideal-self ratings in relation to cultural variables. Using Osgood's system for assessing total affective meaning again, they found that the self concepts of men and women were more affectively differentiated in countries lower in socio-economic development, lower in per centage of Christians, lower in per centage of women employed outside the home and studying at universities, and from more southern latitudes. There was also a +0.78 correlation with Hofstede's (1980) power distance.

This broad and careful programme of research has revealed many universals or consistencies across cultures in gender stereotypes. In addition, it has related the size of these consistent differences to dimensions of country-level variation. It appears then that variability in the differences itself has a pattern.

Generalities or detail?

The studies of gender differences illustrate a principle that will recur in other material that we shall review shortly. If we wish to make statements about universal or etic aspects of social behaviour, they need to be phrased in highly abstract ways. Conversely, if we wish to highlight the meaning of these generalizations in specific or emic ways, then we need to refer to more precisely specified events or behaviours. In this way we can find some possibility of etic statements about mate preferences and gender role differentiation. But we also find frequent examples of the ways in which these generalizations are expressed in quite different ways in different national cultures. The more detailed is the description of behaviour, the greater becomes the likelihood of finding significant variation.

For instance, the Buss study found that the second most highly desired attribute of a mate, world-wide, was dependable character. However, Christensen (1973) found very large variations in attitudes to marital infidelity in nine national cultures. The per centage of students disapproving of infidelity varied from 10 per cent in the Danish sample to 90 per cent of mid-Western Americans. Presumably the way in which Buss's and Christensen's findings are to be reconciled is to say that infidelity is thought of as being a sign of undependability in some cultures but not in others. However, this line of reasoning can be extended even further: what specific behaviour is it that is thought of as amounting to infidelity? Buunk and Hupka (1987) compared reactions to various forms of sexual behaviour by one's partner toward a third party in each of seven national cultures. It was found that in Hungary, kissing and hugging evoked strong jealousy, while dancing together in Russia, flirting in the former Yugoslavia and having sexual fantasies about another in the Netherlands were reported to be the most upsetting. If one looks at behaviours in this degree of detail, it could turn out that almost every national culture gives unique meanings to general principles.

Emotional expression

Many researchers using procedures popularized by Ekman (1972) have found that photographs of faces carefully posed to depict different social emotions can be interpreted accurately by people from many parts of the world. In the early studies (reviewed by Izard, 1980), subjects were shown a series of photographs and asked to choose which of a list of emotions each face portrayed. Results from twelve countries showed that at least six emotions could be reliably discriminated in all countries. The 'universal' emotions proved to be enjoyment, sadness, anger, disgust, surprise and fear.

Ekman, Sorenson and Friesen (1969) provided the most stringent test of the robustness of these findings, by repeating them among pre-literate societies in New Guinea. They found that the results held up, even when Americans judged New Guinean faces and New Guineans judged American faces. Ekman *et al.* (1987) improved their design even further by asking for ratings of the intensity with which each emotion was portrayed. Sampling across ten countries, they again found high consensus on which of the six emotions was being portrayed. They also found agreement on which emotions were the most intense, and on variations in the intensity of the six emotions.

Decoding emotion

These studies are frequently cited as an instance of a universal ability to decode emotions in the same manner. Some caution is required before such a conclusion could be accepted, however. Firstly, in these studies subjects are provided with a list of names for emotions from which to choose. Furthermore, the list of named emotions all derived from English language names for emotions, translated into the subjects' languages. Translation of such emotion words is vulnerable to the challenge of inequivalence (van Goozen and Frijda, 1993). Although the results show that choices are far above the level that would be achieved by guessing randomly, the 'imposed-etic' provision of the names for emotions makes the task very much easier. Izard (1971) also used photographs, but asked subjects in the United States, the United Kingdom, France and Greece to describe the emotions portrayed in their own words. The per centages of responses that the researchers judged to be correct in these circumstances were very much lower, and they varied sharply among the different emotions. Joy and surprise were consistently recognized, while interest and shame were the least identifiable.

Russell (1994) reviewed the mass of extant literature and challenged the use of 'forced choice response format[s], within-subject design, [and] preselected photographs of posed facial expressions' (p. 102) which inflate accuracy figures. He criticized the reliance on a standard method and encouraged researchers to pay more attention to the ecological validity of the stimuli, methods and measures used in such decoding research. He concluded that much more work is needed before any universality thesis could be supported.

Russell (1991) argued that, 'Rather than ask whether a given culture agrees with one preformulated hypothesis, we might more usefully ask how members of that culture conceptualize emotions and facial behaviour' (p. 137). In this regard Markus and Kitayama (1991) report on Japanese studies in which subjects were asked to rate the similarity between all possible pairs of twenty different emotions specified by the Japanese language. While the majority of emotions could be mapped in a manner that replicated the relations found in similar English language studies, some could not. These were emotions that were differentiated along a dimension measuring engagement versus disengagement in a social relationship. They argue that this dimension of engagement/disengagement is salient in a culture, such as that of Japan, which emphasizes interdependence and harmony (Kitayama, Markus and Kurokowa, 1995). A thorough review of how emotions are conceptualized in various cultures led Russell (1994) to conclude, that, '. . . people of different cultures and speaking different languages categorize the emotions somewhat differently. The boundaries around the domain appear to vary, as do the divisions within the domain' (p. 444).

In generalizing about the recognition of emotion then, we should bear in mind the likelihood that we are speaking only about the recognition of those emotions that prove to have relatively high cultural generality.

Matsumoto (1989) reanalyzed the results of several of the early studies of facial emotion recognition, in a way that relates them more closely to the theme of this book. He computed correlations between the per centage of subjects in each of fifteen countries correctly identifying each emotion, and scores for those countries on Hofstede's (1980) four dimensions. He found that happiness was more readily identified in national cultures that are high on individualism and low on power distance. Sadness on the other hand was more identifiable in collectivist cultures. Recently, Schimmack (1996) has found that fear and sadness are more accurately identified by persons from cultures high in uncertainty avoidance. Once again, we discover that the variability within a generalization may itself be explicable.

Matsumoto (1989) was not able to provide a clear explanation of why this particular pattern of differences should be found, although one could speculate. However, in a further study, Matsumoto (1992) compared the ability of US and Japanese judges to recognise six emotions. He used faces of both nationalities and both genders, showing real rather than posed emotions. His American subjects proved significantly better at identifying anger, disgust, fear and sadness, whereas respondents from both nationalities did equally well at recognizing happiness and surprise. Matsumoto concluded that the Japanese were less good at identifying negative emotions because it is socially less desirable to express such emotions in Japan than in the United States. The Japanese judges did better at judging female faces than male faces, which is consistent with somewhat greater tolerance for the expression of emotion by Japanese women compared with men.

This research points the way toward more fruitful research in this area. Rather than considering solely the recognition of facial expressions across cultures, what is needed is a careful comparison across cultural groups of each of the stages entailed in the experience of an emotion (Mesquita and Frijda, 1992). We must consider what triggers the emotion, how it is experienced and whether or not it is shared with others. What the early studies established is that there is some generality in the manner in which certain facial emotional expressions can be *decoded* in different cultures. Of equal or greater interest is the question of whether there are differences in the frequency with which these emotions are *actually experienced and displayed* in different national cultures. While the decoding studies can tell us something about universal, biologically rooted processes which may underlie certain types of emotion, studies of experience and display can tell us in what ways culture may channel these processes.

Experiencing emotion

Scherer and others undertook a survey of reported emotions in twenty-seven countries (Wallbot and Scherer, 1986). In each country, students and young professionals were asked to report on naturally occurring emotions. In the sample as a whole it was found that anger and joy were consistently reported as the most frequent emotions. However, there were significant variations across samples in the frequency, intensity and duration of reported emotions.

Scherer, Wallbot and Summerfield (1986) reported that differences across the eight European countries included in the overall study were less than expected. Unfortunately, the differences found are reported qualitatively and not related to theoretical models such as that of Hofstede. However, Gudykunst, Ting-Toomey and Chua (1988) reanalyzed some of these findings in terms of Hofstede scores for the relevant countries. They examined the situations in each national culture that were most frequently reported to trigger the emotions of enjoyment, sadness, fear and anger. Even within the relatively homogeneous sample of European data, substantial differences were found. Fear, for example, was associated with *novel situations* in cultures that were high on masculinity but low on power distance and uncertainty avoidance. Gudykunst *et al.* argue that this finding is consistent with the Hofstede perspective, since cultures that are high on power distance and uncertainty avoidance will have developed well-established procedures that would reduce the fearfulness, indeed the likelihood, of novel situations.

A comparison of the American and Japanese data deriving from this same project is reported by Matsumoto *et al.* (1988). They found that, compared with

Japanese students, US students reported emotions that lasted longer, were more intense, and were accompanied by more bodily symptoms. The US students also described themselves as reacting more positively to the emotions they described, and expressing more verbal reactions to them. In contrast to the European study, these findings not only suggest that different triggers to emotion occur in different cultures, but also that Americans actually react more emotionally than do Japanese, in general (see also Dion, in press).

Kitayama, Markus and Kurokawa (1995) distinguish the types of emotion experienced. With students from collectivist Japan the 'interpersonally engaged emotions (e.g., friendly feelings, feelings of indebtedness) were experienced more frequently than disengaged emotions (e.g., pride, anger)' (p. 2). With students from individualistic America, positive emotions were experienced much more frequently than negative emotions. These contrasting patterns of emotion-experiencing were explained as arising from the different requirements for effective functioning in collectivist as opposed to individualistic cultural systems.

Whether or not one accepts such a conclusion must depend upon whether one thinks the Americans and Japanese were equally forthright in describing their emotions. In cross-cultural comparisons, it is difficult to disentangle reports of emotions from cultural display rules as to what emotions may be expressed and when, even to supposedly neutral researchers.

Emotional display and the 'inscrutable oriental'

Westerners have long stereotyped Japanese and other East Asians as 'inscrutable'. A much discussed but unpublished study by Friesen (1972) illustrates how the results of Matsumoto *et al.* (1988) might be explained. Friesen showed short films to Japanese and American students, either when they were on their own, or when there was a 'scientist' present. The film presented was either a stress-inducing film about body mutilation or a neutral film. The reactions of the film watchers were themselves filmed as they watched. When they viewed the films alone, both Japanese and Americans registered similar reactions of disgust as they watched the body mutilation film. However when the scientist was present, the Japanese no longer indicated disgust, but were found to smile more instead. Display rules about how to behave in the presence of an authority can thus override more spontaneous emotions. It is possible that the reports of emotions by the Japanese in the Matsumoto *et al.* study could have been affected by similar factors. In other words, we still have only rather partial evidence that persons in some countries *experience* more emotion than others, but have much stronger evidence that display rules vary from culture to culture.

Gudykunst *et al.* (1988) undertook further re-analyses of the European data that bear upon the matter of display rules. They found that both verbal and non-verbal reactions to experienced emotions were significantly stronger in national cultures high on individualism. This finding is consistent with the Matsumoto *et al.* (1988) finding, since Hofstede (1980) locates the United States much higher on individualism than Japan. In a similar way, Argyle *et al.* (1986) found that rules restraining the social expression of anger and distress were more strongly endorsed in Japan and Hong Kong, which score higher on collectivism than in Italy or the United Kingdom, which score higher on individualism.

Almost all the data on emotional expression in collectivist cultures that we have so far considered are drawn from East Asian cultures. We need therefore to check whether our conclusions hold up in other collectivist cultures. Using data from Costa Rica and the United States, Stephan, Stephan and De Vargas (1996) confirmed their prediction that the Costa Ricans were less comfortable expressing negative emotions. Furthermore, Mandal, Bryden and Bulman-Fleming (1996) found that Indians reacted more negatively when confronted with negative emotional displays than did Canadians. It may be the case that when negative emotions are activated in persons from collectivist cultures, they are transformed into the socially more acceptable emotions of shame (Kitayama, Markus and Matsumoto, 1995) or sorrow (Kornadt *et al.*, 1992).

The data on emotional expression are thus rather clear. The decoding of emotional expressions has some generality, but our experience and expression of emotions is much more culturally bounded. People in individualist, low-power distance cultures may be more reactive and expressive because in such cultures there is a greater need for such cues in guiding our reactions to one another. In collectivist cultures, role and context will provide a greater share of the necessary cues. Particularly important in such cultures will be avoidance of experiencing or expressing emotions that may disrupt social harmony (Bond, 1993).

Event appraisal and emotions

Ellsworth (1994) has provided an elegant middle way between the opposing positions that emotion is culturally constituted or that emotion is biologically based, by integrating theory and research on appraisal theories of emotion. In her view,

> Emotions consist of patterned processes of *appraisal* of one's relation to the environment along specified dimensions, such as novelty, valence, certainty, control, attribution of agency, and consistency with social norms, along with associated physiological responses and action tendencies. (p. 45, emphasis added)

Research indicates that, within a given culture, a particular emotion arises from a particular pattern of appraisals (Smith and Ellsworth, 1985). So, how the perceiver appraises the situation determines which emotion is activated. In addition, there is now considerable evidence to suggest that the dimensions used to assess emotion-arousing situations are identical across cultures (e.g. Gehm and Scherer, 1988; Mauro, Sato and Tucker, 1992). Ellsworth concludes,

> Attention to changing conditions; a sense of pleasure or distaste; a sense of uncertainty (or certainty); the perception of an obstacle; the sense of being in control or out of control; the attribution of agency; a sense of the likely praise,

Box 4.1 **A clash of display rules**

In the interchange between Chan and Mrs Robertson, Chan gave no direct expression to his feelings in Mrs Robertson's presence. When talking to his sister, he expressed some qualified distress, but the reaction was still fairly muted by Western standards. In contrast, Mrs Robertson did express some of her irritation directly, both by way of what she said, but also through a changing tone of voice, sighs and various facial expressions. However, she was much more forthright when discussing the episode afterwards with her department chairman. Both parties had adhered to the display rules of their respective cultures, and most probably neither knew how distressed the other was. Chan's feeling was more likely shame, Robertson's anger.

censure, or ridicule of one's group; and an ultimate judgment of the value or fitness of what has happened – these [dimensions of appraisal] turn up with remarkable consistency in the emotional worlds of different cultures. (p. 30)

Culture then exercises a decisive influence on the emotion experienced by shaping how a given event is interpreted or appraised. So, if one is socialized to believe that one could have controlled a negative outcome, one might feel guilty. If different cultural training led one to perceive that exercising control was impossible, then one might instead feel sad. Culture will also shape whether people evaluate the resultant emotional feeling as socially acceptable or not. If not, then this emergent appraisal may itself help transmute the emotion, say from shame to anger or vice versa (Kitayama, Markus and Kurokawa, 1995). Finally, cultures will influence the way in which the emotion is displayed and responded to in a given situation (Mesquita and Frijda, 1992). Some cultures, for example the Chinese, may value moderation in the expression of any emotion, believing any departure from the mean to have negative consequences for physical health (Bond, 1993). Others, for instance Latin American cultures, favour the expression of positive, but not negative emotions (Triandis *et al.*, 1984).

The appraisal approach thus uses universal dimensions of situation appraisal to explain the experience of emotions. Where the resultant pattern of appraisal is the same, the emotional feeling will also be identical. However, culture is likely to influence both the appraisal process and the expression of the resulting emotion. The observed emotional life of people from different cultural traditions is thus likely to be different even in apparently identical situations.

Personality traits

A variety of personality researchers have considered the question of whether particular personality traits or groups of traits and their relationships are found universally. This interest has frequently involved taking a personality measure first developed in the United States and testing whether it has predictive validity else-where. For instance, Kelley *et al.* (1986) compared those who scored high and low on Rotter's (1966) external locus of control scale. This measure assesses the degree to which one believes that various types of events are outside one's personal control. In the United States, those who believe in an external locus of control have been found also to score high on a chronic self-destructiveness scale, as well as on reports of heavy drinking, excessive smoking and dangerous driving. Kelley *et al.* asked students in Hong Kong, India, Venezuela and the United States to complete both questionnaires. It was found that in India and Hong Kong, but not in Venezuela, those scoring high on external control also scored high on chronic self-destructiveness. However, no check was made on whether the chronic self-destructiveness scale was a valid predictor of behaviour outside the United States, so it is difficult to interpret the result of this imposed-etic study.

A clearer result was obtained by Evans, Palsane and Carrere (1987), who used the measure of Type A personality (Glass, 1977). This identifies the type of person who is competitive, aggressive and compulsively active. They found that in India as in the United States, Type A bus drivers had more accidents. In India, Type A drivers also blew their horns more often, overtook more often and braked more frequently. This illustration of cross-cultural predictive validity despite the use of an imposed-etic measure is encouraging, but we need to look at more systematic tests done in a wider range of countries.

A more basic concern involves discovering whether the pattern of personality variation itself is universal. That is, do the various components of personality relate to one another in the same way across cultural groups? Once that issue has been addressed, researchers can start comparing the strength of personality traits in people from different cultures and to explore universal predictors and conse-quences of these personality traits (e.g., McCrae, Costa and Yik, 1996).

Extraversion–introversion

Eysenck and Eysenck (1982) put forward the view that their personality model has cross-cultural validity, on the basis of the use of their personality questionnaires by many researchers in twenty-five countries. The Eysenck model specifies three separate personality dimensions – introversion–extraversion, neuroticism–stability and psychoticism – each of which they argue has a biological basis. The first of these is a particularly interesting personality dimension from our point of view, since we might expect that an introvert would tend to stay with established membership groups and hence endorse allocentric values, while an extravert would enjoy meeting new people and hence endorse idiocentric values. In fact, a measure of idiocentric self-construal (see Chapter 5) is predicted by a measure of extro-version. Allocentrism is not, however, predicted by introversion (Kwan, Bond and Singelis, 1997).

The evidence for cross-cultural validity put forward by Eysenck and his associates is based upon the results of separate factor analyses of responses to his questionnaire in each country. They report that closely similar factors emerge in all the countries where it has been used. Eysenck's conclusions have been challenged by Bijnen, Van der Net and Poortinga (1986), who argue that the statistical tests used to judge the similarity of factor structures are unreliable. Bijnen *et al.* were able to show that they could in some cases detect an equally high level of similarity between sets of numbers that had been generated randomly by a computer. Eysenck (1986) contested this conclusion, citing further statistical analyses, but Bijnen and Poortinga (1988) cast doubt on these analyses also. It appears that the tests used continue to show an apparently 'good' match between two data sets even when up to eighteen out of twenty-one questionnaire item responses have been replaced by random data.

The doubts cast upon Eysenck's analyses do not of course imply that extraversion or other personality traits do not have some etic generality. This remains perfectly possible, but alternative research methods are likely to be needed to test whether or not they do. The Eysenck Personality Questionnaire was originally devised in the United Kingdom and its use in many other countries falls into Berry's (1969) category of imposed etic. The data from other countries are tested to see whether they fit the original UK pattern. Munro (1986) summarizes a decade of research with the Eysenck Personality Questionnaire and other personality tests such as the Rotter scale in Zimbabwe. He found that in his samples some questionnaire items correlated poorly with the intended dimensions. Munro concludes that a better strategy is to start by building an emically valid questionnaire within any one national culture (e.g. Cheung*et al.*, 1998; Tsuji *et al.*, 1996), and then examining convergences with Western-based personality theories.

Starting from the emic

A series of studies from the Philippines shows how this strategy can be fruitfully applied in the field of personality research. Church and Katigbak (1988) asked Filipino students to provide descriptions of the qualities they would expect to find in healthy and unhealthy persons. A scale on which to describe one's own personality was constructed from the items provided. This indigenous scale was then presented to further students, along with several well-known US personality measures. It was found that the responses to the scale did not correlate very well with the US measures, and furthermore that the items on the US scales did not cluster together for Filipino students in the way that they had done for American students.

Thus far we have a somewhat dispiriting set of results, which might imply that all we can hope to do is to make emic studies within cultures and give up trying to find dimensions with etic validity. However, Church and Katigbak (1989) report further analyses that were based upon a thorough implementation of Berry's view as to what is the appropriate way to link emic and etic findings. They argue that rather than use the same standard questionnaires in each country, one should first look at the inter-relations *among* the emic data sets from within each culture. The inter-relations found can then be compared with proposed etic generalizations derived from broader theorizing. In this case the etic generalization that they drew on was the proposal of Costa and McCrae (1985) that the various traits proposed by Western researchers can be reduced to five major dimensions of personality. These are identified as extraversion, agreeableness, conscientiousness, emotional stability and openness to experience.

Using the character traits provided by their Filipino subjects, Church and Katigbak (1989) tested whether these traits also would be clustered by Filipinos into similar groupings. Several tests were used, in one of which subjects were asked to sort the traits into groups of those that 'go together'. In a second study, subjects were asked to rate their fellow students, and their ratings were then factor-analyzed. Each of these methods supported the cross-cultural validity of the Costa and McCrae 'Big Five' personality dimensions. After further data collections, Katigbak, Church and Akamine (1996) report that, 'all of the Big Five . . . higher order dimensions were represented by the Philippine dimensions, and none of the Philippine dimensions were [sic] largely culture-specific.' It is interesting to note that Eysenck's dimensions do themselves overlap with some of the Big Five. The Church and Katigbak studies thus support Eysenck's views, but do so through a more cross-culturally sensitive research procedure.

In a parallel series of studies in Hong Kong, Yang and Bond (1990) found that the Big Five dimensions of personality as measured by Norman's (1963) imposed etic instrument correlated well with four out of five factors derived from Chinese person perception scales, but not in a one-to-one fashion. The fifth dimension appeared functionally similar to that of the American, but required assessment in an emically sensitive manner.

Studies supporting the generality of the Big Five factors have also been reported from Israel, Germany and Japan (Digman, 1990). More recently, McCrae and Costa (1997) have reported that very similar structures to the Big Five have been found in nations representing six different language families (as spoken in Germany, Portugal, Israel, China, Korea and Japan) using their NEO PI-R measure (see also Paunonen *et al.*, 1996). The fact that the Big Five are proving to be replicable across a broad range of cultures does not of course exclude the possibility that other dimensions having only local importance may be detected. For instance, some suggestive evidence for culture-specific dimensions in China is available from Cheung *et al.* (1998). They found evidence for an additional factor, Chinese tradition, beyond the Big Five dimensions as defined by the NEO PI-R. This indigenous factor adds predictive power over and above the Big Five dimensions in explaining, for example, filial piety (Zhang and Bond, 1996).

Evaluating the Big Five

This series of studies suggests that there is considerable cross-cultural generality in the way in which personality traits are clustered together into dimensions by respondents who are asked to rate questionnaire items about their own or others' personality. This need not surprise us, since as we saw earlier there is also some generality in ability to recognize expressed emotions, which presumably provide the basis for many personality judgements (e.g. Borkenau and Liebler, 1992). Many personologists conclude that this similarity in personality structure supports an evolutionary, biological basis for the organization of personality (Buss, 1991; Hogan, 1996).

Similarity in structure does not, of course, mean similarity in importance. Church's series of emic studies of Filipino personality also led him to discuss which personality concepts were most central to Filipino culture. The concept of '*pakikisama*', which translates as 'going along with or conceding to the in-group' has often been identified as particularly important. Church points out the similarity between this concept and emic concepts reported by other researchers into societies that are as highly collectivist as the Philippines. He notes in particular the concept of '*sympatia*' which is given great importance in many Hispanic cultures and '*philotimo*' within Greek culture. In a similar way Filipino emphasis on dependence and loyalty to superiors has parallels with the Japanese concept of '*amae*', which describes the process of being nurtured by a powerful superior and being reciprocally obligated to him (Church, 1987). Thus, while Church's results indicate that Filipinos are able to perceive one another in ways that are consistent with an etic formulation of the 'Big Five' personality traits, they may give more importance to one of those big five, namely agreeableness. Members of many other high-collectivist, high-power distance cultures may do likewise, as Bond and Forgas (1984) found when comparing Australians and Hong Kong Chinese. The Chinese weighted agreeableness information more strongly than the Australians when developing intentions to behave in an associative, friendly way towards the target (see also Chang, Lin and Kohnstamm, 1994; Watkins and Gerong, 1997, on the salience of conscientiousness in Chinese culture).

If the 'Big Five' personality traits do underlie personality judgements in a wide variety of national cultures, then it becomes important to examine how far the Big Five correspond with the dimensions of personal values identified by Schwartz (1992) which we have been using to support Hofstede's characterization of different cultures. Presumably one's values reflect one's needs, which in turn arise from the socialization process in each cultural group (Bilsky and Schwartz, 1994). Bilsky and Schwartz found that in Israel the two higher order dimensions of extroversion and emotionality located themselves as hypothesized on the Schwartz value circumplex: extroversion in hedonism and self-direction; emotionality, undefined. Luk and Bond (1993) used the NEO PI-R and, as Table 4.1 shows, found that all the Big Five dimensions were related to Schwartz's (1992) value domains among Hong Kong Chinese respondents. Particularly noteworthy is the strong positive association of agreeableness with the self-transcendent value domains and the negative association with the self-enhancing value domains. Multicultural research of this sort is needed in order to assess the universality of these various linkages, as some may be specific to Israeli or Chinese culture.

Table 4.1 ● Schwartz's value domains and the Big Five measures of personality				
Schwartz's value domains	Neuroticism	Extroversion	Openness to experience	Agreeable-ness	Conscientious-ness
Self-direction					−0.23
Stimulation		0.25			
Hedonism				−0.37	−0.20
Achievement				−0.40	
Power	0.20		−0.26	−0.36	
Security					
Conformity				0.29	0.20
Tradition		−0.20		0.40	
Benevolence		0.24		0.45	
Universalism			0.37		

Only correlations 0.20 or above are shown. Source: from Luk and Bond (1993), with permission.

Self-efficacy

The concept of self-efficacy was introduced by Bandura (1977, 1986) as a central component in his social-cognitive theory of behaviour. It refers to a person's belief that he or she can perform a particular activity or, more generally, succeed in performing the various activities he or she may undertake. A person's sense of self-efficacy may be derived from personal experiences of mastery, vicarious experiences from observing others, verbal persuasion by knowledgeable others, or from physiological feedback.

Self-efficacy is a central concept in human agency:

> People's beliefs in their personal efficacy influence their aspirations and the outcomes they expect for their effort, what courses of action they choose to pursue, how much effort they will invest in activities, how long they will persevere in the face of obstacles and failure experiences and their resiliency following setbacks. People do not regard options in domains of low perceived efficacy worth considering whatever benefits they may hold . . . Regardless of the sphere of activity, a high sense of efficacy pays off in performance accomplishments and personal well-being. (Bandura, 1996, p. 105)

Such strong claims are based upon extensive research, some of it performed outside the United States. For instance, Schwartzer has developed a measure of general self-efficacy, showing high levels of consistency and reliability in a variety of cultures (Schwartzer, 1993). Schwartzer *et al.* (1997) report that self-efficacy scores correlate positively with optimism and negatively with depression and anxiety among students in Costa Rica and Germany. In Hong Kong it correlates positively with optimism about handling the 1997 transition to Chinese rule.

Bandura (1997) has pointed out that, 'Because efficacy beliefs involve self-referent processes, self-efficacy is sometimes inappropriately equated with individualism.' He argues, however, that,

> Personal efficacy is valued not because of reverence for individualism but because a strong sense of personal efficacy is vital for successful adaptation and change regardless of whether they are achieved individually or by group members putting their personal capabilities to the best collective use. (p. 32)

In other words, Bandura sees a sense of self-efficacy as a universally important component of individual and group functioning.

This universality of function is illustrated in Earley's (1993, 1994) work on social loafing, which was discussed in Chapter 2. His 1993 study examined social loafing effects across collective and individualistic cultural groups when persons worked alone, with ingroup or with outgroup members. He found that,

> The performance of individualists who thought they were working in an ingroup or an outgroup was lower than the performance of individualists working alone, whereas collectivists' performance was lower in an individual or outgroup context than in an ingroup context. (p. 319)

These same outcomes, however, could be explained by measures that Earley also collected of how efficacious the participants believed they (and their group) were in these various conditions, *regardless of the participant's national culture*.

Despite this cultural generality in self-efficacy effects, culture influences how efficacy beliefs are moulded, the activities that self-efficacy serves, and 'the social arrangements through which they are best manifested' (Bandura, 1996, p. 106). Those from collectivist societies 'display lower personal and group efficacy and low productivity when they have to perform in a culturally mixed group' (p. 106). Again, we can discover a pattern of cultural difference against a backdrop of universal similarity in function (see also Oettingen *et al.*, 1994).

Aggression

Another aspect of personality to have received a good deal of attention from cross-cultural researchers is aggressiveness. In terms of personality traits, we can assume aggressiveness to be negatively related to Big Five agreeableness and also to the angry hostility facet of neuroticism as operationalized by Costa and McCrae (1992). However, it has quite often been thought of as a behaviour rather than as a more consistent personality trait, so it is appropriate to consider it separately. Faced with a great diversity of definitions, Segall *et al.* (1990) propose that we define aggression simply as 'any behaviour by a person that inflicts harm upon another'.

In his review of the literature, Geen (1994) summarized the (mostly US) research on aggression into a two-step model: first, some provocation increases negative affect. Second, this affect elicits a tendency to fight or to flee. Which option is exercised will depend on '(1) the person's genetic endowment, (2) prior conditioning and learning, and (3) the recognition of aspects of the situation that facilitate or inhibit aggression' (p. 3).

The latter two points are summarized using an expectancy-value framework (Feather, 1988): 'Aggression that is rewarded produces an increased expectancy that such behaviour will be useful in the future under similar conditions and also enhances the perceived value of the behaviour' (p. 5). So, for example, men perceive their aggression as instrumental, whereas women perceive their aggression as lack of control (Campbell, 1993). These gender differences in the perception of aggression's usefulness and value may be a factor in the universal finding that males are more aggressive than females (Barry, Child and Bacon, 1959; Whiting and Edwards, 1973). This general framework will be useful in examining the topics of homicide and insults.

Murder

Archer and Gartner (1984) lamented the absence of a comparative, data-based perspective in studies of crime and violence. 'The empirical poverty and provincialism of the field' (p. 5) makes it impossible to draw causal inferences based on controlled observations which allow one to generalize across societies and historical periods. Such comparative research is indeed difficult, plagued as it is by problems of under-reporting and the use of different indicators. Where these issues of access and data quality can be addressed, the yield is encouraging.

While a number of theorists argue that aggression is instinctually or biologically rooted, they must contend among other things with extremely large variations in expressed aggression among the different cultures of the world. The murder rate for instance is currently seven times higher in the United States than in Britain, and in South Africa it is thirty-five times higher. At the very least, we must argue that aggression is channelled in different ways within different cultures.

An attempt to detect the uniformities between cultures that affect murder rates is reported by Landau (1984). Landau predicted that murder rates would rise in countries where stress was increasing and social support systems were failing. He compared reported statistics for murder and other crimes for thirteen countries over a decade. As a measure of stress he used rate of inflation and as a measure of failing social support he relied upon the ratio of divorces to marriages. The predictions were supported in all countries except Japan, where he found a rising suicide rate rather than a rising murder rate.

It is tempting to give a psychological explanation to these culture-level findings. So, one could argue with Landau (1984) that higher stress and lower social support induce frustration which leads to aggression. Or, one could argue with Geen (1994) that they lead to more negative affect, the first of the two steps in his model. Regardless, taking such an approach commits the 'aggregative fallacy', i.e.

'the error of assuming that associations found among events when one has studied aggregates will also be found – to the same degree or in the same direction – when one studies individuals' (Nettler, 1984, p. 101) or, in the terms we discussed in Chapter 3, the ecological fallacy. It is, of course, very difficult to study homicide except by aggregating across social units because the event is so rare. When we do study aggregated scores, however, then our results are about those units (cities, provinces, countries) rather than about individuals. The findings may be suggestive about psychological processes, but not necessarily. Culture-level and individual-level phenomena need to be linked.

This is by no means impossible to accomplish. For example, societal differences in homicide are correlated with mean temperature ratings, with hotter and more humid climates showing higher murder rates (Robbins, DeWalt and Pelto, 1972). Anderson and Anderson (1996) have shown the same result for states within the United States. At the individual level, Anderson, Deuser and DeNeve (1995) showed that higher temperatures increased hostile affect, hostile cognitions and physiological arousal but decreased positive affect. They hypothesize that these outcomes bias the processing of social events in a hostile direction. Extending this process to a larger social arena, one could then easily explain the higher overall homicide rates in hotter climates.

A history of war is another important culture-level variable. Archer and Gartner (1984) analyzed homicide data from combatant and non-combatant nations from World War 2. They found an increase for the post-war homicide rates in the combatant nations, regardless of whether they had won or lost the war, regardless of whether their economies had improved or not, and regardless of age or gender groups of the perpetrators. They concluded,

> The one model that appears to be fully consistent with the evidence is the legitimation of violence model, which suggests that the presence of authorized or sanctioned killing during war has a residual effect on the level of homicide in peacetime society. (p. 96)

These results are compatible with those of Ember and Ember (1994a). They studied 186 societies from the ethnographic records of the Human Relations Area Files (a reference bank of anthropological data) and concluded that war was a major cause of increased internal homicide. Their multiple regression analyses showed that 'socialization for aggression in boys in late childhood predicts higher rates of homicide and assault' (p. 620). This socialization for male aggression was a likely consequence, not itself a cause, of war.

War was found to be more likely when a society had a history of uncontrollable disasters that reduced food supplies. Warfare then became an expansionary activity to ensure future security against hunger (Ember and Ember, 1994b). Environmental protection and careful management of food supplies become even more pressing concerns (World Commission on Environment and Development, 1987) in light of these conclusions about war and homicide.

Socialization for aggression appears to be supported by a society's legal institutions. Cohen (1996) argued that certain states in the United States had developed cultures favouring violence for self-protection because of their frontier heritage. Southern states had, in addition, an enhanced culture of violence because of their history of disciplining, controlling and punishing Black slaves. These cultural legacies are reflected in laws relating to the owning and use of guns, to the defence of self and property, to spousal abuse, to corporal and capital punishment. These weaker legal constraints provide a backdrop for attitudes more approving of violence than are found in other states (Cohen and Nisbett, 1994). Both legally and socially, then, higher rates of homicide in the South and West may be sustained by the lower expectancies for punishment accorded such crimes (Geen, 1994).

Knauft (1987) has pointed out that norms of interpersonal harmony characterize many societies, such as the Gebusi of New Guinea or the !Kung of South Africa, or the Central Eskimo, which nonetheless have remarkably high homicide rates. These are highly egalitarian, decentralized groupings little studied by social scientists. Socialization theories for violence do not seem applicable in these societies, given their cultural norms of peaceableness. Instead, violence tends to flare up because of male disputes over women. In the absence of status markers among men to organize sexual access to women and against a normative structure emphasizing harmony, these disputes escalate tempestuously. Murder often results. Surprisingly, 'this violence . . . is perceived as outside the realm of cultural control altogether or else as functioning to support commonality and egalitarianism' (p. 478). Knauft's analysis of rarely studied cultures alerts us to the potential myopia of theories about aggression derived only from studying people in more complex social systems (see also Keuschel, 1988).

Insults

North American experimental research has indicated that even at the individual level, aggression does not in fact inevitably follow frustration (Berkowitz, 1989). This conclusion opens the way for investigating a host of cultural influences upon whether and how aggression is expressed. Although murder would no doubt be included in just about everyone's definition of aggression, there is much more scope for differences across cultures in interpreting whether or not different forms of more minor harm do or do not constitute aggression. Strong criticism from one's boss, for instance, might be judged much less aggressive in a high power distance culture than in a low power distance culture. Bond et al. (1985b) tested this idea in a study of students in Hong Kong and the United States. Students were asked to evaluate an episode in which a manager insults either a superior or a subordinate, who is either inside or outside their own department. The judgements made by the Chinese students were much more dependent upon who it was that was receiving the insult than were the US judgements. The Chinese saw the insult delivered to a subordinate within one's own department as less illegitimate, and saw less reason to dislike the superior who delivered it. The Chinese also differentiated more between insults to in-group members and out-group members. This is likely to be related to the higher collectivism of Hong Kong compared with the United States. In fact, Chinese often label in-group insults as 'scoldings', a description that accords them more legitimacy.

Considerable anthropological writing has focused on 'cultures of honour'. In such cultures a critical remark can quickly provoke counter-attack and retribution out of all proportion to someone from a different culture. Such violent counter-attacks will then be justified by a whole ideology about the need to protect oneself, one's honour or one's reputation (see also Felson, 1978).

Anthropologists have noted that cultures of honour are associated with herding economies (Peristiany, 1965) where the frequent absence of legal redress for theft meant that herders had to be socialized to condone and undertake violence against thieves. Cohen and Nisbett (1994) have used this logic to explain the greater endorsement of some forms of violence in the southern United States and its higher levels of gun ownership and homicide. They have also shown that contemporary descendants of these immigrant herdsmen are more likely than their compatriots in the northern United States to react to an insult as a threat to their masculine reputation, to be physiologically aroused, to be cognitively more primed for aggression, and to counter-attack or assert dominance (Cohen et al., 1996). This 'hyper-sensitivity' is sustained through legal codes and socialization practices, even though its economic basis in herding has long since passed.

Expressing or suppressing aggression

A number of other studies support the view that whether or not negative affect leads to aggressive behaviour has a good deal to do with social norms concerning aggression in a given cultural setting. Whether one is willing to commit aggressive acts oneself will also depend upon how much social support there is for such actions. We saw in Chapter 2 that obedience in the Milgram experiment was shown in several countries to be heavily influenced by whether others joined in the process of administering shocks or refused to do so.

Some researchers have argued that groups are always more aggressive than individuals. Jaffe and Yinon (1983) in Israel, for instance, replicated US findings that groups were more willing to administer shocks to subjects in an experiment than were individuals. However, Rabbie (1982), summarizing a series of experiments on aggression done in the Netherlands, concludes only that groups are *more sure* of themselves, as we might expect following the discussion of group polarization in Chapter 2. Where norms favour aggression, a group will indeed be more aggressive than individuals, but where norms favour restraint, it will be less so. We thus find a broad range of evidence that both the expression of aggression and the form in which it is expressed varies with the social context, as has also been found within North America. This conclusion is consistent with the cross-cultural variation in display rules for other types of emotion, which we considered earlier in this chapter.

Pro-social behaviour

A contrast with studies of aggression is provided by studies of people's willingness to help one another in situations where some distress or difficulty has arisen. Studies have usually been conducted in public places, and involve asking for directions, asking for small change from a larger denomination coin or the staging of some minor emergency, such as dropping something on the street. Studies in the United States, Canada, Australia and Turkey have all shown that help is more forthcoming in rural districts than in large cities. In the Netherlands, however, helpfulness was equally high in all city districts and in rural areas, and Korte, Ympa and Toppen (1975) attribute this outcome to a strong norm for 'civility' in Dutch society. In Turkey, less help was given in suburban districts, whereas elsewhere it was lowest in the city centre (Korte and Ayvalioglu, 1981).

Rather few studies have been reported that make direct comparisons of pro-social behaviours using identical procedures in different countries. Hedge and Yousif (1992) selected the United Kingdom and Sudan as contrasting countries, and found that although the previously obtained urban–rural differences again appeared in both countries, there was no overall difference in the per centages of helpful responses given between the two countries. Yousif and Korte (1995) also found urban–rural differences in attitudes toward helping in the United Kingdom and Sudan.

An ambitious cross-cultural comparison of helping behaviours has been conducted by Norenzayan and Levine (1994). They computed an overall helping index from three behaviours (picking up papers dropped by a man on crutches, helping a blind person across the street, and picking up someone's dropped pen) in the main or capital cities of eighteen countries. They then correlated the helping index with a host of demographic, environmental-economic, and psycho-social-cultural variables. A number of correlations were found, all indicating 'a general trend where cities in wealthy countries are less likely to offer help to strangers compared to cities in poor countries' (p. 13).

This outcome was regarded as consistent with Milgram's (1970) system over-load theory, the notion that life in advanced economies 'exerts tremendous pressure on the cognitive capacities of individuals and leads to the screening out of stimuli that are not essential to one's needs, including help required by a stranger' (Norenzayan and Levine, 1994, p. 3). This conclusion is compatible with the rural-urban differences noted before, with Levine et al.'s (1994) comparison of helping in thirty-six US cities, and with Yousif and Korte's (1995) finding that helping behaviour has no correspondence to a person's attitudes towards helping. Rather, one helps if one is cognitively available to do so.

There is thus some evidence that responding helpfully to strangers in the street is at least widespread, if not universal. However, we have to consider more closely what we mean by 'responding helpfully'. In each of the studies of helping so far mentioned, the persons seeking help were local nationals of the country where the study was done. From these studies we know how many people received a response coded as helpful, but not what was the nature of that help nor the reasons why it was given or withheld. As Fiske (1991b) points out, pro-social behaviour may be found within almost all cultures studied by anthropologists, but its meaning may vary widely. One may help another out of obligation to a group seen as similar to one's own, out of deference, out of politeness, out of a wish to impress and so forth.

Two studies that compared responses to locals and foreigners making the same requests illustrate some of this variability. Greece is one country well known to offer a welcome to foreigners, at least until the current tourist invasion. Feldman (1967) found that foreigners who asked a favour in Athens received *more* help than did Greeks who asked the same favour in the same place. The reverse was true in Paris and Boston. In a similar way, Collett and O'Shea (1976) had foreigners ask directions to two non-existent sites, as well as two that did exist. In Teheran and Isfahan (both in Iran), the foreigner was frequently given directions as to how to reach the non-existent sites. This did not occur in London. The *format* of helpfulness was thus preserved by the Iranians, although of course it is no help at all to be given fictitious directions. In some collective cultures therefore it appears that foreigners or outsiders are not treated in the same manner as those who are local. Instead they are treated in a manner that could imply that they are in some way more important and worthy of help.

The simple distinction between giving help and withholding it thus has its limitations. In cultures that welcome strangers, we need to look carefully to see what it is about the stranger that leads to him or her being accorded at least a semblance of help. Probable answers will include age, gender, skin colour, demeanour, presumed cultural identity and of course the nature of the culture's own norms about what types of behaviours are thought admirable. The format of helpfulness, like that of aggression, is culturally mediated.

Organizational structures

There remains one further area in which some writers have asserted that there are cultural universals. It is suggested that just as culture constrains the expression of personality in particular ways, so may organizations be pressed to adopt particular structures. This might occur, for instance, through a Darwinian process of natural selection. Organizations that adopt particular structures may be more likely to succeed, where those that do not will fail. Success and failure may ultimately be determined by economic criteria, but we need also to consider the likelihood that an organization's success will be mediated by the degree to which it can accommodate the personalities, attitudes and values of those working within it.

The view that there are universal structural requirements for an organization to survive was first put forward by a group of researchers centred upon the University of Aston in the United Kingdom (Hickson *et al.*, 1974; Hickson and McMillan, 1981). Their thesis has most often been tested upon business organizations, although government and educational organizations have also been included in some surveys. Business organizations survive if they meet the needs of their customers and other key constituencies, such as their shareholders or owners. The Aston thesis was that as an organization increases in size, efficiency can only be accomplished by setting in motion the processes of specialization, centralization and formalization. For instance, we might expect organizations to set up separate departments concerned with sales, production, research, personnel and many other functions. They will also need to put in place procedures to coordinate the work of these separate functions, which could include sets of formal rules as well as specifications as to who has authority over whom. The model therefore asserts that if organizations in any part of the world are sampled, their size will be positively correlated with measures of specialization, formalization and centralization.

Support for the Aston model has been obtained within samples of organizations in many countries, including not just those in Western Europe and North America, but also Poland, Egypt, Iran, India, Jordan, Israel and Japan (Donaldson, 1986). However, there are two important qualifications that must be made to this support, each of them close to themes that recur throughout this book. Firstly, the propositions advanced by the Aston group, and the measures used in testing their model, fall into the imposed-etic category. They assume that the processes of growth and subsequent bureaucratization that have been well-studied in Western nations over the past hundred years are the only possible way to run an organization. For instance, it is assumed that if an organization is successful it will grow in size. Secondly, the model also assumes that specification of the roles and duties of individuals and departments within an organization will actually determine how people behave in practice. Let us examine these two points in turn.

Developments in the world economy over the past two decades have forced a reappraisal of conventional thinking about organizational effectiveness. Organizations from the nations of the Asian Pacific rim have challenged and questioned the prior dominance of organizations from Western nations. We shall discuss what goes on within these organizations in more detail in Chapter 8, so for the present let us simply note that this success has been accomplished within the context of a series of collectivist cultures in which teamwork is stressed more than individual achievement and long-term stability is valued over short-term growth or profit. The development of economies based upon family-based ethnic Chinese businesses is particularly instructive (Redding, Norman and Schlander, 1994). The phenomenal economic growth of Hong Kong, for instance, has been accomplished not by the creation of a relatively small number of world-renowned organizations, but through the creation of networks of tens of thousands of small family businesses. The tendency within Chinese family businesses is for organizations that start to grow in size to fragment into a series of additional small businesses (Redding, 1990).

Thus, while the Aston model is built around the assumption that economic success will lead to growth in organization size, with the predictable effect of subsequent bureaucratization, Chinese family businesses have an entirely different way of handling success. Redding and Wong (1986) found that even when they equated the size of organizations from the United Kingdom and Hong Kong, the Hong Kong firms had less defined roles, less standardization, fewer specialist positions and more centralization. We cannot say for sure that in the long run, large-scale Chinese business organizations will not emerge. If they do, they too may need to be structured in the manner specified by the Aston model. However, it is only likely that this will happen if the global processes of modernization prove so powerful that the distinctively Chinese values that sustain the present pattern are substantially eroded. We discuss whether or not this outcome is likely in Chapter 12.

The second reason for questioning the Aston thesis is that its predictions are formulated in terms of a number of rather general processes, such as centralization and formalization. Some writers have questioned whether the measures used to assess these processes are sufficiently sensitive to detect much of what actually happens within an organization (Maurice, 1976). For instance, the measure of centralization is based upon an assessment of who in the organization actually takes certain key decisions. However, no account is taken of whether in practice the decision-maker consults others or not before taking each decision. In consequence, a great deal of variance in behaviour across different cultures is likely to go undetected. Tayeb (1988) compared samples of UK and Indian organizations. The Aston measure for centralization showed them to be similar to one another. However, she found that the UK managers consulted others much more than did the Indian managers, as we should expect for managers from a lower power distance culture. Thus it may be the case that rather generalized measures of organizational behaviour show universal patterns, whereas more specific assessments reveal cultural differences, just as we have noted in earlier sections of this chapter.

Some interim conclusions

The previous chapter explored culture and related concepts. It was argued that the best hope for cross-cultural social psychology is to locate a means of classifying national cultures, in order that we can test the limits of the knowledge we already have. The most prominent candidate to emerge from the studies so far has proved to be the distinction between cultural collectivism and cultural individualism.

As a first test of the usefulness of this distinction we have now surveyed several areas in which it has been proposed that there are cultural universals. In each of these areas, we have found some evidence that it is indeed possible to formulate broad, universal generalizations. There *are* gender differences that transcend cultures. We *can* all decode certain facial expressions. Personality traits *do* cluster in similar ways. Humans *are* all capable of both aggression and pro-social behaviour. Dimensions of organizational structure *are* relatively invariant. It is possible that most of these generalizations have some type of biological basis. Poortinga (1990) suggests that the degree to which attributes prove to be universals will depend upon whether they are genetically transmitted or culturally acquired, as shown in Figure 4.1. Thus, universals will be most obvious for physiological and perceptual

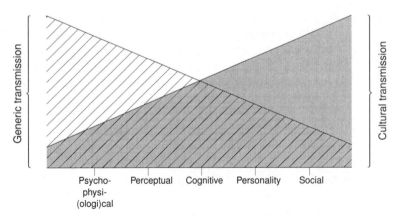

Figure 4.1. Poortinga's model of genetic and cultural transmission. (Source: Poortinga, 1990.)

aspects of behaviour, while cultural variations are more probable in the areas of personality, social and organizational behaviour.

It is consistent with the Poortinga model that in each of the areas of social behaviour examined, we have found that the general principles are expressed in ways that are given shape by more specific cultural referents. Furthermore, in most of these areas it has turned out that by looking at measures of cultural variation, such as individualism–collectivism, we can illuminate substantial amounts of variance in the results which had in some cases eluded the original investigators.

Some cautions

We shall therefore be making further and more systematic tests of the individualism–collectivism concept within each of the major research fields of social psychology in the remainder of this book. Before we do so, we need to insert a few cautions. We have argued already that there is a need to be clear about levels of explanation in cross-cultural social psychology. We shall speak of idiocentrism–allocentrism wherever it is clear that researchers are referring to differences among individuals rather than differences among cultures.

However, this semantic precision will not wholly protect us from the accusation that our discussion is too polarized between the concepts of individualism and collectivism. Indeed, Sinha and Tripathi (1994) argue that the propensity to make yes/no splits between exclusive pairs of concepts is itself a distinctively Western way of theorizing. As Kagitçibasi (1994) points out, it is quite possible that someone could be idiocentric and allocentric at the same time, as indeed has been confirmed by empirical research (e.g. Singelis, 1994). For instance, office workers may pursue largely idiocentric career goals at work, but when relaxing at home, they may take on a much more allocentric set of values.

We also need to ensure that we do not stereotype particular cultures or groups of cultures. Numerous national cultures are heterogeneous. Countries such as Australia, the United States and Brazil are very ethnically heterogeneous, but most other national cultures also contain substantial diversity by race, ethnicity and region. It is the purpose of science, however, to test out the value of simplifications, and so we shall for the time being stay with our chosen concepts, in order to assess their strengths and limitations.

We run yet one further risk of seeming to bracket together cultures that scored relatively similarly on the Hofstede (1980) or Schwartz (1994) measures. It is patently obvious that, although for instance Chinese societies, India and Brazil are all classified as relatively high on collectivism, these countries differ in many other respects, some of which are reflected in their scores on the other Hofstede dimensions of uncertainty avoidance, masculinity/femininity and so forth. The Schwartz studies suggest that we shall ultimately need to take into account still further dimensions of cultural variation. At the least, we need studies that enable us to make clearer distinctions among those nations where the values of horizontal collectivism, vertical collectivism and particularism are most strongly endorsed. Within the existing literature these nations are mostly treated simply as different exemplars of collectivism.

Japan is often cited as a collectivist society, but Hofstede (1980) found it only moderately high and the collectivism there is much more focused upon the work group than in many other cultures (Nakane, 1970). In Chinese societies, collectivism is more strongly integrated with the family (Bond and Hwang, 1986). In Latin America, the Hispanic concept of *sympatia* between peers expresses a core value of collectivism (Triandis *et al.*, 1984), but power distance is frequently also high. However, Marin and Marin (1982) caution against assumptions that Hispanic communities are culturally all similar. Hofstede noted in particular that in Costa Rica power distance was much lower than elsewhere in Latin America. In India, whether one behaves individualistically or collectivistically is said to depend on the context, since Indians are reported to be more tolerant of contradictions than are members of other national cultures (Sinha, 1992).

In concluding this chapter, it only remains for us to address a little further the issue of methodology. The debate about methodology often reduces to a polarization between those who favour etic approaches and those who favour emic approaches. Etic researchers look for general principles, and by the way we have chosen to write this book we show some sympathy with them. Emic researchers seek to build indigenous psychologies. This approach also has importance, but may take time before it bears substantial fruit, as we shall see when we explore this approach more fully in Chapter 11. The debate between the two positions is like an imaginary debate on which we sometimes ponder: one faction points out that almost everyone in the world wears clothes (a universal); the other investigates the types of clothing worn at particular places or times (emic expressions of the universal). One faction has a not very useful generalization. The other has a mass of descriptive data. What is needed is a way of linking the two approaches – an etic way of being emic! For this synthesis to be possible, a theory is required that predicts why variation occurs from one culture to another. In the case of clothing, the theory would no doubt be based on climatic variation. In the more general case of social behaviour, individualism–collectivism appears at present to be the front-running candidate from among the various contenders. However, the concepts of individualism and collectivism, no less than other cultural concepts, have generally arisen from within Western psychology. We must consider further how compatible they may be with emic concepts which have found favour in other parts of the world.

Summary

Psychologists seek to identify the universals of human behaviour. There is indeed substantial evidence, particularly for the universality of gender differences, of emotional expressions and of dimensions of personality. However, in order to establish these universals, theorists have needed to formulate their concepts at a relatively high level of abstraction. When one asks how these universals are to be expressed and interpreted within specific cultural contexts, one finds ever increasing cultural specificity. Whether it is the generality or the specificity that can offer greater value to psychology remains open to debate.

The self and social cognition

**Man is the measure of all things
– of what is, that it is; of what is not, that it is not.**

Protagoras

In this chapter we will focus upon the subject as knower, as a constructor of sense-making categories of the personal and interpersonal worlds. How may the self be described? How do we perceive the other actors in our social world? How do we explain our actions? Theirs? How do we derive a sense of esteem about ourselves? And how do we compare ourselves with them? Although these questions are intrinsically interesting, one purpose for discovering answers has been to make better predictions of the behaviour of the knowing subject.

Some authors (e.g. Sampson, 1981) would argue that it is a typically individualistic presumption that a person's self-conception is an important factor in shaping his or her behaviour. Landrine (1992) characterizes this 'referential' view of the self by the belief that, 'The self in Western culture is the final explanation for behavior and is responsible for behavior' (p. 404). By contrast, the self in sociocentric cultures 'has no enduring, trans-situational characteristics, no traits or desires or needs of its own in isolation from its relationships and contexts' (p. 406). In such collectivist cultures, then, social variables like norms may be more powerful predictors of behaviour than self-derived variables such as attitudes.

In Chapter 3, we argued that cultures can best be classified as falling within four types, namely horizontal collectivist, vertical collectivist, universalist and particularist. Cross-cultural researchers into social cognition, however, have almost all derived their hypotheses from the simpler distinction between individualist and collectivist cultures. We prefer to see that as a distinction between the universalist cultures within which most social and organizational psychology has been conducted and the more heterogeneous set of cultures that constitute the rest of the world. For clarity, we will continue for the most part to refer to cultures as individualist and collectivist. Finer distinctions must await the time when sufficient studies are available to compare studies from cultures that are, for instance, vertically collectivist rather than horizontally collectivist.

So, as we have discussed, the science of psychology is largely the product of individualistic cultures, especially that of the United States. In consequence, certain topics become the focus of psychologists' attention to the relative exclusion of others (Hogan and Emler, 1978; Markus and Kitayama, 1994). Given the dynamics of the profession, these culturally salient topics along with their associated research paradigms and instruments are then likely to form the basis of cross-cultural studies. The self is one such topic. We begin by examining the self in its physical context.

The self in its physical context

The substantial element of choice about whom we associate with in individualist cultures is likely to find expression in how we manage the spatial relationships between ourselves and others. One might expect that in individualist cultures, people would prefer to emphasize their independence by keeping others at a greater physical distance, or by protecting distinctive areas of personal space. In collectivist cultures on the other hand, people might on average prefer to be closer to other members of the group with whom they will share their future and thus prefer to share space with them. On the other hand, members of collectivist cultures might prefer to keep a greater distance from those with whom they are not linked. However, other matters such as relative status and gender are also very important in determining preferred spatial relations, so that we should not expect an oversimple picture.

Proximity

An early study by Little (1968) asked people in five countries to indicate how close two persons should be when having conversations on eighteen different types of topic. He found some cultural differences which held up across all topics. Those who favoured greatest proximity were Greeks, followed by Italians, Americans, Swedes and Scots, in that order. However, Little's study combined across conversations between friends, between acquaintances, and between strangers. Some important distinctions may thus have been submerged.

We look now at a series of studies that specify more closely how people are acquainted. Watson and Graves (1966) had Arab and American students in America who were friends talk to each other in pairs, with each set of pairs coming from the same country. They were instructed to speak in their own language. The results for Iraqis, Saudis, Kuwaitis and Egyptians were all closely similar. Compared with Americans, the Arabs all faced each other more directly, sat closer, had more eye-contact and talked louder. Watson (1970) extended his sample to include students at the University of Colorado from thirty-one countries, although he was able to locate no more than one pair from many of these countries. He found that those from Arab countries, India and Pakistan sat closest, followed by Latin Americans and South Europeans, East Asians and finally Northern

Europeans, among whom he included Americans and Australians. Watson also had all his subjects rate how close was their friendship with each other, and it turned out that the Arabs, Indians and Pakistanis, who were the groups that had sat closest, also rated their friendships most highly. One could argue that this finding undermines the validity of his conclusions. Many studies have shown that we sit nearer to those whom we like. If different degrees of liking can account for how close the friend-pairs sat, we would not need to invoke cultural explanations for the results. However, it is just as likely that the different ratings of friendship were themselves influenced by cultural differences.

As we discussed in Chapter 3, comparing mean scores on questionnaires completed by different cultural groups is a perilous enterprise, since the members of some cultures are much more prone to use the extremes on rating scales than are others (Chen, Lee and Stevenson, 1995). Watson could have resolved this doubt by looking at the relationship between proximity and liking *within* each cultural group, but he did not take this important step. In a somewhat similar study, also in America, Sussman and Rosenfeld (1982) reported that in conversation previously unacquainted Japanese sat further apart than Americans, while Venezuelans sat closer still, an outcome pattern that is consistent with Watson's findings. Graham (1985) found that Brazilian negotiators not only looked at one another more and but also touched one another more than did Americans or Japanese. Shuter (1977) observed pairs of people talking to one another on the street in Venice, Heidelberg and Milwaukee. All-male pairs stood closest in Italy and furthest apart in the United States. Mixed sex pairs were also most distant in the United States, but did not differ between Germany and Italy.

There are also a number of studies focusing upon positioning by strangers in situations where there is no requirement that they speak to one another.

Box 5.1) **Comparing rating scale data cross-culturally: a cautionary research note**

Chen, Lee and Stevenson (1995) showed that Americans and Canadians were less likely than Japanese and Taiwanese students to use the mid-point of self-report rating scales. Furthermore, this 'moderation bias' was itself correlated moderately with individual-level measures of allocentrism in all four cultural groups. Reconstructing the response scales into an agree/disagree format did not, however, eliminate the cultural differences across groups. Nonetheless, this work indicates that researchers would be wise to control for this moderation bias in their cross-cultural work. One could, for example, use forced-choice, agree vs. disagree items. Alternatively, one could ensure that positive and negative items measuring the constructs in a study are equally represented in all one's scales. Researchers who do neither of these things and continue to use self-report rating scales will often need to use within-subject data standardization before comparing mean scores from different samples (see Leung and Bond, 1989, for a detailed exploration of this complex issue).

Noesjirwan (1977) found that in doctors' waiting rooms, Indonesians were likely to choose a seat near to a stranger of the same sex, while Australians chose seats that separated them maximally from others. The Indonesians also more often started a conversation with the person whom they sat beside. Presumably shared gender was a sufficient reason for the Indonesians to treat one another as related. Sanders, McKim and McKim (1988) found that students from Botswana in Southern Africa preferred to keep a greater distance from strangers than did American students. Mazur (1977) compared the distance apart of unacquainted men sitting on park benches in San Francisco, Seville in Spain and Tangier in the Arab country of Morocco. He found no differences, despite the fact that Arabs are widely reported to favour close proximity and frequent eye-contact. Perhaps these differences only emerge with friends. Sanders, Hakky and Brizzolara (1985) found differences in distance *preferences* between Egyptian and American students only among women. Preferences were determined by asking subjects to position markers on a chart representing an imaginary room. The Egyptian women students required both male friends and male strangers to keep rather distant, while according to this data collection method, the Egyptian men showed a pattern similar to that for both American men and women.

These results indicate that the generalizations advanced by Hall (1966) and others about the existence of overall cultural differences in preferred spatial positioning are well supported for those who are well acquainted. Among strangers the findings are less clear and it is also evident that factors such as gender substantially affect preferences. The significance of physical proximity presumably lies in what behaviours proximity permits. Watson's (1970) study showed that those who sat closer also touched one another. Similarly, Shuter (1976) found that Latin Americans show frequent touching as well as close proximity. Close proximity also makes it easier to maintain eye-contact and to judge whether one's partner is doing so.

These differences in preferred levels of contact are of course not just matters of academic interest. As soon as someone from one country visits another, they encounter the need to adapt their spatial behaviour to local preferences, if they wish to give the desired impression. Collett (1971), for instance, reports a programme in which Englishmen were trained to stand closer to Arabs, make more eye-contact, touch more and smile more. Trainees were better liked by Arabs than the untrained controls. When Chan Chi Lok approaches too close to Mrs Robertson in our example, she motions him to sit at a more 'proper' distance.

Marriott (1993a) observed meetings between Japanese and Australian business persons. She found marked differences between the spatial relationships preferred by each party. The Japanese typically used separate meeting rooms or meeting areas, even if only two or three persons were involved in the meeting. They would not entertain visitors in their offices, which were often shared with other managers. A meeting room would contain a rectangular low table. The Japanese would sit nearest to the door, with the senior person either closest to the door or at the centre of his side of the table. The other Japanese present would sit in rank order of their seniority. The Australians would be invited to mirror this pattern. A similar arrangement was observed within Japanese offices in Melbourne. In contrast, Australian managers paid much less attention to seating position if a large room was used for a meeting. Meetings with individuals took place within the Australian manager's office, with the Australian sitting behind his or her desk. The Australians were aware of the Japanese emphasis upon the importance of positioning, and attempted to accommodate to it. However, in Marriott's view, although they were aware of the importance of seniority, they did not fully understand the Japanese etiquette of modestly waiting to be invited to take an appropriate seat. These spatial preferences can be seen as clear expressions of the relatively high collectivism and power distance of Japanese business culture, and the low power distance, low collectivism of Australian business culture.

Homes and territories

Altman and Gauvain (1981) observe that in individualist cultures homes tend to be clearly demarcated. Doors, gardens, fences and gates indicate a relatively small internal 'home' area, which is furnished in a distinctive manner. In collectivist cultures on the other hand, physical boundaries may be less clearly marked, and the 'inner' area may be centred on a courtyard or other open space. Some of these differences no doubt derive from climatic variations, but climatic differences themselves may well be related to the social structures to be found in different parts of the world. While the boundaries of homes in collectivist cultures may thus appear more physically permeable, Gudykunst, Ting-Toomey and Chua (1988) point out that the boundaries are nonetheless there and that they are based on rules about who has access to what space. Altman and Chemers (1980) review a series of studies showing that even in conditions of considerable poverty and consequent crowding, rules are found that provide some degree of privacy.

One way of studying the nature of such rules is to see what happens when they are violated. Gudykunst, Ting-Toomey and Chua (1988) propose that in individualist cultures, violation leads to an active, aggressive response, whereas in collectivist cultures there is more likely to be some kind of passive withdrawal. Violation of cultural rules about appropriate positioning by visitors from other cultures is likely to be an extremely frequent event. However, it is only easy to detect a violation in the types of situation where rule violation precipitates an observable response.

The meaning of spatial positioning

At present our knowledge of the relation between spatial positioning and culture is rather incomplete. One reason for this is that many of the studies so far done have used rather crude and simple measures, such as verbal preferences about one's distance from others, whereas the processes operating are probably much more subtle. A second difficulty is that because physical proximity is readily measurable, it has been easy to assume that it is given the same meaning in all cultures. It could be the case, for example, that in some of the highly collectivist Arab and Latin cultures proximity signals intimacy, whereas in some of the higher power distance cultures in East Asia proximity could signal a lack of deference. Interviews by Watson (1970) with his subjects support this view. High eye-contact was reported to have positive connotations by Arabs, Latins, Indians and Pakistanis. But Africans and East Asians described high eye-contact as conveying insubordination or anger. We shall explore additional aspects of the ways in which non-verbal aspects of our behaviour convey messages to others in Chapter 6.

Possessions

A further, much-neglected aspect of the physical aspect of self has to do with possessions. We might expect that in individualist cultures ownership would be clearly delineated and that a person's material possessions would be seen as an expression of their identity. Conversely, in a collectivist culture, possessions would more likely be shared among the group and be seen as indicative of the group's identity. Wallendorf and Arnould (1988) compared attitudes toward possessions of adults in Arizona and in the Niger republic, an Islamic Hausa society to the North of Nigeria. The comparison was between urban Americans and rural inhabitants of Niger, so that we are looking at differences that might also be found between town and country within a single culture. Overall, the Americans rated themselves as more attached to their possessions than did respondents in Niger. One respondent in Niger reflected local values by pointing out that if one had too many possessions, they might be lost through divine intervention, thereby indicating that for him possessions were related to religious beliefs surrounding attachment to material objects.

The favourite possessions most frequently reported by the Americans were functional items, sources of entertainment, personal nicknacks, pieces of art and photographs. Asked why they valued these objects, 60 per cent responded that they reflected attachments based on personal memories, for instance, of friends or family members. The American responses thus emphasized one's individualized life history. In Niger, some difficulty was found in conveying the interviewer's understanding of what a possession was. Disallowed responses included 'my children', 'my fields' and 'my Koranic studies'. Once these difficulties were overcome, the women's favourite possessions proved to be almost all related to marriage or domestic goods. The men listed religious and magical objects as well as livestock and tools. The reasons given for valuing possessions did not emphasize the owner's distinctive personal history, but rather more the requirement for maintaining one's own and one's family's position within society. This contrast in the meaning attached to one's possessions suggests that they allow one to make more socially salient themes important in one's cultural group.

Dittmar, Singelis and Papadopoulou (1996) extend this line of analysis by demonstrating linkages between the self-concepts of British, Greek and Americans and the way in which they valued their possessions. US respondents described themselves more idiocentrically (i.e. in terms of beliefs about the self as independent) and saw their possessions as expressing their individual self. British and Greek respondents saw their possessions as reflecting their social position and sentimental associations with others.

Clothing the self

Jahoda (1982) provides related material from another part of the world. He contrasts the wearing of the *chadoor*, or full-length veil, by women in certain Islamic countries with Zimbardo's (1970) experiments in the United States. Zimbardo showed that when subjects in his experiments were asked to wear a full-length robe, their behaviour became 'deindividuated', that is to say, they were more likely to act in aggressive or socially irresponsible ways. Zimbardo postulates that since they were no longer individually identifiable, they no longer felt so responsible for their actions. In contrast, Jahoda points out that in countries where it is the norm for women to be veiled, rather than setting free one's individual impulses, the veil (a garment of rather similar dimensions to Zimbardo's robes) very precisely specifies one's social obligations. In a similar way, we saw in Chapter 2 that being an identified member of a group in collectivist cultures inhibited social loafing rather than enhancing it.

Interestingly enough, the role of clothing in defining one's group identity also proved crucial in an attempt by Zimbardo to replicate his findings in Belgium. While he had used student subjects in his US studies, in Belgium he used soldiers. When the soldiers donned Zimbardo's robes, they proved *less* aggressive than when in regular uniform, which was the reverse of Zimbardo's prediction. It appears that rather than deindividuating the soldiers, the robes made them feel more identifiable, whereas in regular uniform they felt less so.

If Zimbardo had used soldiers in the United States, we might expect that he would have obtained results similar to the Belgian ones. Armies, even in predominantly individualist countries, encourage an allocentric value system, within which one's obligations to one's military unit are publicly spelled out through the wearing of uniforms. To step out of uniform is to become an independent actor, just as it would be for an Islamic woman in an Arab country to renounce the veil.

The self in its cultural context

If our focus of attention is upon the self, we must clearly move from the cultural level of analysis to the individual level of analysis. A recent seminal contribution towards psychologizing about culture's impact on the self was made by Markus and Kitayama (1991). They drew the distinction between an independent conception of the self fostered by many individualistic cultural systems and an interdependent conception of the self fostered by many collectivist cultural systems (see also Oerter *et al.*, 1996).

The independent self

The perception of oneself as an independent agent has been a major emphasis in the life of Western industrial nations in recent times. Values such as freedom and self-determination are highly esteemed and many members of these nations will, if asked, characterize themselves as possessing traits and abilities, such as intelligence, friendliness, modesty or what you will. It is by no means certain that this was always so. In mediaeval times, the word 'individual' had a decidedly different meaning in the English language. It was used to refer to each of the members of the Trinity, that is to say God-the-Father, God-the-Son and the Holy Spirit (Williams, 1961). In other words, in the religious imagery that was predominant at the time, an individual was not a separate entity, but was indissolubly linked to others, whose identity was collectively defined.

More recent Western conceptions of the individual as being in some way autonomous or separate from the social context parallel the type of analytic thinking that has been highly valued since the time of Descartes in Western countries. This way of thinking often polarizes pairs of concepts as a basis for construing the world. Frequently used concept pairs in social psychology would include: self/others, individual/group, leader/follower, environment/heredity and of course individualism/collectivism. An instance of the way in which this type of thinking finds a ready home within Western psychology is provided by the widespread use of versions of the semantic differential questionnaire, in which subjects are asked to evaluate themselves or others on a series of bipolar rating scales.

This oppositional way of construing individuals and their environments is certainly not the only possible approach to adopt. As Geertz (1974) emphatically puts it:

> The Western conception of the person as a bounded, unique, more or less integrated motivational and cognitive universe, a dynamic centre of awareness, emotion, judgment and action organized into a distinctive whole and set contrastively both against other such wholes and against its social and natural background is, however incorrigible it may seem to us, a rather peculiar idea within the context of the world's cultures. (p. 225)

As Figure 5.1 shows, Calvin and Hobbes have also explored some of the limitations of perceiving oneself as an independent entity.

The interdependent self

Thinking about oneself as interdependent is consistent with a more holistic, less analytic way of thinking. Within this approach, the inter-relatedness of objects and concepts is more salient. In discussing Western and Chinese science in historical times, Needham (1978) writes:

> We are driven to the conclusion that there are two ways of advancing from primitive truth. One way was the way taken by some of the Greeks: to refine the

Figure 5.1 Rampant idiocentrism?

ideas of causation in such a way that one finished up with a mechanical explanation
of the universe, just as Democritus did with his atoms. The other way is to
systematize the universe of things and events into a structural pattern which
conditioned all the mutual influences of its different parts. (p. 166)

Anthropologists have documented a variety of 'Eastern' cultures in which the
self is defined in this more contextually, multiply shaped manner (Marsella, De
Vos and Hsu, 1985). This type of interdependent conception of self in contemporary societies has only recently been studied empirically by psychologists.
Markus and Kitayama (1991) propose that an individual with interdependent
values regards the preservation of harmonious relations with the other key people
in his or her life as the primary goal. It follows from this proposition that an
interdependent person will not necessarily maintain a consistent core of actions
towards other people in general. It may well be necessary to behave in different
ways at different times in order to accommodate different others. One's actions
toward a shopkeeper, one's boss, one's maternal uncle, a neighbour's child or a
fellow-passenger on a bus will all be bounded by the obligations defining that
particular type of relationship with that particular person. Indeed, interdependent
(or allocentric) persons are more likely to report that they are more influenced in
their behaviour by contextual factors, including norms (Trafimow and Finlay,
1996) and context (Singelis and Brown, 1995).

Some Western theorists have also pointed out that situations affect how individuals behave (Mischel, 1968; Argyle, Furnham and Graham, 1981). However,
after a good deal of debate, most Western theorists now envisage a process of
person–situation interaction (Epstein and O'Brien, 1985). That is to say, while
everyone may be less friendly when standing in a queue than when attending a
party, certain people will be more friendly than others in both settings. However,
ways of being friendly while in a queue and while at a party may also differ subtly,
so recent theorists speak of the *coherence* of behaviour across situations rather than
a more precisely defined consistency.

For a person with interdependent values, maintaining a coherent core around
any trait, for instance friendliness, would be less important. What would count

more strongly is the immediate requirements of each specific situation and the people who make up that situation. Hence, if persons with interdependent values are asked to describe themselves, they may well find it difficult to do so, if the context for their actions is not specified.

Describing oneself

This rationale is supported by the findings of Markus and Kitayama's own studies, (1994). Japanese respondents were found to make distinctions among emotions based upon how engaged or disengaged they were with the person toward whom the emotion was relevant. One might expect similar findings from other relatively collectivist societies, since the degree of engagement could be crucial to the experience of emotion in such settings, whereas in individualist societies, the degree of engagement with another would be less decisive, and one's emotions would be seen as more autonomous. A study by Stipek, Weiner and Li (1989) also supports this view. Chinese and Americans were asked to describe situations in which they had become angry. The Americans were found to be more likely to describe events that had happened to them personally. The Chinese on the other hand referred to a higher proportion of events that had happened to other people they knew.

Bond and Cheung (1983) asked Japanese, Hong Kong Chinese and American students to describe themselves. They used a familiar procedure in Western studies, known as the Twenty Statements Test (TST). This simply asks respondents to provide twenty answers to the question 'Who Am I?' As expected they found that Americans used many more generalized trait descriptions than the Japanese. However, the results for the Hong Kong students were rather more similar to those from the United States. They concluded that the Hong Kong students were more Westernized, having been educated in English with more Western curricula.

Another possibility is that the coding system they employed to analyze references to social roles was too global to detect differences between US and Hong Kong descriptions of one's relations with others. In the scheme that they used, both an independent (or, following the terms used in this book, idiocentric) self-statement 'I am a student' and an interdependent (allocentric) self-statement 'I am a member of the second-year psychology class' would have been coded as a reference to role. Triandis, McCusker and Hui (1990) also used the TST, comparing student responses from mainland United States, Hawaii, Greece, Hong Kong and China. They found that references to oneself as a member of a social category were much higher for the Chinese responses than for those from elsewhere. Similar differences between Koreans and Americans were found by Rhee *et al.* (1995) and between members of different ethnic communities in Australia (Bochner, 1994).

A more precise test of differences in self-concept was that reported by Cousins (1989) who asked Japanese and American students to describe themselves.

Initially he used the familiar version of the TST. As expected, he found that the Americans came up with many more generalized (i.e. situation-free) trait labels in describing themselves, while the Japanese were more likely to qualify their characterizations by specifying the context within which they behaved in a given way. For instance one respondent described himself or herself as 'one who plays Mah Jongg on Friday nights'. Cousins then modified the TST so that respondents were asked to describe how they were in a series of specific settings, for example at home, with their friends and so forth. Under these conditions, the pattern was reversed. Japanese students were now able to use more generalized trait labels about themselves. American students on the other hand used fewer traits and were more inclined to add qualifications. For instance one respondent wrote, 'I am often lazy *at home*'. Cousins concludes that the Americans' need to preserve an independent, context-free self-concept led them to assert that although they might behave in a certain way in a particular setting, this would not necessarily reflect their 'real' self. The American respondent quoted above implies that he or she is not *really* lazy, just often lazy at home, thereby preserving the image of independence from the context. The Japanese respondents, on the other hand, show that they are better able to characterize themselves when the nature of their interdependence is specified.

If we imagine that a researcher managed to intercept Mrs Robertson and Mr Chan, we can note as in Box 5.2 some similar contrasts that we might find in their responses to a test of self-concept. Mrs Robertson uses broad traits and generalized roles to describe herself. Mr Chan specifies the settings in which he is engaged, and indicates how he behaves in some of them.

Structured trait descriptions. A more widely used method of assessing the self-concept involves asking respondents to report their psychological traits on adjective check lists (e.g. Gough's Adjective Check List). Often these adjectives are derived from sampling words in daily use by culling them from newspaper reports,

---

Box 5.2 **Who am I? – some answers from Mrs Robertson and Mr Chan**

Mrs Robertson:

● A teacher
● Divorced
● Scottish
● A long way from home
● Does not suffer fools gladly
● Active
● Lonely

Mr Chan:

● A student at Hong Kong University
● I come from the Chan family
● I try to work hard at my lessons
● I joined the Pokfulam basketball team
● I care for my sister
● I visit my mother in the hospital every day
● Anxious when talking to Mrs Robertson

dictionaries or novels. This lexical approach (Saucier and Goldberg, 1996) yields a comprehensive set of trait self-descriptors used by literate members of a culture.

This approach to assessing one's personality has helped contribute to the growing consensus about the Big Five factor model of personality (Digman, 1990, discussed in Chapter 4); the initial work on trait descriptors in the United States identified five factors along which people perceived themselves to vary, viz. surgency, agreeableness, conscientiousness, emotional stability and intellect (Goldberg, 1990). Similar work has been done in other cultural groups using different languages and have likewise identified a similar five factors (e.g. in Dutch and German by John, Goldberg and Angleitner, 1984; in Russian by Shmelyov and Pokhil'ko, 1992; in Taiwanese by Yang and Bond, 1990; in Japanese by Isaka, 1990; in Spanish by Benet and John, 1996).

Inspired in part by such apparent consensus, Williams, Satterwhite and Saiz (in press) set out to compare the varying psychological importance attached to these five factors of self-description by students in twenty countries. Across all countries, extroversion and agreeableness were rated as the most important; emotional stability and openness to experience the least; conscientiousness fell in between these extremes. This pancultural finding may derive from the key role of extroversion and of agreeableness in guiding our social behaviours (Wiggins, 1979). Country-specific patterns were also found. So, for example, Singaporeans rated emotional stability highest and agreeableness the lowest. Such divergent patterns may derive from societal concerns which are then reflected in the psychological importance attached to various dimensions of self-perception.

Recently, studies have surfaced from some cultures which report more than five factors in self-perceptions of indigenous traits. Yik and Bond (1993) found six in Hong Kong, while Narayan, Menon and Levine (1995) also found six in India; Benet and Waller (1995) found seven in Spain, as did Almagor, Tellegen and Waller (1995) in Israel. Church and Katigbak (1989) found eight in the Philippines. There is, of course, some degree of arbitrariness associated with extracting factors from a matrix of correlations. Theoretical positions to defend may then lead investigators to extract the number of factors their theory leads them to expect. It may be, however, that particular cultural dynamics do lead people of a given culture to differentiate more finely around a common theme. So, for example, Yik and Bond detected three separate components of conscientiousness in Chinese self-perceptions – restraint, application and intellect. This relative emphasis on conscientiousness is reinforced by noting the emphasis by Chinese respondents on this dimension in the unstructured TST mentioned earlier (Ip and Bond, 1995; Watkins and Gerong, 1997). In other cultures, distinctions may be drawn within other dimensions, e.g. with agreeableness among Filipinos (Church, 1987).

Another issue may be addressed using this research approach – how closely do imported trait scales, translated into the local language, reproduce the dimensions of self-perception produced by locally developed or indigenous trait scales (Church, Katigbak and Reyes, 1996)? Results from this type of research show a similar number of dimensions from each type of instrument, but that each local dimension involves combinations of the imported dimensions (e.g. Yik and Bond, 1993). In other words, the 'imposed-etic' scales divide up the pie of self-perceived personality differently; the local instruments may therefore prove to be more effective in predicting local categories of behaviour than are scales from overseas.

Some implications of independent/interdependent self-construals for social cognition

A number of cross-cultural psychologists have been stimulated by this distinction between cultural constructions of the self. They have extended its logic to traditional topics in social psychology. For example, Heine and Lehman (1997) argued that the cognitive dissonance arising from knowing that one has done something bad or foolish should be greater in cultures where an independent self is socialized. In cultures socializing for interdependence, 'the behavior of individuals is largely governed by situational constraints and obligations, and consequently, behavior is not typically seen as an accurate reflection of the individual's thoughts and attitudes.' (p. 7) (see also Kashima *et al.*, 1992). In such a society individuals should experience less dissonance when performing self-inconsistent actions. This prediction was confirmed in a Japanese–Canadian comparison. Carr (1996) reviews studies from several African nations and argues that in that region 'cognitive tolerance' is a better descriptor of response to inconsistency than cognitive dissonance.

Moving into new areas, Campbell *et al.* (1996) examined the concept of self-concept clarity which they defined as 'the extent to which an individual's specific self-beliefs are clearly and confidently defined, internally consistent, and temporarily stable' (p. 142). They argued that those from cultures with an independent but not an interdependent construction of the self should have higher levels of self-concept clarity. This prediction was confirmed by comparing Canadian with Japanese respondents.

Measuring independent/interdependent self-construals

Singelis (1994) was the first to develop a measure for these two types of self-construal, followed closely by Gudykunst *et al.* (1994). This multicultural group of collaborators consulted to develop culturally decentred scales and produced a derived-etic instrument (see Box 5.3). Both Singelis and Gudykunst discovered that independent and interdependent self-construals were unrelated to one another, not bipolar opposites, as their verbal labels might imply.

It is important to note that the 'decade of collectivism' from the mid 1980s spawned a host of measures for allocentric and idiocentric dispositions. Yamaguchi's (1994) collectivism scale, Hui's (1988) indcol scale, Triandis *et al.*'s (1995) allocentrism/idiocentrism measures, Matsumoto, Kudoh and Takeuchi's (1996) individualism–collectivism assessment inventory and Hamaguchi's (1987)

Box 5.3 Assessing independent and interdependent self-construals

Independent items	Interdependent items
I should be judged on my own merit.	I consult with others before making important decisions.
Being able to take care of myself is a primary concern for me.	I consult with co-workers on work-related matters.
My personal identity is very important to me.	I will sacrifice my self-interest for the benefit of my group.
I prefer to be self-reliant rather than depend on others.	I stick with my group even through difficulties.
I am a unique person separate from others.	I respect decisions made by my group.
If there is a conflict between my values and the values of groups of which I am a member, I follow my values.	I will stay in a group if they need me, even when I am not happy with the group.
I try not to depend on others.	I maintain harmony in the groups of which I am a member.
I take responsibility for my own actions.	I respect the majority's wishes in groups of which I am a member.
It is important for me to act as an independent person.	I remain in the groups of which I am a member if they need me, even though I am dissatisfied with them.
I should decide my future on my own.	I try to abide by customs and conventions at work.
What happens to me is my own doing.	I give special consideration to others' personal situations so I can be efficient at work.
I enjoy being unique and different from others.	It is better to consult with others and get their opinions before doing anything.
I am comfortable being singled out for praise and rewards.	It is important to consult close friends and get their ideas before making a decision.
I help acquaintances, even if it is inconvenient.	My relationships with others are more important than my accomplishments.
I don't support a group decision when it is wrong.	

Source: Gudykunst et al. (1994). Reprinted with permission.

kanjin-shugi ('between-people-ism') scale and others are all tapping aspects of this complex contrast based on collective and individualistic cultural systems. They are inter-related in complex ways (Triandis, 1996) and each scale may be appropriate for addressing different questions about self-construal and behaviour. Most scales assume that allocentric or idiocentric values apply equally to all domains of one's life. However, some scales (e.g. Hui, 1988, Matsumoto *et al.*, 1996) allow that one can have allocentric responses in relation to family, for instance, and idiocentric responses in relation to work.

An important refinement has emerged from this psychometric work across cultures: Singelis *et al.* (1995) presented evidence that the personality dimension of allocentrism/idiocentrism could be differentiated into horizontal and vertical components. That is, people in a variety of cultures can be allocentrics (or idiocentrics) with either an egalitarian or a hierarchical bent (see also Gelfand, Triandis and Chan, 1996). At the individual level, then, researchers are drawing a parallel distinction to that which was drawn at the cultural level by Smith, Dugan and Trompenaars (1996), as we noted in Chapter 3: cultures can vary in terms of hierarchy and equality while also varying in universalism and particularism.

So, there has been an outpouring of measures all related to thinking about the psychological dynamics of individualism and collectivism. One very important opportunity has resulted from all this psychometric activity: the measurement of these various types of self-construals has enabled psychologists to move from the cultural level of analysis to the individual level of analysis. Cultural collectivism can be hypothesized to press for generally higher levels of interdependent self-construals, but for lower levels of independent self-construals. These self-construals can then be linked to other variables across cultural groups to reveal pancultural processes. So, for example, Gudykunst *et al.* (1994) reported that more interdependent persons in both Japan and the United States endorsed the Schwartz (1992) value domains of restrictive conformity, security and prosociality more strongly; while more independent persons favoured self-direction. Likewise Singelis *et al.* (1996) showed that for Hong Kong Chinese and Americans higher interdependent self-construals are related to greater other-based embarrassability, while higher independent self-construals go with lower self-based embarrass-ability. Furthermore, Singelis (1997) found that in a multicultural group of students, cultural collectivism was related to holding a more interdependent self-construal, which was in turn related to greater sensitivity and responsiveness to others' emotions. Previous work (e.g. Heine and Lehman, 1997, on dissonance) had presumed that interdependent Japanese were less disturbed by their behavioural inconsistencies than were the independent Canadians. Now, respondents' self-construals could be individually measured and the links of these self-construals to dissonance could be directly assessed in members of both cultural groups. Surmise about the processes operative within individuals can now be directly assessed at the psychological level.

The case of self-monitoring. The above studies provide some support for the distinction between independent and interdependent self-concepts, though few of them included a measure of what values the subjects actually endorsed. Further evidence comes from a series of studies by Gudykunst, which focused upon the concept of self-monitoring. This concept was first defined by Snyder (1979) who devised a test of the degree to which his US subjects monitored their own behaviour. Gudykunst, Gao and Franklyn-Stokes (1996) and Gudykunst *et al.* (1990) propose that Snyder's scale measures only that type of self-monitoring to be expected in individualist cultures. After conducting interviews with Japanese and Chinese respondents, Gudykunst *et al.* created a new self-monitoring scale, which they claimed had derived-etic properties. They were able to show that American and British respondents score high on items measuring monitoring of *one's own* behaviour, whereas Japanese and Chinese respondents scored high on items measuring monitoring of *others'* behaviour (in order to determine what is socially appropriate behaviour). Furthermore, they showed that these differences were stronger for those who endorsed interdependent values than for those who endorsed independent values.

The Gudykunst studies bridge the gap in the other studies between culture-level interpretations of the data and the actual values endorsed by their respondents. This linkage gives us added confidence in our interpretation of the differences we have reported in self-concept and how they link to individual social behaviour. In this case, those with a more independent self-construal monitor themselves more during social interaction; those with more interdependent self-construals monitor the reactions of others more.

Self-construals and personality

Self-construals are understandings we develop about ourselves – our traits, beliefs, motivations, values and behavioural style. Reports on such features of our personality are precisely what is measured by the tests of personality discussed in the last chapter. If one compares the items in Gudykunst *et al.*'s (1990) self-construal scale with those on self-report measures of personality such as the NEO PI-R, they appear remarkably similar. In fact correlations between Singelis' (1994) Self-construal Scale and Costa and McCrae's (1992) Five Factor Inventory are significant for both US and Hong Kong Chinese respondents (Kwan, Bond and Singelis, 1997). Independence is predicted by extroversion, conscientiousness, neuroticism (negatively), and openness to experience; interdependence is less well accommodated, relating only to agreeableness (cf. Yamaguchi, Kuhlman and Sugimori, 1995).

This sort of finding is not surprising: McCrae, Costa and Yik (1996) have recently presented a model that locates self-construals as one characteristic adaptation shaped by cultural influences. These characteristic adaptations are also determined by the bed-rock of the underlying five personality factors. This theoretical linkage, supported by such empirical correlations as those shown above, brings the field close to the spirit of the culture and personality school (Barnouw, 1985). This approach, popular in the 1940s, regarded a given cultural system as pressing for a particular personality type in that culture. Evidence, however, was weak. Current instruments for assessing personality have higher reliabilities and substantial validities compared with previous tools based on psychoanalysis. So, personality traits and their derivative self-construals can now be shown to differentiate cultural groups from one another (e.g. Kashima *et al.*, 1995) and be used to explain differences between cultural groups (e.g. Kwan, Bond and Singelis, 1997). This use will increase; it is to be hoped that researchers will anchor their specific measures in the basic measures of personality that show universal properties. It is variation in levels of these five dimensions which may account for some of the behavioural differences across cultures (Bond, 1996b).

Perceiving others

Explaining the causes of others' behaviour

If divergences between how independent and interdependent people describe themselves and their physical environment are rooted in the processes of social cognition, we should expect to find similar differences when we examine the process by which they perceive others. Shweder and Bourne (1982) compared free descriptions of their peers by seventy Indian and seventeen US adults. Some 72 per cent of the US statements about their peers were context-free personality trait attributions, whereas only 50 per cent of the Indian statements fell into this category. As we might expect, a larger proportion of the Indian statements were those that specified the social context of the characteristic described. A typical American statement could thus be 'he is selfish', while an equivalent Indian statement might be 'he is hesitant to give money away to his family'. In another early study, Korten (1974) compared perceptions of others by US and Ethiopian students. The Americans characterized others in terms of abilities, knowledge and emotional style. The Ethiopians made much more use of descriptions of the person's interactions with others ('he likes to talk with his room-mates'), and of their opinions and beliefs ('he is against this country's form of government'), both of which are more context-related descriptors.

More recently, J. G. Miller (1984) also compared Indian and American free descriptions of others, and found an even stronger divergence between the two countries in the use of context-free and context-specific descriptions. Her American sample used three times as many trait attributions, while the Indians used twice as many context-bound traits. She also presented her subjects with a series of one-paragraph incidents and asked them to explain why they thought the key person in the incident acted as they had done. An example appears in Boxes 5.4 and 5.5. Once again, the Americans gave significantly more dispositional explanations while the Indians gave more contextual ones.

In yet another Indian–American comparison, L'Armand, Pepitone and Shanmugam (1981) asked matched samples to make ratings of who was to blame in a case history of a rape incident which was put before them. Although most respondents in both countries blamed the man, twice as many Americans as Indians assigned blame to the woman – a person attribution. On the other hand,

---

Box 5.4 **Why did the motorcyclist act as he did? (1)**

The episode below was contributed by one of Miller's (1984) subjects. She asked both her Indian and her American subjects why they thought the motorcycle driver acted as he did.

> This concerns a motorcycle accident. The back wheel burst on the motorcycle. The passenger sitting on the rear jumped. The moment the passenger fell, he struck his head on the pavement. The driver of the motorcycle – who is an attorney – as he was on his way to court for some work, just took the passenger to a local hospital and went on and attended to his court work. The driver left the passenger there without consulting the doctor about the seriousness of the injury – the gravity of the situation – whether the passenger should be shifted immediately – and he went on to court. So ultimately the passenger died.

Miller cites three reasons provided by Americans and three provided by Indians as typical of the responses she found. Consider your own explanations before you look at Box 5.5, on page 116.

---

the Indians were five times more influenced than the Americans by information about the prior sexual history of the woman. Whether she was previously chaste or not was seen as crucial – a contextual factor concerning relations with others, which would have a major effect upon her perceived responsibility and upon her future marriage prospects.

It is noticeable that while each of these studies shows significant differences between the Indian and the American samples, the differences are simply differences in the *frequency* of using trait attributions and context-specific attributions. In other words, some Americans did provide situational explanations of behaviour and some Indians did use personality traits as explanations. We could not consequently argue plausibly that the processes of social cognition were fundamentally different in the samples from the two countries. A more probable explanation would be that people in the two cultural groups tend to direct their attention differentially. According to this view, those with idiocentric values would focus primarily on the actions of themselves and of others. Those with allocentric values would give more attention to the context of actions and to how different actions mesh together.

Consistent with this reasoning, Newman (1993) compared the attribution processes of American allocentrics and idiocentrics. He found that allocentrics were less likely to give internal, trait explanations for the behaviour of others (see also Trafimow and Finlay, 1996). People from collectivist cultures are more likely to be allocentrics and to have interdependent self-construals. So, they are more likely to make external attributions for the behaviour of others (e.g. Lee, Hallahan and Herzog, 1996; Morris and Peng, 1994).

A further illustration of this phenomenon is provided by Miller, Bersoff and

Harwood (1990) who asked Indian and American students and children on what basis they would decide whether to intervene in various emergencies. They found that Indians reported much more frequently that it would be a matter of the moral obligations inherent in their social role to respond, whereas the Americans saw most situations as a matter for personal choice. Only in life-threatening emergencies did the US responses come close to the Indian pattern. The differences found were less sharp among younger children. These results led Miller *et al.* to infer that the different response patterns are acquired as one is gradually socialized to prevailing cultural patterns. Markus and Kitayama (1991) see this socialization process as deriving from the gradual internalization of different rules that lay out the priorities as to what one should attend to in any situation.

Selecting what we attend to

If the manner in which we learn to direct our attention does underlie cultural differences in social cognition, then it is interesting to examine what happens if we are asked to redirect our attention for a while. Trafimow, Triandis and Goto (1991) asked Caucasian and Chinese students attending the University of Illinois to focus their attention in one of two ways for two minutes and then to complete the TST. In one experimental condition they were asked to think of all the things that linked them with their family. In the other condition they were asked to think about all the things that separated them from their family. These experimental manipulations did have a substantial effect on how subjects subsequently chose to describe themselves, as shown in Table 5.1. Thinking about oneself as separate caused the Chinese to use more trait attributions, and thinking about one's family caused the Caucasians to use more role attributions.

Differences in where people direct their attention by those with independent and interdependent values may help to explain some limitations on what Ross

Table 5.1 ● **Responses to the Twenty Statements Test after different attention-focusing instructions**				
	Statements about oneself that were:			
	Independent		Interdependent	
Respondents	US	Chinese	US	Chinese
Think about what makes you different from family and friends	86	68	6	19
Think about what you have in common with family and friends	71	59	21	34
Source: adapted from data reported by Trafimow, Triandis and Goto (1991).				

Box 5.5) **Why did the motorcyclist act as he did? (2)**

US responses:
1. He was obviously irresponsible.
2. He must have been in a state of shock.
3. He was aggressive in pursuing his career success.

Indian responses:
1. It was his duty to be in court for the client he was representing.
2. He might have become nervous or confused.
3. The injured man might not have looked as seriously injured as he was.

(1977) termed the 'fundamental attribution error'. By this phrase he meant the tendency found in many studies for people to explain the behaviour of others in terms of the others' traits and abilities rather than in terms of the context that may evoke it. The studies reviewed in this chapter so far indicate that it is an error that is absent or at least reduced in collectivist cultures and in allocentric persons. It is, then, hardly fundamental.

Some choice language

Differences in where people focus their attention are unlikely to provide the sole consequence of idiocentric and allocentric value orientations. An extensive line of research derives from the propositions put forward by Whorf (1956) to the effect that the way in which culture members think would be bounded by the structure and nature of the language they use. There is some debate as to whether the language of a culture determines or reflects the behaviour patterns within it. The aspect of interest here is in whether the type of language use that is current in individualist and collectivist cultures can be shown to reflect these differences in values.

Semin and Rubini (1990) examined cultural variations in the language employed in describing people in Italy, using rather different methods from those employed in the studies so far described. They compared the types of insults available in northern and southern Italy. Southern Italians are said more often to endorse allocentric values, while in northern Italy idiocentric values are more favoured. Their hypothesis that students from Sicily would report a larger proportion of 'relational' insults than those from Bologna and Trieste in the north was upheld. Swear-words and certain types of individualistic insult were reported more from the north. Some of the less graphic examples of these insult types are given in Box 5.6. The importance of choosing the culturally appropriate type of insult for maximal effect is underlined by the work of Bond and Venus (1991). They found that in Hong Kong their subjects responded more strongly to insults addressed to them as group members than to insults addressed to them as individuals.

> **Box 5.6** **A choice of culturally-rooted insults**
>
> Individualist insults (distinctive to northern Italy)
>
> ● You are stupid
> ● You are a cretin
> ● Swear-words referring to religious figures
> ● Swear-words referring to sexual nouns
>
> Collectivist insults (distinctive to southern Italy)
>
> ● I wish a cancer on you and all your relatives
> ● Your sister is a cow
> ● You are queer and so is your father
> ● You are a Communist
> ● Insults relating to incest

The impact of physical characteristics

In 1983, McArthur and Baron presented an ecological theory of social perception. This theory

> holds that social perceptions serve an adaptive function – either for the survival of the species or for the goal attainment of individuals. It further holds that a person's directly perceptible attributes, such as movements, vocal qualities, and facial appearance, provide useful knowledge about that person's behavioral 'affordances' which are the opportunities for acting and being acted upon that the person provides. The particular affordances that are detected are assumed to depend upon the perceiver's attunements, which may be innate or conditioned by the perceiver's social goals, behavioral capabilities, or perceptual experience. (Zebrowitz-McArthur, 1988, p. 245)

This theoretical position has stimulated considerable cross-cultural work which explores whether a given physical cue communicates the same impression in various cultures.

So, comparative studies between Korea and the United States have shown that information concerning *physical* qualities of stimulus persons may convey similar affordances in both cultures (McArthur and Berry, 1987; Montepare and Zebro-witz-McArthur, 1987). In both countries, very similar reactions were found to various qualities of relatively baby-shaped adult faces, i.e. those with large eyes, full lips, smooth skin, small noses and round faces. Similarly, in both countries, a soft voice was rated as weak, incompetent and warm (Peng, Zebrowitz and Lee, 1993). Keating (1985) asked judges in eleven countries to say which of a series of paired photographs was the more dominant. There was good consensus that the more dominant persons had broad chins, thin lips and receding hairlines.

Such results are explained in terms of the 'age overgeneralization effect' (Zebrowitz and Collins, 1996). This is a universal pattern of responding to physical cues associated with babies as opposed to more mature members of our species. Since babies everywhere are dependent, weak and submissive, adults possessing baby-like physical characteristics are presumed to possess baby-like psychological attributes. In contrast, those with more mature physical characteristics are perceived as assertive and dominant. Such social perceptions are universal because people in all cultures are familiar with age-related physical changes and more mature persons are socialized to nurture young members of the species. Such age overgeneralizations may account for the perceptions of fatter (chubbier) persons as agreeable and dependent (Sleet, 1969) or for the lower status achieved by shorter persons (Collins and Zebrowitz, 1995).

Physical attractiveness. Our biological heritage would predispose us to seek out healthy, youthful persons for mating. Those possessing features that universally connote 'reproductive fitness' will then be perceived as more attractive. So, for example, Montepare and Zebrowitz (1993) found that those persons with youthful gaits were perceived as sexier. Similarly, women endowed with thick, long hair, full lips, high cheekbones and glowing skin are regarded as more physically attractive (Gangestad, 1993). Men with strong chins and prominent cheekbones are regarded as physically attractive, both within and across cultures (Cunningham, Barbee and Pike, 1990). These qualities all confer a selective advantage in mating with such young and fit partners. Given the universality of such cues, it is not surprising that judgements of facial physical attractiveness across cultural groups are highly correlated (e.g. Bernstein, Tsai-Ding and McClelland, 1982, for Taiwanese and Americans; Cunningham et al., 1995, for Blacks, Whites and Asians in the United States).

Most research on physical attractiveness uses photographs of the face as stimulus material. Attempts have been made to specify the measurable parameters of such faces and it is their physical averageness that appears to make them attractive within many cultural groups (Gangestad and Thornhill, 1994) and also across cultural groups (Jones and Hill, 1993). The debate continues, however, as recent research shows that departures from average favouring higher cheekbones, a thinner jaw and larger eyes are seen as even more attractive than the average composites both within and across cultures (Perrett, May and Yoshikawa, 1994).

The stereotyping of physical attractiveness. The physical attractiveness stereotype is known as the 'beautiful is good' schema, since meta-analyses of such studies consistently show that beautiful people are regarded more positively across a range of socially desirable traits (e.g. Feingold, 1992). The only qualification in this stereotype lies in the judged vanity of the physically attractive (Eagly et al., 1991). Almost all of the studies on the beauty stereotype, however, have been done in North America. Dion, Pak and Dion (1990) tested the hypothesis that the beauty stereotype should be more potent in individualistic cultures where personal attributes are regarded as more informative about the individual's personality. Among Canadian Chinese, they found that more idiocentric respondents (as measured by community involvement) showed greater effects of the beauty stereotype on their personality trait ratings of others.

Recently, the beauty stereotype has been tested cross-culturally by having respondents rate persons from their own and from other cultural groups. In all cases, the 'beautiful is good' schema has been confirmed (Albright *et al.*, 1997; Chen, Shaffer and Wu, 1997; Wheeler and Kim, 1997). Cultural variation, however, appears to lie not in the strength of the stereotype, but rather in what is regarded as 'good'. So, for example, Wheeler and Kim found that collectivist Koreans 'did not perceive attractive targets as higher in potency, as North American participants do, and did perceive attractive targets as higher in integrity and in concern for others, as North American participants do not' (p. 2). Further work in other cultures is needed to confirm the universality of the physical attractiveness stereotype, and also to assess the extent to which its content can be explained socio-culturally.

Feeling good about oneself

Self-esteem

The motive to develop and sustain an overall sense of self-worth and self-regard is a fundamental component in many Western theories of personality development. The loss of self-esteem and efforts to regain it play key roles in theories of social behaviour (e.g. Solomon, Greenberg and Pyszczynski, 1991) and in the origins of psychopathology (e.g. Taylor and Brown, 1988).

How might culture influence the development of self-esteem? Proponents of terror management theory (Solomon, Greenberg and Pyszczynski, 1991) argue that one comes to feel good about oneself to the extent that one meets the cultural imperatives defining one's social group. So, those in collectivist and individualistic cultures should have a sense of personal worth based on different attributes. Thus,

> with independence as the central cultural imperative, identifying, creating, and affirming positive features of the self while avoiding, ignoring, or discounting negative features of self, should be directly linked to self esteem . . . within an interdependent framework, the identification of one's problems, shortcomings, or deficits is an integral part of the cultural task of fitting in. (Kitayama, Markus and Lieberman, 1995, p. 539)

The measurement problem. Direct measures of self-esteem require the respondent to endorse positive self-statements and reject negative self-statements, be they general or specific. If Kitayama, Markus and Lieberman (1995) are correct in their assertions, then respondents from collective cultures should show less self-esteem than respondents from individualistic cultures. At the cultural level, however, the data are not supportive: a general measure of self-satisfaction does not correlate with cultural individualism (Diener and Diener, 1995); also, a measure of specific, positive self-statements from the TST showed respondents from the collectivist Philippines making more (50 per cent) than respondents from the individualistic United States (38 per cent), who in turn gave more than those from collectivist Hong Kong (27 per cent) (Watkins and Gerong, 1997).

A more direct test of the Kitayama, Markus and Lieberman (1995) hypothesis can be made by associating measures of independent/interdependent self-construals with self-esteem in both collectivist and individualistic cultures. When this design is followed, an independent self-construal is found to be positively correlated with self-esteem in both a collectivist and an individualistic cultural group, as Kitayama *et al.* would predict. However, an interdependent self-construal is negatively associated with self-esteem *only* in the individualistic cultural group; in the collectivist group, self-esteem is unrelated to interdependent self-construal, whether the positive or the negative items of the Rosenberg (1965) self-esteem scale are used to assess the connection (Kwan *et al.*, 1997).

This result suggests that interdependence is a liability in individualistic cultural systems, perhaps because an other-orientation and its attendant self-sacifice under-cuts personal success in such settings. In collectivist cultures, this trade-off is not in force; interdependence becomes neutral for one's self-esteem. This line of reasoning is consistent with cross-cultural work on the unrealistic optimism bias, i.e. the self-protective tendency to believe one is more likely than others to experience positive events and less likely than others to experience negative events (Weinstein, 1980). Canadians, presumably more independent, show this self-enhancing bias; Japanese, presumably more interdependent, do not (Heine and Lehman, 1995).

An alternative role for culture. Culture may shape the *type* of self-esteem that is emphasized, rather than its overall level. When one begins to sub-divide into types of self-esteem, then one faces the problem of metric equivalence of the self-esteem components across cultures. Fortunately, evidence is supportive of measurement robustness across these various components in many cultures (Watkins and Dong, 1994).

Tafarodi and Swann (1996) distinguished between generalized self-liking and generalized self-competence. They argued for and confirmed a 'cultural trade-off' hypothesis whereby respondents from collectivist China would be relatively higher in self-liking, while respondents from the individualistic United States would be relatively higher in self-competence. A more direct test of this, and other future models of this sort, will require the inclusion of individual-level measures of allocentrism and idiocentrism.

Self-esteem and psychological processes. Levels of self-esteem or types of self-esteem may differ across cultures, but self-esteem itself may have the same effect within every culture. So, for example, those higher in self-esteem are less likely to favour the humbling of high achievers in both Japan and Australia

Box 5.7 **Self-esteem and decision-making**

The optimism bias is probably stronger in those with an independent self-construal. Work on decision-making by Mann *et al.* (1997a,b) suggests that this rosy view of one's outcomes is related to one's self-esteem, which is higher in those with independent self-construals (Kwan *et al.*, in press). Mann *et al.* administered the Melbourne Decision Making Questionnaire to US, Australian, New Zealand, Japanese, Taiwanese, and Hong Kong university students. They found that respondents from the individualistic cultures reported higher decision-making self-esteem. This self-esteem correlated negatively in all cultural groups except the Japanese with 'passing the buck' to others, procrastination, and hypervigilance – three aspects of decision-making where the collectivist cultural groups all scored higher.

Once having made decisions, however, those from collective cultures may display greater confidence in their correctness. Yates *et al.* (1989) asked subjects in Japan, China, Malaysia and the United States to choose between the truth of pairs of factual statements. They were then asked to estimate the probability that they had chosen correctly. Both US and Japanese optimistically rated the probability over 50 per cent. However the Chinese and Malays were even more confident, thereby contradicting the prediction that they would express a more modest expectation. Yates, Lee and Shinotsuka (1996) suggest that while U.S. (individualistic?) cultural values encourage one to think of as many explanations for events as possible, Chinese (collectivistic?) values do not include such a strong spirit of enquiry. They proposed that Chinese respondents were therefore more confident because they had not thought of so many reasons for alternative possibilities. Asked to list possible reasons why their decisions might be wrong, the Chinese respondents produced many fewer reasons than the US respondents. Given the similarity of Japanese to US probability ratings, however, some cultural variable other than individualism may be involved. The use of self-construal or other individual-level measures in future work will help pinpoint the dynamics involved in producing confidence with one's decisions.

(Feather and McKee, 1993). Or, the negative relationship between self-esteem and delinquency may be found with Hong Kong Chinese (Leung and Lau, 1989), just as it is in the United States (Kaplan and Robbins, 1983). No evidence has yet been presented to show that self-esteem functions differently from culture to culture in relating to some other variable. Such an outcome would require a radical rethinking in our theories of human functioning.

Collective self-esteem. One problem with self-esteem measures to date is that they are so self-focused. A host of self-esteem questionnaires originated in the United States where an individualistic ideology may have predisposed psychologists towards exploring self-esteem in the first place (Hogan and Emler, 1978), as well as 'biased coverage' (Kitayama, Markus and Lieberman, 1995) by emphasizing independent aspects of oneself.

As we shall discuss more fully in Chapter 7, social identity theory defines the collective self as 'that aspect of an individual's self-concept which derives from his knowledge of his memberships in a social group (or groups) together with the value and emotional significance attached to that membership' (Tajfel, 1981, p. 255). Our group memberships are one aspect of our interdependent selves and may contribute to our psychological well being over and above that contributed by more independently focused self-measures. Crocker and her colleagues have developed a collective self-esteem scale and shown that it predicts measures of life satisfaction and hopelessness over and above self-esteem predictions alone (Crocker *et al.*, 1994). This outcome was especially true for their Asian (and presumably more allocentric) Americans. Our theories of psychological well being may need to be broadened to include more interdependent elements to accommodate less individualistic cultures.

Subjective well-being

A construct related to self-esteem is subjective well-being (SWB) defined by Diener *et al.* (1996) simply as 'peoples' evaluations of their lives.' (p. 1). SWB is a composite measure including these components: positive affect, lack of negative affect, life satisfaction, and satisfaction with domains of activity such as work and recreation. These measures have been drawn from self-report surveys of both college students and probability samples of adults in forty-one nations.

A number of conclusions were drawn from analyses of this survey data:

1. 'Nations differ substantially in their mean levels of reported subjective well-being, and these differences tend to be stable across surveys and across time. The mean levels in most nations are, however, above the neutral point' (Diener *et al.*, 1996). Of course, surveys such as this one are impractical to distribute in nations experiencing international conflict, famine, or plague. Under normal conditions, however, most people report positive levels of SWB.
2. 'Both economic development and cultural norms for feelings correlate with mean levels of reported well-being. 'Cultural norms for feelings' refers to how desirable it is for a person to experience certain emotions, in this case positive emotions. Norms continue to correlate with mean reported subjective well-being even when national income is controlled.' (Diener *et al.*, 1996, p. 13). A cluster of national variables associated with economic development such as human rights observance (Humana, 1986), individualism and basic need fulfilment are positively associated with SWB. These correlations with economic development are not confined to satisfaction with material aspects of life; 'The economic development syndrome also appears to be correlated with better social relationships.' (Diener *et al.*, p. 8), as measured by satisfaction with home life and with jobs. Note that country heterogeneity (ethnic diversity), murder rates and population density did *not* correlate with SWB.
3. 'Despite variables such as income that do correlate with the average subjective

well-being across nations, there are also differences in how strongly various factors correlate with subjective well-being within different cultures. For example, self-esteem correlates with life satisfaction more strongly in individualistic nations than in collectivistic ones' (Diener *et al.*, p. 13). This important finding raises the interesting question of which other individual-level measures may be more strongly associated with SWB in collectivist nations. One answer follows.

4. 'Affect (moods and emotions) appears to be weighted more highly in life satisfaction judgments in individualistic nations, whereas cultural norms are weighted more heavily in collectivistic cultures' (Diener *et al.*, p. 13). This conclusion is exactly what one would expect from applying the logic of independent/interdependent self-construals associated respectively with individualistic/collectivist cultural logics – those in collectivist cultural systems pay relatively more attention to external sources (viz. cultural norms about feeling) in assessing their SWB.

Perceived quality of life

Veenhoven (1993, 1996a) has argued that people in a variety of nations can reliably and meaningfully rate their happiness. These ratings may be found in the World Database of Happiness (Veenhoven, 1996b). By multiplying this rating with the country life expectancy average, she calculated a 'happy life-expectancy' (HLE) index in forty-eight nations. By this measure, India and Nigeria show the lowest 'apparent quality of life'; Iceland and the Netherlands score highest.

HLE correlates positively with a number of country-level indicators: gross domestic product (GDP) per capita, gender equality, literacy rate, perceived freedom at work, membership frequency in voluntary associations, absence of corruption and infrequency of prejudice; other indicators, such as measures of religiosity, population density and military expenditure do not. Given the high correlation of HLE with GDP per capita ($r = 0.78$), one might argue that 'apparent quality of life' is a reflection of economic modernity. Indeed, many of the above relationships between HLE and the social indicators disappear if GDP per capita is controlled statistically.

However, some significant relationships remain: absence of corruption, infrequency of prejudice and perceived freedom at work predict HLE regardless of per capita income level. These country-level phenomena suggest that societal norms which can develop independently from economic advancement are also important in shaping the perceived quality of life from nation to nation. These factors, along with those attached to economic modernity, provide a societal context within which each citizen can thrive with a long and happy life.

Attributing success and failure

In addition to studying perceptions of oneself and of others, cognitive social psychologists have also been very interested in the explanations we put forward when we do better or worse than others on some task. Nisbett and Ross (1980) identified a 'self-serving bias' whereby subjects in experiments are often found to attribute successes to their own skills and abilities, but are more inclined to explain failures in terms of contextual factors. The studies we have discussed in earlier sections of this chapter strongly suggest that we need to consider whether these effects will only be found in individualistic cultural groups.

In evaluating the 'self-serving bias' hypothesis, we must bear in mind the findings of cross-cultural studies on the self-concept. As Cousins (1989) reported, the Japanese describe themselves dispositionally when the situation is clearly specified, while Americans do so when it is not. Since respondents in other collectivist cultures frequently also refer to social context in describing themselves, it is likely that if Cousins' study were to be repeated there, a similar effect would be found. How then might we expect interdependent subjects to account for their successes and failures? The research design typically employed in this type of study presents subjects with a series of *specific* tasks upon which they do or do not do well. This would lead us to expect that interdependent subjects would account for their successes and failures in terms of personal attributes at least as much as do independent subjects.

In search of the self-serving bias in attributions

Kashima and Triandis (1986) compared explanations given by Japanese and American students, all of them studying in America, for their successes and failures. A free response format was first employed, to ensure that types of explanation not found among Western samples were not overlooked. It was found that the free response categories elicited were in fact readily classifiable into the four categories originally distinguished by Heider (1958), namely ability, effort, task difficulty and luck. Kashima and Triandis' experimental task required subjects to remember details of slides they were shown of scenes in unfamiliar countries. The task was a difficult one, and subjects from both countries tended to explain successes in terms of situational factors such as luck or familiarity, and failures in terms of task difficulty. As the self-serving hypothesis would predict, the American subjects explained their successes more in terms of ability than they did their failures. However, the Japanese subjects showed the reverse pattern – they attributed their failures to a greater lack of ability more than they attributed their successes to ability, a 'self-effacement bias'. Overall, there was no difference in the frequency with which ability constructs were used to explain performance, but they were clearly used in a very different way.

These studies illustrate the need for us to distinguish between two issues. Firstly, we need to look at how often interdependent subjects use dispositional trait terms to explain their performance. Secondly, we need to look at whether they use dispositional traits in the same manner as the self-serving bias hypothesis proposes. There is fairly general evidence that terms classifiable as effort and ability are widely used by subjects to account for success and failure. For instance, Munro (1979)

Figure 5.2 A becoming modesty? (Source: Feign, 1986.)

compared white Zimbabweans, black Zimbabweans and black Zambians. For all three groups the most frequently endorsed explanations were 'actions', 'personal' and 'chance', which are presumably similar to effort, ability and luck, respectively. Separate means are not presented for success and failure.

Boski (1983) compared responses of students belonging to the three main tribal groups in Nigeria: Ibo, Yoruba and Hausa. He found effort and ability frequently used to explain success and contextual factors more endorsed as reasons for failure. Within these overall effects, he predicted that each cultural group would show a different pattern, based upon prevailing cultural values within that group. In particular, Ibos are believed to endorse idiocentric values more frequently, whereas the Muslim and more traditional Hausa are thought to hold more allocentric values. Boski did indeed find that his Hausa subjects explained their success significantly less than did Ibos in terms of ability and more in terms of contextual factors such as the nature of the task and luck. Few differences were found in explanations for failures. Lee and Seligman (1997) found a self-serving bias on both success and failure outcomes for presumably idiocentric white Americans but a self-effacing bias for presumably allocentric Chinese from the People's Republic of China. Similarly, Fry and Ghosh (1980) compared the attributions for success and failure of matched samples of white Canadian and Asian Indian Canadian children aged between 8 and 10. The white children showed the usual pattern of self-serving attributions, rating effort and ability higher for success, and contextual factors such as luck and an unfair experimenter higher for failure. In contrast, the Asian Indian children saw luck as relatively more important in their successes and ability as more important in their failures than did the white children.

Limitations on the modesty bias in attributions

Each of the four studies reviewed above included samples likely to score relatively high on allocentrism and each found that after working on an experimental task, there was little evidence of self-serving attributional bias among allocentric subjects. This conclusion appears to be contradicted by the results of one further study, that by Chandler *et al.* (1981), who asked students in the United States, Japan, India, South Africa and the former Yugoslavia to complete a structured questionnaire asking questions about the reasons for academic successes and failures. They found that in all countries except Japan subjects did rate themselves as more personally responsible for their successes than for their failures, although the effect was stronger in some countries than others.

In order to reconcile the findings of Chandler *et al.* with the other cross-cultural studies of success and failure, we can consider the different procedures that they employed. Chandler *et al.* used a questionnaire containing items which are relatively context-free. An example from the scale they used is: 'I feel that my good grades reflect directly on my academic ability'. In the other studies, experimenters contrived that their subjects did in fact succeed (or fail) on a specific task immediately before they filled out their ratings. As we saw earlier in the chapter, members of collectivist cultures often find it difficult to describe themselves or others unless they are able to specify the context. It is clear that the experimental studies do provide a specific setting and a particular person (the experimenter) who is asking for explanations of behaviour. The explanations given are more likely to be emically valid representations of how subjects wished to account for their behaviour to the experimenter. The Chandler *et al.* measure, on the other hand, is an imposed etic measure, which, at least in the more collectivist countries sampled, is likely to have evoked what might have been thought to be an ideal student's self-perception and self-presentation. Even despite these limitations, it is notable that Chandler *et al.* found no self-serving bias in Japan. Another study using imposed-etic measures, Watkins and Regmi (1990), also found no self-serving bias among Nepalese students, when they were asked to make ratings accounting for the actual grades they had obtained.

Several studies with Chinese subjects support the view that valid tests for self-serving bias are those which specify the context. Wan and Bond (1982) found that the attributions for success and failure made by Hong Kong Chinese varied, depending upon the circumstances under which they were asked to provide their explanations. Where explanations were made to a specific, known experimenter, a reversal of the self-serving bias was found for attributions to the factor of luck. Where the explanations were provided in a more context-free, anonymous questionnaire, the effect was reversed. Consistent with this pattern of attribution, the students who gave modest or self-effacing rather than self-serving attributions proved to be those who were better liked by their peers (Bond, Leung and Wan, 1982b). Not surprisingly then, Stipek, Weiner and Li (1989) found that their Chinese subjects were much less likely to express pride in success than were American subjects.

It should come again as no surprise to us that the attributions provided by those with allocentric values depend upon whom they are addressing. It is of course central to allocentric values that someone who endorses those values will adjust their words and actions to what is appropriate in relation to specific others. Mizokawa and Ryckman (1990) illustrate another aspect of the ways in which such adaptations may be made. They administered a questionnaire to Asian American children in the United States, comparing those from varying ethnic origins. The forty-item questionnaire asked for ratings of success and failure in specific academic subjects. They too found evidence for modesty effects as well as self-serving biases, but the effects varied between one cultural group and another. Southeast Asians for instance showed a modesty effect for ability ratings, but a self-serving bias for effort ratings, whereas the Japanese–American children showed the reverse pattern.

Thus we should not assume that a modesty bias will obtain uniformly across all the domains within which members of collectivist groups account for their actions. Indeed it is probably also the case that the manner in which 'effort' and 'ability' are conceptualized, itself varies by culture (e.g. Watkins and Cheng, 1995). A series of studies in India has shown that where Indians are asked to predict the performance of someone of known ability and motivation, their predictions are arrived at *additively* (Singh, 1981). That is to say they expect performance to depend simply on the level of ability and on the amount of effort. This contrasts with the predictions originally formulated by Heider (1958) and supported by studies in the United States, which sees performance as a function of ability *multiplied* by effort. The Heider model implies that a good level of both motivation and effort are required if performance is to be high. The Indian results indicate that at least in Singh's (1981) samples, which were extensive, it was believed that sufficient effort can compensate for lack of ability. One could speculate that this belief is more likely to be true in collectivist cultural groups, since if one member contributes ability and another effort, group performance could be high. Displays of effort seem to be important strategies for conveying group loyalty and commitment to one's group in collectivistic cultures and a 'cult of effort' is often found in such settings (e.g. Holloway *et al.*, 1986).

Linking ability attributions to performance

Little *et al.* (1995) have isolated three belief systems that children use to explain their school outcomes: means–ends beliefs are conceptions of what factors (e.g. teacher's help) are important in achieving an outcome; agency beliefs refer to whether one possesses a given means to achieve that outcome; control expectancies refer to a general belief that one can achieve an outcome. Little *et al.* compared East German, Russian and American students on these three types of beliefs and on the linkage of these beliefs to actual performance.

Means–ends beliefs show a similar structure across cultures and are rated at similar levels. The association of these beliefs with actual performance was weak in all three cultural groups. However, agency beliefs and control expectancies showed different results across cultures. First, American students rated their own agency and control as higher than did students in the other cultures. The lower ratings of the German and Russian students was explained in part by the practice of giving critical, comparative, public feedback to students in these school systems, especially before the recent changes in Soviet bloc countries. There was thus less opportunity for self-enhancing tendencies to operate. In addition, the Russian and German students showed a much stronger correlation between their agency or control ratings and their actual performance than did the American children. The authors explained this tighter linkage by noting that the German and Russian children were given performance-based feedback in class, so that their beliefs and expectancies came to map their academic output more closely (see also Oettingen et al., 1994).

As Little et al. (1995) argue, these educational practices surrounding student evaluation reflect broader cultural emphases. So, for example, the use of private, supportive feedback which characterizes American classrooms is consistent with its individualistic, optimistic orientation. These practices then have implications on how these students evaluate their performance-related capacities and how closely those self-ratings correspond to actual performance.

Comparing oneself with others

The way in which we compare our attitudes and behaviours with those of other people has long been given a central role in social psychology. However, the reasons for comparing oneself with others may differ, depending upon whether one endorses idiocentric or allocentric values. In an individualist cultural group, social comparison could provide feedback as to one's personal qualities and abilities, and hence reinforce or undermine one's sense of a distinctive, unique self. In a collectivist cultural group, social comparison can take on different meanings depending on the target of one's comparisons. In relation to other members of one's own group, social comparison will provide guidelines enabling the group member to sense what is the group consensus and to detect possible dangers of future disagreement. In relation to strangers or members of other known groups, social comparison is likely to emphasize differences, enhancing the prestige of one's group or else not to occur at all, since these others are outside one's network of relationships.

Takata (1987) asked Japanese students to solve anagram problems. They were then asked to compare their performance with that of another subject, supposedly picked at random, who had done better or worse. Where they had done worse than others, the Japanese expressed more confidence that the estimate of their ability was accurate, whereas when they had done better they were more doubtful. A 'self-effacing' bias was thus again found. Takata then asked subjects whether they would like to seek further information. Those who had received low estimates of their abilities were less interested in obtaining more information, presumably because they were content with the evaluation they had received.

Endo (1995), however, has shown that with Japanese a modesty bias in comparative appraisals emerges only with known reference to others; when comparisons are made with 'most other people', a self-enhancement bias occurs. This contrasting outcome underscores the sensitivity to the relationship with the other that is fundamental in collectivist cultures among (presumably) allocentric respondents.

These findings contrast with the positive value placed on assertiveness and self-confidence in more individualist cultures. Markus and Kitayama (1991) reported a direct comparison between Japanese and American students. Subjects were asked to estimate what proportion of students in their university would score higher than them on various traits and abilities, such as athletic ability, sympathy, intellectual ability, memory and so forth. On average, the Americans estimated that only 30 per cent would be above them, whereas the Japanese estimates were close to the (presumably correct) 50 per cent mark. Similarly, Yik, Bond and Paulhus (1997) show that Hong Kong Chinese rate themselves lower in desirable personality attributes than others rate them; Canadians rate themselves higher than others rate them.

Reasons for valuing achievement

The achievement motive has often been thought of as a fundamental human need (McClelland, 1961). While it may well be the case that both those with idiocentric and allocentric values do compare their achievements with those of others, their motives for doing so are not likely to be identical. Church and Katigbak (1992) asked college students in the United States and the Philippines to make ratings as to their motivations for doing well in their academic work. The American students ranked personal achievement and getting good grades higher than the Filipinos did. The Filipinos endorsed allocentric goals more often, particularly preparing to get a good job, and gaining the approval of others. In a similar way, Yang (1986) proposes that in order to understand the Chinese orientation toward achievement we must distinguish between achievement defined in an idiocentric and an allocentric manner (see also Yu, 1996).

The studies examined in this brief section all concern East Asian orientations toward achievement. Although numerous other studies of achievement motivation have been conducted from other parts of the world, these studies used an imposed-etic format, which does not permit a culturally sensitive analysis of why members of particular cultures do or do not favour achievement. The findings of the studies that we have examined are relatively clear, but we must be careful not to draw conclusions about collectivist cultures in general from such a restricted range of examples. Further studies from additional cultural groups will be required before it would be wise to assert that the modesty found in these studies is part of collectivist cultures in general. We shall discuss in the next chapter some examples from the Arab world and elsewhere of communication styles in which exaggeration rather than modesty is positively valued. In addition, it would be most helpful if researchers measured the individual-level variables thought to be important in generating these overall cultural differences. So, for example, Kwan (1997) has found that self-enhancement in rating one's personality is related positively to an independent self-construal, extroversion, conscientiousness and emotional stability. This type of linkage suggests the individual-level variables that may be responsible for differences across cultural groups.

Progress review

In this chapter we have commenced the task laid out at the end of Chapter 4. In reviewing studies in the area of the self and social cognition we have focused upon some of the research fields currently attracting greatest interest in social psychology. Our task has been to see how far the individualism/collectivism concept helps us to tease out a clear strand among results obtained from different parts of the world. Since most studies of social cognition are based upon studies of individuals rather than of whole cultures, we have for the most part used the concepts of idiocentrism and allocentrism, together with the related notion of independent and interdependent self-concepts to analyze the findings.

We have found substantial evidence that studies undertaken in more collectivist cultures do yield rather different results. Subjects in these parts of the world perceive themselves and others in more situational terms, demarcate themselves from others less sharply, and less often make self-serving ratings and attributions. However, in only a minority of the studies that we have cited were any individual-level measures of the subject's values or self-construals actually taken. Consequently, explanations of why these differences are found cannot be wholly conclusive.

A number of recent studies suggest that greater progress in defining valid individual-level measures of values and self-concept will be required before this ambiguity can be resolved. Some critics (e.g. Kagitçibasi, 1997) have suggested that individuals may define themselves as allocentric in particular domains of their life and idiocentric in other domains. For instance, in some cultures, one might sustain allocentric values in relation to family and idiocentric values at work. Data supporting this view have been obtained in the United States and Japan (Matsumoto, Kudoh and Takeuchi, 1996).

A second possibility is that endorsement of idiocentrism–allocentrism will vary markedly between different sectors within a national culture. Marshall (1997) found for instance that although New Zealanders endorsed idiocentrism more than Indonesians, as one would expect, a greater amount of variance in these scores was explained by social class variations within each nation. Furthermore, Watkins et al. (1996) recently found variations in response to the TST measure of self-concept between students in nine nations unrelated to presumed levels of individualism–collectivism. Cultural differences are most probably greater among non-student populations, but this is nonetheless a challenging finding.

Empirically based critiques of these kinds can help to sharpen our understanding of the ways in which culture-level differences can explain the results of individual-level studies. By doing so they will strengthen the bridge that is required between North American theories of social cognition and relevant studies from the rest of the world.

The theories of social cognition that are most strongly supported in current work in the United States rest upon models of the individual's information-processing (Markus and Zajonc, 1985; Sampson, 1985). It would be consistent with such models to propose that the differences surveyed in this chapter could be explained by postulating that those with idiocentric and allocentric orientations are socialized to *direct their attention in somewhat different ways*. An idiocentric person would seek to identify the active element in any situation and to discern its effect on other elements, in something like the manner clearly laid out in Kelley's (1967) formulation of attribution theory. Rather than proceed in this way, an allocentric person would attend to the configuration of elements in any situation, and infer causation by looking at what most often goes with what. The British philosopher John Stuart Mill (1872/1973) already identified these two alternate procedures for determining causation, which he termed the 'method of difference' and the 'method of association'. Most probably all of us can and do infer causation in both ways on occasion. All that is required to explain the differences found between cultural groups is to postulate that each of us does it more often one way than the other. Clear evidence for the lack of correlation between interdependent and independent self-construals supports this line of reasoning (Gudykunst *et al.*, 1994; Singelis, 1994).

However, reducing cultural differences in social cognition to an analysis of differences in where individuals direct their attention would be a serious over-simplification. As we saw in Chapter 3, a culture is a system of *shared* meanings. This implies that any differences there may be in how we as individuals direct our attention, or behave in other distinctive ways, is not just a matter of something that we as individuals happen to do. It occurs because we grow up in particular groups, which teach us how to construe the world.

A model of social cognition that sees the optimum level of analysis as being at the level of individual choices about the direction of attention and the processing of information is likely to command more interest in individualist cultures than elsewhere and also to be of greatest value in studying the behaviour of individuals. We turn next to the key question of the individual's relation to other group members.

Summary

Exploration of cultural differences in the processes of social cognition has been greatly helped by the development of individual-level constructs which parallel culture-level differences in individualism–collectivism. While not all studies have included direct measures of idiocentrism–allocentrism or independent/inter-dependent self-construals, an increasing number have done so. Individuals who endorse allocentric values or have an interdependent self-concept evaluate themselves and their social world in significantly different ways from those who have been the typical research subjects of mainstream social psychological study. The consequences of this difference for social behaviour are explored in the next three chapters.

Communication and interpersonal relations

'When I use a word,' Humpty Dumpty said, in a rather scornful
tone, 'it means just what I choose it to mean – neither
more nor less.'
'The question is,' said Alice, 'whether you can make words
mean so many different things.'
'The question is,' said Humpty Dumpty, 'which is to be
master – that's all.'

(Lewis Carroll, *Through the Looking Glass*)

In the previous chapter we focused upon cognitive processes presumed in individualistic cultures especially to be the basic bed-rock upon which social interaction is built. As we have seen already, however, the social environment of those living within cultures that are predominantly collectivist or particularistic differs substantially from that found in the individualistic or universalistic cultures where most psychology has been done. This variation in the values, beliefs, expectancies and behaviours of those around one will have a major influence upon the types and amount of information that is available in a particular location. In this chapter we will take further our exploration of how this variation affects the way in which people get to know one another and influence one another's behaviour. We start by examining differences in the styles of communication that occur, and in related attitudes toward time. We shall then be in a position to consider how different types of social relationship evolve.

Communication style

The variety of ways in which English is spoken in everyday life can make it difficult for a native English speaker to accept the idea that there is something unified about the communication patterns found within, for instance, white Anglo cultural groups. There is of course a rich variety of forms of spoken English within any one of countries such as the United States, the United Kingdom, Australia or Canada.

Such variations often serve to demarcate sub-cultural groups in terms of class, ethnicity or regional location. For instance, the manner in which Mrs Robertson spoke to Mr Chan marks her out as a lowland Scot. Several of the phrases which she used would make it particularly difficult for other native speakers of English, let alone Chan, to understand her. When she said 'I doubt you are twenty minutes late', she meant that she was sure that he was twenty minutes late. However, she had failed to think through the fact that although her meaning would be clear enough in Edinburgh or Glasgow, particularly if delivered with an appropriate accent, it would confuse most English speakers from outside Scotland.

Regional dialects pose difficulties in Chinese or any other language just as much as they do in English. However, the emphasis in the present context is more upon the issue of whether there are distinctive aspects of communication *style* across cultures generally and which can be related to idiocentric or allocentric orientations in particular. To address this level of generality, we need to consider those aspects of communication that transcend the specific language being spoken.

The cultural context of language and its use

Munroe, Munroe and Winters (1996) propose that the types of language that evolve in different cultures will be influenced by the physical environment within which people live. In particular, where people live in warm parts of the world, they will spend more time outdoors than those living in cold climates. They will therefore need to communicate with one another across longer distances and against a background of greater extraneous noise. To do so effectively they will need languages with simpler, less ambiguous structure. Munroe *et al.* predict that words in hot countries will more often have a pattern of regularly alternating consonants and vowels (e.g. 'Panama' or 'matador'). Words that do not follow this sequence (e.g. 'screech' or 'stick') are harder to decode and they therefore expect them to be more frequent in cold climates. Their hypothesis was upheld, using samples of words from fifty-three societies, forty-seven of which were non-literate. The study did not include enough languages from literate cultures to show whether this effect still obtains within modern societies, after taking into account the extensive importation into local languages of words from English and other widely spoken languages. This extension of the Munroe *et al.* hypothesis would be most helpful.

Leaving aside phonetic structure, Hall (1976) has proposed that the actual usage of language in different cultures can be classified as high context or low context. For Hall, a low-context culture is one in which speech is explicit and the message intended is largely conveyed by the words spoken. In contrast, a high-context culture is one in which a good deal of the meaning is implicit and the words spoken will often be indirect and convey only a small part of the message. The remaining part of the message is to be inferred by the listener on the basis of past knowledge of the speaker, the setting of the particular conversation, and any other contextual cues available. Hall classifies numerous countries around the world as falling into one or the other category, on the basis of his observations.

Hall (1976) thought of high- and low-context cultures as spread along a continuum, rather than as polar opposites. Gudykunst, Ting-Toomey and Chua (1988) point out that there is a close match between Hall's classification and where different national cultures were located by Hofstede (1980) along his empirically derived scale of individualism–collectivism. Gudykunst *et al.* go on to investigate how high- and low-context communication may serve to sustain individualist and collectivist cultures.

They propose that discourse in individualist countries can be characterized as direct, succinct, personal and instrumental. This contrasts with the indirect, elaborate, contextual and affective emphases of communication in collectivist societies. From this general proposition one may derive predictions such as that in individualist cultural groups: speech will be more focused, briefer, will involve more reference to 'I' and to specific goals. In collectivist societies, speech will be more discursive and will include more qualifiers such as 'maybe', 'perhaps', 'probably', 'slightly', 'somewhat' and 'rather'. It will also be adapted to reflect the status of the persons addressed and will involve the speaker in scanning the listeners for affective cues as to how they are responding to the message they are receiving.

Empirical testing of such propositions will be a massive project. What are already available are piecemeal comparisons of communicative styles in specific pairs or groups of cultures. Katriel (1986), for example, compares communicative styles of Jews and Arabs in Israel. She contrasts the relatively individualistic Jewish Sabra (native-born) preference for 'straight talk', with the collectivist preference in Arab languages for *'musayra'*, which is translated as '. . . going with the other, . . .

Box 6.1   Use of personal pronouns in different languages

One linguistic phenomenon that sustains cultural emphasis is the 'pronoun-drop'. In many languages, it is possible to drop or elide the first and second person singular pronouns (i.e. 'I' and 'you') in speech. Such linguistic elision short-circuits the separation between speaker and interlocutor, thereby supporting a sense of 'we-ness' in the interactants. Kashima and Kashima (in press) studied thirty-nine languages, spoken in seventy-one cultures. They found that pronoun-dropping is characteristic of languages used by those in collectivist cultures where reinforcing relatedness is important; in individualistic cultures, the distinctiveness of individuals is important, and such separations are reinforced by using the words for 'I' and 'you'.

They also studied the number of different first and second person singular pronouns in each language. Their prediction was that cultures with more of these pronouns would be those that made more distinctions on the basis of status or role, as measured by the culture-level characterizations of Hofstede (1980), Schwartz (1994), the Chinese Culture Connection (1987) and Smith, Dugan and Trompenaars (1996). Hypotheses using each of these data sources were supported.

humouring, . . . accommodating oneself to the position or situation of the other' (Katriel, 1986, p. 111). The contrast she describes is in agreement with the predictions about directness of Gudykunst, Ting-Toomey and Chua (1988). More systematic evidence is provided by the work of M. S. Kim. She proposed that speakers within collectivist cultures will be guided by the requirement to not impose on the hearer and to not hurt the hearer's feelings, whereas in individualist cultures speakers will be constrained by the requirement for clarity. Her hypotheses were tested by asking respondents from different cultures to rate the importance of these constraints. At the culture-level the requirement to not impose on and to not hurt the other was rated higher in Korea and Hawaii, whereas the requirement to be clear was rated higher in the mainland United States (Kim, 1994). A parallel study using individual-level measures of self-concept showed that those with interdependent self-concepts sought not to impose on or hurt others, whereas those with independent self-concepts sought to be clear (Kim, Sharkey and Singelis, 1994; M. S. Kim et al., 1996). Despite these differences, in all cultural groups the use of various constraints in communication is related to assessments of their perceived effectiveness in promoting the interaction (Kim and Bresnahan, 1994).

Similarly, Gudykunst, Gao and Franklyn-Stokes (1996) developed self-report measures of high- vs. low-context styles of communication. They discovered eight factors of communication common to five different cultural groups: ability to infer others' meanings, use of direct vs. ambiguous communication, interpersonal sensitivity, use of dramatic communication, use of feelings to guide behaviour, openness in discourse, precision and positive perceptions of silence. These investigators also developed individual-level measures of self-construal and of values consistent with theorizing about cultural individualism/collectivism. Independent self-construals and values positively predicted reported ability to interpret indirect messages, use of dramatic, feeling-oriented, open and precise communication; while they negatively predicted the use of indirect messages. Interdependent self-construals and values positively predicted sensitivity and negatively predicted favourable attitudes towards silence. In general, then, most hypotheses about the mediation of high- and low-context styles of communication by self-construals were confirmed in this ambitious study.

Of course, direct and explicit communication is required at certain times in all cultural groups, just as is indirect and allusive communication (Levine, 1985; Miller, 1994). Yeung (1996), for example, analyzed transcripts from participative decision-making meetings in Australian and Hong Kong banks. She found both forms of communication in both cultural groups. In such task-focused settings with their evaluative pressures, participants want their individual inputs to be understood and acknowledged. So, Yeung noticed that members of both cultures disagreed equally often but did so in different ways: Australians used the 'yes, but . . .' form more; Hong Kong Chinese asked more rhetorical questions. Also, participants from both groups moderated direct assertions of their position on an issue so as not to be perceived as pushy, but did so in different ways – the

Australians used more verbal hedges, e.g. 'somewhat', 'I think that . . .', 'hopefully'; the Hong Kong Chinese used more questions, especially of the 'can we . . .?' form when stating their positions. Similarly, Beebe and Takahashi (1989) also found that Japanese could be just as direct and explicit and disagreeing in their speech as Americans, albeit using different semantic formulas.

In some languages, the pronoun 'we' can be strategically used to blur boundaries between speaker and hearer(s). Mao (1996) identified four different, sometimes inter-related, meanings of 'we' in Chinese communication: singular we, humbleness, politicking, and evasion. We can expect that such rich potentials for the 'we' pronoun will be found in the languages of all collective cultures.

This focus on 'we' rather than 'I' echoes a collectivist theme found in comparisons of how Hong Kong Chinese and Germans structure letters of complaint (Laucken, Mees and Chaussein, 1992). First, Chinese were more likely to write the letters anonymously, thereby dissociating the complainant from the complaint, so as to protect relations with the complainee. Also, the Chinese were much more likely to point out that several others were affected by the problem, not only themselves. Finally, the Chinese were much less likely to level a personal accusation at a guilty perpetrator than were the Germans. All of these tactics combine to give the Chinese letters a less assertive, more harmony-oriented quality. This collective approach generates less contention by de-personalizing the exchanges. It is in this sense that communication in collective cultures may be construed as less 'direct'.

Self-disclosure

Disclosure of personal information about oneself can be thought of as one type of direct communication. Won-Doornink (1985) compared self-disclosure in the United States and Korea and found as she expected that it was higher in the United States. After reviewing other studies, she concludes that the difference she found is typical of differences between Eastern (collectivist) and Western (individualist) cultures. Mutual self-disclosure would be of greater value in individualist cultures since it will enable the making of choices as to whether one wishes to get to know

---

Box 6.2 **Direct and indirect communication**

Some characteristics of direct and indirect talk are illustrated in the exchange between Mrs Robertson and Mr Chan. Mrs Robertson gives an explicit order for Chan's friend to wait in the hall; she confronts him openly about his lateness and his lying. Chan presents his position as the class's position, frequently using the pronoun 'we'; he uses a rhetorical question when defending his absence from classes while watching his sister; he phrases his request for a compassionate pass negatively, thereby giving Mrs Robertson more latitude to refuse (not that she needs much!).

another person further. In a collectivist culture, it would be less crucial to know a person's particular history or personality, and more important to be clear about the other person's affiliations and status, and the rules governing the immediate context. Disclosure is something that would only have greater value within already established in-group relationships.

Goodwin (1995) reported low willingness to self-disclose personal information among Russian students and entrepreneurs. Goodwin and Lee (1994) found British students more willing to disclose to their friends than were a sample of Singapore Chinese students. Derlega and Stepien (1977) compared willingness to self-disclose in Poland and the United States. The Poles, who were presumably somewhat more collectivist, made a stronger distinction between disclosure to a friend and to a stranger than did the Americans. Taking this line of analysis further, Gudykunst *et al.* (1992) compared how sharply distinctions were drawn between in-group relationships and out-group relationships by students in the United States, Japan, Hong Kong and Taiwan. They found that in the three more

---

Box 6.3   Culture and the Internet

As new media of communication are created, we may expect that they will evolve in ways that express the cultural priorities of those who use each medium. It is estimated that some 85 per cent of electronic mail is currently in the English language (Naisbitt and Aburdene, 1990). However, this relative verbal and linguistic uniformity cannot accommodate the full range of ways that people like to use in communicating with one another. In particular, e-mail lacks the non-verbal accompaniments of other modes of communication. This has been remedied to be the creation of 'emoticons', with which communicators can emphasize their feelings about the content of the messages they are sending and receiving. The best known emoticon is the smiley :-) . Emoticons most probably originated in North America and have been widely adopted by e-mail communicators. Japanese users of e-mail are said to use emoticons more frequently than Western users, possibly because of their greater resemblance to kanji characters.

Japanese e-mail users found the smiley hard to comprehend because the 'face' portrayed by the smiley is turned to one side. They have consequently devised an alternative form (^-^) , which appears much more like a face. Since there is no keyboard character that can produce an upward curve, the Japanese smiley is somewhat more 'expressionless', unless one knows how to read it. Just as Japanese language differs for men and women, so the emoticon given above is the male version. Women would use (^.^) , since it would traditionally be immodest for a Japanese woman to bare her teeth as widely as is implied by the male version. Other Western emoticons for anger and sadness are rarely used in Japan, but emoticons for apology ^o^;> and 'cold sweat' (^ ^;) are in use. Thus can the Internet contribute to the cross-cultural study of emotion.

Source: *New York Times*, 10 August 1996.

collectivist countries there was more self-disclosure and more questioning of the other within in-group relationships than in out-group relationships. In the United States on the other hand there was no significant differentiation between in-group and out-group on these measures.

The preservation of face

A more general account of the functions of the differing styles of communication in individualist and collectivist cultures is provided by Ting-Toomey's (1988) theory of face. She argues that in all cultures we seek to save face, but the concept has different referents in individualist and collectivist cultures. In all cultural settings we are concerned with both 'positive face' and 'negative face' (Brown and Levinson, 1987). 'Negative face refers to an individual's desire to have one's autonomy prerogatives respected, whereas positive face consists of the desire to have one's presented image approved . . . Brown and Levinson assumed that people usually cooperate to minimize face threat, because both parties' face wants are vulnerable to the actions of the other party' (Leichty and Applegate, 1991, pp. 452–3). Concern about face needs are regarded as a universal concern during interaction (Ho, 1976).

In fact, 'face' is a broad metaphor encompassing all those behavioural considerations regarded as important in nurturing a relationship, or preventing its disruption. It is related to the concept of 'politeness' in that impolite behaviours threaten the face of both the impolite person and the recipient of the impolite behaviour. Politeness theory (Brown and Levinson, 1987) has been developed to explain variations in the strategies, both verbal and non-verbal, that interactants use to communicate appropriate degrees of politeness.

Speakers who use deferential language are rated as more likeable, more influential, and less dominant (Liska and Hazelton, 1990). Such deferential language addresses the social universal identified by Goody:

> the basic constraints on effective interaction appear to be essentially the same across cultures and languages; everywhere a person must secure the cooperation of his interlocutor if he is to accomplish his goals. To secure cooperation he must avoid antagonizing his hearer. . . . (1978, p. 6)

Politeness theory predicts that, universally, speaker politeness increases with the power of the target over the speaker, the social distance of the target from the speaker, and the degree of imposition a speaker makes on a target. Using both Korean and US respondents, Holtgraves and Yang (1990, 1992) confirmed the importance of these variables in shaping verbal politeness in both cultures; Ambady et al. (1996) also found that non-verbal politeness markers increased in both Korean and US role-plays as a function of power differences and degree of imposition. So, evidence is accumulating that in various cultures persons vary the politeness of their behaviour towards another as a function of the same relationship and content variables. Such concern about honouring the face needs of both parties allows the interaction to proceed.

In an individualist culture the focus of face, however, is primarily the 'I', who is concerned that his or her positive qualities be seen and their negative qualities be hidden or excused. The work of Goffman (1959) for instance emphasizes procedures for 'facework', or avoiding the loss of negative face in Western countries. In collectivist cultural groups, says Ting-Toomey (1988), the preservation of harmony is the major goal and positive face is sustained where this result is accomplished. When there is a danger of conflict, the concern is not that 'I' specifically would be embarrassed, but that 'We' need to ward off that danger by reading the indirect communication cues sufficiently early that a conflictful situation may be averted. In a comparison of informal rules about how one should relate to others, Argyle *et al.* (1986) found greater endorsement of rules for restraining emotional expression, preserving harmony and avoiding loss of face in Japan and Hong Kong than in Italy and the United Kingdom. These rules cover a much broader range of conversational topics than simple self-disclosure and also involve differences in communication style.

So, many people in individualist cultures will seek to avoid embarrassing others, but in terms of Ting-Toomey's model, this concern would derive from somewhat different reasons from those in a collectivist setting. Choi and Choi (1992) present an analysis of the Korean concepts of *noon-chi* and *che-myun*, which they translate respectively as 'tact' and 'face-saving'. They point out that tact in English has overtones of interpersonal diplomacy or manipulation, whereas in Korean the meaning is more collective and focused on the avoidance of conflict. They quote an example of *noon-chi*, where A wishes B to leave his office. A therefore asks B what is the time. Being used to indirect communication, B correctly infers that A would like him to leave and does so, leaving the harmony of their relationship intact. The intent of this tactful behaviour is to protect the relationship rather than to demonstrate interpersonal diplomacy.

Of course, even across collectivist cultures the tactics of facework may vary. Tsai (1996) reports that Chinese and Japanese ways of handling face-threatening situations differ. She claims that Japanese people will save face by apologizing if they know they will be unable later to meet an obligation, while the Chinese are more likely to give face by promising help even if they will not be able to do so. Thus, even within cultures in which face is regarded as a major concern, there appear to be cultural differences in the strategies whereby face is maintained.

Despite our best efforts, situations do arise from time to time where we lose face. Under these circumstances, we engage in 'facework'. Ting-Toomey's (1988) theory predicts that in individualist cultures, someone who is insulted is more likely to seek to repair face by rebutting the insult, particularly if others have witnessed the insult. Bond and Venus (1991) examined what happened when Hong Kong students were insulted by an experimental stooge who was role-playing as their teacher in an experimental task. If the insult was addressed to them personally, the Chinese subjects resisted the insult *less* when there was a group member present than when they were alone. Bond and Venus interpret this reversal as showing that subjects were more concerned to avoid open conflict that would bring shame upon their group than they were to save personal face. In a separate experimental condition, the insult was directed not just to them but also to their group. In this condition subjects defended themselves more vigorously, but they were also noted to glance much more frequently at the other member of their group who was present, perhaps in the hope that they could learn how their colleague was responding to the insult.

Counter-attacking insults is only one, rather direct, form of facework. Cocroft and Ting-Toomey (1994) have developed a culturally balanced typology of facework strategies using Japanese and American respondents. They identified seven independent factors: anti-social, self-presentation, self-attribution, hint, order, pro-social and indirect strategies. Americans used the first four strategies more frequently; the Japanese used the last more frequently. Unfortunately, the researchers did not relate the use of facework strategies to individual-level measures of idiocentrism or allocentrism. They also acknowledge that the different strategy types may not be conceptually equivalent. So, the fact that Americans use self-attribution (i.e. taking personal blame) more as a way of protecting the other's face may not be applicable to Japanese who are less concerned about their (or other's) negative face needs. So, understanding the cultural dynamics of facework is complex (see also Imahori and Cupach, 1994), but at very least it is clear that behavioural strategies differ across culture.

Is silence golden?

Giles, Coupland and Wiemann (1992) compared the beliefs of Chinese and Americans about talking. The Americans described talking as pleasant and important, and as a way of controlling what goes on. The Chinese were more tolerant of silence and saw quietness as a way of controlling what goes on. Studies of negotiation have shown that the Japanese also tolerate silence and frequently use it strategically to control how negotiation proceeds (Graham, 1985; Hasegawa and Gudykunst, 1997). Australians show a lesser willingness to communicate verbally than Americans. This difference appears to arise because of the Australians' higher apprehension and lower self-perceived competence (Barraclough, Christophel and McCroskey, 1988). Even among more individualist countries the meaning of silence and of talk may vary. In Finland, for instance, it is said that silence often conveys attentiveness and encouragement to the speaker to continue, whereas in some other countries the speaker is more likely to continue only where there is active verbal or non-verbal acknowledgment that the message is being heard (Wiemann, Chen and Giles, 1986).

Scherer (1979) found that in both Germany and the United States, dominance may be expressed through talking, but that the dominant person's manner of speaking differs between the two countries. Dominant Americans spoke more loudly and with a greater range of expressiveness; dominant Germans showed a lesser range of expressiveness but high verbal fluency. Everyday experience suggests that persons from different nations often differ in predictable ways in how loudly or softly they speak. There appears to be no published research into whether these variations are associated with the value-types which are most endorsed in a given nation.

Peng, Zebrowitz and Lee (1993) compared the responses of Koreans and Americans to recordings of recitations of the alphabet in English and Korean. Both samples of listeners equated loudness with power. Americans also associated speed of speaking with competence and power, but Koreans did not. In addition, Peng *et al.* predicted that speaking in a tight rather than a relaxed voice would convey high status to Koreans, but not to Americans. This effect was not obtained, possibly because tightness and loudness were found to be highly correlated within the speech samples that were used.

The varieties of truthfulness

A further aspect of communication style has to do with what is considered to be 'truthful' and what is considered to be deceitful communication in different cultures. In universalist cultures, truth is thought of as an absolute state, just as laws are thought of as in principle equally applicable to all citizens. In more particularist or collectivist cultures, communication is always thought of as occurring within a social context. Social sensitivity and tact are required in determining what it is appropriate to say in a given setting. Even in universalist cultures the telling of 'white lies' (untrue statements designed to preserve social harmony) is widely condoned. We may expect, however, that the frequency of such statements to be higher in particularist and collectivist cultures (McLeod and Carment, 1988).

Christie and Geis (1970) reported a series of studies of what they termed 'Machiavellianism' in the United States. Machiavellians are those who seek to manipulate others through a variety of deceitful strategies. Studies of Machiavellianism and ingratiation have been reported from various countries, some of them using Christie and Geis' questionnaire measures. Tripathi (1981), for example, showed that the Machiavellianism scale had some validity in India, since those who scored high on it proved to be those candidates who told lies while attempting to obtain university scholarships. No direct cross-cultural comparisons of Machiavellianism have yet, however, been made.

Almaney and Ahwan (1982) discuss the practice of *mubalagha*, translated as 'exaggeration', in Arab language countries. They argue that if an Arab does not make statements in a form that Westerners would call exaggerated, other Arabs would not believe that they meant what they are saying, and might even infer that they meant the opposite. The kinds of cross-cultural misunderstanding that this belief about sincerity may generate between Arabs and Westerners were all too vividly illustrated during the 1990–91 Gulf War crisis. At that time, the Iraqi government did not heed the warnings of US Secretary of State James Baker that incursion into Kuwait would lead to massive retaliation. Subsequent analyses by commentators suggested that the reason was because Baker did not deliver his threats with sufficient extravagance. In consequence, Iraqi Foreign Minister Aziz did not believe that his threats were sincere. An earlier instance of US–Arab failure to communicate during diplomatic negotiations is given in Box 8.5 (p. 219).

These examples illustrate the principle expounded in Chapter 3, that while there may well be etic principles with transcultural validity, the emic means by which they are expressed will vary from culture to culture. In the present case, it may well be true that in all cultures people wish to impress certain others, but the means of doing so will be culturally specific.

Complimenting and responding

Praising another is a form of associative behaviour found in all cultures (Triandis, 1978), and is designed to enhance solidarity among interactants. Compliments are reinforcing, so by analyzing their content one can gain a window into what is valued in a culture (Nelson, El Bakary and Al Batal, 1993). By analyzing their form, one can learn about cultural styles of communicating.

Barnlund and Araki (1985) pioneered the comparative work in this area, using exhaustive interviews by native speakers with Japanese and Americans to help them design a culturally balanced questionnaire about complimenting behaviour. Consistent with theorizing about high-context cultures, the Japanese respondents show a preference for indirect forms of flattery (non-verbal forms, via a third party, etc.). The Americans also endorse a number of indirect forms, but at a lesser frequency. Americans praise others more frequently (see also Beebe and Takahashi, 1989), are more fulsome in their praise and focus on physical appearance more than Japanese. Americans flatter those closer to them (e.g. spouses, friends) more than those more distant (e.g. strangers, acquaintances); Japanese reverse this pattern.

Arab culture is also high-context, and research by Nelson, El Bakary and Al Batal (1993) can illuminate similarities as well as differences with the Japanese. Using the interview-questionnaire approach of Barnlund and Araki (1985), Nelson *et al.* confirmed that Arabs, like Japanese, complimented less than Americans. Egyptian compliments, however, are equally direct. When given, they are longer and more elaborate than the American variety, often including metaphors. They praise physical appearance equally often, but focus more on natural attributes (e.g. eyes) not effort-derived attributes (e.g. hairstyle). Egyptians, like the Americans, praise personality traits relatively more than the Japanese (when they do praise), but like the Japanese, praise skill and work relatively more than the Americans. Clearly, information from other high- and low-context cultures is needed before reliable patterns of difference may be detected. It is equally true that we will need considerable instruction in how to compliment most effectively across cultural lines (Wolfson, 1989).

There is also variability in responding to compliments. In modesty-valuing cultures, one may be embarrassed by flattery (see Figure 5.2). Loh (1993), for example, found that Hong Kong Chinese tend to deflect or even deny compliments more frequently than the British, who are more likely to accept the praise, for example by saying, 'Thank you'. Loh believes that for the British, the agreement norm is the more polite option; for Chinese, the modesty norm dominates. Again, the potential for cross-cultural misunderstanding is considerable (see Chapter 9).

The non-verbal component

Communication involves more than the verbal components discussed above. As people talk and listen, they also gaze, smell, gesture, emit facial cues such as smiles, position their bodies *vis-à-vis* one another, and shift their postures. These non-verbal behaviours help manage the six social functions of expressing intimacy, regulating interaction, exercising social control, providing information, managing affect, and facilitating service and task delivery (Patterson, 1991).

These broad functions are applicable in any cultural setting, so that it is appropriate to examine non-verbal behaviours cross-culturally. A considerable amount of such work has been done (e.g. Poyatos, 1988), some of it covered earlier (e.g. proxemics in Chapter 5). The problem is that much of this research has been descriptive and atheoretical.

Gestures. The study of gestures cross-culturally is a case in point. In the video 'A world of gestures', Archer (1991) documents the variety of gestures used in different cultures to communicate information around topics such as sex, suicide, conflict, friendship, beauty and so forth. Of course there is considerable cultural variation in whether a concept has a gesture and, if so, how it is signalled. Cultural fluency requires that one masters this 'vocabulary' of manual signals; one can easily offend people from different cultures by incorrectly using, for example, the 'thumbs up' or 'V for victory' signs in cultures where they have a different meaning!

Gestures that can be used independently of speech are called emblems (Kendon, 1988). They are a language unto themselves, but are difficult to relate to any theory of culture. In fact, contemporary research on gestures distinguishes a variety of gesture types. Bavelas (1994), for example, separates conversational, topical, and interactive gestures. Interactive gestures constitute between 10 and 20 per cent of those used in Canadian conversations, but fulfil the essential need 'for the speaker to include and involve the addressee without yielding the floor' (p. 212).

How is this basic function accomplished in other cultural groups and how can this variability be related to culture? Wakushima (1996), for instance, reports that fewer such interactive gestures are used in Japan, where their use is regarded as impolite. Instead, verbal mechanisms are deployed. Why? Anderson and Bowman (1985) argue that people from cultures high in power distance show more bodily tension as a way of appeasing superiors. This habit may generalize to other interactions, inhibiting gestures generally, and forcing people into using other channels to achieve the goals of including and involving the addressee without yielding the floor.

The concern of some researchers has shifted to an 'effectiveness' approach for understanding non-verbal behaviours (Hecht, Andersen and Ribeau, 1989). The capacity to achieve a given outcome by using the various types of non-verbal behaviour such as gazing and proxemics must now be considered along with gestures. 'By linking nonverbal messages to meanings, functions, and outcomes, the researcher identifies a range of behavior, provides a means of assessing utility, and develops explanations as well as descriptions of cultural patterns and differences' (p. 178). Using such an approach requires that researchers stop grouping non-verbal behaviours by origin, e.g. the eyes, the hands, the vocal cords, and begin measuring functions achieved.

It is how these functions are achieved across cultures that then becomes the proper pursuit of researchers. A shift to this concern will move cross-cultural work on non-verbal behaviour away from its fascination with cataloguing local peculiarities into theory-building focused on communicative functions.

Body odour. Face-to-face communication brings people into olfactory as well as visual and aural contact. Hannigan (1995) underscores the importance of such contact:

> smell is the most directly connected of the human senses to the limbic system – the part of the brain that deals with emotion and memories. The limbic system is also able to trigger the hypothalamus and the pituitary gland which release hormones related to sex, appetite and body temperature. Thus, odors can be a back door to a human being's most intimate and emotional aspects of self. (p. 499)

Because of its primitive power, smell and words associated with pleasant and repulsive smells are used to mark both social and cultural boundaries (Largey and Watson, 1971; Almagor, 1990), dividing our interpersonal world into acceptable and unacceptable groupings.

Given its immediacy of impact, one's body odour can then become an early factor in attracting or repelling others. This topic is, however, rarely researched in science. As Ackerman (1990) points out,

> There's been so much anecdotal evidence about different races having distinctive odors – because of diets, habits, hairiness or lack of it – that such claims are difficult to discount, even though the topic scares most scientists, who are understandably concerned about being called racist. (p. 22)

In one of the rare studies on olfaction across cultures, Schleidt, Hold and Attili (1981) had Japanese, German and Italian participants assess armpit odour from worn clothes belonging to persons from all three cultural groups. Women classified their own gender's odour as less unpleasant than did men, regardless of cultural group (a gender universal?). However, Japanese classified all the odours as more unpleasant than did the Germans or the Italians. Ackerman (1990) points out that Caucasians (and Negroids) have more apocrine (sweat) glands at the base of hair follicles and are hairier. Hence racially different groups may smell 'riper' to Mongoloids. Also, Japanese odour thresholds may be lower, given their scrupulous concern for personal cleanliness.

What is true across cultures for the smell of sweat is also probably true for the smell of breath. Knapp (1978) observes that,

> Arabs consistently breathe on people when they talk. However, this habit is more than a matter of different manners. To the Arab good smells are pleasing and a way of being involved with each other. To smell one's friend is not only nice but desirable, for to deny him your breath is to act ashamed. (p. 171)

One's breath odour will be a function of one's diet and one's dental hygiene, both variables strongly influenced by cultural socialization. Again, research on this topic is rare and none compares cultural groups, despite travellers' notes that breath odour is a powerful repellent (Hannigan, 1995).

In the context of interpersonal attraction, it is noteworthy that Schleidt, Hold and Attili (1981) found that Italian and German women classified their marital partner's axillary odour as unpleasant; Japanese women did not. The authors suggest therefore that marital choice in Japan may be more influenced by sexual attraction than by socio-economic factors (as in Germany or Italy). This fascinating speculation places great importance on the role of body odour; given the paucity of research on this powerful sense modality, however, it would be wise to explore the issue during interpersonal interactions to assess its impact, particularly in cross-cultural interactions (see Chapter 9).

Smiling. In a carefully balanced experiment, Matsumoto and Kudoh (1993) showed photos of smiling vs. unsmiling models to both Japanese and American raters who rated both within and across cultural lines. In all conditions a smiling face was judged as more sociable. Likewise, Albright *et al.* (in press) have found that Mainland Chinese and American judges associate the non-verbal cue of smiling with the sociability components of optimism and honesty. Given the universal association of smiling with happiness (see Chapter 4), these perceptions will probably be found anywhere.

However, smiling communicates culturally different perceptions as well. Albright *et al.* (1997) found that the Chinese also associated smiling with a lack of self-control and calmness, an outcome consistent with Chinese socialization for emotional self-restraint (Bond, 1993). Matsumoto and Kudoh (1993) found that smiling increased American judgements of intelligence, but did not affect the Japanese judgements. These authors also point out that there are varieties of smiles depending on which facial muscles are innervated and by how much. The subtleties involved in the perception of a cue as simple as a smile are likely to be complex and affected by cultural dynamics surrounding the issue of emotional expression.

Time perspective

A key element in defining collectivist cultures is that one will have less choice over the groups to which one belongs. As a result allocentrics are likely to have a different perspective on time. If I know that within all or most of my lifetime I shall be a member of a particular group, my thinking about that group will extend further – both into the future and into the past – than if there is a possibility of my moving to another group next week or next year. It will also be less important that I deal with interpersonal issues now, since what is not taken care of today could be handled another time. Little attention has been given to time perspective by psychologists until recently (e.g. Levine, 1997), although anthropologists have been much more interested in this important issue.

Monochronic time and polychronic time

Hall (1983) distinguishes cultures that view time monochronically from cultures that view time polychronically. A monochronic view of time sees it as a scarce resource which must be rationed and controlled through the use of schedules and appointments and through aiming to do only one thing at any one time. In monochronic cultures people sometimes see spare time or time spent waiting as something that needs to be 'killed'. We should expect to find a conception of time as monochronic in many individualist cultures. A polychronic view of time sees the maintenance of harmonious relationships as the important agenda, so that use of time needs to be flexible in order that we do right by the various people to whom we have obligations. We should expect this concern to be characteristic of many collectivist cultures. While there is a good deal of plausibility to Hall's model, there are other attributes of cultures which are also likely to be important in relation to time. For instance, Hofstede's dimension of uncertainty avoidance is most probably linked to the degree to which we plan our time usage carefully in advance. The dimension of Confucian work dynamism identified by the Chinese Culture Connection (1987) researchers is also strongly linked with time. As Hofstede (1991) stresses, Confucian values stress perseverance and thrift in obtaining long-term goals, and he therefore relabelled Confucian work dynamism as long-term orientation.

An initial series of studies by Levine, West and Reis (1980) and Levine and Bartlett (1984) compared various aspects of time management in seven countries. They found substantial correlations between the accuracy of clocks in public places, the speed at which people walked down the street and the speed at which a post office clerk completed the sale of a small-denomination postage stamp. Using these three measures as components, Levine and Norenzayan (submitted) have more recently computed a 'Pace of Life' index for thirty-one nations, as shown in Box 6.4.

The results of Levine and Norenzayan's (submitted) study thus shows a strong link between a country's economic affluence and its citizens' typical pace of life.

Box 6.4) The pace of life in thirty-one nations

Levine and Norenzayan (submitted) studied the speed with which solitary walkers in large (mostly capital) cities walked in summer weather, postage clerks sold a postage stamp and the accuracy of public clocks. The three measures combined to form a pace of life index. The pace of life appears to be fastest in Northern and Western Europe, with the addition of Japan. Levine and Norenzayan showed that their index correlated strongly with high per capita gross domestic product (GDP), low average annual maximum temperature and values presumed to be individualist. The GDP measure was the strongest predictor and the measures of temperature and values did not account for any additional variation in the pace of life.

Fast-moving nations	Moderate nations	Slow-moving nations
Switzerland	Hong Kong	Greece
Ireland	France	Kenya
Germany	Poland	China
Japan	Costa Rica	Bulgaria
Italy	Taiwan	Romania
England	Singapore	Jordan
Sweden	United States	Syria
Austria	Canada	El Salvador
Netherlands	Korea	Brazil
	Czech Republic	Indonesia
		Mexico

However, we should not be tempted to infer direct causal links from correlations. To do so, we should need to look at whether pace of life changes as economic development increases. No data of this type are yet available. There are likely to be other facets of existing social structures that will serve to maintain differences in pace of life despite changes in a culture. For instance, in further comparisons between Brazil and the United States, Levine and Bartlett (1984) found that in Brazil someone who always arrived late for appointments was rated as more likeable, happy and successful than someone who did not, whereas in the United States someone who always arrived early was more likely to be seen in this way.

Looking ahead

Time perspective has to do not only with how fast one does things but also with how far ahead one thinks it valuable to plan. Hofstede (1991) proposes that the essence of long-term orientation (referred to earlier as Confucian work dynamism) is a focus on the future rather than on the short-term present. We should expect this contrast to show up in comparisons between Americans on the one hand and Chinese or Japanese on the other. Doktor (1983) made observational studies of Japanese managers at work. He found that within his sample of observations, 41 per cent of Japanese managers undertook tasks which lasted more than one hour, compared with only 10 per cent of US managers. In a similar way, 49 per cent of US managers did tasks that lasted less than nine minutes compared with only 18 per cent of the Japanese managers. These outcomes imply that the Japanese managers interacted out of longer time perspectives, but does not provide a direct measure of this important construct at the individual level.

A study of the duration of activities was also made by Wheeler, Reis and Bond (1989) who asked students in the United States and Hong Kong to keep diaries of their activities over a period of two weeks. The Chinese spent more time in groups and less in dyads. They spent longer on their activities and did them with a narrower range of other people. The result for the Chinese is consistent with the polychronic emphasis on people rather than activities, but again does not directly measure orientation toward the future.

Two studies did obtain direct measures, but unfortunately these studies have data only from countries which vary in their level of collectivism but which all score low on long-term orientation (Hofstede, 1991). Sundberg, Poole and Tyler (1983) surveyed 15-year-old adolescents in small towns in India, Australia and the United States. They were asked to list seven future events to be chosen by themselves. The average time into the future of these seven events was significantly longer for the boys from the more collectivist India than for the boys from more individualist Australia and the United States. However, the Indian girls had the shortest time perspective of all. Only in India was there a significant difference in the perspectives of the boys and the girls. The prediction of longer time perspectives in collectivist cultures is thus upheld for boys but not for girls. Such findings underline for us the hazards of generalizing about national cultures as a whole. In countries such as India where gender roles are more sharply differentiated than in the United States or Australia, the study highlights the importance of subcultural variations. Sundberg *et al.* point out that entry into the Indian school studied was more selective for girls than for boys. These girls may therefore have been more idiocentric in orientation than females elsewhere in India. Unfortunately, no individual-level measures were taken.

Meade (1972) also compared time perspectives between Americans and various Indian samples. His respondents, who were all male, were asked to write short stories, starting with single sentences provided by him. One of these was: 'L. B. is beginning his new job . . .'. The stories were analyzed to determine whether the major theme referred to the future or to the past. No separate coding was provided for references to the present. He found that while 62 per cent of American stories were set in the future, future reference in his Indian samples varied from 8 per cent among Brahmins and 16 per cent among Muslims to 56 per cent among Parsees and 58 per cent among Kshatriya Hindus. Before we could know whether these substantial differences are related to variations in cultural values, we would need separate measures of values from each of the cultural groups sampled. The results again underline the heterogeneity of Indian culture, and the dangers of hasty generalizations based upon single ethnic groups from a given country.

Many more studies will be required before it is clear how precisely differing time perspectives are correlated with differences in cultural values. The evidence thus far is inconclusive. What we need is a valid and reliable measure of time perspective at the individual level. Trompenaars (1993) collected data on time perspective from his sample of business employees in forty-three nations, using measures devised by Cottle (1976). For instance, respondents are asked to draw circles which represent the past, the present and the future. The size of the circles and the degree of their interrelatedness are then coded. However, the results have not been published.

Intimate relationships

If cultures differ in the ways in which their members communicate with one another and in their attitudes towards time, we might expect that these different emphases would have a major effect upon the types of relationship that develop among culture members. This general prediction should be illustrated nowhere more vividly than in the field of intimate relationships. We will discover that both the conception and the manifestations of intimacy are shaped by culture. Continuing developments are to be expected, since intimacy is the most recent component of the universal dimensions in social behaviour to have evolved (Adamopoulos, 1991).

Marriages are of course contracted in numerous different ways in different cultures, and in many countries there is currently a decline in the occurrence of arranged marriages along with an increase in 'love' marriages. Xu and Whyte (1990) interviewed women in the city of Chengdu in China who had married between 1933 and 1987. The per centage who reported having chosen their husband themselves rose steadily from 17 to 57 per cent over this time period. Even the remaining 43 per cent reported that they had exercised some degree of choice in the selection of their partner. Similarly, Sprecher and Chandak (1992) found that between a third and a half of their sample of young adults in India believe that they should have freedom in choosing their partner. Since these changes indicate an increasing element of choice, we might presume that this shift is related to the emergence of increasingly idiocentric values.

Is romantic love a culture-bound concept?

Romantic love has often been seen as an integral consideration in the free choice of one's partner. As such, we might expect it to be endorsed most strongly in individualist nations. When Sprecher et al. (1994) asked students in the United States, Japan and Russia, 'Are you in love right now?', the majority in all three nations answered that they were, with the highest scores from Russia rather than the presumably more individualist United States. Levine et al. (1995) asked students in eleven nations, 'If a man (woman) had all the other qualities you desired, would you marry this person if you were not in love with him (her)?' Respondents in India, Pakistan and Thailand were significantly more likely to answer yes than were those in the remaining countries. The proportion answering yes in each country was significantly correlated with Hofstede's (1980) collectivism scores.

However, the use of such simple and straightforward questions risks masking cultural differences in what people actually mean by 'being in love'. Shaver, Wu and Schwartz (1991) found that young people in the United States and Italy associated love with happiness whereas their interviews with Chinese showed positive linkage between love and sadness. Rothbaum and Tsang (in press) analyzed the content of US and Chinese love songs. The Chinese songs had more references to sadness, to the future and to the context within which love occurred, while the US songs focused more directly upon the object of the singer's love. However, there was no difference between the samples in the intensity of emotion expressed. We noted in Chapter 3 Sagiv and Schwartz's (1995) finding that 'friendship' also had a somewhat different meaning in Japan than elsewhere. To contend with this problem we need measures that differentiate understandings of what love is.

Doherty *et al.* (1994) distinguish between romantic love and companionate love. They compared responses of four ethnic groups in Hawaii: Chinese, Pacific Islanders, Japanese and Caucasian Americans. Doherty *et al.* conclude that the Caucasians endorsed romantic love less than the other three groups. However, they did not take account of possible cultural differences in questionnaire response bias. If one looks at the ratio of responses to the romantic love items and the companionate love items, the Chinese come out as most romantic, followed by the Caucasians.

Another frequently used measure has been the Love Attitude Scale of Munro and Adams (1978). This scale provides a measure of how strongly respondents endorse three dimensions identified as romantic power, romantic idealism and conjugal love. The romantic power items portray love as a powerful force affecting one's life and dispersing obstacles. The romantic idealism items assert that loving is the essence of life. The conjugal love items state that love should have a calming and sobering effect, which demands careful consideration. The scale was developed in Canada, where the three dimensions were found to be reliably separable. High-school and college students have completed the scale in the Caribbean (Payne and Vandewiele, 1987), Senegal (Vandewiele and Philbrick, 1983), Uganda (Philbrick and Opolot, 1980), the United States (Philbrick, 1987) and in numerous populations of Blacks and Whites in South Africa (Stones and Philbrick, 1991). No checks were made upon the validity of the scale outside North America, so we are dealing here with an imposed etic measure.

In this case also, it is not appropriate to compare means between country samples, since they may be biased by cultural differences in predisposition to use extreme points in responding to the various items. However, we can overcome this problem by comparing which of the dimensions is most strongly endorsed within each sample. After correcting for the fact that one dimension has fewer items, we do find some differences of emphasis. The conjugal love scale was favoured most by the Ugandans, the Senegalese and by US engineering students. The romantic idealism scale was most favoured by the Caribbeans. The romantic power scale is strongly favoured by all of the South African samples, both Black and White. The Canadian sample included a wider age range, but among the younger respondents romantic idealism scored highest. These differing results show no clear pattern: more active theorizing is necessary in order to give greater structure to future studies.

A somewhat similar approach was followed by Simmons, von Kolke and Shimizu (1986) and Simmons, Wehner and Kay (1989), except that they used different measures to assess romantic love. They found that on the Hobart (1958) scale of romantic love, French and German students scored highest, with Japanese somewhat lower. One sample of Americans scored above the Japanese and another sample was below them. However, analyses of responses to individual items on the scale indicate here also that romantic love is given a somewhat different meaning in each country. For instance, the statement 'Lovers should freely confess everything of personal significance to each other' was accepted by 75 per cent of Germans, 53 per cent of Americans and 25 per cent of Japanese.

This series of results fits readily into the same pattern that emerged from the studies of mate preferences by Buss (1989) and Buss *et al.* (1990), which we considered in Chapter 4. There are relatively universal ways in which people speak about their attachment to others. However, the more detail we add to the measures, explicating exactly what attitudes and behaviours are entailed within the generalized notion of love or of romance, the more differences we start to find.

Hatfield and Rapson (1996) draw together the results of eighteen different surveys of premarital sexual behaviour from nineteen countries. Relatively low frequencies were found among Japanese, Korean, Israeli, Hong Kong and Chinese American respondents. Much higher per centages are found in European, African, Latin American and North American respondents. No theories have yet been formulated that could account for this pattern of differences.

Established intimate relationships

Cross-cultural studies of existing intimate relationships are scarce indeed. Ting-Toomey (1991) asked large samples of students in the United States, France and Japan to make ratings about their current relationship with an opposite sex, close friend. The Americans reported more 'love commitment' and more open disclosure, but also more ambivalence about whether to continue the relationship, as one might expect in an individualist culture. The French reported a lower level of conflict than either the Americans or the Japanese. Ting-Toomey attributes this result to high uncertainty avoidance in France, but this explanation is unconvincing, since Japan scores even higher on this cultural dimension. It is quite likely that one could not fully understand the differing results for conflict level without examining also whether there are differences between the three countries in how important other peer relationships are at the same time. It might be the case for instance that conflict is not so much surprisingly low in France, but surprisingly high in Japan. This could be because many male Japanese will have strong commitments to same-sex work-related peer groups, which may generate conflict with their opposite-sex relationships. Consistent with this speculation, Ting-Toomey found that Japanese women respondents reported more conflict than did Japanese males, an effect not found in the other two countries.

We noted in Chapter 4 that the behaviours that are most likely to precipitate partners' jealousy vary by culture (Buunk and Hupka, 1987). Hupka and Ryan (1990) extend this line of analysis by seeking to predict in which societies reactions to adultery would be most strongly expressed. Drawing upon data files accumulated from numerous earlier anthropological studies, they compared 150 tribal societies. Very wide variations were found in husbands' response to female infidelity, ranging from indifference to murder. Hupka and Ryan conclude that these differences can be predicted from variations in the importance given to marriage and to property ownership in each society. Levinson (1989) surveyed data files across an even wider range of societies, examining the incidence of violence within marital relationships. Over 330 societies, husbands were reported to beat wives in 84 per cent, and wives beat husbands in 27 per cent, usually much less violently. This type of data gives us no information on the frequency of violent episodes, nor on whether it is declining in recent times.

Van Yperen and Buunk (1991) considered a more general aspect of our understanding of intimate relationships, by comparing the levels of satisfaction of Dutch and American couples. A number of US theorists have applied adaptations of Adams' (1965) equity theory, which we discuss more fully in Chapter 8, to this field. Van Yperen and Buunk examined whether equity theory could explain couples' satisfaction with their relationship in the way that has been demonstrated in US studies. They found that among their US subjects those who were most satisfied with their relationship were those who felt that they and their partners were putting an equal amount into the relationship. However, in the Netherlands the most satisfied were those who were 'overbenefited', in other words who felt that their partner was putting more into the relationship than they were themselves. Overbenefited Americans were less satisfied than those who felt the benefits were equal.

These results are particularly interesting from our point of view because Van Yperen and Buunk (1991) also asked their subjects to complete a measure of what they called 'communal orientation', which may well tap allocentric values. The US sample in the study was drawn from Pennsylvania and Hawaii, where more than half the respondents were Asians. Van Yperen and Buunk show that in the sample as a whole it was the subjects who were high on communal orientation whose responses departed from equity theory predictions. Thus they lead us away from a stereotyped conclusion that relationships in the Netherlands differ from those in the United States. The alternative explanation is that relationships differ between those individuals who endorse allocentric values and those who do not. In fact they found that the link between endorsement of communal orientation and departure from equity theory predictions was stronger in their US results, probably because their US sample was more diverse.

The diversity of the US sample could be not only caused by ethnic diversity but also by gender differences. Van Yperen and Buunk (1991) paid some attention to Hofstede's characterization of the Netherlands as 'feminine'. Hofstede's labelling of this dimension leaves something to be desired, since it encourages us to confuse the characterizations of cultures and individuals. However, his characterization of a feminine culture is one in which communal values predominate, whereas masculine cultures are those in which achievement (usually by men) is more highly prized. Hofstede found the Netherlands and the Scandinavian countries to be the most 'feminine' by this definition. Feminine cultures are also characterized by Hofstede as encouraging more equal relations between men and women. In line with this grouping of countries, Van Yperen and Buunk found no difference between the evaluations of relationship contribution by the Dutch men and women, whereas there were significant gender differences in the US sample. In both countries the women were more communally oriented. The most likely overall explanation of the findings is therefore that the Dutch score mostly scored moderate to high on communal orientation, whereas the Americans' scores varied much more widely, on account of both gender and ethnic background.

So why should the responses of couples with allocentric values not adhere to equity theory? Within an intimate relationship, we might expect that allocentric values would lead partners to assess the relationship as a unit rather than calculating individual contributions separately. Indeed, US research suggests that, even in individualist cultures, the degree to which partners start to keep count of who they see as the cause of difficulties can predict relationship breakdown (Bradbury and Fincham, 1990). Furthermore, Dion and Dion (1993) suggest that although romantic love may be seen as the ideal in individualist nations, persons with strongly idiocentric values will be the ones most likely to terminate a relationship. Dion and Dion (1991) found support for this proposition in Canada, while Doherty et al. (1994) found measures of romantic love and individualism negatively correlated in Hawaii. We need to take care here to distinguish levels of analysis. It appears that within cultures where most persons endorse idiocentric values, those who are relatively in favour of allocentric values will be the ones who are more committed to their relationships.

Established relationships frequently lead, of course, to the creation of families, and families provide one of the cornerstones of any culture, but more especially of cultures built upon collectivist values. It is perhaps unsurprising that researchers in low-context cultures have devoted more attention to the creation of dyadic love relationships than to the broader context of family relationships within which such dyadic relations are likely to be contained. We may also expect greater emphasis upon the dynamics of the nuclear family and less upon the role of the extended family within individualistic cultures. Cross-cultural studies of either type of family have mostly been conducted by clinical and developmental psychologists: as such they do not find a place in this volume and must be sought elsewhere (Kagitçibasi, 1996b; Berry, Dasen and Saraswathi, 1997).

Studies of relationship termination within relatively collectivist cultures are rare. Hortaçsu and Karançi (1987) found that Turkish students attributed the end of their relationships to their partner's personality and to incompatibility, much as might be expected in the United States. However, these were students at the Middle East Technical University in Ankara, where teaching is in English, and they may well have had relatively idiocentric values. In the eleven-nation survey by Levine *et al.* (1995), students were also asked whether, 'If love has completely disappeared from a marriage . . . it is best to make a clean break and start new lives'. Responses varied widely, but the culture-level means were unrelated to the Hofstede (1980) collectivism scores. The factors leading to the dissolution of a marriage thus seem more likely to be affected by social structures and legal factors than by culture-level values.

Same-sex friendship

Interpersonal intimacy is also found in same-sex relationships, but there are very few cross-cultural studies of this topic. Such work is clearly important, though, since cross-cultural friendships will succeed or fail in part because the parties involved share or diverge in their conceptions of friendship. Verkuyten and Masson (1996) studied the perception of same-sex friendships across a number of different ethnic groups living in the Netherlands. They attempted to understand ethnic group differences by using an individual-level measure of idiocentrism and allocentrism.

Verkuyten and Masson (1996) found that their ethnic groups did not differ on idiocentrism (see also Kashima *et al.*, 1995). The Mococcans and Turks, however, were higher than the Dutch and Southern Europeans on allocentrism. Higher allocentrism was in turn related to 'more perceived similarity of self to friends than friends to self', use of 'social or ascribed characteristics such as ethnicity, gender, and religion more often in describing their friends', reports of 'having fewer best friends than low allocentrics' (p. 215). Higher allocentrics 'saw their friendship with their best friend as more close' and 'had fewer other-than-best friends' (p. 215). Finally 'high allocentrics endorsed friendship rules about the relation with third parties more than low allocentrics did . . . , consistent with the idea that allocentrism involves mutual face-saving and regulation by ingroup norms to a greater extent' (p. 215).

This sophisticated study showed that all the ethnic group differences could be 'unpackaged' or explained by the individual-level variable of allocentrism. Furthermore, it extended our understanding of interdependent self-construals into the domain of close, personal relationships. This understanding is consistent with the cross-cultural literature discussed before on the self-concept, intensity of in-group relations and concerns for interpersonal harmony.

Cooperation and competition

Having looked at some of the issues surrounding the development of intimate relationships, we now turn to the more general question of what overall factors might determine whether individuals will cooperate or compete with one another in a broader range of social settings. As may have been the case in other research areas, researchers' universalistic assumptions did not initially lead them to see it as crucially important to specify who exactly is the other person with whom you as experimental subject must choose to compete or to cooperate. Furthermore, the types of study we shall now discuss used tightly controlled experimental designs, allowing minimal communication between the parties, and frequently giving the participant little information about the other party. These studies have adopted a particular operational definition of cooperation which is embedded within various experimental games. Each of these games provides the subject with a finite series of options, which the experimenter labels as cooperative or competitive. In the light of what was said earlier (in Chapter 3), we need to scrutinize these studies to determine whether the way the experimenter defines what is going on is also the way that the experimental subject perceives the situation. This potential difference is characteristic of imposed-etic research, that is to say research that takes a concept or procedure from one culture and uses it in other cultures without allowing any possibility of examining its meaning within those other cultures. This is of course a danger with many of the studies discussed in this book, but it is particularly acute with the studies now to be reviewed, because they are so tightly structured, and because many of them involve subjects in playing games where they neither speak to one another nor provide the experimenter with any direct feedback on how they experience what is happening.

Of the experimental games that became popular in the study of cooperation and competition in the United States, the most widely used was certainly the 'Prisoner's Dilemma'. This game involves two players making one or more simultaneous choices. Depending upon how the players' choices are coordinated, both may benefit, either one may prosper at the expense of the other, or both may lose. A typical payoff matrix is shown in Table 6.1. Each player has the choice of cooperating (C) or defecting (D). The numbers in the table represent the money or other rewards that each party will receive when both decisions have been made. Thus, if both players choose C, both receive a reward of 3. But if player 1 chooses C while Player 2 chooses D, then Player 1 receives only 1 and Player 2 gets 4. Each party can therefore prosper at the expense of the other if they can induce the other to make 'cooperative' choices while they themselves defect. Of course, if both players defect then both do less well than if they had both cooperated. The closely related Maximizing Differences game, which makes it easier to see whether a subject is trying maximize winnings or to outdistance the other player, is also illustrated in the table.

McClintock and McNeel (1966) and McNeel, McClintock and Nuttin (1972) compared the performance of US and Flemish Belgian students on the

Table 6.1 ● Typical gaming matrices				
		Game 1: Prisoner's dilemma matrix		Game 2: Maximizing difference matrix
		Player 2		Player 2
		Choice C	Choice D	Choice C	Choice D
Player 1	Choice C	3 \ 3	1 \ 4	3 \ 3	1 \ 3
	Choice D	4 \ 1	2 \ 2	3 \ 1	1 \ 1

The first figure in each cell gives Player 1's payoff and the second figure gives Player 2's payoff.

Maximizing Differences game. They reported that the Belgians were much more competitive. However, Faucheux (1976), who is French, published an extensive critique of what he saw as the pro-American bias of the data analysis. He pointed out that the Belgians had behaved more competitively only when they were losing, whereas the Americans had been competitive when they were winning. His interpretation of the data was thus that the Americans were more truly competitive, whereas the Belgians were trying to utilize the structure of the game in a manner that preserved the equality of the participants.

The same type of ambiguity in interpretation emerged from a series of studies by Marwell and his colleagues. Marwell and Schmitt (1972) found Norwegians to be much more competitive than Americans when they were faced with the risk of exploitation. However Marwell, Schmitt and Boyesen (1973) found that when the risk of exploitation was eliminated, the Norwegians became much more cooperative than the Americans. Through these studies we are introduced to the notion that a supposedly objective record of cooperative and competitive behaviour by this or that cultural group is in fact open to alternative interpretations upon closer inspection.

A similar study by Carment (1974) found 35 per cent competitive responses among Canadian students as against 55 per cent among Indian students. The implication that Indians are more competitive than Canadians was contradicted by Alcock (1974) who found Canadians to be more competitive than Indians when time pressure was introduced into a different game. In a further study Alcock (1975) found that when Indians felt that they were in a strong position they became more competitive, whereas under these conditions Canadians became less competitive. These studies suggest that rather than labelling this or that national group as more or less competitive, it is better to look at what situations evoke competitive behaviour from each national sample.

A final study in this series by Carment and Alcock (1984) strengthens this assessment. In a Maximising Differences game, Indians were again found to be

more competitive than Canadians. However, when the gaming matrix was modified to make much higher winnings available to one player than to the other, a
complex series of effects was found. Canadians became more competitive, that is to
say the player who could receive the extra winnings was inclined to take them,
while the disadvantaged player sought to prevent this outcome. Among the
Indians, the reverse pattern appeared: the advantaged player was likely to avoid the
extra winnings, while the disadvantaged player tried to make sure that the advantaged player did receive the bonus. One way of interpreting this outcome would be
to say that the Canadians perceived the situation as becoming more competitive,
whereas the Indians acted as they might in a hierarchical situation, with subordinates showing deference and superiors showing magnanimity. Again, we need
to learn how the experimental subjects were interpreting the situation in order to
understand the meaning of their responses.

In another study also involving Indians, L'Armand and Pepitone (1975) found
that American students were willing to reward a stranger when it cost them little,
but not when it reduced their own rewards. For Indian students this contrast made
little difference: they were not willing to give much reward in either condition.
Some clarification as to why is provided in the study by Pandey (1979), which
showed that the willingness of Indians to give to others is heavily dependent upon
the status of the groups to which both the donor and the recipient belong. In
L'Armand and Pepitone's experiment, the stranger who was to receive the rewards
was visible to subjects but they could not speak to him. However, they would have
been able to see that he was a high-status Brahmin. Further analyses by L'Armand
and Pepitone showed that those among the Indian subjects who were also
Brahmins were more willing to reward the stranger than were the non-Brahmin
subjects.

The last two studies reviewed demonstrate how experiments which have a
relatively clear structure in an individualist culture such as the United States or
Canada yield puzzling findings when they fail to take account of the collectivist
basis upon which Indians might decide how to allocate rewards in the experimental
procedure.

Putting competitiveness into context

The experiments reviewed so far in this section have all involved comparisons of
the cooperativeness or competitiveness of North Americans with others. Table 6.2
summarizes some consistencies in what was found. In each case the investigators,
who were all North Americans, found the 'foreign' group to be more competitive.
In five of the six studies they then went on to amend the circumstances of the
experiment in some way, and found that while the competitiveness of the foreign
group declined, that of the North American group rose. This way of looking at the
results fits in well with the proposition that the experimental subjects from outside
North America are more 'context-sensitive' than the North Americans. Of course
the North Americans did respond to the changed circumstances as well, but usually

Table 6.2 ● Gaming studies comparing North Americans and others

Study	Overall effect	Effect of changed context
McClintock and McNeel (1966)	Belgians compete more	Belgians compete less* Americans compete more*
Carment (1974)	Indians compete more	
Alcock (1974, 1975)	Equal	Indians compete less Canadians compete more
Carment and Alcock (1984)	Indians compete more	Indians redefine situation as superior–subordinate? Canadians compete more
Marwell and Schmitt (1972), Marwell, Schmitt and Boyesen (1973)	Norwegians compete more	Norwegians compete least Americans compete less
Rapoport, Guyer and Gordon (1971)	Danes compete more	Danes compete less Americans compete more

* In this case the experimenters did not make a change, but they provided subjects with feedback that enabled them to see how they were faring as the experiment proceeded, thus enabling subjects to adapt to the changing context.

to a lesser degree. We should expect subjects from more collectivist cultures to be more context-sensitive, but it is notable that three of these five studies were comparing Europeans with North Americans. Belgium, Denmark and Norway were ranked eighth, ninth and thirteenth on individualism by Hofstede (1980) compared with the United States and Canada at first and fourth. We might therefore expect even larger differences in results from cultures that fall further toward the high-context end of the spectrum, so long as we continue to bear in mind that whether a member of a collectivist culture chooses to compete or cooperate will depend very much on who is the other party to the transaction.

This analysis provides a hypothesis with which we can now examine further studies from other parts of the world. Bethlehem (1975) proposed that Westernization would increase competitiveness. He compared traditional and Westernized members of the Tonga tribe in Zambia, as well as Asian students also resident in Zambia. As expected, he found the traditional Tongans played a modified version of the Prisoner's Dilemma game in a much more cooperative manner than did the more Westernized groups.

In another study conducted in Africa, Foley Meeker (1970) compared Westernized and traditional members of the Kpelle tribe in Liberia. It is likely that the Westernised Kpelle would have a more idiocentric value orientation than the traditional Kpelle. When using a version of the Prisoner's Dilemma game, it was again found that the traditional players were much more cooperative. However, in this case Foley Meeker also used an adaptation of the Maximizing Differences game, and the results for this interaction structure showed traditional and non-traditional players to be equally and highly competitive. Once again we find that as a way of measuring cultural competitiveness, experimental games give confusing results. We do not know why Foley Meeker's subjects responded to the two games in a different manner. She suggests that in the Maximizing Differences game each subject receives a clear message from the other as to whether they are seeking to compete or cooperate, and both groups reciprocate competition with competition. However, in the Prisoner's Dilemma it is less easy to get a clear picture of what the other party is doing. In these circumstances, Foley Meeker suggests that Westernized game players tend to compete, whereas traditional players decide to trust the other party.

An interestingly similar pattern of results was found in a study concerning ethnic groups within the United States by Cox, Lobel and McLeod (1991). Using a Prisoner's Dilemma design and student subjects, they found Anglo students more competitive than Hispanic, Black and Asian Americans. Furthermore, when given feedback that the other party was making cooperative choices, the Anglos became still more competitive, while the Hispanics, Blacks and Asian Americans became more cooperative. Gabrenya (1990) has shown that this higher cooperation from those with collective cultural backgrounds is reversed when strangers are partners. In contrast to this pattern with the Taiwanese, his participants from an individualistic culture (the United States) showed more cooperation with a stranger than with a friend. The nature of one's relationship with a partner thus appears to be an important moderator of cooperative behaviour across the cultural dimension of collectivism.

Cooperation among children

A slightly different approach to the cross-cultural study of cooperation has been used by Madsen and his colleagues in their studies of children around the world. Madsen devised an experimental apparatus upon each of which groups of two to four children work. They are required to steer a ball, guide a marble or open a box collaboratively by pulling on strings. If they coordinate their efforts, the tasks are fairly simple; but if they compete, they rapidly become impossible. The world-wide series of studies by Madsen and others using his experimental methods has shown that in many countries where group rewards are offered, cooperation becomes established. However, when individual rewards are offered, the children find it much less easy to cooperate. Table 6.3 summarizes what has been found to occur under these circumstances. It is clear from the table that rural children are more cooperative than urban children. However, the only differences between countries apparent from direct comparisons in this series of studies – those between Mexico and the United States – could equally well be explained as due to urban–rural differences, since Madsen's studies compared children from Los Angeles with those from a small town in Baja California.

Table 6.3 ● Results of studies using the Madsen apparatus

Study	Location	Results
Sommerlad and Bellingham (1972)	Australia	Aboriginals more cooperative
Thomas (1975)	New Zealand	Polynesians and rural Maoris more cooperative than urban Maoris or Whites
Munroe and Munroe (1977)	USA, Kenya	Kikuyus more cooperative
Miller and Thomas (1972)	Canada	Blackfoot Indians more cooperative than Whites
Shapira (1976)	Israel	Kibbutz more cooperative than urban
Shapira and Madsen (1969)	USA, Israel	Urban children, no difference
Shapira and Lomranz (1972)	Israel	Arabs less cooperative than Jewish kibbutz, more than Jewish urban
Madsen and Yi (1975)	Korea	Rural more than urban
Madsen (1971)	USA, Mexico	Mexicans more cooperative
Madsen (1967)	Mexico	Rural more cooperative than urban
Madsen and Shapira (1970)	USA, Mexico	Mexicans more cooperative
Kagan and Madsen (1972)	USA, Mexico	Mexicans more cooperative
Madsen and Lancy (1981)	Papua New Guinea	Rural more cooperative than urban
Marin, Mejia and Oberle (1975)	Colombia	Rural more cooperative than urban
Hullos (1980)	Hungary	Rural more cooperative than urban

A study by Kagan, Knight and Martinez-Romero (1982) also found rural Mexican children more cooperative than Americans or Mexican-Americans. However in this case, an interview method was used, with children being asked what they would do if a toy were taken from them, or if they were hit by another child. The study therefore confirms the previous finding by showing that the same differences in level of cooperation can be obtained by a quite different research method.

Strube (1981) subjected all available studies of children's competitiveness to meta-analysis, in order to determine how uniform were any gender differences that had been reported. He concludes that boys are more competitive in Anglo-American and Indian cultures, while there is a trend in the opposite direction in Israel. As we found in Chapter 4, gender differences may well vary by culture.

The differences found between boys and girls and between urban and rural populations leave us with the question of whether this series of studies has also detected any differences between samples that could be confidently attributed to the effects of culture. Table 6.4 shows the results of four studies, which all used the marble-pull apparatus with urban children aged between 9 and 11, before they had been given any explicit coaching on ways of using the apparatus to cooperate. It is evident that the American children were rather less cooperative than those in the other three countries, presumably because of their more idiocentric orientation.

Cooperation and the identity of the partner

More recent research into aspects of cooperation and competition has taken greater account of the likelihood that your behaviour in experimental games will not just be a function of your values or cultural background, but also of your perception of your partner. Van Lange and Liebrand (1991) compared the willingness to contribute to a group bonus of students who were characterized as individualistic–competitive or as pro-social–altruistic. They found in both the Netherlands and the United States that, when subjects were led to believe that the other player was intelligent, pro-social players became more cooperative, whereas individualists did not. Thus, even in two of the national cultures that Hofstede (1980) characterized as most individualist, we find some subjects whose behaviour assumes the interdependent pattern once they know they are relating to a cooperative partner.

A similar issue was addressed by Yamagishi and Sato (1986). They found that willingness of Japanese students to make individual contributions to a group bonus depended both on whether the five-person experimental groups were composed of friends or strangers and on what were the rules as to how the bonus would be calculated. If the bonus was to be at the level of the lowest individual contribution or else at the level of the average contribution, friends contributed more than did strangers. If the bonus was to be at the level of the highest individual contribution, the behaviour of friends and strangers did not differ. Thus even in a

---

Table 6.4 ● Cooperative behaviour in the Madsen marble-pull apparatus

Study	Country	Average number of cooperative trials
Madsen (1971)	USA	0.2
Shapira (1976)	Israel	1.67
Madsen and Yi (1975)	Korea	1.44
Madsen and Lancy (1981)	Papua New Guinea	2.2

All studies used ten trials, except Shapira's which used twelve. The Israeli mean has been reduced to make it comparable with the others.

collectivist culture, knowing that the other players were friends only enhanced cooperative behaviour when the rules of the game also enhanced interdependence.

These recent studies of cooperative behaviour emphasize, just as did the series of studies on children's cooperation, that cooperative behaviour is affected by many factors within cultures as well as by differences across cultures. What we now need are studies that do not confound these different effects. The studies also illustrate how cultural pressures can be over-ridden when strong, contextual factors push in opposing directions. Furthermore, we should not forget that individualism–collectivism is unlikely to be the only culture-level variable relevant to levels of cooperation. Several of the Prisoner's Dilemma studies involved comparisons between members of North American cultures, which Hofstede (1980) character-ized as culturally masculine, and Northern European, which mostly score high on cultural femininity. According to Hofstede's data, members of feminine cultures may be expected to put less emphasis on winning and more emphasis on develop-ing good relations with the other party.

Behaviour in small groups

Having considered pair relationships, we can now extend our coverage to the way in which people relate to others within small groups. This assessment will involve us in referring back to some of the replications of classic studies that we reviewed in Chapter 2. In each case it is fruitful to do so in the light of the conceptual framework that we have now advanced.

Another look at social loafing

We noted in Chapter 2 that a complete reversal of social loafing effects had been obtained in several East Asian nations as well as in Israel. The studies by Earley (1989, 1993) provide some of the strongest evidence for this reversal. In addition to the details described earlier, we can now add that each subject in these studies also completed brief measures assessing their idiocentrism/allocentrism.

Earley's measures confirmed that the US managers did in fact have values that were much more idiocentric than were those of the Israeli and Chinese managers. Furthermore, individual-level analysis showed that regardless of culture it was the individuals with the most allocentric values whose work was increased by the presence of others and those with idiocentric values who loafed in the presence of others. In addition, the Earley (1993) study included a further experimental manipulation. Subjects were either led to believe that they were working alone, or that they were working with their in-group or with an out-group. Idiocentrics were found to loaf whatever the nature of the group in which they were working. Allocentrics enhanced their performance when working with their in-group, but not when working with an out-group. This study thus underlines how crucial it is in analyzing behaviour within collectivist cultures to distinguish social influences within the in-group and behaviour toward strangers.

Conformity revisited

If members of collectivist groups spend their time in fewer but more stable groups and hence seek in-group harmony, then we should expect that social influence processes would lead them toward greater levels of conformity than those reported from groups in individualist cultures. In Chapter 2, we described some aspects of the results of R. A. Bond and Smith's (1996) meta-analysis of the various replications of the Asch (1951) studies of conformity in making judgements of line length. These studies are not ideal for our present purpose, since we cannot be sure that judgements of physical stimuli of this kind are responsive to social pressure in the same way as are social stimuli such as attitudes or social representations. However, researchers have attempted precise replications of the Asch experiment in a much wider range of countries than is available for any other social psychological study, so that they provide us with the firmest data available.

Bond and Smith (1996) extended their analysis by first estimating what variations in experimental design influenced the number of judgement errors made within the studies that had been conducted in the United States. For instance they found that more errors were made when the number of judges was greater, when the naïve subject was female, and when subjects were in face-to-face contact. Having accounted for the variance in results due to these design variations which could therefore be expected world wide, they then sought explanations for the remaining cultural variations. They found that the conformity levels from different nations reported in Table 2.2 (see p. 19) could be predicted from culture-level value scores for the relevant nations. In particular, conformity level was related to collectivism scores derived from Hofstede (1980) and Trompenaars (1993) and conservatism scores from Schwartz (1994).

In interpreting what these results mean, we need to think more about who the subjects were in these studies. The original Asch studies were undertaken with students who were mostly strangers to one another. While most of the studies reported following the same procedures as did Asch, hardly any of them specify whether subjects were or were not strangers to one another. This is crucial information, since we would expect a member of a cultural group with allocentric values to conform if the pressure came from in-group members, but not if it came from strangers. The studies from Japan are particularly interesting in this connection. Frager (1970) used students who were strangers to one another and to his considerable surprise found a low level of conformity. Indeed, he also recorded high levels of anti-conformity, which is movement *away* from the majority opinion. This reversal may have been related to the high level of student unrest and rebellion at the time in Keio University, where the study was undertaken. The more recent Japanese study by Williams and Sogon (1984) showed a much higher error rate for pre-existing intact groups, and a lower rate for unacquainted students. This result supports the view that conformity rates for allocentric subjects are strongly influenced by their relationship to the other judges in the experiment, with greater conformity within long-term groups and less, or even anti-conformity, with strangers.

Looking at specific studies more carefully, we can discover that some of the other high conformity rates are also recorded where the subjects may have had some strong reason to hold allocentric values which linked them to other members of their in-group. For instance, conformity was particularly high among un-employed Blacks in Britain (Perrin and Spencer, 1981), and among members of the minority Indian population in Fiji (Chandra, 1973). This way of looking at the findings encourages us to think not so much about levels of conformity in different national cultures, but about conformity as a consequence of allocentric values, whether those values characterize a whole culture or particular sub-cultures within a larger society.

However, conformity need not necessarily stem from some long-lasting set of values, but may arise from experimental manipulations of social categorization. The recent British study by Abrams *et al.* (1990) found much greater conformity when subjects were led to believe that the other judges were fellow students of psychology than when they were told that they were students of a different major, ancient history. Of course, we would expect that the effect of such categorizations would be stronger for those with an allocentric orientation.

We thus have a range of experimental results ranging from Berry's (1967) ecological studies of conformity in agricultural and hunting societies (discussed in Chapter 2) to laboratory studies in individualist and collectivist cultures, which all

---

Box 6.5 **Fitting in with the group**

Mr Nakagawa Takehiro was very honoured to have obtained admission to a prestigious graduate school in the United States. He was not familiar with the work of the professor he was to be working with, but had been advised that the university he was going to had the highest status of those that had made him offers, and had chosen to go there on that basis. He had never been outside Japan before and was naturally apprehensive about his first meeting with his professor, and keen to give the right impression.

Soon after settling in, Mr Nakagawa located the professor's office and, finding her at her desk, presented his card. She shook his hand warmly and glanced briefly at his card.

'Oh, my goodness', she said, 'we're going to have a hard time with your name. How would it be if we call you Taki?'

She went on to explain that she was holding open house the following Sunday, and that would give him a chance to meet colleagues and other students. After instructing him on how to reach the house, she said that he should come whenever he would like. Mr Nakagawa wondered whether this was to be a formal occasion, but his professor reassured him that he should wear whatever he found most comfortable. Mr Nakagawa quickly told his professor that he would be coming and left her office. As he walked away he reflected that it was going to be very difficult to find out how to do the right thing. He thought that perhaps his imperfect English had caused him to miss his professor's guidance as to when he should come and what he should wear.

support a similar conclusion. The more one's fate is interdependent with that of others, the greater is one's likelihood of conforming.

Minority influence

The Asch experiments have been taken by most researchers as an opportunity to look at the way that the majority could induce a minority to conform. In recent years, a reversal of approach has developed among some researchers, who examine the circumstances under which a minority may influence the majority to change its views. Originally proposed in France (Moscovici and Faucheux, 1972; Moscovici, 1976), this approach has taken root much more firmly in Europe than in North America. Moscovici regards minority influence as more 'indirect' than majority influence. By this designation he means that a minority may *gradually* induce changes in a majority by maintaining its deviant position with a high level of consistency. The change created in this way will most probably not appear on direct measures of influence, but may only be detected by looking for changes in related attitudes. Moscovici also asserts that the effects of minority influence will persist longer than will those achieved by majority influence, because the changes that occur will not be a superficial conformity but will be more deeply internalized.

In one of their more striking experiments, Moscovici and Personnaz (1980) showed that the minority was able to influence the judgements of the majority when evaluating the colour of a series of blue–green slides, by consistently stating them to be green. This experiment had two stages. Firstly, majority and minority members made their colour judgements together. Subsequently, each group member was asked to report privately what colours were the after-images they saw after viewing each slide. (The after-image is the colour that appears when one looks at a white screen after concentrating one's vision on a bright colour for a time.) In this stage of the experiment, majority members never heard the judgements of after-image colour made by the minority, but they nonetheless reported that they were seeing red–purple, which is the after-image of green. The effect persisted even on further trials after the consistent minority was no longer present. The process of minority influence is thus not actually at all 'indirect', since it is based on the consistent statement of dissent, but its lasting effects may sometimes only be detected indirectly.

Positive results of this type have been repeatedly obtained by Moscovici and his colleagues in Paris, and by researchers in other European countries. Most North American researchers were initially sceptical of the replicability of these effects, preferring the view that majority and minority influence are both explained by the same influence process. They asserted that minority influence just happened more rarely than majority influence, because there are fewer people arguing for the minority view. Wood *et al.* (1994) conducted a meta-analysis of all available minority influence studies. They concluded that minority influence effects were replicable on both sides of the Atlantic as well as in Japan. However, their analysis also showed an interesting variation across nations in the types of effect that were obtained. Since studies from further countries have been published subsequent to the analysis by Wood *et al.*, these differences can be examined to see whether it can be explained in terms of cultural difference. As Table 6.5 shows, data from studies comparing influence towards the minority in comparison to control data are now available from studies in ten nations.

The most crucial test of Moscovici's hypothesis is given by private indirect measures of compliance. As the table shows, strong support was obtained in France, Switzerland, Italy and Greece but not in the United States or Northern Europe. However, in the Southern European countries direct measures of compliance, both public and private, showed a lesser effect, as Moscovici's model also predicts. Contrary to Moscovici, direct measures showed larger effect sizes within the United Kingdom and the United States. In most of the remaining nations an insufficient number of studies is available to be confident that the differences in the table are consistent or meaningful.

Where should minority influence be strongest? Examined from a cultural perspective, Moscovici's work is interesting in two particular ways. Firstly, there is the question of what it is about the cultures of European countries that has led to greater interest in the topic of minority influence and greater success in supporting Moscovici's hypotheses that minorities would achieve their influence

Table 6.5 ● Studies of minority influence

	Public compliance		Private direct compliance		Private indirect compliance	
	Number of effects	Effect size	Number of effects	Effect size	Number of effects	Effect size
USA	14	−0.46	29	−0.24	4	−0.07
UK	3	−0.73	6	−0.89		
France	10	−0.17	13	−0.35	11	−0.45
Belgium	6	−0.10	4	−0.18	1	−0.21
Italy			7	−0.18	1	−0.61
Spain			6	−0.10		
Switzerland	2	−0.70	6	−0.07	6	−0.63
Greece			5	−0.20	3	−0.78
Japan	3	−0.26	1	−0.34		
Netherlands			1	−0.08	1	−0.15
Australia			4	−0.21		

A negative effect size indicates that subjects changed their opinions in the direction advocated by the minority, as compared to no-influence control subjects. The data in this table are derived from Wood *et al.* (1994) and R. Bond, Smith and Wood (1997).

in indirect ways. Secondly, and in the long run more importantly, Moscovici's emphasis upon minority influence can be related to the notion that in collectivist cultures influence and indeed communication will be more indirect, in order to avoid the loss of harmony that might otherwise ensue. It appears that although indirect minority influence may be widespread in collectivist cultures, the means by which it would be accomplished would not be through the type of rigidly consistent and vocal deviance that Moscovici found to be effective in France. In contrast, in cultures that are more individualist than France, such as the United Kingdom and the United States, the evidence suggests that if frustrated minority members suppress their wish to leave the group and persist with the presentation of their views they can indeed accomplish a measure of direct as well as indirect influence.

The only tests of Moscovici's hypotheses from outside Western Europe, North America and Australia have been reported from Japan. Koseki's (1989) study reported substantial minority influence in groups judging the numbers of dots projected on a screen. However, her results illustrate some of the difficulties of arriving at research procedures with equivalent meaning in different cultures. In Koseki's initial study the confederate 'always spoke first or at a very early stage, disregarding precedence and in a confident fashion'. The significance of this sequencing is that who speaks first in Japanese society is often a strong indicator of high status. We may therefore be looking here at the effects of high status rather than of minority status. In further studies, Koseki systematically varied when her confederate spoke. She found that when the confederate spoke last, minority influence was very much weaker, although still significantly present.

Yoshiyama (1988) also found minority influence, this time on a task involving the matching of line lengths. He reported that the majority perceived the minority to be less competent than themselves but more confident, particularly when the gap between majority and minority was wide. Atsumi and Sugiman (1990) used a discussion task and found that both the majority and the minority exerted some influence. Where the gap between majority and minority was small, the minority was more likely to prevail, whereas when the gap was wider, it yielded to the majority. Furthermore, as Moscovici's model predicts, where minority influence did occur its effects were more persistent.

All the Japanese findings are consistent with the view that subjects may have been seeking the optimal way of maintaining group harmony. The minority appears to achieve their influence because, as in the West, consistent behavioural style is perceived as a sign of confidence. However, the Japanese studies indicate that the majority will only rely upon this confidence where the majority are closer to the minority in the first place. Parallels to these experimental findings may be seen in the proceedings of the Japanese Diet. The majority Liberal Democrats fairly frequently compromise with the views of the minority political parties, instead of voting them down as would occur in Western legislatures. The minority parties often reinforce this tendency by threatening to withdraw if a compromise is not reached.

We have now reviewed three types of social influence that occur within small groups. Each of these is a form of influence that is conceptualized as occurring among peers. The notable omission is that of influence deriving from some aspect of position in a hierarchy, namely leadership. We shall reserve this issue until Chapter 8, since it has most typically been studied within the context of organizational behaviour. We should nonetheless resist the implicit assumption that hierarchical influence only occurs in organizations. In cultures where values of equality are more strongly endorsed than values of hierarchy, organizations may indeed be where hierarchical relations are most evident. However, in cultures where hierarchy is a dominant value, we should expect influence based on that value to be widespread in all relationships, be they intimate or work-based.

Individual contributions to small groups

It is difficult to study the behaviour of participants in groups: careful categorization of target activities and extensive training of observers are needed. Cross-cultural studies pose even greater problems in creating equivalent situations and measures.

In addition, theories about cultural influences on communication processes must be developed to help understand comparative results. What, for example, can be concluded from the fact that Americans ask relatively more questions during unstructured, leaderless group discussions than do Mainland Chinese or Hong Kong Chinese (Ho, 1996)? Are Americans extending greater freedom of action to their co-discussants? Or perhaps avoiding direct confrontation of opinions?

Oetzel (1995, 1996) tried to address this linkage between theory and outcome by using 'effective decision-making theory' to understand individual inputs to a group discussion. The theory focuses on turn-taking and expressed disagreement, both of which will affect the task and maintenance dimensions of group behaviour (Bond and Shiu, 1997). Oetzel argues that collectivist cultural dynamics would favour more equality in turn-taking and more avoidant strategies for conflict management (Ting-Toomey *et al.*, 1991). These cultural-level differences would then be mirrored at the individual level: those with interdependent self-construals would show the collectivist style of verbal inputs; those with independent self-construals, the individualistic.

Oetzel (1996) compared Japanese group discussants with American. He found no differences across cultures in homogeneous groups. He did, however, confirm his prediction that those with independent self-construals, be they American or Japanese, would take a greater number of turns and engage in more competitive strategies when dealing with conflict situations during the group discussion. Scores on interdependence did not predict either behaviour, but Oetzel argues that in groups that lasted longer, interdependence would become more salient and would then predict the use of avoidant and cooperative conflict strategies.

Small group processes

The previous section considered the behaviour of individuals in groups or in sub-groups as the object of inquiry; the present section focuses on the group itself as the phenomenon to be understood. At this level, research may, for example, target the degree of equality in member conversation or group turnover in membership as outcomes to study.

Group efficacy

When people must work together to accomplish interdependent tasks, a new perception emerges to motivate their performance as group members. Bandura (1997) labels this construct 'perceived collective efficacy', defined as 'a group's shared belief in their conjoint capabilities to organize and execute the courses of action required to produce given levels of attainments' (p. 478). The interactive dynamics required for effective group functioning result in collective efficacy's tapping a different construct from that of the summed self-efficacies of a group's members. These interactive considerations include: 'the mix of knowledge and competencies in the group, how groups are structured and its activities coordinated, how well it is led, the strategies it adopts and whether members interact with one another in mutually facilitory or undermining ways' (p. 478). Perceptions of group efficacy have been shown to predict group performance across a wide variety of interdependent tasks.

How might culture affect perceived group efficacy? Earley (1993) argued that persons are socialized in collectivist cultural systems to believe that they are more efficacious when working in in-groups and that their in-groups are more effi-cacious than are groups composed of outsiders. Consequently,

> collectivists will anticipate receiving more rewards and feel more efficacious, both alone and as group members, and thus will perform better, while working in an ingroup context than while working in an outgroup context or working alone. Individualists will anticipate receiving more rewards and feel more efficacious, and thus perform better, while working alone than while working in an ingroup or an outgroup context. (pp. 324–5)

We noted earlier that Earley's study did obtain the predicted pattern of social loafing effects. Earley also showed that the levels of loafing obtained in the differ-ent experimental conditions were strongly linked to individual participants' ratings of both self and group efficacy.

This field study provides evidence for the predictive power of collective efficacy beliefs. In addition, it provides a model for how cultural values may operate to influence this important judgement of group 'potency' (Guzzo et al., 1993). Similarly, we might anticipate linkages between masculinity–femininity (Hofstede, 1980) and the efficacy of task and social role allocation; hierarchy (Schwartz, 1994) and the efficacy of authoritarian styles of leadership; and long-term orientation (Hofstede, 1991) and the efficacy of short- versus long-term groupings.

Group performance

P. B. Smith *et al.* (in press) compared the way managers from twenty-three nations handled disagreements both within the group and across different groups. Managers from high power distance nations showed low reliance on subordinates in resolving in-group problems. This result can be explained in terms of the centralization of authority within and loyalty towards the group in high power distance cultures. The handling of in-group disputes also differed as a function of individualism–collectivism. In collectivist cultures there was greater reliance on formal rules and procedures, consistent with the cultural aversion to interpersonal conflict. In individualistic cultures, team members reported greater reliance on their own experience and training, consistent with the cultural emphasis on self-reliance.

These results suggest that culture exercises an impact on the group procedures by which teams function and generate their outputs. These culture–process links may be integrated with the broader model of team performance developed by Helmreich and Schaefer (1994), shown in Figure 6.1, which explicitly acknow-ledges the role of national culture. In the case of the Smith *et al.* study, national culture becomes an input factor shaping the values of team members, who then undertake different decision processes for resolving problem events. These procedures then relate to different outcomes, such as increased frequency of inter-departmental disputes.

National culture has also been related to norms concerning leader–member responsibilities and communication procedures. In an effort to improve aircrew functioning, Merritt and Helmreich (1996) administered a Cockpit Management Attitudes questionnaire to pilots and flight attendants from eight nations. The attitudes of respondents from the five Asian nations clustered together, indicating an endorsement of 'top-down communication and coordination, a preference for

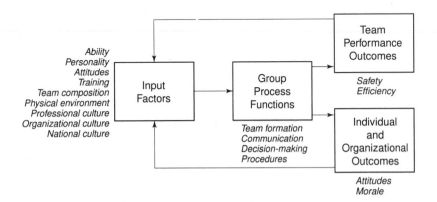

Figure 6.1 A model of team performance. (Source: adapted from Helmreich and Schaefer, 1994. Provided by Robert Helmreich, and used with permission.)

autocratic leadership, a willingness to monitor others' performance, and a disregard for stress' (p. 17). This approach to managing the flight deck was in contrast to that of the American groups, especially the pilots. Given that these attitudes are related to American operational behaviour and crew effectiveness, it becomes essential to relate these differences to their cultural context (Helmreich, Merritt and Sherman, 1996). Thus, the distinctive Asian set of attitudes may be functional in an Asian cockpit because Asian team process differs from the American, even though it yields equally effective outcomes. Or it may not. Answers to these cultural questions become important in training flight crews from different cultural backgrounds to handle emergencies with greater effectiveness (Merritt, 1996).

A sophisticated linkage of culture to group performance was provided by Erez and Somech (1996) in their analysis of social loafing. They argued that social loafing would disappear in teams when 'performance in the presence of familiar others, the use of specific goals, intra-group communication, and incentives strengthened evaluation apprehension' (p. 26). However, those team members with the independent self-construal that is promoted in individualistic cultures would feel less evaluation apprehension in the absence of goals, communication and incentives, and thus would loaf more, relative to those with the interdependent self-construals that are promoted in collectivist cultures. The results from a study with Israeli managers confirmed their hypotheses.

This study succeeded in unpackaging culture's effect on group behaviour through a careful linkage of culturally derived self-construals to the incentives informing performance. Different types of group tasks in different contexts will likewise have to be connected to culture through psychological processes in future research. This is demanding work, but necessary to give cross-cultural psychology greater external validity.

Summary

Communication in collectivist cultures is more indirect, less succinct and less interpretable without knowledge of its context than that typically found in individualist cultures. Time perspectives are longer, and more attention is given to the maintenance of harmonious relationships. Despite recent changes, romantic love is still somewhat less strongly endorsed in more collectivist nations, at least in East Asia. Social influences in collective cultures are stronger, but they rest on a mutual search for harmony rather than on unilateral imposition. Some progress has been made in showing how predominant cultural values can be validly linked to the incidence of cooperative behaviours and to variations in small group processes.

Intergroup relations

If the enemy's troops march up angrily and remain facing
ours for a long time without either joining battle
or taking themselves off again, the situation is one
that demands great vigilance and circumspection.

Sun Tzu, *The Art of War*

In the two preceding chapters we have generally looked at social behaviour from a perspective that reflects the predominantly individualistic emphasis of many contemporary North American researchers. In this chapter we move toward a perspective that remains focused upon individual behaviour, but that takes group membership as the determinant of that behaviour. The individualistic approach sees group behaviour as an aggregated result of the social cognitions and resultant behaviours of its members. The present approach reverses this presumed causal chain of events: the individual's identity and consequent behaviour is seen as defined by his or her group memberships. The principal theorists proposing this perspective have been Europeans, but the influence of their ideas is now widely diffused.

The Swiss psychologist Doise (1986) has explored the question of how many different levels of explanation are required for a valid social psychology. Most probably, all would agree that social psychology should be able to offer explanations both of individual and of small group behaviour. The more European flavour to Doise's formulation is provided by his inclusion of explanations at the level of intergroup relations and of society as a whole. It is through an emphasis upon these more macroscopic levels of influence that recent European work has become distinctive.

The analysis of social cognition that we presented in Chapter 5 portrays the individual for the most part as an isolated processor of social information. Attributions about oneself and others are seen as dependent upon where we direct our attention and how we process the information we extract from our immediate social environment. In 1972, Israel and Tajfel edited a volume in which a number of European social psychologists argued that social psychology should become more 'social' than this, broadening its approach so as to encompass the continuing network of social affiliations, past and present, that influence our behaviour. In other words, they argued that we need to attend more fully to *the manner in which social information in the environment is created and maintained over time*, rather than focusing exclusively on how that information may subsequently be processed by individuals. For instance, there exist in society relatively stable understandings of what it means to be a member of the middle class, or to be someone who plays golf, or who works for IBM. If we join one of these groupings, we may categorize and define ourselves in the eyes of others.

Social identity theory

Tajfel's (1981) social identity theory proposed that the social part of our identity derives from the groups to which we belong. By favourably comparing attributes of our own groups with those of out-groups, he suggests that we acquire both a positive sense of who we are and a clear understanding of how we should act toward in-group and out-group members. While this biased categorizing might seem to be axiomatic in a collectivist culture where a sharp distinction is made among people as a result of their group memberships, Tajfel's proposition was intended to apply equally to individualist cultural groups where his initial experiments were run.

The minimal group paradigm

Tajfel devised an experimental procedure known as the minimal group paradigm which was designed to test rigorously whether the simple fact of belonging to a group was enough to affect one's behaviour towards other groups. Tajfel *et al.* (1971) assigned English schoolboys randomly to two groups. Each boy was told that he had been assigned either to a group called Klee or a group called Kandinsky, on the basis of a test that supposedly measured their artistic preferences. The seating positions of group members were intermingled, and no boy knew which others had been assigned to the same group as himself. They were then asked to allot rewards to members of their own group and to members of the other group, choosing pairs of rewards from a series of possibilities such as the ones in Table 7.1. These pairings had been constructed in such a way as to make it possible to choose between various hypotheses as to why particular choices were made. The four possibilities examined were that the payoffs chosen would be those which: (A) maximized the rewards assigned to one's own group, or (B) maximized the total rewards allocated overall, or (C) maximized the difference between the two groups, in favour of one's own group or (D) treated both groups equally.

As Table 7.1 shows, the average allocations of rewards made by group members clustered toward the centre of the scales. This makes clear that subjects were not seeking to maximize their own group's rewards, nor were they seeking to maximize

Table 7.1 ● Sample reward allocation matrices used by Tajfel et al. (1971)

Matrix 1													
Member 74 in Klee group	25	23	21	19	17	15	13	<u>11</u>	9	7	5	3	1
Member 44 in Kandinsky group	19	18	17	16	15	14	13	<u>12</u>	11	10	9	8	7
Matrix 2													
Member 74 in Klee group	11	12	13	14	15	16	17	18	<u>19</u>	20	21	22	23
Member 44 in Kandinsky group	5	7	9	11	13	15	17	19	<u>21</u>	23	25	27	29

Within each matrix, the subject must choose one of the *pairs* of numbers that are above/below one another. The underlined numbers show the choices most typically made by members of the Kandinsky group.

the overall rewards paid out by the experimenter. These goals could have been much better accomplished by using the ends of the scales. A closer match with the data is provided by option C, that subjects were trying to maximize the difference between their group's rewards and the other group's rewards, with some tendency also toward option D, equality.

When we consider the arbitrary and artificial way in which these groups were constructed, this is a remarkable finding. In other similar experiments in this series, group membership was determined by the toss of a coin. It appears that simply being told that one belongs to a particular group category causes one to discriminate in favour of that group. Tajfel argued that this favouritism arises because the differentiation between one's group and another group serves to create a meaningful definition of one's social identity in that situation. Of course, in such an oversimplified experimental situation there are few other ways in which one could mark out a distinctive identity. In more typical, everyday settings, he considered some subset of one's relevant longer-term group memberships as defining one's situational identity, and therefore as shaping the way in which one will think and act in that situation.

The results of studies using the minimal group paradigm have been quite frequently replicated in Britain, and in certain other predominantly individualist countries. Mullen, Brown and Smith (1992) reported a meta-analysis of 137 tests of in-group bias effects, drawn from some studies using the minimal group paradigm and others using real groups. The studies included in their analysis had been conducted in seven nations and Table 7.2 compares the average effect sizes reported for each of these nations. It can be seen that effect sizes were rather larger in the United States, Germany and the Netherlands than they were in the other

Table 7.2 ● In-group bias effect sizes by nation

Nation	Number of effects	Mean effect size
UK	82	0.12
USA	33	0.22
Germany	11	0.27
Netherlands	4	0.59
Ireland	3	0.14
Switzerland	2	−0.01

three countries. Mullen *et al.* report that variations in the designs of these studies also caused significant differences in effect size. In particular, there was no evidence for in-group bias among members of artificially created groups that had been assigned low status. Indeed, members of these groups showed a significant degree of out-group bias. These effects illustrate the need for more precisely specified predictions from Tajfel's theory (Jost and Banaji, 1994), which we will consider later in this chapter. The effects found with groups having lower status membership make more difficult the comparison of degree of typical in-group bias across nations. There were twenty effect sizes of this type, seventeen of them from UK studies. If one eliminates these studies from the UK sample, the mean UK effect size becomes 0.24, comparable to the figures for the other North European and North American nations. The range of nations included within this meta-analysis does not permit us to tell whether broader sampling would show greater diversity of effect. Additional minimal group studies have been reported by Hogg and Sunderland (1991) using Australian students as subjects.

The replicability of minimal group effects

Minimal group effects in cultural groups likely to have more collectivist values have been successfully replicated by Kakimoto (1992) from Japan. Wetherell (1982) reported rather more complex results from New Zealand. Her first study compared 8-year-old children from low socio-economic backgrounds of European and of Polynesian origin. Both groups were found to favour maximizing differences between the in-group and the out-group, but the effect was significantly stronger for the European children. The Polynesian responses also reflected some wish to maximize joint rewards. In a second study, Wetherell examined this effect more fully. By increasing her sample she was able to compare children of European, Maori and Samoan origin. She found that the Europeans once again sought to maximize the in-group/out-group difference. The Samoans' choices favoured maximizing joint rewards, while the Maoris' responses were intermediate between those of the Europeans and the Samoans.

The results for the Samoan children are of particular interest, since they derive from a cultural group that has traditionally been strongly collectivist. On the surface, the results contradict Tajfel's theory and suggest that its validity may be restricted to more individualist cultural groups. However, the use of Tajfel's research procedures in a rather different setting from that in which they were first developed provides us with little information as to how the Samoan children perceived the situation. One possibility that Wetherell (1982) considers is that they were relatively unaffected by her telling them which group they had been assigned to. Their allocentric values would more likely tell them that the salient groups in the study were the overall group of Samoans on the one hand and the Pakeha (white European) experimenter on the other (Bochner and Perks, 1971). On this line of analysis, they were maximizing in-group rewards, with these rewards accruing to both groups of Samoans. A second possibility also discussed by Wetherell is that within traditional Polynesian culture the giving of gifts to others is highly esteemed. Thus, by rewarding the out-group a Polynesian child could in fact be acquiring a positive social identity in the Samoan social calculus. This interpretation would be consistent with the 'modesty bias' found in other studies from East Asia, as discussed in Chapter 5. The difficulty in choosing between these interpretations underlines the importance of using indigenous experimenters in studies comparing different cultural groups. It can also remind us that even in studies of the minimal group paradigm within Western nations, we have very little information as to how participants in this type of experiment perceive what is going on.

Broader tests of social identity theory

The value of social identity theory does not rest solely upon the outcome of studies using the minimal group paradigm. A further development of social identity theory, by a group of British and Australian researchers, is known as social categorization theory (Turner *et al.*, 1987). This theory distinguishes between personal identity and social identity and proposes that the degree to which one categorizes oneself as a member of a particular social category will predict both the nature of the in-group influence processes that will occur and one's orientation towards out-groups. More specifically, social categorization theorists propose that group processes such as conformity, minority influence, group polarization and in-group bias can all be explained as member responses to the social reality of being categorized. It is expected that someone categorized as a group member will generally seek to approximate their understanding of the way in which a 'proto-typical' member of that group would behave.

Being categorized as a group member can be either temporary or permanent. The social categorization theorists mostly test their propositions on the basis of short-term experimental manipulations of categorization (e.g. Abrams *et al.*, 1990), where it is the experimenter who provides the range of possible categories for categorization. However, the message of this book is that members of collectivist cultures are frequently categorized by themselves and by others as members of certain groups permanently, whereas members of individualist cultures can experience much greater social mobility in and out of the groups within which they are categorized. It follows that we should expect group dynamic effects to be stronger within long-term groups than within *ad hoc* experimental groups, especially within collectivist cultures. In Chapter 6, we examined studies of conformity and of minority influence, finding some evidence that these effects are indeed stronger in collectivist cultures. We now consider a further range of studies looking this time at the behaviour of in-group members towards out-group members.

In-group bias: a broader view

In reviewing the achievements of social identity theory and social categorization theory, Mummendey (1995) suggests that the further one moves away from the minimal group paradigm, the more it becomes the case that factors additional to the mere fact of social categorization affect group members' behaviour. Indeed, she suggests that minimal group effects may be strengthened precisely because members who are categorized by the experimenter have no other information about their own or other groups. In real-world interactions, one may categorize the other person in many ways, thereby qualifying the effect of any one category on subsequent behaviour as Dorai (1993) has shown in France as well as Islam and Hewstone (1993b) in Bangladesh. Nonetheless, studies from a broad range of nations have shown that members of different ethnic groups do often maintain biased systems of beliefs about the positive qualities of their own group and the negative qualities of other groups. Indeed it was the abundant everyday evidence of inter-ethnic stereotyping that led Tajfel and others to develop their theories in the first place. Data from other research areas in psychology confirm the effect. For instance, in the field of consumer psychology, Peterson and Jolibert (1995) reported a meta-analysis of studies of the 'country-of-origin' effect. They found that products described as coming from one's own country are rated higher on quality and reliability than when the same products are described as coming from other countries.

Group-serving attributions

Some studies illustrate the manner in which the mere fact of group membership can completely reverse the pattern of attributions made about an individual's behaviour. For instance, Taylor and Jaggi (1974) asked thirty Hindu clerks in India to evaluate a series of desirable and undesirable events, for example a shopkeeper who either cheated customers or was generous. The actions presented to subjects were said to have been performed either by a fellow Hindu or by an out-group Muslim. It was found that the positive behaviours performed by members of one's own group were believed to arise from internal dispositions, while their negative behaviours were seen as the result of external forces. However, Hindu evaluations of these *same* behaviours when performed by a Muslim were strikingly different. In this case the desirable behaviours were seen as externally caused, and some of the undesirable ones as internally caused! Taylor and Jaggi's demonstration of group-serving attribution (Hewstone, 1990) is thus consistent with social identity theory: the Hindu clerks would have been able to sustain a positive social identity, since they perceived the causes of behaviours by in-group and out-group members in ways that favoured their group over the other. Pettigrew (1979) labelled this prejudice-sustaining style of explaining outcomes 'the ultimate attribution error'.

Another study showing somewhat similar results compared attributions by Saudi and US students (Al-Zahrani and Kaplowitz, 1993). Subjects from both nations were asked to attribute the causes of various behaviours shown by family members and by strangers. As one would expect, the US students made more internal attributions, but when subjects were rating behaviours by members of the other nation, a marked contrast was found. Saudi subjects showed the same pattern of out-group attributions as Taylor and Jaggi reported from India: negative American behaviours were seen as internally caused and positive behaviours as externally caused. Subjects from the United States did not show this pattern of attribution when rating Saudi behaviours, however. This lack of bias could be because, for an American, comparing oneself to a Saudi is probably a much less relevant act than it is for a Saudi to compare to an American. Al-Zahrani and Kaplowitz also obtained measures of idiocentrism and allocentrism from their subjects. Scores on these measures did not, however, correlate with the degree of out-group bias shown by Saudi respondents. Further studies will be required to determine whether this was due to some specific circumstance, for instance the uniformity of Saudi feeling toward the United States, or whether this type of in-group bias cannot be accounted for by variations in allocentrism. The former explanation is the more likely one, as the literature on group-serving attributions reveals tremendous complexity in determining factors (Hewstone, 1990).

This complexity increases when the measurement of group-serving attribution is itself differentiated. Weber (1994) has distinguished the protective function of group attributions (i.e. attributing in-group negative or out-group positive behaviour to external causes) from the enhancement function (i.e. attributing in-group positive and out-group negative behaviour to internal causes). The former maintains group esteem, whereas the latter enhances it. Under normal intergroup conflict, only protective bias is found. Weber speculates that the group enhancement bias in attributions will only be found under the rare conditions of acute conflict.

Tajfel (1981) acknowledged that under certain circumstances it may be impossible for members of a group to find a positive basis upon which to compare their group with other groups. This might occur for instance in groups that had low status in society. Under these circumstances, he envisaged that group members would do one of three things. Firstly, they might seek new bases for comparison which would give a more favourable outcome, such as emphasizing the beauty of traditional clothing or the liveliness of the group's language, an option that he termed social creativity. Secondly, they might leave the group and join another with more positive qualities, an option which he termed social mobility. Individualistic cultures with their emphasis on equal opportunity and freedom of association may provide more opportunities and support for such an option! Thirdly, they might seek to change the attributes of their group so that it would command more favourable evaluations in future, an option that he termed social change.

The social mobility option is also likely to be somewhat more practicable in individualist cultural groups than in collectivist groups, although even in individualist cultures categories such as skin colour and gender do not permit such a strategy to be used. The social change option is likely to be a slow and difficult process everywhere, since changes in the attributes of one whole social group may well threaten the position of other social groups with vested interests in the status quo and take time to mobilize.

The implications of this discussion are that, just as Mullen, Brown and Smith (1992) found with artificial laboratory groups, we might expect to find some examples of real groups whose members *do not* rate their own group higher than others. They should be most frequent within vertical collectivist societies. In this type of society one could expect that disadvantaged groups would be more inclined to accept as legitimate that higher status groups were more deserving of their higher rewards.

In-group derogation

Hewstone and Ward (1985) modified the experimental design used by Taylor and Jaggi (1974) to obtain attributions from Chinese and Malay subjects located in Malaysia. The Chinese form a substantial ethnic minority in Malaysia, and are restricted from entering certain occupations. It was found that the dominant group, the Malays, made ethnocentric attributions similar to those found by Taylor and Jaggi in India. Malays saw positive acts by other Malays as more internally caused than if the same act had been carried out by a Chinese. Likewise, they saw negative acts by a Malay as more situationally caused than if they were done by a Chinese. The Chinese, however, showed a pattern of out-group favourit-ism in their attributions. This reversal was hypothesized to arise possibly because of the subordinate status accorded to the Chinese in Malaysia, and acknowledged by them so as to be acceptable to the Malaysian majority (see also Feather, 1995, for similar results with minorities in Australia).

Hewstone and Ward (1985) then repeated their study in Singapore, where the political power relations between the two ethnic communities are substantially reversed and where inter-ethnic harmony is politically pursued. In this changed social context, the numerically dominant Chinese showed neither in-group favouritism or denigration in their group attributions; the numerically weaker Malays continued to show in-group favouritism, albeit less so than in Malaysia.

In this carefully balanced, cross-cultural study, we may sense the complexity of the factors involved in intergroup attributions. In-group derogation by the subordinate Chinese in Malaysia did not reappear as in-group favouritism in Singapore where they dominate. Are we then dealing with a general Chinese pattern of relative group effacement in attributions *vis-à-vis* the Malays? Or with the effects of institutionalized racism in Malaysia versus mandated racial harmony in Singapore? Or with both?

In-group derogation using attributions provided by social psychologists may be replaced by in-group favouritism when group members choose the categories for comparison. Several European studies have illustrated the way in which disadvantaged groups use social creativity in choosing alternative criteria upon which to evaluate themselves. For example, van Knippenberg and van Oers (1984) compared the perceptions of two different categories of nurses in the Netherlands. The more highly trained group saw themselves as superior in theoretical insight, while the less trained group saw themselves as more friendly. Likewise, Mummendey and Schreiber (1984) found that members of different political parties in Germany each evaluated their party more positively on those attributes that they considered to be the more important.

Group identification and in-group bias

An alternative approach to social identity theory which links it directly to the theme of this book has been made in Britain by Brown and his colleagues. Hinkle and Brown (1990) reason that a central tenet of social identity theory is that one will discriminate against an out-group if one identifies with the in-group. Social identity theorists do not all accept this derivation, but it is nonetheless a useful line of investigation within a cross-cultural context, since as Hinkle and Brown point out, their prediction is much more likely to be supported in the case of people endorsing allocentric values than in the case of those holding idiocentric values. Field studies in hospitals, factories, a paper-mill and a bakery, however, have indicated that there is in fact a *highly variable* relationship between identification with the group and favouring one's in-group. Roccas and Schwartz (1993), for example, find that higher intergroup similarity strengthens the relationship between group identification and in-group bias.

Hinkle and Brown (1990) conclude that this variation must be due to the fact that comparing one's group with other groups is not *always* important to one's identity. In some groups, such as sports teams, their very reason for existence is to compare their success with that of others. Hinkle and Brown call these 'relational' groups. These are contrasted with 'autonomous' groups, such as juries or close-knit families where there is much less reason to engage in intergroup comparisons. Their reconceptualization of social identity theory is shown in Figure 7.1. An empirical study by Brown *et al.* (1992) obtained measures of allocentrism and of relational orientation from members of various British groups. As their model predicts, they found that identification with the in-group and bias against the

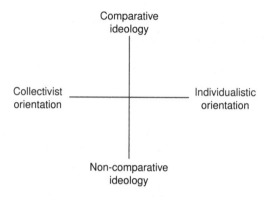

Figure 7.1 Hinkle and Brown's reformulation of social identity theory. (Source: Hinkle and Brown, 1990.)

out-group were highly correlated *only* where both allocentrism and relational orientation were high. Feather (1994a) provided further evidence with a study in Australia. He found a positive relationship between in-group bias toward Australia and identification with being an Australian. As Hinkle and Brown would predict, this relationship was stronger among subjects who endorsed the Schwartz value domains of conformity, security and (low) hedonism. These can be considered equivalent to allocentric values.

As we pointed out earlier, social identity theory was formulated by Europeans who were concerned to make 'social psychology more social'. There is a certain irony about this intention, insofar as most commentators would agree that its hypotheses are more likely to be supported in collectivist cultures. Field tests of theory, mostly in Europe, have yielded rather mixed results, and it may be that Hinkle and Brown's (1990) explanation will enable us to understand why. However, we have little information at present as to whether a relational orientation is also important within collectivist cultures. Triandis (1992) suggests that members of collectivist cultures are not interested in comparing themselves with out-groups and instead are characterized by 'in-group centrism'. Torres (1996) made a series of comparative tests of the Hinkle–Brown model in Brazil and the United Kingdom. Using schoolchildren as subjects, she found that the correlation between identification with one's own social class and bias against other social classes was stronger in Brazil than in the United Kingdom. However, in both countries this effect was unrelated to endorsement of allocentric values or relational orientation. Thus she obtained the type of country-level effect that we might expect, but her individual-level measures were unable to explain it. Possibly this was because she selected social class as the group upon which she focused, a rather different type of group from those upon which Hinkle and Brown had earlier focused.

In order to clarify her findings, Torres (1996) then selected four types of groups to which students belong in Brazil and the United Kingdom. Accepting the criticisms of imposed-etic measures of idiocentrism/allocentrism, she designed measures specific to each type of group. Her analysis then revealed that her student samples described religious groups to which they belonged in terms of high allocentrism and high involvement. In these groups, but not in the other three types of groups, identification and in-group bias were strongly correlated. With some modification, Hinkle and Brown's (1990) theory thus proved able to make successful predictions within two quite different cultures.

It might be the case that in individualist cultures people make a distinction between groups with which they do and do not wish to compare themselves. In collectivist cultures, on the other hand, greater awareness of the contextual embeddedness of all behaviour might mean that a comparative orientation is part of the values characterizing allocentrism. However, the social comparison in which allocentrics engage may not be quite the same as that envisaged by social identity theorists. As an allocentric group member, I am not going to be so preoccupied with my identity as a group member: that is securely established. I will be focused instead upon my group as a whole and upon any threats to its well-being, whether they come from within or without. My behaviour will thus adapt to the presence or absence of either in- or out-group members. A study by Bond *et al.* (1985a) illustrates this possibility. They compared the effects of having an audience present or absent on explanations given for typical gender behaviours. In the United States, the presence or absence of an audience had no effect on the explanations provided. However in Hong Kong, with more allocentric participants (Kwan, Bond and Singelis, 1997), if a same-sex audience was absent, the explanations given became more biased against the out-group.

Perhaps the most interesting aspect of the studies by Hinkle and Brown's (1990) group is that their studies have shown sufficient variability in the endorsement of idiocentrism/allocentrism to enable intracultural tests of their hypothesis. Thus, variables that arose from comparative studies made *across* cultures have also proved to have some validity in understanding variations in behaviour both *within* a Western culture and cross-culturally.

Social dominance theory

At the beginning of this chapter it was suggested that the study of intergroup relations moved us away from the individualistic emphasis of more current research into social cognition. However, it is notable that the studies so far discussed in this chapter mostly have to do with the behaviour of particular individuals within a group context. The individual's group membership is seen as affecting his or her behaviour towards in- or out-group members. This progression away from a focus upon individual behaviour can be taken one step further. Social dominance theory, developed by Sidanius and Pratto, asserts that the members of high- and low-status groups will differ from one another in consistent and predictable ways (Sidanius, 1993). In particular, high-status groups will endorse a 'social dominance orientation' (SDO), that is to say, they will maintain a set of beliefs that legitimize their dominance, and an endorsement of social dominance will be linked with close attachment to their group. In contrast, in low-status groups these measures will not correlate well with each other. In other words, those members of low-status groups who endorse an SDO will not feel closely attached to their groups, while those who are closely attached will not endorse an SDO.

This acceptance or rejection of lower status will have implications for minority group attributions: accepted minority group status may lead to attributions unfavourable to one's own group (e.g. Milner, 1975), whereas resented minority group status may sharpen the ultimate attribution error (Amabile and Glazebrook, 1982). Tajfel's (1981) social identity theory also considered relations between high- and low-status groups, and Sidanius and Pratto's theory reflects the several alternative options that Tajfel saw as open to individual members of low-status groups, such as social mobility or social creativity.

Sidanius, Pratto and Rabinowitz (1994) showed support for their model as applied to gender differences among US students in Euro-American and Afro- and Hispanic-American students. Among males and Euro-Americans, an SDO and in-group attachment were linked, whereas among the lower-status groups they were not (see also Sidanius, Levin and Pratto, 1996). Recently, Pratto et al. (1996) have extended this work into three new cultures. They find that SDO can be reliably measured in other cultures, that men generally score higher than women, that high SDO is associated with sexism, and most importantly for our present purposes, it predicts ethnic prejudice in the local intergroup hegemony (except in China). The global differences in values that we have noted in earlier chapters would lead us to expect that SDO would be more strongly endorsed in some nations than others. For instance, the effect should be stronger in nations espousing hierarchy than in those espousing egalitarian commitment (Schwartz, 1994).

In essence what social dominance theory asks us to do is to consider data that are often interpreted to terms of individual differences, and see that they are equally well accounted for by a group-level theory. Whether we find it more useful to study phenomena at the individual or the group level is open to continuing debate, but one certain contribution of group-level analysis is that it requires us to focus on the continuity of the mostly negative ways in which groups view one another, regardless of changing group memberships. The 'orientation' which in Sidanius and Pratto's model is perceived by dominant groups to legitimize their dominance comprises a variety of attitudes and beliefs, which other researchers often refer to as prejudice.

Stereotypes

In the next two sections we shall discuss stereotypes and prejudice. The two concepts are often used interchangeably and with insufficient precision. A stereotype is a group of beliefs about persons who are members of a particular group, whereas prejudice can better be thought of as an attitude, usually negative,

> ### Box 7.1　Stereotypes of people from different countries
>
> Peabody (1985) asked samples of students from six European nations to make ratings as to how likely it was that a man from a given country would have certain qualities. Ratings were made on thirty-two judgement scales (intelligent–stupid, etc.). Judgements were made for a typical person from France, Germany, Italy, England, Russia and America (thus providing heterostereotypes) as well as from one's own country (providing an autostereotype). Some subjects from each country refused to make such judgements, or relied heavily on the neutral scale points. Their data were discarded. When the remaining data were analyzed, it was found that the heterostereotypes provided by judges from different nations were in quite strong agreement. The traits shown below are those that were most strongly and consensually agreed, in order of strength of effect. The data were collected in around 1970, and the meaning of the adjective 'gay' should probably be read as the opposite of 'grim', rather than in its contemporary sense.
>
> | Americans | English | French | Germans | Italians | Russians |
> | --- | --- | --- | --- | --- | --- |
> | Self-confident | Self-controlled | Gay | Hard-working | Gay | Serious |
> | Active | Tactful | Active | Firm | Impulsive | Hard-working |
> | Spontaneous | Calm | Self-confident | Forceful | Agitated | Firm |
> | Conceited | Selective | Likable | Persistent | Spontaneous | Cautious |
> | Forceful | Persistent | Conceited | Active | Thrifty | |
> | Generous | Cautious | Self-confident | Intelligent | | |
> | Extravagant | | | | | |

toward the members of a group. Gender, ethnicity, age, education, wealth and the like may form the basis for a stereotype, as indeed can any identifiable social marker. Stereotypes vary in many aspects: they may be widely shared by others, even by the stereotyped persons themselves, in which case they assume the characteristics of Moscovici's (1981) social representations (Augoustinos and Walker, 1995), or they may be idiosyncratic to the individual holding them; they may involve beliefs about the traits, values, behaviours, opinions or indeed the beliefs of typical persons from that other group; they may be simple or differentiated, positive or negative, confidently or unsurely held (Triandis *et al.*, 1982).

The early work on stereotypes was dominated by an interest in groups that typically shared a history of conflict, abuse, or atrocity. Against such a background, stereotypes about the out-group were extreme, simple, negative and symmetrical, with members of each group rating their own group members positively while denigrating members of the out-group (Schwartzwald and Yinon, 1977). The elimination of stereotypes was widely believed to be a prerequisite for intergroup harmony (Taylor, 1981). This liberal distaste for stereotyping was held by many social scientists and reinforced by the cultural emphasis on personal uniqueness (Snyder and Fromkin, 1980), characteristic of the individualist societies where most research into stereotypes is conducted.

Recently, however, psychologists have been developing a more balanced appreciation of stereotypes. Many have noted the 'kernel of truth' (Mackie, 1973) that stereotypes possess; others have observed that interacting social groups often hold positive stereotypes about one another (Berry, Kalin and Taylor, 1977). In established multi-ethnic communities, trait stereotypes of out-group members become more positive the more secure the in-group raters are about their own group and culture (Lambert, Mermigis and Taylor, 1986). Furthermore, stereotypes of some groups may be defined across many dimensions, giving opportunity for judges to ascribe a broad, differentiated identity to their own and other group members (e.g. Bond, 1986). Taylor (1981) has argued that this last outcome of the stereotyping process may in fact be an important component in sustaining harmonious intercultural relations. For example, Ben-Ari, Schwarzwald and Horiner-Levi (1994) showed that consensually accepted stereotypes about the intelligence of Western Jews and the social competence of Middle Eastern Jews overrode the tendency for each group to make potentially divisive, group-serving attributions for its own behaviour.

The functions of stereotypes

Stereotypes consist of pre-established expectations about members of other groups. They allow those who hold them to reduce their uncertainty about what members of other groups are likely to want, to believe and to do. As such, they are one form of cognitive schema (Rummelhart, 1984). They reduce the need to attend to and process individual information about the other (Hamilton and Trolier, 1986), so that attention may be devoted to other aspects of the interaction. 'Consistent with the dominant information processing approach to cognition, stereotypes are now seen to be an inevitable product of the need to categorize and simplify a complex social world' (Augoustinos and Walker, 1995, p. 1).

Additionally, stereotypes assist individuals to maintain a positive sense of self-esteem deriving from their group memberships (Weinreich, Luk and Bond, 1996). As we noted earlier in this chapter, Tajfel (1981) argued that people's memberships in various groups constitute one aspect of their self-concept. They strive to establish a sense of esteem in part by differentiating their groups from other groups along dimensions that yield favourable comparisons.

A key dimension identified in all ethnic or cultural stereotypes of character is the 'beneficence' dimension (Giles and Ryan, 1982), involving such traits as honest, kind, loyal and trustworthy. This dimension appears to be a combination of the conscientiousness and agreeableness factors of the 'Big Five' components of personality (Digman, 1990). Generally, group members rate their own group members higher on beneficence than they rate out-group members. Out-group members do the same, resulting in the 'mirror image' (Bronfenbrenner, 1961) pattern of intergroup perceptions. Such 'in-group enhancement' is probably a basic feature of all socialization in any viable cultural group (Bond, Chiu and Wan, 1984). The critical question for intergroup harmony is the *size* of the gap between the in-group and the out-group rating, especially on perceived values (Feather, 1980) and perceived humanity (Schwartz, Struch and Bilsky, 1990). A moderate difference may be socially necessary for a group to remain viable; a large difference, socially destructive.

An additional basis of comparison often appears in real-life stereotypes, a 'competence' dimension (Giles and Ryan, 1982). This dimension involves such traits as intelligent, successful, wealthy, educated and so forth. Ratings on this dimension have some basis in intergroup social reality, as these groups have considerable shared history to use in anchoring their judgements. Not surprisingly, there is often agreement between the groups about the relative standing of their own and other group members on competence-type dimensions. For example, a decade ago, both British and Hong Kong Chinese in Hong Kong acknowledged the higher average status of the British (Bond and Hewstone, 1988). It would be interesting to know how long this image will persist, given the recent change in Hong Kong's status.

Other dimensions of comparison may appear if the measurement scales provided to the respondents are sufficiently comprehensive. Neuroticism, extroversion and openness have all been isolated in stereotype research (e.g. Bond, 1986). So, simply at the level of stereotyped perceptions of character, group members have a wide array of dimensions which they may use to derive an adequate measure of self-esteem.

Stereotypes have a further important function for groups in contact, which is that they guide the behaviour of people from these different groups when they interact. Gibson (1979) has argued that 'perception is for doing' and research has shown that perception of another's personality relates to the behaviour that one undertakes with that other person. So, for example, both Chinese and Australians are more likely to associate in various ways with someone they regard as 'beneficent' (Bond and Forgas, 1984). Conversely, they will avoid and probably criticize or attack people they regard as evil-natured. It is this view of the enemy as evil that sustains all group conflict.

Members of different groups can interact in more harmonious ways, of course. Here, perceptions of out-group members on competence dimensions will probably guide subordination behaviour. In a similar way, perceptions of neuroticism will guide formal as opposed to self-disclosing and intimate behaviour, and perceptions of extroversion will guide initiating, sociable behaviour (Bond, 1983).

So, stereotypes of the out-group can further reduce uncertainty by guiding our behavioural choices towards members of the out-group. When groups have some experience of interacting, they may come to agree on the stereotypes they hold about one another. At the Chinese University of Hong Kong, for example, both local Chinese and American exchange students believe that the Americans are more extroverted, the Chinese more introverted (Bond, 1986). This shared perception guides behaviour in a complementary fashion – typically the American initiates and the Chinese responds. It is probable that mutual, interaction-facilitating stereotypes arise among all groups that work together (e.g. Everett and Stening, 1987), thereby easing the uncertainty and anxiety of encountering a stranger from a different group.

Augoustinos and Walker (1995) argue that stereotypes also serve the societal function of acting as 'ideological representations that are used to justify and legitimize existing social and power relations within a society' (p. 1). Jost and Banaji (1994) elaborate on this position, asserting that stereotypes 'justify the exploitation of certain groups over others, and . . . explain the poverty or powerlessness of some groups and the success of others in ways that make these differences seem legitimate and even natural' (p. 10). This position predicts the acceptance of relatively negative own-group stereotypes by socially disadvantaged groups. It would appear to apply most strongly with respect to the competence rankings of social groups, a dimension of stereotypes where there is typically much greater agreement than on the beneficence dimension.

The origin of stereotypes

The early work on stereotypes (Katz and Braly, 1933) revealed that people can hold intense stereotypes about persons from other cultural and ethnic groups, even though they had never met such persons. These polarized attitudes probably arise out of a generalized distrust of persons foreign and their reinforcement at home, by the media and in educational curricula. Stereotypes are likely to be particularly clear and consensually held if one's own group has a long history of dealings with an out-group within one's borders. In this type of situation, the anxiety surrounding intercultural encounters can be attenuated by the high predictability the stereotype affords.

National stereotypes

Earlier in this chapter we noted Peabody's (1985) study of the national stereotypes that European students held about thirty years ago. Using much more recent data, Linssen and Hagendoorn (1994) found a rather similar set of heterostereotypes for seven Western European nations. A question of interest is from what types of relatively objective information these persistent stereotypes might be constructed. The traits attributed to other nations in Linssen and Hagendoorn's study were summarized by them in terms of efficiency, dominance, empathy and emotionality. Perceived efficiency was found to be best predicted by level of economic development, while political power predicted dominance. One can see some kind of logical basis for such connections. However, empathy was best predicted by country size, and emotionality by southerly latitude. Further studies will be required from other regions of the world, to determine whether or not these are chance effects.

Although Linssen and Hagendoorn (1994) did not include Russia in their study, their results could help to explain why Peabody's subjects described Russians as they did, even leaving to one side influences derived from media coverage of the Cold War. Russia is large and northerly and, at the time the data were collected, politically powerful and economically successful. Consistent with Linssen and Hagendoorn's findings, Russians were characterized by Peabody's respondents in ways that are consistent with dominance and efficiency. More recent data, however, show that the Russian autostereotype is now very different (Stephan *et al.*, 1993; Peabody and Shmelyov, 1996). The traits they see as most typical of themselves are: generous, frank, rash, impractical, likeable and broad-minded. Times change, national dominance declines and stereotypes follow suit.

An additional finding from the Peabody (1985) study was that the students' auto-stereotypes of their own nation were on average no more positive than their heterostereotypes of other nations. Earlier studies of national or ethnic group stereotypes have almost always found in-group bias. For instance, Brewer and Campbell (1976) found that among thirty ethnic groups in Kenya, Tanzania and Uganda, virtually all showed in-group bias. Peabody's results might seem to suggest some difficulty for social identity theory, but the alternative is that the lack of in-group bias was because nationality was not an important sense of identity for the student respondents. Koomen and Bähler (1996) analyzed opinion poll data from the general population which, although published recently, was collected at about the same time as Peabody's, and in a fairly similar range of European nations. Consensus upon heterostereotypes was once more found, but there was also a markedly more positive autostereotype.

However, there are further studies that do not find in-group bias in stereotyping. Mlicki and Ellemers (1996) found Polish students markedly negative about Polishness and more positive toward the Dutch. The traits most frequently attributed to Poles by Poles were 'boozy', quarrelsome and disordered. Negative autostereotypes have also been reported for Hungarians (Larsen *et al.*, 1992) and Venezuelans (Salazar, 1997). The Polish data are particularly interesting, since Mlicki and Ellemers established that despite attributing such negative qualities to their nation, Poles identified strongly with being Polish.

We need to consider how these results can be accounted for by the two theories that we have outlined in this chapter – social identity theory and social dominance theory. Social identity theory would assert that if one is a member of a low-status group – in this case, a nation – the options are social mobility or social creativity. Leaving aside mobility, the most obvious form of social creativity is to consider oneself a member of a larger, more socially valued, grouping. Consistent with this strategy, Mlicki and Ellemers (1996) found that their Polish subjects identified with being Europeans more strongly than did their Dutch subjects. Salazar (1997) found an analogous result in Latin America. Venezuelans, Peruvians, Mexicans, Colombians and citizens of the Dominican Republic all identified more strongly with being Latin American than with being a member of their own nation. Within Salazar's sample only Brazilians showed a stronger identification with their

---

Box 7.2 **The complexities of measuring national identity and in-group bias**

Most studies of national identity have been based upon asking samples of respondents to select adjectives to characterize their own and others' qualities. A good deal may be missed by the use of such procedures. Condor (1996) used a more qualitative approach to assess social identity of the English. She reports that most other British respondents (the Welsh, Scottish and Northern Irish, from among the population of the United Kingdom) have little hesitation in identifying themselves as Welsh, Scottish or Northern Irish. However, the English were unsure how to identify themselves. Are they British or English? Do they live in Great Britain, the United Kingdom or England?

Furthermore, they rather often engaged in a form of false modesty. Those interviewed by Condor acknowledged that they saw many negative attributes of Englishness. However, they felt that the English were in fact better than other national groups, because this willingness to be self-critical showed that they were less prejudiced against other nations. Thus their in-group bias was justified by asserting a lack of in-group bias! It remains to be seen whether this effect can be found in other nations also.

---

nationality. Personnaz (1996) also found French students identified more with Europe than with France. Social identity theory can thus accommodate most aspects of the results of the study of national stereotypes. Where autostereotypes are negative, nation-members can choose alternative superordinate identities. However, social identity theory has real difficulty in accounting for Poles' high identification with being Polish, unless their identification with some superordinate identity was even stronger.

Social dominance theory would assume that there exists a generally accepted hierarchy of national identities and that we could predict from a knowledge of that hierarchy the nations in which positive self-image and national identification would be high and linked with one another. If it were the case that Central Europeans feel envious of Western Europeans, or that Latin Americans feel overshadowed by the United States, theory could predict most of the effects that are found. But no direct measures are available as to whether this ranking is in fact the case. A test of whether social dominance theory could account for the Polish results would require a correlational analysis, which Mlicki and Ellemers (1996) do not provide.

Accurate stereotypes?

If we are to make use of the concept of stereotype accuracy in aiding intergroup relations, we must first define it. Ottati and Lee (1995) consider three possibilities that might demonstrate stereotype accuracy: heterostereotype convergence, heterostereotype–autostereotype convergence and convergence between stereotypes and objective indicators. If we were to accept the first of these as valid, we could conclude from Peabody's (1985) study of national stereotypes that, because Western European students from different nations were largely agreed as to what Russians were like, their perceptions must be valid. Since later data, discussed above, indicate that the Russian autostereotype is very different, this conclusion would be hard to defend. Some studies do show heterostereotype–autostereotype convergence. For instance, US and Chinese students agree that the Chinese are more inhibited and less varied than Americans (Bond, 1986; Lee and Ottati, 1993; Lee and Ottati, 1995). Of course, the Chinese respondents evaluated these qualities positively, whereas the US respondents saw them negatively. Nonetheless the data provide evidence of stereotype accuracy in terms of auto/heterostereotype convergence.

Lee and Duenas (1995) provide a case study of meetings between US and Mexican businessmen. Each had a stereotype of the other's orientation toward time which was essentially accurate in terms of behaviour. Both groups agreed that the Mexicans were polychronic, or as the American businessmen put it, '*mañana* people'. On the other hand, both groups agreed that the Americans were mono-chronic, or as the Mexicans put it, 'machines'. Times of arrival for meetings and compliance with deadlines provide objective and less emotive data on stereotype accuracy. Despite this agreement, however, the two parties were unable to do business together until each had understood why the other group perceived them as they did and collective decisions had been achieved as to how to manage time. Accurate stereotypes are thus an aid to effective management of intergroup relations, but are not in themselves sufficient to guarantee success.

Prejudice

Baron and Byrne (1994) define prejudice as, 'an attitude (usually negative) toward the members of some group, based solely on their membership in that group' (p. 218). It is distinguished from discrimination which involves actions (again usually negative) towards those individuals. As an attitude, prejudice functions like other cognitive schemas (Fiske and Taylor, 1991) such that prejudice-consistent information is attended to and rehearsed more frequently and remembered more accurately than is inconsistent information.

Ethnocentrism

Sumner (1906/1940) defined ethnocentrism as, 'the view of things in which one's own group is the center of everything, and all others are scaled and rated with reference to it' (p. 13). This rather neutral definition of a probably universal cognitive process has assumed more volatile connotations over time; more contemporary definitions treat ethnocentrism as favouritism of one's in-group and rejection of the out-group (Levine and Campbell, 1972).

Triandis (1994) identifies four generalizations about this universal tendency:

1. What goes on in our culture is seen as 'natural' and 'correct', and what goes on in other cultures is perceived as 'unnatural' and 'incorrect'.
2. We perceive our own in-group customs as universally valid.
3. We unquestionably think that ingroup norms, roles, and values are correct.
4. We believe that it is natural to help and cooperate with members of our in-group, to favor our in-group, to feel proud of our in-group, and to be distrustful of and even hostile toward out-groups. (pp. 251–2)

From this perspective, our in-group defines the standard that anchors our assessment of other groups and our ethnocentrism guides our willingness to associate with them (Lambert, Mermigis and Taylor, 1986). The more we believe out-groups are similar to our in-group standard, the less hostile we are towards them (Brewer and Campbell, 1976).

The measure of ethnocentrism as an individual trait began with the work on authoritarianism by Adorno *et al.* (1950). Altemeyer (1981) criticized the psychometric deficiencies of this and other early measures and developed a more defensible measure called right wing authoritarianism (RWA). This construct taps the inter-related components of submission to legitimate authorities, willingness to aggress against others if authorities approve, and conventionalism. This scale has demonstrated its cross-cultural validity in a number of studies (Altemeyer, 1988; Rubinstein, 1996). It seems to tap a general conventionality in one's ideology and, not surprisingly, is negatively related to the Big Five dimension of openness to experience (Trapnell, 1994). Even in situations where most citizens have dropped their nationalistic bias, those high in RWA continue to show favouritism (Altemeyer and Kamenshikov, 1991).

In light of the above, it is noteworthy that Triandis (1996) has found that among respondents from the United States RWA is positively associated with vertical collectivism (allocentrism). Similarly, Lee and Ward (in press) found that it was only those Malays and Chinese in Singapore who were high in allocentrism that showed in-group favouritism in their intergroup attitudes. Could it be that many individual-level measures of collectivism (i.e. allocentrism) tap into the ethnocentrism that is a part of RWA ideology? Given the emphasis on the in-group that is a feature of collective cultural dynamics, this overlap is likely.

In this regard it is probable that ethnocentrism, however measured, shows variability from country to country (Ramirez, 1967). Bond (1988b) identified significant differences among students in twenty-two countries along a value dimension of social integration versus cultural inwardness. Social integration was defined by values such as tolerance of others and harmony with others, whereas cultural inwardness was defined by values such as a sense of cultural superiority and respect for tradition. We believe that persons from countries where the typical individual is high in cultural inwardness will be more likely to avoid contact with out-group members and discriminate against them in various ways (e.g. Bond, 1991a, on human rights).

Box 7.3 **On decentring one's worldview**

How culturally sensitive is your usage of the ways that you identify nations and ethnic groupings? Here are some examples of labels that cut across the preferences of those thus labelled:

● Citizens of the United States are frequently referred to as Americans, thereby marginalizing all the other inhabitants of the Americas. The authors of this book have not entirely escaped this habit.

● Citizens of the United Kingdom are frequently referred to as English, thereby marginalizing the Welsh, Scottish and Northern Irish, who also belong to the United Kingdom.

● Citizens of the Netherlands are often said to come from Holland, which is the name of two provinces within the Netherlands.

● Pacific Asia is often referred to as the Far East. To the Chinese, China is the Middle Kingdom.

● Former Soviet bloc countries are often referred to as located in Eastern Europe. Czechs, Hungarians and Poles point out that they are located in Central Europe.

● Restaurants serving South Asian cuisine in the United Kingdom are typically described as Indian restaurants. They are mostly owned by Pakistanis and Bangladeshis.

Although it may appear as if ethnocentrism is a uniformly baleful concept, it too can have positive aspects. Feshbach's (1987) factor-analytic study of political attitudes, for instance, showed a distinction between nationalism and patriotism. Nationalism taps the divisive, chauvinistic orientation towards other groups that is the focus of most research on authoritarianism. Patriotism taps the integrative, sustaining component of appreciation for one's own group that is necessary to sustain a viable, cooperative group, whatever its size. As we shall see in Chapter 10, this positive form of ethnocentrism appears to be a necessary component of a harmonious, multicultural society.

The opposite of ethnocentric attitudes is tolerance. Berry and Kalin (1995) developed an individual measure of tolerance that was used in a Canadian survey of ethnic attitudes. They found a shared ranking of ethnicities across Canada, based on Europeanness of background. As might be expected, however, 'Tolerant individuals show little differential preference for various groups. Intolerant individuals on the other hand show relatively great positive preference for those groups that are generally preferred by the population, and great negative preference for groups least preferred' (p. 315). As expected, then, those with lower ethnocentrism are much less rejecting of out-group members.

Predicting intergroup prejudice

Prejudicial judgements about various types of out-groups may be predicted in part by stereotypes held about those groups. Most work of this type has used stereotypes about the *character* associated with out-group members; beliefs about the *values* of out-group members are also important. Bond and Mak (1996), for example, found that perception of an out-group's position on Schwartz's (1992) dimension of self-transcendence (i.e. benevolence and universalism) was associated with lower rejection of those group's members.

Values termed 'symbolic beliefs' (Esses, Haddock and Zanna, 1993) seem particularly important. These are stereotypes about whether members of the out-group promote or undermine the in-group's cherished social traditions. These symbolic beliefs are only moderately correlated with beliefs about character, and, more importantly, are more powerful than beliefs about character in predicting negative attitudes towards a given group and its members (Esses *et al.*; Haddock, Zanna and Esses, 1993). The strength of the connection between symbolic beliefs and prejudice is especially strong for those high in RWA (Esses *et al.*).

The values held by majority and by minority group members are also important in generating or counteracting prejudice. Sagiv and Schwartz (1995) have examined 'readiness for out-group social contact' in both dominant-group Jews and minority-group Arabs in Israel. For the Jewish group they found that readiness was positively associated with universalism and self-direction domains of values and negatively with tradition, security and conformity values. For the Arab groups, the decisive value domain was achievement. These results show the role of one's values in guiding behaviour across group lines, but need to be confirmed in culturally different intergroup contexts. Such work may incorporate the related variable of similarity in values, as Feather's (1980) research has suggested the importance of closer value matches in guiding social interaction.

Emotions may be associated with various out-groups as a result of previous intergroup histories, media portrayals and individual experiences. These emotions, both positive and negative, relate to prejudice (Dijker, 1987), over and above that predicted by cognitions about the group (e.g. Stephan *et al.*, 1994). Esses, Haddock and Zanna (1993) argue that, 'stereotypes (about character) in part determine our emotional reactions to members of other groups which then more directly influence our attitudes towards the groups' (pp. 152–3). Once the effects of emotions have been assessed, information about stereotypic character of out-group members adds nothing further in predicting prejudice (Haddock, Zanna and Esses, 1994).

From prejudice to discrimination

There is a strong automaticity to stereotyped cognitions about out-group members (Devine, 1989). Emotional responses based on prior learning may also be activated during an out-group encounter. Their translation into action, however, depends on personal and social factors. Devine *et al.* (1991) asked US respondents to distinguish between how they should feel and how they would (or do) feel towards various out-groups. Respondents also evaluated how they responded to the discrepancy between how they should and would (or did) feel towards members of these various groups. Highly prejudiced persons showed less well-internalized personal standards about avoiding discriminatory behaviour and reported less need to behave in accordance with these already weaker restraints. In addition, they felt less guilt and shame about the discrepancies between their internal standards and their actual behaviour.

In short, prejudiced individuals appear to experience less ambivalence about their feelings towards out-group members. Lacking such internal conflict, their prejudices are more easily translated into discriminatory practices (e.g. Haddock, Zanna and Esses, 1993). Less prejudiced individuals are self-critical about their departures from more egalitarian standards. Such cognitive constraints may then motivate a search for strategies that short-circuit discrimination. Gaertner *et al.* (1989, 1993) have advanced a common in-group identity model whereby the us/them distinction is dissolved by an appeal to a shared identity or fate. We might expect that such a defusing recategorization would be a strategy appealing to less prejudiced individuals.

Of course there is more to discrimination than personal proclivities. We live in social groups that may feel under political and economic threat by other groups, for instance former East and West Germans in contemporary Germany (Ripple, 1996); or be fuelled by 'ideologies of antagonism' (Staub, 1988) passed down from the past and sustained by racist talk common to in-group members (Wetherell and Potter, 1992). These social inducements to discrimination may be further unrestrained by any wider political ideology of intergroup harmony (e.g. Canada's policies of multiculturalism and human rights observance; Humana, 1986). Such a volatile mix can be exacerbated by some of the societal factors related to aggression in Chapter 4 (e.g. a recent history of environmental disasters or warfare) and cultural values supporting a sense of cultural superiority.

It must be noted in passing that the vast majority of research on intergroup issues (stereotyping, prejudice, discrimination) is carried out in those societies that are low on cultural measures of hierarchy (Schwartz, 1994), power distance (Hofstede, 1980) and conservatism (Smith, Dugan and Trompenaars, 1996). Such social systems tolerate considerable public discussion about inequalities and their legitimacy, citizens are conversant with such discourse and many actively participate in the civic dialogue on issues such as racism, homophobia, ageism and sexism. Given the egalitarianism of such societies, one must question the generalizability of some of the psychological processes that have been identified. For example, the phenomena of tokenism and of reactions to being favoured on the basis of one's out-group status are probably unlikely events and irrelevant processes in hierarchical cultures. Legitimizing ideologies justify group hierarchies in such systems, short-circuiting the motivation for reverse discrimination policies, such as deliberately compensating members of discriminated groups.

Intergroup conflict

Discriminatory behaviour need not result in open intergroup hostilities. The social ideology surrounding differential access to material and social resources may be accepted by members of all competing groups. In societies high in hierarchy (Schwartz, 1994), for example, the SDO of members from all groups may be high and occur without the loss of in-group attachment. In such a social system, the group status ranking would be accepted and justified by all parties without either guilt or resentment.

Alternatively, unequal group access to resources may prevail and be resented by members of groups discriminated against. The consequences of challenging this order, however, may be too destructive to contemplate, as in colonial regimes, or the social bases for group mobilization may be lacking. Further, members of the groups in question may be part of a society characterized by 'cross-cutting ties', i.e. where residential, political or social group memberships are shared by members of competing groups. Conflict behaviour is less in societies with cross-cutting ties than in societies with ties that reinforce polarization between groups. Under various combinations of the above conditions, and especially if upward individual mobility is possible, intergroup conflict will be reduced. Culture-general norms of benign redress for violations to the order (DeRidder and Tripathi, 1992) would be endorsed and followed, muting the potential for violence.

Of course, a cursory glance over the front page of any newspaper suggests that there are many intergroup situations where these happier conditions do not obtain and instead that violence is the order of the day. Relative inequalities between the groups may be great (Wilkinson, 1996), group interests may be perceived to conflict (Tzeng and Jackson, 1994), norms of physical retribution for perceived injustice, such as blood revenge among the Northern Albanians, may be strong (Dragoti, 1996), perceptions of group potency (Guzzo et al., 1993) may be high and shared among group members, material conditions of existence may be deteriorating, and scapegoating ideologies concerning the out-group may be firmly entrenched (Staub, 1996) along with dehumanizing beliefs held about the values that characterize out-group members (Schwartz, Struch and Bilsky, 1990). Each of these factors will exacerbate the potential for intergroup violence, especially for those identifying strongly with their in-group (Struch and Schwartz, 1989).

This concludes for the moment our coverage of studies that focus upon the most direct consequences for individuals of belonging to one group rather than to another. However, there are numerous other aspects of intergroup relations that are important to cross-cultural psychologists. As we shall note in the next chapter, organizations are usefully thought of as multigroup systems, and the types of formal and informal negotiations which occur within and between organizations are crucial to their success. Furthermore, a clear understanding of intergroup relations can facilitate the processes of immigration and acculturation, which we discuss in Chapter 10.

Summary

Belonging to a group can define one's social identity, not just by defining who one is, but also who one is not. Defined group membership provides one with a prototype of how one should behave. This is particularly likely to occur where the group has relational goals and the members have allocentric values. Where one's group membership does derive from allocentric values, a sharper distinction is likely between behaviour toward in-group members and out-group members.

Membership in dominant groups is associated with high group identification and high in-group bias. Members of most nations favour their own nation, but there is also evidence that identification with a regional identity is preferred to a national identity in some European and Latin American nations. Not all stereotypes are inaccurate or negative and they may arise because of observable characteristics of the nations concerned. Stereotyping may reflect prejudice in favour of one's own group and against out-groups. Under social conditions and with predisposed persons, this prejudice may lead to discriminatory behaviour. Social and cultural considerations will then shape whether discriminatory intergroup practices result in intergroup violence.

Organizational behaviour

Japanese and American management is 95 percent the same and differs in all important respects

T. Fujisawa, co-founder, Honda

Some large organizations have existed for very long periods indeed. The Catholic Church can most probably claim greatest longevity. However, until recently only a tiny proportion of the population of most countries spent the majority of their waking hours within medium to large-sized organizations. With the growth of mass education, technology-based health care and the consumer economy, that proportion is now rapidly increasing. This process occurred earliest in Western Europe and North America, and in consequence most formulations of how best to manage organizations were advanced by writers and researchers from those regions. We have explored in earlier chapters the ways in which the values and social behaviours of North Americans and Western Europeans differ from those most typically found elsewhere. This suggests two questions that will concern us throughout the present chapter: What happens when Western approaches to the management of organizations are used in other parts of the world? Can cross-cultural psychology contribute to the explanation of why organizations from the Pacific Asian region have become so successful recently? To answer the first of these questions we need to consider in turn some of the traditional topic areas within organizational psychology.

Selection and assessment

A core element in Western theories of organization is that procedures are required to assess the skills and personalities of individuals, in order that those with the required attributes may be hired and assigned to roles within which their measured expertise will be optimally utilized. Further similar procedures are required in order to appraise whether individuals are performing their specific jobs adequately and whether they require training, promotion or sacking. The implicit orientation

198

of this approach to the management of organizations is toward conceptualizing the individual as a separate entity, whose attributes can be evaluated apart from his or her social context. A great deal of effort has been invested in the development of reliable and valid procedures for testing whether or not job applicants have the attributes required by the organization. While some Western organizations do rely substantially upon psychometric tests and complex procedures such as assessment centres, the most widespread bases for recruitment are interviews and biographical data.

It is clearly the case that organizations in all parts of the world need to recruit new members. However, we might predict that with increasing culture distance from the individualist assumptions of Western selection techniques, other procedures would find greater favour. Consider first variations within Europe. Shackleton and Newell (1991, 1994) surveyed the selection procedures employed by 250 companies within each of five European nations. Table 8.1 shows that there were wide variations in the most frequent procedures. Interviews were normally used, though less so in Germany. In the United Kingdom and Germany, application forms and references provided the principal additional bases for assessment. In France and Belgium, interviews and application forms were more likely to be supplemented by personality and cognitive tests as well as by handwriting analysis. The relatively low per centage of companies reporting that they 'always' relied on handwriting analysis masks the fact that 77 per cent of French companies, 44 per cent of French-speaking Belgian companies and 21 per cent of Dutch-speaking Belgian companies used it at least sometimes. In Italy, interviews alone were the favoured procedure and these were much less frequently conducted by personnel specialists than in the other countries surveyed. To interpret the meaning of these differences we need also to consider a recent content analysis of 1,400 newspaper advertisements for executives in eight West European nations (Tollgerdt-Andersson, 1996). This study found that around 80 per cent of newspaper advertisements in Sweden, Norway and Denmark specified personal and social abilities that would be required of the person appointed. This figure reduced to around 65 per cent in Germany and the United Kingdom and 50 per cent in France, Italy and Spain. The requirements most frequently specified are also given in Table 8.1.

The high emphasis on necessary relationship skills in Scandinavian managers is consistent with Hofstede's characterization of these nations as holding 'feminine' values. In Germany and the United Kingdom the traits most often specified gave less emphasis to the interpersonal skills required for collaboration. In the nations further south, which Hofstede found somewhat higher on power distance, age becomes an important criterion. Thus, while there is no doubt a good deal in common between the qualities sought in managers within the European Union, there are nonetheless differences of emphasis which reflect the likely cultures of organizations at differing locations.

Turning now to regions of the world where collectivist and hierarchical values are more strongly espoused, we find a markedly different approach to selection.

Table 8.1 ● Percentage of European companies 'always' using each selection technique and qualities most often specified in advertisements

Country	Inter-views	Application forms	Refer-ences	Personality tests	Cognitive tests	Handwriting analysis	Qualities most often specified
Belgium (Flemish)	91	74	15	35	30	2	–
Belgium (Walloon)	100	92	12	25	32	12	–
France	94	89	11	17	7	17	Age
Italy	96	45	32	8	8	0	Age
Spain	–	–	–	–	–	–	Age
Germany	60	83	76	2	2	0	Leadership
UK	91	70	74	10	12	0	Communication
Sweden	–	–	–	–	–	–	Cooperation
Denmark	–	–	–	–	–	–	Cooperation
Norway	–	–	–	–	–	–	Results and cooperation orientation

Source: abstracted from Shackleton and Newell (1994) and Tollgerdt-Andersson (1996).

Huo and von Glinow (1995) report that interviews are rarely used for selection purposes in Taiwan or in China. More important selection criteria will be at what institution candidates received their training and whether they come from a nearby location or ethnic sub-grouping. In a collectivist culture, especially a vertically collectivist one, it can safely be assumed that a graduate of a high-prestige institution will be highly able, since admission criteria are very competitive. Personal qualities and relationship skills are not seen as something that could be validly assessed within a short interview or test. Since the candidate appointed can expect to remain an organization member indefinitely there will be plenty of opportunity to socialize them to the behaviour patterns required by the organization. Similar views on graduate selection procedures are found also in other East Asian nations such as Japan and Korea. In the case of the appointment of more senior managers, Child (1994) notes that in China the most frequent procedure would be recommendation by other senior managers on the basis of *guanxi* relationships (see Chapter 11), followed by informal interviews not with the candidate, but with those with whom he or she is currently working.

One other issue concerning selection has to do with whether an organization seeks candidates for a position by internal promotion or by external recruitment. Here too we find substantial differences in procedures. Child (1981) compared the practices of a large sample of British and German firms. He reports that in Germany senior managers prefer to keep in constant touch with what is happening in the organization. This preference has the disadvantage that (in the view of the senior managers) it leads to 'trained incapacity' among middle managers. The senior managers therefore prefer to make senior appointments from outside. In contrast, British senior managers prefer that their subordinates handle more routine events and only consult them when difficulties arise. This encourages the development of the talents of more junior managers so that in time British organizations are able to select senior appointees internally.

Once an employee has joined an organization, Western management theory assumes that his or her performance will be optimized if regular evaluative feedback is received. This may be formalized as a performance appraisal system, or simply be part of regular meetings between employees and their superiors. Remuneration may be contingent upon the outcome of this process. Seddon (1987) identifies some of the reasons why such systems may not work well in non-Western organizations. To have one's work appraised on an individual basis assumes that there exist separate sets of individual work roles within the organization. In collectivist cultures work is more likely to be team-based and it will be difficult to discern each individual's contribution. Furthermore, as we noted in Chapter 6, collectivist cultures are mostly not characterized by direct and open communication. Open and critical feedback could destroy group harmony or cause serious loss of face to both parties. If they exist at all, appraisal systems are therefore likely to be used in quite different ways in different cultures. In individualist cultures, an appraiser could be defined as a coach, helping the individual to define his career goals and work progress, or as an overt and direct critic of poor previous performance. In collectivist cultures, an appraiser is more likely to become a benevolent provider of instructions as to what is to be done in the future. Consistent with this distinction, Seddon (1987) found that only 10 per cent of Swedish managers thought that the manager should be more knowledgeable than themselves, compared with 66 per cent of Italian and 65 per cent of Hong Kong managers. The collectivist appraiser's instructions are also likely to be focused upon the group as well as the individual. Chow (1994) found over 90 per cent of her respondents in Hong Kong and China agreed that a person's ability to function effectively as part of the group should be a very important basis for appraisal. Black and Porter (1991) found that dimensions of managerial behaviour which correlated with the receipt of positive appraisals in the United States did not do so when US managers working in Hong Kong were appraised, nor did they find this emphasis with Chinese managers working in Hong Kong. This result could have occurred because the measurement dimensions used were invalid in Hong Kong, or because the behaviours required for a manager to be effective in Hong Kong are in fact different. At least in the case of the American managers working in Hong Kong, the latter explanation is the more likely one. If appraisals of the Chinese managers were to be valid, they would need to be based on criteria of known emic validity.

Our knowledge of the ways in which selection and appraisal are carried out in different parts of the world is rather incomplete. Nonetheless, what information is available indicates that even though the processes identified by these names are a central and continuing feature of organizational life, they are likely to be carried out in widely varying ways in different contexts.

Work motivation

It will come as no surprise to careful readers of this book that work motives vary by culture in systematically predictable ways. Two of the four dimensions of culture identified by Hofstede (1980) were of course based upon variations in endorsement of a series of work goals by IBM employees. One of these dimensions (individualism–collectivism) has become the major organizing concept for many subsequent studies, while the other (masculinity–feminity) has received much less attention. Hofstede *et al.* (1996) report data concerning Hofstede's original work goals questions from students in ten European nations. They found that endorsement of the different work goals did not follow the same patterns as they had among IBM employees thirty years earlier. For instance, in those nations where a high value had been placed on 'earnings', 'advancement' was also endorsed. However, among the student groups of the 1990s, the nations where earnings were most endorsed were opposite to those where advancement was most endorsed. Of course this change may be due to many factors: different nations sampled, different types of person sampled, different points in history, different economic circumstances and so forth.

The important point that this contrast illustrates is that while there is good evidence for continuity across cultures in the overall structure of values, specific work goals may well vary, depending on the circumstances of individuals and of nations. What is or is not considered to be work may itself also vary across cultures. For instance, there are wide variations in the definition of what activities constitute work, rather than say, helping a friend. Child-minding, assisting a tourist or teaching someone English may or may not be considered work depending upon who does it and where it is done. While work is typically seen as activity for which one receives financial compensation, there exists a range of studies indicating that this is at best a simplification. The Meaning of Working International Team (1987) asked employees in eight industrialized nations whether they would continue working after winning a large amount of money in a lottery. The percentage who replied that they would varied from 93 per cent in Japan and 88 per cent in the United States to 70 per cent in Germany and 69 per cent in the United Kingdom. Adigun (1997) asked a similar question in two less industrialized nations, Turkey and Northern Cyprus, and around 70 per cent of respondents said 'yes'. In Malawi, Carr *et al.* (in press) found that 64 per cent said yes to the same question. These data indicate the substantial importance of non-financial motives in work, and also suggest that work motivation may be higher in some parts of the world than in others.

The Meaning of Working International Team (1987) provided further evidence that work motivation is particularly high in Japan. Asked to divide 100 points between work, home life, hobbies, religion and other interests, the Japanese gave more points to work than did respondents from any other nation. These data may be more valid than answers to the lottery question, since there is less scope for cultural differences in response bias to affect the answers given. One's work obligations in Japan may include going drinking after hours and sharing in other recreational activities with one's work colleagues, whereas in other cultures this could be more a matter of choice, and would most usually be thought of as something more separate from work. Shwalb *et al.* (1992) compared the values of large samples of Japanese and US managers. They found that the Japanese gave greater emphasis to task involvement, achieving excellence and financial reward, while the US respondents stressed affiliation, social concern and recognition. These results are interesting since an incautious reading of Japan as collectivist and the United States as individualist might lead one to have expected the opposite pattern. One possible explanation is that each sample stressed as goals those aspects of work that were less readily available to them.

Schwartz (in press) proposes that cultural differences in work motivations can be predicted on the basis of his surveys of values endorsed by students and teachers. One can expect for instance that work centrality will be high in nations where mastery and hierarchy are strongly endorsed, and low where affective autonomy, egalitarianism, harmony or conservatism are favoured. Furthermore, quite apart from the centrality of work in a culture, it is likely that the strongly endorsed values in a culture will provide insight into the types of motivator which will prove most effective. Ruiz Quintanilla and England (1996) make a distinction between those who see work as an individual entitlement that should be provided by employers and by the state and those who see work as an obligation owed by the individual to the wider society. They found that Belgians and Germans favour the view of work as an entitlement, whereas in Japan both views were equally endorsed and in the United States work was seen more as an obligation. This is consistent with Schwartz's view that work will be seen as an entitlement in nations endorsing the values of egalitarianism and intellectual autonomy.

The idea that there are cultural differences in work motivation has a long history. The nineteenth-century German sociologist Max Weber (1921/1947) saw the existence of the Protestant work ethic as a major contributor to the rise of capitalism in certain Western European nations. Interestingly, contemporary data indicate that the Protestant work ethic now has a surprising distribution. Giorgi and Marsh (1990) drew upon the results of an earlier opinion survey of over 12,000 respondents in nine West European countries. They found that endorsement of work as a positive value was indeed still higher in the countries with a higher proportion of Protestants. However, they go on to report that it is no longer the Protestants who represent work in this way. The highest scorers were those who described themselves as atheists in the predominantly Protestant countries. Thus the social representation of hard work as a virtue has not shown much movement over the past century within Europe geographically, but it has become detached from its origins in a particular religious belief.

Some researchers have followed this line of thinking further. If the Protestant work ethic is no longer firmly linked to Protestant religious beliefs, then it is plausible to examine where else in the world the work ethic is strongly endorsed. Furnham, Kirkcaldy and Lynn (1994) report an analysis of questionnaire

Box 8.1) Trends in job satisfaction in seven European nations

The company known as International Survey Research has sampled job satisfaction among employees of work organizations in Western Europe for more than a decade. The table below shows the per centages of employees who described their current situation favourably in 1985 and again in 1997.

	1985	1997	Change
Italy	53	56	+3
Switzerland	65	66	+1
Belgium	58	58	0
France	60	57	−3
Netherlands	70	65	−5
Germany	67	61	−6
United Kingdom	64	54	−10

The samples upon which these figures are based were sufficiently large that all the changes shown, except for those in Switzerland and Italy, are statistically significant. The trend toward reduced job satisfaction in Northern European nations is marked, especially in the United Kingdom. It is associated with reduced feelings of job security and lower identification with the interests of the organization.

Source: International Survey Research (1995, 1997).

responses by 12,000 students in forty-one countries. The measure included some items referring to work ethic. Unfortunately, no account was taken of the likelihood of cultural bias in the answering of questionnaire items (see our discussion of how to do this in Chapter 3). The mean scores obtained are therefore likely to be misleading. Furnham *et al.* (1993) summarize the administration of several rather longer measures of Protestant work ethic in thirteen nations, and conclude that it is currently highest in nations that score high on power distance and collectivism. However, this study too used no correction for response bias, so its conclusions require independent verification, as the authors acknowledge.

There is an additional danger in using measures of Protestant work ethic away from its original context. Most items assessing the construct are implicitly or explicitly individualistic, and we may expect that endorsement of these items by respondents from collectivist cultures will fail to pick up some of the key reasons why they might choose to work hard. We discussed in Chapter 3 the measure of Confucian work dynamism that emerged from the study conducted by the Chinese Culture Connection (1987). The elements within the Confucian work dynamism factor are less individualistic and give greater emphasis to continuity of purpose and obligations to others. Redding titled his 1990 study of overseas Chinese entrepreneurs in Southeast Asia *The Spirit of Chinese Capitalism*, deliberately echoing the title of Weber's study of European entrepreneurs a century earlier. However, the content of the entrepreneurial values of the two groups shows some marked contrasts. Yu (1996) underlines the way in which Chinese achievement motivation is socially oriented, not individualistic. In studies in Taiwan, a measure that he devised of socially oriented achievement motivation had much higher validity in predicting task performance than a measure of individually oriented achievement orientation. McClelland's (1961) claim that achievement motivation was highest in Western societies is vulnerable to the same criticism. Indeed, the superior academic performance and business success of recent migrants from a number of Asian nations into Western societies has confirmed the presence of strong and persistent achievement motivation, which may often, though not always, be socially motivated. A further possible line of research is opened up by Ali's (1988, 1990) development of a measure of Islamic work beliefs.

The implications of this section are clear: we can only hope to understand the ways in which organization members respond to the various issues that are important in organizations if we draw upon concepts and measures that are not imposed-etic in nature. Organizations everywhere face problems such as how to train employees, how to allocate rewards, how to coordinate work, how to reach agreement with other parties and how to introduce change. We shall review work in each of these areas in turn. Consider first a clear example from the field of training. Earley (1994) compared training programmes intended to increase managers' self-efficacy and performance. The study was conducted in the United States, Hong Kong and China. Earley found that subjects who had endorsed a

---

Box 8.2) Putting Russia back on the map

Although Russia has a large population, it has figured in few cross-cultural studies. Ralston *et al.* (1997) compared the Schwartz individual-level value types endorsed by samples of around 200 managers in the United States, Russia, Japan and China. The three most strongly endorsed values in each nation's sample was as follows:

	First	Second	Third
USA	Self-direction	Achievement	Benevolence
Russia	Security	Self-direction	Benevolence
Japan	Achievement	Self-direction	Universalism
China	Benevolence	Security	Achievement

These results indicate that despite stereotypic expectations in the West derived from the Soviet period, contemporary Russian managers do not espouse collectivist values to the same extent as do those in China.

measure of idiocentric values responded better to training focused upon individual achievement, whereas those who had endorsed allocentric values responded better to efficacy training which emphasised contribution to the group. Earley conducted a further experiment, this time just in the United States and China, in which he followed up managers' actual work performance six months later. Again, the efficacy treatments succeeded better if they were well-matched to the trainee managers' values.

Reward allocation

A central element in the process whereby organizations transform the individual motivations of employees to productive work is the allocation of rewards. Many studies have been made of this process, most typically contrasting preferences for the use of different criteria in allocating reward. Unfortunately, many studies of what is usually referred to as distributive justice have been done by researchers who do not always make clear who exactly are the parties between whom resources are to be allocated. Furthermore, allocations are usually to be made to individuals rather than to groups. These types of research design have most probably occurred because researchers, whose own values are universalistic, see principles of justice as being universally applicable, and more easily studied by looking at individuals rather than at groups. This leaves us with some difficulties in linking studies of distributive justice to studies of resource allocation in organizational contexts.

Nonetheless, there is some linkage between the notion of in-group bias and the notion that in a situation of scarcity, resources should go to those who are most deserving, either because they worked hardest or because they are the most needy. While social identity theory and its derivative, social categorization theory, assumes that resources will go to oneself or to one's group, distributive justice researchers have compared preferences for equity or equality as criteria of fairness. The equity theory developed by Adams (1965) in the United States proposes that we will favour an allocation of rewards that matches the 'inputs' and 'outputs' of different work team members. Thus, Adams' theory has a clearly universalist emphasis in that it implies that rewards will be differentially allocated among different group members on the basis of their distinguishable inputs. While there has been substantial debate about the validity of equity theory as formulated by Adams, it continues to command substantial support within US studies. It appears that while Americans do on the whole favour reward allocation on the basis of equity, there are a variety of circumstances under which they would evaluate an allocation based on equality as being fairer. For example, Elliott and Meeker (1984) studied supervisors in the United States, who were asked to allocate rewards among five members of an imaginary work team who were likely to continue working together. Under these circumstances, more than 60 per cent of allocations were based on exact equality rather than equity.

The greater emphasis upon harmony within collectivist and particularist cultural groups would lead one to expect that fairness would more frequently be judged to arise from equality rather than equity. However, we also have to remember that within these types of cultural groups, members are more permanently committed to their membership groups. We must therefore maintain a distinction between how those with allocentric values would distribute rewards within their membership groups and how they would distribute them to strangers or outsiders.

In-group preferences

In order to study reward allocation within one's group, Leung and Bond (1982) asked students in Hong Kong and the United States to consider how grades should be assigned in hypothetical groups of students taking a course. Although students in both countries favoured a group member who had made competent task contributions, the Chinese distributed their grades around the group more equally than did the Americans. In a further study Bond, Leung and Wan (1982a) found the same effect both for task contributions but also for contributions toward maintaining group harmony. Kim, Park and Suzuki (1990) replicated this study, using students in the United States, Japan and Korea. They found that equity was important in all three countries, but less so in Korea, the more collectivist country.

Collectivist cultural logic further suggests that reward allocation to out-group members would be made differently from that to in-group members. In a third study, Leung and Bond (1984) used two scenarios, involving either friends or strangers. They found that with the in-group friend, the Chinese shared the rewards more equally through the group, but with the out-group stranger the Chinese adhered to the equity norm more closely than did the Americans. In collectivist cultures, crossing group boundaries thus appears to switch the allocation rule in force.

Two studies have examined the in-group allocation of bonuses or pay cuts in India and the United States (Murphy-Berman et al., 1984; Berman, Murphy-Berman and Singh, 1985). In this case three criteria for allocation were compared: equity, equality and need. We might expect that as with equality, allocation within the in-group according to need would be used more in collectivist settings, so as to promote the welfare of in-group members. Presumably need as a criterion could be expected to outweigh equality, the greater the inequalities existing within the group. In both studies the Indians were found to be more likely to allocate higher bonuses and lower pay cuts to those most in need than were the Americans. The effect was stronger for the allocation of bonuses. Thus, the findings show that in both countries the effects of need may to some extent outweigh a preference for equity or equality, but that the effect is stronger in the more collectivist country.

Leung and Park (1986) consider the possibility that what one considers fair will depend upon one's goals in belonging to a group. If one's prime motive is to promote task accomplishment, then equity would seem to provide the fairest basis for reward. If the preservation of group harmony is more important, then equality becomes a more attractive criterion. Comparing Korean and American subjects, they found that allocations were indeed influenced by goal orientation in both countries. Nonetheless, overall the Koreans favoured equality more than did the Americans. Likewise, Kashima *et al.* (1988) reported a stronger preference for equality than equity among Japanese than among Australians who were asked to evaluate the fairness of bonus payments at work. Finally, in a study of 12-year-old Japanese and Australian schoolchildren, Mann, Radford and Kanagawa (1985) examined preferences as to who should do the allocating of rewards in the group. As we might expect, the Japanese favoured sharing the task around equally, whereas the Australians preferred giving the power to allocate differential rewards to a sub-group.

The impressive consistency of these studies is balanced by Marin (1985) who failed to find any difference in allocation preferences between Indonesian students in America and Americans. However, the Indonesians had been in the United States for nearly two years. More surprisingly, Leung and Iwawaki (1988) failed to find any differences in in-group allocations among Japanese, Korean and American students in their respective countries. In this case the authors had also collected data on the preference for idiocentric or allocentric values of the Japanese and American students within their sample. They were surprised to find that their Japanese sample scored no higher on average than the Americans on allocentrism, and suggest that this may account for the failure of their study to find national differences in allocation preference. Consistent with the argument about collectivism, however, they did find that in each country, the students who favoured allocentric values were those whose allocation preferences were more towards equality. A further test of the link between allocentric values and preference for equality is provided by Hui, Triandis and Yee (1991). They found that Hong Kong students shared rewards for work done more equally than did American students and that this average difference across cultural groups was accounted for by the levels of allocentric values that they had endorsed.

The comparisons between Asian countries and the United States thus make it clear that equality is relied upon more frequently in more collectivist countries in the case of in-group reward allocation. As one might expect, the differences are not so marked in comparisons between the United States and West European countries, many of which also score quite highly on individualism. In a complex study, Pepitone *et al.* (1967) studied reward distribution by American, French and Italian students playing an experimental game. The US and French students allocated rewards on the basis of equity, taking more for themselves when they were led to believe that their ability was high. The behaviour of the Italians was less clear, possibly because there is said to be much higher collectivism in southern Italy than in the north. A further study by Pepitone *et al.* (1970) showed that the Italians did favour equality to a greater extent, reducing their allocations to themselves when they had already been given a monetary reward before the experiment started. In these studies and in others comparing Americans with Austrians (Mikula, 1974) and Germans (Kahn, Lamm and Nelson, 1977), it appears that situational factors may have been more important than cultural factors in determining preferences for equity or equality.

Out-group preferences

If we turn now to the fair allocation of rewards to those outside one's own group, we find a series of studies supporting the view that members of collectivist cultures do not extend the same principles to such allocations. Aral and Sunar (1977) demonstrated that Turkish students favoured the equity norm more than Americans in dividing rewards between two architects. Mahler, Greenberg and Hayashi (1981) asked students in Japan and America how rewards should be divided in a set of stories describing two workers. In one of the stories where the two workers did the same work the Japanese favoured equality more strongly but they found no difference where the story presented implied that the two workers were not strongly connected. Marin (1981) compared Colombians and Americans and found the Colombians favoured equity more strongly in allocating rewards to subjects in a psychological experiment. We have mentioned already the study by Leung and Bond (1984) which found that when dealing with an out-group, Hong Kong Chinese were closer to the equity norm than were Americans.

The studies of distributive justice thus yield a fairly clear picture. In more collectivist countries there is greater reliance on the criteria of equality *within* the in-group, but greater use of the equity criterion *outside* the group. This conclusion rests on the assumption that most people within a country labelled as collectivist will themselves hold more allocentric values. In one of the two studies so far reported in which measures of subjects' values were obtained, this cultural difference was not found, but in both of these studies subjects' values did actually accord with their behaviour. The variability of values within countries should help us to understand why occasional studies have been reported in which differences between countries do not fit the overall pattern.

The clarity of this conclusion derives from studies comparing allocation on the basis of equity and equality criteria. When other criteria are introduced, the results are slightly different. The studies discussed earlier by Murphy-Berman *et al.* (1984) and Berman, Murphy-Berman and Singh (1985) showed that need had a stronger effect on in-group allocations in India than in the United States. Murphy-Berman and Berman (1993) found that need also had a stronger effect in Germany than in the United States, even though in this case the student subjects were asked to make allocations to factory workers, who would presumably be considered as out-group members. Berman and Murphy-Berman (1996) develop their analysis further by examining how those who make particular allocations in Germany and the United States are perceived by others. Germans favoured those who allocated on the basis of need in all conditions, while Americans favoured those who allocated on the basis of equity when a bonus was to be allocated and on the basis of need when a pay cut was required. Americans saw the allocator who distributed bonus on the basis of equity as intelligent but unlikeable, and the allocator who distributed on the basis of need as likeable but not intelligent. Thus the Germans relied on a single general principle (favour the collective good), while the Americans' evaluations were more situation-specific (judge each individual's situation on its merits). Singh and Pandey (1994) compared allocation decision by students from different caste backgrounds in India. The decisions to be taken concerned admission of students to a class, granting of financial support and of a job. Low-caste students favoured allocation on the basis of merit, while middle-caste students gave greater priority to need. Upper-caste students varied their ratings according to circumstance. These studies all suggest that need is a criterion that has been given insufficient attention, particularly in the many contexts where economic adversity is widespread.

A further possible criterion for resource allocation has only recently been included in studies of this type, namely seniority. It is possible that the egalitarian values of many US researchers encouraged them to see other criteria as more important. Rusbult, Insko and Lin (1993) hypothesized that seniority-based reward allocation would be stronger in the more hierarchical Taiwan than in the United States. However, what they found was that in Taiwan there was a significant tendency to allocate more bonus on the basis of seniority only among their male subjects. In contrast, in the United States female subjects allocated more bonus on the basis of seniority. Thus these results are clearly confounded by differences in gender roles in the two samples. Chen (1995) compared Chinese and US managers on preferences as to how reward allocations should be made. The Chinese laid greater emphasis upon seniority and rank as criteria than did the Americans. In a further study, Chen, Meindl and Hunt (1997) developed separate measures for vertical collectivism and horizontal collectivism. They found that preference for seniority-based resource allocation was positively related to endorsements of vertical collectivism and negatively related to endorsements of horizontal collectivism. These more recent results suggest that although the in-group–out-group distinction in reward allocation by members of collectivist cultures is well established, it most probably rests upon endorsement of horizontally collectivist values. In regions of the world where vertical collectivism is more strongly favoured, we may expect allocation criteria such as seniority to be important.

The extensive range of empirical results now available concerning reward allocation has to some extent outrun the theories that were formulated by earlier researchers. We are now concerned not simply with differentiation between in-groups and out-groups in relation to individualism–collectivism, but must take account also of issues such as the salience of need, of seniority, and of variations in the role of the allocator. Leung (1997) has formulated a 'contextual' model of resource allocation, which postulates that different allocation rules become salient within the different possible social contexts. According to this model, the differentiation in the way that allocentrics allocate rewards within the in-group and towards out-groups will only be found when the allocator is him- or herself among the candidates to receive some of the rewards. Within the in-group, the allocator may seek to enhance harmony by allocating on the basis of need or to maintain harmony by allocating on the basis of equality. Where the allocator is in a supervisory role, allocation is predicted to be on the basis of equity in all cultures. We shall return to Leung's model later in this chapter.

Hierarchy and leadership

This chapter has so far mostly discussed relations between members of organizations as though there were no status differentiation within them. Even within low-power distance Western nations, this is a considerable simplification of the nature of relationships within most work organizations. Furthermore, as we saw in Chapter 3, those countries that score high on Hofstede's measure of cultural collectivism typically also score high on power distance. We should therefore look to studies of the process of leadership to aid our understanding of organizational dynamics. Western theorists, from Lewin, Lippitt and White (1939) onwards, have long been in the habit of contrasting autocratic with democratic leadership and thinking of hierarchy as the opposite of participation. When we find that, in many parts of the world, power distance and hierarchy are part of a social structure that is also collectivist and participative, we must then begin to look carefully at the generality of the Western model.

Leadership functions and leadership roles

In individualist cultures a group member's position in a work team will be bounded by choice processes – the group member's choice to have joined the organization, and the group's valuation of the contribution that he or she makes to the work of that team. In a collectivist culture there will be less reason for each member to have a clearly delineated role, since their identity is defined not by what they do in the team but by the fact that they belong to it. In a classic series of studies in the United States, Bales (1951) showed how discussion groups of students developed separate 'task' and 'socio-emotional' leaders. While the task leader took on the function of organizing the task, the socio-emotional leader cracked jokes or defused conflicts in a manner that enabled the group to function smoothly even when the task was unrewarding. If the above reasoning is correct, we should expect this type of fixed role differentiation to be less frequent in collective cultures.

Box 8.3　Signifying hierarchy

Mrs Robertson and Mr Chan are both aware that their relationship is based upon hierarchy. Mrs Robertson reflects her position and feeling of superiority by referring to Mr Chan simply as Chan. She interrupts him and terminates the meeting. Mr Chan is unsure what is the best way to express deference to Mrs Robertson, particularly as she is a woman, and he avoids naming her, except when he calls her 'teacher', an important honorific in Chinese culture. He also allows her to interrupt him without protesting.

Krichevskii (1983) found that such role differentiation did occur among sports teams and student groups in the (former) Soviet Union. However, since no firm data on the level of collectivism of Soviet society are available, this result is equivocal. Smith (1963) using groups of British students and managers on training courses, and Koomen (1988) using Dutch groups of students, showed that the amount of differentiation between task roles and socio-emotional roles varied depending upon how strongly members were attracted to the group. This fits the pattern of Bales's original US findings. No empirical studies are available from more collectivist societies, but it is widely reported that members of work teams in Japanese organizations do not have precisely differentiated roles, with all members responsible for fulfilling whatever functions are required at a particular time.

When is leadership needed?

A leader within an individualistic culture may perhaps best be seen as an individual who provides to the group whatever task or relationship-oriented functions are lacking. Some US theorists (e.g. Kerr and Jermier, 1978; Manz, 1983) point out that in certain circumstances, which they attempt to specify, a work team may be almost entirely self-managing. In other words it would require virtually no input from an externally appointed leader, although of course the necessary leadership functions would be provided by the various members of the team.

In contrast, it would be most unlikely that one would find a team without a leader within a collectivist culture, since the principle of seniority or power distance is embedded within such cultures. An effective leader in a wide variety of collectivist cultures is more likely to be one who is seen as having all the required task and group maintenance attributes and does not have a role which differentiates separate functions of leadership.

However, we should not assume that the presence of a seniority system indicates that leadership in such groups is autocratic in the sense understood in Western cultures. The manner in which leaders and their group members will relate to one another will be determined by the communication style prevailing in each cultural setting, as discussed in earlier chapters. The leader will be owed deference, but in one culture this deference might be conveyed by waiting to be told what to do and in another it might be conveyed by coming up with suggestions as to what to do. By differentiating these two different ways of showing deference, we may hope to understand some of the diversity of the results of the studies of group decision in collective cultures which were touched upon in Chapter 2.

As we saw there, a number of studies from Japan have shown that group decision-making is highly effective in that culture. The continuing central role of group discussion in Japanese culture is confirmed by the extensive use of 'Quality Circles' and other methods of group decision-making, such as the *ringi* procedure for consulting all concerned, in Japanese manufacturing firms (Smith and Misumi, 1989). Japan can be seen as an example of a culture that is hierarchical, but in which one expresses deference to one's superior by active participation and the making of numerous suggestions. Significantly, the leader often does not participate in these meetings but receives their output after the consultation is over. In contrast, the experiments in group decision reported from Puerto Rico (Marrow, 1964; Juralewicz, 1974) were failures. In Hispanic cultures, decision-making is more likely to be seen as the prerogative of the leader and to be too active in group participation would be to challenge or doubt his or her authority.

Leadership is thus likely to be embedded in group structure to a greater degree in collective cultures than in individualistic cultures. The functions of effective leadership will nonetheless be exercised within each type of culture through the distinctive style of communication appropriate to that setting. There is currently a good deal of difficulty in determining how true is this general proposition. This is because the numerous published studies of leadership vary greatly in how specifically they characterize what leaders do.

Leadership effectiveness

We shall consider first the work of researchers who have focused upon rather global attributes of leaders and leadership. Some recent theorists identify the leader's key capacity as being the creation of a 'charismatic' vision which is shared between leader and organization members as to what they are trying to accomplish. Bass (1985), for instance, designed a questionnaire in the United States which distinguishes the 'transformational' leader from the leader whose links with organization members is more mundanely 'transactional'. The transformational leader is considered to be one who creates and sustains an emotional bond with the work team, not simply based on liking, but on shared vision of the desired state that they are trying to create. The Bass questionnaire has been used in subsequent studies in the United States, Japan, Singapore, Italy, Canada, Spain, New Zealand, Germany and India. In each case the leaders who were seen by their subordinates as transformational were the ones most highly evaluated by them (Bass and Avolio, 1993).

Even more extensive evidence is becoming available from the current, very large-scale 'GLOBE' research project (House and Wright, 1997). Samples of organization employees in fifty-six nations have completed a questionnaire describing their superior and other aspects of their organization's culture. Although full results are not yet available, the conceptualization of leadership agreed by House's research team is 'the ability to influence, motivate and contribute toward the effectiveness of the organizations of which they are members'. Preliminary indications are of cross-cultural uniformities in endorsement of transformational or 'value-based' leadership, rather than differences by nation in results.

There is thus some likelihood that we can specify in a broad manner the universal qualities of a successful leader within an organizational context. However, the measures used in these studies are imposed-etic in nature, and we need to examine carefully what it is that causes respondents to fill them out in a particular way in different cultural contexts. Dorfman (1996) notes that when responses to the Bass questionnaire were factor-analyzed, the factors that emerged from studies in Singapore, the Netherlands and the Dominican Republic were all rather different from the original factors obtained in Bass's US studies. To gain a clearer understanding of just what it is that effective leaders do, we may need to look at measures that help us to understand why the factor structures vary in this way. These measures will most probably be ones that focus upon more specific attributes of leader behaviour.

The best known Western theories of leadership have frequently differentiated leader styles that emphasize the task function from those that emphasize the socioemotional or group maintenance function. For example, Fiedler (1967) differentiated task- and relationship-oriented leadership, while Vroom and Yetton (1973) distinguish, autocratic, consultative and group-oriented styles. Tests of these and related models in the United States have found different effects of these styles on productivity in different settings (Smith and Peterson, 1988; Yukl, 1994). A series of 'contingency' theories have then been advanced in an attempt to explain the circumstances under which this or that style of leadership is more effective.

In contrast, studies of leadership within collectivist cultures have come up with markedly different results from those obtained in more individualist countries. Among the most extensive studies are those of Misumi (1985) in Japan. Misumi's studies have included such varied organizations as coal mines, banks, shipyards, bus companies and local government offices. Over a period of more than thirty years Misumi has found that in a wide variety of Japanese groups and organizations the most effective leaders are those who are simultaneously high on both task *and* relationship behaviours. Although Misumi terms his two aspects of leadership style as 'performance' and 'maintenance', they have a good deal in common with formulations of the two leader styles most often studied in the United States.

Misumi's findings are echoed in other countries with collective cultures. Bond and Hwang (1986) review studies of leadership in Taiwan. Studies using translated versions of the Ohio State leadership scales developed in the United States again showed that leaders high on both task and relationship dimensions were the most effective. Sinha (1995) reports findings on effective leadership in India. The most effective style is characterized as high on both task behaviour and on nurturance of subordinates. Ayman and Chemers (1983) obtained a similar result in Iran, as did Farris and Butterfield (1972) in Brazil. Although all of these studies support the importance of two similar-sounding dimensions of leader behaviour, the specific questionnaire items making up the scales reflect the different cultural values which are emically important in each location.

In more individualist countries, such as those of Western Europe, studies of leadership have yielded results that are more similar to those obtained in the United States. Different types of leader style are found effective in different settings (Smith and Tayeb, 1988). Zhurvalev and Shorokhova (1984) from the former Soviet Union also report findings favouring contingency theory. They reported that Lewin's distinction between autocratic, democratic and *laissez-faire* styles was insufficient to distinguish all the approaches found in Soviet enterprises. They observed also managers whose styles were intermediate between Lewin's styles, and some who combined elements of all three styles. Their findings were that all of these styles of leadership, except the passive style, could be effective in particular circumstances. They also list some of the environmental circumstances that affect leadership effectiveness.

Many of the studies that we have reviewed of the effects of leader style in different nations have relied upon the conceptualizations of task- and group-oriented styles that were first developed in the 1950s. Ekvall and Arvonen (1991) suggest that the changing context of leadership in many if not all cultural contexts requires investigation of additional dimensions of leader style. They devised a measure that added a 'change-centred' style to the two more traditional dimensions of leader style. In doing so, they made a connection with the more recent emphasis upon transformational leadership. Their measure showed that change-orientation was independent of the task- and group-oriented styles, among managers in the United States, Sweden and Finland.

Howell *et al.* (1997) tested the predictive validity of several of the characterizations of leader style discussed above, within electronics plants in the United States, Mexico, Taiwan, Korea and Japan. They found that leaders who were supportive and who made rewards contingent on performance were rated positively in all five samples. Leaders who were perceived as charismatic were rated positively in all countries except Japan. Directive leadership had positive effects in Mexico, Korea and Taiwan, but not in the United States or Japan. Participative leadership had positive effects only in the United States. Thus, some effects are culture-general and some are culture-specific, with the more global characterizations of leadership being culture-general, and the more specific ones proving less universal in effect.

While the effects of different leader styles have thus been frequently surveyed within nations, few researchers have used experimental methods to make direct cross-national comparisons of the effectiveness of leader behaviour. Box 8.4 examines a direct comparison between Israel and the United States, in which the experimenter portrayed different leadership styles.

Evidently, studies that have focused upon more specific aspects do detect cultural differences in leaders' behaviours and their consequences. If the arguments advanced earlier in this book are valid, then it should be possible to relate such variation to previously established dimensions of cultural variance. Several studies have attempted to do this. Jago *et al.* (1993) asked managers how they would handle a series of standard work problems. Polish and Czech managers chose the most autocratic procedures, followed by US and French managers, while German, Austrian and Swiss managers relied on greatest participation. Jago *et al.* argued that this outcome reflected varying endorsement of power distance in the seven nations sampled. Smith *et al.* (1994) asked managers from fourteen nations to rate how they handled eight relatively routine work events. They found that reported

Box 8.4) Group participation in Israel and the United States

Erez and Earley (1987) compared the response of three groups of students to different ways of setting goals. The students were asked to construct as many class schedules as possible for their colleges, such that no student would have conflicting obligations. In one experimental condition, the student groups were *assigned* their goal by the experimenter. In the second condition they appointed a *representative* who negotiated a goal for the group, while in the third, the group *participated* in reaching a decision. By 'guiding' the groups as to what goals were realistic, the experimenters ensured that in all three experimental conditions similar goals were set. The students compared were from the US Midwest, from Israeli cities, and from Israeli kibbutzim. In Phase 1 of the experiment low goals were set, while in Phase 2, higher goals were set. The figure below shows that the Israelis were much more strongly affected by the goal-setting procedures, especially in Phase 2. They reacted against assigned goals and responded positively to participative decision-making.

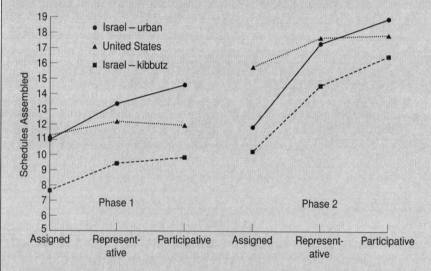

Erez and Earley propose that this difference in results is to be explained by the difference in cultural values obtaining in the United States and Israel. They collected measures of the students' values about allocentrism and power, and showed that higher endorsement of allocentric values and lower endorsement of power distance by the Israelis went along with the way they responded to the experimental manipulations. Thus, response to different styles of group leadership at the cultural level is predicted by differences in the individual cultural values of the subjects in the study.

reliance on one's own experience and training was strongly correlated with the Hofstede (1980) rankings for high individualism, whereas in high-power distance nations reported reliance on formal rules and procedures was greater.

Broader perspectives on leadership

There are further possibilities to explore concerning leadership. As we have seen, most theorists in this area of research have characterized a limited number of leadership 'styles' and investigated how much leaders who emphasize each style influence their subordinates' performance. Such a view of leadership may cause us to miss several other aspects of effective leader behaviour, including flexibility over time, the use of different behaviours in different contexts, and targeting of specific behaviours toward particular individuals. There are a few cross-cultural studies that provide evidence on some of these aspects.

Peterson *et al.* (1995) compared the types of challenge faced by samples of managers in twenty-two nations. They found that role overload was highest in nations scoring high on Hofstede's (1980) measure of power distance, whereas a measure of role ambiguity was higher in low-power distance nations. This study gives us a picture of the Western manager as faced with handling considerable amounts of uncertainty and ambiguity. Effective leadership in this situation would require the ability to reach decisions on the basis of inadequate or incomplete information and to make links with others who could reduce the uncertainties. In contrast, the manager in a high-power distance nation is at the centre of a net of relationships which is more likely to create overload than ambiguity. Effective leadership in this situation will require the capacity to prioritize and maintain a clear vision of important goals.

If leaders face different organizational and environmental challenges in different nations they are also likely to use different ways of handling their relations with others. Luthans, Welsh and Rosenkrantz (1993) observed managers at work in Russia and compared their results with earlier samples studied in the United States. They found that the Russian managers spent proportionately more time on 'traditional' leadership, i.e. planning, deciding and coordinating, whereas the US managers devoted a higher proportion of their time to networking with others both in and outside the organization. This is the type of difference that we might expect between the activities of leaders in high- and low-power distance contexts. A similar, but small-scale, study by Boisot and Liang (1992) found Chinese managers spent much more time with their superiors and much less of it with outsiders or peers than did US managers, as one would expect within a higher-power distance culture.

Schermerhorn and Bond (1991) compared upward and downward influence behaviours among managers in Hong Kong and the United States. Both samples showed similar large differences in how they would approach superiors compared with subordinates. However, the Hong Kong managers endorsed the use of assertiveness more strongly, while the US managers scored higher on use of rational arguments, ingratiation and exchange of favours. Schmidt and Yeh (1992) compared downward influence strategies favoured by managers in the United States, Australia, Japan, UK and Taiwan. The strongest factor from the United Kingdom and the United States was identified as 'bargaining', whereas 'reasoned friendliness' prevailed in Australia, 'assertive reasoning' in Japan and 'sanctions' in Taiwan. However, as we might expect, the specific behaviours found to define each of these factors varied somewhat across the cultural samples. Thus, once again, as we move to more specific operationalizations of measurement, we find more and more cultural distinctiveness. What one needs to do in order to be considered as charismatic, transformational, participative or autocratic is to some extent context-specific (see Box 1.2, p. 6, for a further example of this proposition).

Negotiation

Although one might usefully think of leadership as a particular kind of negotiation, there are numerous other processes occurring both within and between organizations that also involve some type of attempt at resolving differences of opinion or achieving joint commitment to actions. Negotiation usually involves communication that is explicit, either through face-to-face interaction or written communication, which makes it easier to study. Typically, it occurs between persons who are not within one's in-group.

Setting the goals of negotiation

Systematic attempts to understand negotiation in different cultures require that we refer once more to the concepts of individualism and collectivism. One would expect that within individualist cultures, negotiators would take as their main priority that agreements are reached on the basis of the logical requirements of the tasks to be accomplished at the present time. In contrast, we could expect that within collectivist cultures negotiators would be particularly concerned about the continuing harmony of their relations with other parties. This would not necessarily mean that members of collectivist cultures would be any more generous to their opposite numbers. We have seen already that those with allocentric values are just as likely as those with idiocentric values to be competitive towards out-group members. However, we should expect allocentric subjects to prefer methods of negotiation that preserve the harmony of the relationship. For instance, they are likely to prefer mediation and indirect communications rather than overt argument or other adversarial procedures. Of course, negotiators in both types of culture would have some regard for both task criteria and the maintenance of the relationship: the difference would be a matter of relative emphasis.

Negotiating styles

Glenn, Witmeyer and Stevenson (1977) studied styles of international negotiation by analyzing transcripts of meetings of the Security Council of the United Nations. They propose that the excerpt shown in Box 8.5 illustrates the difference between what they call the factual and the intuitive styles of discourse. The factual style, used by the US representatives, concentrates on what they perceive as the key issue

Box 8.5   Negotiating cross-culturally as a representative

US ambassador: 'The representative of Syria made a statement in reference to a remark of mine. I will recall the circumstances of this remark. The remark was made in the context of a malicious and false accusation that United States aircraft from carriers had participated in the attack. And I said, with respect to that remark, that people ought to put up evidence that such an accusation was true. There has been no evidence offered. There can be no evidence offered of that, because there is no basis for that accusation. That accusation was a false and malicious and scandalous one. That is the remark I made, and I was impelled to make, because of the dangers of indicating to anybody involvement on the part of the United States, which has never been the case in this particular situation.'

Syrian ambassador: 'I would not reply to the distinguished representative of the United States were it not for some of the very words he used in reference to my statement, when he said, referring to a previous statement, that it was a false, malicious and scandalous accusation. I confirm categorically that the United States has helped Israel in its invasion of the United Arab Republic and Jordan and is to be held responsible for whatever destruction and killings have taken place in the United Arab Republic and Jordan, and are taking place right now in my own country, Syria. If anything is scandalous, it is the policy of the United States, which has been shameful for the last twenty years *vis-à-vis* the Arab world and *vis-à-vis* the Arab nations.'

US ambassador: 'Ambassador Tomeh's personal comments, which are in violation of every type of diplomatic usage, are beneath contempt, and I would not purport to dignify them with an answer. The remark to which I referred and which I said was utterly false and malicious was the remark that carrier planes from the Sixth Fleet had intervened in this conflict, and I challenge anybody, including the Ambassador, to bring evidence before the Council to this effect.'

Syrian ambassador: 'I shall ignore the venomous attack made personally against me by the representative of the United States. I would merely say this, that it is not enough to belong to a Great Power. The United States with one bomb can destroy the whole of Syria. But it is much greater and much stronger to belong to a great cultural and intellectual tradition. And this I am proud of.'

Source: Glenn, Witmeyer and Stevenson (1977) pp. 63–4.

and plays down the context of the alleged incident. The intuitive style, used by the Syrian representatives, addresses the broad context of US–Arab relations and resists US attempts to focus on specific detail. The difference in styles is consistent with what we might predict from the fact that allocentric values are likely to be more strongly espoused in Arab societies than in Western societies. The exchange is a rather heated one, explained by the fact that it occurred at the time of the 1967 Arab–Israeli war. Similar differences of style are apparent during much more recent interchanges between representatives of Arab and Western countries.

Private negotiations may of course prove more fruitful (and be conducted differently) from those conducted in the full glare of publicity, but even in private the differences of style are likely to persist.

Kimmel (1994) reviews reasons for a more recent failure in US–Arab negotiations – the meeting between US Secretary of State Baker and Iraqi Foreign Minister Tariq Aziz, prior to the Gulf War of 1990. Baker's approach was to present a definite demand for Iraqi withdrawal from Kuwait, in the form of a written letter containing a short time deadline. In other words the demand was task-oriented, impersonal, abstract, definite and time-constrained. Aziz's preference was to get to know the US negotiators, to propose later direct meetings between national leaders, to review the historical context of present actions, to take further time and to consider a broader range of issues. In other words, consistent with Arab styles of relating, Aziz favoured slow-paced, relationship-based, initially indefinite discourse, leading to direct meetings of more senior figures. The failure to achieve a basis on which the two parties could negotiate led, of course, to the loss of tens of thousands of lives.

Porat (1970) compared simulated union–management bargaining in five European countries. Both the management role and the union role were in fact played by managers who were attending training courses. Table 8.2 shows that the more adversarial targets were set by those from countries that Hofstede characterized as more individualist. However, all five countries represented score relatively high on individualism. Harnett and Cummings (1980) found that buyers from the United States, Finland, Spain, France and Belgium all used their bargaining power to extract maximum profit. In contrast, buyers from more collectivist Thailand and Japan were more inclined to share the profit equally between buyer and seller, presumably because they expected that this egalitarian stance would benefit longer-term relations with the seller.

The most extensive series of cross-cultural studies of negotiation is that conducted over the past fifteen years by Graham and his colleagues (Esteban *et al.*, 1993; Graham, Mintu and Rodgers, 1994). A simulation of buyer-seller negotiations is used, with managers attending business courses randomly assigned to act as either buyer or seller. A parallel series of studies has now been completed in sixteen

Table 8.2 ● Adversarial target-setting and individualism

Country	Percentage of negotiators setting adversarial goals	Hofstede ranking on individualism
United Kingdom	43.6	3
Sweden	33.3	10
Denmark	25.0	9
Switzerland	21.1	14
Spain	12.5	20

> ### Box 8.6 Negotiating cross-culturally on behalf of oneself
>
> The negotiation between Mrs Robertson and Mr Chan was clearly a failure. Mrs Robertson's negotiating position was based upon rigid adherence to an abstract principle which she considered logical: that failed exams must be retaken. Chan explored various bases for compromise, drawing on a wider range of circumstantial factors, such as his effort, his mother's illness, etc. He was also inventive in devising new means of reaching agreement, as illustrated by his proposal of a 'compassionate pass'. Each had a different idea as to the key issues and as to the means by which the dispute should be resolved.

countries, with sample sizes from country to country ranging between forty and eighty. Data were obtained in the United States, Mexico and Canada (Adler, Schwarz and Graham, 1987), the United Kingdom, France and Germany (Campbell *et al.*, 1988), Japan, Korea and Taiwan (Graham *et al.*, 1988), and Russia (Graham, Evenko and Rajan, 1992). More recent data were obtained from China, the Philippines and Czechoslovakia. In summarizing these studies, Graham's initial orientation was to test the cross-cultural generality of a series of findings from US studies, in other words to use an imposed-etic approach. The central proposition was that negotiators who used a 'problem-solving approach' (PSA) would obtain less advantageous results. However, use of a PSA approach was predicted to influence one's fellow negotiator also to adopt a PSA approach, and if this outcome does occur then the prediction is that PSA negotiators will be more successful than negotiators who are more self-interested. Measurement of the PSA approach is accomplished though rating scales completed by the negotiators at the end of a one-hour negotiation session. Esteban *et al.* (1993) found that when they pooled the data from all thirteen nations, the predicted effects were obtained. It was also found that PSA was higher among negotiators from nations that obtained higher collectivism scores in Hofstede's (1980) study. Although these results were as predicted, we need to interpret them with caution, since no account is taken of possible cultural differences in questionnaire response bias.

Movement toward a more emic set of data analyses is accomplished by testing the hypotheses within each country sample separately (Graham, Mintu and Rodgers, 1994). Doing so shows marked differences between the results from different countries, a finding that may partly be due to the rather small samples used. However, Graham *et al.* are able to show that some of the variability in results can be predicted by reference to Hofstede country scores, thereby giving us confidence that they are not random effects. It was found for instance that negotiators' behaviour in the high-power distance samples was significantly affected by the role to which they had been assigned. Sellers tend to defer to buyers. In low-power distance, low-context cultural groups there is no suggestion that negotiators take any note of what is their role: they are oriented toward the payoff matrices

Figure 8.1 Differing approaches to conflict resolution. (Source: Feign, 1987.)

provided by the experimenters. The more individualistic, low-PSA approach was more effective within the individualistic nations, whereas in Taiwan and Korea this relationship was significantly reversed.

As is the case in other areas of study, we can be most confident of results obtained by investigators who also measured the values of those who participated in their studies. The Esteban *et al.* (1993) study did include a measure of allocentric values derived from the Rokeach Value Survey and values were found to vary between the samples in the manner that we would expect. A more direct analysis of the relationship between values and negotiation was made by Chan *et al.* (1995). Comparing intracultural negotiations among Hong Kong and US students, they found that the reaching of agreements in Hong Kong occurred more frequently with friends than with strangers, while among US subjects it made no difference with whom they were negotiating. As expected the Hong Kong subjects endorsed more allocentric values than the US subjects, so their behaviour is consistent with our expectation that they would adapt their negotiation strategy to the context.

In the series of studies by Graham and his colleagues, six pairs of negotiators from most of the nations that they sampled were also videotaped (Graham, 1993). Analysis of the videotapes indicated that there was much greater divergence in the non-verbal aspects of negotiation behaviour than in the verbal aspects. Negotiation in all cultures proceeded primarily on the basis of questions, disclosure of information about one's position, and the making of commitments. Use of the direct negative 'No' varied between an average of twice among the Japanese to forty-two times among the Brazilians. Direct facial eye-contact was highest in Taiwan, France and Brazil and low in the United Kingdom and Japan. Silences longer than ten seconds occurred in Russia, Japan, the United Kingdom and China. Interruptions were most frequent in Korea, Germany and France. Since these are all behaviours that can be reliably coded, studies of this type using larger samples have considerable promise. It appears that the variations in negotiator toughness found within the series of studies by the Graham group may be communicated within each culture more by non-verbal behaviours than by verbal behaviours. Within each culture the meanings of these ·non-verbal behaviours are likely to be well understood. In negotiations between members of different cultures this cannot be assumed.

The studies that we have considered in this section concern direct negotiations between buyers and sellers. Similar processes may be expected to operate in the more indirect process whereby advertisers attempt to influence consumers. Han and Shavitt (1994) analyzed the content of magazine advertisements in Korea and the United States. As we might expect, the US advertisements were found to contain more appeals to idiocentric values and less appeals to allocentric values. The researchers then conducted an experiment in which students were asked to read advertisements and rate their persuasiveness. The results showed that idiocentric appeals were rated equally effective in both countries when advertising for products that one uses on one's own. However, for products that are used with others, the Koreans responded better to allocentric appeals, while the US subjects responded better to idiocentric appeals.

Conflict resolution

Having considered some studies that focus primarily on the relative 'toughness' of negotiation styles, we turn now to look at the various processes by which agreement can be achieved. Kirkbride, Tang and Westwood (1991) surveyed nearly 1,000 Hong Kong managers and management students. Their preferred conflict management styles were compromising and avoiding. Ohbuchi and Takahashi (1994) asked Japanese and US students to describe conflict situations they had experienced and how they had resolved them. The Japanese most frequently reported avoidance, whereas the Americans had used direct bilateral confrontation of the issues. Focusing on legal conflicts, Lind *et al.* (1978) surveyed samples of students and found that adversarial ways of resolving the issues are preferred in individualist countries such as France, Germany, the United Kingdom and the United States. Leung and Lind (1986) asked students in Hong Kong and the United States to evaluate which of several methods would be best in resolving various hypothetical conflict situations with which they were presented. The Chinese favoured an inquisitorial type of investigation, that is to say, the appointment of a senior figure such as a judge, who sifts the evidence and apportions blame. The Americans preferred the adversarial system, whereby separate accounts are put forward by prosecutors and defenders.

In a further study, Leung (1987) presented additional data designed to clarify why these different preferences were held. One needs to remember that both Hong Kong and the United States have British style adversarial justice systems, so that in preferring the inquisitorial mode the Chinese respondents were actually rejecting the system already existing in their society. Leung found that the modes of conflict resolution favoured by his Chinese subjects were those that they thought most likely to reduce animosity. Although inquisitorial investigation was preferred over adversarial adjudication, more informal procedures such as mediation and bargaining were even more strongly preferred. These studies therefore favour the view that the preservation of harmony is a major goal in collectivist cultures such as Hong Kong. Indeed, Leung went on to show that those of his subjects who scored higher on a measure of allocentric values were those who saw mediation and bargaining as more likely to lead to the reduction of animosity.

A similar result was achieved by Trubisky, Ting-Toomey and Lin (1991) who compared the preferences of Taiwanese and American students as to how a conflict within a student group should be resolved. The Taiwanese students favoured the use of conflict resolution styles identified as 'obliging', 'avoiding', 'integrating' and 'compromising'. In the United States the use of these styles was lower, while preference for the style identified as 'dominating' varied, depending upon the personality of each individual American. Trubisky *et al.* point out that Hofstede identified the United States as strongly individualist and Taiwan as strongly collectivist, but found little difference between these two countries on his other three dimensions. They argue that the differences found must therefore be explained by the varying levels of collectivism of the two countries. However, Trubisky *et al.* failed to correct for cultural differences in questionnaire response bias. When this correction is made, the US students are found to be highest on 'contending' and the Taiwanese are much higher on 'avoiding'.

Leung *et al.* (1990, 1992) took this sequence of studies one step further. They compared the preferred methods of conflict resolution of students in two relatively individualist cultures, the Netherlands and Canada, and two relatively collectivist cultures, Spain and Japan. The Spanish and Japanese preferred negotiation and compliance more and accusing less than did the Canadians and Dutch.

Refinements to conflict theory

Just as was the case when we considered studies of reward allocation, the literature now available requires theoretical reformulation. A simple contrast between preferences predicted for idiocentrics and allocentrics is now too crude to account for existing results. While idiocentrics may have conflict resolution preferences which they apply to all situations, the context sensitivity of allocentrics may be expected to lead them to vary their preferences depending upon circumstance. Leung (1997) proposes that in collectivist cultures there are two separable concerns, animosity reduction and disintegration avoidance. Animosity reduction will be the prime concern in situations of relatively intense conflict. Given the

Figure 8.2 A typical cross-cultural negotiation?

preference within collectivist cultures for the preservation of in-group harmony, intense conflicts are likely to be with out-groups. Where more moderate disagreements arise, affecting relationships either within the in-group or with out-groups with which one has a continuing relationship, disintegration avoidance will be a stronger concern. Leung predicts that where the goal is animosity reduction, problem-solving and compromising will be favoured in collectivist cultures. However, when the goal is disintegration avoidance, yielding and avoiding will be preferable strategies. It is not entirely clear which of the studies reviewed may have concerned relatively moderate disagreements. Leung's (1987) study concerned disputes likely to go to a court of law. Consistent with his later model, Leung's (1987) subjects favoured those modes of conflict resolution that they believed would lead to animosity reduction.

More direct tests of this new formulation are now required. In particular, many of the studies in this area of research have focused upon Chinese and Japanese subjects as exemplars of collectivist cultures, and we need to know whether the explanations that have been achieved hold up in other parts of the world. Gire and Carment (1993) compared preferred conflict resolution procedures of Canadian and Nigerian students, using the same interpersonal and intergroup conflicts employed by Leung *et al.* (1990, 1992) in their four-nation comparison. Both groups preferred negotiation, but the Nigerians were significantly more inclined to issue threats, especially in the intergroup conflict. The Canadians perceived only negotiation as likely to lead to animosity reduction, whereas the Nigerians saw both negotiation and the use of threats as leading to animosity reduction. Thus the specific detail of Leung's predictions are not upheld for the Nigerian sample, but his general principle that specific behaviours seen as leading to animosity reduction will be favoured gains further support. The Nigerians' expectation that the use of threats could contribute to animosity reduction is particularly interesting since it is opposite to findings obtained with Hong Kong Chinese and Israeli students (Bond, Leung and Schwartz, 1992). The Israelis were more inclined to make threats than the Hong Kong Chinese, but their preference was for arbitration, and it was arbitration that they most strongly expected to lead to animosity reduction.

The generality of Leung's model can be further tested by Bierbrauer's (1994) comparison of conflict resolution procedures favoured by Germans and by two groups seeking asylum in Germany, Lebanese Arabs and Turkish Kurds. Vignettes depicting rather serious disputes were presented to respondents. The Germans preferred that the disputes be resolved on the basis of law, and they saw the main purpose of the procedures that they favoured as being to uphold the rule of law and to provide guidance on future behaviour. The Kurds and Arabs favoured informal procedures based on tradition or morality, administered by the parties involved or their families. They saw the main value of these procedures as upholding moral values and animosity reduction. These findings also are consistent with the Leung model.

Organizational cultures

In this chapter we have surveyed some of the principal ways in which organizational behaviour has been studied. In order to do so, we have focused in turn upon a series of organizational processes, at many points considering those processes outside of the context of actual organizations. It is worth pausing to note that in doing so, we are following the procedure most frequently used by researchers from individualist nations. We fragment the object that we wish to study into a series of seemingly more manageable elements and look at them separately from one another. In doing this, we gain something and we lose something. Consider for a moment what is lost. Organizations are powerful social systems, within which many people spend the majority of their waking hours. They constitute one of the major building blocks of social systems. In this book, we have repeatedly explored the difference between analyzing cultural differences at the level of national cultures and at the level of individuals within those national cultures. But a case can be made out for a third level of analysis: the level of organizational culture.

The senior managements of most large organizations devote considerable time and money on attempts to mould the culture of their organization. Some such attempts may succeed and others may fail, but the important point is this: organizations have cultures, just as do nations. Organizational and national cultures may overlap, but there is no logical certainty that they will do so. Just as the population of a particular region within a nation may come to endorse certain values in contrast to those endorsed in other regions, so may employees of a given organization come distinctively to favour certain attitudes and values. The organizational cultures of multinational firms may indeed transcend the national boundaries of countries within which they operate. It is now widely known that IBM, the company from which Hofstede (1980) derived the data for his pioneering study, expected that he would find no national differences, since they had invested heavily in creating a transnational company culture. Instead, the variations found across nations were substantial, arguing strongly for the robustness of the dimensions he found (Hofstede and Bond, 1988).

More recently, Hofstede has developed measures that summarize variations in organization culture among twenty companies in Denmark and the Netherlands

(Hofstede *et al.*, 1990). In order to do so, one aggregates the data provided across individuals within each organization, just as dimensions of national cultures rest upon aggregation of data across populations from each nation. In the case of the Hofstede *et al.* (1990) study, data were collected both on the values endorsed by organizational members and on their perceptions of organizational practices. The measures of practices proved more useful in identifying distinctions between the cultures of different organizations. Six factors representing organizational practices were identified, of which the principal one contrasted emphasis on results with emphasis on organizational processes. Other factors contrasted employee-orientation versus job-orientation, parochialism versus professionalism, open system orientation versus closed system orientation, loose control versus tight control and normative versus pragmatic orientation.

In making sense of the variations in selection practices, work motivations, resource allocation, leadership, negotiation and conflict resolution that we have discussed in this chapter, we might expect that analysis in terms of variations in organizational rather than national cultures would provide a more fine-grained analysis. Such studies lie in the future, since well-validated measures of organizational culture are currently few and far between. The more usual procedure of defining organizational culture on the basis of simple pooling of individual-level data from within an organization mixes up individual and organization-level variance (Hofstede, Bond and Luk, 1993).

Van Muijen and Koopman (in press) compared perceptions of the cultures of industrial organizations within ten European nations. They found that descriptions of *actual* reliance on rules and level of innovation were not closely correlated with predictions derived from Hofstede's (1980) scores for the values endorsed in these nations. There was, however, some link between *preferences* for rules or for innovation and the Hofstede scores. They find this divergence to be consistent with the conclusions reached in Hofstede *et al.*'s (1990) study: differences in national cultures are best understood in terms of endorsement of different values, but differences in organizational cultures rest more closely on differences in actual practices. Thus there may be a broad consensus within a nation that certain values are highly esteemed, but particular organizations can over time develop distinctive sets of assumptions about how to implement those values in practice.

Organizational practices

A more delimited approach to organizational culture is to examine one or more specific practices comparatively. For instance, organization members may provide different types of explanation for specific behaviours. Johns and Xie (1995) compared estimates of absenteeism obtained from employees of organizations in Canada and China. When asked how often they were absent, employees from both nations mostly responded that they were absent less often than the average employee (an instance of the self-serving bias). However, when asked to estimate absenteeism among their work group, the Chinese again mostly estimated absences as below average (an instance of the group-serving bias), whereas the Canadians did not. This study therefore neatly illustrates the need for culture-sensitive measures in detecting cultural differences in organizational behaviour.

Morris, Davis and Allen (1994) compared the endorsement of entrepreneurial behaviour within samples of companies in the United States, Portugal and South Africa. They predicted that entrepreneurial behaviour would be most evident in organizations within which values were neither extremely idiocentric nor extremely allocentric. They expected that where idiocentrism prevailed individuals would be unable to gain sufficient cooperation from others, whereas when allocentrism predominated less dramatic innovation would be expected. They succeeded in finding the predicted curvilinear relationship in the United States and in South Africa, but not in Portugal, the most collectivist of their three samples. Since entrepreneurial activity is clearly strong in some collectivist cultures, such as Hong Kong, it may be that the measure of entrepreneurial behaviours used by Morris et al. did not have sufficient validity for use within progressively more collectivist cultures.

Organizational justice

Several researchers have become interested in whether employees' feelings that they have been treated fairly by their organization will affect the way that they respond to the incentives and leadership behaviours provided by the organization. Leung, Earley and Lind (no date) compared supermarket employees in the United States and Hong Kong. Among their US sample, perceived injustice weakened the link between supervisor behaviour and perceptions of job security, commitment to the organization and 'organizational citizenship' (willingness to make contributions to the organization additional to those required; Organ, 1988). Similar weakening of links was found in Hong Kong between supervisor behaviour and organizational commitment. In both countries, perceived injustice also weakened the link between satisfaction with pay, job security and organizational commitment. In Hong Kong, perceived injustice was much more influential in reducing the effects on satisfaction with pay, whereas in the United States, the strongest effects were those derived from perceptions of the supervisor. Leung et al. conclude that the effects of justice perceptions are mediated by the different motivations that are salient at each location. Pay was more of an issue for the Hong Kong employees and hence the effects of injustice were more marked in that area, whereas quality of supervision was more salient in the United States.

Some of the difference in findings within the Leung et al. (no date) study may have been due to the use of imposed etic measures. A further study by Farh, Earley and Lin (1997) devised a measure of organizational citizenship that had greater validity for Chinese respondents. Upon surveying employees of eight companies in Taiwan, they found that perceived justice predicted enhanced levels of four organizational citizenship behaviours: altruism toward colleagues, conscientiousness, interpersonal harmony and protection of company resources. This study thus represents the first successful attempt outside the United States to devise emically valid measures for testing the linkage between organizational justice and organizational citizenship. This type of study provides no information as to the extent of variation in the cultures of the eight companies sampled, but it does suggest the applicability of the concept of organizational justice outside North America.

A related study also suggesting differences between the United States and other locations was completed by Borges-Andrade (1994) in Brazil. Earlier US studies have reported significant links between satisfaction with one's immediate supervisor and organizational commitment. He found that within Brazil factors concerning the organization as a whole were stronger predictors of commitment. High commitment was predicted by the overall reputation of the organization, by the priority given to human resource management in the overall organization and by the perception that the organization treated employees in a just and fair manner. Thus, while the US studies show managers responding to their immediate individual environment, the Brazilians were more influenced by the broader collective context.

Decision-making procedures

We reviewed earlier studies of the consequences of particular styles of leadership. The focus here is upon the way in which organizations (or particular functions within organizations) in a culture may be characterized as favouring distinctive ways of taking decisions. The most extensive study of this type compared the levels in the organization at which particular types of decision were taken in twelve European nations (Industrial Democracy in Europe International Research Group, 1981). Large differences were found across different nations, especially in relation to major decisions. These variations partially reflected different laws regulating consultation with trade unions and other concerned parties (see e.g. Brewster, 1995). This study was replicated more recently (Industrial Democracy in Europe International Research Group, 1993), revealing continuing substantial differences, though with some attenuation. The adoption of the Social Charter (which specifies standard requirements for employment practices) by the European Union may be expected to reduce these differences further over the next decade.

A related series of studies has shown that in a wide range of European nations, managers believe that the next level down in the hierarchy does not have the expertise to participate more fully in decision-making (Heller and Wilpert, 1981). In this and later studies, it was found that there was more variation in the level at which specific decisions were taken across organizations and across functions within those organizations than there was across the United Kingdom, the Netherlands and the former Yugoslavia (Heller et al., 1988) as well as across the United Kingdom and China (Wang and Heller, 1993). This pattern of results is consistent with the view discussed above that organizational cultures are differentiated by variations in endorsement of specific practices, rather than values.

There may also be national differences in the degree to which upward initiatives are welcomed within organizations. Carr and MacLachlan (1997) refer to what they call 'motivational gravity' in organizations, in other words the degree to which members of an organization generally support and encourage individual initiative. They asked a sample of Malawian managers how their organizational colleagues would mostly react to a worker who performed well, came up with bright ideas or regularly earned a bonus. They found that most respondents predicted a negative, discouraging response from peers and colleagues. Similar evaluations have been identified as 'red-eye disease' in Hong Kong (Bond, 1993) or the need to 'cut down tall poppies' in Australia (Feather, 1994b). In contrast, Carr (1994) found that Japanese managers would predict a positive, encouraging response in the same circumstances. More studies are required to enable us to understand the distinctive qualities of the types of organizational culture that fosters what we might think of such 'motivational buoyancy' rather than gravity. As we noted above, Morris, Davis and Allen (1994) detected cultural variations in entrepreneurial behaviour within organizations and this may be sustained by the same phenomenon.

Putting organizations back together

One further possible way of exploring particular organizational cultures is to do so via emically based case study material from different nations and we shall provide some instances of this approach in Chapter 11. This approach has the virtue of giving us a more vivid picture of how organizations operate in a given context, but like other emic approaches it is vulnerable to the way in which the analytic approach adopted may itself vary from one culture to another. Even more so than in the case of social psychological theories, the theories of organization that have been advanced by writers from different countries tend to take different points of departure and thereby encourage the researcher to look for different types of phenomena. Üsdiken and Pasadeos (1995), for instance, note that US and European theorists only rarely refer to each other's work. Hofstede (1996a) suggests that US theories are mostly focused upon the individual and upon the creation of participation and harmony, while European theorists are more interested in systems and assume the presence of conflicts, and the need for rules and procedures to regulate them. However, the division among theorists may be as much linguistic as it is regional. Chanlat (1994), who is French-Canadian, details the rather separate emphases of French-language organizational analysis over the past half-century. While there are certainly also different emphases between North American and European English language theorists of organization, there has been greater interchange between them than across the linguistic divide.

Throughout this chapter, we have discussed organizations as though they were culturally homogeneous. This has been a necessary simplification in order to explore some basic aspects of the processes occurring within organizations. In the next chapter we consider what happens when persons from different cultures inter-act together, as happens with great frequency within multinational organizations, joint-venture organizations and many types of business negotiations.

Summary

Each of the elements that contribute to the effectiveness of organizations is conducted in a somewhat different manner in different parts of the world. Employees' work goals vary and in consequence they respond to leaders, negotiate with others and resolve conflicts in ways that reflect these differing priorities. Effective methods of selection and appraisal require measurement procedures that take account of these differences. The process of working together in organizations leads over time to distinctive organizational cultures, characterized by particular ways of seeking to accomplish the organization's goals. Leaders who propound a charismatic vision of their organization's purpose may have a substantial impact upon the practices employed within that culture, but will succeed in doing so only if their vision is transmitted in a manner that accords with the values and practices endorsed by organization members.

9

The characteristics of cross-cultural interaction

'What kind of a bird are you if you can't sing?', chirped the bird.
'What kind of a bird are you, if you can't swim?',
retorted the duck.

Sergei Prokofiev, *Peter and the Wolf*

The abstractions and niceties of cultural analysis become quickly focused on practical concerns when people from different cultures meet. Such encounters are becoming ever more frequent in a world where the forces of trade, migration, the media, travel and human rights are pushing people and governments to confront and accommodate ethnic diversity ever more frequently (Naisbitt and Aburdene, 1990).

Social scientists are increasingly being asked to examine interactions occurring across cultural lines. In what ways do people of different cultures behave differently? Which of these differences are important when people of different cultures live and work together? How do these differences have an impact on the communication process? In attempting to answer these sorts of questions, we are fortunate to enjoy the legacy of considerable work on intergroup behaviour done *within* nations sharing a broader single culture (see Chapter 7). Much of this work can be extended to encounters across different cultural lines.

This chapter provides a test for the preceding chapters by discussing our present understanding of the challenges inherent in cross-cultural contact. We shall begin by examining the process of relationship development in its universal aspects. An encounter with anybody unknown produces anxiety and a need to develop expectations for their behaviour in order to interact effectively with them. The process of person perception is the first step in this direction. The initial identification of the other often elicits stereotypes associated with the other's group or cultural membership. We then use this set of assumptions about the other to guide our behaviour towards them and to structure our interpretation of their behaviour towards us, often negatively.

When the stranger is from a different cultural background, his or her communicative behaviour will often puzzle or irritate us because it counters our expectations and we interpret it as inappropriate. This confusion is reciprocal and may be complicated by language differences. Each party attempting to repair the situation may do so in ways that are culturally different, further compounding the difficulties. As a way of grounding our presentation of these various problems, we will conclude this chapter with an analysis of the unhappy encounter between Chan Chi Lok and Mrs Robertson.

Meeting others

Encountering the stranger

As originally described by Simmel (1950), a stranger is a person simultaneously 'within' and 'without'. Although physically present and sharing the same environment, the newcomer is not acquainted with the others present and does not know how they are likely to respond, either verbally or non-verbally. As Herman and Schield (1961) analyzed such encounters,

> The immediate psychological result of being in a new situation is lack of security. Ignorance of the potentialities inherent in the situation, of the means to reach a goal, and of the probable outcomes of an intended action leads to insecurity. (p. 165)

Furthermore, the physique, dress, mannerisms, and speech of the stranger may suggest to observers that he or she belongs to a different group from the observers' group. They may believe that the stranger's group follows a different life-style and is aggressively disposed towards their own group. Furthermore, observers often worry that their own group members may interpret interacting with an out-group stranger as disloyalty to their own group. These intergroup considerations (Stephan and Stephan, 1985) increase the anxiety already attendant upon encounters with strangers (Gudykunst and Hammer, 1988).

The probable outcome of such an encounter is avoidance, especially if the observer is introverted and anxious in personality; for most persons, it is generally too effortful and dangerous to construct a bridge from the known to the unknown. Role constraints, however, may preclude this option. The stranger may be a customer, or a guest, or a teacher, or an employer. Furthermore, we may be curious and open to novel experience as persons, find the stranger physically attractive, or come from a culture that encourages accommodation to diversity (e.g. those high on Schwartz's, 1994, egalitarian commitment). Such factors may lead us to interact, despite the uncertainty. In such cases how do people proceed?

Uncertainty reduction

As Berger (1987) has proposed,

> To interact in a relatively smooth, coordinated, and understandable manner, one must be able both to predict how one's interaction partner is likely to behave, and,

based on these predictions, to select from one's own repertoire those responses that will optimize outcomes in the encounter. (p. 41)

In meeting a stranger, then, Berger would argue that concern for gathering useful information about the other is heightened because one knows so little about him or her.

Sharing the other's culture is extremely helpful in filling this need, of course, because people from the same culture have been socialized to share similar role expectations (e.g. Tyler, 1995), situational understandings (Forgas and Bond, 1985), implicit theories of personality (Yang and Bond, 1990) and communication scripts (Wierzbicka, 1994). As Forgas (1981) has written,

It is the unique capacity of human beings for symbolic processes which allows them to build up expectations and internal representations about their daily interactions with one another. These representations, in turn, are the elementary building blocks of both socialized personalities and social systems. (p. 168)

If strangers come from the same cultural system, then their capacity to anticipate the other's responses will be greatly increased. When interactants are from different cultures, the normal uncertainty at meeting strangers is exacerbated (Gudykunst and Shapiro, 1996). The culturally socialized guidelines for relationship development are no longer shared. Simard (1981), for example, reports that,

when focusing on a potential friend from the other group, [French and English interactants] perceive it as more difficult to know how to initiate a conversation, to know what to talk about during interaction, to be interested in the other person, and to guess in which language they should talk, than when they considered a person from their own group. (p. 183)

Such perplexity is common when meeting persons from different cultural groups. In consequence, anxiety in such encounters is greater than that already attendant on intracultural encounters with strangers.

Fortunately, the context of the encounter (perhaps a political rally or a classroom) will eliminate many behaviours as possibilities and help to focus each party's anticipations on interaction scripts relevant to the situation. Thereafter, Berger (1987) argues, we undertake a variety of 'knowledge acquisition strategies', which include passive, active and interactive techniques, to learn about the other person. Passive techniques involve unobtrusive observation with preference given for social, informal settings where a target's real personality is believed to be more apparent. Active techniques involve manipulating the social environment without directly interacting with the target, such as by asking members of the target's social network for information. Interactive techniques involve direct, face-to-face contact and include question asking, disclosure elicitation and relaxing the target to obtain more accurate information. The use of these strategies yields information about one's particular interaction partner, further reducing uncertainty and its attendant anxiety as intercultural interactions extend across time (Hubbert, Guerrero and Gudykunst, in press).

It has been confirmed in Korea, Japan, and the United States that lower levels of uncertainty about the other are associated with greater attraction across a number of different relationships – acquaintance, friendship, and dating (Gudykunst, Yang and Nishida, 1985). Given the breadth of these findings across relationships, it seems reasonable to accept as universal the proposition that persons are motivated to reduce their levels of uncertainty about strangers and that increased certainty is one aspect of viable relationships with others. 'Getting to know you' is essential in un-becoming strangers to one another. The first step in this process is identifying who the stranger is.

Identifying the other

Much of our daily life is spent interacting with others in a state of 'mindlessness' (Langer, 1989). In many contexts we relate to others in routine, automatic ways determined by social scripts. As defined by Abelson (1976), a script is a coherent sequence of events expected by the individual and involving him as a participant or observer. Scripts are learned throughout the individual's lifetime both by participation in event sequences and by vicarious observation. By relying on shared scripts, people in various roles, such as passengers, ticket vendors, librarians and telephone operators, can process normal exchanges without paying any attention to the special qualities of those persons requiring their services.

When some novel exchange is initiated or when one of the parties wants to move outside the role relationship, however, the situation changes. Novel but appropriate action must be taken, so the individuals become 'mindful'. One feature of that elicited mindfulness involves ascertaining information about one's interaction partner.

Identity cues

A number of psychologically useful cues are immediately apparent when interacting with others. Gender, age, race, physical attractiveness, body shape, baby-facedness and so forth are all visually apparent. When the other talks, speech volume, speed, fluency and accentedness are likewise quickly available in addition to the content of the other's speech. Additional non-verbal behaviours, such as clothing, proxemics, body odour, posture, kinesics and patterns of gazing, can also be monitored.

Each of these characteristics in others is informative about their personality. Categorical cues, such as gender, provide information about the other through the mediation of stereotypes. Individual cues, such as speech volume, can be directly informative and allow us to make 'snap judgements' (McArthur and Baron, 1983) about the other's mood and personality. Together, this information allows us to reduce our uncertainty about people, generate expectations about how they will respond, and develop a clear behavioural orientation towards them. In short, we are better able to act. Of course, as we have discovered in previous chapters, people from different cultures may focus on different cues and interpret these cues differently in order to direct their behaviour. So, when they then interact across cultural lines, they may be starting with very different assumptions about one another than would be the case for a within-culture encounter!

Out-group identification

A key issue in initial perceptions of the other is concerned with whether he or she is categorized as an out-group member. There are many categories possible for distinguishing people from one another such as gender, age, ethnicity and so forth. Which of these categories becomes salient, indeed whether categories of difference or similarity become salient, is an important issue for much of what follows in this chapter (see Zarate and Smith, 1990).

Procedures used in studies of social perception often simplify the stimulus conditions so as to focus respondents on the variable of interest to the researcher. So, for example, subjects may be asked to imagine a particular group of people, say Blacks, and asked to rate their characteristics (e.g. Quattrone and Jones, 1980). Such procedures sharpen experimental control but they blunt ecological validity by begging the question of whether people would notice the other's Blackness outside the laboratory. What then *is* noticed in natural settings?

A number of factors appear to influence the salience of categories in everyday person perception. First, it may be that certain categories assume universal salience. Brewer (1988), for example, has hypothesized that both gender and race constitute 'primitive' categories of social perception. As such, these categories immediately assume salience in interpersonal encounters and are accorded priority over all other possible categories.

Secondly, the distinctiveness of the category in the social field is another factor (McGuire et al., 1978). The lower the proportion of perceptually different persons within a group, the more likely they will be perceived as members of that group. Behaviour of such 'distinctives' will be better remembered, perceived as more influential, and interpreted in terms of their group stereotype (Taylor et al., 1978).

Thirdly, a person's 'prototypicality' (Cantor and Mischel, 1978) as a physical exemplar of a group probably influences the likelihood of categorizing that person as a group member. Atypical persons are harder to place and are less likely to be categorized into a particular group.

Fourthly, it is possible that deviations from normal speech in the form of accent, syntax or grammar are salient cues for out-group membership. Speech is an important component of effective task completion and those speaking to one another must quickly gauge each other's productive competence (Coupland et al., 1988) in order to manage their discourse smoothly. The probability that one must adjust to the other's manner of speaking to coordinate effectively is increased when the other departs from normal speech patterns, so one's anxiety is increased. The need for uncertainty reduction is sharpened and informative social categories, such as ethnicity, then become salient (Gallois et al., 1988).

The most dramatic divergence of speech occurs when the other uses a foreign language. In this case the first step is to identify correctly *which* language is being spoken, so that one can decide if the language is within one's repertoire and in what way speech norms in the situation permit one to accommodate to the other's language. Additional cues about the other's culture or ethnicity become prominent in guiding such a linguistic categorization.

Finally, a history of conflict between one's group and the other's group will serve to 'educate the observer's attention' (McArthur and Baron, 1983), heighten the sense of threat, and make the other's group membership salient (Giles and Johnson, 1986). It is also probable that persons from economically, socially or politically powerful groups (e.g. colonialists) will be more salient and categorizable. Personality dispositions of the observer enter the picture here with ethnocentric, aggressive and insecure persons being more prone to notice the other's membership in an out-group (Scott, 1965). In this situation the responses of the parties, starting with their perceptions, is shifted towards the intergroup end of the interpersonal vs. intergroup continuum (Hewstone and Brown, 1986). Each person then responds to the other almost exclusively in terms of the other's group membership, ignoring his or her distinctive personal characteristics in guiding their behaviour.

Certainly more needs to be known about the conditions leading to a person's being categorized as an out-group member. Even more important is the need to discover when additional, non-category-based information about the other also becomes salient. This latter consideration is critical because research indicates that subjects do not always apply category-based stereotypes to a person when additional personality information is available (Pratto and Bargh, 1991), or when they are motivated to attend to individual differences (Zebrowitz, Montepare and Lee, 1993).

Let us assume, then, that the result of contact between two persons of different cultures, races or ethnicities has led one or both parties to classify the other as an out-group member. At this point, the categorization will elicit the stereotype associated with that group along with the emotional feelings associated with that group (see Chapter 7). These cognitions and emotions will then provide a background to the interaction, structuring our behaviour towards the other and our interpretation of his or her behaviour towards us.

Communicating with foreigners

The act of communicating has components and dynamics which are basic to the process anywhere. How these components are weighted and evaluated and how these dynamics are engaged, however, show important cultural differences (see summaries by Gudykunst, Ting-Toomey and Nishida, 1996; Gudykunst and Kim, 1997). These differences must be accommodated in some way if cross-cultural exchanges are to remain viable. This section examines the challenges inherent in communicating across cultural lines.

Communication

Briefly, the act of communication involves transmitting messages to another person, who translates those messages by giving them meaning. These messages may be sent by conscious intent or not and include information about both the content of the message and the relationship between those communicating (Watzlawick, Beavin and Jackson, 1967). Much communication behaviour is scripted so that exchanges proceed in a routine manner and lead to desirable, expected outcomes. Verbal communication involves a number of instrumental skills. The more similar one's partner is perceived to be in the use of these skills, the more attractive that partner is regarded, both within one's ethnic group (Burleson, Kunkel and Birch, 1994) and across ethnic groups (Lee, 1996).

For communication to succeed, interactants

> need to coordinate both the content and the process of what they are doing . . . they cannot even begin to coordinate on content without assuming a vast amount of shared information or common ground – that is, mutual knowledge, mutual beliefs, and mutual assumptions. . . . And to coordinate on process, they need to update their common ground moment by moment. (Clark and Brennan, 1991, p. 127)

This on-line affirmation of understanding is called grounding. The less common ground interactants share, the narrower the range of usable discussion topics (Chen, 1995) and the more they will need to ground their communications as they proceed in order to ensure that they have reached the same point of understanding in their exchange.

Cross-cultural communication is a demanding process requiring high levels of interaction involvement. This is defined as engagement in a conversation through being sensitive to the give and take of the conversation, integrating one's thoughts, feelings and behaviours into the process of the exchange (Cegala, 1981). Ironically, interaction involvement is lower in intercultural conversations, at least initially (Chen, 1995).

Occasionally, the communication process breaks down. A partner may disrupt the normal routine, for example by saying, 'I have an excruciating headache' when asked, 'How are you?'; or the outcome of the exchange may not be what one or both of the parties anticipated, as when an appointment is not kept. At this point one or both parties to the communication become 'mindful' (Langer, 1989) of their communication and must decide how to respond. They may withdraw from the interaction, adopt a new routine, or process the impasse by explicitly confronting the difficulty – 'meta-communicating' as Watzlawick, Beavin and Jackson (1967) describe the repair process.

These forms of response themselves meet with responses from the other and together they constitute an ongoing negotiation of the relationship. Communications are steps in this negotiation process. Accurate communication occurs when both parties to the communication agree about the meaning of the various communications exchanged. Such accuracy is tested by the outcome of events and is typically only addressed when a breakdown occurs and the parties together engage in conscious 'repairs' (Schwartz, 1980). Considerable inaccuracy probably exists during most communication exchanges (Figure 9.1) but is never assessed, because the outcome is either acceptable to the parties involved or else not worth confronting even though it is unacceptable.

Effective communication, then, means that the outcome of the process continues to meet the needs and intentions of the parties involved. As Wish (1979) has shown, stable relationships in the United States are perceived to vary across five dimensions:

1. Cooperative to competitive.
2. Intense to superficial.
3. Task oriented to socio-emotional.
4. Hierarchical to egalitarian.
5. Formal to informal.

These dimensions probably apply to relationships in all cultural systems (Adamopoulos, 1988; Lonner, 1980), although no empirical work has addressed this important question.

Cultural groups probably vary in their frequency of, and preference for, certain types of relationship. Such differences should not lead us as social scientists, however, to define as effective communication that which leads to the type of relationships idealized in our own cultural group. Communications between two parties can be effective *regardless* of how their relationship may be characterized, providing that each party is achieving a desired sort of relationship.

Figure 9.1 The cultural meanings of 'Yes'. (Source: Feign, 1987.)

On occasion one or both parties to a communication may wish to change the nature of their relationship. So, for example, the subordinate in a hierarchical relationship may wish for more egalitarian exchanges. Such a desire may temporarily disturb the relationship, but their communications may continue to be accurately understood and effective in communicating their dissatisfaction with the *status quo*. In short, effective communication does not entail agreement about the nature of a relationship or current satisfaction with that relationship.

As will become apparent, these issues of common ground, grounding procedures, communication accuracy, breakdown confrontation, repair strategies, and type of desired relationship become especially critical in exchanges *across* cultural lines (Tannen, 1985; Scollon and Scollon, 1995; Wiseman, 1995; Gudykunst *et al.*, 1996).

The social context for communication

Persons from different cultural groups come into contact with one another in a variety of contexts – a French graduate student doing fieldwork for her thesis meets a Chinese peasant at a factory, a Zulu reports for work to his Afrikaner boss at a diamond mine in the Transvaal, a Turkish child of immigrant parents attends her first day of classes at a German primary school. The possibilities are legion, whether contacts take place between members of the same society or between members of different societies. In an attempt to organize this variety, Bochner (1982) conceptualized cross-cultural contacts as shown in Table 9.1.

Many of these contact variables have been widely researched in social psychology. For example, the variable of time span has been examined by Kiesler, Kiesler and Pallak (1967). They found that when those in contact expected no future interactions with the other, they were more extreme in their dislike of 'inappropriate' actions by those others. Similarly, Bond and Dutton (1975) found that those anticipating no future interaction with others aggressed against them more freely. These findings have obvious implications for interactions between locals and foreign tourists, a dynamic that may be exacerbated by their resentment of the relative wealth displayed by the tourists.

Likewise, each of the other contact variables in Table 9.1 will set social psychological processes into motion. They will operate whether those interacting are members of the same or of different cultures, unless the consciousness of one or both groups is engaged to resist the pattern (e.g. Devine, 1989). The work of Dutton (1973) on reverse discrimination, for example, shows that under certain conditions members of minority groups are given preferential treatment by members of the dominant majority. Each of the variables that form the context for intergroup contact helps structure background considerations for examining any such interaction which then has the added complication of occurring across cultural lines. Complexity is added to this complication when it is appreciated that each pairing of two cultural groups has its own 'culture of relationships' (Triandis *et al.*, 1993). This specific 'pair-culture' must be factored into predictions about an outcome.

Table 9.1 ● Types of cross-cultural contact

Contact variables:	Between members of the same society		Between members of different societies	
	Type	Example	Type	Example
On whose territory?	Usually joint	Black and white Americans	Home or foreign territory	Tourists Overseas students Immigrants and their respective hosts
Time span	Long term	Black and white Americans	Short term Medium term Long term	Tourists Overseas students Immigrants
Purpose	Make a life in	Black and white Americans	Make a life in Study in Make a profit Recreation	Immigrants Overseas students Workers Tourists
Type of involvement	Participate in society	Black and white Americans	Participate Exploit Contribute Observe	Immigrants Workers Experts Tourists
Frequency of contact	High	Black and white Americans	High Medium Low	Immigrants Overseas students Tourists
Degree of intimacy between participants	High to low social distance (variable)	Black and white Americans	High to low social distance (variable)	Immigrants Overseas students Tourists
Relative status and power	Equal to unequal (variable)	Black and white Americans	Equal Unequal	Tourists Overseas students Immigrants
Numerical balance	Majority–minority Equal distribution	White and black Americans, Chinese, Japanese and Caucasian Hawaiians	Majority–minority	Host and students Immigrants Tourists
Visible distinguishing characteristics	Race Religion Language	Black and white Americans Ireland India Canada	Race Religion Language	Immigrants Overseas students Tourists

Construing situations from culture to culture

All encounters between people take place in what Barker (1968) called 'behavior settings', where the participants have some type of relationship with one another. So, classmates meet in the school canteen, an employer joins his employees at a company wedding, spouses discuss their day's events while preparing dinner. An understanding of these social episodes is shared by the participants (i.e., they hold common ground), so that their interaction may proceed according to script, with both parties focusing on the issues at hand (Forgas, 1979).

If the respondents to a social episode come from different cultures, however, there is a high probability that their initial understanding of that event will differ. To demonstrate this likelihood, Forgas and Bond (1985) had Australian and Chinese students evaluate a number of episodes common to both groups, such as arriving late to a tutorial. What emerged from this study was that persons from each cultural group used four criteria for evaluating this set of situations. Both Australians and Chinese evaluated the episodes in terms of whether they were involving or not and whether they were task or social in nature. The problem was that the same situation elicited different levels of response along these two shared dimensions. For example, giving directions was more involving for Australians than for Chinese, but studying was more task-oriented for Chinese than for Australians. In terms of the remaining two dimensions of evaluation, there was no overlap of meaning at all between the Australians and the Chinese. Australians considered the episodes in terms of whether they elicited competitive responses or confident responses. In contrast the Chinese considered whether the episodes elicited egalitarian responses or happy responses.

At the very least, this study demonstrates that the same situations can mean very different things to persons of different cultural backgrounds. The behaviours evoked by these different situational representations are thus also likely to differ (Furnham, 1982), so that the participants' initial responses to the same behaviour setting often disconfirm one another's expectations. Coordinating behaviour quickly becomes difficult because participants lack initial common ground and attention must be shifted towards negotiating shared meanings about the situation if the relationship is to continue.

Role relationships. An important feature of social situations is the role relationships among the participants. People from different cultures may agree that they are in a friend–friend relationship or an employer–employee relationship. However, they may differ in terms of how much power or intimacy constitutes that relationship. The research on politeness theory (Brown and Levinson, 1987) shows that both these variables influence the level of politeness behaviours required in the role relationship. If, however, the cross-cultural interactants differ in their assumptions about the power differentials or degree of intimacy characterizing a given relationship, they are likely to be denying adequate face or giving too much face to their partner.

For example, Scollon and Scollon (1981) point out that native Athabascans (a group of North American Indians) assume greater distance in employment situations than do English-speaking Americans. In consequence, Athabascans tend to be more polite in work settings. English-speaking Americans, presuming more familiarity, show less politeness and are hence regarded as acting superior by the Athabascans (Holtgraves, 1992). As another case-in-point, Spencer-Oatey (1997) showed that the tutor–tutee relationship is construed to be much closer in China than in the United Kingdom. Chinese students may then evince insufficient politeness when 'imposing' on UK tutors and hence be regarded as presumptuous. In these and other similar ways, cross-cultural relationships may be put at early risk because of these differing constructions of the same role relationship (see also Tyler, 1995).

The above analysis presumes that both parties understand a given behaviour, e.g. thanking the other, as communicating the same thing, i.e. politeness. This is not always the case across cultures, as we discuss next.

Communication breakdown

Disconfirmed expectations and misattributions

Living across cultural lines constantly produces surprises for those involved. People are late for appointments, or early, or do not make appointments at all and simply arrive. People stand too close or too far away; talk too much, or too little, or too fast, or too slow, or about the wrong topics. They are too emotional, or too moderate, show too much or too little of a certain emotion, or show it at the wrong time or fail to show it at the right time. The list of possible surprises in people's verbal and non-verbal behaviours is as long as the list of domains where cultural differences have been documented (see especially Chapter 6).

The human response to surprise is to search for explanations (Pyszczynski and Greenberg, 1981). The discovery of an explanation for the unusual behaviour of the other will reduce our uncertainty, as Berger (1987) has argued, and make the other's behaviour more predictable. The intercultural problem, of course, is that the person explaining the other's behaviour has his or her own cultural guidelines for interpreting the surprising behaviour. Often these guidelines will lead to an unfavourable personality attribution about the other. So, the American business-man who gazes intently at a prospective Malaysian partner and addresses him by his first name may well be regarded as 'disrespectful' (see also LaFrance and Mayo, 1976). Or, the Briton who interrupts the Japanese, a much more frequent event in English than in Japanese conversations (Murata, 1994), may well be regarded as 'aggressive' (see also Box 9.1).

Such negative attributions are likely because there is a normative aspect to many of our expectations about behaviour from others (Burgoon and Walther, 1990). We generally prefer behaviour that is typical of our own cultural group. In the perceiver's culture, behaviour that deviates from expectation often violates social

> ### Box 9.1 US–Japanese negotiations
>
> Graham (1993) videotaped simulated buyer–seller negotiations between Japanese and US businessmen, using the procedures described in Chapter 8 for his mono-cultural studies. The negotiators were then asked to review the tapes along with the researchers and to comment on 'focal points' when negotiations had become difficult. The difficulties that arose were mostly those one might expect from Graham's earlier monocultural data. Japanese negotiators were uncomfortable with a high rate of interruptions, with direct rejections of their offers and when the seller took the initiative rather than allowing the buyer to do so. US negotiators incorrectly interpreted head nods as agreement, became angry when high initial selling prices were proposed, and became confused when they could not discern whether a 'final' offer really was final.
>
> Okumura and Brett (1996) used a similar format. They predicted and found that because of the Japanese norm that sellers should defer to buyers, US negotiators got better deals when they were buyers and worse deals when they were sellers. This result may cast some light on the difficulties US and other Western companies have encountered in entering Japanese markets.

rules and is diagnostic of somebody as rude, neurotic, ignorant, or simply uncivilized. This last attribution is commonly employed after intercultural encounters and is actually quite fitting. As assessed against the cultural standards of the observer, the behaviour of the other is indeed 'uncivilized' (Burgoon, 1989), since someone socialized according to your cultural norms would rarely behave in such a way. The other person is probably behaving, however, in ways that are situationally appropriate to his or her own cultural training.

The net result is a cross-cultural 'misattribution', i.e. an attribution about the reason for an event given by a foreigner which differs from that typically given by a member of the host culture (see Brislin *et al.*, 1986). The other person may intend to communicate friendliness by asking you about your family, but is instead perceived as 'nosey'; may spontaneously be communicating respect by lowering his or her eyes, but instead be regarded as 'indifferent'. The outcome of the attribution process is determined by the cultural programme used to decode the behaviour. Where these codes differ as they so often do, misattributions will be rife.

Positive misattributions? Not all misattributions arising from atypical behaviour are negative, of course (Burgoon, 1995). For example, an Australian teacher may be delighted with the extent of the courtesy shown by the principal when he gives a guest lecture at a Japanese high-school. This departure from expectation would be incorrectly explained, however, if the teacher made an attribution such as, 'The principal behaved in this way because he considers me a talented academic'. For the principal would simply have been observing Japanese academic etiquette towards a visitor, and not communicating special deference to the Australian teacher. The teacher would have misinterpreted the principal's courtesies.

If the teacher uses his culturally appropriate attribution to guide his future behaviour towards the principal, some negative surprises may then begin arising. Should the teacher request a job, or invite the principal to dinner, or offer a further lecture, the response to these initiatives may not confirm his Australian expectations about how a talented academic is treated. At this point the frustrated teacher may begin to regard the principal as inconsistent, inscrutable or un-civilized.

With respect to violations of expectancies surrounding non-verbal behaviours, Burgoon (1989) has shown that certain forms of departure from expectation are positively evaluated, at least within the United States. For instance, where a communicator came closer, made more eye-contact or used more of some forms of touch than expected, the reactions of the other party were found to be more positive. Given these findings, the first issue cross-culturally is to discover which types of non-verbal violation by what types of communicator are positively evaluated in other cultures. Then one needs to know if *foreigners* are allowed to violate the norm with the same positive reactions as locals. A double standard may well be applied, especially when other members of the host culture are present. Currently, social scientists know nothing about either of these two issues despite our need to learn (Burgoon, 1995). It seems judicious to presume, however, that most violations by foreigners of the host's non-verbal code will be negatively evaluated by locals (see, e.g. Vrij and Winkel, 1992; Jones *et al.*, 1994), regardless of whether the perpetrator is from one's own or a different cultural group (Drew and Ward, 1993). The same is probably also true for most cases of violations in the expected verbal code (e.g. Lee, 1996).

In conclusion then, until people from different cultures become more knowledgeable about the other's cultural codes, the cycle of misattributions will continue. This cycle will sooner or later result in distressing experiences which set a withdrawal dynamic into motion.

The language barrier

Language is an efficient means of transmitting symbolic information to achieve instrumental and affective goals. Cultural conventions regulate basic features of language use from microscopic issues, such as syntax, vocabulary, sentence structure and accent, to macroscopic considerations such as how much one speaks, about what topics, and with whom. Within the same culture there are striking differences in these aspects of language use and how these differences are evaluated (e.g. Elwell, Brown and Rutter, 1984, on the impact of accent variation); across cultural groups, these differences are further compounded.

The first cross-cultural consideration is that a language casts a net of mutual intelligibility around those who use it and becomes a unifying force for group cohesion. As Fishman (1972) has argued, one's mother tongue assumes a powerful, emotional resonance and for people of many cultural groups a defining characteristic of a valued national identity (Smolicz, 1979).

Speech accommodation. A second problem arises in cross-cultural interactions and is most obvious when partners to the exchange speak different mother
tongues. Who will accommodate to whom, so that they can communicate
effectively? Speech accommodation involves shifting one's speech patterns (e.g.
accent, dialect, discourse style) towards those of one's interlocutor, so that greater
similarity of language use is achieved (Thakerar, Giles and Cheshire, 1982). That
accommodation may be one way or mutual depending on the interpersonal
attraction and relative power of the parties concerned (Giles and Johnson, 1981).

If the two cultural groups are antagonistic towards one another and if group
membership is a salient component of the interaction, divergence of speech style or
language used will probably occur (e.g. Bourhis *et al.*, 1979). Participants may
refuse to speak the other party's language, effectively isolating one another behind
a wall of inscrutability. Given the close perceived association between language
and culture, members of one cultural group may even refuse to learn the other
group's language. They may believe that including it in their educational
curriculum would subtract from their own cultural heritage (Lambert, 1967), or
perpetuate the dominance of a resented cultural group over their own (Giles and
Byrne, 1982).

Even if relations between the two cultural groups are positive and stable, the
issue of whose speech moves towards whose must still be negotiated. The roles of
the interactants are a key consideration, as is the relative status of the ethnic groups
involved and their solidarity, the ethnolinguistic vitalities (see Box 9.2) of each
speech community, and the interaction goals of each party (see Gallois *et al.*, 1988,
for a review). This negotiation is a socially delicate task for both participants. The
effort they put into accommodation will be appreciated and reciprocated by
members of the other language group (Giles, Bourhis and Taylor, 1977), but can
be interpreted negatively by their own group members who are present. Those
who switch into a second language, for example, may be perceived to hold political
preferences more like those endorsed by members of the other language
community (Bond, 1985) and may evoke more ethnic affirmation from members
of their own speech community in response (Bond and Cheung, 1984).

In addition, those who use a second language may discover that they are
experiencing cognitive, valuational and interpersonal shifts when they are using
their first language (e.g. Hoffman, Lau and Johnson, 1986). Kolers (1968)
showed that word associations become more dissimilar as bilinguals move from
concrete to abstract words and feelings. This finding has obvious implications for
translation issues. Less obvious is the political/social impact of shifting into a
second language. For example, Guthrie and Azores (1968) used a sentence
completion test in the Philippines and found that respondents answering the
Tagolog version mentioned traditional values and attitudes more frequently than
did those responding in their second language, English. Similarly, Chinese
bilinguals responded to compliments in a more accepting, less deflecting manner
when responding in English than when responding in Chinese (Loh, 1993). The
general conclusion from such work is that one shifts towards the position of the

Box 9.2　Ethnolinguistic vitality

The 1970s ushered in a renewed interest in the study of ethnicity and intergroup relations around the world. In order to conceptualize and integrate these studies, it became necessary to analyze the features of the socio-structural context in which intergroup behaviour occurred. Language use came to be regarded as an important reflection of inter-group relations. A group's ethno-linguistic vitality was defined as 'that which makes a group likely to behave as a distinctive and collective entity in the inter-group context' (Giles, Bourhis and Taylor, 1977, p. 308). Factors proposed to influence group vitality were as follows:

● *Demographic* – the numbers and concentration of ethnolinguistic groups within a political unit.
● *Institutional control* – the degree of formal and informal representation of the ethnolinguistic group within the social apparatus of government, education, business, mass media, religion, and so forth.
● *Status* – a speech community's prestige – historically, culturally and linguistically, as ascribed both locally and also internationally.

A group's ethnolinguistic vitality may be assessed both subjectively or objectively. Subjective assessments may show variable levels of consensus both within a given group and across the various groups in a society. How people perceive their group's ethnolinguistic vitality is related to their attitudes towards second-language learning and to their degree of speech accommodation in cross-linguistic encounters.

Source: from Harwood, Giles and Bourhis (1994).

out-group when using its language, though this does not always happen (Bond and Yang, 1982).

Clearly, language is an important medium for eliciting ethnically charged responses both for those who use it and for those who hear it. The increasing use of English as 'the language of wider communication' (Naisbitt and Aburdene, 1990) may defuse this dilemma somewhat, as the English language becomes more detached from the ideology and motivations of any particular cultural group. In the case of other language groups, however, the question of language choice for competent bilinguals will continue to be an important one, helping to determine how the interpersonal situation is itself defined (Gallois and Callan, 1991; Giles and Hewstone, 1982). This fact of intercultural life adds another layer of difficulty to cross-cultural interactions.

Second-language ability. The language competence of the interacting parties is another important issue to consider. Regardless of other factors, they must find a common language they can both use if they are to work effectively. Across different language communities, the general outcome is that one of the two parties must use his or her second language. This requirement introduces cognitive strain

---

Box 9.3) The perils of translation

Getting one's translation *almost* right can lead to amusing ambiguities for native speakers encountering the results. These ambiguities would be problematic for research purposes, but can be criticized, indulged or even cherished, when they occur in everyday cross-cultural interaction.

Airline advertisement:	We take your bags and send them in all directions.
In a hotel:	You are invited to take advantage of the chambermaid.
In a shop:	For your convenience, we recommend courteous efficient self-service.
Clockwork toy:	Guaranteed to work through its useful life.
Another hotel:	In case of fire, do your utmost to alarm the hotel porter.
Tourist agency:	Take one of our horse-driven city tours – we guarantee no miscarriages.
Newspaper report:	A new swimming pool is rapidly taking shape, since the contractors have thrown in the bulk of their workers.

Source: Davies (1989).

---

on the second-language user who may already be contending with heavy demands in dealing with the task that brought the parties together in the first place.

Additionally, second-language users face an issue of impression management; they are likely to be rated as higher in competence-related traits the more proficient they are in a foreign tongue (Hui and Cheng, 1987; Wible and Hui, 1985). This issue of appearing competent will be even more acute for a second-language speaker who is of lower status in the relationship, which is frequently the case. In fact his or her second-language ability may be one of the criteria by which performance is evaluated in the organization where he or she is working. It will affect people's willingness to entrust them with important tasks (Hui and Cheng, 1987). These concerns add further tension to the encounter for the second-language speaker. They may also lead to inaccurate communication if language uncertainties produced by higher status speakers go unchallenged because the second-language user is reluctant to appear incompetent by asking for clarifications. Not surprisingly, interactants in such cross-cultural exchanges engage in less rather than more grounding behaviour to clarify their communication. In consequence, less effective task performance is achieved (Li, 1994).

There is evidence that first-language speakers in a cross-language interaction are responsive to the lower linguistic competence of their partner (Pierson and Bond, 1982). They modify aspects of their speech, such as using more filled pauses, a slower rate of speech, a reduced complexity of sentence structure, and so forth (see also Gass and Varonis, 1985; Varonis and Gass, 1985a, on 'foreigner talk'). These 'interpretability strategies' (Coupland *et al.*, 1988) make their actual speech easier to understand, as does familiarity with non-native speech in general, a specific

Figure 9.2 Linguistic accommodation. (Source: Feign, 1986.)

non-native accent, and a particular non-native speaker (Gass and Varonis, 1984). To effect this modification, however, they must adopt a greater 'addressee focus' (Gallois *et al.*, 1988) than is normal, so that they can monitor the intelligibility of their speech for their partner. Again, this requirement shifts attention from the task at hand to the communication process itself. Ironically, there may be less redundancy of content in these vulnerable intercultural exchanges than in the less demanding intracultural conversations (Li, 1994).

As a further concern, the first-language speaker must create an interpersonal environment where confusion signals (and communication grounding!) are acceptable, even encouraged. If not, the second-language speaker may pretend that he or she understands in order to avoid embarrassment or to appear competent, with negative consequences later when events reveal otherwise (e.g. Li, 1994). Of course, the first-language speaker must be able to read these confusion signals (e.g. embarrassed laughter, nodding, furrowing of the brow, slackening of the jaw, uttering an ambiguous 'Oh?', etc.). These signals, too, are culturally variable, so the first-language speaker must attend to, and interpret, them correctly.

The net result of these various considerations is that a cross-language encounter may be equally demanding for the native language speaker as for the second-language speaker, though for different reasons. Both must pay more attention than normal to the vehicle of communication. Misunderstanding of one another's speech and failed expectations are more likely (Varonis and Gass, 1985b), with the attendant danger that negative stereotypes of one another's group will be confirmed.

In addition they must each balance a host of delicate personal, social, and cultural factors in deciding whether, and how, and how much they will accommodate to one another linguistically. Not surprisingly, most bilinguals follow the law of least effort and avoid second-language encounters outside the workplace. Instead, they socialize within their own linguistic communities.

Speech pragmatics. In faultless English, Mr Chan greets his teacher Mrs Robertson with, 'Have you had your lunch yet?' In faultless Thai, a French engineer contributes to a planning session in Bangkok with, 'Permit me to demonstrate to you several ways in which your conclusions are mistaken.' In faultless Portuguese, a Dutch visitor asks his Brazilian host, 'What time should I *really* arrive for dinner?' In faultless English, a Chinese professor states to a visiting teacher from Ireland, that his wife (who is present) did not attend university because, 'She's not very clever' (Wei and Yue, 1996). In each of these cases the speaker has accommodated linguistically to the other's language and has used that language fluently. In each case, however, they have violated the code of language *usage* in the other's culture. In Scotland one does not ask one's teacher about her eating activities; in Thailand one does not publicly contradict one's business associates; in Brazil one does not confront one's host with a demand for precision about time; in Ireland one does not make pejorative references to others about one's family members in their presence.

Speech pragmatics refers to the characteristic communication patterns, values and attitudes governing the use of language. As was discussed in Chapter 6, each culture has a normative communication style. The way in which an argument is developed (Scollon and Wong-Scollon, 1991), the directness of the presentation (Yeung, 1996), the amount of self-disclosure (Gudykunst and Kim, 1997), and the topics of conversation are all bound by convention from culture to culture (Thomas, 1983; Blum-Kulka, House and Kasper, 1989). Violation of these conventions will set into motion the misattribution cycle described earlier (Riley, 1989).

Indeed, the negative consequences may be even more dramatic if one speaks the other's language fluently. We speculate that in this case the other party will probably assume that because you know the language, you 'should have known better'. If this reasoning occurs, the other will more likely construe your talk as 'insulting' rather than simply 'ignorant', and then counter-attack (Felson, 1978). Competence in another's language can thus become a two-edged sword if one handles it unwisely.

Corrective feedback

So far, we have suggested that people from different cultures are likely to understand the same situation differently. In consequence they will behave towards one another in ways that violate one another's culturally based scripts for those situations. Such disconfirmations lead to surprise, attempts at correction, and eventually to frustration and often to the confirmation of negative stereotypes about the other's group. Where choice is involved, each party may then choose not to interact further.

Choice is often not available, as in a work setting. People may also be strongly motivated to forge a viable relationship with people from other cultures for personal reasons. In order to coordinate their behaviours more smoothly with one another then, they must learn to confront disfluencies and engage in repairs (Schwartz, 1980). Here further cultural problems are lurking.

It is worth noting before we proceed that this feeling of interaction discomfort may be vague and unfocused. So, for example, as mentioned in Chapter 6, Japanese use fewer interactive gestures than Canadians in conversations with friends or strangers (Wakushima, 1996). When interacting cross-culturally, the Canadian may then find too few interactive gestures coming from a Japanese interlocutor; the Japanese, too many. Both may be made uneasy by the departure from baseline, but unable to identify the source of their 'dis-ease'. In such a case, it is unlikely that they could remedy the situation themselves without explicit instruction on the source of the problem by informed persons. So, the following discussion applies only to problems that can be identified by the participants.

Embarrassment. Goffman (1956) defined 'face' as, 'the positive social value a person effectively claims for himself by the line others assume he has taken during a particular contact' (p. 213). When that line is brought into question by developments during encounters with others, we feel embarrassed. Embarrassment is an acute social pain which quickly spreads its 'dis-ease' to others present. It is a universal phenomenon (Ho, 1976) and highly aversive, especially for those high in self-consciousness and social anxiety (Yuen, 1991).

Cupach, Metts and Hazelton (1978) distinguish two major types of embarrassment as 'improper identity' situations and 'loss of poise' situations. The former occur when one's actions violate a social expectation associated with a role; the latter, when one's composure is undermined by events. Both abound in cross-cultural interactions.

There is some evidence that persons from certain cultural groups feel more embarrassment across a wider range of social situations than do those from other cultural groups (Yuen, 1991). As we discovered in Chapter 6, one's face is more closely tied to the behaviour of one's group members in a collectivist culture, making one more broadly vulnerable (Ting-Toomey, 1988). Singelis *et al.* (1996) administered Modigliani's (1966) Embarrassability Scale to Hong Kong Chinese, Asian American and Caucasian American respondents. They found two factors for all samples, one measuring self-embarrassability (i.e. the shame one feels at violating social expectations) and the other measuring empathetic embarrassability (the shame one feels for others who violate social expectations). Caucasian Americans reported less of either embarrassment than Asian Americans or Hong Kong Chinese. More importantly for our understanding of these differences was the fact that respondents higher in an independent self-construal reported less of either type of embarrassment; those higher in interdependent self-construals reported more of both types of embarrassment. Evidently cultural logics in how the self relates to others is the factor that determines the amount of embarrassment we experience (see also Singelis and Sharkey, 1995).

The first consequence of these cultural differences is that collectivists will tend to avoid interactions likely to lead to embarrassment more than individualists. This avoidance applies especially to cross-cultural interactions and to interactions with superiors. Secondly, they will tend to mask their embarrassment more than individualists, and so 'smooth over' the situation. Both of these tendencies will reduce the probability of generating the feedback necessary for interacting parties to know that something is amiss (e.g. Li, 1994). Without feedback, no correction will occur.

Remedial strategies. Once embarrassment has been felt and communicated, people take steps to restore face and put the interaction back 'on track' (Felson, 1978). Strategies range from apologizing, justifying and excuse-giving to ignoring the event, making a joke out of the *contretemps*, or attacking the other.

The choice of strategy is influenced by a variety of factors, including the culture of the interactants. Sueda and Wiseman (1992), for example, found that Americans were more likely to use humour and justification, while the Japanese used more apologies. These differences were explained in terms of cultural demands, which emphasize autonomy protection in individualist cultures but relationship protection in collectivist cultures (Ting-Toomey, 1988).

Both these remedial actions are normative within their own cultural context. The cross-cultural question is how they will be interpreted by members from the other cultural group. As the repair strategies occur at a critical juncture in the relationship, the outcome of this attribution process may well be decisive. With the groups described above, the danger is that the Japanese may interpret the American's humour as insincerity, just as the American may interpret the Japanese person's apology as acceptance of responsibility. Both would probably be wrong. A failure to understand the culturally based style of remediation could then set in motion a further set of embarrassing failures to communicating successfully.

Even when it is normative in both cultural groups to offer an apology, the form of the apology may vary. Garcia (1989) compared American and Venezuelan apologies following the failure to attend an American friend's party. She found

> the Americans were deferential and self-effacing towards the offended American host (using negative politeness strategies), the Venezuelans, in line with their sociocultural rules of language use, were friendly but not contrite, expressing themselves in terms of familiarity and solidarity with the host (using positive politeness strategies). (p. 3)

The Venezuelan style of apologizing is consistent with the greater closeness characterizing relations between friends. It is, however, inconsistent with the greater formality characterizing the host–guest relationship in American culture.

In consequence, the American hosts were in fact offended by the apologies professed by the Venezuelans, regarding them as callous and impolite – hardly the impression the Venezuelans wished to convey!

Similar differences arise when Japanese and Americans apologize (Barnlund and Yoshioka, 1990). The Japanese are more likely to say directly, 'I am very sorry', but are less likely to repeat the apology than the Americans. When they do apologize, the Japanese are less likely to offer explanations for their mistake and more likely to compensate the offended party by doing something for him or her. Furthermore, the Japanese are more likely to vary their mode of apologizing in response to the status of the offended party. One can easily imagine the potential for cross-cultural misunderstanding which arises from such different ways of redressing the situation!

Incompetence in one's second language may further reduce one's success at remediation. One may have been socialized to apologize in the same way as one's cross-cultural interlocutor, or one may have learned the correct way to apologize in that person's culture. One may simply not be able, however, to produce the complex linguistic utterance required (Trosborg, 1987). Negative attributions may then result.

Giving feedback. A definition of the meaning and function of feedback in communication is given by Haslett and Ogilvie (1988). Feedback refers to 'the response listeners give to others about their behavior. . . . Feedback from others enables us to understand how our behavior affects them, and allows us to modify our behavior to achieve our desired goals' (p. 385). Grounding inputs are a form of feedback. No feedback, no correction.

Feedback comes in many forms, verbal or non-verbal. It also comes at different removes from the event, immediately or some time later, as subsequent events indicate to the participants that something unintended was in fact transmitted. Feedback may also be conveyed from different sources, by the person involved or by some third party. It may be communicated in person or more impersonally, perhaps by letter. However feedback arises, it is essential for effective communication. By using it, interacting parties can engage in 'a series of diminishing mistakes – a dwindling series of under- and over-corrections converging on the goal' (Deutsch, 1968, p. 390). The cross-cultural problem, of course, is whether people from different cultural groups notice the feedback they are being given and whether they can decode it correctly.

Feedback is often negative. Nomura and Barnlund (1983) define criticism as 'the expression of dissatisfaction concerning the personal qualities or behavior of another person that is offered in face-to-face dyadic encounters' (p. 2). In light of the foregoing discussion in this chapter, it is easy to imagine how frequently these two forms of dissatisfaction may be experienced across cultural lines! But how is such criticism communicated? Nomura and Barnlund developed a culturally balanced Interpersonal Criticism Scale using interviews with both US and Japanese respondents. Responses were ordered along a dimension ranging from more passive (e.g. attempt not to show, express to a third party, respond ambiguously) to more active (e.g. make constructive suggestions, pass sarcastic remarks, insult) forms. Across genders and across many types of dissatisfactions, the US respondents expressed more active forms of criticism than did the Japanese. This outcome is consistent with Hall's analysis of high- and low-context styles of communication. As is consistent with the relational sensitivity of those from high-context cultures, the Japanese varied their (more passive) forms of criticism more in response to the status of their targets than did Americans.

When critical or other feedback is provided in a culturally different way, the potential for misunderstanding it is considerable. One may miss it entirely or translate it incorrectly. Such failures may initiate a new round of ineffective coordination and subsequent embarrassment. Even when a culturally different form of feedback is correctly understood, it may be resented. The other party may be regarded as 'blunt' or 'inscrutable' because he or she is providing feedback in a manner that deviates from the cultural conventions used by the receiver. The cultural divide widens. . . .

Accommodating one's style

Miller (1995) provides evidence of some of the ways in which Japanese and US co-workers overcome some of these difficulties in practice. All her subjects had worked together for at least a year. Sharing of jokes and complaining about others were frequent. Switching back and forth between English and Japanese speech was also used to check on clear communication. Two other procedures are more distinctive to Japanese speech than to English: 'echoing', that is to say frequently repeating a word that the other party has just spoken; and active listening, which in Japanese is expressed by frequent interjections of acknowledgement. Thus, both parties had incorporated some aspects of the other's behavioural styles into their own. Thomas and Ravlin (1995) demonstrated the benefits of such accommodation experimentally. US employees of a Japanese firm in the United States were played videotapes showing a Japanese manager who either did or did not adapt his behavioural style to the US context. The manager who did adapt was perceived as more effective and more trustworthy.

Rao and Hashimoto (1996) showed that behavioural adaptation by Japanese is widespread. They surveyed 202 Japanese managers working in Canada. They were asked to indicate which types of influencing behaviours they used with fellow Japanese and with Canadians. With Canadians they reported more assertiveness, more appeals to reason, more threats and more appeals to higher authority. These managers had thus moved substantially from the more indirect modes of influence that they found effective within their own culture. Weldon *et al.* (1996) compared the adaptations made by Chinese and US managers when disagreeing cross-culturally, rather than intraculturally. The Chinese showed greater changes than did the US managers. Intraculturally, the Chinese sought to embarrass the other party and teach them a lesson. However, cross-culturally they focused upon attempting to rectify the situation while maintaining the relationship.

Pushing for preferred relationships

As described earlier, Wish (1979) identified five dimensions of relationship variation found in the United States. We expect that these variations can be identified in all cultural groups. Furthermore, we believe that cultural systems vary in the extent to which they encourage various forms of relationship and are characterized by such different types of relationships. Although no direct evidence exists to support this belief, Hofstede's (1991) five dimensions of cultural variation suggest some testable conjectures. We hypothesize that cultural uncertainty avoidance is related to greater formality in relationship, masculinity to greater task-orientation, power distance to greater hierarchy, individualism to greater superficiality, and long-term orientation to greater competitiveness.

If these conjectures are sound, then an additional difference must be confronted by those interacting across cultural lines. Even if each party has learned to translate the other's behaviour correctly, each may be pushing the relationship in different directions. The American housewife may want a less hierarchical relationship with her Sri Lankan maid, the Swedish teacher may wish a less formal relationship with her Arab student, the English businessman may want a more cooperative relationship with his Chinese supplier, a Filipino may want a more friendly relationship with his Canadian colleague, and a Brazilian husband may want a more intense relationship with his Finnish wife. Of course, all relationships must be negotiated over time. Barriers to this negotiation may arise, however, when cultural backgrounds discourage certain forms of relationship relative to others.

Humour

Humour in corporate life helps to create an amiable atmosphere, improves worker camaraderie, removes intimidation, encourages communication and creates more productive environments. It exercises a powerful binding force in social encounters for many cultural groups (e.g. Fine, 1976). Shared humour is a potential antidote to the anxiety, tension and irritations that characterize much cross-cultural interaction. Creating humour would help compensate interactants for the effort and skill acquisition required to sustain and make intercultural exchanges more effective.

Analyses of humorous cultural products such as Alden, Hoyer and Lee's (1993) work on television advertising, finds that incongruent cognitive elements characterize humour in various cultural groups. What becomes incongruous, however, will depend on a culture's particular codes (Berger, 1975). When such codes (or common ground) are lacking, creating humour cross-culturally will be difficult. This will be particularly true when joking is language-dependent (Jordan, 1988), as in the case of punning.

Furthermore, cultural groups vary in the value placed on a sense of humour. For example, Weller, Amitsour and Pazzi (1976) reported that Israeli Jews of Eastern descent found absurd jokes less funny than did Jews of Western descent. The authors argued that Western Jews come from a culture emphasizing rational logic and hence enjoy absurdities more because they offer a temporary release from rational thought. Obviously people from a culture that is 'dour' or serious for whatever reasons will derive less social reinforcement from joking, even if they do understand the joke in the first place.

Considerable work is needed on this subtle topic of humour in particular, and 'having fun' more generally. Despite the difficulties of cross-cultural living, it often succeeds, as we shall discover in Chapter 10. We need to know much more about how people can delight one another across cultural lines.

Cross-cultural teams

We turn now to some specific instances of cross-cultural work experiences on which empirical data are available. Some types of work teams are fairly frequently composed of members of different cultural groups. For instance, student teams working on projects in North America are often ethnically very heterogeneous. How do the processes described in this chapter affect the performance of these teams?

Kirchmeyer and Cohen (1992) constructed four-person discussion groups of business students in Canada. Each group contained one ethnic minority group member. Minority group members felt less competent at communicating (Kirchmeyer, 1993), and their contributions were rated lower than those of other group members. However, Kirchmeyer suggests that diversity can become an advantage rather than a disadvantage, if conflicting viewpoints are constructively elicited. The 1992 study showed that where this elicitation had occurred, discussion quality was rated higher and the contributions of minority members were more positively evaluated. Whether these advantages of diversity can be achieved or not is likely to depend upon many variables, including the nature of the task, the leadership and language skills of those in the team and the duration of the team's work together.

For instance, McLeod, Lobel and Cox (1996) found that culturally heterogeneous groups of US students produced more ideas on how to get tourists to visit the United States than did homogeneous, Anglo-only groups. However, this task requires only the production of ideas, whereas teams are more typically required to reach agreement on some issue, and it is at this point that minority views are likely to be at risk. Watson, Kumar and Michaelsen (1993) compared culturally homogeneous and heterogeneous groups of US business students who discussed a series of case studies over a seventeen-week period. Initially the homogeneous groups were rated more effective by judges. However, by the end of the study and following consultation on improving intragroup process the heterogeneous groups were superior on the range of perspectives employed and the alternative solutions generated. Thus over time, heterogeneity evolved from a handicap to an advantage. Thomas, Ravlin and Wallace (1994) also studied business student groups discussing case studies, but their study was conducted over ten weeks in Japan. The homogeneous Japanese-only groups were rated more positively, but again there was a reduction in the difference between the ratings made by the homogeneous and the heterogeneous groups over time.

Oetzel (1996) compared student groups that were either all Japanese, all US Anglo or mixed. He also collected measures of his subjects' independent and interdependent self-construals. The groups were required to reach a decision on a case involving plagiarism in forty minutes. Those with independent self-concepts were found to speak more often and to act more competitively in all types of group. In addition, within the heterogeneous groups, the propensity of the US students to speak more and the Japanese to speak less was accentuated. This study gives us a more precise picture of some of the determinants of problematic group processes in heterogeneous teams, but the short group life-span precludes the emergence of ways of handling these problems over time.

The studies of student teams that we have surveyed in this section tell us something of what may happen in newly formed teams, but leaves wide open what happens in teams that last longer, or in teams that are not composed of students, or in teams where not everyone is reasonably fluent in English. Few studies are available of other, more long-lasting, work teams. Bilbow (1996) made video recordings of departmental meetings within a multinational business firm in Hong Kong. During the time reserved for formal reports, Chinese participants spoke almost as frequently as did Western participants. However, in free discussion periods, the Westerners spoke more than twice as frequently as the Chinese. Furthermore, two-thirds of all the contributions from Chinese team members were reactive to earlier talk, whereas only one-quarter of Western talk was reactive. These figures were based on those members of the teams who had similar status.

This type of analysis cannot give us direct evidence on whether this pattern of speaking impeded the effectiveness of the teams. Bilbow (1996) suggests that Chinese and Westerners have different perceptions of the purpose of meetings, as we may expect from the discussion of how culture shapes the perception of situations. Another possibility is that the distribution of talk was influenced by the fact that meetings were conducted in English. Du-Babcock *et al.* (1995) studied teams of students in Hong Kong participating in a business game. Some sessions were videoed with the teams working in English while in others they worked in Cantonese. They found that in the English language sessions there was a marked reduction in non-verbal feedback provided by the less proficient English speakers. Presumably the stress of producing coherent discourse short-circuits or freezes normal channels for non-verbal feedback to others, thus impeding effective communication within the team, especially about confusion being experienced by members.

Another form of multicultural work team whose members typically interact with one another for relatively short periods of time is the airline flight crew. Since the language used globally for air traffic control is English, a number of airlines from non-English speaking nations use pilots whose first language is English, while remaining flight crew are mostly recruited locally. Merritt (1995) interviewed expatriate and local pilots as to the benefits and frustrations they experienced while working in three such multicultural airlines. The most frequent reported frustrations were language problems and strained cockpit atmosphere. Some pilots reported that where speech is too rapid or unclear, valuable time must be spent on clarifications, to the detriment of safety. Strained cockpit atmosphere can be explained by differences in the values of cockpit crew members. Merritt and Helmreich (1996) found that respondents from Asian flight crews endorsed deference to authority, while US pilots expected team members to speak up if they perceived the pilot to be acting incorrectly. These value differences can contribute not just to strained atmosphere, but to increased risks to safety in emergency situations. Even with a monocultural crew, Helmreich (1994) provides evidence of the serious consequences of poor communication both within the crew and between the crew and traffic control. Analyzing the causes for the crash of a Colombian airline flight that ran out of fuel while waiting to land at New York, he found that language difficulties and failures to communicate within the crew owing to high-power distance values were the key elements in a wholly avoidable disaster.

While value differences may accentuate risk in some circumstances, Bochner and Hesketh (1994) detected other undesirable consequences among those working together over longer time periods. Within an Australian bank, they found that non-Anglo employees endorsed greater levels of allocentrism and power distance than did Anglo employees. Furthermore they felt more discriminated against and were more in favour of policies promoting multiculturalism within the bank.

The studies reviewed in this section have suggested that multicultural teams face certain initial problems which make it likely that they will operate less effectively than monocultural teams. Over time this situation may reverse, if teams evolve structures and procedures that harness the potential benefits of their diversity (e.g., Watson, Kumar and Michaelson, 1993). Smith and Noakes (1996) present a model of a series of four phases that teams will need to pass through in order to achieve this synergy:

1. *Establishing fit*. In this phase, the team will need to become aware that the differences between team members are not simply personality differences, but arise from the variance in values and the meanings placed on behaviours that members bring to the team.
2. *Tasks and procedures*. Next, the team will need to work out ways in which the team can do its work, despite the fact that there is wide divergence in preferred ways of proceeding. This will include not just the basic elements of the assigned task, but more fundamental issues such as the management of time and the language(s) to be used.
3. *Associations among individuals*. As time passes, it is likely that sub-groups will arise within the team of those who find one another most congenial. These sub-groups will probably reflect divergences in cultural values, and the team needs to find ways of ensuring that emerging cliques do not impede the effectiveness of the team as a whole.

4. *Participative safety*. A multicultural team will be taking maximum benefit from its diversity when it arrives at the point where all members feel safe to contribute to task accomplishment without social or professional risk to themselves or others.

The study of Watson, Kumar and Michaelson (1993) indicated that some student groups were well on their way to this goal after seventeen weekly meetings. However, whether effective working can be accomplished in this time, or indeed at all, will depend upon the magnitude of diversity, the quality of a team's leadership structure and many other variables. Programmes of diversity training are also widely employed in an attempt to enhance the prospects of success. However, the success of such programmes may depend upon whether they too are implemented in ways that respect the varying values of those who attend. Kirkbride, Durcan and Tang (1990) for instance suggest that team members from a vertical collectivist culture such as Hong Kong respond better to didactic input and instruction by senior persons, rather than the highly participative training designs favoured by persons from individualist cultures. Effective training programmes for multi-cultural teams are therefore likely to be those that do not press team members to work in a particular way, but that focus instead upon the specific problems that arise and how they may best be overcome.

Multinational and joint-venture business organizations

Improvements in transportation and communication over the past two decades have ensured that among the larger business organizations, those that prosper will be those that conduct their business on a global basis. In consequence, manufacturing firms from wealthy countries are increasingly choosing to locate their production facilities in countries where labour costs are low. Thus we find an explosive growth in the creation of factories in certain key regions of the world. US firms have created a range of '*maquiladora*' (Spanish for 'factories') in Northern Mexico. US, Japanese, Hong Kong and Western European firms have invested heavily in China and in other Southeast Asian nations. There has also been substantial investment in Central and Eastern Europe.

In some instances, these investments are made directly by the foreign-owned multinational business firm. However, there is a growing trend for firms to negotiate 'joint-venture' partnerships with local organizations. This is seen as an attractive option by investing firms because local partners are thought likely to have a much better understanding of local conditions affecting employment, as well as negotiations with governments, marketing arrangements and so forth. The scale of these recent changes is enormous. By 1994, there were around 45,000 foreign direct investments and joint ventures in China, whereas a decade earlier there were hardly any. Even within the small nation of Hungary there were over 15,000 by the same date (United Nations Commission on Trade and Development, 1995). These two nations and Mexico are the three developing nations in which investment has been greatest in recent years. Although the ownership structures of joint ventures and direct investments by multinational firms differ, in both cases the result is that a relatively small number of expatriate managers work with a much larger number of local employees, most of whom work at the more junior organizational levels.

These developments derive from economic pressures, and multinational firms are often well aware of the cultural problems that such investments entail. Trevor (1983), for instance, entitled his study *Japan's Reluctant Multinationals*. If we consider what might be the nature of these problems, we must change the level at which we pitch our analysis. When considering multicultural teams in the preceding section, we focused upon the ways in which divergence in the values of individual team members can affect the success or failure of a team. There will be many multicultural teams within joint-venture organizations and these types of value divergence will be much in evidence. However, when we focus upon the culture of whole organizations, different issues come to the fore. In particular, what differentiates one organizational culture from another is not so much value difference but difference in specific practices. We can therefore expect that joint-venture organizations will experience difficulty in meshing their favoured practices. As we saw in Chapter 8, organizational practices such as selection, reward allocation and negotiation procedures are conducted in rather different ways within different nations. The joint-venture partners who invest in a particular project must determine whether they will attempt to impose the procedures with which they are most familiar or whether to accept guidance from local partners as to what will work best within the local culture.

Studies of joint ventures and multinational firms indicate that when they seek to impose globally uniform procedures they are at best only partially successful in doing so. Child (1994) reports on interviews conducted with expatriate managers within joint ventures in Northern China during the late 1980s. The principal area in which problems were reported were in those aspects of human resource management that are most directly linked to cultural value differences. For instance, attempts to use rule-based procedures for selecting those to be promoted or to be trained abroad, to introduce or extend pay differentials and to introduce appraisal systems were all to some extent problematic. US firms were found to push most strongly for the imposition of these systems. Japanese managers were more inclined to report that aspects of normal Japanese practice do not work well in China. In consequence they were more directive and made less use of the participative techniques that are widespread in Japanese organizations. European managers reported having attempted similar changes to those espoused by US management, but were more inclined to compromise when difficulties arose. Worm (1996) provides more recent information on a rapidly changing scene, based on interviews with both Scandinavians and Chinese. He summarizes the numerous cultural differences facing twenty-one Scandinavian firms operating in China in terms of a contrast between universalism and particularism. Worm concludes that universalist Western management techniques can operate successfully, provided that they are introduced in ways that preserve face, give respect to elders and include the building of trust-based personalized relationships.

One way in which companies seek to overcome cultural problems within joint ventures is by appointing local managers whose cultural background is more similar to that of the joint venture partner. For example, Smith, Wang and Leung (1997) found that many Hong Kong managers had been appointed by Western companies as managers of joint venture hotels in China. The cultural problems reported in these hotels were substantially fewer than in the hotels with Japanese or Western managers. However, senior local Chinese managers were more dissatisfied when working with a Hong Kong Chinese manager than with a Japanese or Western manager (Leung *et al.* 1997), perhaps because they believed that they were more able to replace a Hong Kong manager than a Japanese or Western one.

Child and Markoczy (1993) examined joint ventures in Hungary. There they found that Japanese firms had encountered more difficulties than US firms. The idiocentric Hungarian employees found the Japanese emphasis on teamwork problematic, just as the allocentric Chinese had trouble with the individualistic assumptions of their US partners. The contrast between idiocentric and allocentric values can also be helpful in understanding the problems that arise when Japanese and other Pacific Asian firms operate in Western countries. White and Trevor (1983) report that among Japanese firms in the United Kingdom, there is a marked contrast in the attitudes of UK employees within manufacturing plants and banks. Manufacturing plants have been established in predominantly working-class areas with strong communitarian values. Japanese locations were in areas where working-class employees hold predominantly allocentric values. Management in these areas is well respected and the plants are productive. In contrast, within banks in the City of London, a predominantly middle-class workforce with more idiocentric values feels much less loyalty to their foreign-owned bank, and frequently changes employers if there is a career advantage in doing so. This job-hopping conflicts with Japanese conceptions of lifetime employment and company loyalty.

The analysis thus far might give the impression that joint ventures only encounter culture-based difficulties if they are based upon partnership between Pacific-Asian nations and Western nations. The differences in such instances may be particularly large, but that does not mean that they are absent from other collaborative ventures. Shenkar and Zeira (1992) surveyed the levels of role conflict and role ambiguity experienced by chief executives of forty-four Israeli joint ventures. They defined a measure of 'culture distance' based upon Hofstede's (1980) scores for the nations represented in the joint ventures. Role conflict was found to be unrelated to culture distance, but role ambiguity was highest when culture distance scores were low for power distance and masculinity and high for individualism and uncertainty avoidance.

Even within Europe, joint ventures between nations with relatively similar value profiles can be problematic. Laurent (1983) surveyed the values of French managers and found that those working in multinational firms endorsed values that were closer to the overall mean for his French sample than those who were working in domestic French enterprises. Presumably the difficulties encountered in the multinational firms had pressed the French managers within these to reassert their core French values. Suutari (1996) asked managers working in a Finnish multinational firm to characterize the behaviours of their partners in several different European nations. In most cases the characterizations they provided were consistent with predictions derived from Hofstede (1980), thereby supporting the view that the organizational culture of this particular multinational firm sampled still does not transcend national differences.

Lichtenberger and Naulleau (1993) summarized a survey of 216 French–German joint ventures. More than half of those surveyed reported that cultural differences caused tensions. Specific issues reported as problematic included differences in work methods, differences in hierarchical relationships and different perspectives on time. Ironically, the most frequently reported problem was the difficulty of convincing company headquarters that cultural differences were important! It is clear that multinational firms and joint ventures face many of the difficulties outlined in this chapter, and that they will continue to struggle to find the best ways of handling them.

One more time: Mr Chan and Mrs Robertson

Having read our analysis of different types of cross-cultural interaction in this chapter, readers may find a review of the encounter between Chan Chi Lok and Jean Robertson in Chapter 1 revealing. Many typical areas of cross-cultural difficulty related to the themes identified in this chapter can be detected in their exchange.

Before extracting some of the key problem domains, it is worth noting that the prognosis for Mr Chan and Mrs Robertson is at present not hopeful. Both appear unaware of the capacity of culture to influence behaviour pervasively. They know that the other comes from a different culture, but appear not to understand any of the conventions associated with the behaviour of people from the other culture. In consequence every act is interpreted by the other 'culturo-centrically', i.e. in terms of the receiver's cultural norms. Confusion and irritation are the inevitable results. Not until they become culturally mindful (Langer, 1989) is any progress possible.

Such mindfulness may develop, of course. Their many and various types of frustration may prompt them to search for more sophisticated attributions than merely labelling the other 'troublesome' or 'uncivilized'. They may express their grievances to a knowledgeable cultural mediator (Bochner, 1980), pick up an informative book on the other's culture, see an illuminating movie, or hear a stimulating lecture on cultural differences in behaviour – there are many potential resources for cultural awakening. Certainly Mrs Robertson will need to receive some feedback on the linguistic difficulties she creates cross-culturally or her job is in jeopardy! Given the increasing appreciation of the cultural component in second-language learning (Valdes, 1986), Mrs Robertson has a good chance of developing cultural awareness should she continue teaching English in Hong Kong. As for Mr Chan, it is hoped that an internationalizing university curriculum (Featherman, 1993) will both stimulate him to broaden his cultural awareness and teach him some skills for dealing with people from different cultures.

Anxiety

Mr Chan is worried about this meeting; his course grade and possibly his graduation plans are at stake. These are extremely important concerns in Chinese culture (Stevenson and Lee, 1996). Partly for interpersonal support, he brings his friend to the appointment. After Mrs Robertson insists the friend wait outside, Mr Chan's anxiety increases. He has greater trouble concentrating on his teacher's English and he begins to stutter. Robertson's confrontive words and interruption further disrupt his sense of control in the situation. His performance declines further, so that he has no words to resist Mrs Robertson's abrupt termination of their meeting.

Mrs Robertson seems without anxiety during this cross-cultural encounter. We believe that her sense of security-in-the-world is sustained by her total innocence about cultural difference and by the mutual use of her mother tongue throughout the encounter. Mrs Robertson acts in fact as if she were dealing with a difficult kindergarten child in Scotland.

Language

One can only hope that Mrs Robertson speaks more slowly and less colloquially in class than she does in her office. Expressions such as 'a wee bit slippery', 'never bother' and others place extraordinary demands on second-language speakers and the statement, 'I doubt you are twenty minutes late' is in fact a literal disclaimer of what Mrs Robertson actually believes. Peculiar questions like, 'You don't get it, do you?' are a perplexing construction for learners of English with their apparently contradictory stance towards the same issue. Chan's 'yes' affirms that he does *not* understand; the English convention is to say 'no' in that case, so Mrs Robertson is surprised by Chan's unexpected answer. Many languages, like Chan's native Cantonese, present questions both positively and negatively, requiring responders to affirm or to deny in their answer. Ambiguities are thereby reduced (see Fig. 9.1).

Mr Chan also creates a few problems for his teacher. He makes many common errors in grammar and vocabulary, as one would expect. The connotations of English are too much to master at this stage of his English language acquisition and his statement that Mrs Robertson 'stinks' produces a dramatic reaction indeed! The pragmatics of his English usage are similarly undeveloped and Chan's question about whether his teacher has yet eaten lunch is judged as impertinent by Mrs Robertson. It is a direct translation from a typical Cantonese greeting around noon-time and an appropriate conversational opener from Chan's perspective. Even when Mrs Robertson learns this Chinese convention, she may well continue to regard it as too personal a greeting, especially from lower-status students.

Proxemics

Doors are boundary markers of personal territory in individualist cultures. To knock and enter before receiving permission is to insult and challenge the occupant. Chinese, indeed collectivist, conventions about doors and territory are different. Chan knows Mrs Robertson is expecting him, so he announces his arrival by knocking and immediately opens the door. Mrs Robertson spends much of the remaining encounter seeking to re-establish her authority, an authority Chan does not realize he has challenged.

His direct physical approach to Mrs Robertson's chair further offends her. Chan does not detect the coldness with which his teacher directs him to sit, but finds it unusual to be positioned so far from someone he is addressing one-to-one. Chinese comfort zones are much closer than Scottish, and Chan begins the process of confirming the stereotype that Westerners such as Mrs Robertson are '*mo yan ching*' (strict, without compassion).

Time

One way people from individualist cultures protect their freedom and deperson-alize control issues is to insist on careful scheduling of time. Given the power disparities in collectivist cultures, people have a more flexible attitude towards commitments generally, and about appointments in particular. By being twenty minutes late, Mr Chan has insulted Mrs Robertson and put her under time pressure, since she has a lunch appointment with her departmental chairman. This sense of pressure leads her to usher Chan out of her office before their business can be concluded, in turn offending him.

Attributional style

The 'cult of effort' is very important in collectivist cultures (Stevenson *et al.*, 1985), since by trying hard or appearing to do so no one challenges the existing order or shows their lack of loyalty (Bond, 1991c). In individualist cultures, greater explanatory emphasis is given to the ability factor (Stevenson and Lee, 1996). Variations in ability are consistent with the uniqueness theme in individualist cultures (Snyder and Fromkin, 1980) and justify individual resistance to group pressure for conformity. Consequently, Mr Chan emphasizes his effort in Mrs Robertson's class, while she stresses his lack of ability, in their negotiation about Chan's performance.

Chan also makes a group-level attribution about the task difficulty when he tells Mrs Robertson that, 'We all found your test very difficult.' His teacher interprets this statement as an influence strategy that uses the tactic of coalition formation (Kipnis, Schmidt and Wilkinson, 1980). This cognition generates reactance (Brehm, 1966) and leads to the individual-focused retort that Chan should assume personal responsibility and not rely on others. Mrs Robertson also believes that Chan is using his family responsibilities, a heavy burden in collectivist cultures, as an excuse by attributing his absence from class to his duties as son and elder brother. She rejects the priority given to family over school.

Lying. External attributions are common in collectivist cultures as strategies for saving superiors' and subordinates' faces when potential conflict arises (Ting-Toomey, 1988). Often a palpable lie will be mutually accepted by both parties in order to preserve harmony. In individualist cultures lying violates the social contract and is condemned when it is detected. Mrs Robertson's statement that Mr Chan is 'a wee bit slippery' is in fact a mild assertion of her belief that he is speaking falsely.

Praise and compassion

In collectivist cultures superiors have considerable authority and discretion. Subordinates attempt to soften the use of this power by allying themselves with their superior through demonstrations of loyalty, praise, respect markers and other tokens of appreciation. In individualist cultures, leaders are bound by established rules and procedures which are negotiated in some detail by those involved. Objective criteria and the facts assume a legitimizing function in this process. Those led are expected to inform themselves of the rules (criteria, schedules, standards) and work accordingly.

When Mr Chan correctly detects his teacher's resistance to passing him, he continues praising Mrs Robertson. She interprets this move as a form of inter-personal bribery and focuses Chan back on the issue of ability. Chan responds by informing his teacher about the difficult family circumstances in which he must function. Mrs Robertson is adamant about Chan's prime duty to his 'job' and incredulous when he openly asks for a 'compassionate pass'. For Mrs Robertson to do so would constitute a betrayal of her 'professionalism'.

Politeness issues

This encounter is fraught with mutual politeness violations. We have already mentioned how Chan breaks Western time and space codes. Linguistically, he uses the impolite 'huh?' rather than the more polite 'pardon'; he says that his teacher 'stinks'; he raises 'irrelevant' issues, such as the class party; and he offends against Scottish pragmatics by asking if Mrs Robertson has eaten and by addressing her throughout as 'teacher' rather than using her given name.

Mrs Robertson violates Chinese codes of communication by the directness of her speech and her blunt disagreements with Chan. She also interrupts him. Mrs Robertson may also appear impolite by her 'bossiness', ordering Chan's friend to leave and terminating the interview so quickly. Ironically, Chan regards such behaviour as acceptable, given the higher status of teachers in Chinese culture.

Indeed, from his cultural perspective Chan is being polite in the extreme: he uses the honorific 'teacher' throughout; he smiles and gazes attentively at Mrs

Robertson, praises her teaching directly but also indirectly by reporting the class' evaluations; refers to her time as 'precious'; and accepts her every topic shift without verbal resistance. Unfortunately, these behaviours are regarded as impolite by Mrs Robertson or misconstrued as ingratiation attempts.

Other issues?

The above are some of the main problem areas for Mr Chan and Mrs Robertson. There are others that readers will be able to detect as their sensitivity develops. All these differences produce palpable consequences, and are difficult for both parties to resolve satisfactorily. To do so requires sustained uphill effort by both parties.

Summary

The prognosis for effective communication across cultural lines does not appear to be good. Freedle (1979) has defined culture as 'a set of interactive schemata for habitual ways in which interacting individuals can dynamically discover what each person intends to convey given the immediate context' (p. xiii). When cultural backgrounds differ, the interacting parties are cast adrift from these shared schemata, including language. The use of different systems for decoding meaning frequently results in mutual misattributions and consequent difficulties in coordinating interaction.

These misattributions will often reinforce and justify pre-existing negative stereotypes about the cultural out-group member that function to separate the parties further. Despite these centrifugal forces, they may still be motivated to commit themselves to the added time, attention, embarrassment and repair work necessary for understanding one another's communications accurately and hence coordinating effectively. Having done so, they may discover that they do not share similar goals for the relationship. In the face of such obstacles to communication, one might wonder if relationships are ever successful across cultural borders! If so, how can satisfactory outcomes be accomplished? We take the issue further in the next chapter.

The consequences of cross-cultural contact

**The people of this world have been brought together
technologically, but have not yet begun to understand what
that means in a spiritual sense.
We have to learn to live as brothers or we will perish as fools.**

Martin Luther King

In the previous chapters we have discussed many features of cross-cultural contact that make it a difficult challenge for all parties concerned. Despite its complexity, effortfulness and danger, however, many people continue to live their lives interculturally. Indeed, multiculturalism is fast becoming a fact of life as we approach the twenty-first century. It is important for us to know what happens to people when they interact with persons from different cultural traditions over long periods of time. Migration is increasing, presenting us with serious social psychological issues worldwide (Bierbrauer and Pedersen, 1996) and offering rich and plentiful opportunities for researchers to assess the course of human adaptation (Rogler, 1994).

Cross-cultural adaptation

In a comprehensive review, Anderson (1994) examines the four models of the adaptive process that have dominated the literature since the 1950s. The first is the recuperation model, based on the concept of 'culture shock' (Oberg, 1960). More recently the medical connotations of this model have been elaborated with a variant focusing on psychological crisis and identity diffusion (Garza-Guerrero, 1974). The second type is the learning model which emphasizes the need to accrue the knowledge and skills necessary to function in a new set of socio-cultural reinforcement contingencies (Guthrie, 1975; Taylor, 1994). Appropriate communication skills and social routines must be learned through the mechanisms of operant conditioning. The third is the 'journey' model, charting the process of moving from ignorance and rejection of the foreign culture to understanding

---

Box 10.1 Tourism and its impact

Tourism is big business. In 1986, 287 million persons spent at least one night overseas for purposes other than making money. This tourism generated official receipts of US$94,600 (World Tourism Organization, 1986). These numbers are increasing and constitute an important component of globalization (Robertson, 1990).

Domestic immigration is also relevant for our purposes, as it may bring persons from one cultural group into contact with those of another. As Bochner (1982, Box 9.1) indicates, however, most tourism to any destination is characterized by contact that is short term, recreational, infrequent, numerically unequal and observational. Often even this rather superficial contact is buffered by tour guides who act as mediators, interfacing with locals on behalf of the tourists (Cohen, 1985).

Despite the sheer amount of tourism there has been little research on its psychological and social impact. Pearce (1981) has noted that tourists experience 'environment shock' (i.e. minor health problems arising from ecological relocation). Cort and King (1979) have documented 'culture shock' in tourists, especially older tourists and those with intolerance for ambiguity.

The reactions of hosts to tourists vary from delight to hostility – they may bring valued foreign currency or the 'poisoned chalice' of environmental degradation (Sisman, 1994), cultural destruction (Smith, 1989), prostitution, crime and gambling (Mathieson and Wall, 1982). Community backlash against tourists and tourism is common (Pearce, Moscardo and Ross, 1991). Pearce (1982) summarizes the consequences of tourism for the host culture:

> tourists appear to have maximum social and psychological impact on their hosts where the host communities are small, unsophisticated and isolated. This impact may be a powerful one, either in direct inter-personal encounters or in subtle indirect influences on the visited community. When the receiving society is technologically more advanced and the affluence gap between tourists and hosts narrower, the contact experience has less impact. In this instance tourists may develop friendships with the hosts and the visitors can sustain local social institutions as well as prompting pride in the visited community. The negative effects are not restricted to interpersonal friction, but also include indirect stress to the hosts through noise, pollution and environmental degradation. (p. 208)

Urry (1990) notes the potent effects of the 'tourist gaze'. Since tourists value being away from their normal context, they seek out situations and experiences that emphasize differentness. This creates a demand for 'staged authenticity', which may focus upon landscape, buildings, museums, revived folklore or various types of interpersonal encounter. This in turn places increasing demands for personal and cultural change on those who live and work at tourist destinations.

---

and acceptance (e.g. Bennett, 1986). The fourth is the equilibrium model. It conceptualizes cross-cultural adaptation 'as a dynamic process of tension reduction' produced when manifested cultural differences disrupt the person's internal balance. The disturbed person then modifies cognitive schemes, behaviour, or the

Box 10.2 The transition experience

Some writers have argued that the cross-cultural experience does not shatter ego integrity, but instead leads to a higher level of maturity (e.g. Adler, 1987). In describing this transition, Adler (1975) points out that it may be stimulated by the confrontation between different cultural systems:

> The dynamics of the cross-cultural experience at the personal level represents the process of positive disintegration. Such experiences can occur whenever new environments of experience and perception are encountered. Although many different reactions and responses can take place in this confrontation of cultures, the greatest shock may be the encounter with one's own cultural heritage and the degree to which one is a product of it. In the encounter with another culture, the individual gains new experiential knowledge by coming to understand the roots of his or her own ethnocentrism and by gaining new perspectives and outlooks on the nature of culture. Throughout the transitional experience the individual is presented with differences and complexity. When differences cannot be ignored, they become distorted. This distortion gives rise to emotions that each person must come to understand experientially. In so doing, learning, self-awareness and personal growth take place. (p. 22)

Anecdotal evidence suggests that such inspirational personal outcomes can emerge from the intercultural encounter (Storti, 1990). Indeed many outstanding social scientists believe that the stimulus for their cross-cultural research and theorizing derives from their personal experience of living and working in different cultures (Bond, 1997). Certainly the hope of such change motivates some exploration across cultures, and fuller scientific documentation of it would be most useful in helping us to understand the cross-cultural experience.

relationship with the new culture until a readjustment to subjective harmony has been achieved (e.g. Grove and Torbiörn, 1985).

As Anderson (1994) notes, each of these models has shortcomings. In place of a careful analysis of the steps involved in adapting to a new culture, researchers have focused pragmatically on outcomes or have indulged themselves in extravagant prose about romantic ordeals and character-building experiences. In place of these alternatives, Anderson proposes that, 'cross-cultural adaptation is a commonplace process of learning to live with change and difference – in this instance, a changed environment and different people, different norms, different standards, and different customs' (p. 299). As such, cultural adaptation may be linked to the literature on general adjustment and constitutes just one type of 'transition experience' (Bennett, 1977). The process may thus share much in common with adapting to bereavement, starting college or giving up alcohol.

Anderson (1994) uses this assessment of previous work as a basis for proposing a model for cross-cultural adaptation. It involves a lengthy series of adjustments, each involving a motive to achieve an outcome, a thwarting of that desired outcome, the production of varied new responses to achieve that outcome, until satisfaction is achieved. When adapting to a new culture, these thwartings are many, simultaneous and unending, often leading to frustration and other negative reactions including apathy, temporary withdrawal or departure. Host nationals are involved in this process, of course, by either rewarding or punishing the culture learner. The learner is processing their reactions and also dealing with the consequences of mastering new skills elicited from his or her in-group members. Both types of response to the culture learner may be negative, making the adaptation process even more aversive.

As Anderson (1994) concludes, 'Cross-cultural adaptation is cyclical, continuous, and interactive' (p. 307). What sustains the culture learner is '(a) a willingness to open oneself up to new cultural influences, (b) a willingness to face obstacles head-on by the use of instrumental strategies, and (c) and perhaps most crucial of all, a resolve not to run away' (p. 313). These motivations require time and peer support (Smith *et al.*, 1963) for their sustained deployment. Anderson believes that,

> How any of us responds at any moment depends on our current appraisals of the stimulus situation. These appraisals in turn depend on both personal and situational factors. . . . The pattern and strength of our motivations, our current emotional state, commitments, beliefs and expectations, the degree of our interaction with host country inhabitants, and the relative power of our personal resources, for instance, all have an influence on the coping responses that are chosen. They interact with such features of the situation as its novelty, imminence, potency, or uncertainty to induce selection of a particular response to a particular stimulus at a particular time. (p. 314)

Not surprisingly in light of the above complexity, there are many possible 'endpoints' to this process. Anderson (1994) identifies six types of adapters:

1. The Returnees: these leave the new culture quickly, abandoning their attempt to cope with early frustrations.
2. The Escapers: these remain in the new culture and minimize contact with an aversive, alien reality by immersing themselves in familiar activities already mastered in their culture of origin.
3. Time Servers: these stay at their post, adapt well enough to do their job passably, but are mildly and chronically depressed, eager to return.
4. The Beavers: bury themselves in the task-related aspects of their work, and achieve at high levels. Interpersonal adaptation is minimal and they avoid social contact with the host culture and its members.
5. The Adjusters: do well at work, mix with members of the host culture, have an intellectual understanding of the host culture, but are still actively striving to cope, to achieve a better fit.
6. The Participators: these have overcome the manifold obstacles to mastering a new culture, have mastered its cognitive, affective and behavioural

requirements, and have become full, effective participants in the life of their new culture.

This is a loose categorization of the outcomes to a complex process. As Anderson points out, 'From a survey of the literature, it is clear that there are probably as many kinds, and levels of adaptation as there are situations and individuals adapting' (p. 318). The resocialization required of cultural migrants is no different in its demands from more typical resocializations throughout life (Taylor, 1994), and it produces as many varied outcomes.

Acculturation

Whereas models of cross-cultural adaptation focus more on processes of adjustments over time, models of acculturation focus more upon the contents or outcomes of that complex process. Acculturation concerns the changes that result in both people and groups of people as a result of contact among people of different cultures. It is most often examined in people who relocate, such as exchange students and immigrants, but has also been studied in indigenous groups within plural societies (Berry and Kim, 1988).

Outcome measures

A plethora of acculturation measures has been used. Ward (1996) summarizes this range:

Church's (1982) review of sojourner adaptation detailed the investigation of acculturative outcomes, including broader worldview, reduction in ethnocentrism, and greater self-awareness and self-esteem. Empirical studies have also relied on attitudes toward host culture (Ibrahim, 1970), psychological distress (Masuda, Lin and Tazuma, 1982), perceptual maturity (Yoshikawa, 1988), mood states (Stone Feinstein and Ward, 1990), health evaluations (Babiker, Cox and Miller, 1980), feelings of acceptance and satisfaction (Brislin, 1981), the nature and extent of interaction with hosts (Sewell and Davidsen, 1961), the acquisition of culturally appropriate, behaviors and skills (Bochner, Lin and McLeod, 1979, 1980), academic competence (Perkins, Perkins, Guglielmino and Reiff, 1977), and job performance (Harris, 1972) as assessments of sojourner and immigrant adaptation. (pp. 126–7)

Some attempts have been made to simplify this array through the use of factor analysis to group similar outcomes empirically into coherent concepts. Ward and her colleagues have carried forward a sustained programme of research focused on two separate dimensions of adaptation, psychological adjustment and socio-cultural adaptation (e.g. Ward and Kennedy, 1993). The first set of outcomes refers to intra-psychic consequences of coping with novel, demanding environments and is characterized by physical and psychological well-being. The second set of outcomes refers to the interpersonal consequences of this coping and is characterized by social and behavioural competencies.

Empirically, these dimensions are moderately and positively related. This inter-relation is understandable, since successful social adaptation arises in part from psychological well-being and leads to a feeling of greater self-efficacy which enhances psychological well-being, and vice versa. Ward (1996) argues, however, that these two factors must be separated because 'they are largely predicted by different types of variables and show different patterns of variation over time' (p. 127). Other investigators have drawn similar distinctions between the psycho-logical/somatic and social/task domains of acculturation (e.g. Hammer, Gudy-kunst and Wiseman, 1978; Kealey, 1989).

Acculturation outcomes across time

The complexity of the assessment issue becomes clearer when acculturation is examined across the variable of time-in-new-culture. Lysgaard (1955) first proposed the 'U-curve' model of adjustment, later elaborated by Oberg (1960) in his stages of honeymoon, crisis, recovery and adjustment. These discussions of 'culture shock' constituted the early 'recovery' models of adaptation mentioned earlier, and were subsequently extended to re-entry problems when sojourners returned to their cultures of origin (Gullahorn and Gullahorn, 1963).

Evaluating such models requires longitudinal research that charts the psychological and socio-cultural dimensions over time in the same subjects. Cross-sectional research is inappropriate here, since short-stayers may be those, such as

Box 10.3 **Perceived domains of intercultural effectiveness**

Different observers have offered different lists of attributes and skills regarded as important in successful adaptation across cultural lines (Ruben, 1976; Furnham and Bochner, 1982). Recently, Hammer (1987) has integrated these various lists of abilities and presented his questionnaire to sojourners, that is to say people who have lived abroad for various periods of time. He concluded that there are three basic skill domains perceived to be involved in effective cross-cultural living. The first has an intra-psychic focus and involves the ability to tolerate and manage the stress that arises from relocating to a novel physical and social environment. The second skill domain involves the capacity to establish and nurture relationships with strangers from a different culture. The third involves the skills of effective communication, such as the ability to deal with miscommunications and make repairs, to understand the other's point of view, and so forth. Readers may wish to relate these three dimensions of perceived competencies to Ward's (1996) two factors of measured outcomes.

tourists, whose type of contact with the culture would not be likely to produce the same types of reactions. Ward (1996) reviews such research and concludes,

> in the main, then, longitudinal research suggests that sociocultural adjustment follows a learning curve, with adaptation problems decreasing steadily, and that psychological adjustment difficulties peak in the early stages of transition . . . and are more variable over time. (p. 132)

The U-curve model is, then, simply wrong – there is no initial euphoria for those who are staying for any length of time, but rather psychological malaise. Recovery is variable – some do, some do not. On the other hand, socio-cultural adjustment follows an upward-sloping curve, probably levelling off as the sojourner achieves an adequate fit with the new cultural environment.

Cultural identity

What is the price of cross-cultural adaptation for one's cultural identity? The historical legacy of colonialism has left many people worried about the potential of intercultural contact for the destruction of native heritages. In extreme forms there is genocide or ethnic cleansing; in other forms, there is assimilation, whereby a stronger cultural group absorbs the weaker, so that its distinctive organization, rituals, dress, architecture, crafts and so forth simply disappear.

At the individual level there are spirited concerns expressed about the loss of cultural identity which may arise out of intercultural contact. Alatas (1972) has identified the 'captive mind syndrome' where a person rejects his or her traditions and uncritically swallows those of another, more powerful cultural group. Others have lamented the rejection of their traditions by people eager to 'pass' into a different cultural group, as sometimes happens with immigrants (Taft, 1973). Park (1928) introduced the term 'marginal man' to designate a person torn between two incompatible traditions and consigned to the periphery of each. This problem is especially acute for returnees who find themselves rejected by their own cultural group members when they return 'home' (Kidder, 1991).

Not all contact leads to rootlessness or cultural loss. Threatened groups may segregate themselves from other groups and their members adopt chauvinistic, ethnocentric attitudes towards these other groups. In effect their cultural identity has been reinforced through cross-cultural contact. Such strengthening of identity may then lead to a spirited assertion of one's own cultural forms, such as a use of the mother tongue rather than the *lingua franca* (e.g. Giles and Viladot, 1994). That contact thereafter becomes limited to specialized 'middle-men' and confined geographical areas in order to contain the potential for cultural degradation (e.g. Pye, 1991).

There are obvious emotional and political overtones to many of the concerns voiced about loss of cultural identity. To assess this question scientifically, one must first ascertain those beliefs, values or attitudes, and behaviours that distinguish people of one cultural group from those of another. Persons can then be said to have 'lost' their original cultural identities to the extent that they endorse a position removed from that of their own group, and approach the position of another cultural group.

Work by Rosenthal and Feldman (1992) indicates how multifaceted this approach to the construct of ethnic or cultural identity can be. It includes subjective self-evaluation (by which ethnic label does one choose to describe oneself?); the evaluative meanings given to one's ethnic group membership (positive or negative?); the cultural practices of one's group (friendship choices, language use, food preferences, attendance at festivals and so forth); and finally, the importance one attaches to these practices. If these aspects of identity are not highly correlated, then cultural contact may affect only certain aspects of one's ethnic or cultural identity.

To evaluate this reasoning, Rosenthal and Feldman (1992) assessed each of these elements of identity among first and second generation Chinese immigrants to Canada and Australia, in comparison with Chinese students in Hong Kong. As expected, they found only moderate linkage between their various measures of ethnic identity. Cultural practices and labelling oneself as Chinese declined in the first generation, but fell no further in the second. Subjective evaluation of one's identity and the importance attached to Chinese cultural practices did not decline at all (see also Keefe and Padilla, 1987). The authors conclude that behavioural aspects of cultural identity may change slowly over time, but that the internal components are more resistant to change.

Many extant measures of cultural/ethnic identity have this multidimensional character. For example, one factor analysis of the Suinn–Lew Asian Self-Identity Acculturation Scale (Suinn, Ahuna and Khoo, 1992) isolated five interpretable factors: (1) reading/ writing/cultural preferences, (2) ethnic interaction choices, (3) ethnic pride, (4) generational identity, and (5) food preferences (Wang *et al.*, 1993, provide another example). Even if researchers confine themselves to behavioural markers of identity, similar complexity energies. Horvath, Marsella and Yamada (in press) developed an Ethnocultural Identity Behavior Index reflecting participation in various ethnocultural traditions. They isolated three related, but separable, factors of behavioural cultural identity: cultural activities, social interaction and language opportunities.

With such differentiation, there is considerable potential for each individual to develop a unique profile of cultural identity. However, researchers all too often combine these separate aspects of ethnic or cultural identity into a single index, thereby precluding discovery of distinctive relationships for each aspect of identity (e.g. Cuellar, Harris and Jasso, 1980; Kodama and Canetto, 1995; Leong, 1996). So, for example, Ward's (1996) measures of psychological and socio-cultural adjustment will probably be associated with different aspects of one's cultural identity (see Ward and Kennedy, 1994, for related findings).

This multidimensionality of acculturation domains suggests a better approach: instead of conceptualizing adaptation to a new culture as a zero-sum process necessitating loss of one's heritage culture, it could be conceptualized as adding to one's existing repertoire. LaFromboise, Coleman and Gerton (1993) call this the 'alternation' model 'which posits that an individual is able to gain competence within two cultures without losing his or her cultural identity or having to choose one culture over the other' (p. 395). Under this approach, a person's willingness or ability to engage in behaviours typical of both one's own and the other cultural group is assessed. One then may be high or low in identification with either cultural group. Horvath and Singelis (in press) took just this approach to classifying their Hawaiian student respondents as Western, traditional, culturally alienated or bicultural. They found, as predicted that biculturals had as high an interdependent self-construal as the traditionals, and as high an independent self-construal as the Western(er)s. This bidimensional approach has also been used among Hispanic Americans (Szapocznik, Kurtines and Fernandez, 1980) and Israeli Arabs (Zak, 1976).

The bidimensional approach is compatible with Berry's (1990) work on acculturative attitudes (see p. 283), and suggests a resourceful, situation-responsive individual who may have one set of behaviours available for use with members of the heritage culture and one for use with members of the host culture. We expect that inconsistencies in the literature about cultural identity and psychological/socio-cultural adaptation arise in part because of whether researchers have construed and scored cultural identity as a unidimensional or bidimensional construct (Ward, 1996).

The self and cultural identity. Weinreich (1986) has defined cultural or ethnic identity as 'that part of the totality of one's self-construal made up of those dimensions that express the continuity between one's construal of past ancestry and future aspirations in relation to ethnicity' (p. 308). This is a phenomenological approach that requires the respondent to locate his or her heritage cultural traditions with respect to his or her self. Other cultural traditions may be located in this perceptual space as well, so that this approach is ideal for examining the impact of many relevant cultural groups in relation to the person's self (Weinreich, 1996). These various identifications can then be related to indices of psychological functioning, such as self-esteem, which may also be derived from Weinreich's (1989) Identity Structure Analysis (ISA). This technique has been applied to a number of situations where multiple cultural influences may be at work, e.g., for children of immigrant parents (Kelly, 1989), or for those involved in intergroup hostility (Weinreich, 1992).

ISA is also applicable to those growing up in peaceful, multicultural societies. Weinreich, Luk and Bond (1996) examined the identity patterns of university students in Hong Kong who are exposed to a variety of Western, Chinese and other cultural groups including Vietnamese refugees. Through ratings of personality constructs, these respondents showed equal degrees of identification with Westerners and with Hong Kong Chinese and lesser degrees with other Chinese or Asians. Greater identification with Hong Kong Chinese was associated with parental and peer identification along with higher levels of self-esteem, as one might expect. However, greater identification with Westerners was also associated with peer identification and self-esteem. Identification with other Chinese groupings was correlated with parental identification, again as one might expect, but also with identity diffusion, the 'lack of a completely coherent sense of cultural grounding' (Weinreich *et al.*, 1996, p. 109). The authors use these results to argue that cultural identifications are multiple, connected to a variety of socializing influences, and fashioned by the individual in light of his or her aspirations and the cultural influences on offer in a multicultural setting.

Acculturation of values. Many social scientists regard values as the fundamental variable distinguishing one cultural group from another and we have adopted a similar perspective in this book. Not surprisingly then, researchers have often studied value change as a measure of acculturation (e.g. Feather, 1979). The typical procedure is to study differences in values across generations of immigrants. Feldman, Mont-Reynaud and Rosenthal (1992) examined differences across first and second generation Chinese immigrants to the United States and Australia, comparing their values on eight domains with those of their host Anglos and with Chinese who stayed in Hong Kong. Change towards host values was rapid in the first generation, slower thereafter. The rate and extent of the acculturation depended on the value domain, however, with tradition showing rapid change and integrity of the family unit showing little change. Given that this value change is away from those held in one's culture of origin towards one's new host culture, this shift could be labelled a loss of cultural identity.

Georgas *et al.* (1996) have found evidence for such loss in family values when Greeks emigrate. They show, however, that the loss is greater for females and younger migrants than for males and older migrants. In addition, the loss is less in Canada where integrationist policies are in force than in European countries where assimilationist ideologies dominate. So, both social and political factors appear to moderate the acculturative impact of the immigrant experience.

As Weinreich (1986) has argued, one may also examine acculturation in values by asking respondents from different generations of immigrants to compare their values with those of other groups. Cameron and Lalonde (1994) compared such similarity ratings for first and second generation Italians in Canada. First generation respondents grouped themselves with family, friends and other immigrants holding Old World values; second generation respondents used a more complex patterning of values and located themselves further from Italians and closer to Canadians. Again, immigration appears to result in culture loss, at least from the perspective of one's heritage cultural group.

The complex pattern of identifications seen in second generation immigrants may also be found, however, with adolescents in multicultural societies. Bond and Mak (1996) had Hong Kong students rate their own values along with those ascribed to typical group members from various Chinese and Western cultures. These normal adolescents rated themselves as more similar in values to Singaporeans than to Hongkongese, their in-group, who in turn were more similar than

Chinese from Taiwan or the People's Republic of China (excluding Hong Kong). In this sense, it may be possible to find evidence for cultural 'loss' without the experience of emigration. Enough cultural alternatives are on offer in ethnically diverse societies to permit a creative acculturation to occur.

Acculturation of personality. The ideal approach to studying acculturation in personality is longitudinal. However, to our knowledge no such studies have been done. Cross-sectional studies using immigrant cohorts and comparing their scores with profiles of those from the immigrants' culture of origin and the immigrants' host culture are a second best. Using this approach it is essential to ensure that one is using equivalent personality measures across the cultures.

McCrae *et al.* (1997) assured such equivalence by first checking for structural equivalence of the NEO PI-R (McCrae *et al.*, 1996). They then compared the responses of bilinguals to the English and Chinese versions of the questionnaire to ensure translation equivalence. With these checks in place, they were able to assess acculturation effects. By comparing ratings of Hongkong- and Canadian-born Chinese made by *both self and other raters*, they found that Canadian-born Chinese were higher in total extroversion, in total openness, and in the trust, altruism and tender-mindedness facets of agreeableness. They conclude, 'Canadian culture appears to promote prosocial behavior and attitudes and openness to some aspects of experience more than does Hongkong Chinese culture' (p. 24).

By then comparing Canadian- and Hongkong-born Chinese with Canadians of European ancestry, McCrae *et al.* (1997) are able to make defensible assessments of ethnic differences in personality. They find that, 'Chinese undergraduates, regardless of country of origin [and length of residence in Canada], score somewhat lower than North Americans of European ancestry on measures of E and especially E3: Assertiveness and E4: Activity' (p. 29). So, this complex design and careful analysis enables one to draw conclusions about both acculturation and ethnicity on a comprehensive, universally applicable measure of personality. We hope that it sets the standard for future research involving other cultural pairings.

Predicting cross-cultural outcomes

Outcome studies

The contact hypothesis (Amir, 1969) maintains that interaction between members of different groups can reduce intergroup prejudice and hostility. Subsequent research addressed to this hypothesis however has progressively narrowed the range of circumstances under which this improvement is likely to occur (Amir, 1976; Hewstone and Brown, 1986). In fact, Stroebe, Lenkert and Jonas (1988) found that student exchanges can lead to a sharpening of negative rather than positive stereotypes. This is likely when the quality of contacts is negative, as shown by Haddock, Zanna and Esses (1994) among ethnic groups in Canada and

---

Box 10.4 **Remigration – going 'home' again**

Many persons return to their heritage cultures from another country where they have been living for a period of time, in some cases all their lives. The motives for their return may be economic, political, or socio-cultural; in most cases such a return is voluntary, but in the case of the returnees' children, they typically have no say in the decision to relocate.

The experience of these remigrants is often difficult (Harvey, 1983; Kidder, 1991), especially for children. Tamura and Furnham (1993) found that girls encountered more adjustment problems than boys and that complaints/difficulties increased the longer the child had been overseas. Georgas and Papastylianou (1996a) discovered that negative attitudes held by these children about their new countrymen increased with time, rather than decreasing. Many opted for a strategy of integration (Berry, 1990), rather than assimilating back to their heritage cultural practices and identity (Georgas and Papastylianou, 1996b).

Empirical studies of elder returnees are few. Despite the numbers and importance of returning students (Westwood and Lawrance, 1988), little is known about their re-adjustment. Business people have been more frequently studied (Harvey, 1989). In a comprehensive study of US managers and their spouses, Black and Gregersen (1991) found that younger persons, those who have spent more time overseas, and those whose social status and housing conditions decline experience greater adjustment difficulties at work, with home nationals, and with the general environment.

More careful conceptualization and subsequent research is needed on remigration (Martin, 1984).

---

by Islam and Hewstone (1993a) among religious groups in Bangladesh. Discrimination is then likely to occur.

At the intergroup level open hostility is sometimes found; where clashes are suppressed, resentment and hatred may be simmering beneath the surface. Even in harmonious intergroup climates, such as that in Canada, a national ethnic hierarchy exists in the preferences citizens hold about the various cultural groups in the country (Berry and Kalin, 1979). Ethnocentrism is present, with all groups favouring their own group (along with the dominant Anglo group), relative to other out-groups. Negative perceptions of other groups are reciprocated in the perceptions reported by those groups. Many social scientists, however, would regard such an attitudinal configuration as the best that could be expected in any multi-ethnic situation.

At the interpersonal level, a scattered selection of results is available for different types of contact. For example, Furnham and Bochner (1986) conclude that 'The evidence is overwhelming that many overseas students do not know a single host national intimately, even after many years of residence in the country being visited, and are therefore quite isolated socially from the host society' (p. 16). After a year in Australia, Japanese exchange students had acquired very low levels of sociolinguistic competence (Marriott, 1993b); Asian students in Australia report a wide range of difficulties in everyday social situations (Barker *et al.*, 1991). Minority racial and ethnic group members make fewer contributions than Anglo majority group members in decision-making teams (Kirchmeyer, 1993). Concerning intercultural marriages, divorce rates tend to be higher than those for mono-cultural marriages (Carter and Glick, 1970; Ho and Johnson, 1990). Research on helping behaviour generally shows compatriots receiving more assistance than foreigners (Bochner, 1982, pp. 21–2).

Such results appear rather piecemeal and uncoordinated. Also, they typically involve persons of one culture interacting with persons from another culture in a host society. So, their interactions and outcomes are influenced by a host of factors specific to the intergroup history and cultures of the groups involved and the political-social context of their encounter. Generalization thus becomes difficult. Fortunately, studies which sample from more than a single nation are beginning to emerge (Berry and Kwak, 1996), which will enable more robust conclusions to be drawn. Nonetheless, the existing results generally support the expectation that cross-cultural relationships are more difficult to manage than are mono-cultural relationships. However, social scientists with a pragmatic agenda have moved beyond the issue of average outcomes to ask which are the specific predictors of successful outcomes when people interact across cultural boundaries.

Cultural predictors. One might expect that persons socialized in stable, exclusive collectivities would suffer more intensely when culturally relocated than would those socialized for greater self-direction and interactional flexibility. The former have more to lose, and the latter more to gain, from new environments.

A study by Carden and Feicht (1991) supports this reasoning. They examined 'homesickness' in Turkish and American females who were living in campus dormitories away from their home towns. The more collectivist Turkish women reported being much more homesick than did the American women. These reactions occurred within the respondents' own culture. It is probable that a similar pattern of homesickness would occur when people travel overseas, particularly more allocentric persons and those from more collectivist cultures.

Additionally we can use Hofstede's (1980) dimensions of culture (or those of any other multicultural study of values, e.g. Schwartz, 1994) to advance a more broad-brush hypothesis. Cluster analysis of his results revealed that some countries, such as Denmark and Sweden, had closely similar profiles; other pairs such as Italy and Mexico were much more dissimilar. A simple prediction would be that persons travelling to nations with greater cultural dissimilarity in values will experience more difficulties. This hypothesis could be further refined by examining each dimension of cultural difference separately. Areas of difficulty and ways of overcoming them could be derived from knowledge of each underlying dimension of difference. Triandis, Brislin and Hui (1988) used just such a strategy for guiding training 'across the individualism–collectivism divide'. Other Hofstede dimensions could be similarly treated.

Other approaches (e.g. stages of economic development – Harbison and Myers, 1959) could be taken to measure the degree of cultural difference. The general findings from research in this vein is, however, consistent: greater similarity, less adaptive difficulty (Ward and Searle, 1991). This outcome also holds for *perceived* degrees of cultural difference (Furnham and Erdmann, 1995; Osbeck, Moghaddam and Perreault, 1997). The distinction between psychological and socio-cultural adaptation should be retained in this work, as culture distance has been shown to affect these two outcomes differently (Phalet and Hagendoorn, 1996). Finally, language differences could be included as a type of culture predictor, since language difficulties are routinely correlated with psychosomatic problems (Chataway and Berry, 1989) and positive attitudes towards the host group (Smith, Griffith, Griffith and Steger, 1980).

Political predictors. There is little research on the effects of political policies on the adaptation of refugees, immigrants and other sojourners (Berry, 1984). However, 'Empirical findings suggest that the probability of acculturative stress can be reduced if participation in the larger society and maintenance of one's heritage culture are welcomed by the policy and practice of the larger society' (Berry, 1991b, p. 17). These practices might include government-sponsored language-learning or cultural orientation programmes, temporary housing and health-care provisions, job training and placement assistance, the easy granting of citizenship, etc. We speculate that such buffering provisions are more likely to be provided in countries characterized by extensive observance of human rights (Humana, 1986), itself correlated with a country's individualism (Hofstede, 1980), integration (Chinese Culture Connection, 1987), or egalitarian commitment and low scores on hierarchy (Schwartz, 1994) (see Bond and Chan, 1995).

Demographic predictors. Results from recent work are consistent with those found earlier in predicting the personality dimension of authoritarianism:

> In all cases higher status respondents held more positive attitudes (towards other cultural groups) than did those of lower socio-economic status. These differences were particularly evident for educational level, but the same pattern was generally exhibited for the occupational status and income measures as well.' (Berry, Kalin and Taylor, 1980, p. 275).

Similarly, groups of higher status within a country's social hierarchy held more positive intergroup attitudes. The authors interpret these results in terms of the greater security felt by members of these privileged status cultural groups. We expect that one's group security in the social hierarchy, especially economic security, will be related to measures of out-group prejudice in *any* cultural setting. This prejudice will then be reflected in measures of perceived discrimination towards ethnic out-groups, which is then related to problems in their socio-cultural adaptation (Aycan and Berry, 1996).

Box 10.5 Perceived discrimination

One can experience discrimination being directed towards oneself as an out-group member, or towards one's group. In a series of studies, Dion (1986) has shown that 'perceiving discrimination being directed against oneself leads to stress and negative affect, as well as heightened identification with one's ingroup' (p. 176). Such an identification may then lead to a sense of one's group being relatively deprived and discriminated against. This sense of group discrimination is predictive of militant protest (Dion and Kawakami, 1996) and is associated with ethnic segregation, at least among visible minorities (Moghaddam, 1994).

Aycan and Berry (1994) show that higher perceived discrimination assessed from Turkish migrants to Canada is associated with their poorer socio-cultural adaptation. Dion, Dion and Pak (1992) find that problems in psychological adaptation are associated with perceived discrimination by those who are lower in hardiness, a composite personality syndrome involving a sense of control, adventure, and commitment (Kobasa, 1979). Women who are members of visible minorities are more likely to have lower self-esteem, perhaps because they are in a position of 'double jeopardy' by virtue of both their culture and their gender (Pak, Dion and Dion, 1991).

As Phalet and Hagendoorn (1996) argue,

The relation between acculturating group and dominant cultural group is very often (though not always) an unequal one. Many newly arrived immigrants lack the financial, social, and cultural resources to compete for success in the host society. Limited resources and low status or prestige together install and perpetuate social inequality between immigrants and their hosts. . . . (p. 134)

As in Aycan and Berry's (1996) study, this social inequality exercises its impact on external (socio-cultural) adjustment when international, as opposed to internal, migration is assessed.

Social inequality also makes adaptation more difficult for females (e.g., Carballo, 1994). The status accorded to women by a receiving country will open or close the opportunity for women to take on new roles (Population Crisis Committee, 1988). New opportunities may then bring them into conflict with the role expectations of their heritage culture, thereby putting them at greater psychological risk, as Naidoo and Davis (1988) found among South Asian women in Canada. Age also affects adaptive outcomes. Acculturation before primary school usually proceeds smoothly (Beiser *et al.*, 1988). Thereafter, difficulties increase (Ebrahim, 1992), as it becomes progressively more difficult to learn the skills necessary to adapt.

Social factors. Considerable effort has been made in social psychology to identify the social conditions conducive to positive intergroup contact. Stephan (1985) reviewed this extensive literature and extracted thirteen features of the

---

Box 10.6 **Social factors promoting intergroup harmony**

1. Cooperation within groups should be maximized and competition between groups should be minimized.
2. Members of the in-group and the out-group should be of equal status both within and outside the contact situation.
3. Similarity of group members on non-status dimensions (beliefs, values, etc.) appears to be desirable.
4. Differences in competence should be avoided.
5. The outcomes should be positive.
6. Strong normative and institutional support for the contact should be provided.
7. The intergroup contact should have the potential to extend beyond the immediate situation.
8. Individuation of group members should be promoted.
9. Non-superficial contact (e.g. mutual disclosure of information) should be encouraged.
10. The contact should be voluntary.
11. Positive effects are likely to correlate with the duration of the contact.
12. The contact should occur in a variety of contexts with a variety of in-group and out-group members.
13. Equal numbers of in-group and out-group members should be used.

Source: from Gudykunst (1991), p. 80.

---

contact situation which facilitate positive attitude change towards the out-group when individuals interact across group lines.

This list was culled from intergroup research conducted for the most part with persons from individualist cultures and sharing the same national culture. Some propositions will need to be modified in other cultural systems and across cultural lines. For example, contact across status lines (2), where competence differences exist (4) is commonplace in collectivist cultural settings. When such intergroup contact is normative, as in multicultural organizations, positive rather than negative outcomes could well be expected (see also Gudykunst, 1988). Stephan's (1985) list, is, however, a useful starting point in developing research hypotheses and in structuring more fruitful outcomes.

The most widely studied social factor relating to personal, as opposed to group, outcomes is social support. Psychological adjustment is related to the quality of support from co-nationals (Ward, 1996), especially that provided by one's spouse (Torbiörn, 1982). Support from members of the host culture is also related to psychological well-being (Stone Feinstein and Ward, 1990), although the quality rather than the quantity of that contact is probably the key factor (see also Islam and Hewstone, 1993a) Those who have more contact with members of the host culture, however, are better placed to learn the necessary interaction skills and so often show higher socio-cultural adaptation (Ward and Kennedy, 1993).

Personality predictors. Church (1982) summarizes a host of studies that examined the impact of personality measures on different types of outcome measures. As the measures had been taken from various sources and provided by various types of sojourners interacting in various contexts with various host cultures during various decades since 1950, the consequent yield of results is understandably complex!

Some simplification can be achieved by using the broad taxonomy of Big Five personality dimensions (see Chapter 4) and Ward's two dimensions of accultur-ation. Conscientiousness, which includes facets related to internal locus of control, self-efficacy and achievement orientation, is consistently related to psychological adjustment (Ward, 1996), and sometimes socio-cultural adaptation (e.g. Phalet and Hagendoorn, 1996). Extroversion yields conflicting results, which Ward (1996) attributes to the importance of a personality fit with host culture norms for this dimension. Neuroticism has been less widely examined despite its link to the intercultural anxiety that retards intercultural adaptation (Gao and Gudykunst, 1990). Of course, neuroticism impedes adaptation, especially psychological adap-tation, to any life change. Neurotics are thus often screened out from programmes involving voluntary cross-cultural interaction.

Less work has been done on agreeableness. Ruben and Kealey (1979), however, found that in a carefully conducted study that (non) self-centred role behaviour and display of respect before departure were both predictive of loss of both psychological adjustment and effectiveness (socio-cultural adaptation?). Each of these characteristics is related to certain facets of agreeableness (e.g. modesty, altruism), so the results are suggestive.

Openness to experience has probably been tapped by earlier measures of toler-ance for ambiguity which Ruben and Kealey (1979) found to predict effectiveness. Openness also relates negatively to measures of intolerance. So, we can expect that high openness promotes the contact across intercultural lines that leads to the learning of adaptive social skills (i.e. socio-cultural adaptation).

Attitudinal predictors. Berry has developed a typology of acculturative atti-tudes by identifying two basic orientations, the first towards one's own cultural group, the second towards other cultural groups:

> One pertains to the maintenance and development of one's ethnic distinctiveness in society, deciding whether or not one's cultural identity and customs are of value and to be retained. The other issue involves the desirability of inter-ethnic contact, deciding whether relations with other groups in the larger society are of value and to be sought. (Those familiar with multiculturalism policy will recognize two of the key elements in the policy: heritage maintenance, and social participation and sharing). (1990, p. 14)

If one dichotomizes both orientations, a four-fold classification of attitude constellations can be developed: Integration, where both groups' cultural traditions are valued; assimilation, where one rejects the heritage culture and embraces other cultures; separation, where one clings to the heritage culture and rejects others; marginalization, where one rejects both. Berry and his colleagues have developed culture-specific measures of these four attitude constellations (Berry, 1990, 1997). The constellations of integration and assimilation are positively related to psychological adjustment; separation and marginalization to maladjustment and psychosomatic problems (e.g. Berry *et al.*, 1989). Extending this work, Ward and Kennedy (1994) showed that stronger identification with host nationals predicted better socio-cultural adaptation.

Berry's acculturative attitude constellations thus appear to be implicated in both forms of adjustment, psychological and socio-cultural. We expect, however, that these constellations exercise their effects through the basic personality dimensions of neuroticism (Schmitz, 1992) and openness to experience (Schmitz, 1996). Specific facets of these dimensions may be especially important, e.g. vulnerability in neuroticism and values in openness. Psychometric improvements now permit the assessment of adaptive outcomes as they relate to personality through a variety of mediators, such as acculturative attitudes (see McCrae and Costa, 1996, for such a model).

Skills. Bochner (1986) and Furnham (1989) have approached the problem of cross-cultural adaptation from a skills perspective. Depending on which particular cultural groups are involved (Triandis, 1995b), people will need specific knowledge about the rules of interaction with their hosts. This can be gleaned from a variety of information sources and may include guidance about being less presumptuous that one is correct (Schneller, 1989) and about making culturally correct attributions (Bhawuk, 1996; Brislin *et al.*, 1986) for the many unexpected interpersonal behaviours that occur in the new cultural context.

Knowledge about these normative patterns of behaviour in the new culture will then have to be put into practice. Argyle (1979) has identified seven social skills that can be developed in persons: perspective-taking, expression, conversation, assertiveness, emotionality, anxiety control and affiliation. Many of these skill areas involve aspects of non-verbal behaviour, which are so important in regulating interaction. Once a culture's position on these interpersonal dimensions is known, people with 'deficits' can learn to respond differently in various contact situations. So, for example, Collett (1971) successfully taught Arab non-verbal skills to normally 'stand-offish' Englishmen, thereby enhancing the impressions they gave to Arabs later. Wolfgang (1992) has created a manual for the training of non-verbal behaviours. Deshpande and Visweswaran (1992) review the evidence that various types of cross-cultural training for expatriate managers can be effective. Some persons will already have culturally fitting skills through personality or previous cross-cultural experience (Parker and McEvoy, 1993). Where requisite

Box 10.7 The culture assimilator

The culture assimilator is a resource for teaching people to improve the accuracy of their cross-cultural attributions. Brislin *et al.* (1986) developed a culture-general assimilator by collecting a variety of cross-cultural misunderstandings that arose in connection with each of eighteen universal themes in social interaction (e.g. dominance–submission). Readers are presented with a number of these detailed 'critical incidents' and invited to choose the correct interpretation for the impasse between the participants. Informed commentary is then provided on each of the possible choices, so that students improve their understanding of the cultural logics involved. An example follows. Read through and work out your own answer before you look at the box on the next page:

OH! SO PROPER!

The English class that Martha Anderson is helping to teach is going very well. The Vietnamese, Cambodian and Central American students seem to enjoy one another and are adjusting to each other well. The men and women frequently help one another. Having very little exposure to other cultures, Martha is amazed at their ease of interaction and often asks the instructor about the different behaviour she observes in the classroom. They are all very polite to each other even when they do not seem to be able to understand each other. They are also especially polite when they are talking to her or to the other instructors, always addressing them in very formal polite titles. Martha would like to develop relationships with some of the students and to make them feel more at home. In one particular instance she is in private talking with Vien Thuy Ng. She asks him to call her by her first name, saying, 'My name is Martha, please call me Martha!' Vien responds by acknowledging that he does indeed know her name but, 'Would it not be good to call you by your proper title?' She persists by saying that is too formal and that they can just be good friends and go by first names. Vien just smiles and nods, but he does not return to the English class the next week.

What could explain this kind of situation?

1. Vien Thuy Ng thought that Martha was too aggressive and forward to him, as women do not talk to men.
2. Martha should not have singled out one individual person. Vien did not like being singled out.
3. English class is too complicated for Vien and he does not really know what is going on.
4. Martha violated a rather intricate system of hierarchy that exists in South Asian countries.

skills are already present or have been successfully enhanced, greater socio-cultural adaptation will be possible (Ward and Searle, 1991).

This is a more microscopic approach to cross-cultural adaptation than the personality approach and must take into account situation-specific requirements (Dinges and Lieberman, 1989) and features arising from the particular pairing of

---

Box 10.8 The culture assimilator – explanations

Rationales for the alternative explanations:

1. In many Southeast Asian countries, the roles of women may be restricted in some ways, such as approaching men. However, this class is in the United States and there are some students from other countries as well as the instructors interacting together. The fact that the class is mixed and that the students seem to get along fairly well suggest that this is really not the reason for Vien's disappearance from the class. There is a better answer; please select again.
2. It is true that individuals from Asian societies do not like to be singled out. However, in this instance, this minor correction was not a singling out. Martha was talking with Vien alone so there would be no great embarrassment involved since others were not present. There is more going on; please select again.
3. This conclusion can hardly be drawn as the scenario states that all seemed to be going well in the class. Please select again.
4. This is the best answer. Southeast Asians have a very intricate system of status hierarchy. Martha violated it by trying to downplay her role or perceived status. Her attempt may not have been the total cause for Vien not wanting to return, however. Probably if she had just suggested it and left it open for Vien to choose he may have felt more comfortable. Her persistence in the matter forced Vien into a situation where he had to relinquish a value that affected his whole worldview or lifestyle.

Source: taken from Brislin et al. (1986).

---

cultures involved (Triandis et al., 1993). It is very useful for focused training programmes, but does, however, require accurate knowledge about the various skills required for adaptation to a specific culture and a detailed assessment of the sojourner's level of these skills.

Communication skills will be an important component of such programmes (Kealey, 1989). Milhouse (1993) identified five, culturally equivalent components of conversational skills: expressiveness, composure, altercentrism (focus on the other), interaction management, and 'vocalics' (paralinguistic considerations). Higher ratings on these components were associated with higher assessed quality of interaction by both Germans and Americans. Of course, each of these skill components must be judged in culture-specific ways, suggesting that skill training will have to be very detailed and accurate. Martin and Hammer (1989) identified additional communication skill components.

One important skill worth identifying separately is language competence. Greater fluency in the mother tongue of the other cultural group increases socio-cultural adjustment (Ward, 1996). This outcome probably arises because such fluency reduces the uncertainty and anxiety we experience with out-group members (Gudykunst, 1995), thereby facilitating interaction across cultural lines. Through this interaction, we are better able to master the correct pragmatics of language use and avoid setting up misattributions about our intentions.

Of course, as the vast majority of cultural sojourners or immigrants will have no access to any training programmes, they will have to adapt as best they can. It is here we believe that broad personality dispositions will influence their willingness and ability to learn these necessary skills during their daily encounters across cultural lines. Broad dispositions such as agreeableness and extroversion will enable them to find 'culture friends' or mediators to guide them and form a support network to sustain them while they are learning to function effectively.

Meta-cultural awareness in mediating outcomes

Marriage is an intense and continuous relationship that demands all our skills and commitment to sustain. The potential for misunderstanding and conflict is enormous. Not surprisingly, cross-cultural marriages have higher divorce rates than within-culture marriages (Ho and Johnson, 1990). This outcome undoubtedly arises because the whole range of cultural differences already discussed becomes relevant in this comprehensive relationship, engaging considerable conflict (Ting-Toomey, 1994a).

Fontaine (1990) argues that viable intercultural marriages provide a useful case study for intercultural relations generally, because 'the partners must have developed workable strategies for dealing with diversity and/or be receiving benefits that offset the greater losses.' (Fontaine and Dorch, 1980, p. 230). Fontaine maintains that such couples create 'inter-cultural microcultures' that permit them to negotiate a shared life. These microcultures emphasize a focus on the ecological context of the tasks at hand, as one way of avoiding a power confrontation between 'my' cultural way versus 'your' cultural way. When differences do arise, partners often attribute their difficulties to a different cultural background rather than to the personality of their spouse. This attributional style accords culture an external reality that becomes one feature of the task constraints to be considered and accommodated. Fontaine reports that what develops in time is an intercultural microculture that has significant departures from either spouse's cultural heritage – a creative synthesis without a sense of cultural loss (see also Ting-Toomey, 1994b).

Fontaine's (1990) analysis of intercultural marriages identifies two key components to their success. Firstly, partners must be cognizant of their partner's cultural heritage and, secondly, they must accord that heritage legitimacy in their dealings with one another. Both developments enhance the process of externalizing culture. It becomes a separable aspect of oneself, as does the cultural heritage of one's partner. When one becomes capable of considering culture as a distinct component of an individual's heritage, one has developed 'meta-cultural' awareness.

Such awareness arises out of personal or direct cross-cultural experience that has induced mindfulness (Langer, 1989) and led one to understand the importance of culture in shaping behaviour. Subsequently, when dealing with people from different cultural traditions, one begins factoring in their cultural background. Their traditions can be understood as explaining their 'idiosyncrasies'. One is thereby able to accommodate to the other's heritage when it is appropriate and to make allowances for otherwise 'inappropriate' behaviour from one's partner. Defensiveness in communication decreases and negative attributions are softened.

We believe that meta-cultural awareness is an important, emergent discovery moderating successful cross-cultural outcomes. If studies of cross-cultural interaction involved those with such awareness, the typically negative outcomes could well be different. Such projects will have to be quite sophisticated, however, since meta-cultural awareness is a two-handed process: many have seen the cartoon of the Japanese man's extended hand hitting the bowing American's head as they first meet. Each is demonstrating his meta-cultural awareness and the result is a failed first step in their interaction! Since both parties are cross-culturally knowledgeable and now know that their partner is also, they will have to negotiate which culture's rules to use and when. A new layer of complexity has been added to the communication process. Meta-cultural awareness, however, will probably make them more patient and forgiving in this negotiation.

Improving cross-cultural outcomes in organizations

A cautionary note is in order here, before psychologists wrestle further with how to enhance cross-cultural interactions in any context:

> Clearly no amount of psychological engineering is going to make poverty-stricken ethnic groups inclined to welcome or even accept interactions with representatives of wealthy or powerful cultures. Nor are members of the better-placed cultures likely to feel comfortable in the presence of persons from grossly disadvantaged societies. However, psychology can make a contribution in instances where there is a minimum of realistic conflict, and yet a great deal of mutual distrust, hostility and even violence. (Bochner, 1982, p. 37)

We agree with the spirit of Bochner's assessment that certain historical, political, economic and social situations drastically limit the impact of whatever psychological knowledge can be applied to improve an intercultural encounter. These other factors often contribute to the unsupportive intergroup environment identified by Stephan (1985) and discussed earlier. They must generally be addressed politically and may require the reallocation of resources in a more egalitarian way.

Some of these political questions need to be addressed at the international level where they involve disputes between nations or common fate problems, such as environmental degradation. Such issues are beyond our mandate of this book. Instead, we shall focus on cross-cultural issues as they surface in organizational life, both within-country and in international operations. Ruben (1989) has pointed out that the work on cross-cultural adaptation and competence has been driven by a pragmatic focus: the need to explain failures in overseas placements, to develop strategies for personnel selection, and to test methods for preparing sojourners. These needs reflect the task concerns of the diplomatic corps, international aid agencies, multinational corporations and other organizations.

The practitioner-focus of these needs has meant that careful, published research has either not been carried out or only published in-house rather than publicly. Growing concern about human rights, especially in North America, has however, added an urgency for guidance about how to address cultural issues in organizational life. This interest has fuelled the publication of many books on the effective management of diversity (e.g. Cox, 1993; Hoecklin, 1993). We add our input to this ground swell, using the analyses in the previous chapters to support our suggestions.

Organizational culture-in-action

The basic issue here is whether the organization is aware that culture shapes interpersonal behaviour and institutional practices with consequent effects on newcomer adaptation. If so, the question then is whether the organization is willing to negotiate its policies and procedures or whether it will expect its personnel to 'cut their toes to fit the shoe', as the Chinese adage puts it. It will be appreciated that the policies and procedures of any organization may advantage persons of certain cultural groups. They will generally be in senior positions and reluctant to negotiate what they expect to be their own disempowerment. It is probable that organizations established and maintained by people from cultures low in power distance will, however, be less resistant in these respects (Bond, 1991b).

Given a supportive organizational culture (Hofstede *et al.*, 1989), how can its members be assisted to work more effectively across cultural lines? A number of factors are important (Tung, 1981; Black, Gregersen and Mendenhall, 1992). We will consider the issues facing the local workforce and the overseas placement separately.

The diverse workforce. This requires the following:

1. An organizational policy explicitly supporting cultural pluralism.
2. Top management that endorses and models cultural accommodation (Thomas and Ravlin, 1995).
3. Practices that reinforce a common organizational identity (Gaertner *et al.*, 1993) and thereby make superordinate goals salient.
4. Provision of training programmes (Landis and Bhagat, 1996), so that members of particular ethnic groups can achieve positions throughout the status levels of the organization, thereby promoting cross-cutting of ethnic boundaries.
5. Use of objective, behaviourally anchored criteria in assessing performance across a variety of job functions. These criteria should include the ability to work effectively across diverse cultural lines.
6. Institution of procedures designed to enhance mutual perceptions of procedural and interactional justice (Tyler and Bies, 1990).
7. Implementation of these procedures in a manner that includes members from the cultural/ethnic groups involved.

8. The use of consultants specialising in group processes within multicultural teams to overcome the inevitable problems of cross-cultural coordination (Watson *et al.*, 1993). This consultation should include knowledgeable input about cultural deference codes (Scollon and Scollon, 1983).

Berry (1991a) provides a detailed case-study of thoughtful planning for and managing of diversity policies in a university setting.

Expatriate support systems. It now appears that premature return rates for business placements are not as high as the 25–40 per cent rates for developed countries or 70 per cent for developing countries as were earlier claimed (Harzing, 1995). Nonetheless, a number of inputs can be provided by the organization to preclude early repatriation. These are expected to strengthen both commitment to stay and productivity by enhancing the 'psychological contract' perceived by expatriates (Guzzo, Noonan and Elron, 1994). These include the following:

1. Availability of fellow culture members for newcomers at work or outside work to provide familiar social support.
2. Attention to factors important in the critical consideration of spouse adjustment (Torbiörn, 1982), such as consulting with them before the assignment (Black and Gregerson, 1991).
3. Training in the effective use of the organization's common language, often English, for *both* native and non-native speakers.
4. In-depth pre-departure training on cultural as well as environmental features of the new posting.
5. Provision of an 'in-house' cultural mediator to advise and mentor the newcomer about issues related to cultural adjustment.
6. Consideration of the re-entry problems facing someone after an overseas posting (Adler, 1981), especially ensuring that the former posting fits the member's future career path within the organization (Mendenhall, Dunbar and Oddou, 1987).
7. Mid-term cultural training (Brislin and Yoshida, 1994) to maximize the impact of the teaching input.
8. Use of criteria for performance evaluation that include aspects of cross-cultural effectiveness, such as the ability to resolve misunderstandings harmoniously.
9. Use of locals to give input in evaluating the performance of the expatriate.

Personnel selection

For the diverse work team. The first priority is to reduce the fragmenting force of prejudice by selecting for high levels of openness to experience. Thereafter, it would be sensible to compose multi-cultural teams with persons high on agreeableness, in order to maximize patience, cooperation, and modesty among team members. Communication competence (Kirchmeyer, 1993), probably associated with extroversion, would also increase the level of contributions from minority group members.

For the overseas placement. When organizations do have a field of candidates from which to choose, the personality factors mentioned above should also be used. In addition, low levels of neuroticism are recommended to help buffer the stress reactions to living in a foreign environment and culture. It is wise to select persons whose cultural background is maximally similar to that of the new host culture, using some scheme such as Schwartz's (1994) mapping of values for matching the expatriate's and the hosts' country. Culturally relevant skills, such as language or knowledge of the host culture's history and literature are also an asset. Finally, a track record of success in other cross-cultural settings, such as having completed a university degree overseas, augurs well for any future assignment. Black, Gregersen and Mendenhall (1992) identify additional selection considerations.

Conclusion

Our world is changing. Cross-cultural contact is increasing, as global interdependencies inexorably expand. Historically, the outcomes of intercultural contact are chequered at best. An enhanced set of skills and dispositions will be required of us all if, as the novelist Faulkner put it, mankind is not merely to survive, but to prevail. In response to this changing *Zeitgeist*, for example, competency in dealing with people from different cultural backgrounds has been included as an ethical standard by both the American and Canadian Psychological Associations; cross-cultural literacy is increasingly regarded as an educational priority (Luce and Smith, 1986); and psychologists are developing programmes to enhance multi-cultural awareness. This chapter has identified the key intercultural processes and outcomes along with the factors that influence them. They must be carefully considered as we negotiate our future.

Indigenous psychologies

The fact that most of us are blind to our own cultural heritage, except when we become aware of contrasting practices, makes the explicit study of culture an essential resource for studying the human condition.

Rogoff and Morelli (1989)

As we noted in Chapter 3, the goal of most psychological researchers has been to identify aspects of human behaviour and experience that are universal, and that can be explained parsimoniously in terms of general principles. This book has adopted the same perspective, seeking to identify whether or not general dimensions of cultural variation can account for observed differences in the various domains that we have discussed. In exploring this perspective, we have encountered many instances of what Sinha (1997) calls 'content-indigenisation', that is to say the testing of theories developed elsewhere using locally generated data. This chapter is devoted to an exploration of what evidence there may be that we are wrong to emphasize these types of study. Some authors have proposed that there are distinctive forms of emotions, values and behaviours that occur uniquely within specific cultural groups. To the extent that these phenomena occur frequently, locally indigenous theories will be required to account for them.

Since most of the studies that we have discussed have relied upon measures that are imposed-etic in nature, it is quite possible that we have overlooked instances of studies with a more explicitly indigenous focus. Researchers are only likely to detect indigenous effects if both the theories that guide them and the measures that they use permit the discovery of phenomena which are outside the range of those encountered in the nations where most psychology has been done. We can consider the probability of this oversight occurring by examining the content of the existing research literature. Öngel and Smith (1994) made a content analysis of 721 papers published during the first twenty-four years of publication of the *Journal of Cross-Cultural Psychology*. Only seven of these papers were coded as having used a 'derived-etic' research method. In other words, only in these seven studies did the researchers develop emically valid measures of the concepts they studied in each of the cultures that they sampled before testing the generality of their findings across cultures. Furthermore, Öngel and Smith found that in most instances, the theories that had guided researchers had been North American (or in a few cases, Western European) in origin.

Content analyses of other journals have confirmed the predominance of Western theories and measures in studies conducted around the world. Adair *et al.* (1993) found that in Indian psychology journals only a few researchers relied upon theories or measures developed within India. Adair *et al.* (1995) found even less evidence of indigenization in Bangladesh. Öngel and Smith (1996) compared content analyses of the *Turkish Journal of Psychology* and the English language journal, *Soviet Psychology*, which prints translated papers taken from a broad range of Russian psychology journals. There was no evidence for the indigenization of psychology in Turkey, but the results for Russia were quite different. During the Soviet period, Russian psychologists did indeed rely upon indigenous theories and measures, although it is not clear to what extent they continue to do so. We discuss the theories that they favoured later in this chapter.

Before taking this discussion further, we need to reflect on why it might be thought a good thing for researchers to rely on locally generated theories or measures. Should not any open-minded scientist draw upon theories regardless of where in the world they were first formulated? In general, we endorse the pursuit of this type of open-mindedness, but for the specific purpose of this chapter it is locally developed theories that are most likely to lead us to locally distinctive or indigenous phenomena. The types of theory employed by psychologists from different parts of the world are of course also strongly influenced by their reading of the research priorities in their local context. In nations that are increasingly different from those in which most social psychology is done, the priority given to the development of a scientific psychology is often lower than is the priority given to understanding and attempting to resolve distinctive social dilemmas. For instance, Adair *et al.* (1997) surveyed researchers in Latin America as to what they saw as the strongest research priorities. In Mexico and Brazil, education was seen as the key priority for scientific attention, whereas in Puerto Rico it was violence, and in Venezuela it was poverty and the quality of life.

We now consider in turn studies from different regions of the world from which indigenous phenomena have been described or proposed. We shall reserve our own judgements as to whether the evidence is or is not compelling that these phenomena are in fact distinctively local until we have finished describing them.

Latin America

In an extensive research programme commencing in 1955, Diaz Guerrero (1995) has proposed an approach to the development of indigenous psychology in Mexico which has also attracted considerable interest from other Latin American nations. Diaz Guerrero's basic proposition is that a culture may be characterized in terms of a series of 'historic socio-cultural premises' (HSCPs). These are culturally significant statements that are endorsed by a substantial majority of the members of a nation or group. HSCPs are distinguished from attitudes as 'more a priori, supra-individual, clearly societal determinants of thinking constituting a group language' (Diaz Guerrero, 1995, p. 54). Within Mexico, 123 HSCPs were identified, which were reduced to nine meaningful factors through factor analysis. These were identified as: affiliative obedience, machismo, virginity, consent, fear of authority, family status quo, respect over love, family honour and cultural rigidity (Diaz Guerrero, 1993).

More recently the focus of Mexican ethnopsychologists has been upon exploring the relationship between their culture-level characterization using HSCPs, individual-level measures of Mexican personality and the ways in which Mexicans define their self-concept. La Rosa and Diaz Loving (1988) asked Mexican students to describe themselves on semantic differential rating scales. The dimensions of self-concept that emerged showed considerable consistency with the HSCP factors. More specific connections have been also been hypothesized and confirmed. Avendano Sandoval and Diaz Guerrero (1992) showed that Mexicans who endorsed the HSCP of 'affiliative obedience' scored high on the personality trait of abnegation. That is to say they were disposed to grant others precedence or to sacrifice themselves for others' benefit.

In Puerto Rico, a series of ethnopsychological studies have identified 'respect' as a key HSCP, and imposed-etic personality tests are said to be unable to detect this construct (Pacheco and Lucca, 1996). In Colombia, Ardila (1996) notes strong emphases upon the family, upon machismo and upon the value of education. Further ethnopsychological studies of self-concept have been reported from Spain (Laguna Reyes, Valdez and Wagner, 1996). This type of research method tends to produce different factor structures for the self-concept within each nation sampled.

Ethnopsychological research thus currently flourishes within a series of Spanish-speaking nations. Despite its current focus upon personality traits and self-concept measurement, it differs from the Big Five studies and the TST self-concept studies discussed earlier in that its basis for prediction is a culture-level concept, and in that its practitioners expect their findings to have an emic and therefore primarily local validity.

Triandis *et al.* (1984) proposed that the concept of *sympatia* plays a central role in peer relationships within Hispanic cultures. They asked Hispanic naval recruits in the United States what types of behaviour they would expect to occur among Hispanics. Results were similar to the indigenous attributes noted in the Mexican studies. Much recent applied social psychology in the region can be seen as resting upon the potential that the presence of *sympatia* provides for the development of community action projects. Sanchez (1996a) describes the way in which replications of basic studies in social psychology fell out of favour among social psychologists. Instead, they focused upon locally pressing social problems, such as overcrowding, unemployment, violence and illiteracy. The basic procedure was to encourage deprived groups to 'problematize' their situation. In other words, meetings were organized to encourage those in deprived circumstances to think about their situation as something that needed change and improvement rather than passive acceptance. Sanchez describes community action projects of this type from seven South American nations. Typically these projects involve groups within the shantytowns (*barrios* and *favelas*) working together to improve their environment, either through building projects or by pressing the authorities for improved services. A particularly vivid instance of more widespread community participation in Venezuela is provided by Sanchez (1996b). Two psychologists conducted a daily radio programme that focused for a week upon a proposed strike by schoolteachers. Air time was given to all parties concerned, including teachers, management, union officials and parents. Listeners were encouraged to brainstorm ways in which the situation could be handled constructively, and their ideas were then put before the central figures in the dispute. There is thus a more widespread radical element within Latin American social psychology than is found in many other regions, leading to active involvement with deprived communities.

Sub-Saharan Africa

Carr (1996) reviews evidence in favour of distinctive attitudes and behaviours from studies conducted in a number of sub-Saharan nations. He suggests that they indicate widespread 'cognitive tolerance', that is to say the maintenance of attitudes or behaviours that are logically inconsistent with one another. In a series of studies in Malawi, he found that endorsement of modern medical explanations of illnesses such as malaria, AIDS (acquired immune deficiency syndrome), epilepsy and schistosomiasis was not negatively correlated with endorsement of traditional explanations. Even among nurses administering Western medical treatments, protective spells were sometimes employed as a defence against fellow nurses' envy of their having been promoted. Thus, belief systems that are for the most part conceived in Western nations as mutually exclusive were not assessed in this way by Malawians. Carr cites a range of earlier studies from East and West Africa that yielded similar findings.

Carr *et al.* (1996) explore a second aspect of proposed cultural difference. They note that in Western studies greater similarity has been found to lead to stronger interpersonal attraction. However, in the selection of expatriates to work in donor agencies and universities in Africa, they note that the black selectors frequently chose more culturally distant white Western candidates in preference to equally well-qualified candidates from other African or Asian nations and in preference to black candidates from Western nations. Clearly, some criterion other than similarity is being favoured here. The legacy of colonial respect may perhaps still linger.

A further distinctive aspect of organizational behaviour in some African nations is what Munene (1995) identifies as the 'not-on-seat' phenomenon. This refers to behaviour that is widespread in organizations in Nigeria, Uganda and neighbouring nations, whereby a manager arrives for work in the morning, puts his jacket on his chair and then goes elsewhere for a substantial part of the day. He attributes this phenomen to low endorsement of organizational citizenship and greater prioritization of family obligations. Munene (1991) provides detailed illustration of some of the difficulties Nigerian organizations face, partly due to the slow pace at which decisions can be made, owing to the 'not-on-seat' phenomenon, but partly due to adverse environmental circumstances. He found that it was not unusual for a company to have to wait up to two years before receiving payment for a service that had been provided.

Mpofu (1995) surveyed the view of self-concept held by student teachers in Zimbabwe. Sixty-eight per cent of open-ended responses to the question 'How does self express itself in your culture?' were coded as collectivistic, which gives us no direct evidence as to whether there may be indigenous attributes of African self-concept, in contrast to the much more extensive studies of self-concept in Pacific Asian cultures. Durojaiye (1993) suggests that there is nothing that is distinctive or indigenous in African psychology. However, he reports a study of conceptions of intelligence held by the Yoruba (from Nigeria) and the Baganda (from Uganda). His findings replicated those of a number of earlier African studies (e.g. Dasen, 1984): intelligence is seen in a way that is similar to how it is defined in Western nations, except that strong emphasis is also placed upon social skills. Dahl (1995) studied the concept of time in Madagascar. He concludes that time is conceived as event-related rather than linear. That is to say that events occur not according to chronological time but when they are ready to happen. A bus leaves when it is full; a meeting commences when enough people are assembled.

The small number of studies reported in this section indicate that a series of possibly distinctive phenomena have been rather tentatively identified, each one of which may prove to be distinctive to particular sub-Saharan cultures or to be more general. No indigenous theories addressing these phenomena have yet been advanced. Howitt and Owusu-Bempah (1994) have documented the manner in which many past characterizations of black Africans have been implicitly or explicitly racist. The discipline will need to evaluate whether any of the phenomena outlined above fall within this category. Alternatively, they may be explicable in more general terms. For instance, are they attributable to the incidence of widespread poverty? Or, are they also characteristic of collectivist or high-power distance nations elsewhere in the world?

India

Although the majority of researchers in India have continued to rely upon Western theories, there is a growing trend toward the introduction of indigenous concepts (Sinha, 1986, 1996). Sinha and Tripathi (1994) suggest that Indians are more tolerant of dissonance than are Westerners, and are able to behave in ways that are a blend of both individualistic and collectivistic orientations. They supported this contention by constructing a questionnaire in which students were asked to indicate whether they would be guided by an idiocentric or an allocentric preference in each of twenty-one specific settings. For instance they were asked whether they would vote for an election candidate on merit or on the basis of personal relationships. They were also permitted to respond by indicating that both preferences would be important. The 'both' option was the one most frequently selected on almost all items. No data exist as to how this would compare with responses from other cultures, and comparative results especially from individualistic cultural groups would be most revealing.

Several groups of researchers have drawn upon traditional Hindu writings as the source of hypotheses for their studies. For instance Palsane and Lam (1996) note that while Western researchers define stress in terms of negative affective states, classic Indian sources emphasize that suffering is a consequence of intensity of desire, and that consequently pleasure and as well as pain can be a source of stress. A reading of the *Bhagavadgita* thus leads to the prediction that detachment (*dharma*), rather than the active coping advocated by Western theorists, will lead to stress reduction. As applied to the carrying out of a task, this line of reasoning suggests that if one carries through a task conscientiously, stress will be unrelated to whether task performance was a success or a failure. Pande and Naidu (1986, 1992) tested these predictions empirically by surveying several hundred Indian adults. Having developed measures of detachment, effort and outcome, they found that those scoring high and low on detachment experienced an equal number of potentially stressful life events. The outcome of these events also did not differ between the two groups, but as predicted those who were more detached scored lower on a standard stress measure. This result shows an interesting convergence with the results of Singh (1981), discussed in Chapter 5, which showed that in India effort is valued highly even if the outcome of that effort is negative.

Krishnan (1992) explored the conception of justice in traditional Indian writings. While Western researchers have mostly contrasted allocations of reward on the bases of equity or equality, the studies by Murphy-Berman *et al.* (1984) and Berman, Murphy-Berman and Singh (1985), reviewed in Chapter 8, found greater emphasis upon the criterion of need. Krishnan concludes that justice is defined in the Indian context not simply in terms of need but of 'deservingness', which is partly a matter of one's current actions and circumstance, but also of what is one's position in society. The effects of this culturally different understanding of what are just or unjust allocations is illustrated for instance in Singh and Pandey's (1994) study of resource allocation by members of different social castes (also discussed in Chapter 8).

Other Indian researchers have explored aspects of social behaviour that are consistent with Sinha and Tripathi's (1994) characterization of Indians as concurrently both individualistic and collectivistic. Pandey (1981b, 1986) made a series of studies of the use of ingratiation techniques in India. He found that they occurred most frequently in relation to one's boss. In these circumstances, ingratiation was expected rather than deviant. Several of the tactics he noted are additional to those identified by US researchers. For instance he found self-degradation, emphasizing one's dependence on the superior, name-dropping and changing one's opinion to gain favour. These techniques can be thought of as ways of seeking to advance one's individual goals while operating within a bounded hierarchical and collective context. A complementary development has been J. B. P. Sinha's (1995) 'nurturant-task' leadership theory, discussed in Chapter 8. Sinha's perspective is that, within the collective context, effective leaders are those who find ways to encourage their subordinates to take on more individual responsibility.

East Asia

As has been apparent throughout this book, comparisons between samples drawn from East Asia and North America have become the most widespread form of cross-cultural study in recent years. These studies have enabled substantial progress in broadening the conceptual base of the field. However, they mostly do not address the degree to which East Asian cultures differ from one another. To address this issue we must examine further studies aimed more directly at indigenous concepts.

Japan

Doi (1973) identifies the Japanese term *amae* (translated as indulgent dependence) as a key characteristic of social relationships within Japan. *Amae* typically occurs between an indulgent senior, parent-like figure and a more junior person who seeks help or support. U. Kim *et al.* (1996) surveyed 847 students and adults in Japan and found this type of relationship to be widespread. They characterise *amae* as unlike childish dependency and as sustaining intimate, trusting and viable relationships. Capacity to *amae* was positively evaluated. Young Japanese were found to *amaesuru* (i.e. to make an *amae* relationship) most with their mother and older Japanese with their spouse and friends.

The Japanese business organization or *kaisha* has also been frequently described as distinctive. The sense of loyalty and commitment of the traditional Japanese family (referred to as *ie*) has to some extent been transposed to business life, at least within the larger and most successful organizations (Kashima and Callan, 1994). The loyalty of employees to the company, and of the company to employees is illustrated by employees' reluctance to take holidays and the company's reluctance to fire employees even in times of severe recession. Japanese organizations are thus not family-based, but are family-like, and we may also expect *amae* relationships to exist between superiors and their subordinates.

China

Chinese persons constitute one-third of the world's population. The recent publication of *The Handbook of Chinese Psychology* (Bond, 1996a) indicates that there is now substantially more data available than in times past, and we have cited a considerable number of studies including Chinese respondents in this book. However, we should beware of overgeneralizing: the data derived from the

Chinese Culture Connection (1987) showed that the values of different Chinese nations differed substantially. Here we simply note that Chinese societies are widely held to endorse Confucian values such as filial piety and industriousness, to value the giving and protecting of face, and to favour socially oriented achievement. In contrast to the organizational forms found in Japan and Korea, the astonishing economic success in recent years of overseas Chinese business firms in Southeast Asia has been accomplished through a myriad of small family-based firms (Redding, Norman and Schlander, 1994). These firms, like many other elements within Chinese societies, operate within networks of personal relationships built upon *guanxi* (relationships), or the exchange of personal favours (*ren ching*). These interpersonal networks are most often built upon family relationships or shared ethnic origin.

Korea

Choi, Kim and Choi (1993) asked samples of Korean students to answer a series of questions about their understanding of two key Korean concepts *woori* (translated as we or us) and *cheong* (translated as human affection). They concluded that when a Korean uses 'we', the pronoun does not just convey an aggregation of persons, as it does in Western languages. It also conveys that there is a unity and lack of differentiation between those who are referred to as 'we'. *Cheong* is seen as the fundamental basis of Korean emotionality, to be expected especially in families, but also among those who have lived in close proximity for long periods of time. It is associated with unconditionality, sacrifice and empathy. In a further study, Choi, Kim and Kim (1995) used a similar method to define the Korean concept of *chem'yon* (translated as social face). The results showed that maintenance of social face is required of those in senior positions in formal and public situations. Maintenance of social face is not seen solely as the responsibility of the senior individual, but also of those around him or her.

While the family is thus a major focus of Korean collectivism, the *chaebol* (large business firm) also has a distinctive quality. It differs from the Japanese *kaisha* in that it is frequently based upon an actual extended family, but resembles it only insofar as a 'family' of collaborating manufacturing firms, banks and government agencies establish very close links (Redding, Norman and Schlander, 1994).

Philippines

Filipino psychologists have proposed that central concepts relevant to social behaviour are *pakikisama* (going along with the majority), *kapwa* (fellow being), *hiya* (sense of shame) and *bahala-na* (stoical resignation) (Enriquez, 1988; Mataragnon, 1988). These authors have strongly espoused the view that intrusive Western research methods are inappropriate within Filipino culture and that valid information can only be accomplished through the use of more culturally congruent research procedures. They favour a form of community group discussion known as *pagtatanung-tanong*, which lends itself to unobtrusive observation. Their goal is to develop *Sikolohiyang Pilipino* or an indigenous Filipino psychology.

The Filipino group is also aware of the danger that Western writers (such as the authors of this book!) will lose the essence of the ways in which Filipino social reality has been characterized by them. A simple translation of a Tagalog phrase may completely change its meaning, and lose its contextual referents. For Enriquez (1993), *kapwa* is the essence of Filipino social relations, embracing the other concepts cited above. *Kapwa* is usually translated as 'fellow being'. He then explains how this translation can mislead:

> The closest English equivalent of kapwa is 'others'. However, the Filipino word kapwa is very different from the English word 'others'. The English word denotes a boundary between self and other: it is an exclusionary term. Kapwa, however, is an inclusionary term, emphasising the unity of the self with others. In the English language, 'others' is used in contrast to 'self' and suggests the recognition of the self as a separate and distinct identity. Kapwa, in contrast, recognises shared identity. (p. 160)

While there are clearly translation hazards in all cross-cultural studies, we noted in Chapter 4 the series of studies by Church and Katigbak (1988, 1989), which found considerable convergence between emically elicited Filipino personality descriptors and the Big Five personality factors. The work of Church (1987) in fact provides the most detailed attempt yet available to interrelate imposed-etic and indigenous data from a non-Western culture.

Russia

We noted at the start of this chapter that the literature of Russian psychology during the Soviet period was found to be substantially indigenous, thus probably providing the only example in the world (aside of course from the United States) where this local development was the case. We need to consider the reasons for this markedly different instance. Soviet Russia was distinctive in that for a period of several decades there existed a society containing a substantial number of psychologists, within which it could be dangerous to one's career, perhaps even one's life, to express deviant views. Radzikhovski (1991) provides a vivid account of the ways in which these pressures moulded the development of the subject. The emphases of the founding fathers of Soviet psychology, Vygotsky and Pavlov, were upon learning and development, an orientation much more compatible with Marxism than biological or determinist views.

However, as Marx asserted, 'The essence of man is not an abstraction inherent in an individual; it is in reality the aggregate of all social relations'. It thus became unacceptable to analyze behaviour in ways that might be seen as individualistic rather than collectivistic. Radzikhovski cites the manner in which Vygotsky addressed this difficulty in 1930:

Modifying Marx's well-known postulate somewhat, we might say that the psychological nature of man is the totality of social relations transferred to an inner plane, and becoming the functions of the personality and the forms of its structure. (Vygotsky, 1930, cited in Radzikhovski, 1991, p. 89)

Thus Vygotsky was able to argue that subjective experience and individual behaviour were part of social relations, and that once an event was experienced it could be in some way internalized. After Vygotsky's death and with increasing pressure on academic life, adherence to his theories were substantially superseded and his student Leontiev developed 'activity theory', which asserts a direct but rather imprecisely specified link between sensory activity and psychological phenomena. Radzikhovski asserts that until *perestroika* occurred, Soviet psychologists continued citing the works of established theorists such as Vygotsky, Pavlov and Leontiev, rather than risk developing new formulations or drawing on non-Soviet sources.

They also focused their concerns predominantly upon the fields of education and developmental psychology, rather than the concerns explored in this book. Within Soviet social psychology, there was certainly some awareness of and citation of Western theorists during the 1970s and 1980s (Strickland, 1979, 1984). By 1990, there was an explicit desire to explore new research topics and develop new theories (Zhurvalev, 1990), and a blending of theoretical orientations is now apparent (Koltsova *et al.*, 1996). For example, Western models of acculturation have been used in developing a Russian 'ethnic psychology', which explores relations between Russians and the various other ethnic groupings within the former Soviet Union (Lebedeva, 1996).

Russian psychology thus cannot be considered to have developed a unified core of accepted indigenous theory. Indeed, it is ironic that Vygotsky's ideas probably now attract more interest in Western nations than in Russia. Van der Veer (1996), for instance, traces the development of Vygotsky's conceptualization of culture, and a Vygotskyan perspective is frequently employed by Western cultural psychologists (Cole, 1990; Valsiner and Lawrence, 1997). Searle-White (1996) even draws on Vygotsky to interpret the findings of his comparison of the ways in which Russian and US students differ in defining the boundaries of personal friendship.

Western Europe

Although social and organizational psychologists in Western Europe have been less distant from the development of the subject as a whole, it remains the case, as Hofstede (1996c) notes on the basis of his earlier data, that cultural diversity within Europe is almost as great as it is within the whole of the world (see also Schwartz and Ros, 1995; Schwartz and Bardi, 1997). Within the field of psychology, this diversity is accentuated by the existence of substantial research literatures that are published in different languages. We shall note just three examples of this divergence.

Spanish 'perverse norms'

Fernandez Dols (1992) has proposed that Spanish society is characterized by the existence of a number of what he calls 'perverse norms'. These are norms that are widely agreed as ethically desirable, but from which deviance is not usually punished. An example would be the presence of traffic speed limits which are mostly accepted as necessary, frequently ignored and only occasionally enforced. Other examples will be more specific to the culture of specific institutions. For instance, it would be regarded as normative in Spain that a candidate for a chair in a university should be able to answer questions on any subject. This enables a member of an appointing committee to victimize a particular candidate by asking questions on an impossibly obscure or irrelevant topic.

Fernandez Dols (1992) suggests that perverse norms are rather more frequent in Spain than in the United States or the United Kingdom. He goes on to propose that in a culture characterized by a high frequency of perverse norms, alternative structures of power will arise that capitalize upon the fact than many persons are vulnerable to accusations that they have transgressed accepted norms. A boss can therefore capriciously victimize those who do not do what he wants, or can favour those whom he has private reasons for promoting. 'Families' or 'clans' will arise within or outside of existing power structures to implement their favoured actions. Those who are punished for their deviance will see themselves as capriciously victimized, even though the norm they have transgressed is accepted as valid. Oceja and Fernandez Dols (1992) have tested these predictions by presenting students with descriptions of instances where individuals were punished for transgressing perverse norms, and asking them to evaluate the actions of punishers and those punished. Their predictions were supported. Fernandez Dols does not propose that this pattern of behaviour is wholly distinctive to Spain, and there are certainly other Southern European nations, such as Italy, in which similar behaviour is popularly believed to be widespread. Indeed, it may occur to some extent in all cultures, but be greater where power distance is larger.

Moscovici's theory of social representations

Within French social psychology, the work of Serge Moscovici has been central to many recent developments. We have noted already in Chapter 6 his studies in the area of minority influence. His more general formulation is known as the theory of social representations. According to this theory, everyday events do not have any particular inherent social meaning. What happens to each of us as we are socialized is that we gradually learn that particular events or situations are understood in certain ways within our culture. As we come to understand things in these ways, we become better able to coordinate with the social activities of our cultural group members, and as we do so, we share in transmitting these meanings to those who join us. The meanings of events are thus not constructed by the individual, but are culturally shared social representations.

Social representations of what it is appropriate to eat and when to do so vary greatly. In many Western industrial countries the eating of cows, pigs and chickens is widely approved, while the eating of horses and dogs is not. The Chinese not only eat dogs, but also monkeys, pangolins, owls and snakes. In Hindu cultural groups cows may not be eaten, while Jews may not eat pigs. Numerous other variations in what is edible may be found and have been the object of much study by anthropologists.

Such variations in beliefs and values have most often been analyzed by social psychologists as variations in attitudes towards various objects. However, Moscovici (1981) would argue that this categorization misses the point. An attitude is a property of an individual. Social representations are collectively created and collectively maintained. Because many of the most fundamental representations exist in our cultural group long before we are born, there is a very slim chance that any one individual will create substantial change in the social representations prevalent within a cultural group. One could argue that major historical figures such as Hitler, Stalin, Gandhi and Martin Luther King did create such major changes. But even in these exceptional cases there remains room for debate as to whether or not these figures achieved prominence precisely because they articulated an already existing or emerging representation. Other social representations may be much more volatile and fluid. Sperber (1985), for instance, distinguishes three types of social representation, which he refers to as culture, tradition and fashion. Cultural representations would be the most lasting. Traditional representations would last through some generations, while fashions encompass the type of rapidly changing representations which have become highly characteristic of contemporary societies dominated by the mass media.

Moscovici's earliest work (1961) on social representations was focused upon the question of how the explanations of behaviour advanced by psychoanalysts were passing into everyday explanations of behaviour used by the lay public in France. He found that 45 per cent of students in his sample reported trying to understand their colleagues through the use of explanations such as 'having a complex'. In more recent work (Farr and Moscovici, 1984), the focus has broadened to encompass the whole range of ways in which 'common-sense' meanings are attributed to persons, groups and events in a cultural group. Moscovici points out that the nineteenth century French sociologist Durkheim (1898) already proposed a social psychology based upon what he called 'collective representations', and work within this tradition was active in the early part of this century.

So how could the social representations approach add to what other types of study have already told us about attitudes, prejudice, stereotyping and so forth? Since social representations are collectively defined and collectively transmitted, it follows that we can best study them by looking at instances of communication among members of a cultural group. The criticism has been advanced that the theory does not specify in advance how one should select the members of a group to be included in one's sample. Moscovici specifies only that the group *is* the people who hold a shared social representation. This definition need not be problematic if one is studying widely shared social representations, but can become more difficult where smaller groups and more transient representations are concerned.

Data on communications among group members can be collected through questionnaires and interviews, administered by members of the same cultural group, but better still may be examples of more spontaneous speech. If we can find clear themes from analyzing suitable samples, we should be better able to understand the representations that underlie them. So, for example, a detailed study of this kind by Herzlich (1973) in France found evidence of three types of social representation of illness: illness as destructive of one's customary activities, illness as a liberation from obligations and illness as an 'occupation' or pastime. Jodelet (1993) also used similar methods to determine the social representations of mental illness and learning difficulties among French peasant communities.

As was the case with the theory of perverse norms, there is no suggestion that a social representations approach to social psychology is in some way restricted to France, or that it necessarily tells us anything thought to be indigenous to France. For instance, similar types of discourse analysis have become popular in several countries of Western Europe (Potter and Wetherell, 1987), as well as among some cultural psychologists in North America (Stigler, Shweder and Herdt, 1990). However, the approach is perhaps most strongly endorsed in Francophone nations.

The principle of honour

As we noted in Chapter 8, there has been little integration of English-language and Francophone organizational theories. Aside from explanations that rest upon many researchers' lack of language skills, this divergence may also have occurred because different concepts prove useful in accounting for organizational behaviour at different locations. An interesting instance of this contextualization is d'Iribarne's (1994) *La Logique de l'Honneur*. In a French organization, this concept defines the way in which managers and employees fulfil the role obligations inherent in the positions to which they have been appointed. Role assignment and promotion in French organizations are much more strongly influenced by the prestige and orientation of the educational institution that one attended than by on-the-job performance. Reflecting this criterion, the principle that d'Iribarne identifies gives emphasis to the way in which a French organization member repays the trust placed in him or her by upholding the dignity and prestige of the professional group with which he or she is identified. In more individualistic cultures a manager might be evaluated simply in terms of individual achievement of specified goals, and in wholly collectivist cultures a manager's success would be synonymous with the work team's success. The principle of honour identifies an intermediate position, within which the individual's performance brings credit to his or her professional reference group. This has the effect of restricting the degree to which senior French managers can inspect or control the work of their subordinates without calling into question their professionalism, with consequent mutual loss of face. More studies are required of the nature of this type of leader–follower relation, and of the extent to which it characterises organization behaviour both within France and in other nations whom Hofstede categorized as relatively high on power distance.

Progress review: indigenous psychologies

This concludes our search for studies that may provide guidance as to what is being missed by the types of investigation that have preoccupied us in earlier chapters. It is apparent that the work done by proponents of indigenous psychology varies greatly. Some researchers have developed research methods which they apply at a particular location, but which could in principle be used just as validly elsewhere. Ethnopsychology and research based upon the theory of social representations fall clearly into this category.

Other researchers have identified phenomena that are particularly marked at a certain location, but that may occur in more moderate degree elsewhere. These phenomena are of particular interest from our perspective, since they can provide a conduit through which emic studies could feed the etic orientation that we have presented. However, here we encounter the problem that will continue to test cross-cultural psychologists: how do we know whether or not phenomena that sound similar between different cultures can be considered as alternative forms of the same basic process? When Fernandez Dols identifies the incidence and properties of perverse norms in Spain, is he addressing the same phenomena as Triandis (1994) is when he characterizes nations as varying along a dimension of 'tightness' or 'looseness'? Or when Carr (1996) identifies cognitive tolerance in Malawi, while Sinha and Tripathi see tolerance of dissonance in India, are these manifestations of what Hofstede (1980) would term low uncertainty avoidance? How similar and how unique are the conceptualizations of 'groupness' from Korea, Japan, China, the Philippines and Latin America that we have discussed? It will only be possible to attempt answers to these and similar questions when we have studies that take each of these phenomena, as emically formulated, and test out their incidence and properties elsewhere.

Most probably we shall find some possibility for assimilation of emic expressions of related phenomena into the emerging general framework of cross-cultural psychology, and some more specifically delineated phenomena which defy such incorporation. Such a conclusion must, however, await the careful scientific attention that we have been describing and advocating throughout this book.

Discerning the future

Chaos/complexity theory forces one to question both the
normality of any given social order as well as the presumption
of directionality and finality in social evolution.
As theory and technology develop by which to explore the
infinite variety of social life, even less may one offer privilege
to given social forms as product of the 'iron laws' of nature,
society or the gods, since human beings increasingly have
the knowledge and the means to shape the world as they
would have it.

Young (1995)

The world we all inhabit is changing at a dizzying pace. Economic development, political realignments, technological progress and media globalization are leading us towards greater modernity and interdependence. Global social change organizations (Cooperrider and Pasmore, 1991) are emerging along with multinational corporations to exert a homogenizing influence on cultural diversity. Some social scientists contend that these parallel processes will result in a convergence at the societal and psychological levels that will render cross-cultural psychology an irrelevant shard of intellectual history. Others perceive potential for continued, even expanding, diversity, as peoples of different cultural traditions confront the realities of development. Coupled with this belief in future diversity is a conviction about the viability of the cross-cultural contribution within social psychology. This chapter explores this debate in the light of our previous chapters, especially their emphasis on the role of individualism–collectivism.

Social psychology as history?

In a seminal paper, Gergen (1973) argued that social psychologists were engaged in examining contemporary historical developments rather than discovering behavioural principles that would remain valid across time and place. Gergen asserted that, 'If we scan the most prominent lines of research during the past decade, we soon realize that the observed regularities, and thus the major theoretical principles, are firmly wedded to historical circumstances' (p. 315). In discussing Festinger's (1954) theory of social comparison processes, for example, Gergen suggested that its fundamental tenet of people wishing to evaluate their opinions and abilities accurately was a historically driven disposition. 'In effect, the entire line of research appears to depend on a set of learned propensities, propensities that could be altered by time and circumstance' (p. 315).

Further complicating the search for scientific regularities was the impact of our disseminating the results of work in contemporary social psychology. As such information circulated, it could become an important new element in the equation predicting behaviour. People might accept the findings as prescriptive guidelines or protect their freedom of action by reacting against the implied prescriptions. In either case, a current result could not be used to predict a future outcome, because people's knowledge of the scientific 'law' now entered the equation.

Implications

In Gergen's (1973) view, the consequences of the historical embeddedness and the reactive effects of knowledge are twofold. First, 'Principles of human interaction cannot readily be developed over time, because the facts on which they are based do not generally remain stable' (Gergen, 1973, p. 309). Social psychology could not, therefore, aspire to the scientific status of, say, physics or biology. The future would be negotiable and open, not predicated on knowledge derived from the past.

Secondly, Gergen concludes that, 'We must think then in terms of a *continuum of historical durability*, with phenomena highly susceptible to historical influence at one extreme and the more stable processes at the other' (p. 318). This conclusion led Gergen to encourage the study of historical and literary documents from the past, as a way of assessing the continuity of interpersonal processes and concerns. In this vein Adamopoulos and Bontempo (1987) have scanned a variety of ancient literary sources for three themes of social behaviour – association, superordination and intimacy. Adamopoulos (1988), for example, detects an early example of egocentric individualism in the exchanges between Agamemnon and Achilles documented in *The Iliad*, a 3,000-year-old classic of Greek literature. Similarly, Simonton (1975) has examined data across 127 generations of European history and found that creative development is influenced by role model availability and by political instability.

Gergen's (1973) argument also led him to encourage the study of cross-cultural social psychology and is consistent with the quantum leap in the amount of cross-cultural psychology that has been undertaken in the past three decades. In his words, 'Although cross-cultural replication is fraught with difficulty, similarity in a given function from across widely divergent cultures would strongly attest to its durability . . .' (p. 318). This book has described many of the universal patterns that have emerged from this accumulation of research. In addition, we have identified dimensions of cultural variation that can be used to bring some degree of order out of the apparent discrepancies in results from different cultural systems.

Nevertheless, we are still left with Gergen's warning that our capacity to use present knowledge to predict future realities is questionable. The world is changing and social-psychological issues and possibly processes are changing as a result. How can our knowledge from the past help us to understand the interpersonal environments of tomorrow? The remainder of this chapter presents speculations and data from social scientists that bear on this issue.

How do cultures change?

In Chapter 3, we defined culture with Hofstede (1980) as the 'collective programming of the mind', with that programming being operationalized in terms of value dimensions. Hofstede argued that these cultural values originated from both external and internal factors operating within each society. The internal factors were labelled 'ecological' and included aspects of a nation's geography, economy, hygiene, demography, gene pool, history, technology, urbanization and material resources. The external influences included forces of nature, such as climate changes or environmental disasters, and forces of man, such as trade, scientific discovery, invasion and the internationalization of the media.

Hofstede (1980) maintains that societal norms and cultural values do change in response to changes in these internal and external factors. In order to anticipate future developments in the 'collective programming of the mind' and hence in social behaviour, it is important to examine the structure of these change agents and their evolution over time.

The convergence hypothesis

Nations, like people, develop over time. Cattell (1953), for example, factor-analyzed a number of macro-level variables descriptive of Great Britain from 1837 to 1937. He extracted ten dimensions along which Britain had changed over the 100 years analyzed. One of these ten he labelled 'cultural pressure', which was essentially a factor of economic modernization whose strength increased mono-tonically during this period.

The diffusion of scientific discoveries and industrial technology since the eighteenth century has driven economic development in all countries of the world. Common characteristics of this global transformation are the specialization of labour, the globalization and impersonality of market-places, the exploitation of natural energy sources, and the concentration of capital resources. Political life has also been transformed. As Yang (1988) has described it:

> political modernization is composed of three major processes: the replacement of a large number of traditional authorities by a single national political authority, the emergence of new political functions that must be managed by new administrative

hierarchies chosen on the basis of achievement rather ascription, and increased participation in politics by social groups throughout society, along with the development of new institutions such as political parties and interest groups to organize this participation. (p. 67)

Similarly, socio-cultural modernization is proceeding in parallel: 'Sociocultural changes are reflected in such processes as the expansion of education, the diversification of occupations, the secularization of religion, the intensification of urbanization, and the development of mass communications' (Yang, 1988, pp. 67–8).

Economic determinists maintain that the political and social changes described above are consequences of the changes in modes of production. Given the wide and increasing diffusion of such economic developments, convergency theorists conclude with Kerr et al. (1960) that, 'the logic of industrialization will eventually lead us all to a common society where ideology will cease to matter' (p. 12). Ideology will cease to matter, presumably, because we will all share a common ideology. To the extent that ideology or values drive behaviour, then differences across people of different cultural heritages will, in time, cease to exist. Such is the putative psychological consequence of the societal convergence produced by modernization.

Convergency theorists believe, then, that given sufficient time for diffusion of technology, training and capital to occur, all countries will be drawn into the vortex of a common modernity. Inglehart (1977), for example, surveyed values in a variety of European countries and the United States, identifying two major factors. The first factor he identified as materialist–post-materialist. This dimension spanned the transition from Maslow's (1954) security and social needs to his self-actualization needs. The wealthier the country, the higher would the

---

Box 12.1 **The spread of the English language**

Naisbitt and Aburdene (1990) present some provocative information about the widespread use of English:

● It is the native language of 400 million people.
● Another 400 million speak English as a second language.
● English enjoys official or semi-official status in 60 countries.
● 250 million Chinese study English.
● 80–90 per cent of Berlitz language students study English.
● English is the dominant language of media, transportation, information storage/transmission, international business, diplomacy, science and youth culture.
● By 2000 there will probably be 1.5 billion persons who speak English.

Given these figures and the continued growth of English usage, English is and will remain the dominant language for cross-cultural interaction and will increase in its pre-eminence for such exchanges.

proportion of post-materialists become. Analysis of the 'Eurobarometer' opinion surveys conducted annually in Western European nations over the past fifteen years shows steady year by year increases in endorsement of post-materialist values in all nations (Inglehart, 1990). However, we should note that by the late 1980s, no more than one-third of respondents were categorized as post-materialists. Nonetheless, based on these sorts of results, some social scientists would argue that a gradual increase of wealth in all countries will make people similar and render our current enchantment with cross-cultural differences in behaviour an archeological curiosity, a historical digression. Interestingly, this academic assessment of contemporary development has filtered down to public awareness and generated ideological reactions from developing nations.

Modernization and Westernization. The scientific aspects of the debate about convergence are complicated by a political agenda, namely, the need of people in many developing countries to assert their cultural uniqueness by distinguishing their culture from that of the West. Politicians in some countries can forge a unity out of disparate ethnic communities by rallying their supporters against the spectre of Westernization. For their part, citizens of such emerging nations may derive some cultural pride by differentiating themselves from Western traditions, as Tajfel's (1981) theory would predict. So, for example, we have the following news release from the *South China Morning Post* (5 January 1991):

> SINGAPORE, Fri. – Singapore outlined today five 'shared values' it said would help the country develop a national identity and combat Western influence. 'The shared values should help us develop a Singaporean identity,' a government white paper said. Schools and parents should inculcate the values in young people, it added. It identified the values as: nation before community and society above self, family as the basic unit of society, regard and community support for the individual, consensus instead of contention and racial and religious harmony.

Particularly worrisome in the minds of many political leaders is the growing self-centredness and erosion of civil harmony that they believe will follow in the wake of Western-inspired modernization.

There are many rational shortcomings to this line of argument, politically useful as it may be (Weinberg, 1969). First, the depiction of 'the West' is very broad, including a host of mostly North American and northern European countries that are themselves culturally different in many respects. We have noted earlier that the values and social organization of these nations are by no means uniform (Hofstede, 1991; Rummel, 1972; Schwartz, 1994). Secondly, critics of the West typically identify the negative features of its social life, ignoring its many positive features, such as broad social welfare, the relatively high status of women and the observance of human rights (Bond, 1991a). Thirdly, they confuse origin with outcome. True, the industrial revolution originated in the West and many of its refinements have developed there. As Yang (1988) has pointed out, however, modernization, is new to all societies, Western and non-Western. The major modern features created by such a new process cannot be found in traditional non-Western ones. It is in this sense that modernization is not Westernization in its strict and narrow sense – the acceptance of traditionally Western things by a non-Western society. (p. 68)

Only rigid economic determinists would conclude that grafting modernization on to Asian, African or South American societies would turn them into Western clones. There is good empirical evidence that these new hosts for modernity will transform this developmental impetus in distinctive and varied ways (e.g. Tsurumi, 1992). Let us then turn to the scientific evidence regarding convergence.

The constellation of individual modernity

Effective participation in modern society is hypothesized to require a core syndrome of cognitions and motivations. To assess this core, sociologists such as Kahl (1968) and Inkeles and Smith (1974) have developed comprehensive batteries of standardized questions and administered these questionnaires to adult samples in a variety of developing countries. Other researchers have focused on single countries, comparing the responses of people from groups at different presumed stages in the modernization process, such as city dwellers versus rural inhabitants (e.g. Armer and Youtz, 1971; Guthrie, 1977).

These instruments, whether they use questions that are imposed etic or derived-emic, show a high degree of agreement in their outcomes. This overlap suggests that a common denominator of psychological characteristics is emerging across these many studies, as may be seen in Box 12.2.

Is idiocentrism another name for modernity? Alert readers will note some conceptual similarity between modernity and idiocentrism as psychological profiles. Yang (1988) contends that about two-thirds of the above characteristics overlap with the profile of idiocentrics. If individualism and collectivism are conceptualized as opposite ends of a continuum, then increasing modernization would lead to a gradual idiocentrism of psychological processes.

One could take the economic index of GNP per capita as a rough approximation of societal modernization. If this step is taken, then Hofstede's (1980) research shows a strong correlation of $+0.82$ between modernity (as measured by wealth) and cultural individualism. Bond's (1988b) work demonstrates a similar link between wealth and average levels of idiocentrism, labelled social integration vs. cultural inwardness. Furthermore, Hofstede's (1980) longitudinal research across a four year span indicated that individualism was the only one of his four dimensions to increase on average across his entire sample of forty countries during that period.

These lines of work thus suggest that economic development, which is generally increasing, goes hand in hand with a change in certain broad patterns of individual

> ### Box 12.2 The profile of a modern person
>
> Yang (1988) has synthesized the results from both the cross-cultural and intracultural studies and produced the following profile of the modern person:
>
> - A sense of personal efficacy (antifatalism).
> - Low social integration with relatives.
> - Egalitarian attitudes towards others.
> - An openness to innovation and change.
> - A belief in sex equality.
> - High achievement motivation.
> - Independence or self-reliance.
> - Active participation in social organizations.
> - Tolerance of, and respect for, others.
> - Cognitive and behavioural flexibility.
> - Strong future orientation.
> - Empathetic capacity.
> - A high need for information.
> - The propensity to take risks in life.
> - Secularization in religious belief.
> - A preference for urban life.
> - An individualistic orientation toward others.
> - Psychological differentiation.
> - A non-local orientation.

behaviour. These patterns are central to the contrast between collective and individualistic cultures that has informed and unified much of our presentation in this text. Should we then conclude that much of its contents may become a historical artefact, doomed to obsolescence?

Internationalism. An additional factor is emerging in conjunction with global development which may add a further homogenizing influence to cultural variation. This is the increasing awareness of humanity's interdependence. As many commentators (e.g. Brown *et al.*, 1990; Mesarovic and Pestel, 1974) have clamoured for people to realize, our growing technological sophistication has brought in its wake the potential for ecological destruction. Mankind's depletion of energy sources, over-harvesting of the oceans, assault upon the atmosphere, destruction of the rain-forests, and erosion of fertile soil are bringing us closer to global disaster. Our headlong pursuit of personal and national affluence has resulted in a 'commons dilemma' (Dawes, 1980) where the very support systems of life on this planet are at risk.

One consequence of these recent developments is the growth of internationalism, a constellation of attitudes with important implications for behaviour towards people of different races, nations and cultures. Sampson and Smith (1957) labelled this concept 'world-mindedness' which they defined as 'a frame of reference, or value orientation favouring a worldview of the problems of humanity, with mankind, rather than the nationals of a particular country, as the primary reference group' (p. 105). They showed that within their American sample this international orientation was a coherent clustering of beliefs on social, political, economic and religious questions, a cluster that was stable within persons, and negatively related to authoritarianism. In a refinement of this early work, Kosterman and Feshbach (1989) have shown that internationalism is not the bipolar opposite of either nationalism (chauvinism) or patriotism (love of one's country), but that these three constructs are independent of one another.

Internationalism was once the preserve of futurists, political factions, and certain religious groups, but has lately been accorded wider currency by economic developments. Psychologists are beginning to develop cross-culturally equivalent measures of world-mindedness (Der-Karabetian, 1992) and relate it to global, ecological concerns (Der-Karabetian, Stevenson and Poggi, 1996). What are the possible consequences of growing internationalism for cultural diversity?

Schwartz's (1994) work is helpful in this regard. One of the seven, culture-level domains of value measured in his international survey was 'harmony', consisting of the following value items: unity with nature, protection of the environment, and a world of beauty. This value type incorporates a set of concerns that form one part of internationalism. Teacher samples from thirty-six countries showed considerable variation in levels of endorsement of harmony values. Many would argue that such variation must decrease over time, as the planet's citizens become more aware of the need to sacrifice present economic demands for future environmental safety. As argued by Schwartz and Bilsky (1990), the increase in overall endorsement of 'harmony' will be purchased at the expense of the value type which stands in opposition to it, viz. mastery. That value type emphasizes success, ambition, independence, and so forth, the acquisitive values that many commentators believe have fuelled our current crisis (Laslo, 1989). The overall consequence of environmental developments, then, is likely to be a reduction in variation across one of Schwartz's major axes of value differences among nations.

This assumption is of course speculative, but is exactly the same sort of argument about the future as was the argument surrounding modernity in the past. The repeated administration of the Schwartz value survey currently in progress will enable us to assess this hypothesis empirically. In the meantime let us look at the arguments opposing convergence.

The evidence against convergence

As is common in science, a strongly stated universal proposition begins to disintegrate upon closer scrutiny. A number of approaches to the convergence hypothesis themselves converge to suggest that the thesis must be questioned and modified. These approaches are discussed below.

Economic development and values

As mentioned earlier, Inglehart (1990) detected a trend in North American and European countries whereby citizens' values were shifting from materialist to post-materialist. As other countries modernized, Inglehart hypothesized that the values of their populace would likewise shift.

Research in other industrialized countries does not, however, support such a conclusion. If we take wealth as a rough measure of modernity, only one of Hofstede's four (1980) or five (1991) dimensions of cultural variation shows any relationship with wealth. The other multicultural studies of value that we discussed earlier likewise extract from two to seven dimensions of national variation in values and only one of these dimensions correlates substantially with measures of economic development (Rummel, 1972; Chinese Culture Connection, 1987; Schwartz, 1994). This frequent finding suggests that values are free to vary in a number of ways independent of a country's level of modernization. These 'modernity-free' domains of value are probably related to the other dimensions of variation in national 'character' discussed earlier and exert their impact on social behaviour just as does individualism.

The fate of individualism–collectivism. Of course the cultural dimension that does most closely associate with wealth and therefore with modernity appears to be the various formulations of individualism–collectivism. In this regard a number of points can be made. Firstly, the strength of the relationship between wealth and various indices of individualism varies from study to study, and in some cases (e.g. Schwartz, 1994) is small. Countries at the same level of economic development may thus vary considerably in their levels of individualism, however measured. Secondly, the only study to assess individualism–collectivism across time actually reported an increase in variation of country scores across a four year span (Hofstede, 1980, Chapter 8). Thirdly, over the past twenty-five years it has not been a country's level of individualism that best predicts its economic development; rather it is the unrelated measure of values called Confucian work dynamism (discussed in Chapter 3) that now predicts growth rates in GNP (Hofstede and Bond, 1988), whatever may have been the case in the past. A country's level of Confucian work dynamism is unrelated to its actual wealth or to its level of individualism, a finding that suggests continued variation across countries in their wealth and hence in their level of individualism–collectivism.

At the very least, then, we must conclude that there is no inexorable convergence of countries towards greater individualism in values with the march of time and of progress. Variations in individualism and collectivism will continue to be an important tool for interpreting cross-cultural differences in behaviour, just as it is an important tool for understanding individual variation within a culture (e.g. Earley, 1989).

Variability of the modernization syndrome

If modernization is a uniform, linear process, then the pattern of modernization across its many components (increased exposure to the mass media, greater secularization, etc.) should be the same from country to country. The evidence indicates that it is not. Studies of the modernization syndrome *across* cultures (e.g. Sack, 1973) and *within* cultures (e.g. Chiu, 1979) reveal a multifaceted phenomenon which takes different forms in different places. Sack, for example, borrowed twenty-nine items tapping the modernity complex from previous studies and administered them to over 1,000 Tunisians. Careful analysis did not reveal a single, underlying, dimension of modernism uniting these measures. Instead, eight unrelated components of the process were revealed: activism, rejection of the white collar syndrome, universalism, low integration with relatives, sense of personal trust and autonomy, rejection of the past, preference for urban life, and family modernism. As Yang (1988) concludes, 'The evidence . . . unequivocally points to the fact that modern psychological characteristics simply do not cohere to form a well-unified syndrome. Individual modernism may be composed of separate components. . .' (p. 81). Individuals and groups within different countries can therefore modernize in different ways, at different rates and with different outcomes.

Traditionalism and modernity as unrelated

The anxiety voiced by some politicians about the spread of modernism is based in part upon the worry that traditional values will be eroded. They set cultural heritage in opposition to economic progress using a zero-sum logic – more of one, less of the other.

Many social scientists, however, maintain that cultural systems are innovative and can synthesize traditional and modern elements in unique ways, so that both traditional and modern elements may co-exist without tension (Abraham, 1980). Psychological data from Taiwan (Yang, 1986), Japan (Ike, 1973) or Chinese societies generally (Yang, 1996) support precisely such a conclusion. In describing Trommsdorff's (1973) survey research in Japan, Yang, for example, (1988) concludes that

> strong traditional values such as group solidarity, interpersonal harmony, paternalism, and familism are coexisting with quite modern values such as achievement and competition, and that along with democratic values exist beliefs in hierarchical social structures and in authority, obedience, and inequality of men and women. (p. 82)

One might thus just as well talk about 'Easternization', rather than Westernization, in this psychological response to the forces of modernity (Marsella and Choi, 1993)!

Reports about lay conceptualizations of modernity are consistent with a position of fruitful, supportive co-existence of national cultures (Bond and King, 1985). The basic, organizing principles involved are two-fold: first, a distinction is made between modernization and Westernization. This contrast enables one to undertake change without feeling indebted or subservient to the West. Secondly, one differentiates the beneficial from the retrogressive aspects of both traditional culture and modern culture. The positive elements of the past and present are embraced; the negative, discarded. Hong Kong Chinese, for example, believe that they retain their tradition of respect for authority, but discard its fatalism; they adopt modern competitiveness, but reject its sexual promiscuity. This cognitive strategy enables one to forge a desirable identity for the future while retaining a connection to one's historical legacy and demonstrates the operation of social creativity in the face of intergroup threat (Tajfel, 1981).

Migration and psychological change

One of the strongest challenges to one's cultural distinctiveness occurs when one emigrates to a country with different cultural traditions. The power of modernization would be demonstrated if people from less modernized countries were found to assimilate to the thought and behaviour patterns characteristic of their more modernized hosts. As we have discovered in Chapter 10, acculturation is a complex problem to explore, requiring attention to such sociological and political issues as the specific cultural groups involved, the status of the immigrants, their relative numbers and dispersion in the host country, constitutional protection for multiculturalism, effective enforcement of legislation against discrimination and so forth. The research is difficult to do, requiring access to often closed communities and to samples across a number of generations.

One of the best examples of such work is by Feldman and Rosenthal (1990). They assessed changes in parental restrictiveness and compliance across two generations of Chinese immigrants from Hong Kong to the United States and to Australia. Expectations for autonomy in first and second generation teenagers were compared with those of their Anglo hosts and Chinese counterparts back in Hong Kong. Their first conclusion was that cultural adaptation appears to be very slow, with even second generation Chinese responding more like their Hong Kong counterparts than their host Caucasians. Secondly, they found that this cultural resilience was more marked in certain domains than in others. So, for example, Chinese in host countries adapted more to local norms about social activities, such as spending time with friends, but not to norms for heterosexual activities, such as early dating or overnight trips with mixed-sex friends. The authors conclude that

> Although Chinese family patterns undergo modest changes when Chinese families live in the West, they nonetheless remain different from their Western counterparts, in terms of the amount of structure they provide and the extent to which they use child-rearing practices which promote autonomy. (p. 277)

Parental restrictiveness is one characteristic of collectivist family structure (Barry, Child and Bacon, 1959; Kagitçibasi, 1990). Although independence from parental influence is connected to the modernity syndrome, there is good evidence for the persistence of traditional socialization practices despite residence in modern, individualistic nations (see also Hines, 1973). As we have found in Chapter 10, cultural homogenization does not occur among immigrants in most psychological domains or in most societies.

A middle way between convergence and divergence

The convergence hypothesis is slippery – adamant proponents may dismiss the opposing evidence by declaring that insufficient time has elapsed for modernizing influences to work their homogenizing effect. Given each country's unique background and different entry points into the process, they could argue, the process in each is bound to be varied, but the eventual outcome will be the same.

This is a linear, simplistic stance that resists those contemporary developments in science that emphasize *systems* of influence and the subtle but complex inter-dependencies of inputs (Gleick, 1987; Young, 1995). We believe that it is more realistic to posit an openness in the modernization process. Different developing societies enter the modernization process with different traditional and contem-porary inputs, making it risky to apply historical precedents to their development. Changing systems continue to be changed by the outcomes of the change process itself. The various modern cultures will themselves evolve in unpredictable ways, making the notion of convergence towards some common end point implausible. More probably we will continue to observe islands of convergence within a sea of diversity.

Specific functional convergence

Yang (1988) has argued that various behaviours and dispositions are adaptive to the imperatives of industrial societies. The value of certain characteristics in agrarian, hunting, gathering or pastoral communities will be lost and they will be replaced by characteristics that function more easily in technological environ-ments. Convergence should thus occur only for those attributes that can serve a *specific function* in adapting to modernization. Some of these characteristics have been identified in the psychological syndrome of modernization and the increase in their frequency represents the 'kernel of truth' in the literature on psychological convergence.

However, this kernel of truth is smaller than often portrayed and it can flourish in varied cultural soils. As Lauterbach (1974) puts it, 'In other words, there is not any one pattern or model of modernization which each modernizing nation must or can follow; beyond a certain technical point, it will inevitably be left to its own devices' (p. 147). Stylistic, expressive and goal-directed characteristics that have no functional relation to industrial–technical performance will remain and evolve in accordance with each culture's internal logic. In addition, Yang (1988) points out that, 'It is of course also possible that new, unique, non-functional characteristics are formed during the process for the society to advance to its modern phase' (p. 84). So, variety can continue despite modernization, and it may even be fostered by the process of growth.

There will continue to be a need to explore the impact of cultural variation on social behaviour. The dimensions of cultural variation may themselves evolve and be replaced, requiring new concepts to be identified in the quest to explain the whole range of human behaviour. One important element in that evolution will be periodic sampling of cultural groups using established value surveys (e.g. that of Schwartz, 1992) which may be expanded. Such projects will enable social psychologists to monitor cross-cultural changes in value endorsements as humanity evolves. Emerging value dimensions, such as internationalism, may be grafted on to these established instruments in order to determine their relationship to existing dimensions.

Particular major events and political upheavals will no doubt continue to provide occasional opportunities to assess the malleability of values and behaviour. For instance, the reunion of the former East Germany with West Germany has yielded data showing a relatively rapid trend toward West German norms in idiocentrism among East German schoolchildren (Oettingen *et al.*, 1994), and in initiative among East German workers (Frese *et al.*, 1996).

Future contributions

Cross-cultural social psychology has a short history, one that approximately parallels that of trans-oceanic flight. Its primary role to date has been that of a gadfly, prodding the mainstream to be more cautious in its generalizations (Bond, 1988a) and less naive about its culturally shaped biases (Sampson, 1978; Furby, 1979). But more is possible.

Expanding our theories

The early European explorers searched for the Spice Islands in order to enhance their local cuisine. Cloves, pepper, cardamom, ginseng and so forth greatly enlarged the culinary range of European chefs and were often found to have additional uses in medical treatment. Similarly, cross-cultural work in social psychology may unearth concepts, processes and theories that broaden our appreciation of what factors influence behaviour by providing a forum for psychologists from outside the mainstream. As Moghaddam (1987) expresses this hope, 'the growth of an indigenous third-world psychology could potentially lead to fresh ideas that could only spring from the work of third-world psychologists, with beneficial results for all of psychology' (p. 917). Given the 'Americo-centrism' of most social science (Featherman, 1993), this broadening in the cultural base out of which psychology is generated will help universalize our discipline. A few examples will illustrate this potential.

Conflict resolution. Beliefs about potential for *animosity reduction* are important in determining how people choose among various strategies for resolving conflict (e.g. Bond, Leung and Schwartz, 1992). This important theoretical construct was introduced to the psychological community by a Chinese psychologist, Leung (1987). Before then, the classical text on conflict resolution by Thibaut and Walker (1975), two Americans, had identified control over the process of conflict as the fundamental factor influencing strategy choice for resolving social disputes.

Given our previous discussion of collectivism and individualism, it will appear plausible that a Chinese psychologist would focus on the outcome of the conflict for the parties concerned whereas American psychologists would focus on the process of its resolution. Similarly, for example, in discussing intercultural marriage, Ting-Toomey, a Chinese social scientist, proposes that

> more culturally-sensitive relational outcome variables such as relational acceptance, relational fatalism, relational longitudinal viewpoint (i.e., adding to the already existing variables of relational satisfaction, quality, and commitment) should be incorporated in the study of relationship between intercultural intimate conflict and intimate conflict outcomes. (1994a, p. 74)

The important consideration here is that many factors probably contribute towards explaining how people decide to resolve conflict in many national cultures, be they Dutch, Indian, Canadian, Korean, Spanish or Japanese. The combined input of psychologists from different cultural traditions can yield theoretical synergy. Like blind and deaf travellers, we can assist one another on our way.

Models of maturity. Kagitçibasi, a Turkish social psychologist, has been in the vanguard of those pointing out the consistent value bias among Western psychologists towards individualism. This bias is strongly expressed in the area of developmental psychology where 'It is taken for granted that the development of autonomy and independence is a prerequisite for optimal personality, cognitive, and moral development' (Kagitçibasi, 1988, p. 31). Challenging this assumption, she describes a variety of social situations and cultural milieux where people's 'innate sociality' (in the terms we are using, their allocentrism) are cornerstones to a functional, adaptive life-style. Kagitçibasi concludes that, 'Such socialization values and practices cannot be adequately studied with a theoretical orientation based on Western, individualistic ideology, emphasizing autonomy and self-reliance in child development' (p. 34).

Consistent with our previous discussion on convergence, Kagitçibasi (1988) notes that, 'A family culture of relatedness and interdependence . . . is not incompatible with socio-economic development' (p. 36). Parading data from a variety of cultures, she asserts that, 'It is possible for individual loyalties to co-exist with communal-familial loyalties and relations, in a new synthesis, rather than being mutually exclusive . . .' (p. 36). An *interdependent* interpersonal perspective does not pit the individual against the group and can thus provide scientists with a fruitful base to explore the 'psychology of relatedness' (Kagitçibasi, 1990, 1996a).

A psychology of relatedness would propose a different view of maturity from that of a psychology of independence. Such a theory would honour both the human requirements for 'agency' (autonomy, independence) *and* for 'communion' (relatedness, interdependence). Research by Kagitçibasi, Sunar and Bekman (1988) and by others (e.g. Lin and Fu, 1990) shows that *both* these orientations may be promoted simultaneously in certain cultural settings. The results of the Lin and Fu research suggest that this outcome is achieved by parental support of interdependence within the family setting, coupled with strong pressures for autonomy and achievement outside the family. The conception of the ideal adult that is suggested by such investigations will differ from that emphasized in individualistic cultural settings because it will accord the orientation towards relatedness a more pivotal role in the fully functioning person. This perspective can also contribute to currently active debates about gender roles and about cultural diversity in Western societies.

Universalizing our measures

The dominance of Americans in the social sciences and the reliance on English for scientific communication has led to the result that almost all our questionnaires used in social psychology are written in English by native speakers of that language. As Wierzbicka (1993) argues, however, many English words, such as 'self', 'emotion', 'mind', etc., carry rich meanings that are difficult to translate fully into other languages. Although such translation is done, much is lost.

Instead of using English, Wierzbicka (1993) has identified 'conceptual universals and . . . a language that can be used for comparing cultures without an ethnocentric bias', giving 'a crucial role . . . to the universals of language and, in particular, to lexical universals' (p. 208). She uses this universal system to develop a number of 'cultural scripts' which she describes as simple sentences or short 'sequences of sentences that attempt to capture a society's tacit cultural norms "from a native's point of view" and, at the same time, to express these norms in terms of universal human concepts' (p. 221). So, for example, the Anglo-American 'feel good' script may be phrased, 'It is good to feel something good all the time'. It is easy to imagine how questionnaires, e.g. the self-construal scales of Chapter 5, could be constructed out of such a universal system. Comparisons across cultural groups would then stand on firmer footing – the results would not simply tell us how members of culture X differ from, say, Americans, on some instrument suffused with Anglo cultural niceties and presumptions; rather the comparison would yield information on how some truly universal concepts or processes are perceived by members of the cultural groups sampled. This would be a considerable advance!

Diversifying our inputs

As Öngel and Smith (1994) point out, North American authors predominate in the major outlet for cross-cultural research, the *Journal of Cross-Cultural Psychology*. Even when they work in multicultural teams, it is probable that these North American authors play the major conceptual role. If the discipline is to open up theoretically and methodologically, then we as practitioners must become more adept cross-cultural team players (Faucheux, 1976; Taft, 1976) in our research. We must manage, indeed be managed, in those ways that we advocate for any effective multicultural team or organization (see Chapter 10).

As cross-cultural psychologists, it will also be necessary to open ourselves up to the contributions of other disciplines such as sociology, political science, history, anthropology and linguistics (Featherman, 1993). Cross-cultural work on speech accommodation theory (see Chapter 9) has been exemplary in this regard (e.g. Giles *et al.*, 1991). Developing this intellectual breadth may seem a tall order, but doing cross-cultural psychology is not for the faint-of-heart (Gabrenya, 1988)! This learning from other disciplines may involve us in new approaches to gathering 'data'. Ethnographic methods, for example, may be particularly important for detecting indigenous understandings (e.g. Mouer, 1995, on Japanese conceptions of work).

Emerging dimensions of cultural variation

By this point readers will appreciate how strongly the cultural dimension of individualism/collectivism has dominated the past two decades of work in cross-cultural social and organizational psychology. Now there are a number of individual-level measures of this construct, here labelled as idiocentrism/allocentrism, by which psychologists can unpackage the cultural dimension. This imbalanced focus on collectivism has in part been fuelled by the emergence of a viable group of researchers in Asian (collectivist) cultures who are interested in comparative work.

Recently, researchers have begun examining other, relatively neglected dimensions of cultural variation. Hofstede has convened a series of symposia focused upon cultural masculinity/femininity at recent congresses of the International Association of Cross-Cultural Psychology. For instance, Hofstede (1996b) presented a paper examining the relationship between cultural masculinity/femininity and measures of religiosity, gender-related beliefs and ideology, and sexual norms and behaviours. In a carefully controlled study, Van de Vliert *et al.* (1997) have also found that cultural masculinity mediates the curvilinear, country-level association between ambient temperature and domestic political violence. An important next stage in developing cross-cultural work on this dimension is to create individual-level measures of the construct, as it reveals itself psychologically. Such measurement will also be required to stimulate comparative work on the revived construct of cultural tightness/looseness (Chan *et al.*, 1996). In this case established individual-level measures such as tolerance for ambiguity (Furnham, 1994) may be brought to bear. Likewise the measure of social dominance orientation (Sidanius, Pratto and Rabinowitz, 1994) is one possible way to unpackage power distance (Hofstede, 1980) or hierarchy (Schwartz, 1994). This seems a pressing need, now that Smith, Dugan and Trompenaars (1996) have shown the probable independence of collectivism from hierarchical social structuring.

The extensive and well-validated values data bank of Schwartz (1994) opens up the possibility of a variety of studies at both the individual level and at the culture level which were not previously feasible. For instance, Barnea and Schwartz (1994) showed that the association between individual values and voting behaviour varies between nations in ways that can be predicted from each country's value profile. Sagie and Schwartz (1996) examined the correlates of differences in value consensus within teacher samples from thirty-seven nations. They found that high consensus was associated with a high rate of socio-economic development but a low degree of political democratization.

The field also needs to move beyond its preoccupation with values. Other psychological constructs, such as beliefs and expectancies (e.g. Bond, Leung and Schwartz, 1992), may be of greater use in predicting individual behaviour. Innovative approaches to conceptualizing culture and its mechanisms of impact on humans could be explored. Eco-cultural theories (Georgas and Berry, 1995) can be developed to the point where their predictive validity can be tested against value-based theories. For instance, is the incidence of role overload among managers in different nations better explained by power distance (Peterson *et al.*, 1995; Peterson and Smith, 1997) or by mean daily temperature (van de Vliert *et al.*, 1996)?

Recent work in the area of environmental psychology (e.g. Stokols, Clitheroe and Zmuidzinas, 1996) is also suggestive in this regard, especially that which contrasts 'normal' with 'abnormal' environments (Suedfeld, 1996). Similarly, Wilkinson (1996) has advanced data showing that a country's relative equality of income distribution is related to the key variables of country health and economic growth. He believes that income equality operates on these outcomes through the agency of social cohesion, surely a variable begging for use by social psychologists!

Conclusion

These and other innovations are only now beginning to emerge, to be conceptualized and integrated into the psychological literature. Were such ideas slow in coming? We think not. Their emergence had to await the diffusion of 'Western' psychology to different cultural milieux and the nurturing of local psychologists who are capable of challenging the biases of the discipline in its own terminology, using its established procedures.

We have now reached this stage. The development of cross-cultural social psychology is one of its manifestations. Its consequences will be an intellectual synergy that will enable us to transcend the limitations imposed by our different cultural origins. We may then be able to claim that we have a more truly universal understanding of humanity's social behaviour.

> And the end of all our exploring
> Will be to arrive where we started
> And know the place for the first time.

> T. S. Eliot, *Four Quartets*

References

Abelson, R. (1976) 'Script processing in attitude formation and decision making', in J. Carroll and J. Payne (eds.), *Cognition and Social Behavior*, Hillsdale, NJ: Erlbaum.

Abraham, M. (1980) *Perspectives on Modernization: Toward a general theory of third world development*, Washington, DC: University Press of America.

Abrams, D., Wetherell, M., Cochrane, S., Hogg, M. A. and Turner, J. C. (1990) 'Knowing what to think by knowing who you are: Self-categorisation and the nature of norm formation, conformity and group polarisation', *British Journal of Social Psychology*, 29, 97–119.

Ackerman, D. (1990) *A Natural History of the Senses*. New York: Random House.

Adair, J. G., Puhan, P. N. and Vohra, N. (1993) 'Indigenisation of psychology: Empirical assessment of progress in Indian research', *International Journal of Psychology*, 28, 149–69.

Adair, J. G., Pandey, J., Begum, H. A., Puhan, B. N. and Vohra, N. (1995) 'Indigenisation and development of the discipline: Perceptions and opinions of Indian and Bangladeshi psychologists', *Journal of Cross-Cultural Psychology*, 26, 392–407.

Adair, J. G. *et al.* (1997) 'Empirical studies of discipline development and indigenisation in Latin America', Symposium presented at Interamerican Congress of Psychology, São Paulo, Brazil.

Adamopoulos, J. (1988) 'Interpersonal behavior: Cross-cultural and historical perspectives', in M. H. Bond (ed.), *The Cross-cultural Challenge to Social Psychology*, Newbury Park, CA: Sage.

Adamopoulos, J. (1991) 'Diachronic and cross-cultural processes in the evolution of intimacy', in S. Ting Toomey and F. Korzenny (eds.), *Cross-cultural Interpersonal Communication*, London: Sage.

Adamopoulos, J. and Bontempo, R. (1987) 'Diachronic universals in interpersonal structures: Evidence from literary sources', *Journal of Cross-Cultural Psychology*, 17, 169–89.

Adams, J. S. (1965) 'Inequity in social exchange', in L. Berkowitz (ed.), *Advances in Experimental Social Psychology*, Volume 2, New York: Academic Press.

Adelman, I. and Morris, C. T. (1967) *Society, Politics and Economic Development: A Quantitative Approach*, Baltimore, MD: Johns Hopkins University Press.

Adigun, I. (1997) 'Orientations to work: A cross-cultural approach', *Journal of Cross-Cultural Psychology*, 28, 352–5.

Adler, N. J. (1981) 'Re-entry: Managing cross-cultural transitions', *Group and Organizational Studies*, 6, 341–56.

Adler, N. J., Schwarz, T. and Graham, J. L. (1987) 'Business negotiations in Canada (French and English speakers), Mexico and the United States', *Journal of Business Research*, 15, 411–29.

Adler, P. S. (1975) 'The transitional experience: An alternative view of culture shock', *Journal of Humanistic Psychology*, 15, 13–23.

Adler, P. S. (1987) 'Culture shock and the cross-cultural learning experience', in L. F. Luce and E. C. Smith (eds.), *Toward Internationalism: Readings in cross-cultural communication*, Cambridge, MA: Newbury House.

Adorno, T. W., Frenkel-Brunswick, E., Levinson, D. J. and Sanford, N. (1950) *The Authoritarian Personality*, New York: Harper Row.

Ajzen, I. (1988) *Attitudes, Personality and Behavior*, Milton Keynes, UK: Open University Press.

Alatas, S. H. (1972) 'The captive mind in development studies: Some neglected problems and the need for an autonomous social science tradition in Asia', *International Social Science Journal*, 24, 9–25.

Albright, L., Malloy, T. E., Qi, D., Kenny, D. A. *et al.* (1997) 'Cross-cultural consensus in personality judgments', *Journal of Personality and Social Psychology*, 73, 270–80.

Alcock, J. E. (1974) 'Cooperation, competition and the effects of time pressure in Canada and India', *Journal of Conflict Resolution*, 18, 171–97.

Alcock, J. E. (1975) 'Motivation in an asymmetric bargaining situation: A cross-cultural study', *International Journal of Psychology*, 10, 69–81.

Alden, D. L., Hoyer, W. D. and Lee, C. (1993) 'Identifying global and culture-specific dimensions of humor in advertising: A multinational analysis', *Journal of Marketing*, 57, 64–75.

Ali, A. (1988) 'Scaling an Islamic work ethic', *Journal of Social Psychology*, 128, 575–83.

Ali, A. (1990) 'Islamic work ethic in Arabia', *Journal of Psychology*, 126, 507–19.

Allport, F. H. (1924) *Social Psychology*, Boston, MA: Houghton Mifflin.

Almagor, M., Tellegen, A. and Waller, N. G. (1995) 'The Big Seven model: A cross-cultural replication and further exploration of the basic dimensions of natural language trait descriptors', *Journal of Personality and Social Psychology*, 69, 300–7.

Almagor, U. (1990) 'Odors and private language: Observations on the phenomenology of scent', *Human Studies*, 13, 253–74.

Almaney, A. and Ahwan, A. (1982) *Communicating with the Arabs*, Prospect Heights, IL: Waveland.

Altemeyer, B. (1981) *Right-wing Authoritarianism*, Winnipeg: University of Manitoba Press.

Altemeyer, B. (1988) *Enemies of Freedom: Understanding right-wing authoritarianism*, San Francisco: Jossey-Bass.

Altemeyer, B. and Kamenshikov, A. (1991) 'Impressions of American and Soviet behaviour: RWA images in a mirror', *South African Journal of Psychology*, 21, 255–60.

Altman, I and Chemers, M. M. (1980) 'Cultural aspects of environment–behaviour relationships', in H. C. Triandis and R. W. Brislin (eds.), *Handbook of Cross-Cultural Psychology*, Volume 5, Boston, MA: Allyn and Bacon.

Altman, I. and Gauvain, M. (1981) 'A cross-cultural dialectic analysis of homes', in L. Liben, A. Patterson and N. Newcombe (eds.), *Spatial Representation and Behavior across the Life-span*, New York: Academic Press.

Al-Zahrani, S. S. A. and Kaplowitz, S. A. (1993) 'Attributional biases in individualist and collectivist cultures: A comparison of Americans with Saudis', *Social Psychology Quarterly*, 56, 223–33.

Amabile, T. M. and Glazebrook, A. H. (1982) 'A negativity bias in interpersonal evaluation', *Journal of Experimental Social Psychology*, 18, 1–22.

Ambady, N., Koo, J., Lee, F. and Rosenthal, R. (1996) 'More than words: Linguistic and nonlinguistic politeness in two cultures', *Journal of Personality and Social Psychology*, 70, 996–1011.

Amir, Y. (1969) 'Contact hypothesis in ethnic relations', *Psychological Bulletin*, 71, 319–42.

Amir, Y. (1976) 'The role of intergroup contact in change of prejudice and ethnic relations', in P. A. Katz (ed.), *Towards the Elimination of Racism*, New York: Pergamon.

Amir, Y. and Sharon, I. (1987) 'Are social–psychological laws cross-culturally valid?', *Journal of Cross-Cultural Psychology*, 18, 383–470.

Ancona, L. and Pareyson, R. (1968) 'Contributo allo studio della aggressione: la dinamica della obbedienza distincttiva', *Archivio di Psicologia Neurologia e Psichiatria*, 29, 340–72.

Andersen, P. A. and Bowman, L. (1985) 'Positions of power: nonverbal cues of status and dominance in organizational communication', paper presented at the annual convention of the International Communication Association, Honolulu, HI.

Anderson, C. A. and Anderson, K. B. (1996) 'Violent crime rate studies in philosophical context: A destructive testing approach to heat and southern culture of violence effects', *Journal of Personality and Social Psychology*, 70, 740–56.

Anderson, C. A., Deuser, W. E. and DeNeve, K. M. (1995) 'Hot temperature, hostile affect, hostile cognition, and arousal: Tests of a general model of affective aggression', *Personality and Social Psychology Bulletin*, 21, 434–48.

Anderson, L. E. (1994) 'A new look at an old construct: Cross-cultural adaptation', *International Journal of Intercultural Relations*, 18, 293–328.

Andreeva, G. (1982) 'Common activity as a factor of causal attribution in a small group', in H. Hiebsch (ed.), *Social Psychology*, Amsterdam: North-Holland.

Andreeva, G. (1984) 'Cognitive processes in developing groups', in L. H. Strickland (ed.), *Directions in Soviet Social Psychology*, New York: Springer.

Aral, S. O. and Sunar, D. (1977) 'Interaction and justice norms: A cross-national comparison', *Journal of Social Psychology*, 101, 175–86.

Archer, D. (Producer) (1991) A world of gestures: Culture and nonverbal communication [Video]. Available from the University of California Extension Media Center, 2176 Shattuck Avenue, Berkeley, CA 94704.

Archer, D. and Gartner, R. (1984). *Violence and Crime in Cross-national Perspective*. New Haven: Yale University Press.

Ardila, R. (1996) 'Ethnopsychology and social values in Colombia', *Interamerican Journal of Psychology*, 30, 127–40.

Argyle, M. (1979) 'New developments in the analysis of social skills', in A. Wolfgang (ed.), *Non-verbal Behavior*, London: Academic Press.

Argyle, M., Furnham, A. and Graham, J. A. (1981) *Social Situations*, Cambridge: Cambridge University Press.

Argyle, M., Henderson, M., Bond, M. H., Iizuka, Y. and Contarello, A. (1986) 'Cross-cultural variations in relationship rules', *International Journal of Psychology*, 21, 287–315.

Armer, M. and Youtz, R. (1971) 'Formal education and individual modernity in an African society', *American Journal of Sociology*, 76, 604–26.

Asch, S. (1951) 'Effects of group pressure on the modification and distortion of judgments, in H. Guetzkow (ed.) *Groups, Leadership and Men*. Pittsburgh, PA: Carnegie.

Atsumi, T. and Sugiman, T. (1990) 'Group decision processes by majority and minority: Decision and implementation, *Japanese Journal of Experimental Social Psychology*, 30, 15–23 (English abstract).

Augoustinos, M. and Walker, I. (1995) 'Stereotypes as social representations', paper presented at the 5th European Congress of Psychology, Athens, Greece.

Avendano Sandoval, R. and Diaz Guerrero, R. (1992) 'Estudio experimental de la abnegacion', *Revista Mexicana de Psicología*, 9, 15–19.

Aycan, Z. and Berry, J. W. (1996) 'Impact of employment-related experiences on immigrants' psychological well-being and adaptation to Canada', *Canadian Journal of Behavioural Science*, 28, 240–51.

Ayman, R. and Chemers, M. M. (1983) 'Relationship of supervisory behavior ratings to work group effectiveness and subordinate satisfaction among Iranian managers', *Journal of Applied Psychology*, 68, 338–41.

Babiker, Z. E., Cox, J. L. and Miller, P. M. (1980) 'The measurement of cultural distance and its relationship to medical consultations, symptomatology, and examination of performance of overseas students at Edinburgh University', *Social Psychiatry*, 15, 109–16.

Bakan, D. (1966) *The Duality of Human Existence*, Chicago: Rand McNally.

Bales, R. F. (1951) *Interaction Process Analysis: A method for the study of small groups*, Reading, MA: Addison-Wesley.

Bandura, A. (1977) 'Self-efficacy: Toward a unifying theory of behavioural change', *Psychological Review*, 84, 191–215.

Bandura, A. (1986) *Social Foundation of Thought and Action: A social cognitive theory*, Englewood Cliffs, NJ: Prentice-Hall.

Bandura, A. (1996) 'A sociocognitive view on shaping the future', in S. C. Choi (ed.), *Proceedings of the Korean Psychological Association 50th Anniversary Conference*. Seoul, Korea: Hak Mun Publishing.

Bandura, A. (1997) *Self-efficacy: The exercise of control*, San Francisco: Freeman.

Barker, M., Child, C., Gallois, C., Jones, E. and Callan, V. J. (1991) 'Difficulties of overseas students in social and academic situations', *Australian Journal of Psychology*, 43, 79–84.

Barker, R. C. (1968) *Ecological Psychology: Concepts and methods for studying the environment of human behavior*, Stanford, CA: Stanford University Press.

Barnea, M. and Schwartz, S. H. (1994) 'Values and voting', unpublished paper, Hebrew University of Jerusalem.

Barnlund, D. C. and Araki, S. (1985) 'Intercultural encounters: The management of compliments by Japanese and Americans', *Journal of Cross-Cultural Psychology*, 16, 9–26.

Barnlund, D. C. and Yoshioka, M. (1990) 'Apologies: Japanese and American styles', *International Journal of Intercultural Relations*, 14, 193–206.

Barnouw, V. (1985) *Culture and Personality*, 4th edn, Belmont CA: Wadsworth.

Baron, R. A. and Byrne, D. (1994) *Social Psychology: Understanding human interaction*, 7th edn, Boston, MA: Allyn and Bacon.

Barraclough, R. A., Christophel, D. M. and McCroskey, J. C. (1988) 'Willingness to communicate: A cross-cultural investigation', *Communication Research Reports*, 5, 187–92.

Barry, H., Child, I. and Bacon, M. (1959) 'Relation of child training to subsistence economy', *American Anthropologist*, 61, 51–63.

Bass, B. M. (1985) *Leadership and Performance Beyond Expectations*, New York: Free Press.

Bass, B. M. and Avolio, B. J. (1993) ' Transformational leadership: A response to critiques', in M. M. Chemers and R. Ayman (eds.), *Leadership Theory and Research: Perspectives and directions*, San Diego, CA: Academic Press.

Bateson, N. (1966) 'Familiarisation, group discussion and risk-taking, *Journal of Experimental Social Psychology*, 2, 119–29.

Baumrind, D. (1964) 'Some thoughts on ethics of research: After reading Milgram's "Behavioral study of obedience"', *American Psychologist*, 19, 421–3.

Bavelas, J. B. (1994) 'Gestures as part of speech: Methodological implications', *Research on Language and Social Interaction*, 27, 201–21.

Beebe, L. M. and Takahashi, T. (1989) 'Sociolinguistic variation in face-threatening speech acts. Chastisement and disagreement', in M. R. Eisenstein (ed.), *The Dynamic Interlanguage: Empirical studies in second language variation*, New York: Plenum.

Beiser, M., Barwick, C., Berry, J. W. *et al.* (1988) *Mental health issues affecting immigrants and refugees*, Ottawa: Health and Welfare Canada.

Bell, P. R. and Jamieson, B. D. (1970) 'Publicity of initial decisions and the risky shift phenomenon', *Journal of Experimental Social Psychology*, 6, 329–45.

Ben-Ari, R., Schwarzwald, J. and Horiner-Levi, E. (1994) 'The effect of prevalent social stereotypes on intergroup attribution', *Journal of Cross-Cultural Psychology*, 25, 489–500.

Benet, V. and John, O. P. (1996) 'Los cinco grandes across cultures and ethnic groups: Multi-trait, multi-language analyses of the Spanish Big Five Inventory', manuscript submitted for publication.

Benet, V. and Waller, N. G. (1995) 'The Big Seven factor model of personality description: Evidence for its cross-cultural generality in a Spanish sample', *Journal of Personality and Social Psychology*, 69, 701–18.

Bennett, J. (1977) 'Transition shock: Putting culture shock in perspective', *International and Intercultural Communication Annual*, 4, 45–52.

Bennett, M. J. (1986) 'A developmental approach to training for intercultural sensitivity', *International Journal of Intercultural Relations*, 10, 179–96.

Berger, A. A. (1975) 'What makes people laugh? Cracking the cultural code', *Etc*, 32, 427–8.

Berger, C. R. (1987) 'Communicating under uncertainty', in M. E. Roloff and G. R. Mitter (eds.), *Interpersonal Processes*, Newbury Park, CA: Sage.

Berkowitz, L. (1989) 'Frustration–aggression hypothesis: examination and reformulation', *Psychological Bulletin*, 106, 59–73.

Berman, J. J., Murphy-Berman, V. and Singh, P. (1985) 'Cross-cultural similarities and differences in perceptions of fairness', *Journal of Cross-Cultural Psychology*, 16, 55–67.

Berman, J. J. and Murphy-Berman, V. A. (1996) 'Cultural differences in perceptions of allocators of resources', *Journal of Cross-Cultural Psychology*, 27, 494–509.

Bernstein, I. H., Tsai-Ding, L. and McClelland, P. (1982) 'Cross- vs. within-racial judgments of attractiveness', *Perception and Psychophysics*, 32, 495–503.

Berry, J. W. (1967) 'Independence and conformity in subsistence-level societies', *Journal of Personality and Social Psychology*, 7, 415–18.

Berry, J. W. (1969) 'On cross-cultural comparability', *International Journal of Psychology*, 4, 119–28.

Berry, J. W. (1980) 'Introduction to methodology', in H. C. Triandis and J. W. Berry (eds.), *Handbook of Cross-Cultural Psychology*, Volume 2. Boston, MA: Allyn and Bacon.

Berry, J. W. (1984) 'Multicultural policy in Canada: A social psychological analysis', *Canadian Journal of Behavioural Science*, 16, 353–70.

Berry, J. W. (1989) 'Imposed etics – emics – derived etics: The operationalisation of a compelling idea', *International Journal of Psychology*, 24, 721–35.

Berry, J. W. (1990) 'The role of psychology in ethnic studies', *Canadian Ethnic Studies*, 22, 8–21.

Berry, J. W. (1991a) 'Towards diversity and equity at Queen's: A strategy for change', *Queen's University Gazette*, 23 (1), Supplement (8 April 1991).

Berry, J. W. (1991b) 'Understanding and managing multiculturalism: Some possible implications of research in Canada', *Psychology and Development Societies*, 3, 17–49.

Berry, J. W. (1997) 'Immigration, acculturation, and adaptation', *Applied Psychology: An International Review*, 46, 5–34.

Berry, J. W. and Annis, R. C. (1974) 'Ecology, culture and psychological differentiation', *International Journal of Psychology*, 9, 173–93.

Berry, J. W., Dasen, P. and Saraswathi, T. S. (eds.) (1997) *Handbook of Cross-cultural Psychology*, 2nd Edn, Volume 2, *Basic Processes and Human Development*, Boston, MA: Allyn and Bacon.

Berry, J. W. and Kalin, R. (1979) 'Reciprocity of inter–ethnic attitudes in a multicultural society', *International Journal of Intercultural Relations*, 3, 99–112.

Berry, J. W. and Kalin, R. (1995) 'Multicultural and ethnic attitudes in Canada: An overview of the 1991 national survey', *Canadian Journal of Behavioural Science*, 27, 301–20.

Berry, J. W., Kalin, R. and Taylor, D. M. (1977) *Multiculturalism and Ethnic Attitudes in Canada*, Ottawa: Ministry of Supplies and Services.

Berry, J. W., Kalin, R. and Taylor, D. M. (1980) 'Multiculturalism and ethnic attitudes in Canada', in J. E. Goldstein and R. M. Bienvenue (eds.), *Ethnicity and Ethnic Relations in Canada*, Toronto: Butterworth.

Berry, J. W. and Kim, U. (1988) 'Acculturation and mental health', in P. Dasen, J. W. Berry, and N. Sartorius (eds.), *Health and cross-cultural psychology*, Newbury Park, CA: Sage.

Berry, J. W. and Kwak, K. (1996) 'International comparative study of ethnocultural youth', paper presented at the 13th Congress of the International Association for Cross-Cultural Psychology, Montreal.

Berry, J. W., Kim, U., Power, S., Young, M. and Bujaki, M. (1989) 'Acculturation attitudes in plural societies', *Applied Psychology*, 38, 185–206.

Best, D. L. and Williams, J. E. (1994) 'Masculinity/femininity in the self and ideal self descriptions of university students in fourteen countries', in A. M. Bouvy, F. J. R. van de Vijver, P. Boski and P. Schmitz (eds.), *Journeys into Cross-cultural Psychology*, Lisse: Swets and Zeitlinger.

Bethlehem, D. W. (1975) 'The effect of Westernisation on cooperative behaviour in Central Africa', *International Journal of Psychology*, 10, 219–24.

Bhawuk, D. P. S. (1996) 'The role of culture theory in cross-cultural training: A multimethod study of culture-specific, culture general, and culture theory-based assimilators', paper presented at the Academy of Management Meeting, Cincinnati.

Bierbrauer, G. (1994) 'Toward an understanding of legal culture: Variations in individualism and collectivism between Kurds, Lebanese and Germans', *Law and Society Review*, 28, 243–64.

Bierbrauer, G. and Pedersen, P. (1996) 'Culture and migration', in G. R. Semin and K. Fiedler (eds.), *Applied Social Psychology*, London: Sage.

Bijnen, E. J., van der Net, T. Z. J. and Poortinga, Y. H. (1986) 'On cross-cultural comparative studies with the Eysenck Personality Questionnaire', *Journal of Cross-Cultural Psychology*, 17, 3–16.

Bijnen, E. J. and Poortinga, Y. H. (1988) 'The questionable value of cross-cultural comparisons with the Eysenck Personality Questionnaire', *Journal of Cross-Cultural Psychology*, 19, 193–202.

Bilbow, G. (1996) 'Requesting strategies in the cross-cultural business meeting', *Pragmatics*, 5, 45–55.

Billig, M. (1976) *Social Psychology and Intergroup Relations*, London: Academic Press.

Bilsky, W. and Schwartz, S. H. (1994) 'Values and personality', *European Journal of Personality*, 8, 163–81.

Birth, K. and Prillwitz, G. (1959) 'Fuhrungsstile und Gruppen Verhalten von Schulkindern', *Zeitschrift fur Psychologie*, 163, 230–301.

Black, J. S. and Gregerson, H. B. (1991) 'When Yankee comes home: Factors related to expatriate and spouse repatriation adjustment', *Journal of International Business Studies*, 22, 671–94.

Black, J. S., Gregersen, H. B. and Mendenhall, M. E. (1992) *Global assignments: Successfully expatriating and repatriating international managers*, San Francisco, CA: Jossey-Bass.

Black, J. S. and Porter, L. W. (1991) 'Managerial behaviors and job performance: A successful manager in Los Angeles may not succeed in Hong Kong', *Journal of International Business Studies*, 22, 99–113.

Blackler, F. (ed.) (1983) *Social Psychology and Developing Countries*, Chichester: Wiley.

Blum-Kulka, S., House, J. and Kasper, G. (eds.) (1989) *Cross-cultural Pragmatics: Requests and apologies*, Norwood, NJ: Ablex.

Bochner, S. (ed.) (1980) *The Mediating Person: Bridges between cultures*, Cambridge, MA: Schenkman.

Bochner, S. (1982) 'The social psychology of cross-cultural relations', in S. Bochner (ed.), *Cultures in Contact: Studies in cross-cultural interaction*, Oxford: Pergamon.

Bochner, S. (1986) 'Training inter-cultural skills', in C. R. Hollin and P. Trower (eds.), *Handbook of Social Skills Training: Vol. 1. Applications across the life span*, Oxford: Pergamon.

Bochner, S. (1994) 'Cross-cultural differences in the self concept: A test of Hofstede's individualism/collectivism distinction', *Journal of Cross-Cultural Psychology*, 25, 273–83.

Bochner, S. and Hesketh, B. (1994) 'Power distance, individualism–collectivism and job-related attitudes in a culturally diverse work group', *Journal of Cross-Cultural Psychology*, 25, 233–57.

Bochner, S., Lin, A. and Macleod, B. M. (1980) 'Anticipated role conflict of returning overseas students', *Journal of Social Psychology*, 110, 265–72.

Bochner, S., Lin, A. and McLeod, B. M. (1979) 'Cross-cultural contact and the development of an international perspective', *Journal of Social Psychology*, 107, 29–41.

Bochner, S. and Perks, R. W. (1971) 'National role evocation as a function of cross-national interaction', *Journal of Cross-Cultural Psychology*, 2, 157–64.

Boisot, M. and Liang, X. G. (1992) 'The nature of managerial work in the Chinese enterprise reforms: A study of six directors', *Organization Studies*, 13, 161–84.

Bond, M. (1983) 'Linking person perception dimensions to behavioral intention dimensions: The Chinese connection', *Journal of Cross-Cultural Psychology*, 14, 41–63.

Bond, M. H. (1985) 'Language as a carrier of ethnic stereotypes in Hong Kong', *Journal of Social Psychology*, 125, 53–62.

Bond, M. H. (1986) 'Mutual stereotypes and the facilitation of interaction across cultural lines', *International Journal of Intercultural Relations*, 10, 259–76.

Bond, M. H. (ed.) (1988a) *The Cross-cultural Challenge to Social Psychology*, Newbury Park, CA: Sage.

Bond, M. H. (1988b) 'Finding universal dimensions of individual variation in multi-cultural studies of values: The Rokeach and Chinese value surveys', *Journal of Personality and Social Psychology*, 55, 1009–15.

Bond, M. H. (1991a) 'Chinese values and health: A cross-cultural examination', *Psychology and Health*, 5, 137–52.

Bond, M. H. (1991b) 'The process of enhancing cross-cultural competence in Hong Kong organizations', *International Journal of Intercultural Relations*, 16, 395–412.

Bond, M. H. (1991c) 'Cultural influences on modes of impression management: Implications of the culturally diverse organization', in R. A. Giacolone and P. Rosenfeld (eds.), *Applied Impression Management: How image-making affects managerial decisions*, Newbury Park, CA: Sage.

Bond, M. H. (1993) 'Emotions and their expression in Chinese culture', *Journal of Nonverbal Behavior*, 17, 245–62.

Bond, M. H. (ed.) (1996a) *The Handbook of Chinese Psychology*, Hong Kong: Oxford University Press.

Bond, M. H. (1996b) 'Social Psychology Across Cultures: Two ways forward', Keynote lecture, International Congress of Psychology, Montreal.

Bond, M. H. (ed.) (1997) *Working at the Interface of Cultures: Eighteen lives in social science*, London: Routledge.

Bond, M. H. and Chan, S. C. N. (1995) 'Country values and country health', paper presented at the 7th European Congress Psychology, Athens, Greece.

Bond, M. H. and Cheung, M. K. (1984) 'Experimenter language choice and ethnic affirmation by Chinese trilinguals in Hong Kong', *International Journal of Inter-cultureal Relations*, 8, 347–56.

Bond, M. H. and Cheung, T. S. (1983) 'The spontaneous self-concept of college students in Hong Kong, Japan, and the United States', *Journal of Cross-Cultural Psychology*, 14, 153–71.

Bond, M. H., Chiu, C. K. and Wan, K. C. (1984) 'When modesty fails: The social impact of group-effacing attributions following success or failure', *European Journal of Social Psychology*, 14, 335–8.

Bond, M. H. and Dutton, D. G. (1975) 'The effect of interaction anticipation and experience as a victim on aggressive behavior', *Journal of Personality*, 43, 515–27.

Bond, M. H. and Forgas, J. P. (1984) 'Linking person perception to behavioral intention across cultures: The role of cultural collectivism', *Journal of Cross-Cultural Psychology*, 15, 337–52.

Bond, M. H. and Hewstone, M. (1988) 'Social identity theory and the perception of intergroup relations in Hong Kong', *International Journal of Intercultural Relations*, 12, 153–70.

Bond, M. H. and Hwang, K. K. (1986) 'The social psychology of Chinese people', in M. H. Bond (ed.), *The Psychology of the Chinese People*, Hong Kong: Oxford University Press.

Bond, M. H. and King, A. Y. C. (1985) 'Coping with the threat of Westernization in Hong Kong', *International Journal of Intercultural Relations*, 9, 351–64.

Bond, M. H., Leung, K. and Schwartz, S. H. (1992) 'Explaining choices in procedural and distributive justice across cultures', *International Journal of Psychology*, 27, 211–25.

Bond, M. H., Leung, K. and Wan, K. C. (1982a) 'How does cultural collectivism operate? The impact of task and maintenance contributions on reward allocations', *Journal of Cross-Cultural Psychology*, 13, 186–200.

Bond, M. H., Leung, K. and Wan, K. C. (1982b) 'The social impact of self-effacing attributions: The Chinese case', *Journal of Social Psychology*, 118, 157–66.

Bond, M. H. and Mak, A. L. P. (1996) 'Deriving an intergroup topography from perceived values: Forging an identity in Hong Kong out of Chinese tradition', invited paper, Korean Psychological Association's 50th Anniversary Conference, Seoul.

Bond, M. H. and Shiu, W. Y. F. (1997) 'The relationship between a group's personality resources and the two dimensions of its group process', *Small Group Research*, 28, 194–217.

Bond, M. H. and Venus, C. K. (1991) 'Resistance to group or personal insults in an in-group or out-group context', *International Journal of Psychology*, 26, 83–94.

Bond, M. H. and Yang, K. S. (1982) 'Ethnic affirmation versus cross-cultural accommodation: The variable impact of questionnaire language on Chinese bilinguals in Hong Kong', *Journal of Cross-Cultural Psychology*, 12, 169–81.

Bond, M. H., Hewstone, M., Wan, K. C. and Chiu, C. K. (1985a) 'Group-serving attributions across intergroup contexts: Cultural differences in the explanation of sex-typed behaviours', *European Journal of Social Psychology*, 15, 435–51.

Bond, M. H., Wan, K. C., Leung, K. and Giacolone, R. A. (1985b) 'How are responses to verbal insult related to cultural collectivism and power distance?', *Journal of Cross-Cultural Psychology*, 16, 111–27.

Bond, R. A. and Smith, P. B. (1996) 'Culture and conformity: A meta-analysis of studies using the Asch's (1952b, 1956) line judgment task',*Psychological Bulletin*, 119, 111–37.

Bond, R., Smith, P. B. and Wood, W. (1997) 'Culture and minority influence', paper given at conference of the British Psychological Society, Social Psychology section, University of Sussex, September.

Borges Andrade, J. E. (1994) 'Comprometimento organizacional na administração pública e em seus segmentos meio e fim', *Temas de Psicologia – Psicologica Social e Organizacional*, 1, 49–61.

Borkenau, P. and Liebler, A. (1992) 'Trait inferences: Sources of validity at zero acquaintance', *Journal of Personality and Social Psychology*, 62, 645–57.

Boski, P. (1983) 'A study of person perception in Nigeria: Ethnicity and self versus other attributions for achievement-related outcomes', *Journal of Cross-Cultural Psychology*, 14, 85–108.

Bourhis, R. Y., Giles, H., Leyens, J. P. and Tajfel, H. (1979) 'Psycholinguistic distinctiveness: Language divergence in Belgium', in H. Giles and R. N. St Clair (eds.), *Language and Social Psychology*, Baltimore, MD: University Park Press.

Bradbury, T. N. and Fincham, F. D. (1990) 'Attributions in marriage: A review and critique', *Psychological Bulletin*, 107, 3–33.

Brehm, J. W. (1966) *A Theory of Psychological Reactance*, New York: Academic Press.

Brewer, M. B. (1988) 'A dual process model of impression formation', in R. Wyer and T. Scrull (eds.), *Advances in Social Cognition*, Volume 1, New York: Erlbaum.

Brewer, M. B. and Campbell, D. T. (1976) *Ethnocentrism and Intergroup Attitudes: East African evidence*, New York: Wiley.

Brewster, C. (1995) 'Toward a "European" model of human resource management', *Journal of International Business Studies*, 26, 1–22.

Brislin, R. (1981) *Cross-cultural Encounters*. Elmsford, NY: Pergamon.

Brislin, R. and Yoshida, T. (1994) *Intercultural Communication Training: An introduction*, Thousand Oaks, CA: Sage.

Brislin, R., Lonner, W. and Thorndike, R. M. (1973) *Cross-cultural Research Methods*, New York: Wiley.

Brislin, R., Cushner, K., Cherrie, C. and Yong, M. (1986) *Intercultural Interactions: A practical guide*, Beverly Hills, CA: Sage.

Bronfenbrenner, U. (1961) 'The mirror image in Soviet–American relations: A social psychologist's report', *Journal of Social Issues*, 17, 45–56.

Brown, L. R. *et al.* (1990) *State of the World 1990*, New York: Norton.

Brown, P. and Levinson, S. (1987) *Politeness: Some universals in language use*, Cambridge: Cambridge University Press.

Brown, R. J., Hinkle, S., Ely, P. C., Fox-Cardamone, L. *et al.* (1992) 'Recognising group diversity: Individualist–collectivist and autonomous–relational social orientations and their implications for intergroup processes', *British Journal of Social Psychology*, 31, 327–42.

Burgoon, J. K. (1989) 'Comparatively speaking: Applying a comparative approach to non-verbal expectancy violations theory', unpublished manuscript, University of Arizona.

Burgoon, J. K. (1995) 'Cross-cultural and intercultural applications of expectancy violations theory', in R. L. Wiseman (ed.), *Intercultural Communication Theory*, Thousand Oaks, CA: Sage.

Burgoon, J. K. and Walther, J. B. (1990) 'Non-verbal expectancies and the evaluative consequences of violations', *Human Communication Research*, 17, 232–65.

Burleson, B. R., Kunkel, A. W. and Birch, J. D. (1994) 'Thoughts about talk in romantic relationships: Similarity makes for attraction (and happiness, too)', *Communication Quarterly*, 42, 259–73.

Burley, P. M. and McGuiness, J. (1977) 'Effects of social intelligence on the Milgram paradigm', *Psychological Reports*, 40, 767–70.

Buss, D. M. (1989) 'Sex differences in human mate preferences: Evolutionary hypotheses tested in 37 cultures', *Behavioral and Brain Sciences*, 12, 1–49.

Buss, D. M. (1991) 'Evolutionary personality psychology', *Annual Review of Psychology*, 42, 459–91.

Buss, D. M. and 49 co-authors (1990) 'International preferences in selecting mates: A study of 37 cultures', *Journal of Cross-Cultural Psychology*, 21, 5–47.

Buunk, B. and Hupka, R. B. (1987) 'Cross-cultural differences in the elicitation of sexual jealousy', *Journal of Sex Research*, 23, 12–22.

Cameron, J. E. and Lalonde, R. N. (1994) 'Self, ethnicity, and social group memberships in two generations of Italian Canadians', *Personality and Social Psychology Bulletin*, 20, 514–20.

Campbell, A. (1993) *Men, Women, and Aggression*, New York: Basic Books.

Campbell, J. D., Trapnell, P. D., Heine, S. J. *et al.* (1996) 'Self-concept clarity: Measurement, personality correlates, and cultural boundaries', *Journal of Personality and Social Psychology*, 70, 141–56.

Campbell, N., Graham, J. L., Jolibert, A. and Meissner, H. G. (1988) 'Marketing negotiations in France, Germany, the United Kingdom and the United States', *Journal of Marketing*, 52, 49–62.

Cantor, N. and Mischel, W. (1978) 'Prototypes in person perception', in L. Berkowitz (ed.), *Advances in Experimental Social Psychology*, Volume 12, New York: Academic Press.

Carballo, M. (1994) *Scientific Consultation on the Social and Health Impact of Migration: Priorities for research*, Geneva: International Organization for Migration.

Carden, A. I. and Feicht, R. (1991) 'Homesickness among American and Turkish college students', *Journal of Cross-Cultural Psychology*, 22, 418–28.

Carlson, J. and Davis, D. M. (1971) 'Cultural values and the risky shift: A cross-cultural test in Uganda and the United States', *Journal of Personality and Social Psychology*, 20, 392–9.

Carment, D. W. (1974) 'Indian and Canadian choice behavior in a maximising difference game and in a game of chicken', *International Journal of Psychology*, 9, 213–21.

Carment, D. W. and Alcock, J. E. (1984) 'Indian and Canadian behavior in two person power games', *Journal of Conflict Resolution*, 28, 507–21.

Carr, S. C. (1994) 'Generating the velocity for overcoming motivational gravity in LDC business organisations', *Journal of Transnational Management Development*, 1, 33–56.

Carr, S. C. (1996) 'Social psychology in Malawi: Historical or developmental?', *Psychology and Developing Societies*, 8, 177–97.

Carr, S. C. and MacLachlan, M. (1997) 'Motivational gravity', in D. Munro, J. F. Schumacher and S. C. Carr (eds.), *Motivation and Culture*. New York: Routledge.

Carr, S., MacLachlan, M., Kachedwa, M. And Kanyangale, M. (1997) 'The meaning of work in Malawi', *Journal of International Development*, 9, in press.

Carr, S. C., Ehiobuche, I., Rugimbana, R. and Munro, D. (1996) 'Expatriates' ethnicity and their effectiveness: "Similarity-attraction" or "inverse resonance"?', *Psychology and Developing Societies*, 8, 265–82.

Carter, H. and Glick, P. C. (1970) *Marriage and Divorce: A social and economic study*, Cambridge, MA: Harvard University Press.

Cattell, R. B. (1953) 'A quantitative analysis of the changes in the culture pattern of Great Britain, 1837–1937, by P-technique', *Acta Psychologica*, 9, 99–121.

Cegala, D. J. (1981) 'Interaction involvement: A cognitive dimension of communication competence', *Communication Education*, 30, 109–21.

Chan, D. K. S., Gelfand, M. J., Triandis, H. C. and Tzeng, O. (1996) 'Tightness–looseness revisited: Some preliminary analyses in Japan and the United States', *International Journal of Psychology*, 31, 1–12.

Chan, D. K. S., Triandis, H. C., Carnevale, P. J. *et al.* (1995) 'Culture and negotiation: Effects of collectivism, relationship between negotiators, and opponent's strategy on negotiation behavior', unpublished paper, Chinese University of Hong Kong.

Chandler, T. A., Shama, D. D., Wolf, F. M. and Planchard, S. K. (1981) 'Multiattributional causality: A five cross-national samples study', *Journal of Cross-Cultural Psychology*, 12, 207–21.

Chandra, S. (1973) 'The effects of group pressure in perception: A cross-cultural conformity study', *International Journal of Psychology*, 8, 37–9.

Chang, Y., Lin, W. and Kohnstamm, G. A. (1994) 'Parents free descriptions on children's characteristics – a verified study on the Big Five in Chinese children', paper presented at ISSBD Workshop, Beijing.

Chanlat, J.-F. (1994) 'Francophone organizational analysis (1950–1990): An overview', *Organization Studies*, 15, 47–80.

Chataway, C. J. and Berry, J. W. (1989) 'Acculturation experiences, appraisal, coping, and adaptation: A comparison of Hong Kong Chinese, French, and English students in Canada', *Canadian Journal of Behavioural Science*, 21, 295–309.

Chen, C. (1995) 'New trends in rewards allocation preferences: A Sino–US comparison', *Academy of Management Journal*, 38, 408–28.

Chen, C., Meindl, J. R. and Hunt, R. (1997) 'Testing effects of horizontal and vertical collectivism: A study of rewards allocation preferences in China', *Journal of Cross-Cultural Psychology*, 28, 44–70.

Chen, C. S., Lee, S. Y. and Stevenson, H. W. (1995) 'Response style and cross-cultural comparisons of rating scales among East Asian and North American students', *Psychological Science*, 6, 170–5.

Chen, L. (1995) 'Interaction involvement and patterns of topical talk: A comparison of intracultural and intercultural dyads', *International Journal of Intercultural Relations*, 19, 463–82.

Chen, N. Y., Shaffer, D. R. and Wu, C. H. (1997) 'On physical attractiveness stereotyping in Taiwan: A revised socio-cultural perspective', *Journal of Social Psychology*, 137, 117–24.

Cheung, F. M., Leung, K., Zhang, J. X. *et al.* (1998) 'Indigenous Chinese personality constructs', *Journal of Cross-Cultural Psychology*, 29.

Child, J. (1981) 'Culture, contingency and capitalism in the cross-national study of organisations', in B. M. Staw and L. L. Cummings (eds.), *Research in Organisational Behaviour*, 3, 303–56.

Child, J. (1994) *Management in China During the Age of Reform*, Cambridge: Cambridge University Press.

Child, J. and Markoczy, L. (1993) 'Host country managerial behaviour and learning in Chinese and Hungarian joint ventures', *Journal of Management Studies*, 30, 611–31.

Chinese Culture Connection (1987) 'Chinese values and the search for culture-free dimensions of culture', *Journal of Cross-Cultural Psychology*, 18, 143–64.

Chiu, H. Y. (1979) 'A test of unidimensionality and universality of individual modernity in ten Taiwanese communities', unpublished doctoral dissertation, Indiana University.

Choi, S. C. and Choi, S. H. (1992) 'The conceptualisation of Korean tact, Noon-Chi', in S. Iwawaki, Y. Kashima and K. Leung (eds.), *Innovations in Cross-cultural Psychology*, Lisse: Swets and Zeitlinger.

Choi, S. C., Kim, U. and Choi, S. H (1993) 'Indigenous analysis of collective representations: A Korean perspective' in U. Kim and J. W. Berry (eds.), *Indigenous Psychologies: Research and experience in cultural context*, Newbury Park, CA: Sage.

Choi, S. C., Kim, U. and Kim, K. (1995) 'Multifacted analyses of chemyon (social face): An indigenous Korean perspective', paper presented at first conference of the Asian Association of Social Psychology, Kyoto.

Chow, I. H. S. (1994) 'An opinion survey of performance appraisal practices in Hong Kong and the People's Republic of China', *Asia Pacific Journal of Human Resources*, 32, 67–79.

Christensen, H. T. (1973) 'Attitudes toward marital infidelity: A nine culture sampling of university student opinion', *Journal of Comparative Family Studies*, 4, 197–214.

Christie, R. and Geis, F. (1970) *Studies in Machiavellianism*, New York: Academic Press.

Church, A. T. (1982) ' Sojourner adjustment', *Psychological Bulletin*, 91, 540–72.

Church, A. T. (1987) 'Personality research in a non-Western culture: The Philippines, *Psychological Bulletin*, 102, 272–92.

Church, A. T. and Katigbak, M. S. (1988) 'The emic strategy in the identification and assessment of personality dimensions in a non-Western culture', *Journal of Cross-Cultural Psychology*, 19, 140–63.

Church, A. T. and Katigbak, M. S. (1989) 'Internal, external and self-report structure of personality in a non-Western culture: An investigation of cross-language and cross-cultural generalisability', *Journal of Personality and Social Psychology*, 57, 857–72.

Church, A. T. and Katigbak, M. S. (1992) 'The cultural context of academic motives: A comparison of Filipino and American college students', *Journal of Cross-Cultural Psychology*, 23, 40–58.

Church, A. T., Katigbak, M. S. and Reyes, J. A. S. (1996) 'Toward a taxonomy of trait adjectives in Filipino: Comparing personality lexicons across cultures', *European Journal of Personality*, 10, 3–24.

Clark, H. H. and Brennan, S. E. (1991) 'Grounding in communication', in L. B. Resnick, J. M. Levine and S. D. Teasley (eds.), *Perspectives on Socially Shared Communication*, Washington, DC: American Psychological Association.

Clemence, A., Doise, W., de Rosa, A. S. and Gonzalez, L. (1995) 'La représentation sociale des droits de l'homme: une recherche internationale sur l'étendue et les limites de l'universalité', *International Journal of Psychology*, 30, 181–212.

Coch, L. and French, J. R. P. (1948) 'Overcoming resistance to change', *Human Relations*, 1, 512–32.

Cocroft, B.-A. K. and Ting-Toomey, S. (1994) 'Facework in Japan and the United States', *International Journal of Intercultural Relations*, 18, 469–506.

Cohen, D. (1996) 'Law, social policy, and violence: The impact of regional cultures', *Journal of Personality and Social Psychology*, 70, 961–78.

Cohen, D. and Nisbett, R. E. (1994) 'Self-protection and the culture of honor: Explaining Southern violence', *Personality and Social Psychology Bulletin*, 20, 551–67.

Cohen, D., Nisbett, R. E., Bowdle, B. F. and Schwarz, N. (1996) 'Insult, aggression, and the Southern culture of honor: An "experimental ethnography"', *Journal of Personality and Social Psychology*, 70, 945–60.

Cohen, E. (1985) 'The tourist guide: The origins, structure and dynamics of a role', *Annals of Tourism Research*, 12, 5–29.

Cole, M. (1990) 'Cultural psychology: A once and future discipline?', in J. J. Berman (ed.) *Nebraska Symposium on Motivation 1989: Cross-cultural perspectives*, 37, 279–336.

Collett, P. (1971) 'On training Englishmen in the non-verbal behaviours of Arabs', *International Journal of Psychology*, 6, 209–15.

Collett, P. and O'Shea, G. (1976) 'Pointing the way to a fictional place: A study of direction-giving in England and Iran', *European Journal of Social Psychology*, 6, 447–58.

Collins, M. A. and Zebrowitz, L. A. (1995) 'The contributions of appearance to occupational outcomes in civilian and military settings', *Journal of Applied Social Psychology*, 25, 129–63.

Condor, S. (1996) 'Unimagined community: Some social psychological issues concerning English national identity', in G. M. Breakwell and E. Lyons (eds.), *Changing European Identities: Social psychological analysis of social change*, Oxford: Butterworth-Heinemann.

Cooperrider, D. L. and Pasmore, W. A. (1991) 'The organization dimension of global change', *Human Relations*, 44, 763–87.

Cort, D. A. and King, M. (1979) 'Some correlates of culture shock among American tourists in Africa', *International Journal of Intercultural Relations*, 3, 211–25.

Costa, P. T. and McCrae, R. R. (1985) *The NEO Personality Inventory Manual*, Odessa, FL: Psychological Assessment Resources.

Costa, P. T. Jr. and McCrae, R. R. (1992) *Revised NEO Personality Inventory (NEO PI-R) and NEO Five-Factor Inventory (NEO-FFI)*, Odessa, FL: Psychological Assessment Resources.

Cottle, T. J. (1976) *Time Perspective: A psychological investigation with men and women*, New York: Wiley.

Coupland, J., Coupland, N., Giles, H., and Wiemann, J. (1988) 'My life in your hands: Processes of self-disclosure in intergenerational talk', in N. Coupland (ed.), *Styles of Discourse*, London: Croom Helm.

Cousins, S. (1989) 'Culture and selfhood in Japan and the U.S.', *Journal of Personality and Social Psychology*, 56, 124–31.

Cox, T. Jr. (1993) *Cultural Diversity in Organizations: Theory, research and practice*, San Francisco: Berrett-Koehlor.

Cox, T. H., Lobel, S. and McLeod, P. L. (1991) 'Effects of ethnic group cultural differences on cooperative and competitive behavior on a group task', *Academy of Management Journal*, 34, 827–47.

Crocker, J., Luhtanen, R., Blaine, B. and Broadnax, S. (1994) 'Collective self-esteem and psychological well-being among White, Black, and Asian college students', *Personality and Social Psychology Bulletin*, 20, 503–13.

Cuellar, I., Harris, L. C. and Jasso, R. (1980) 'An acculturation scale for Mexican American normal and clinical populations', *Hispanic Journal of Behavioural Sciences*, 2, 199–217.

Cunningham, M. R., Barbee, A. P. and Pike, C. L. (1990) 'What do women want? Facialmetric assessment of multiple motives in the perception of male facial physical attractiveness', *Journal of Personality and Social Psychology*, 59, 61–72.

Cunningham, M. R., Roberts, A. R., Barbee, A. P. *et al.* (1995) '"Their ideas of beauty are, on the whole, the same as ours": Consistency and variability in the cross-cultural perception of female physical attractiveness', *Journal of Personality and Social Psychology*, 68, 261–79.

Cupach, W. R., Metts, S., and Hazelton, V. (1978) 'Coping with social dis-ease: Remedial strategies and embarrassment', paper presented at the Western Speech Communication Association, Salt Lake City, UT.

Dahl, Ø. (1995) 'When the future comes from behind: Malagasy and other time concepts and some consequences for communication', *International Journal for Intercultural Relations*, 19, 197–209.

Dasen, P. (1984) 'The cross-cultural definition of intelligence: Piaget and the Baoulé', *International Journal of Psychology*, 19, 407–34.

Davies, D. (1989) 'Travellers' tales', *Far Eastern Economic Review*, 28 September, 41.

Dawes, R. M. (1980) 'Social Dilemmas', *Annual Review of Psychology*, 31, 169–93.

De Monchaux, C. and Shimmin, S. (1955) 'Some problems in experimental group psychology', *Human Relations*, 8, 53–60.

Der-Karabetian, A. (1992) 'World-mindedness and the nuclear threat: A multinational study', *Journal of Social Behavior and Personality*, 7, 293–308.

Der-Karabetian, A., Stephenson, K. and Poggi, T. (1996) 'Environmental risk perception, activism and world-mindedness among samples of British and US college students', *Perceptual and Motor Skills*, 83, 451–62.

DeRidder, R. and Tripathi, R. C. (1992) *Norm Violation and Intergroup Relations*, Oxford: Clarendon.

Derlega, V. J. and Stepien, E. G. (1977) 'Norms regulating self-disclosure among Polish university students', *Journal of Cross-Cultural Psychology*, 8, 369–76.

Deshpande, S. P. and Viswesvaran, C. (1992) 'Is cross-cultural training of expatriate managers effective? A meta-analysis', *International Journal of Intercultural Relations*, 16, 295–310.

Deutsch, K. (1968) 'Toward a cybernetic model of man and society', in W. Buckley (ed.), *Modern Systems Theory for the Behavioral Scientist*, Chicago: Aldine.

Devine, P. G. (1989) 'Stereotypes and prejudice: Their automatic and controlled components', *Journal of Personality and Social Psychology*, 56, 5–18.

Devine, P. G., Monteith, M. J., Znwerink, R. J. and Elliot, A. J. (1991) 'Prejudice with and without compunction', *Journal of Personality and Social Psychology*, 60, 817–30.

Diab, L. N. (1970) 'A study of intragroup and intergroup relations among experimentally produced small groups', *Genetic Psychology Monographs*, 82, 49–82.

Diaz Guerrero, R. (1993) 'Mexican ethnopsychology', in U. Kim and J. W. Berry (eds.), *Indigenous Psychologies: Research and experience in cultural context*, Newbury Park, CA: Sage.

Diaz Guerrero, R. (1995) 'Origins and development of Mexican ethnopsychology', *World Psychology*, 1, 49–67.

Diener, E. and Diener, M. (1995) 'Cross-cultural correlates of life satisfaction and self-esteem', *Journal of Personality and Social Psychology*, 68, 653–63.

Diener, E., Shao, L., Diener, C. and Suh, E. (1996) 'Subjective well-being: National similarities and differences', paper presented at 26th International Congress of Psychology, Montreal.

Digman, J. M. (1990) 'Personality structure: Emergence of the five-factor model', *Annual Review of Psychology*, 41, 417–40.

Dijker, A. J. (1987) 'Emotional reactions to ethnic minorities', *European Journal of Social Psychology*, 17, 305–25.

Dinges, N. G. and Lieberman, D. A. (1989) 'Intercultural communication competence: Coping with stressful work situations', *International Journal of Intercultural Relations*, 13, 371–85.

Dion, K. K. and Dion, K. L. (1991) 'Psychological individualism and romantic love', *Journal of Social Behavior and Personality*, 6, 7–13.

Dion, K. K. and Dion, K. L. (1993) 'Individualistic and collectivistic perspectives on gender and the cultural context of love and intimacy', *Journal of Social Issues*, 49, 53–69.

Dion, K. K., Pak, A. W. and Dion, K. L. (1990) 'Stereotyping physical attractiveness: A sociocultural perspective', *Journal of Cross-Cultural Psychology*, 21, 158–79.

Dion, K. L. (1986) 'Responses to perceived discrimination and relative deprivation', in J. M. Olson, C. P. Herman and M. P. Zanna (eds.), *Relative deprivation and social comparison: The Ontario symposium*, Volume 4, pp. 159–79, Hillsdale, NJ: Erlbaum.

Dion, K. L., Dion, K. K. and Pak, A. W. P. (1992) 'Personality-based hardiness as a buffer for discrimination-related stress in members of Toronto's Chinese community', *Canadian Journal of Behavioural Science*, 24, 517–36.

Dion, K. L. and Kawakami, K. (1996) 'Ethnicity and perceived discrimination in Toronto: Another look at the personal/group discrimination discrepancy', *Canadian Journal of Behavioural Science*, 28, 203–13.

D'Iribarne, P. (1994) 'The honour principle in the bureaucratic phenomenon', *Organizational Studies*, 15, 1–15.

Dittmar, H., Singelis, T. M. and Papadopoulou, K. (1996) 'Gender differences in the meaning of personal possessions as reflections of independent versus interdependent aspects of identity in the UK, US and Greece', paper given at 13th Congress of the International Association of Cross-Cultural Psychology, Montreal.

Doherty, R. W., Hatfield, E., Thompson, K. and Choo, P. (1994) 'Cultural and ethnic influences on love and attachment', *Personal Relationships*, 1, 391–98.

Doi, T. (1973) *The Anatomy of Dependence*, New York: Harper Row.

Doise, W. (1986) *Levels of Explanation in Social Psychology*, Cambridge: Cambridge University Press.

Doise, W., Clemence, A. and Spini, D. (1996) 'Human rights and social psychology', *British Psychological Society, Social Psychology Section Newsletter*, No. 35, 3–21.

Doktor, R. (1983) 'Culture and the management of time: A comparison of Japanese and American top management practice', *Asia Pacific Journal of Management*, 1, 65–71.

Donaldson, L. (1986) 'Size and bureaucracy in East and West: A preliminary meta-analysis', in S. Clegg, D. C. Dunphy and S. G. Redding (eds.), *The Enterprise and Management in South-East Asia*, Hong Kong: Hong Kong University Centre for Asian Studies.

Doraï, M. (1993) 'Effets de la catégorisation simple et de la catégorisation croissée sur les stéréotypes', *International Journal of Psychology*, 28, 3–18.

Dorfman, P. (1996) 'International and cross-cultural leadership', in B. J. Punnett and O. Shenkar (eds.), *Handbook for International Management Research*, Cambridge, MA: Blackwell.

Dragoti, E. (1996) 'Ancient crimes return to haunt Albania', *Psychology International*, 7, 1–3.

Drew, A. M. and Ward, C. (1993) 'The effects of ethnicity and culturally congruent and incongruent nonverbal behaviors on interpersonal attraction', *Journal of Applied Social Psychology*, 23, 1376–89.

DuBabcock, B., Babcock, R. D., Ng, P. and Lai, R. (1995) 'A Comparison of Use of L1 and L2 in Small-Group Business Decision-Making Meetings', Research Monograph 6, Department of English, City University of Hong Kong.

Durkheim, E. (1898) 'Representations individuelles et representations collectives', *Revue de Metaphysique et de Morale*, 6, 273–302.

Durojaiye, M. O. A. (1993) 'Indigenous psychology in Africa: The search for meaning', in U. Kim and J. W. Berry (eds.) *Indigenous Psychologies: Research and experience in cultural context*, Newbury Park, CA: Sage.

Dutton, D. G. (1973) 'Reverse discrimination: The relationship of amount of perceived discrimination toward a minority group on the behaviour of majority group members', *Canadian Journal of Behavioural Science*, 5, 34–45.

Eagly, A. M., Ashmore, Makhijani, M. G. and Kennedy, L. (1991) 'What is beautiful is good, but . . .: A meta-analytic review of research on the physical attractiveness stereotype', *Psychological Bulletin*, 110, 109–28.

Earley, P. C. (1989) 'Social loafing and collectivism: A comparison of the United States and the People's Republic of China', *Administrative Science Quarterly*, 34, 565–81.

Earley, P. C. (1993) 'East meets West meets Mideast: Further explorations of collectivistic versus individualistic work groups', *Academy of Management Journal*, 36, 319–48.

Earley, P. C. (1994) 'Self or group? Cultural effects of training on self-efficacy and performance', *Administrative Science Quarterly*, 39, 89–117.

Ebbinghaus, H. (1908) *Abriss der Psychologie*, Leipzig: Veit.

Ebrahim, S. (1992) 'Social and medical problems of elderly migrants', *International Migration*, 30, 179–97.

Ekman, P. (1972) 'Universals and cultural differences in facial expressions of emotion', in J. Cole (ed.), *Science*, 164, 86–88.

Ekman, P., Sorenson, E. R. and Friesen, W. V. (1969) 'Pan-cultural elements in facial displays of emotion', *Nebraska Symposium on Motivation*, Lincoln, NE: University of Nebraska Press.

Ekman, P., and 11 others (1987) 'Universals and cultural differences in the judgments of facial expressions of emotion', *Journal of Personality and Social Psychology*, 53, 712–17.

Ekvall, G. and Arvonen, J. (1991) 'Change-centred-leadership: An extension of the two-dimensional model', *Scandinavian Journal of Management*, 7, 17–26.

Elliott, G. C. and Meeker, B. F. (1984) 'Modifiers of the equity effect: Group outcome and causes for individual performance', *Journal of Personality and Social Psychology*, 46, 586–97.

Ellsworth, P. C. (1994) 'Sense, culture, and sensibility', in S. Kitayama and H. R. Markus (eds.), *Emotion and culture: Empirical studies of mutual influence*, Washington, DC: American Psychological Association.

Elwell, C. M., Brown, R. J. and Rutter, D. R. (1984) 'Effects of accent and visual information on impression formation', *Journal of Language and Social Psychology*, 3, 297–9.

Ember, C. R. and Ember, M. (1994a) 'War, socialization, and interpersonal violence: A cross-cultural study', *Journal of Conflict Resolution*, 38, 620–46.

Ember, M. and Ember, C. R. (1994b) 'Prescriptions for peace: Policy implications of cross-cultural research on war and interpersonal violence', *Cross Cultural Research*, 28, 343–50.

Endo, Y. (1995) 'A false modesty/other-enhancing bias among Japanese', *Psychologia*, 38, 59–69.

Enriquez, V. (1988) 'The structure of Philippine social values: towards integrating indigenous values and appropriate technology', in D. Sinha and H. S. R. Kao (eds.), *Social Values and Development: Asian perspectives*, New Delhi: Sage.

Enriquez, V. (1993) 'Developing a Filipino psychology', in U. Kim and J. W. Berry (eds.), *Indigenous Psychologies: Research and experience in cultural context*, Newbury Park, CA: Sage.

Epstein, S. and O'Brien, E. J. (1985) 'The person–situation debate in historical and current perspective', *Psychological Bulletin*, 98, 513–37.

Erez, M. and Earley, P. C. (1987) 'Comparative analysis of goal-setting strategies across cultures', *Journal of Applied Psychology*, 72, 658–65.

Erez, M. and Somech, A. (1996) 'Group productivity loss – the rule or the exception: The effect of culture and group based motivation', *Academy of Management Journal*, 39, 1513–37.

Esses, V. M., Haddock, G. and Zanna, M. P. (1993) 'Values, stereotypes, and emotions as determinants of intergroup attitudes', in D. M. Mackie and D. L. Hamilton (eds.), *Affect, Cognition and Stereotyping: Interactive processes in group perception*, New York: Academic Press.

Esteban, G., Graham, J. L., Ockova, A., and Tang, S. (1993) 'Hofstede, Rokeach and culture's influence on marketing negotiations', unpublished paper, University of California, Irvine.

Evans, G. W., Palsane, N. and Carrer, S. (1987) 'Type A behavior and occupational stress: A cross-cultural study of blue-collar workers', *Journal of Personality and Social Psychology*, 52, 1002–7.

Everett, J. E. and Stening, B. W. (1987) 'Stereotyping in American, British, and Japanese corporations in Hong Kong and Singapore', *Journal of Social Psychology*, 127, 445–60.

Eysenck, H. J. (1986) 'Cross-cultural comparisons: The validity of assessment by indices of factor comparisons', *Journal of Cross-Cultural Psychology*, 17, 506–15.

Eysenck, H. J. and Eysenck, S. B. G. (1982) 'Recent advances in the cross-cultural study of personality', in J. N. Butcher and C. D. Spielberger (eds.), *Advances in Personality Assessment*, Volume 2, Hillsdale, NJ: Erlbaum.

Farh, J. L., Earley, P. C. and Lin, S.-C. (1997) 'Impetus for action: A cultural analysis of justice and organizational citizenship behavior in Chinese society', *Administrative Science Quarterly*, 42, 421–44.

Farr, R. and Moscovici, S. (eds.) (1984) *Social Representations*, Cambridge: Cambridge University Press.

Farris, G. F. and Butterfield, A. (1972) 'Control theory in Brazilian organizations', *Administrative Science Quarterly*, 17, 574–85.

Faucheux, C. (1976) 'Cross-cultural research in experimental social psychology', *European Journal of Social Psychology*, 6, 269–322.

Feather, N. T. (1979) 'Assimilation of values in migrant groups', in M. Rokeach (ed.), *Understanding Human Values*, New York: Free Press.

Feather, N. T. (1980) 'Similarity of values systems within the same nation: Evidence from Australia and Papua New Guinea', *Australian Journal of Psychology*, 32, 17–30.

Feather, N. T. (1988) 'From values to actions: Recent applications of the expectancy-value model', *Australian Journal of Psychology*, 40, 105–24.

Feather, N. T. (1994a) 'Values, national identification and favouritism towards the in-group', *British Journal of Social Psychology*, 33, 467–76.

Feather, N. T. (1994b) 'Attitudes toward high achievers and reactions to their fall: Theory and research concerning tall poppies', *Advances in Experimental Social Psychology*, 26, 1–73.

Feather, N. T. (1995) 'National identification and ingroup bias in majority and minority groups: A field study', *Australian Journal of Psychology*, 47, 129–36.

Feather, N. T. and McKee, I. R. (1993) 'Global self-esteem and attitudes toward the high achiever for Australian and Japanese students', *Social Psychology Quarterly*, 56, 65–76.

Featherman, D. L. (1993) 'What does society need from higher education?', *Items*, 47 (2/3), 38–43.

Feign, L. (1986) *Fong's Aieeyaaa*, Hong Kong: *Hong Kong Standard*.

Feign, L. (1987) *Fong's Aieeyaaa, Not Again*, Hong Kong: *Hong Kong Standard*.

Feingold, A. (1992) 'Good looking people are not what we think', *Psychological Bulletin*, 111, 304–41.

Feldman, R. E. (1967) 'Honesty toward compatriot and foreigner: Field experiments in Paris, Athens and Boston', in W. W. Lambert and R. Weisbrod (eds.), *Comparative Perspectives on Social Psychology*, Boston, MA: Little, Brown.

Feldman, S. S., Mont-Reynaud, R. and Rosenthal, D. A. (1992) 'The acculturation of values of Chinese adolescents residing in the United States and Australia', *Journal of Research on Adolescence*, 2, 147–73.

Feldman, S. S. and Rosenthal, D. A. (1990) 'The acculturation of autonomy expectations in Chinese high schoolers residing in two Western nations', *International Journal of Psychology*, 25, 259–81.

Felson, R. B. (1978) 'Aggression as impression management', *Social Psychology Quarterly*, 41, 205–13.

Fernandez Dols, J. M. (1992) 'Procesos escabrosos en Psicologia Social: el concepto de norma perversa', *Revista de Psicologia Social*, 7, 243–55.

Feshbach, S. (1987) 'Individual aggression, national attachment, and the search for peace: Psychological perspectives', *Aggressive Behavior*, 13, 315–25.

Festinger, L. (1954) 'A theory of social comparison processes', *Human Relations*, 7, 117–40.

Fiedler, F. E. (1967) *A Contingency Theory of Leadership Effectiveness*, New York: McGraw Hill.

Fine, G. A. (1976) 'Obscene joking across cultures', *Journal of Communication*, 26, 134–40.

Fishman, J. A. (1972) *Language and Nationalism*, Rowley, MA: Newbury House.

Fiske, A. P. (1991a) *Structures of Social Life: The four elementary forms of human relations*, New York: Free Press.

Fiske, A. P. (1991b) 'The cultural relativity of selfish individualism: Anthropological evidence that humans are inherently sociable', in M. S. Clark (ed.), *Prosocial Behavior, Review of Personality and Social Psychology*, 12, 176–214.

Fiske, A. P. (1992) 'The four elementary forms of sociality: Framework for a unified theory of sociality', *Psychological Review*, 99, 689–723.

Fiske, S. T. and Taylor, S. E. (1991) *Social Cognition*, 2nd edn, New York: Random House.

Foley Meeker, B. (1970) 'An experimental study of cooperation and competition in West Africa', *International Journal of Psychology*, 5, 11–19.

Fontaine, G. (1990) 'Cultural diversity in intimate intercultural relationships', in D. Cahn (ed.), *Intimates in Conflict: A communication perspective*, Hillsdale, NJ: Erlbaum.

Fontaine, G., and Dorch, E. (1980) 'Problems and benefits of close intercultural relationships', *International Journal of Intercultural Relations*, 4, 329–37.

Forgas, J. P. (1979) *Social Episodes: The study of interaction routines*, London: Academic Press.

Forgas, J. P. (1981) 'Affective and emotional influences on episode representations', in J. P. Forgas (ed.), *Social Cognition: Perspectives on Everyday Understanding*, London: Academic Press.

Forgas, J. P. and Bond, M. H. (1985) 'Cultural influences on the perception of interaction episodes', *Personality and Social Psychology Bulletin*, 11, 75–88.

Frager, R. (1970) 'Conformity and anti-conformity in Japan', *Journal of Personality and Social Psychology*, 15, 203–10.

Fraser, C., Gouge, C. and Billig, M. (1971) 'Risky shifts, cautious shifts and group polarisation', *European Journal of Social Psychology*, 1, 7–30.

Freedle, R. (ed.) (1979) *New Directions in Discourse Processing*, Volume 2, Norwood, NJ: Ablex.

French, J. R. P., Israel, J. and Ås, D. (1960) 'An experiment on participation in a Norwegian factory: Interpersonal dimensions of decision-making', *Human Relations*, 13, 3–19.

Frese, M., Kring, W., Soose, A. and Zempel, J. (1996) 'Personal initiative at work: Differences between East and West Germany', *Academy of Management Journal*, 39, 37–63.

Friend, R., Rafferty, Y. and Bramel, D. (1990) 'A puzzling misinterpretation of the Asch 'conformity' study', *European Journal of Social Psychology*, 20, 29–44.

Friesen, W. (1972) 'Cultural differences in facial expressions in a social situation: An experimental test of the concept of display rules', unpublished PhD thesis, University of California San Francisco.

Fry, P. S. and Ghosh, R. (1980) 'Attributions of success and failure: Comparison of cultural differences between Asian and Caucasian children', *Journal of Cross-Cultural Psychology*, 11, 343–63.

Furby, L. (1979) 'Individualistic bias in studies of locus of control', in A. R. Buss (ed.), *Psychology in Social Context*, New York: Irvington.

Furnham, A. (1982) 'The message, the context and the medium', *Language and Communication*, 2, 33–47.

Furnham, A. (1989) 'Communicating across cultures: A social skills perspective', *Counselling Psychology Quarterly*, 2, 205–22.

Furnham, A. (1994) 'A content, correlational and factor analytic study of four tolerance of ambiguity questionnaires', *Personality and Individual Differences*, 16, 403–10.

Furnham, A. and Bochner, S. (1982) 'Social difficulty in a foreign culture: An empirical analysis of culture shock', in S. Bochner (ed.), *Cultures in Contact*, New York: Pergamon.

Furnham, A. and Bochner, S. (1986) *Culture Shock: Psychological reactions to unfamiliar environments*, London: Methuen.

Furnham, A. and Erdmann, S. (1995) 'Psychological and socio-cultural variables as predictors of adjustment in cross-cultural transitions', *Psychologica*, 38, 238–51.

Furnham, A., Kirkcaldy, B. D. and Lynn, R. (1994) 'National attitudes to competitiveness, money and work among young people: First, second and third world differences', *Human Relations*, 47, 119–31.

Furnham, A., Bond, M. H., Heaven, P. C. *et al.* (1993) 'A comparison of Protestant work beliefs in 13 nations', *Journal of Social Psychology*, 133, 185–96.

Furuhata, K. (1980) *Ningenkankei no Shakaishinrigaku (Social Psychology of Interpersonal Relations)*, Tokyo: Science Publishers.

Gabrenya, W. K. Jr. (1988) 'Social science and social psychology: The cross-cultural link', in M. H. Bond (ed.), *The Cross-cultural Challenge to Social Psychology*, Newbury Park, CA: Sage.

Gabrenya, W. K. Jr. (1990) 'Dyadic social interaction during task behavior in collectivist and individualist societies', paper presented at the Workshop on Individualism and Collectivism, Seoul, Korea.

Gabrenya, W. K., Wang, Y. E. and Latané, B. (1985) 'Social loafing on an optimising task: Cross-cultural differences among Chinese and Americans', *Journal of Cross-Cultural Psychology*, 16, 223–42.

Gaertner, S. L., Mann, J., Murrell, A. and Dovidio, J. F. (1989) 'Reducing intergroup bias: The benefits of recategorization', *Journal of Personality and Social Psychology*, 57, 239–49.

Gaertner, S. L., Dovidio, J. F., Anastasio, P. A. *et al.* (1993) 'The common ingroup identity model: Recategorization and the reduction of intergroup bias', in W. Stroebe and M. Hewstone (eds.), *European Review of Social Psychology*, 4, 1–26.

Gallois, C. and Callan, V. J. (1991) 'Interethnic accommodation: The role of norms', in H. Giles, J. Coupland and N. Coupland (eds.), *Contexts of Accommodation: Developments in applied sociolinguistics*, Cambridge: Cambridge University Press.

Gallois, C., Franklyn-Stokes, A., Giles, H. and Coupland, N. (1988) 'Communication accommodation in intercultural encounters', in Y. Y. Kim and W. B. Gudykunst (eds.), *Theories in Intercultural Communication*, Newbury Park, CA: Sage.

Gangestad, S. W. (1993) 'Sexual selection and physical attractiveness: Implications for mating dynamics', *Human Nature*, 4, 205–36.

Gangestad, S. W. and Thornhill, R. (1994) 'Facial attractiveness, developmental stability, and fluctuation asymmetry', *Ethnology and Sociobiology*, 15, 73–85.

Gao, G. and Gudykunst, W. B. (1990) 'Uncertainty, anxiety, and adaptation', *International Journal of Intercultural Relations*, 14, 301–17.

Garcia, C. (1989) 'Apologizing in English: Politeness strategies used by native and non-native speakers', *Multilingua*, 8, 3–20.

Garza-Guerrero, A. C. (1974) 'Culture shock: Its mourning and the vicissitudes of identity', *Journal of the American Psychoanalytic Association*, 22, 408–29.

Gass, S. M. and Varonis, E. M. (1984) 'The effect of familiarity on the comprehensibility of nonnative speech', *Language Learning*, 34, 65–89.

Gass, S. M. and Varonis, E. M. (1985) 'Variation in native speaker speech modification to nonnative speakers', *Studies in Second Language Acquisition*, 7, 37–58.

Geen, R. G. (1994) 'Human aggression: Current theories and research', paper presented at the annual convention of the American Psychological Association, Los Angeles.

Geertz, C. (1974) 'From the native's point of view: On the nature of anthropological understanding', in K. Basso and H. Selby (eds.), *Meaning in Anthropology*, Albuquerque: University of New Mexico Press.

Gehm, T. L. and Scherer, K. R. (1988) 'Relating situation evaluation to emotion differentiation: Nonmetric analysis of cross-cultural questionnaire data', in K. R. Scherer (ed.), *Facets of Emotion*, Hillsdale, NJ: Erlbaum.

Gelfand, M., Triandis, H. C. and Chan, D. K. S. (1996) 'Individualism versus collectivism or versus authoritarianism?', *European Journal of Social Psychology*, 26, 397–410.

Georgas, J. and Berry, J. W. (1995) 'An ecocultural taxonomy for cross-cultural psychology', *Cross-Cultural Research*, 29, 121–57.

Georgas, J. and Papastylianou, D. (1996a) 'Acculturation and ethnic identity: The remigration of ethnic Greeks to Greece', in H. Grad, A. Blanco and J. Georgas (eds.), *Key Issues in Cross-cultural Psychology*, Lisse: Swets and Zeitlinger.

Georgas, J. and Papastylianou, D. (1996b) 'Re-acculturation of children of returning migrants to Greece', paper presented at the 13th Congress of the International Association for Cross-Cultural Psychology, Montreal.

Georgas, J., Berry, J. W., Shaw, A. *et al.* (1996) 'Acculturation of Greek family values', *Journal of Cross-Cultural Psychology*, 27, 329–38.

Gergen, K. J. (1973) 'Social psychology as history', *Journal of Personality and Social Psychology*, 26, 309–20.

Gibson, J. J. (1979) *The Ecological Approach to Visual Perception*, Boston: Houghton Mifflin.

Gielen, U. P. (1994) 'American mainstream psychology and its relationship to international and cross-cultural psychology', in A. L. Comunian and U. P. Gielen (eds.), *Advancing Psychology and its Applications: International perspectives*, Milan: Franco-Angeli.

Giles, H., Bourhis, R. Y., and Taylor, D. M. (1977) 'Towards a theory of language in ethnic group relations', in H. Giles (ed.), *Language, Ethnicity, and Intergroup Relations*, London: Academic Press.

Giles, H. and Byrne, J. L. (1982) 'An intergroup approach to second language acquisition', *Journal of Multilingual and Multicultural Development*, 3, 17–40.

Giles, H., Coupland, N. and Wiemann, J. M. (1992) '"Talk is cheap . . . but my word is my bond": Beliefs about talk', in K. Bolton and H. Kwok (eds.), *Sociolinguistics Today: Eastern and Western perspectives*, London: Routledge.

Giles, H. and Hewstone, M. (1982) 'Cognitive structures, speech, and social situations: Two integrative models', *Language Sciences*, 4, 187–219.

Giles, H., and Johnson, P. (1981) 'The role of language in ethnic group relations', in J. Turner and H. Giles (eds.), *Intergroup Behavior*, Chicago: University of Chicago Press.

Giles, H. and Johnson, P. (1986) 'Perceived threat, ethnic commitment, and interethnic language behaviour', in Y. Y. Kim (ed.), *Interethnic Communication: Current research*, Newbury Park, CA: Sage.

Giles, H. and Ryan, E. B. (1982) 'Prolegomena for developing a social psychological theory of language attitudes', in E. B. Ryan and H. Giles (eds.), *Attitudes towards Language Variation*, London: Edward Arnold.

Giles, H. A. and Viladot, A. (1994) 'Ethnolinguistic differentiation in Catalonia', *Multilingua: Journal of Cross-Cultural and Inter-Language Communication*, 13, 301–12.

Giles, H., Coupland, N., Williams, A. and Leets, L. (1991) 'Integrating theory in the study of minority languages', in R. L. Cooper and B. Spolsky (eds.), *The Influence of Language on Culture and Thought*, Amsterdam: Mouton de Gruyter.

Giorgi, L. and Marsh, C. (1990) 'The Protestant work ethic as a cultural phenomenon', *European Journal of Social Psychology*, 20, 499–518.

Gire, J. T. and Carment, D. W. (1993) 'Dealing with disputes: The influence of individualism–collectivism', *Journal of Social Psychology*, 133, 81–95.

Glass, D. C. (1977) *Behavior Patterns, Stress and Coronary Disease*, Hillsdale, NJ: Erlbaum.

Gleick, J. (1987) *Chaos: Making a New Science*, New York: Viking.

Glenn, E. S., Witmeyer, D. and Stevenson, K. A. (1977) 'Cultural styles of persuasion', *International Journal of Intercultural Relations*, 1, 52–66.

Goffman, E. (1956) 'Embarrassment and social organization', *American Journal of Sociology*, 62, 264–71.

Goffman, E. (1959) *The Presentation of Self in Everyday Life*, New York: Doubleday.

Goldberg, L. R. (1990) 'An alternative "description of personality": The Big-Five factor structure', *Journal of Personality and Social Psychology*, 59, 1216–29.

Gologor, E. (1977) 'Group polarisation in a non-risk-taking culture', *Journal of Cross-Cultural Psychology*, 8, 331–46.

Goodwin, R. (1995) 'The privatisation of the personal? 1: Intimate disclosure in modern-day Russia', *Journal of Personal and Social Relationships*, 12, 121–31.

Goodwin, R. and Lee, I. (1994) 'Taboo topics among Chinese and English friends', *Journal of Cross-Cultural Psychology*, 25, 325–38.

Goody, E. N. (1978) 'Introduction', in E. N. Goody (ed.), *Questions and Politeness*, Cambridge: Cambridge University Press.

Gouge, C. and Fraser, C. (1972) 'A further demonstration of group polarisation', *European Journal of Social Psychology*, 2, 95–7.

Graham, J. L. (1985) 'The influence of culture on the process of business negotiations: an exploratory study', *Journal of International Business Studies*, 16, 81–96.

Graham, J. L. (1993) 'The Japanese negotiation style: Characteristics of a distinct approach', *Negotiation Journal*, 9, 123–40.

Graham, J. L., Evenko, L. I. and Rajan, M. N. (1992) 'A empirical comparison of Soviet and American business negotiations', *Journal of International Business Studies*, 23, 387–418.

Graham, J. L., Mintu, A. T. and Rodgers, W. (1994) 'Explorations of negotiation behaviors in ten foreign cultures using a model developed in the United States', *Management Science*, 40, 72–95.

Graham, J. L., Kim, D. K., Lin, C.-Y. and Robinson, M. (1988) 'Buyer–seller negotiations around the Pacific rim: Differences in fundamental exchange processes', *Journal of Consumer Research*, 15, 48–54.

Greenberg, J. and Baron, R. A. (1995) *Behavior in Organizations: Understanding and managing the human side of work*, 5th edn, Englewood Cliffs, NJ: Prentice Hall.

Grove, C. J. and Torbiörn, I. (1985) 'A new conceptualization of intercultural adjustment and the goals of training', *International Journal of Intercultural Relations*, 9, 205–33.

Gudykunst, W. B. (1988) 'Culture and intergroup processes', in M. H. Bond (ed.), *The Cross-cultural Challenge to Social Psychology*, Newbury Park, CA: Sage.

Gudykunst, W. B. (1991) *Bridging Differences: Effective intergroup communication*, Newbury Park: Sage.

Gudykunst, W. B. (1995) 'Anxiety/Uncertainty Management (AUM) theory: Current status', in R. L. Wiseman (ed.), *Intercultural Communication Theory*, Thousand Oaks, CA: Sage.

Gudykunst, W. B., Gao, G. and Franklyn-Stokes, A. (1996) 'Self-monitoring and concern for social appropriateness in China and England', in J. Pandey, D. Sinha and D. P. S. Bhawuk (eds.) *Asian Contributions to Cross-cultual Psychology*, New Delhi: Sage.

Gudykunst, W. B. and Hammer, M. R. (1988) 'Strangers and hosts: An uncertainty reduction-based theory of intercultural adaptation', in Y. Y. Kim and W. B. Gudykunst (eds.), *Intercultural Adaptation*, Newbury Park, CA: Sage.

Gudykunst, W. B. and Kim, Y. Y. (1997) *Communicating with Strangers*, 3rd edn, New York: McGraw-Hill.

Gudykunst, W. B. and Shapiro, R. B. (1996) 'Communication in everyday interpersonal and intergroup encounters', *International Journal of Intercultural Relations*, 20, 19–46.

Gudykunst, W. B., Ting-Toomey, S. and Chua, E. (1988) *Culture and Interpersonal Communication*, Newbury Park, CA: Sage.

Gudykunst, W. B., Ting-Toomey, S. and Nishida, T. (eds.) (1996) *Communication in Personal Relationships across Cultures*, Thousand Oaks, CA: Sage.

Gudykunst, W. B., Yang, S. M. and Nishida, T. (1985) 'A cross-cultural test of uncertainty reduction theory: Comparisons of acquaintance, friend, and dating relationships in Japan, Korea, and the United States', *Human Communication Research*, 11, 407–55.

Gudykunst, W. B., Gao, G., Nishida, T., Nadamitsu, Y. and Sakai, J. (1990) 'Self-monitoring in Japan and the United States', in S. Iwawaki, Y. Kashima and K. Leung (eds.), *Innovations in Cross-Cultural Psychology*, Lisse: Swets and Zeitlinger.

Gudykunst, W. B., Gao, G., Schmidt, K. L. *et al.* (1992) 'The influence of individualism–collectivism, self-monitoring and predicted-outcome value on communication in in-group and out-group relationships', *Journal of Cross-Cultural Psychology*, 23, 196–213.

Gudykunst, W. B., Matsumoto, Y. Ting-Toomey, S., Nishida, T. and Karimi, H. (1994) 'Measuring self-construals across cultures: A derived-etic analysis', paper presented at the International Communication Association, Sydney.

Gudykunst, W. B., Matsumoto, Y., Ting-Toomey, S., Nishida, T., Kim, K. and Heyman, S. (1996) 'The influence of cultural individualism–collectivism, self con-struals, and individual values on communication styles across cultures', *Human Communication Research*, 22, 510–43.

Guerin, B. (1993) *Social Facilitation*, Cambridge: Cambridge University Press.

Gullahorn, J. T. and Gullahorn, J. E. (1963) 'An extension of the U-curve hypothesis', *Journal of Social Issues*, 19, 33–47.

Guthrie, G. M. (1975) 'A behavioural analysis of culture learning', in R. W. Brislin, S. Bochner and W. J. Lonner (eds.), *Cross-cultural Perspectives on Learning*, New York: Wiley.

Guthrie, G. M. (1977) 'A socio-psychological analysis of modernization in the Philippines', *Journal of Cross-Cultural Psychology*, 8, 177–206.

Guthrie, G. M. and Azores, F. M. (1968) 'Philippine interpersonal behavior patterns', *Ateneo de Manila University IPC Papers*, 6, 3–63.

Guzzo, R. A., Noonan, K. A. and Elron, E. (1994) 'Expatriate managers and the psychological contract', *Journal of Applied Psychology*, 79, 617–26.

Guzzo, R. A., Yost, P. R., Campbell, R. J. and Shea, G. P. (1993) 'Potency in groups: Articulating a construct', *British Journal of Social Psychology*, 32, 87–106.

Haddock, G., Zanna, M. P. and Esses, V. M. (1993) 'Assessing the structure of prejudicial attitudes: The case of attitudes towards homosexuals', *Journal of Personality and Social Psychology*, 65, 1105–18.

Haddock, G., Zanna, M. P. and Esses, V. M. (1994) 'The (limited) role of trait-laden stereotypes in predicting attitudes towards native peoples', *British Journal of Social Psychology*, 33, 83–106.

Hall, E. T. (1966) *The Hidden Dimension*, New York: Doubleday.

Hall, E. T. (1976) *Beyond Culture*, New York: Doubleday.

Hall, E. T. (1983) *The Dance of Life: The other dimension of time*, New York: Doubleday.

Hamaguchi, E. (1987) 'Experimental and survey research on the Japanese basic value', Faculty of Human Sciences, Osaka University (in Japanese).

Hamilton, D. C. and Trolier, T. K. (1986) 'Stereotypes and stereotyping: An overview of the cognitive approach', in J. F. Dovidio and S. L. Gaertner (eds.), *Prejudice, Discrimination, and Racism*, Orlando, FL: Academic Press.

Hammer, M. R. (1987) 'Behavioral dimensions of intercultural effectiveness: A replication and extension', *International Journal of Intercultural Relations*, 11, 65–88.

Hammer, M. R., Gudykunst, W. B. and Wiseman, R. L. (1978) 'Dimensions of intercultural effectiveness: An exploratory study', *International Journal of Intercultural Relatives*, 2, 382–93.

Han, S.-P. and Shavitt, S. (1994) 'Persuasion and culture: Advertising appeals in individualistic and collectivistic societies', *Journal of Experimental Social Psychology*, 30, 326–50.

Hannigan, T. P. (1995) 'Body odor: The international student and cross-cultural communication', *Culture and Psychology*, 1, 497–503.

Harbison, F. H. and Myers, C. A. (1959) *Management in the Industrial World*, New York: McGraw-Hill.

Harnett, D. L. and Cummings, L. L. (1980) *Bargaining Behavior: An international study*, Houston, TX: Dame.

Harris, J. G. (1972) 'Prediction of success on a distant Pacific Island: Peace Corps style', *Journal of Clinical and Consulting Psychology*, 38, 181–90.

Harvey, M. (1983) 'The other side of foreign assignments: Dealing with the repatriation problem', *Columbia Journal of World Business*, 17, 53–9.

Harvey, M. (1989) 'Repatriation of corporate executives: An empirical study', *Journal of International Business Studies*, 20, 131–44.

Harwood, J., Giles, H. and Bourhis, R. Y. (1994) 'The genesis of vitality theory: Historical patterns and discoursal dimensions', *International Journal of the Sociology of Language*, 108, 167–206.

Harzing, A. W. K. (1995) 'The persistent myth of high expatriate failure rates', *International Journal of Human Resource Management*, 6, 457–74.

Hasegawa, T. and Gudykunst, W. B. (1997) 'Silence in Japan and United States', manuscript submitted for publication.

Haslett, B. and Ogilvie, J. (1988) 'Feedback processes in small groups', in R. Cathcart and L. Samovar (eds.), *Small Group Communication: A reader*, 5th edn., Dubuque, IA: Brown.

Hatfield, E. and Rapson, R. L. (1996) *Love and Sex: Cross-cultural perspectives*, Needham Heights, MA: Allyn and Bacon.

Hecht, M. L., Andersen, P. A. and Ribeau, S. A. (1989) 'The cultural dimensions of nonverbal communication', in M. K. Asante and W. B. Gudykunst (eds.), *Handbook of International and Intercultural Communication*, Newbury Park, CA: Sage.

Hedge, A. and Yousif, Y. H. (1992) 'The effect of urban size, cost and urgency on helpfulness: A cross-cultural comparison between the United Kingdom and the Sudan', *Journal of Cross-Cultural Psychology*, 23, 107–15.

Heider, F. (1958) *The Psychology of Interpersonal Relations*, New York: Wiley.

Heine, S. J. and Lehman, D. R. (1995) 'Cultural variation in unrealistic optimism: Does the west feel more invulnerable than the east?', *Journal of Personality and Social Psychology*, 68, 595–607.

Heine, S. J. and Lehman, D. R. (1997) 'Culture, dissonance, and self-affirmation', *Personality and Social Psychology Bulletin*, 23, 389–400.

Heller, F., Drenth, P., Koopman, P. and Rus, V. (1988) *Decisions in Organisations: A three-country comparative study*, London: Sage.

Heller, F. and Wilpert, B. (1981) *Competence and Power in Managerial Decision-making*, Chichester: Wiley.

Helmreich, R. L. (1994) 'Anatomy of a system accident: The crash of Avianca flight 052', *International Journal of Aviation Psychology*, 4, 265–84.

Helmreich, R. and Schaefer, H. (1994) 'Team performance in the operating room', in M. S. Bogner (ed.), *Human Error in Medicine*, Hillsdale, NJ: Erlbaum.

Helmreich, R., Merritt, A. C. and Sherman, P. J. (1996) 'Human factors and national culture', *International Civil Aviation Organization Journal*, xxx.

Hendrix, L. and Johnson, G. D. (1985) 'Instrumental and expressive socialization: A false dichotomy', *Sex Roles*, 13, 581–95.

Herman, S. and Schield, E. (1961) 'The stranger group in a cross-cultural situation', *Sociometry*, 24, 165–74.

Herskovits, M. J. (1948) *Man and his Works: The science of cultural anthropology*, New York: Knopf.

Herzlich, C. (1973) *Health and Illness: A social psychological analysis*, London: Academic Press.

Hewitt, J. P. (1994) *Self and Society: A symbolic interactionist social psychology*, 6th edn, Boston: Allyn and Bacon.

Hewstone, M. (1990) 'The "ultimate attribution error"? A review of the literature on intergroup causal attribution', *European Journal of Social Psychology*, 20, 311–35.

Hewstone, M. and Brown, R. (1986) 'Contact is not enough: An intergroup perspective on the contact hypothesis', in M. Hewstone and R. Brown (eds.), *Contact and Conflict in Intergroup Encounters*, Oxford: Blackwell.

Hewstone, M., Stroebe, W., and Stephenson, G. (1996) *Introduction to Social Psychology: A European perspective*, 2nd edn, Oxford: Blackwell.

Hewstone, M. and Ward, C. (1985) 'Ethnocentrism and causal attribution in Southeast Asia', *Journal of Personality and Social Psychology*, 48, 614–23.

Hickson, D. J. and McMillan, C. J. (1981) *Organisation and Nation: The Aston programme IV*, Westmead: Gower.

Hickson, D. J., Hinings, C. R., McMillan, C. J. and Schwitter, J. P. (1974) 'The culture-free context of organizational structure', *Sociology*, 8, 59–80.

Hines, G. H. (1973) 'The persistence of Greek achievement motivation across time and culture', *International Journal of Psychology*, 8, 285–8.

Hinkle, S. and Brown, R. (1990) 'Intergroup comparisons and social identity: Some links and lacunae', in D. Abrams and M. Hogg (eds.), *Social Identity Theory: Constructive and critical advances*, Hemel Hempstead: Harvester Wheatsheaf.

Ho, D. Y. F. (1976) 'On the concept of face', *American Journal of Sociology*, 81, 867–84.

Ho, F. C. and Johnson, R. C. (1990) 'Intra-ethnic and inter-ethnic marriage and divorce in Hawaii', *Social Biology*, 37, 44–51.

Ho, Y. S. (1996) 'Cultural differences in group discussion style', unpublished bachelor's thesis, Chinese University of Hong Kong.

Hobart, C. W. (1958) 'The incidence of romanticism during courtship', *Social Forces*, 36, 362–7.

Hoecklin, L. A. (1993) *Managing Cultural Differences for Competitive Advantage*, London: Economist Intelligence Unit.

Hoffman, C., Lau, I. and Johnson, D. R. (1986) 'The linguistic relativity of person cognition: An English–Chinese comparison', *Journal of Personality and Social Psychology*, 51, 1097–1105.

Hofstede, G. (1980) *Culture's Consequences: International differences in work-related values*, Beverly Hills, CA: Sage.

Hofstede, G. (1983) 'Dimensions of national cultures in fifty countries and three regions', in J. Deregowski, S. Dzuirawiec and R. Annis (eds.), *Expiscations in Cross-cultural Psychology*, Lisse, Netherlands: Swets and Zeitlinger.

Hofstede, G. (1991) *Cultures and Organizations: Software of the mind*, London: McGraw-Hill.

Hofstede, G. (1996a) 'An American in Paris: The influence of nationality on organisation theories', *Organization Studies*, 17, 525–37.

Hofstede, G. (1996b) 'Masculinity, religion, gender and sex', paper presented at 13th Congress of the International Association for Cross-Cultural Psychology, Montreal.

Hofstede, G. (1996c) 'Images of Europe: Past, present and future', in P. Joynt and M. Warner (eds.), *Managing across Cultures: Issues and Perspectives*, London: International Thomson Business Press.

Hofstede, G. and Bond, M. H. (1988) 'The Confucius connection: From cultural roots to economic growth', *Organization Dynamics*, 16, 4–21.

Hofstede, G., Bond, M. H. and Luk, C.-L. (1993) 'Individual perceptions of organizational cultures: A methodological treatise on levels of analysis', *Organization Studies*, 14, 483–503.

Hofstede, G., Neuyen, B., Ohayv, D. D. and Sanders, G. (1990) 'Measuring organisational cultures: A qualitative and quantitative study across 20 cases', *Administrative Science Quarterly*, 35, 286–316.

Hofstede, G., Kolman, L., Nicolescu, O. and Pajumaa, I. (1996) 'Characteristics of the ideal job among students in eight countries', in H. Grad, A. Blanco and J. Georgas (eds.), *Key Issues in Cross-cultural Psychology*, Lisse: Swets and Zeitlinger.

Hogan, R. (1996) 'A socioanalytic perspective on the five-factor model', in J. S. Wiggins (ed.), *The Five-Factor Model of Personality: Theoretical perspectives*, New York: Guilford Press.

Hogan, R. and Emler, N. (1978) 'The biases of contemporary social psychology', *Social Research*, 45, 478–534.

Hogg, M. A. and Sunderland, J. (1991) 'Self-esteem and intergroup discrimination in the minimal group paradigm', *British Journal of Social Psychology*, 30, 51–62.

Hogg, M. A. and Vaughan, G. M. (1995) *Social Psychology: An introduction*, Hemel Hempstead: Prentice Hall.

Holloway, S. D., Kashiwagi, K., Hess, R. D. and Azuma, H. (1986) 'Causal attribution by Japanese and American mothers and children about performance in mathematics', *International Journal of Psychology*, 21, 269–86.

Holtgraves, T. (1992) 'The linguistic realization of face management: Implications for language production and comprehension, person perception, and cross-cultural communication', *Social Psychology Quarterly*, 55, 141–59.

Holtgraves, T. and Yang, J. (1990) 'Politeness as universal: Cross-cultural perceptions of request strategies and inferences based on their use', *Journal of Personality and Social Psychology*, 59, 719–29.

Holtgraves, T. and Yang, J. (1992) 'Interpersonal underpinnings of request strategies: General principles and differences due to culture and gender', *Journal of Personality and Social Psychology*, 62, 246–56.

Hong, L. K. (1978) 'Risky shift and cautious shift: Some direct evidence of the culture-value theory', *Social Psychology Quarterly*, 41, 342–46.

Hortaçsu, N. and Karançi, A. N. (1987) 'Premarital breakups in a Turkish sample: Perceived reasons, attributional dimensions and affective reactions', *International Journal of Psychology*, 22, 57–64.

Horvath, A. M., Marsella, A. J. and Yamada, S. Y. (in press) 'Ethnocultural identity: The psychometric properties of a self-report behavior scale', *Psychological Reports*.

Horvath, A. M. and Singelis, T. M. (in press) 'Biculturalism and self-construal', *International Journal of Intercultural Relations*.

House, R. J. and Wright, N. (1997) 'Cross-cultural research on organizational leadership: A critical analysis and a proposed theory', in P. C. Earley and M. Erez (eds.), *Frontiers of Industrial and Organizational Psychology*, San Francisco: Jossey-Bass.

Howell, J. P., Dorfman, P. W., Hibino, S., Lee, J. K. and Tate, U. (1997) 'Leadership in Western and Asian countries: Commonalities and differences in effective leadership processes across cultures', *Leadership Quarterly*, 8, 233–74.

Howitt, D. and Owusu-Bempah, J. (1994) *The Racism of Psychology*, Hemel Hempstead: Harvester Wheatsheaf.

Hubbert, K. N., Guerrero, S. L. and Gudykunst, W. B. (in press) 'Intergroup communication over time', *International Journal of Intercultural Relations*.

Hui, C. H. (1988) 'Measurement of individualism–collectivism', *Journal of Research on Personality*, 22, 17–36.

Hui, H. C. and Cheng, I. W. M. (1987) 'Effects of second language proficiency of speakers and listeners on person perception and behavioural intention: A study of Chinese bilinguals', *International Journal of Psychology*, 22, 421–30.

Hui, C. H., and Triandis, H. C. (1989) 'Effects of culture and response format on extreme response style', *Journal of Cross-Cultural Psychology*, 20, 296–309.

Hui, C. H., Triandis, H. C. and Yee, C. (1991) 'Cultural differences in reward allocation: Is collectivism the explanation?', *British Journal of Social Psychology*, 30, 145–57.

Hullos, M. (1980) 'Collective education in Hungary: Development of competitive–cooperative and role-taking behaviours', *Ethos*, 8, 3–23.

Humana, C. (1986) *World Human Rights Guide*, London: Pan.

Huo, Y. P. and von Glinow, M. A. (1995) 'On transplanting human resource practices to China: A culture-driven approach', *International Journal of Manpower*, 16(9), 3–13.

Hupka, R. B. and Ryan, J. M. (1990) 'The cultural contribution to jealousy: cross-cultural aggression in sexual jealousy situations', *Behavior Science Research*, 24, 51–71.

Ibrahim, S. E. M. (1970) 'Interaction, perception, and attitudes of Arab students toward Americans', *Sociology and Social Research*, 55, 29–46.

Ike, N. (1973) 'Economic growth and intergenerational change in Japan', *American Political Science Review*, 67, 1194–1203.

Imahori, T. T. and Cupach, W. R. (1994) 'A cross-cultural comparison of the interpretation and management of face: US American and Japanese responses to embarrassing predicaments', *International Journal of Intercultural Relations*, 18, 193–219.

Industrial Democracy in Europe International Research Group (1981) *Industrial Democracy in Europe*, Oxford: Oxford University Press.

Industrial Democracy in Europe International Research Group (1993) *Industrial Democracy in Europe Revisited*, Oxford: Oxford University Press.

Inglehart, R. (1977) *The Silent Revolution: Changing values and political styles among Western publics*, Princeton, NJ: Princeton University Press.

Inglehart, R. (1990) *Culture Shift in Advanced Industrial Society*, Princeton, NJ: Princeton University Press.

Inkeles, A. and Smith, D. H. (1974) *Becoming Modern: Individual change in six developing countries*, Cambridge, MA: Harvard University Press.

International Survey Research (1995) *Employee Satisfaction: Tracking international trends*, London: International Survey Research.

International Survey Research (1997) *Tracking Trends: Employee satisfaction in Europe in the '90s*, London: International Survey Research.

Ip, G. W. M. and Bond, M. H. (1995) 'Culture, values and the spontaneous self-concept', *Asian Journal of Psychology*, 1, 29–35.

Isaka, H. (1990) 'Factor analysis of trait terms in everyday Japanese language', *Personality and Individual Differences*, 11, 115–24.

Islam, M. R. and Hewstone, M. (1993a) 'Dimensions of contact as predictors of intergroup anxiety, perceived outgroup variability, and outgroup attitude', *Personality and Social Psychology Bulletin*, 19, 700–10.

Islam, M. R. and Hewstone, M. (1993b) 'Intergroup attributions and affective consequences in majority and minority groups', *Journal of Personality and Social Psychology*, 64, 936–50.

Israel, J. and Tajfel, H. (eds.) (1972) *The Context of Social Psychology: A critical assessment*, London: Academic Press.

Izard, C. (1971) *The Face of Emotion*, New York: Appleton-Century-Crofts.

Izard, C. (1980) 'Cross-cultural perspectives on emotion and emotion communication', in H. C. Triandis and W. Lonner (eds.), *Handbook of Cross-cultural Psychology: Volume 3 – Basic Processes*, Boston: Allyn and Bacon.

Jaffe, Y. and Yinon, Y. (1983) 'Collective aggression: The group–individual paradigm in the study of collective antisocial behaviour', in H. H. Blumberg, A. P. Hare, V. Kent and M. F. Davies (eds.), *Small Groups and Social Interaction*, Volume 1, pp. 267–75, Chichester: Wiley.

Jago, A. and 5 co-authors (1993) 'Culture's consequence? A seven-nation study of participation', *Proceedings of the 24th Annual Meeting of the Decision Sciences Institute*, Washington DC: Decision Sciences Institute.

Jahoda, G. (1979) 'A cross-cultural perspective on experimental social psychology', *Personality and Social Psychology Bulletin*, 5, 142–8.

Jahoda, G. (1982) *Psychology and Anthropology: A psychological perspective*, London: Academic Press.

Jahoda, G. (1984) 'Do we need a concept of culture?', *Journal of Cross-Cultural Psychology*, 15, 139–52.

Jahoda, G. (1993) *Crossroads between Culture and Mind*, Cambridge, MA: Harvard University Press.

Jahoda, G. and Krewer, B. (1997) 'History of cross-cultural and cultural psychology', in J. W. Berry, Y. Poortinga and J. Pandey (eds.), *Handbook of Cross-Cultural Psychology*, 2nd edn, Volume 1, Needham Heights, MA: Allyn and Bacon.

Jamieson, B. D. (1968) 'The risky shift phenomenon with a heterogeneous sample', *Psychological Reports*, 23, 203–6.

Jesuino, J. C. (1986) 'Influence of leadership processes on group polarisation', *European Journal of Social Psychology*, 16, 413–24.

Jodelet, D. (1993) 'Indigenous psychologies and social representations of the body and the self', in U. Kim and J. W. Berry (eds.), *Indigenous Psychologies: Research and experience in cultural context*, Thousand Oaks, CA: Sage.

John, O. P., Goldberg, L. R. and Angleitner, A. (1984) 'Better than the alphabet: Taxonomics of personality descriptive terms in English, Dutch, and German', in H. Bonarius, G. van Heck and N. Smid (eds.), *Personality Psychology in Europe: Theoretical and empirical developments*, Lisse: Swets and Zeitlinger.

Johns, G. and Xie, J. L. (1995) 'Workgroup absence culture and the social perception of absence: The People's Republic of China vs. Canada', paper presented to Academy of Management meeting, Vancouver.

Jones, D. and Hill, K. (1993) 'Criteria of facial attractiveness in five populations', *Human Nature*, 4, 271–96.

Jones, E., Gallois, C., Barker, M. and Callan, V. J. (1994) 'Evaluations of interactions between students and academic staff: Influence of communication accommodation, ethnic group, and status', *Journal of Language and Social Psychology*, 13, 158–91.

Jordan, D. K. (1988) 'Esperanto – the international language of humor: Or what's so funny about Esperanto?', *Humor: International Journal of Humor Research*, 1, 143–57.

Jost, J. T. and Banaji, M. R. (1994) 'The role of stereotyping in system-justification and the production of false consciousness', *British Journal of Social Psychology*, 33, 1–27.

Juralewicz, R. S. (1974) 'An experiment in participation in a Latin American factory', *Human Relations*, 27, 627–37.

Kagan, S., Knight, G. P. and Martinez-Romero, S. (1982) 'Culture and the development of conflict resolution style', *Journal of Cross-Cultural Psychology*, 13, 43–58.

Kagan, S. and Madsen, M. C. (1972) 'Experimental analyses of cooperation and competition of Anglo-American and Mexican children', *Developmental Psychology*, 6, 49–59.

Kagitçibasi, C. (1970) 'Social norms and authoritarianism: A Turkish–American comparison', *Journal of Cross-Cultural Psychology*, 4, 157–74.

Kagitçibasi, C. (1988) 'Diversity of socialization and social change', in P. R. Dasen, J. W. Berry, and N. Sartorius (eds.), *Health and Cross-cultural Psychology*, Newbury Park, CA: Sage.

Kagitçibasi, C. (1990) 'Family and socialization in cross-cultural perspective: A model of change', in J. Berman (ed.), *Nebraska Symposium on Motivation, 1989*, Lincoln, NE: Nebraska University Press.

Kagitçibasi, C. (1994) 'A critical appraisal of individualism–collectivism: Toward a new formulation', in U. Kim, H. C. Triandis, C. Kagitçibasi *et al.* (eds.), *Individualism and Collectivism: Theory, method and applications*, Newbury Park, CA: Sage.

Kagitçibasi, C. (1996a) 'The autonomous–relational self: A new synthesis', *European Psychologist*, 1, 180–6.

Kagitçibasi, C. (1996b) *Family and Human Development Across Cultures: A view from the other side*, Hillsdale, NJ: Erlbaum.

Kagitçibasi, C. (1997). 'Individualism and collectivism' in J. W. Berry, M. H. Segall and C. Kagitçibasi (eds.), *Handbook of Cross-cultural Psychology*, 2nd edn, Volume 3, Needham Heights, MA: Allyn and Bacon.

Kagitçibasi C., Sunar, D., and Bekman, S. (1988) *Comprehensive Preschool Education Project Final Report*, Ottawa: IDRC.

Kahl, J. A. (1968) *The Measurement of Modernism: A study of values in Brazil and Mexico*, Austin, TX: University of Texas Press.

Kahn, A., Lamm, H. and Nelson, R. (1977) 'Preferences for an equal or equitable allocation', *Journal of Personality and Social Psychology*, 35, 837–44.

Kakimoto, T. (1992) 'Cognitive distraction and the effect of social categorisation', paper presented at the 25th International Congress of Psychology, Brussels.

Kane, T. R. and Tedeschi, J. T. (1973) 'Impressions created by conforming and independent persons', *Journal of Social Psychology*, 91, 109–16.

Kaplan, H. B. and Robbins, C. (1983) 'Testing a general theory of deviant behavior in longitudinal perspective', in K. T. van Dusen and S. A. Mednick (eds.), *Prospective Studies of Crime and Delinquency*, Boston, MA: Kluwer-Nijhoff.

Karau, S. J. and Williams, K. D. (1993) 'Social loafing: A meta-analytic review of social integration', *Journal of Personality and Social Psychology*, 65, 681–706.

Kashima, E. S. and Kashima, Y. (in press) 'Culture and language: A case of cultural dimensions and personal pronoun use', *Journal of Cross-Cultural Psychology*.

Kashima, Y. and Callan, V. (1994) 'The Japanese work group' in H. C. Triandis (ed.) *Handbook of Industrial/Organizational Psychology*, 2nd edn, Volume 4, pp. 609–46. Palo-Alto, CA: Consulting Psychologists Press.

Kashima, Y. and Triandis, H. C. (1986) 'The self-serving bias in attributions as a coping strategy: A cross-cultural study', *Journal of Cross-Cultural Psychology*, 17, 83–97.

Kashima, Y., Siegal, M., Tanaka, K. and Isaka, H. (1988) 'Universalism in lay conceptions of distributive justice: A cross-cultural examination', *International Journal of Psychology*, 23, 51–64.

Kashima, Y., Siegal, M., Tanaka, K. and Kashima, E. S. (1992) 'Do people believe behaviours are consistent with attitudes? Towards a cultural psychology of attribution processes', *British Journal of Social Psychology*, 31, 111–24.

Kashima, Y., Yamaguchi, S., Kim, U. *et al.* (1995) 'Culture, gender, and self: A perspective from individualism–collectivism research', *Journal of Personality and Social Psychology*, 69, 925–37.

Katigbak, M. S., Church, A. T. and Akamine, T. X. (1996) 'Cross-cultural generalizability of personality dimensions: Relating indigenous and imported dimensions in two cultures', *Journal of Personality and Social Psychology*, 70, 99–114.

Katriel, T. (1986) *Talking Straight: Dugri speech in Israeli Sabra culture*, Cambridge: Cambridge University Press.

Katz, D. and Braly, K. W. (1933) 'Verbal stereotypes and racial prejudice', *Journal of Abnormal and Social Psychology*, 28, 280–90.

Kealey, D. (1989) 'A study of cross-cultural effectiveness: Theoretical issues and practical applications', *International Journal of Intercultural Relations*, 13, 387–428.

Keating, C. F. (1985) 'Human dominance signals: The primate in us', in S. L. Ellyson and J. F. Dovidio (eds.), *Power, Dominance and Non-verbal Behavior*, New York: Springer.

Keefe, S. M. and Padilla, A. M. (1987) *Chicano Ethnicity*, Albuquerque: University of New Mexico Press.

Kelley, H. H. (1967) 'Attribution theory in social psychology', in D. Levine (ed.), *Nebraska Symposium on Motivation*, 14, 192–240.

Kelley, K. and 5 co-authors (1986) 'Chronic self-destructiveness and locus of control in cross-cultural perspective', *Journal of Social Psychology*, 126, 573–7.

Kelly, A. F. D. (1989) 'Ethnic identification, association and redefinition: Muslim

Pakistanis and Greek Cypriots in Britain', in K. Liebkind (ed.), *New Identities in Europe. Immigrant ancestry and the ethnic identity of youth*, London: Gower.

Kendon, A. (1988) 'How gestures can become like words', in F. Poyatos (ed.), *Cross-cultural Perspectives in Nonverbal Communication*, Toronto: Hogrefe.

Kenrick, D. T. (1994) 'Evolutionary social psychology: From sexual selection to social cognition', in M. P. Zanna (ed.), *Advances in Experimental Social Psychology*, 26, 75–121.

Kerr, C., Dunlop, J. T., Harbison, F. H., and Myers, C. A. (1960) *Industrialism and Industrial Man: The problems of labor and management in economic growth*, London: Heinemann.

Kerr, S. and Jermier, J. M. (1978) 'Substitutes for leadership: Their meaning and measurement', *Organizational Behavior and Human Performance*, 22, 375–403.

Keuschel, R. (1988) *Vengeance is their Reply: Blood feuds and homicides on Bellona island*, Copenhagen: Dansk Psykologisk Forlag.

Kidder, L. H. (1991) *Japanese Returnees: Loose threads in a tight culture*, unpublished manuscript, Temple University.

Kiesler, C. A., Kiesler, S. B. and Pallak, M. S. (1967) 'The effect of commitment to future interaction on reactions to norm violations', *Journal of Personality*, 35, 585–600.

Kilham, W. and Mann, L. (1974) 'Level of destructive obedience as a function of transmitter and executant roles in the Milgram obedience paradigm', *Journal of Personality and Social Psychology*, 29, 696–702.

Kim, K. I., Park, H. J. and Suzuki, N. (1990) 'Reward allocations in the United States, Japan and Korea: A comparison of individualistic and collectivistic cultures', *Academy of Management Journal*, 33, 188–98.

Kim, M. S. (1994) 'Cross-cultural comparisons of the perceived importance of interactive constraints', *Human Communication Research*, 21, 128–51.

Kim, M. S. and Bresnahan, M. (1994) 'A process model of request tactic evaluation', *Discourse Processes*, 18, 317–44.

Kim, M. S., Sharkey, W. F. and Singelis, T. (1994) 'The relationship between individual's self-construals and perceived importance of interactive constraints', *International Journal of Intercultural Relations*, 18, 1–24.

Kim, M. S., Hunter, J. E., Miyahara, A., Horvath, A. M., Bresnahan, M. and Yoon, H. J. (1996) 'Individual- vs. culture-level dimensions of individualism and collectivism: Effects on preferred conversational styles', *Communication Monographs*, 63, 29–49.

Kim, U., Yamaguchi, S. *et al.* (1996) 'Conceptual and empirical analysis of *amae*', Symposium presented at 13th Congress of International Association for Cross-Cultural Psychology, Montreal.

Kimmel, P. R. (1994) 'Cultural perspectives on international negotiations', *Journal of Social Issues*, 50, 179–96.

Kipnis, D., Schmidt, S. M. and Wilkinson, I. (1980) 'Intraorganizational influence tactics: Exploration in getting one's way', *Journal of Applied Psychology*, 65, 440–52.

Kirchmeyer, C. (1993) 'Multicultural task groups: An account of the low contribution level of minorities', *Small Group Research*, 24, 127–48.

Kirchmeyer, C. and Cohen, A. (1992) 'Multicultural groups: Their performance and reactions with constructive conflict', *Group and Organization Management*, 17, 153–70.

Kirkbride, P., Durcan, J. and Tang, S. F. Y. (1990) 'The possibilities and limits of team training in South East Asia', *Journal of Management Development*, 9, 41–50.

Kirkbride, P., Tang, S. F. Y. and Westwood, R. I. (1991) 'Chinese conflict preferences and negotiating behaviour: Cultural and psychological influences', *Organization Studies*, 12, 365–86.

Kitayama, S., Markus, H. R. and Kurokawa, M. (1995) 'Cultural views of self and emotional experience: Does the nature of good feelings depend on culture?', unpublished manuscript.

Kitayama, S., Markus, H. R. and Lieberman, C. (1995) 'The collective construction of self esteem: Implications for culture, self, and emotion', in J. Russell, J. Fernandez-Dols, A. S. R. Manstead and J. C. Wellenkamp (eds.), *Everyday Conceptions of Emotion: An introduction to the psychology, anthropology and linguistics of emotion*, Dordrecht: Kluwer.

Kitayama, S., Markus, H. R. and Matsumoto, H. (1995) 'Culture, self, and emotion: A cultural perspective on "self-conscious" emotions', in J. P. Tangney and K. W. Fischer (eds.), *Self-Conscious Emotions: The psychology of shame, guilt, embarrassment, and pride*, New York: Guilford.

Klein, K. J., Dansereau, F. and Hall, R. J. (1994) 'Levels issues in theory development, data collection and analysis', *Academy of Management Review*, 19, 195–229.

Kluckhohn, C. (1962) 'Universal categories of culture', in S. Tax (ed.), *Anthropology Today*, Chicago: University of Chicago Press.

Kluckhohn, C. and Murray, H. A. (1948) *Personality in Nature, Culture and Society*, New York: Knopf.

Kluckhohn, F. R. and Strodtbeck, F. L. (1961) *Variations in Value Orientations*, Evanston, IL: Row, Peterson.

Knapp, M. L. (1978) *Nonverbal Communication in Human Interaction*, 2nd edn, New York: Holt, Rinehart and Winston.

Knauft, B. M. (1987) 'Reconsidering violence in simple human societies: Homicide among the Gebusi of New Guinea', *Current Anthropology*, 28, 457–500.

Kobasa, S. C. (1979) 'Stressful life events, personality, and health: An inquiry into hardiness', *Journal of Personality and Social Psychology*, 37, 1–11.

Kodama, K. and Canetto, S. S. (1995) 'Reliability and validity of the Suinn–Lew Asian self-identity acculturation scale with Japanese temporary residents', *Psychologia*, 38, 17–21.

Kogan, N. and Doise, W. (1969) 'Effects of anticipated delegate status on level of risk-taking in small decision-making groups', *Acta Psychologica*, 29, 228–43.

Kolers, P. A. (1968) 'Bilingualism and information processing', *Scientific American*, 218, 78–86.

Koltsova, V. A., Oleinik, Y. N., Gilgen, A. R. and Gilgen C. K. (1996) *Post-Soviet Perspectives on Russian Psychology*, Westport, CT: Greenwood.

Koomen, W. (1988) 'The relationship between participation rate and liking ratings in groups', *British Journal of Social Psychology*, 27, 127–32.

Koomen, W. and Bähler, M. (1996) 'National stereotypes: Common representations and ingroup favouritism', *European Journal of Social Psychology*, 26, 325–32.

Kornadt, H.-J., Hayashi, T., Tachibana, Y., Trommsdorff, G. and Yamauchi, H. (1992) 'Aggressiveness and its developmental conditions in five cultures', in S. Iwawaki, Y. Kashima and K. Leung (eds.), *Innovations in Cross-cultural Psychology*, Lisse: Swets and Zeitlinger.

Korte, C. and Ayvalioglu, N. (1981) 'Helpfulness in Turkey: Cities, towns and urban villages', *Journal of Cross-Cultural Psychology*, 12, 123–41.

Korte, C., Ympa, I. and Toppen, A. (1975) 'Helpfulness in Dutch society as a function of urbanisation and environmental input level', *Journal of Personality and Social Psychology*, 32, 996–1003.

Korten, F. F. (1974) 'The influence of culture and sex on the perception of persons', *International Journal of Psychology*, 9, 31–44.

Koseki, Y. (1989) 'A study of the influence of deviant minority on visual judgments within a small group', *Japanese Psychological Research*, 31 (4), 149–60.

Kosterman, R. and Feshbach, S. (1989) 'Toward a measure of patriotic and nationalistic attitudes', *Political Psychology*, 10, 257–74.

Kravitz D. A. and Martin, B. (1986) 'Ringelmann rediscovered: The original article', *Journal of Personality and Social Psychology*, 50, 936–41.

Krewer, B. and Jahoda, G. (1993) 'Psychologie et culture: vers une solution du Babel?', *International Journal of Psychology*, 28, 367–76.

Krichevskii, R. L. (1983) 'The phenomenon of the differentiation of the leadership role in small groups', in H. H. Blumberg, A. P. Hare, V. Kent and M. Davies (eds.), *Small Groups and Social Interaction*, Volume 1, Chichester: Wiley.

Krishnan, L. (1992) 'Justice research: The Indian perspective', *Psychology and Developing Societies*, 4, 133–51.

Kwan, V. S. Y. (1997) 'Alternative conceptualizations of self-enhancement', unpublished Master's thesis, Chinese University of Hong Kong.

Kwan, V. S. Y., Bond, M. H. and Singelis, T. M. (1997) 'Pancultural explanation for life satisfaction: Adding relationship harmony to self-esteem', *Journal of Personality and Social Psychology*, 73, 1038–51.

LaFrance, M. and Mayo, C. (1976) 'Racial differences in gaze behaviour during conversations: Two systematic observational studies', *Journal of Personality and Social Psychology*, 33, 547–52.

LaFromboise, T., Coleman, H. L. K. and Gerton, J. (1993) 'Psychological impact of biculturalism: evidence and theory', *Psychological Bulletin*, 114, 395–412.

Laguna Reyes, I., Valdez, M. J. and Wagner, W. (1996) 'The self-concept across cultures', paper given at International Congress of Psychology, Montreal.

Lambert, W. E. (1967) 'The social psychology of bilingualism', *Journal of Social Issues*, 23, 91–109.

Lambert, W. E., Mermigis, L. and Taylor, D. M. (1986) 'Greek Canadians' attitudes toward own group and other Canadian ethnic groups: A test of the multiculturalism hypothesis', *Canadian Journal of Behavioural Science*, 18, 35–51.

Lamm, H. and Kogan, N. (1970) 'Risk-taking in the context of intergroup negotiation', *Journal of Experimental Social Psychology*, 6, 351–63.

Landau, S. F. (1984) 'Trends in violence and aggression: A cross-cultural analysis', *International Journal of Comparative Sociology*, 24, 133–58.

Landis, D. and Bhagat, R. S. (eds.) (1996) *Handbook of Intercultural Training*, 2nd edn, Thousand Oaks, CA: Sage.

Landrine, H. (1992) 'Clinical implications of cultural differences: The referential versus the indexical self', *Clinical Psychology Review*, 12, 401–15.

Langer, E. (1989) *Mindfulness*, Reading, MA: Addison-Wesley.

Largey, G. P. and Watson, D. R. (1971) 'The sociology of odors', *American Journal of Sociology*, 77, 1021–34.

L'Armand, K. and Pepitone, A. (1975) 'Helping to reward another person: A cross-cultural analysis', *Journal of Personality and Social Psychology*, 31, 189–98.

L'Armand, K., Pepitone, A. and Shanmugam, T. E. (1981) 'Attitudes toward rape: A comparison of the role of chastity in India and the U.S.', *Journal of Cross-Cultural Psychology*, 12, 284–303.

La Rosa, J. and Diaz Loving, R. (1988) 'Diferencial semantico del autoconcepto en estudiantes', *Revista de Psicologia Social y Personalidad*, 4, 39–57.

Larsen, K. S., Killifer, C., Csepelli, G. *et al.* (1992) 'National identity: A new look at an old issue', *Journal of Social Behavior and Personality*, 7, 309–22.

Laslo, E. (1989) *The Inner Limits of Mankind*, London: Oneworld.

Latané, B., Williams, K. and Harkins, S. (1979) 'Many hands make light the work: causes and consequences of social loafing', *Journal of Personality and Social Psychology*, 37, 822–32.

Laucken, U., Mees, U. and Chassein, J. (1992) 'Beschwerde und normative Ordnung. Eine Kulturvergleichende untersuchung', in U. Mees (ed.), *Psychologie des Ärgers*, Berlin: Hogrefe.

Laurent, A. (1983) 'The cultural diversity of Western conceptions of management', *International Studies of Management and Organization*, 13, 75–96.

Lauterbach, A. (1974) *Psychological Challenges to Modernization*, New York: Elsevier.

Lebedeva, N. (1996) 'Ethnic psychology in Russia', *Cross-Cultural Psychology Bulletin*, 30(4), 14–16.

Lee, C. M. (1996) 'Attraction in initial interethnic interactions', unpublished Master's thesis, California State University, Fullerton.

Lee, F., Hallahan, M. and Herzog, T. (1996) 'Explaining real-life events: How cultural and domain shape attributions', *Personality and Social Psychology Bulletin*, 22, 732–41.

Lee, L. and Ward, C. (in press) 'Ethnicity, idiocentrism–allocentrism, and intergroup perceptions', *Journal of Applied Social Psychology*.

Lee, Y.-T. and Duenas, G. (1995) 'Stereotype accuracy in multicultural business', in Y.-T. Lee, L. J. Jussim and C. R. McCauley (eds.), *Stereotype Accuracy: Towards appreciating group differences*, Washington, DC: American Psychological Association.

Lee, Y.-T. and Ottati, V. (1993) 'Determinants of in-group and out-group perceptions of heterogeneity: An investigation of Sino-American stereotypes', *Journal of Cross-Cultural Psychology*, 24, 298–318.

Lee, Y.-T. and Ottati, V. (1995) 'Perceived in-group homogeneity as a function of group salience and stereotype threat', *Personality and Social Psychology Bulletin*, 21, 610–19.

Lee, Y.-T. and Seligman, M. E. P. (1997) 'Are Americans more optimistic than the Chinese?', *Personality and Social Psychology Bulletin*, 23, 32–40.

Leichty, G. and Applegate, J. L. (1991) 'Social-cognitive and situational influences on the use of face-saving persuasive strategies', *Human Communication Research*, 17, 451–84.

Leong, T. L. F. (1996) 'Acculturation and Asian values in the United States', paper presented at the Conference on Global Organizations, Department of Management, Hong Kong University of Science and Technology.

Leung, K. (1987) 'Some determinants of reactions to procedural models for conflict resolution: A cross-national study', *Journal of Personality and Social Psychology*, 53, 898–908.

Leung, K. (1989) 'Cross-cultural differences: Individual-level and cultural-level analysis', *International Journal of Psychology*, 24, 703–19.

Leung, K. (1997) 'Negotiation and reward allocation across cultures', in P. C. Earley and M. Erez (eds.) *New Perspectives on International Industrial/Organizational Psychology*, San Francisco: Jossey-Bass.

Leung, K. and Bond, M. H. (1982) 'How Chinese and Americans reward task-related contributions: A preliminary study', *Psychologia*, 25, 32–9.

Leung, K. and Bond, M. H. (1984) 'The impact of cultural collectivism on reward allocation', *Journal of Personality and Social Psychology*, 47, 793–804.

Leung, K. and Bond, M. H. (1989) 'On the empirical identification of dimensions for cross-cultural comparison', *Journal of Cross-Cultural Psychology*, 20, 133–51.

Leung, K., Bond, M. H. and Schwartz, S. H. (1995) 'How to explain cross-cultural differences: Values, valences and expectancies?', *Asian Journal of Psychology*, 1, 70–5.

Leung, K., Earley, P. C. and Lind, E. A. (no date) 'Fairness heuristic: A cross-cultural study of organizational justice in the United States and Hong Kong', Chinese University of Hong Kong.

Leung, K. and Iwawaki, S. (1988) 'Cultural collectivism and distributive behavior: A cross-cultural study', *Journal of Cross-Cultural Psychology*, 19, 35–49.

Leung, K. and Lau, S. (1989) 'Effect of self-concept and perceived disapproval of delinquent behavior in school children', *Journal of Youth and Adolescence*, 18, 345–59.

Leung, K. and Lind, E. A. (1986) 'Procedural justice and culture: Effects of culture, gender and investigator status on procedural preferences', *Journal of Personality and Social Psychology*, 50, 1134–40.

Leung, K. and Park, H. J. (1986) 'Effects of interactional goal on choice of allocation rules: A cross-national study', *Organizational Behavior and Human Decision Processes*, 37, 111–20.

Leung, K., Bond, M. H., Carment, D. W., Krishnan, L. and Liebrand, W. B. G. (1990) 'Effects of cultural femininity on preference for methods of conflict processing: A cross-cultural study', *Journal of Experimental Social Psychology*, 26, 373–88. Correction to this paper (1991). *Journal of Experimental Social Psychology*, 27, 201–2.

Leung, K., Au, Y. F., Fernandez-Dols, J. M. and Iwawaki, S. (1992) 'Preferences for methods of conflict processing for two collectivist cultures', *International Journal of Psychology*, 27, 195–209.

Leung, K., Smith, P. B., Wang, Z. M. and Sun, H. (1997) 'Job satisfaction in joint venture hotels in China: An organizational justice analysis', *Journal of International Business Studies*, 27, 947–63.

Levine, D. N. (1985) *The Flight from Ambiguity*, Chicago: University of Chicago Press.

Levine, R. (1997) *A Geography of Time*, New York: Basic Books.

Levine, R. V. and Bartlett, C. (1984) 'Pace of life, punctuality and coronary heart disease in six countries', *Journal of Cross-Cultural Psychology*, 15, 233–55.

Levine, R. A. and Campbell, D. T. (1972) *Ethnocentrism: Theories of conflict, ethnic attitudes and group behavior*, New York: Wiley.

Levine, R. V. and Norenzayan, A. (submitted) 'The pace of life in 31 countries', California State University, Fresno.

Levine, R. V., West, L. J. and Reis, H. T. (1980) 'Perceptions of time and punctuality in the US and Brazil', *Journal of Personality and Social Psychology*, 38, 541–50.

Levine, R. V., Sato, S., Hashimoto, T. and Verma, J. (1995) 'Love and marriage in eleven cultures', *Journal of Cross-Cultural Psychology*, 26, 554–71.

Levine, R. V., Martinez, T., Brase, G. and Sorenson, K. (1994) 'Helping in 36 U.S. cities', *Journal of Personality and Social Psychology*, 67, 69–82.

Levinson, D. (1989) *Family Violence in Cross-cultural Perspective*, Newbury Park, CA: Sage.

Lewin, K. (1947) 'Group decision and social change', In T. M. Newcomb and E. L. Hartley (eds.), *Readings in Social Psychology*, New York: Holt.

Lewin, K., Lippitt, R. and White, R. K. (1939) 'Patterns of aggressive behavior in experimentally created "social climates"', *Journal of Social Psychology*, 10, 271–99.

Li, H. Z. (1994) 'Inter- and intra-cultural information transmission', unpublished Doctoral dissertation, University of Victoria, Canada.

Lichtenberger, B. and Naulleau, G. (1993) 'Cultural conflicts and synergies in the management of French–German joint ventures', in P. S. Kirkbride (ed.), *Human Resource Management in Europe: Perspectives for the Nineties*, London: Routledge.

Lin, C. Y. C. and Fu, V. R. (1990) 'A comparison of child rearing practices among Chinese, immigrant Chinese, and Caucasian–American parents', *Child Development*, 61, 429–33.

Lind, E. A., Erickson, B. E., Friedland, N. and Dickenberger, M. (1978) 'Reactions to procedural models for adjudicative conflict resolution', *Journal of Conflict Resolution*, 22, 318–41.

Linssen, H. and Hagendoorn, L. (1994) 'Social and geographic factors in the explanation of the content of European nationality stereotypes', *British Journal of Social Psychology*, 33, 165–82.

Liska, J. and Hazelton, V. (1990) 'Deferential language as a rhetorical strategy: The case for polite disagreement', *Journal of Social Behavior and Personality*, 5, 187–98.

Little, K. B. (1968) 'Cultural variations in social schemata', *Journal of Personality and Social Psychology*, 10, 1–7.

Little, T., Oettingen, G., Stetsenko, A. and Baltes, P. (1995) 'Children's action–control beliefs about school performance: How do American children compare with German and Russian children?', *Journal of Personality and Social Psychology*, 69, 686–700.

Locke, E. A. and Schweiger, D. M. (1979) 'Participation in decision-making: One more time', in B. M. Staw (ed.), *Research in Organizational Behavior*, Volume 1, Greenwich CT: JAI Press.

Loh, T. W. C. (1993) 'Responses to compliments across languages and cultures: A comparative study of British and Hong Kong Chinese', Research Report No. 30, City University of Hong Kong.

Lonner, W. J. (1980) 'The search for psychological universals', in H. C. Triandis and W. W. Lambert (eds.), *Handbook of Cross-Cultural Psychology: Volume 1 – Perspectives*, 143–204, Boston: Allyn and Bacon.

Lonner, W. J. (1989) 'The introductory psychology text: Beyond Ekman, Whorf and biassed IQ tests', In D. M. Keats, D. Munro and L. Mann (eds.), *Heterogeneity in Cross-cultural Psychology*, Lisse: Swets and Zeitlinger.

Luce, L. F. and Smith, E. C. (1986) 'Cross-cultural literacy: A national priority', in L. F. Luce and E. C. Smith (eds.), *Toward Internationalism: Readings in cross-cultural communication,* 2nd edn, Cambridge, MA: Newbury House.

Luk, C. L. and Bond, M. H. (1993) 'Personality variation and values endorsement in Chinese university students', *Personality and Individual Differences*, 14, 429–37.

Luthans, F., Welsh, D. H. B. and Rosenkrantz, S. A. (1993) 'What do Russian managers really do? An observational study with comparisons to U. S. managers', *Journal of International Business Studies*, 24, 741–61.

Lysgaard, S. (1955) 'Adjustment in foreign society: Norwegian Fulbright grantees visiting the United States', *International Social Science Bulletin*, 7, 45–51.

McArthur, L. Z. and Baron, R. M. (1983) 'Toward an ecological theory of social perception', *Psychological Review*, 90, 215–38.

McArthur, L. Z. and Berry, D. S. (1987) 'Cross-cultural agreement in perceptions of baby-faced adults', *Journal of Cross-Cultural Psychology*, 18, 165–92.

McClelland, D. C. (1961) *The Achieving Society*, New York: Free Press.

McClintock, C. G. and McNeel, C. P. (1966) 'Cross-cultural comparisons of inter-personal motives', *Sociometry*, 29, 406–27.

McCrae, R. R. and Costa, P. T. Jr. (1985) 'Openness to experience', in R. Hogan and E. H. Jones (eds.), *Perspectives in Personality*, Volume 1, Greenwich, CT: JAI Press.

McCrae, R. R. and Costa, P. T. Jr. (1996) 'Toward a new generation of personality theories: Theoretical contexts for the five-factor model', in J. S. Wiggins (ed.), *The Five-factor Model of Personality*, New York: Guilford.

McCrae, R. R. and Costa, P. T. (1997) 'Personality trait structure as a human universal', *American Psychologist*, 52, 509–16.

McCrae, R. R., Costa, P. T. Jr. and Yik, M. S. M. (1996) 'Universal aspects of Chinese personality structure', in M. H. Bond (ed.), *The Handbook of Chinese Psychology*, Hong Kong: Oxford University Press.

McCrae, R. R. and John, O. P. (1992) 'An introduction to the five factor model and its applications', *Journal of Personality*, 60, 175–215.

McCrae, R. R., Zonderman, A. B., Costa, P. T., Bond, M. H. and Paunonen, S. V. (1996) 'Evaluating replicability of factors in the revised NEO Personality Inventory: Confirmatory factor analysis versus Procrustes rotation', *Journal of Personality and Social Psychology*, 70, 552–66.

McCrae, R. R., Yik, M. S. M., Trapnell, P. D., Bond, M. H. and Paulhus, D. L. (1997) 'Interpreting personality profiles across cultures: Bilingual, acculturation, and peer rating studies of Chinese undergraduates', manuscript submitted for publication.

McDougall, W. (1908) *Introduction to Social Psychology*, London: Methuen.

McGuire, W. J., McGuire, C. V., Child, P. and Fujioka, T. (1978) 'Salience of ethnicity in the spontaneous self-concept as a function of one's ethnic distinctiveness in the social environment', *Journal of Personality and Social Psychology*, 36, 511–20.

Mackie, M. (1973) 'Arriving at "truth" by definition: The case of stereotype inaccuracy', *Social Problems*, 20, 431–47.

McLeod, B. A. and Carment, D. W. (1988) 'To lie or not to lie: A comparison of Canadian and Chinese attitudes towards deception', unpublished manuscript, McMaster University.

McLeod, P. L., Lobel, S. A. and Cox, T. H. (1996) 'Ethnic diversity and creativity in small groups', *Small Group Research*, 27, 248–64.

McNeel, C. P., McClintock, C. G. and Nuttin, J. (1972) 'Effects of sex-role in a two-person mixed-motive game', *Journal of Personality and Social Psychology*, 24, 372–8.

Madsen, M. (1967) 'Cooperative and competitive motivation of children in three Mexican sub-cultures', *Psychological Reports*, 20, 1307–20.

Madsen, M. (1971) 'Developmental and cross-cultural differences in the cooperative and competitive behavior of young children', *Journal of Cross-Cultural Psychology*, 2, 365–71.

Madsen, M. and Lancy, D. F. (1981) 'Cooperative and competitive behavior: Experiments related to ethnic identity and urbanization in Papua New Guinea', *Journal of Cross-Cultural Psychology*, 12, 389–408.

Madsen, M. and Shapira, A. (1970) 'Cooperative and competitive behavior of urban Afro-American, Anglo-American, Mexican-American and Mexican village children', *Developmental Psychology*, 3, 16–20.

Madsen, M. and Yi, S. (1975) 'Cooperation and competition of urban and rural children in the republic of South Korea', *International Journal of Psychology*, 10, 269–75.

Mahler, I., Greenberg, L. and Hayashi, H. (1981) 'A comparative study of rules of justice: Japanese versus Americans', *Psychologia*, 24, 1–8.

Makita, M. (1952) 'Comparative study on lecture and group decision in motivating a desired behavior', *Japanese Journal of Educational Psychology*, 1, 84–91.

Mandal, M. K., Bryden, M. P. and Bulman-Fleming, M. B. (1996) 'Similarities and variations in facial expressions of emotions: cross-cultural evidence', *International Journal of Psychology*, 31, 49–58.

Mann, L., Radford, M. and Kanagawa, C. (1985) 'Cross-cultural differences in children's use of decision rules: a comparison of Japan and Australia', *Journal of Personality and Social Psychology*, 49, 1557–64.

Mann, L., Burnett, P., Radford, M. and Ford, S. (1997a) 'The Melbourne decision making questionnaire: An instrument for measuring patterns for coping with decisional conflict', *Journal of Behavioral Decision Making*, 10, 1–19.

Mann, L., Radford, M., Burnett, P. *et al.* (1997b) 'Cross cultural differences in self-reported decision making style and confidence', unpublished manuscript, University of Melbourne.

Mantell, D. M., (1971) 'The potential for violence in Germany', *Journal of Social Issues*, 27, 101–12.

Manz, C. C. (1983) *The Art of Self-leadership*, Englewood Cliffs, NJ: Prentice Hall.

Mao, L. M. R. (1996) 'Chinese first person pronoun and social implicature', *Journal of Asian Pacific Communication*, 7, 106–28.

Marin, G. (1981) 'Perceiving justice across cultures: Equity vs. equality in Colombia and in the United States', *International Journal of Psychology*, 16, 153–9.

Marin, G. (1983) 'The Latin American experience in applying social psychology to community change', in F. Blackler (ed.), *Social Psychology and Developing Countries*, Chichester: Wiley.

Marin, G. (1985) 'Validez transcultural del principio de equidad: el colectivismo–individualismo come una variable moderatora', *Revista Interamericana de Psicologia Occupational*, 4, 7–20.

Marin, G. and Marin, B. V. (1982) 'Methodological fallacies when studying Hispanics', in L. Bickman (ed.), *Applied Social Psychology Annual*, 3, 99–118.

Marin, G., Mejia, B. and Oberle, C. (1975) 'Cooperation as a function of place of residence among Colombian children', *Journal of Social Psychology*, 95, 127–8.

Markus, H. and Kitayama, S. (1991) 'Culture and the self: Implications for cognition, emotion and motivation', *Psychological Review*, 98, 224–53.

Markus, H. R. and Kitayama, S. (1994) 'A collective fear of the collective: Implications for selves and theories of selves', *Personality and Social Psychology Bulletin*, 20, 568–79.

Markus, H. and Zajonc, R. B. (1985) 'The cognitive perspective in social psychology', in G. Lindzey and E. Aronson (eds.), *Handbook of Social Psychology*, Volume 1, New York: Random House.

Marriott, H. (1993a) 'Spatial arrangements in Australian–Japanese business communi-cation', *Journal of Asian Pacific Communication*, 4, 107–26.

Marriott, H. (1993b) 'Acquiring sociolinguistic competence: Australian secondary students in Japan', *Journal of Asian Pacific Communication*, 4, 167–92.

Marrow, A. J. (1964) 'Risks and uncertainties in action research', *Journal of Social Issues*, 20 (3), 5–20.

Marrow, A. J. (1969) *The Practical Theorist: The life and work of Kurt Lewin*, New York: Basic Books.

Marsella, A. J. and Choi, S. C. (1993) 'Psychological aspects of modernization and economic development in East Asian nations', *Psychologia*, 36, 201–13.

Marsella, A. J., De Vos, G. and Hsu, F. L. K. (1985) *Culture and Self: Asian and Western perspectives*, London: Tavistock.

Marsh, R. M. (1967) *Comparative Sociology: A codification of cross-societal analysis*, New York: Harcourt Brace Jovanovich.

Marshall, R. (1997) 'An investigation of variances of individualism across two cultures and three social classes', *Journal of Cross-Cultural Psychology*, 28, 490–5.

Martin, J. N. (1984) 'The intercultural reentry: Conceptualizations and suggestions for future research', *International Journal of Intercultural Relations*, 8, 115–34.

Martin, J. N. and Hammer, M. R. (1989) 'Behavioral categories of intercultural communication competence: everyday communicators' perceptions', *International Journal of Intercultural Relations*, 13, 303–32.

Marwell, G. and Schmitt, D. R. (1972) 'Cooperation and interpersonal risk: Cross-cultural and cross-procedural generalisations', *Journal of Experimental Social Psychology*, 8, 594–9.

Marwell, G., Schmitt, D. R. and Boyesen, B. (1973) 'Pacifist strategy and cooperation under interpersonal risk', *Journal of Personality and Social Psychology*, 28, 12–20.

Maslow, A. H. (1954) *Motivation and Personality*, New York: Harper.

Masuda, M., Lin, K. and Tazuma, L. (1982) 'Life changes among Vietnamese refugees', in R. C. Nann (ed.), *Uprooting and surviving*, Boston, MA: Reidel.

Mataragnon, R. H. (1988) 'Pakikiramdam in Filipino social interaction: A study of subtlety and sensitivity', in A. C. Paranjpe, D. Y. F. Ho and R. W. Rieber (eds.), *Asian Contributions to Psychology*, New York: Praeger.

Mathieson, A. and Wall, G. (1982) *Tourism: Economic, physical and social impacts*, London: Longman.

Matsui, T., Kakuyama, T. and Onglatco, M. L. (1987) 'Effects of goals and feedback on performance in groups', *Journal of Applied Psychology*, 72, 407–15.

Matsumoto, D. (1989) 'Cultural influences of the perception of emotion', *Journal of Cross-Cultural Psychology*, 20, 92–105.

Matsumoto, D. (1992) 'American–Japanese cultural differences in the recognition of universal facial expressions', *Journal of Cross-Cultural Psychology*, 23, 72–84.

Matsumoto, D. and Kudoh, T. (1993) 'American–Japanese cultural differences in attributions of personality based on smiles', *Journal of Nonverbal Behavior*, 17, 231–44.

Matsumoto, D., Kudoh, T., Scherer, K. and Wallbot, H. G. (1988) 'Emotion antecedents and reactions in the US and Japan', *Journal of Cross-Cultural Psychology*, 19, 267–86.

Matsumoto, D., Kudoh, T. and Takeuchi, S. (1996) 'Changing patterns of individualism and collectivism in the United States and Japan', *Culture and Psychology*, 2, 77–107.

Maurice, M. (1976) 'Introduction: Theoretical and ideological aspects of the universalistic approach to the study of organisations', *International Studies of Management and Organization*, 6, 3–10.

Mauro, R., Sato, K. and Tucker, J. (1992) 'The role of appraisal in human emotions: A cross-cultural study', *Journal of Personality and Social Psychology*, 62, 301–17.

Mazur, A. (1977) 'Interpersonal spacing on public benches in 'contact' versus 'non-contact' cultures', *Journal of Social Psychology*, 101, 53–8.

Mead, M. (1935) *Sex and Temperament in Three Primitive Societies*, New York: Morrow.

Meade, R. D. (1967) 'An experimental study of leadership in India', *Journal of Social Psychology*, 72, 35–43.

Meade, R. D. (1972) 'Future time perspectives of Americans and subcultures in India', *Journal of Cross-Cultural Psychology*, 3, 93–100.

Meade, R. D. (1985) 'Experimental studies of authoritarian and democratic leadership in four cultures: American, Indian, Chinese and Chinese–American', *High School Journal*, 68, 293–5.

Meaning of Working International Team (1987) *The Meaning of Work: An international view*, New York: Academic Press.

Meeus, W. H. J. and Raaijmakers, Q. A. W. (1986) 'Administrative obedience: Carrying out orders to use psychological–administrative violence', *European Journal of Social Psychology*, 16, 311–24.

Mendenhall, M., Dunbar, E. and Oddou, G. R. (1987) 'Expatriate selection, training, and career pathing: A review and critique', *Human Resource Management*, 26, 331–45.

Merritt, A. C. (1995) 'Commercial pilot selection and training: The next ten years, some global considerations', paper presented at Royal Aeronautical Society conference.

Merritt, A. C. (1996) 'Facing the issue: Indirect communication in aviation', *Proceedings of the Third Australian Aviation Psychology Symposium*, pp. 135–42, Sydney, 1995.

Merritt, A. C. and Helmreich, R. L. (1996) 'Human factors on the flightdeck: The influence of national culture', *Journal of Cross-Cultural Psychology*, 27, 5–24.

Mesarovic, M. and Pestel, E. (1974) *Mankind at the Turning Point: The second report to the Club of Rome*, New York: Dutton.

Mesquita, B. and Frijda, N. H. (1992) 'Cultural variations in emotions: A review', *Psychological Bulletin*, 112, 179–204.

Mikula, G. (1974) 'Nationality, performance and sex as determinants of reward allocation', *Journal of Personality and Social Psychology*, 29, 435–40.

Milgram, S. (1963) 'Behavioral study of obedience', *Journal of Abnormal Psychology*, 67, 371–8.

Milgram, S. (1970) 'The experience of living in cities', *Science*, 167, 1461–8.

Milgram, S. (1974) *Obedience to Authority: An experimental view*, New York: Harper Row.

Milhouse, V. H. (1993) 'The applicability of interpersonal communication competence to the intercultural communication context', in R. Wiseman and J. Koester (eds.), *International and Intercultural Communication Annual*, Volume 17, pp. 184–203, Newbury Park, CA: Sage.

Mill, J. S. (1872/1973) *A System of Logic*, Volumes 7 and 8 in J. M. Robson (ed.), *Collected Works of John Stuart Mill*, Toronto: University of Toronto Press.

Miller, A. G. and Thomas, R. (1972) 'Cooperation and competition among Blackfoot Indian and urban Canadian children', *Child Development*, 43, 1104–10.

Miller, J. G. (1984) 'Culture and the development of everyday social explanation', *Journal of Personality and Social Psychology*, 46, 961–78.

Miller, J. G., Bersoff, D. M. and Harwood, R. L. (1990) 'Perceptions of social responsibilities in India and in the United States: Moral imperatives or personal decisions?', *Journal of Personality and Social Psychology*, 58, 33–47.

Miller, L. (1994) 'Japanese and American indirectness', *Journal of Asian Pacific Communication*, 5, 37–55.

Miller, L. (1995) 'Two aspects of Japanese and American co-worker interaction: Giving instructions and creating rapport', *Journal of Applied Behavioral Science*, 31, 141–61.

Milner, D. (1975) *Children and Race*, Harmondsworth: Penguin.

Miranda, F. S. B., Caballero, R. B., Gomez, M. N. G. and Zamorano, M. A. M. (1981) 'Obediencia a la autoridad', *Psiquis*, 2, 212–21.

Mischel, W. (1968) *Personality and Assessment*, New York: Wiley.

Misra, S. (1981) 'Excursion from the pure to the applied in experimental social psychology', in J. Pandey (ed.), *Perspectives on Experimental Social Psychology in India*, New Delhi: Concept.

Misumi, J. (1985) *The Behavioral Science of Leadership: An interdisciplinary Japanese research program*, Ann Arbor, MI: University of Michigan Press.

Misumi, J. and Haraoka, K. (1958) 'An experimental study of group decision (1)', *Research Bulletin of the Faculty of Education, Kyushu University*, 5, 61–81.

Misumi, J. and Haraoka, K. (1960) 'An experimental study of group decision (11)', *Japanese Journal of Educational and Social Psychology*, 1, 136–53.

Misumi, J. and Nakano, S. (1960) 'A cross-cultural study of the effects of democratic, authoritarian and laissez-faire atmosphere in children's groups', *Japanese Journal of Educational and Social Psychology*, 1, 10–22 and 119–35.

Mizokawa, D. T. and Ryckman, D. B. (1990) 'Attributions of academic success and failure: A comparison of six Asian–American ethnic groups', *Journal of Cross-Cultural Psychology*, 21, 434–51.

Mlicki, P. and Ellemers, N. (1996) 'Being different or being better? National stereotypes and identifications of Polish and Dutch students', *European Journal of Social Psychology*, 26, 97–114.

Modigliani, A. (1966) 'Embarrassment and social influence', unpublished Doctoral dissertation, University of Michigan.

Moede, W. (1920) *Experimentelle Massenpsychologie*, Leipzig: Hirzel.

Moghaddam, F. M. (1987) 'Psychology in the three worlds', *American Psychologist*, 42, 912–20.

Moghaddam, F. M. (1990) 'Modulative and generative orientations in psychology: Implications for psychology in the three worlds', *Journal of Social Issues*, 46, 21–41.

Moghaddam, F. M. (1994) 'Ethnic segregation in a multicultural society: A review of recent trends in Montreal and Toronto and reconceptualization of causal factors', in F. Frisken (ed.), *The Changing Canadian Metropolis: A public policy perspective*, Volume 2, Berkeley: University of California Press.

Montepare, J. M. and Zebrowitz McArthur, L. (1987) 'Perceptions of adults with child-like voices in two cultures', *Journal of Experimental Social Psychology*, 23, 331–49.

Montepare, J. M. and Zebrowitz, L. (1993) 'A cross-cultural comparison of impressions created by age-related variations in gait', *Journal of Non-Verbal Behavior*, 17, 55–68.

Morris, M. H., Davis, D. L. and Allen, J. W. (1994) 'Fostering corporate entrepreneurship: Cross-cultural comparisons of the importance of individualism versus collectivism', *Journal of International Business Studies*, 25, 65–90.

Morris, M. W. and Peng, K. P. (1994) 'Culture and cause: American and Chinese attributions for social and physical events', *Journal of Personality and Social Psychology*, 67, 949–71.

Moscovici, S. (1961) *La Psychanalyse: Son image et son public*. Paris: Presses Universitaires de France.

Moscovici, S. (1976) *Social Influence and Social Change*, London: Academic Press.

Moscovici, S. (1981) 'On social representation', in J. P. Forgas (ed.), *Social Cognition: Perspectives on everyday life*, London: Academic Press.

Moscovici, S. and Faucheux, C. (1972) 'Social influence, conformity bias and the study of active minorities', in L. Berkowitz (ed.), *Advances in Experimental Social Psychology*, Volume 6, New York: Academic Press.

Moscovici, S. and Personnaz, B. (1980) 'Studies in social influence. V: Minority influence and conversion behaviour in a perceptual task', *Journal of Experimental Social Psychology*, 16, 270–82.

Moscovici, S. and Zavalloni, M. (1969) 'The group as a polariser of attitudes', *Journal of Personality and Social Psychology*, 12, 125–35.

Mouer, R. (1995) 'Work post-modernism or ultra modernism: The Japanese dilemma at work', in Y. Sugimoto and J. P. Arnason (eds.), *Japanese Encounters with Post-modernity*, London: Kegan Paul.

Mpofu, E. (1995) 'Exploring the self-concept in an African culture', *Journal of Genetic Psychology*, 155, 341–54.

Mullen, B., Brown, R. J. and Smith, C. (1992) 'Ingroup bias as a function of salience, relevance and status: An integration', *European Journal of Social Psychology*, 22, 103–22.

Mummendey, A. (1995) 'Positive distinctiveness and social discrimination: An old couple living in divorce', *European Journal of Social Psychology*, 25, 657–70.

Mummendey, A. and Schreiber, H. J. (1984) '"Different" just means "better": Some obvious and some hidden pathways to in-group favouritism', *British Journal of Social Psychology*, 23, 363–8.

Munene J. C. (1991) 'Organisational environments in Africa: A factor analysis of critical incidents', *Human Relations*, 44, 439–58.

Munene J. C. (1995) '"Not on seat": An investigation of some correlates of organisational citizenship behaviour in Nigeria', *Applied Psychology: An International Review*, 44, 111–22.

Munro, B. and Adams, G. (1978) 'Love American style: A test of role structure theory on changes in attitudes toward love', *Human Relations*, 31, 215–28.

Munro, D. (1979) 'Locus of control attribution: Factors among Blacks and Whites in Africa', *Journal of Cross-Cultural Psychology*, 10, 157–72.

Munro, D. (1986) 'Work motivation and values: Problems and possibilities in and out of Africa', *Australian Journal of Psychology*, 38, 285–96.

Munroe, R. L. and Munroe, R. H. (1977) 'Cooperation and competition among East African and American children', *Journal of Social Psychology*, 101, 145–6.

Munroe, R. L., Munroe, R. H. and Winters, S. (1996) 'Cross-cultural correlates of the consonant–vowel (cv) syllable', *Cross-Cultural Research*, 30, 60–83.

Murata, K. (1994) 'Intrusive or co-operative? A cross-cultural study of interruption', *Journal of Pragmatics*, 21, 385–400.

Murphy-Berman, V. and Berman, J. J. (1993) 'Effects of responsibility for illness and social acceptability on reactions to people with AIDS: A cross-cultural comparison', *Basic and Applied Social Psychology*, 14, 215–29.

Murphy-Berman, V., Berman, J. J., Singh, P. *et al.* (1984) 'Factors affecting allocation to needy and meritorious recipients: A cross-cultural comparison', *Journal of Personality and Social Psychology*, 46, 1267–72.

Myers, D. (1996) *Social Psychology*, 5th edn, New York: McGraw-Hill.

Naisbitt, J. and Aburdene, P. (1990) *Megatrends 2000: Ten new directions for the 1990's*, New York: Avon.

Naidoo, J. and Davis, J. C. (1988) 'Canadian South Asian women in transition: A dualistic view of life', *Journal of Comparative Family Studies*, 19, 311–27.

Nakane, C. (1970) *Japanese Society*, London: Weidenfeld and Nicolson.

Narayan, L., Menon, S. and Levine, E. L. (1995) 'Personality structure: A culture-specific examination of the five-factor model', *Journal of Personality Assessment*, 64, 51–62.

Needham, J. (1978) *The Shorter Science and Civilisation of China*, Cambridge: Cambridge University Press.

Nelson, G. L., El Bakary, W. and Al Batal, M. (1993) 'Egyptian and American compliments: A cross-cultural study', *International Journal of Intercultural Relations*, 17, 293–314.

Nettler, G. (1984) *Explaining Crime*, 3rd edn, New York: McGraw-Hill.

Newman, L. S. (1993) 'How individuals interpret behavior: Idiocentrism and spontaneous trait inference', *Social Cognition*, 11, 243–69.

Nicholson, N. (1996) 'Personality, culture and organization: Change and stability dynamics', paper presented at the Conference on Work Motivation in the Context of a Globalizing Economy, Ein-Gedi, Israel.

Nisbett, R. E. and Ross, L. (1980) *Human Inference: Strategies and shortcomings of social judgments*, Englewood Cliffs, NJ: Prentice Hall.

Noesjirwan, J. (1977) 'Contrasting cultural patterns of interpersonal closeness in doctors' waiting rooms in Sydney and Jakarta', *Journal of Cross-Cultural Psychology*, 8, 357–68.

Nomura, N. and Barnlund, D. (1983) 'Patterns of interpersonal criticism in Japan and the United States', *International Journal of Intercultural Relations*, 7, 1–18.

Norenzayan, A. and Levine, R. V. (1994) 'Helping in 18 international cities', paper presented at the annual meeting of the Western Psychological Association, Kona, Hawaii.

Norman, W. T. (1963) 'Toward an adequate taxonomy of personality attributes: Replicated factor structure in peer nomination personality ratings', *Journal of Abnormal and Social Psychology*, 66, 574–83.

Oberg, K. (1960) 'Cultural shock: Adjustment to a new cultural environment', *Practical Anthropology*, 7, 177–82.

Oceja, L. V. and Fernandez Dols, J. M. (1992) 'El reconocimiento de la norma perversa y sus consecuencias en los juicios de las personas', *Revista de Psicologia Social*, 7, 227–40.

Oerter, R., Oerter, R., Agostiani, H., Kim, H. O. and Wibowo, S. (1996) 'The concept of human nature in East Asia: Etic and emic characteristics', *Culture and Psychology*, 2, 9–51.

Oettingen, G., Little, T., Lindenberger, U. and Baltes, P. (1994) 'Causality, agency and control beliefs in East vs. West Berlin children: A natural experiment in the role of context', *Journal of Personality and Social Psychology*, 66, 579–95.

Oetzel, J. C. (1995) 'Intercultural small groups: An effective decision-making theory', in R. L. Wiseman (ed.), *Intercultural Communication Theories*, Newbury Park, CA: Sage.

Oetzel, J. G. (1996) 'Explaining individual communication processes in homogeneous and heterogeneous groups through individualism–collectivism and self-construal', manuscript submitted for publication.

Ohbuchi, K. and Takahashi, Y. (1994) 'Cultural styles of conflict management in Japanese and Americans: Passivity, covertness and effectiveness of strategies', *Journal of Applied Social Psychology*, 24, 1345–66.

Okumura, T. and Brett, J. M. (1996) 'Inter- and intra-cultural negotiation: U. S. and Japanese negotiators', unpublished manuscript, Northwestern University.

Öngel, Ü. and Smith, P. B. (1994) 'Who are we and where are we going? JCCP approaches its 100th issue', *Journal of Cross-Cultural Psychology*, 25, 25–53.

Öngel, Ü. and Smith, P. B. (1996) 'Indigenous psychologies: Where can we find them?', Paper presented at International Congress of Psychology, Montreal.

Organ, D. W. (1988) *Organizational Citizenship Behavior: The Good Soldier syndrome*, Lexington, MA: Lexington Books.

Osbeck, L. M., Moghaddam, F. M. and Perreault, S. (1997) 'Similarity and attraction among majority and minority groups in a multicultural context', *International Journal of Intercultural Relations*, 21, 113–23.

Osgood, C. E., Suci, G. J. and Tannenbaum, P. H. (1957) *The Measurement of Meaning*, Urbana, IL: University of Illinois Press.

Ottati, V. and Lee, Y.-T. (1995) 'Accuracy: A neglected component of stereotype research', in Y.-T Lee, L. J. Jussim and C. R. McCauley (eds.), *Stereotype Accuracy: Towards appreciating group differences*, Washington, DC: American Psychological Association.

Pacheco, A. M. and Lucca, N. (1996) 'Of actions and deeds: Ethnopsychology in Puerto Rico', *Interamerican Journal of Psychology*, 30, 111–17.

Pak, A. W. P., Dion, K. L. and Dion, K. K. (1991) 'Social–psychological correlates of experienced discrimination: Test of the double jeopardy hypothesis', *International Journal of Intercultural Relations*, 15, 243–54.

Palsane, M. N. and Lam, D. J. (1996) 'Stress and coping from traditional Indian and Chinese perspectives', *Psychology and Developing Societies*, 8, 29–53.

Pande, N. and Naidu, R. K. (1986) 'Effort and outcome orientations as moderators of the stress–strain relationship', *Psychological Studies*, 32, 207–14.

Pande, N. and Naidu, R. K. (1992) '*Anasakti* and health: A study of non-attachment', *Psychology and Developing Societies*, 4, 89–104.

Pandey, J. (1979) 'Effect of status of benefactor and recipient on helping behaviour', *Journal of Social Psychology*, 15, 303–11.

Pandey, J. (ed.) (1981a) *Perspectives on Experimental Social Psychology in India*, New Delhi: Concept.

Pandey, J. (1981b) 'Ingratiation as social behaviour', in J. Pandey (ed.), *Perspectives on Experimental Social Psychology in India*, New Delhi: Concept.

Pandey, J. (1986) 'Socio-cultural perspectives on ingratiation', in B. A. Maher and W. B. Maher (eds.), *Progress in Experimental Personality Research*, Volume 14, Orlando, FL: Academic Press.

Park, R. E. (1928) 'Human migration and the marginal man', *American Journal of Sociology*, 33, 881–93.

Parker, B. and McEvoy, G. M. (1993) 'Initial examination of a model of intercultural adjustment', *International Journal of Intercultural Relations*, 17, 355–80.

Parsons, T. and Shils, E. A. (eds.) (1951) *Towards a General Theory of Action*, Cambridge, MA: Harvard University Press.

Patterson, M. L. (1991) 'A functional approach to nonverbal exchange', in R. S. Feldman and B. Rimé (eds.), *Fundamentals of Nonverbal Behavior*, New York: Cambridge University Press.

Paunonen, S. V., Keinonen, M., Trzebinski, J. *et al.* (1996) 'The structure of personality in six cultures', *Journal of Cross-Cultural Psychology*, 27, 339–53.

Payne, M. and Vandewiele, M. (1987) 'Attitudes toward love in the Caribbean', *Psychological Reports*, 60, 715–21.

Peabody, D. (1985) *National Characteristics*, Cambridge: Cambridge University Press.

Peabody, D. and Shmelyov, A. G. (1996) 'Psychological characteristics of Russians', *European Journal of Social Psychology*, 26, 507–12.

Pearce, P. L. (1981) '"Environment shock": A study of tourists' reactions to two tropical islands', *Journal of Applied Social Psychology*, 11, 268–80.

Pearce, P. L. (1982) 'Tourists and their hosts: Some social and psychological effects of inter-cultural contact', in S. Bochner (ed.), *Cultures in Contact: Studies in cross-cultural interaction*, Oxford: Pergamon.

Pearce, P. L., Moscardo, G. and Ross, G. F. (1991) 'Tourism impact and community perception: An equity-social representational perspective', *Australian Psychologist*, 26, 147–52.

Peng, Y., Zebrowitz, L. A. and Lee, H. K. (1993) 'The impact of cultural background and cross-cultural experience on impressions of American and Korean male speakers', *Journal of Cross-Cultural Psychology*, 24, 203–20.

Pepitone, A., and 7 co-authors (1967) 'The role of self-esteem in competitive choice behavior', *International Journal of Psychology*, 2, 147–59.

Pepitone, A., and 10 co-authors (1970) 'Justice in choice behavior: A cross-cultural analysis', *International Journal of Psychology*, 5, 1–10.

Peristiany, J. G. (ed.). (1965) *Honor and Shame: The values of Mediterranean society*, London: Weidenfeld and Nicolson.

Perkins, C. S., Perkins, M. L., Guglielmino, L. M. and Reiff, R. F. (1977) 'A comparison of adjustment problems of three international student groups', *Journal of College Student Personnel*, 18, 382–88.

Perrett, D. I., May, K. A. and Yoshikawa, S. (1994) 'Facial shape and judgments of female attractiveness', *Nature*, 368, 239–42.

Perrin, S. and Spencer, C. P. (1981) 'Independence or conformity in the Asch experiment as a reflection of cultural and situational factors', *British Journal of Social Psychology*, 20, 205–10.

Personnaz, B. (1996) 'European identity and national groups', *International Journal of Psychology*, 37, 5715.

Peterson, M. F. and Smith, P. B. (1997) 'Does national culture or ambient temperature explain cross-national differences in role stress? No Sweat! A response to Van de Vliert and van Yperen', *Academy of Management Journal*, 39, 930–46.

Peterson, M. F. and 22 co-authors (1995) 'Role conflict, ambiguity and overload: A 21 nation study', *Academy of Management Journal*, 38, 429–52.

Peterson, R. A. and Jolibert, A. J. P. (1995) 'A meta-analysis of country-of-origin effects', *Journal of International Business Studies*, 26, 883–900.

Pettigrew, T. (1958) 'Personality and sociocultural factors in intergroup attitudes: A cross-national comparison', *Journal of Conflict Resolution*, 2, 29–42.

Pettigrew, T. F. (1979) 'The ultimate attribution error: Extending Allport's cognitive analysis of prejudice', *Personality and Social Psychology Bulletin*, 5, 461–76.

Phalet, K. and Hagendoorn, L. (1996) 'Personal adjustment to acculturative transitions: The Turkish experience', *International Journal of Psychology*, 31, 131–44.

Philbrick, J. L. (1987) 'Sex differences in romantic attitudes toward love in engineering students', *Psychological Reports*, 61, 482.

Philbrick, J. L. and Opolot, J. A. (1980) 'Love style: Comparison of African and American attitudes', *Psychological Reports*, 46, 286.

Pierson, H. D. and Bond, M. H. (1982) 'How do Chinese bilinguals respond to variations of interviewer language and ethnicity?', *Journal of Language and Social Psychology*, 1, 123–39.

Poortinga, Y. H. (1990) 'Towards a conceptualisation of culture for psychology', *Cross-Cultural Psychology Bulletin*, 24, 2–10.

Population Crisis Committee (1988) 'Country rankings of the status of women: poor, powerless, and pregnant', Population Briefing Paper, No. 20.

Porat, A. (1970) 'Cross-cultural differences in resolving union–management conflict through negotiations', *Journal of Applied Psychology*, 54, 441–51.

Potter, J. and Wetherell, M. (1987) *Discourse and Social Psychology*, London: Sage.

Poyatos, F. (ed.) (1988) *Cross-Cultural Perspectives on Communication*, Toronto: Hogrefe.

Pratto, F. and Bargh, J. A. (1991) 'Stereotyping based on apparently individuating information: Trait and global components of sex stereotypes under attention overload', *Journal of Experimental Social Psychology*, 27, 26–47.

Pratto, F., Liu, J. H., Levin, S., Sidanius, J. *et al.* (1996) 'Social dominance orientation and legitimization of inequality across cultures', unpublished manuscript, Stanford University.

Pye, L. W. (1991) 'The challenge of modernization to the Chinese national identity', *Chinese University Bulletin Supplement*, 22, 12–29.

Pyszczynski, T. A. and Greenberg, J. (1981) 'Role disconfirmed expectancies in the instigation of attributional processing', *Journal of Personality and Social Psychology*, 40, 31–8.

Quattrone, G. A. and Jones, E. E. (1980) 'The perception of variability within ingroups and outgroups: Implications for the law of small numbers', *Journal of Personality and Social Psychology*, 38, 141–52.

Rabbie, J. (1982) 'Are groups more aggressive than individuals?', Henri Tajfel lecture, conference of the British Psychological Society, Social Psychology section.

Radzikhovski, L. A. (1991) 'The historical meaning of the crisis in psychology', *Soviet Psychology*, 29, 73–96.

Ralston, D. A., Holt, D. H., Terpstra, R. H. *et al.* (1997) 'The impact of national culture and economic ideology on managerial work values: A study of the United States, Russia, Japan and China', *Journal of International Business Studies*, 28, 177–208.

Ramirez, M. (1967) 'Identification with Mexican family values and authoritarianism in Mexican Americans', *Journal of Social Psychology*, 73, 3–11.

Rao, A. and Hashimoto, K. (1996) 'Intercultural influence: A study of Japanese expatriate managers in Canada', *Journal of International Business Studies*, 27, 443–66.

Rapoport, A., Guyer, M. and Gordon, D. (1971) 'A comparison of performance of Danish and American students in a "threat" game', *Behavioral Science*, 16, 456–66.

Redding, S. G. (1990) *The Spirit of Chinese Capitalism*, Berlin: De Gruyter.

Redding, S. G., Norman, A. and Schlander, A. (1994) 'The nature of individual attachment to the organization: A review of East Asian variations', in H. C. Triandis (ed.), *Handbook of Industrial/Organizational Psychology*, 2nd edn, Volume 4, Palo Alto. CA: Consulting Psychologists Press.

Redding, S. G. and Wong, G. Y. Y. (1986) 'The psychology of Chinese organisational behaviour', in M. H. Bond (ed.) *The Psychology of the Chinese People*, Hong Kong: Oxford University Press.

Retschitzsky, J., Bossel-Lagos, M. and Dasen P. (1989) *La Recherche Interculturelle*, 2 volumes, Paris: L'Harmattan.

Rhee, E., Ulemann, J. S., Lee, H. K. and Roman, R. J. (1995) 'Spontaneous self-descriptions and ethnic identities in individualistic and collectivistic cultures', *Journal of Personality and Social Psychology*, 69, 142–52.

Riley, P. (1989) 'Well don't blame me! On the interpretation of pragmatic errors', in W. Oleksy (ed.), *Contrastive Pragmatics*, Amsterdam: John Benjamins.

Rim, Y. (1964) 'Personality and group decisions involving risk', *Psychological Reports*, 14, 37–45.

Ripple, S. (1996) 'Does interpersonal contact help to reduce intergroup conflict: The case of the united Germany', paper presented at the 13th Congress of the International Association for Cross-Cultural Psychology, Montreal.

Robbins, M. C., DeWalt, B. R. and Pelto, P. J. (1972) 'Climate and behavior: A biocultural study', *Journal of Cross-Cultural Psychology*, 3, 331–44.

Robertson, R. (1990) 'Mapping the global condition: Globalization as the central concept', *Theory, Culture and Society*, 7, 15–30.

Roccas, S. and Schwartz, S. (1993) 'Effects of intergroup similarity on intergroup relations', *European Journal of Social Psychology*, 23, 581–95.

Rodrigues, A. (1982) 'Replication: A neglected type of research in social psychology', *Interamerican Journal of Psychology*, 16, 91–109.

Rodriguez, A. and Seoane, J. (eds.) (1989) *Creencias, Actitudes y Valores*, Volume 7 of J. Mayor and J. L. Pinillos (eds.), *Tratado de Psicologia General*, Madrid: Alhambra University Press.

Rogler, L. H. (1994) 'International migrations: A framework for directing research', *American Psychologist*, 49, 701–8.

Rogoff, B. and Morelli, G. (1989) 'Section introduction', *American Psychologist*, 44, 341–2.

Rohner, R. (1984) 'Toward a conception of culture for cross-cultural psychology', *Journal of Cross-Cultural Psychology*, 15, 111–38.

Rosenberg, M. (1965) *Society and the Adolescent Self-Image*, Princeton, NJ: Princeton University Press.

Rosenthal, D. A. and Feldman, S. S. (1992) 'The nature and stability of ethnic identity in Chinese youth: Effects of length of residence in two cultural contexts', *Journal of Cross-Cultural Psychology*, 23, 214–27.

Rosenzweig, M. R. (1992) *International Psychological Science: Progress, problems and prospects*, Washington, DC: American Psychological Association.

Ross, E. A. (1908) *Social Psychology*, New York: MacMillan.

Ross, L. (1977) 'The intuitive psychologist and his shortcomings: Distortions in the attribution process', in L. Berkowitz (ed.), *Advances in Experimental Social Psychology*, 10, 173–220.

Rothbaum, F. and Tsang, B. (in press) 'Love songs in the US and China: On the nature of romantic love', *Journal of Cross-Cultural Psychology*.

Rotter, J. (1966) 'Generalised expectancies for internal versus external control of reinforcement', *Psychological Monographs*, 80 (Whole No. 609).

Ruben, B. (1976) 'Assessing communication competency for intercultural adaptation', *Group and Organizational Studies*, 1, 334–54.

Ruben, B. (1989) 'The study of cross-cultural competence: Traditions and contemporary issues', *International Journal of Intercultural Relations*, 13, 229–40.

Ruben, B. D. and Kealey, D. J. (1979) 'Behavioral assessment of communication competency and the prediction of cross-cultural adaptation', *International Journal of Intercultural Relations*, 3, 15–47.

Rubinstein, G. (1996) 'Two peoples in one land: A validation study of Altemeyer's right-wing authoritarianism scale in the Palestinian and Jewish societies in Israel', *Journal of Cross-Cultural Psychology*, 27, 216–30.

Ruiz Quintanilla, S. A. and England, G. W. (1996) 'How working is defined: Structure and stability', *Journal of Organizational Behaviour*, 17, 515–40.

Rummel, R. J. (1972) *The Dimensions of Nations*, Beverly Hills, CA: Sage.

Rummelhart, D. E. (1984) 'Schemata and the cognitive system', in R. S. Wyer and T. K. Scrull (eds.), *Handbook of Social Cognition*, Volume 1, Hillsdale, NJ: Erlbaum.

Rusbult, C. E., Insko, C. A. and Lin, Y.-H. W. (1993) 'Seniority-based reward allocation in the US and Taiwan', *Social Psychology Quarterly*, 58, 13–30.

Russell, J. A. (1991) 'Culture and the categorisation of emotions', *Psychological Bulletin*, 110, 426–50.

Russell, J. A. (1994) 'Is there universal recognition of emotion from facial expression? A review of the cross-cultural studies', *Psychological Bulletin*, 115, 102–41.

Sack, R. (1973) 'The impact of education on individual modernity in Tunisia', *International Journal of Comparative Sociology*, 14, 245–72.

Sagie, G. and Schwartz, S. H. (1996) 'National differences in value consensus', in H. Grad, A. Blanco and J. Georgas (eds.), *Key Issues in Cross-cultural Psychology*, Lisse: Swets and Zeitlinger.

Sagiv, L. and Schwartz, S. H. (1995) 'Value priorities and readiness for outgroup social contact', *Journal of Personality and Social Psychology*, 69, 437–48.

Salazar, J. M. (1997) 'Permanence and change in national identities' in J. G. Adair (ed.) *Advances in Psychological Science*, Hove: Psychology Press.

Sampson, D. L. and Smith, H. P. (1957) 'A scale to measure world-minded attitudes', *Journal of Social Psychology*, 45, 99–106.

Sampson, E. E. (1978) 'Personality and the location of identity', *Journal of Personality*, 46, 552–68.

Sampson, E. E. (1981) 'Cognitive psychology as ideology', *American Psychologist*, 36, 730–43.

Sampson, E. E. (1985) 'The decentralization of identity: Toward a revised concept of personal and social order', *American Psychologist*, 40, 1203–11.

Sanchez, E. (1996a) 'The Latin American experience in community social psychology', in S. C. Carr and J. F. Schumaker (eds.), *Psychology and the Developing World*, Westport, CT: Praeger.

Sanchez, E. (1996b) 'Social psychology applied in a Latin American context', paper given at International Congress of Psychology, Montreal.

Sanders, J. L., Hakky, U. M. and Brizzolara, M. M. (1985) 'Personal space amongst Arabs and Americans', *International Journal of Psychology*, 20, 13–17.

Sanders, J. L., McKim, W. and McKim, A. (1988) 'Personal space among Botswana and American students', *Journal of Social Psychology*, 128, 559–61.

Saucier, G. and Goldberg, L. R. (1996) 'The language of personality: Lexical perspectives on the Five-Factor mode', in J. S. Wiggins (ed.), *The Five-Factor Model of Personality: Theoretical perspectives*, New York: Guilford.

Schachter, S. (1951) 'Deviation, rejection and communication', *Journal of Abnormal and Social Psychology*, 46, 190–207.

Schachter, S., and 7 co-authors (1954) 'Cross-cultural experiments on threats and rejection', *Human Relations*, 7, 403–39.

Scherer, K. R. (1979) 'Personality markers in speech', in K. R. Scherer and H. Giles (eds.), *Social Markers in Speech*, Cambridge: Cambridge University Press.

Scherer, K. R., Wallbot, H. G. and Summerfield, A. B. (eds.) (1986) *Experiencing Emotion: A cross-cultural study*, Cambridge: Cambridge University Press.

Schermerhorn, J. R. and Bond, M. H. (1991) 'Upward and downward influence tactics in managerial networks: A comparative study of Hong Kong Chinese and Americans', *Asia Pacific Journal of Management*, 8, 147–58.

Schimmack, U. (1996) 'Cultural influences on the recognition of emotion by facial expressions: Individualistic or Caucasian cultures?', *Journal of Cross-Cultural Psychology*, 27, 37–50.

Schleidt, M., Hold, B. and Attili, G. (1981) 'A cross-cultural study on the attitude towards personal odors', *Journal of Chemical Ecology*, 7, 19–33.

Schmidt, S. M. and Yeh, R. S. (1992) 'The structure of leader influence: A cross-national comparison', *Journal of Cross-Cultural Psychology*, 23, 251–64.

Schmitz, P. G. (1992) 'Acculturation styles and health', in S. Iwawaki, Y. Kashima and K. Leung (eds.), *Innovations in Cross-cultural Psychology*, Amsterdam: Swets and Zeitlinger.

Schmitz, P. G. (1996) 'Acculturation: The relevance of open-mindedness as a moderator variable', paper presented at the 13th Congress of the International Association of Cross-Cultural Psychology, Montreal.

Schneller, R. (1989) 'Intercultural and intrapersonal processes and factors of misunderstanding: Implications for multicultural training', *International Journal of Intercultural Relations*, 13, 465–84.

Schurz, G. (1985) 'Experimentelle Uberprufung des Zusammenhangs zwischen Personlichkeitsmerkmalen und der Bereitschaft der destruktiven Gehorsam gegenuber Autoritaten', *Zeitschrift für Experimentelle und Angewandte Psychologie*, 32, 160–77.

Schwartz, J. (1980) 'The negotiation for meaning', in D. Larsen-Freeman (ed.), *Discourse Analysis in Second Language Research*, Rowley, MA: Newbury House.

Schwartz, S. H. (1991) 'The universal content and structure of values: Theoretical advances and empirical tests in 20 countries', *Advances in Experimental Social Psychology*, 25, 1–65.

Schwartz, S. H. (1994) 'Beyond individualism/collectivism: new dimensions of values', in U. Kim, H. C. Triandis, C. Kagitçibasi, S. C. Choi and G. Yoon (eds.), *Individualism and Collectivism: Theory application and methods*, Newbury Park, CA: Sage.

Schwartz, S. H. (in press) 'Cultural value differences: Some implications for work', *Applied Psychology: An International Review*.

Schwartz, S. H. and Bardi, A. (1997) 'Influences of adaptation to communist rule on value priorities in Eastern Europe', *Political Psychology*, 18, 385–410.

Schwartz, S. H. and Bilsky, W. (1987) 'Towards a psychological structure of human values', *Journal of Personality and Social Psychology*, 53, 550–62.

Schwartz, S. H. and Bilsky, W. (1990) 'Toward a theory of the universal content and structure of values: extensions and cross-cultural replications', *Journal of Personality and Social Psychology*, 58, 878–91.

Schwartz, S. H. and Ros, M. (1995) 'Values in the West: A theoretical and empirical challenge to the individualism–collectivism dimension', *World Psychology*, 1, 91–122.

Schwartz, S. H. and Sagiv, L. (1985) 'Identifying culture-specifics in the content and structure of values', *Journal of Cross-Cultural Psychology*, 26, 92–116.

Schwartz, S. H., Struch, N. and Bilsky, W. (1990) 'Values and intergroup social motives: A study of Israeli and German students', *Social Psychology Quarterly*, 53, 185–98.

Schwartzwald, J. and Yinon, Y. (1977) 'Symmetrical and asymmetrical interethnic perception in Israel', *International Journal of Intercultural Relations*, 1, 40–7.

Schwarzer, R. (1993) 'Measurement of perceived self-efficacy: psychometric scales for cross-cultural research', Berlin: Freie Universität.

Schwarzer, R., Bässler, J., Kwiatek, P., Schröder, K. and Zhang, J. X. (1997) 'The assessment of optimistic self-beliefs: Comparison of the German, Spanish and Chinese versions of the general self-efficacy scale', *Applied Psychology: An International Review*, 46, 69–88.

Scollon, R. and Scollon, S. (1981) *Narrative, Literacy and Face in Interethnic Communication*, Norwood, NJ: Ablex.

Scollon, R. and Scollon, S. B. K. (1983) 'Face in interethnic communication', in J. C. Richards and R. W. Schmidt (eds.), *Language and Communication*, London: Longman.

Scollon, R. and Scollon, S. (1995) *Intercultural Communication: A discourse approach*, Oxford: Blackwell.

Scollon, R. and Wong-Scollon, S. (1991) 'Topic confusion in English–Asian discourse', *World Englishes*, 10, 113–25.

Scott, W. A. (1965) 'Psychological and social correlates of international images', in H. C. Kelman (ed.), *International Behaviour: A social-psychological analysis*, New York: Holt, Rinehart.

Searle-White, J. (1996) 'Personal boundaries among Russians and Americans: A Vygotskyan approach', *Cross-Cultural Research*, 30, 184–208.

Secord, P. F. and Backman, C. W. (1974) *Social Psychology*, 2nd edn, New York: McGraw-Hill.

Seddon, J. W. (1987) 'Assumptions, culture and performance appraisal', *Journal of Management Development*, 6, 47–54.

Segall, M. H., Dasen, P. R., Berry, J. W. and Poortinga, Y. H. (1990) *Human Behavior in Global Perspective: An introduction to cross-cultural psychology*, New York: Pergamon.

Semin, G. R. (1975) 'Two studies on polarisation', *European Journal of Social Psychology*, 5, 121–31.

Semin, G. R. and Glendon, I. (1973) 'Polarisation and the established group', *British Journal of Social and Clinical Psychology*, 12, 113–21.

Semin, G. R. and Rubini, M. (1990) 'Unfolding the concept of person by verbal abuse', *European Journal of Social Psychology*, 20, 463–74.

Sewell, W. H. and Davidsen, O. M. (1961) *Scandinavian Students on an American Campus*, Minneapolis: University of Minnesota Press.

Shackleton, V. and Newell, S. (1991) 'Management selection: A comparative survey of methods used in top British and French companies', *Journal of Occupational Psychology*, 64, 23–36.

Shackleton, V. and Newell, S. (1994) 'European management selection methods: A comparison of five countries', *International Journal of Selection and Assessment*, 2, 91–102.

Shanab, M. E. and Yahya, K. A. (1978) 'A cross-cultural study of obedience', *Bulletin of the Psychonomic Society*, 11, 267–69.

Shapira, A. (1976) 'Developmental differences in competitive behavior of kibbutz and city children in Israel', *Journal of Social Psychology*, 98, 19–26.

Shapira, A. and Lomranz, J. (1972) 'Cooperative and competitive behavior of rural Arab children in Israel', *Journal of Cross-Cultural Psychology*, 3, 353–9.

Shapira, A. and Madsen, M. (1969) 'Cooperative and competitive behavior of kibbutz and urban children in Israel', *Child Development*, 40, 609–17.

Shaver, P. R., Wu, S. and Schwartz, J. C. (1992) 'Cross-cultural similarities and differences in emotion and its representation: A prototype approach', in M. S. Clark (ed.), *Review of Personality and Social Psychology*, 13, 175–212.

Shenkar, O. and Zeira, Y. (1992) 'Role conflict and role ambiguity of chief executive officers in international joint ventures', *Journal of International Business Studies*, 23, 55–75.

Sherif, M. and Sherif, C. W. (1953) *Groups in Harmony and in Tension: An integration of studies on intergroup relations*, New York: Octagon.

Sherif, M., Harvey, O. J., White, B. J. *et al.* (1961) *Intergroup Conflict and Cooperation: The Robber's Cave Experiment*, Norman, OK: University of Oklahoma Press.

Shirakashi, S. (1984–5) 'Social loafing of Japanese students', *Hiroshima Forum for Psychology*, 10, 35–40.

Shmelyov, A. G. and Pokhil'ko, V. I. (1992) 'A taxonomy of Russian personality-trait names', unpublished manuscript, Moscow State University.

Shuter, R. (1976) 'Proxemics and tactility in Latin America', *Journal of Communication*, 26, 46–52.

Shuter, R. (1977) 'A field study of non-verbal communication in Germany, Italy and the United States', *Communication Monographs*, 44, 298–305.

Shwalb, D. W, Shwalb, B., Harnisch, D. L. *et al.* (1992) 'Personal investment in Japan and the USA: A study of worker motivation', *International Journal of Intercultural Relations*, 16, 107–24.

Shweder, R. A. (1973) 'The between and within of cross-cultural research,' *Ethos*, 1, 531–45.

Shweder, R. A. and Bourne, E. J. (1982) 'Does the concept of the person vary cross-culturally?', in A. J. Marsella and G. M. White (eds.), *Cultural Conceptions of Mental Health and Therapy*. Dordrecht, Holland: Riedel.

Shweder, R. A. and Sullivan, M. A. (1993) 'Cultural psychology: Who needs it?', *Annual Review of Psychology*, 44, 497–523.

Sidanius, J. (1993) 'The psychology of group conflict and the dynamics of oppression: A social dominance perspective', in S. Iyengar and W. McGuire (eds.), *Explorations in Political Psychology*, Durham, NC: Duke University Press.

Sidanius, J., Levin, S. and Pratto, F. (1996) 'Consensual social dominance orientation and its correlates within the hierarchical structure of American society', *International Journal of Intercultural Relations*, 20, 385–408.

Sidanius, J., Pratto, F. and Rabinowitz, J. L. (1994) 'Gender, ethnic status and ideological asymmetry: A social dominance interpretation', *Journal of Cross-Cultural Psychology*, 25, 194–216.

Simard, L. M. (1981) 'Cross-cultural interaction: Potential invisible barriers', *Journal of Social Psychology*, 113, 171–92.

Simmel, G. (1950) 'The stranger', in K. Wolff (ed. and trans.), *The Sociology of George Simmel*, New York: Free Press.

Simmons, C. H., von Kolke, A. and Shimizu, H. (1986) 'Attitudes toward romantic love among American, German and Japanese students', *Journal of Social Psychology*, 126, 327–36.

Simmons, C. H., Wehner, E. A. and Kay, K. A. (1989) 'Differences in attitudes toward romantic love of French, and American college students', *Journal of Social Psychology*, 129, 793–9.

Simonton, D. K. (1975) 'Sociocultural context of individual creativity: A transhistorical time-series analysis', *Journal of Personality and Social Psychology*, 32, 1119–33.

Singelis, T. M. (1994) 'The measurement of independent and interdependent self-construals', *Personality and Social Psychology Bulletin*, 20, 580–91.

Singelis, T. M. (1997) *Culture, self, and emotional contagion*, manuscript submitted for publication.

Singelis, T. M. and Brown, W. J. (1995) 'Culture, self, and collectivist communication: Linking culture to individual behavior', *Human Communication Research*, 21, 354–89.

Singelis, T. M. and Sharkey, W. F. (1995) 'Culture, self-construal, and embarrassability', *Journal of Cross-Cultural Psychology*, 26, 622–44.

Singelis, T. M., Triandis, H. C., Bhawuk, D. P. S. and Gelfand, M. (1995) Horizontal and vertical dimensions of individualism and collectivism: A theoretical and measurement refinement', *Cross-Cultural Research*, 29, 240–75.

Singelis, T. M., Bond, M. H., Lai, S. Y. and Sharkey, W. F. (1996) 'Self construal, self-esteem, and embarrassability in Hong Kong, Hawaii, and Mainland United States', manuscript submitted for publication.

Singh, P. and Pandey, J. (1994) 'Distributive decisions as a function of recipients' need performance variations and caste of allocator', in A.-M. Bouvy, F. J. R. van de Vijver, P. Boski and P. Schmitz (eds.), *Journeys into Cross-cultural Psychology*, Lisse: Swets and Zeitlinger.

Singh, R. (1981) 'Prediction of performance from motivation and ability: An appraisal of the cultural difference hypothesis', in J. Pandey (ed.), *Perspectives on Experimental Social Psychology in India*, New Delhi: Concept.

Sinha, D. (1986) *Psychology in a Third World Country: The Indian experience*, New Delhi: Sage.

Sinha, D. (1992) 'Appropriate indigenous psychology: The Indian trend', in S. Iwawaki, Y. Kashima and K. Leung (eds.), *Innovations in Cross-cultural Psychology*, Amsterdam: Swets and Zeitlinger.

Sinha, D. (1996) 'Culture as the target and culture as the source: A review of cross-cultural psychology in Asia', *Psychology and Developing Societies*, 8, 83–105.

Sinha, D. (1997) 'Indigenising psychology', in J. W. Berry, Y. Poortinga and J. Pandey (eds.) *Handbook of Cross-cultural Psychology*, 2nd edn, Volume 1, *Theory and Method*, Boston, MA: Allyn and Bacon.

Sinha, D. and Tripathi, R. C. (1994) 'Individualism in a collectivist culture: A case of coexistence of opposites', in U. Kim, H. C. Triandis, C. Kagitçibasi *et al.* (eds.), *Individualism and Collectivism: Theory, method and applications*, Newbury Park, CA: Sage.

Sinha, J. B. P. (1995) *The Cultural Context of Leadership and Power*, New Delhi: Sage.

Sisman, R. (1994) 'Tourism: environmental relevance', in E. Cater and G. Lowman (eds.), *Ecotourism: A sustainable option?*, Chichester: Wiley.

Sleet, D. A. (1969) 'Physique and social image', *Perceptual and Motor Skills*, 28, 295–9.

Sloan, T. and Montero, M. (eds.) (1990) 'Psychology for the third world: A sampler', *Journal of Social Issues*, 46(3), 1–165.

Smith, C. A. and Ellsworth, P. C. (1985) 'Patterns of cognitive appraisal in emotion', *Journal of Personality and Social Psychology*, 48, 813–38.

Smith, M. B., Fawcett, J. T., Ezekiel, T. and Roth, S. (1963) 'A factorial study of morale among Peace Corps teachers in Ghana', *Journal of Social Issues*, 19(3), 10–32.

Smith, P. B. (1963) 'Differentiation between sociometric rankings: a test of four theories', *Human Relations*, 16, 335–50.

Smith, P. B., Dugan, S. and Trompenaars, F. (1996) 'National culture and managerial values: A dimensional analysis across 43 nations', *Journal of Cross-Cultural Psychology*, 27, 231–64.

Smith, P. B., Dugan, S. and Trompenaars, F. (1997) 'Locus of control and affectivity by gender and occupational status: A 14 nation study', *Sex Roles*, 36, 51–77.

Smith, P. B. and Misumi, J. (1989) 'Japanese management: A sun rising in the west?', in C. L. Cooper and I. T. Robertson (eds.), *International Review of Industrial and Organizational Psychology*, Volume 4, Chichester: Wiley.

Smith, P. B. and Noakes, J. (1996) 'Cultural differences in group processes', in M. A. West (ed.), *Handbook of Work Group Psychology*, Chichester: Wiley.

Smith, P. B. and Peterson, M. F. (1988) *Leadership, Organizations and Culture*, London: Sage.

Smith, P. B. and Tayeb, M. (1988) 'Organisational structure and processes', in M. H. Bond (ed.), *The Cross-cultural Challenge to Social Psychology*, Newbury Park, CA: Sage.

Smith, P. B., Trompenaars, F. and Dugan, S. (1995) 'The Rotter locus of control scale in 43 countries: A test of cultural relativity', *International Journal of Psychology*, 30, 377–400.

Smith, P. B., Wang, Z. M. and Leung, K. (1997) 'Leadership, decision-making and cultural context: event management within Chinese joint ventures', *Leadership Quarterly*, 8, 413–31.

Smith, P. B., Peterson, M. F., Misumi, J. and Tayeb, M. H. (1989) 'On the generality of leadership styles across cultures', *Journal of Occupational Psychology*, 62, 97–110.

Smith, P. B., Peterson, M. F. and 14 co-authors (1994) 'Organizational event management in 14 countries: A comparison with Hofstede's dimensions', in A. M. Bouvy, F. Van de Vijver, P. Boski and P. Schmitz (eds.), *Journeys into Cross-cultural Psychology*, Lisse: Swets and Zeitlinger.

Smith, P. B., Peterson, M. F., Leung, K. and Dugan, S. (in press) 'Individualism–collectivism and the handling of disagreement: A 23 country study', *International Journal of Intercultural Relations*.

Smith, P. B. and Schwartz, S. H. (1997) 'Values', in J. W. Berry, M. H. Segall and C. Kagitçibasi (eds.), *Handbook of Cross-cultural Psychology*, 2nd edn, Volume 3, Boston: Allyn and Bacon.

Smith, R. J., Griffith, J. E., Griffith, H. K. and Steger, M. J. (1980) 'When is a stereotype a stereotype?', *Psychological Reports*, 46, 643–51.

Smith, V. L. (ed.) (1989) *Hosts and Guests: The anthropology of tourism*, 2nd edn, Philadelphia, PA: University of Pennsylvania Press.

Smolicz, J. J. (1979) *Culture and Education in a Plural Society*, Canberra: Curriculum Development Centre.

Snyder, C. R. and Fromkin, H. L. (1980) *Uniqueness: The human pursuit of difference*, New York: Plenum.

Snyder, M. (1979) 'Self-monitoring processes', *Advances in Experimental Social Psychology*, 12, 85–128.

Solomon, S., Greenberg, J. and Pyszczynski, T. (1991) 'A terror management theory of social behavior: the psychological functions of self-esteem and cultural worldviews', *Advances in Experimental Social Psychology*, 24, 93–159.

Sommerlad, E. and Bellingham, W. P. (1972) 'Cooperation–competition: A comparison of Australian, European and Aboriginal school children', *Journal of Cross-Cultural Psychology*, 3, 149–57.

Spencer-Oatey, H. (1997) 'Unequal relationships in high and low power distance societies: A comparative study of tutor–student relations in Britain and China', *Journal of Cross-Cultural Psychology*, 28, 284–302.

Sperber, D. (1985) 'Anthropology and psychology: Toward an epidemiology of representations', *Man*, 20, 73–89.

Sprecher, S. and Chandak, R. (1992) 'Attitudes about arranged marriages and dating among men and women from India', *Free Inquiry in Creative Sociology*, 20, 1–11.

Sprecher, S., Sullivan, Q. and Hatfield, E. (1994) 'Mate selection preferences: Gender differences examined in a national sample', *Journal of Personality and Social Psychology*, 66, 1074–80.

Sprecher, S., Aron, A., Hatfield, E., Cortese, A. *et al.* (1994) 'Love: American style, Russian style and Japanese style', *Personal Relationships*, 1, 349–69.

Staub, E. (1988) 'The evolution of caring and nonaggressive persons and societies', *Journal of Social Issues*, 44, 81–100.

Staub, E. (1990) 'Moral exclusion, personal goal theory, and extreme destructiveness', *Journal of Social Issues*, 46, 47–64.

Staub, E. (1996) 'Cultural-societal roots of violence: The examples of genocidal violence and of contemporary youth violence in the United States', *American Psychologist*, 51, 117–32.

Stephan, W. G. (1985) 'Intergroup relations', in G. Lindzey and E. Aronson (eds.), *Handbook of Social Psychology*, 3rd edn, Volume 2, New York: Random House.

Stephan, W. G. and Stephan, C. W. (1985) 'Intergroup anxiety', *Journal of Social Issues*, 41, 157–76.

Stephan, W. G., Stephan, C. W. and De Vargas, M. C. D. (1996) 'Emotional expression in Costa Rica and the United States', *Journal of Cross-Cultural Psychology*, 27, 147–60.

Stephan, W. G., Ageyev, V., Stephan, C. W. *et al.* (1993) 'Measuring stereotypes: A comparison of methods using Russian and American samples', *Social Psychology Quarterly*, 56, 54–64.

Stephan, W. G., Ageyev, V., Coates-Shrider, L., Stephan, C. W. and Abalkina, M. (1994) 'On the relationship between stereotypes and prejudice: An international study', *Personality and Social Psychology Bulletin*, 20, 277–84.

Stevenson, H. W. and Lee, S. Y. (1996) 'The academic achievement of Chinese people', in M. H. Bond (ed.), *The Handbook of Chinese Psychology*, Hong Kong: Oxford.

Stevenson, H. W., Stigler, J. W., Lee, S. Y. *et al.* (1985) 'Cognitive performance and academic achievement of Japanese, Chinese, and American children', *Child Development*, 56, 713–34.

Stigler, J. W., Shweder, R. A. and Herdt, G. (eds.) (1990) *Cultural Psychology: Essays on comparative human development*, Cambridge: Cambridge University Press.

Stimpson, D., Jensen, L. and Neff, W. (1992) 'Cross-cultural gender differences in preference for a caring morality', *Journal of Social Psychology*, 132, 317–22.

Stipek, D., Weiner, B. and Li, K. (1989) 'Testing some attribution–emotion relations in the People's Republic of China', *Journal of Personality and Social Psychology*, 56, 109–16.

Stokols, D., Clitheroe, C. and Zmuidzinas, M. (1996) 'Qualities of work environments that promote perceived support for creativity', paper presented at the 26th International Congress of Psychology, Montreal.

Stone Feinstein, B. E. and Ward, C. (1990) 'Loneliness and psychological adjustment of sojourners. New perspectives on cultural shock', in D. M. Keats, D. Munro and L. Mann (eds.), *Heterogeneity in Cross-cultural Psychology*, Lisse: Swets and Zeitlinger.

Stoner, J. A. F. (1961) 'A comparison of individual and group decisions involving risk', unpublished master's thesis, Massachusetts Institute of Technology.

Stones, C. R. and Philbrick, J. L. (1991) 'Attitudes toward love of a small fundamentalist community in South Africa', *Journal of Social Psychology*, 131, 219–23.

Storti, C. (1990) *The Art of Crossing Cultures*, Yarmouth, ME: Intercultural Press.

Strickland, L. H. (ed.) (1979) *Soviet and Western Perspectives in Social Psychology*, Oxford: Pergamon.

Strickland, L. H. (ed.) (1984) *Directions in Soviet Social Psychology*, New York: Springer.

Stroebe, W., Lenkert, A. and Jonas, K. (1988) 'Familiarity may breed contempt: The impact of student exchange on national stereotypes and attitudes', in W. Stroebe, A. Kruglanski, D. Bar-Tal and M. Hewstone (eds.), *The Social Psychology of Intergroup Conflict: Theory, research and applications*, New York: Springer.

Strube, M. J. (1981) 'Meta-analysis and cross-cultural comparison: sex differences in child competitiveness', *Journal of Cross-Cultural Psychology*, 12, 3–20.

Struch, N. and Schwartz, S. H. (1989) 'Intergroup aggression: Its predictors and distinctness from in-group bias', *Journal of Personality and Social Psychology*, 56, 364–73.

Sueda, K. and Wiseman, R. L. (1992) 'Embarrassment remediation in Japan and the United States', *International Journal of Intercultural Relations*, 16, 159–74.

Suedfeld, P. (1996) 'What can abnormal environments tell us about normal people?', *International Journal of Psychology*, 31, 438.

Suinn, R. M., Ahuna, C. and Khoo, G. (1992) 'The Suinn–Lew Asian self-identity acculturation scale: Concurrent and factorial validation', *Educational and Psychological Measurement*, 52, 1041–6.

Sumner, W. G. (1906/1940) *Folkways*, Boston: Ginn.

Sundberg, N. D., Poole, M. E. and Tyler, L. E. (1983) 'Adolescents' expectations of future events – A cross-cultural study of Australians, Americans and Indians', *International Journal of Psychology*, 18, 415–27.

Sussman, N. and Rosenfeld, H. (1982) 'Influence of culture, language and sex on conversational distance', *Journal of Personality and Social Psychology*, 42, 66–74.

Suutari, V. (1996) 'Comparative studies on leadership beliefs and behavior of European managers', *Acta Wasaensia*, 50, University of Vaasa, Finland.

Szapocznik, J., Kurtines, W. M. and Fernandez, T. (1980) 'Bicultural involvement and adjustment in Hispanic-American youths', *International Journal of Intercultural Relations*, 4, 353–65.

Tafarodi, R. W. and Swann, W. B., Jr. (1996) 'Individualism–collectivism and global self-esteem: Evidence for a cultural trade-off', *Journal of Cross-Cultural Psychology*, 27, 651–72.

Taft, R. (1973) 'Migration: Problems of adjustment and assimilation in immigrants', in P. Watson (ed.), *Psychology and Race*, Harmondsworth: Penguin.

Taft, R. (1976) 'Cross-cultural psychology as a social science: Comments on Faucheux's paper', *European Journal of Social Psychology*, 6, 323–30.

Tajfel, H. (1972) 'Experiments in a vacuum', in J. Israel and H. Tajfel (eds.), *The Context of Social Psychology: A critical assessment*, London: Academic Press.

Tajfel, H. (1981) *Human Groups and Social Categories*, Cambridge: Cambridge University Press.

Tajfel, H., Billig, M., Bundy, R. P. and Flament, C. (1971) 'Social categorisation and intergroup behaviour', *European Journal of Social Psychology*, 1, 149–78.

Takata, T. (1987) 'Self-deprecative tendencies in self-evaluation through social comparison', *Japanese Journal of Experimental Social Psychology*, 27, 27–36.

Tamura, T. and Furnham, A. (1993) 'Comparison of adaptation to the home culture of Japanese children and adolescents returned from overseas sojourn', *The International Journal of Social Psychiatry*, 39, 10–21.

Tannen, D. (1985) 'Cross-cultural communication', in T. A. van Dijk (ed.), *Handbook of Discourse Analysis*, Volume 4, 203–15, London: Academic Press.

Tayeb, M. H. (1988) *Organisations and National Culture: A comparative analysis*, London: Sage.

Taylor, D. M. (1981) 'Stereotypes and intergroup relations', in R. C. Gardner and R. Kalin (eds.), *A Canadian Social Psychology of Ethnic Relations*, Toronto: Methuen.

Taylor, D. M. and Jaggi, V. (1974) 'Ethnocentrism and causal attribution in a South Indian context', *Journal of Cross-Cultural Psychology*, 5, 162–71.

Taylor, E. W. (1994) 'A learning model for becoming interculturally competent', *International Journal of Intercultural Relations*, 18, 389–408.

Taylor, S. E. and Brown, J. D. (1988) 'Illusion and well-being: A social psychological perspective on mental health', *Psychological Bulletin*, 103, 193–210.

Taylor, S. E., Fiske, S. T., Etcoff, N. l. and Ruderman, A. J. (1978) 'Categorical and contextual bases of person memory and stereotyping', *Journal of Personality and Social Psychology*, 36, 778–93.

Thakerar, J. N., Giles, H. and Cheshire, J. (1982) 'Psychological and linguistic parameters of speech accommodation theory', in C. Fraser and K. R. Scherer (eds.), *Advances in the Social Psychology of Language*, Cambridge: Cambridge University Press.

Thibaut, J. and Walker, L. (1975) *Procedural Justice: A psychological analysis*, Hillsdale, NJ: Erlbaum.

Thomas, D. (1975) 'Cooperation and competition among Polynesian and European children', *Child Development*, 46, 948–53.

Thomas, D. C. and Ravlin, E. C. (1995) 'Responses of employees to cultural adaptation by a foreign manager', *Journal of Applied Psychology*, 80, 133–46.

Thomas, D. C., Ravlin, E. C. and Wallace, A. W. (1994) 'Effect of cultural diversity in work groups', unpublished manuscript, University of Auckland.

Thomas, J. (1983) 'Cross-cultural pragmatic failure', *Applied Linguistics*, 4, 91–112.

Ting-Toomey, S. (1988) 'A face-negotiation theory', in Y. Kim and W. B. Gudykunst (eds.), *Theory in Intercultural Communication*, Newbury Park, CA: Sage.

Ting-Toomey, S. (1991) 'Intimacy expressions in three cultures: France, Japan and the United States', *International Journal of Intercultural Relations*, 15, 29–46.

Ting-Toomey, S. (1994a) 'Managing conflict in intimate intercultural relationships', in D. Cahn (ed.), *Intimate Conflict in Personal Relationships*, Hillsdale, NJ: Erlbaum.

Ting-Toomey, S. (1994b) 'Managing intercultural conflicts effectively', in L. Samovar and R. Porter (eds.), *Intercultural Communication: A reader*, 7th edn, Belmont, CA: Sage.

Ting-Toomey, S., Gao, G., Trubisky, P., *et al.* (1991) 'Culture, face maintenance, and styles of handling interpersonal conflict: A study in five cultures', *International Journal of Conflict Management*, 2, 275–96.

Toki, K. (1935) 'The leader-follower structure in school classes', *Japanese Journal of Psychology*, 10, 27–56.

Tollgerdt-Andersson, I. (1996) 'Attitudes, values and demands on leadership: A cultural comparison among some European countries', in P. Joynt and M. Warner (eds.), *Managing across Cultures: Issues and perspectives*, London: Routledge.

Torbiörn, I. (1982) *Living Abroad: Personal adjustment and personnel policy in the overseas setting*, Chichester: Wiley.

Torres, A. R. R. (1996) 'Exploring group diversity: Relationships between in-group identification and in-group bias', unpublished doctoral dissertation, University of Kent, UK.

Trafimow, D. and Finlay, K. A. (1996) 'The importance of subjective norms for a minority of people: Between-subjects and within-subjects analyses', *Personality and Social Psychology Bulletin*, 22, 820–8.

Trafimow, D., Triandis, H. C. and Goto, S. G. (1991) 'Some tests of the distinction between the private self and the collective self', *Journal of Personality and Social Psychology*, 60, 649–55.

Trapnell, P. D. (1994) 'Openness versus intellect: A lexical left turn', *European Journal of Personality*, 8, 273–90.

Trevor, M. (1983) *Japan's Reluctant Multinationals: Japanese management at home and abroad*, London: Pinter.

Triandis, H. C. (1976) 'On the value of cross-cultural research in social psychology: Reactions to Faucheux's paper', *European Journal of Social Psychology*, 6, 331–41.

Triandis, H. C. (1978) 'Some universals of social behavior', *Personality and Social Psychology Bulletin*, 4, 1–16.

Triandis, H. C. (1988) 'Cross-cultural contributions to theory in social psychology', in M. H. Bond (ed.), *The Cross-cultural Challenge to Social Psychology*, Newbury Park, CA: Sage.

Triandis, H. C. (1990) 'Cross-cultural studies of individualism and collectivism', in J. J. Berman (ed.), *Nebraska Symposium on Motivation, 1989*, 37, 41–133.

Triandis, H. C. (1992) 'Comments on "Social identity processses: Some limitations and limiting conditions"', *Revista de Psicologia Social, Monografico*, 113–15.

Triandis, H. C. (1994) *Culture and Social Behavior*, New York: McGraw-Hill.

Triandis, H. C. (1995a) *Individualism and Collectivism*, Boulder, CO: Westview.

Triandis, H. C. (1995b) 'Culture-specific assimilators', in S. M. Fowler and M. G. Mumford (eds.), *Intercultural Sourcebook: Cross-cultural training methods*, Yarmouth, ME: Intercultural Press.

Triandis, H. C. (1996) 'Converging measurement of horizontal and vertical individualism and collectivism', unpublished manuscript, University of Illinois.

Triandis, H. C., Brislin, R. and Hui, C. H. (1988) 'Cross-cultural training across the individualism–collectivism divide', *International Journal of Intercultural Relations*, 12, 269–89.

Triandis, H. C., Lisanski, J., Setiadi, B., Chang, B. H., Marin, G. and Betancourt, H. (1982) 'Stereotyping among Hispanics and Anglos: The uniformity, intensity, direction, and quality of auto- and heterostereotypes', *Journal of Cross-Cultural Psychology*, 13, 409–26.

Triandis, H. C., Marin, G., Lisansky, J. and Betancourt, H. (1984) 'Simpatia as a cultural script for Hispanics', *Journal of Personality and Social Psychology*, 47, 1363–75.

Triandis, H. C., Leung, K., Villareal, M. and Clack, F. L. (1985) 'Allocentric vs. idiocentric tendencies: convergent and discriminant validation', *Journal of Research in Personality*, 19, 395–415.

Triandis, H. C., McCusker, C. and Hui, C. H. (1990) 'Multimethod probes of individualism and collectivism', *Journal of Personality and Social Psychology*, 59, 1006–20.

Triandis, H. C., Kurowski, L. L., Tecktiel, A. and Chan, D. K. S. (1993) 'Extracting the emics of diversity', *International Journal of Intercultural Relations*, 17, 217–34.

Triandis, H. C., Chan, D. K. S., Bhawuk, D. P. S. *et al.* (1995) 'Multimethod probes of allocentrism and idiocentrism', *International Journal of Psychology*, 30, 461–80.

Trimble, J. E. (1990) 'Ethnic specification, validation prospects, and the future of drug use research', *International Journal of the Addictions*, 25, 149–70.

Tripathi, R. C. (1981) 'Machiavellianism and social manipulation', in J. Pandey (ed.), *Perspectives on Experimental Social Psychology in India*, New Delhi: Concept.

Triplett, N. D. (1898) 'The dynamogenic factor in pace-making and competition', *American Journal of Psychology*, 9, 507–33.

Trommsdorff, G. (1973) 'Value change in Japan', *International Journal of Intercultural Relations*, 7, 337–60.

Trompenaars, F. (1993) *Riding the Waves of Culture*, London: Brealey.

Trosborg, A. (1987) 'Apology strategies in natives/non-natives', *Journal of Pragmatics*, 11, 146–67.

Trubisky, P., Ting-Toomey, S. and Lin, S.-L. (1991) 'The influence of individualism–collectivism and self-monitoring on conflict styles', *International Journal of Intercultural Relations*, 15, 65–84.

Tsai, H. Y. (1996) 'Concept of 'mien tzu' (face) in East Asian societies: The case of Taiwanese and Japanese', in H. Grad, A. Blanco and J. Georgas (eds.), *Key Issues in Cross-cultural Psychology*, Lisse: Swets and Zeitlinger.

Tsuji, H., Fujishima, Y., Natsuno, Y. *et al.* (1996) 'Standardization of the Five-Factor personality questionnaire', paper presented at the 26th International Congress of Psychology, Montreal.

Tsurumi, K. (1992) 'Aspects of endogenous development in contemporary China and Japan', paper presented at joint symposium, International Associations of Comparative Sociology and of Sociology of Organizations, Kurashiki, Japan.

Tung, R. (1981) 'Selection and training of personnel for overseas assignments', *Columbia Journal of World Business*, 1, 68–78.

Turner, J. C., Wetherell, M. S. and Hogg, M. A. (1989) 'Referent informational influence and group polarisation', *British Journal of Social Psychology*, 28, 135–47.

Turner, J. C., Hogg, M. A., Oakes, P. *et al.* (1987) *Rediscovering the Social Group: A self-categorisation theory*, Oxford: Blackwell.

Tyerman, A. and Spencer, C. (1983) 'A critical test of the Sherifs' Robber's Cave experiments', *Small Group Behaviour*, 14, 515–31.

Tyler, A. (1995) 'The construction of cross-cultural miscommunication: Conflicts in perception, negotiation, and enactment of participant role and status', *Studies in Second Language Acquisition*, 17, 129–48.

Tyler, T. R. and Bies, R. J. (1990) 'Interpersonal aspects of procedural justice', in S. J. Carroll (ed.), *Applied Social Psychology in Business Settings*, Hillsdale, NJ: Erlbaum.

Tzeng, O. C. S. and Jackson, J. W. (1994) 'Effects of contact, conflict, and social identity on interethnic group hostilities', *International Journal of Intercultural Relations*, 18, 259–76.

United Nations (1990) *Demographic Yearbook, 1989*, New York: United Nations.

United Nations Commission on Trade and Development (1995) *World Investment Report, 1995: Transnational Corporations and Competitiveness*, New York: United Nations.

Urry, J. (1990) *The Tourist Gaze*, London: Sage.

Üsdiken, B. and Pasadeos, Y. (1995) 'Organizational analysis in North America and Europe: A comparison of co-citation networks', *Organization Studies*, 16, 503–26.

Valdes, J. M. (ed.) (1986) *Culture Bound*, New York: Cambridge University Press.

Valsiner, J. (1995) 'Editorial: Culture and psychology', *Culture and Psychology*, 1, 5–10.

Valsiner, J. and Lawrence, J. (1997) 'Human development in culture across the life-span', in J. W. Berry, P. R. Dasen and T. S. Saraswathi (eds.), *Handbook of Cross-cultural Psychology*, 2nd edn, Volume 2, *Basic Processes and Human Development*, Boston, MA: Allyn and Bacon.

Van de Veer, R. (1996) 'The concept of culture in Vygotsky's thinking', *Culture and Psychology*, 2, 247–64.

Van de Vijver, F. and Leung K. (1997) *Methods and Data Analysis for Cross-cultural Research*, Thousand Oaks, CA: Sage.

Van de Vliert, E. and van Yperen, N. W. (1996) 'Why cross-national differences in role overload? Don't overlook ambient temperature', *Academy of Management Journal*, 39, 986–1004.

Van de Vliert, E., Schwartz, S. H., Huismans, S. E. *et al.* (1997) 'Temperature, cultural masculinity and domestic political violence: A cross-national study', manuscript submitted for publication.

Vandewiele, M. and Philbrick, J. L. (1983) 'Attitudes of Senegalese students toward love', *Psychological Reports*, 52, 915–8.

van Goozen, S. and Frijda, N. H. (1993) 'Emotion words used in six European countries', *European Journal of Social Psychology*, 23, 89–95.

van Knippenberg, A. F. M. and van Oers, H. (1984) 'Social identity and equity concerns in intergroup perceptions', *British Journal of Social Psychology*, 23, 351–62.

Van Lange, P. A. M. and Liebrand, W. B. G. (1991) 'Social value orientation and intelligence: A test of the goal prescribes rationality principle', *European Journal of Social Psychology*, 21, 273–92.

Van Muijen, J. and Koopman, P. L. (in press) 'The influence of national culture on organisational culture: A comparative study between ten countries', *European Journal of Work and Organisational Psychology*.

VanYperen, N. W. and Buunk, B. P. (1991) 'Equity theory and exchange and communal orientation from a cross-national perspective', *Journal of Social Psychology*, 131, 5–21.

Varonis, E. M. and Gass, S. (1985a) 'Non-native/non-native conversations: A model for negotiation of meaning', *Applied Linguistics*, 6, 71–90.

Varonis, E. M. and Gass, S. M. (1985b) 'Miscommunication in native/nonnative conversation', *Language in Society*, 14, 327–43.

Veenhoven, R. (1993) *Happiness in nations: Subjective appreciation of life in 56 nations 1946–1992*, Rotterdam: RISBO.

Veenhoven, R. (1996a) 'Developments in satisfaction research', *Social Indicators Research*, 37, 1–46.

Veenhoven, R. (1996b) 'Happy life-expectancy: A comprehensive measure of quality-of-life in nations', *Social Indicators Research*, 39, 1–58.

Veiga, J. F. (1991) 'The frequency of self-limiting behavior in groups: A measure and an explanation', *Human Relations*, 44, 877–95.

Verkuyten, M. and Masson, K. (1996) 'Culture and gender differences in the perception of friendship by adolescents', *International Journal of Psychology*, 31, 207–17.

Vidmar, N. (1970) 'Group composition and the risky shift', *Journal of Experimental Social Psychology*, 6, 153–66.

Vrij, A. and Winkel, F. W. (1992) 'Cross-cultural police–citizen interactions: The influence of race, beliefs, and nonverbal communication on impression formation', *Journal of Applied Social Psychology*, 22, 1546–59.

Vroom, V. H. and Yetton, P. W. (1973) *Leadership and Decision-making*, Pittsburgh: University of Pittsburgh Press.

Wakushima, K. (1996) 'The confirmation of interactive gestures: The relationship between interactive gestures and family therapy', *Japanese Journal of Family Psychology*, 10, 91–103 (in Japanese).

Wallbot, H. G. and Scherer, K. R. (1986) 'How universal and specific is emotional experience? Evidence from 27 countries on five continents', *Social Science Information*, 25, 763–95.

Wallendorf, M. and Arnould, E. J. (1988) '"My favourite things": A cross-cultural inquiry into object attachment, possessiveness and social linkage', *Journal of Consumer Research*, 14, 531–47.

Wan, K. C. and Bond, M. H. (1982) 'Chinese attributions for success and failure under public and anonymous conditions of rating', *Acta Psychologica Taiwanica*, 24, 23–31.

Wang, Z. M. and Heller, F. (1993) 'Patterns of power distribution in managerial decision-making in Chinese and British industrial organizations', *International Journal of Human Resource Management*, 4, 113–28.

Wang, A., Silver, N., Wooten, W., Chiddick, M. and Chiddick, B. (1993) 'Development of an ethnic identity scale', paper presented on the 1993 annual meeting of the American Psychological Association, Toronto.

Ward, C. (1996) 'Acculturation', in D. Landis and R. S. Bhagat (eds.), *Handbook of Intercultural Training*, 2nd edn, pp. 124–47, Thousand Oaks, CA: Sage.

Ward, C. and Kennedy, A. (1993) 'Psychological and sociocultural adjustment during cross-cultural transitions: A comparison of secondary students at home and abroad', *International Journal of Psychology*, 28, 129–47.

Ward, C. and Kennedy, A. (1994) 'Acculturation strategies, psychological adjustment, and sociocultural competence during cross-cultural transitions', *International Journal of Intercultural Relations*, 18, 329–43.

Ward, C. and Searle, W. (1991) 'The impact of value discrepancies and cultural identity on psychological and sociocultural adjustment of sojourners', *International Journal of Intercultural Relations*, 15, 209–25.

Watkins, D. and Cheng, C. (1995) 'The revised causal dimension scale: A confirmatory factor analysis with Hong Kong subjects', *British Journal of Educational Psychology*, 65, 249–52.

Watkins, D. and Dong, Q. (1994) 'Assessing the self-esteem of Chinese school children', *Educational Psychology*, 14, 129–37.

Watkins, D. and Gerong, A. (1997) 'Culture and the spontaneous self-concept: A study of Filipino college students and cross-cultural comparisons', *Journal of Social Psychology*, 137, 480–8.

Watkins, D. and Regmi, M. (1990) 'Self-serving bias: A Nepalese investigation', *Journal of Social Psychology*, 130, 555–6.

Watkins, D., Adair, J., Akande, A. *et al.* (1996) 'Individualism–collectivism, gender, and the self-concept: A nine cultural investigation', manuscript submitted for publication.

Watson, O. M. (1970) *Proxemic Behavior: A Cross Cultural Study*, The Hague: Mouton.

Watson, O. M. and Graves, T. D. (1966) 'Quantitative research in proxemic behavior', *American Anthropologist*, 68, 971–85.

Watson, W. E., Kumar, K. and Michaelsen, L. K. (1993) 'Cultural diversity's impact on interaction process and performance: Comparing homogeneous and diverse task groups', *Academy of Management Journal*, 36, 590–602.

Watzlawick, P., Beavin, J. H. and Jackson, D. D. (1967) *The Pragmatics of Human Communication*, New York: Norton.

Weber, J. G. (1994) 'The nature of ethnocentric attribution bias: Ingroup protection or enhancement?', *Journal of Experimental Social Psychology*, 30, 482–504.

Weber, M. (1921/1947) *The Theory of Economic and Social Organisation*, New York: Free Press.

Wehmann, P., Goldstein, M. A. and Williams, J. R. (1977) 'Effects of different leadership styles on individual risk-taking in groups', *Human Relations*, 30, 249–59.

Wei, L. and Yue, L. (1996) '"My stupid wife and ugly daughter": The use of pejorative references as a politeness strategy by Chinese speakers', *Journal of Asian Pacific Communication*, 7, 129–42.

Weinberg, I. (1969) 'The problem of the convergence of industrial societies: A critical look at the state of a theory', *Comparative Studies in Society and History*, 11, 1–15.

Weinreich, P. (1986) 'The operationalization of identity theory in racial and ethnic relations', in J. Rex and D. Mason (eds.), *Theories of Race and Ethnic Relations*, Cambridge: Cambridge University Press.

Weinreich, P. (1989) 'Variations in ethnic identity: Identity structure analysis', in K. Liebkind (ed.), *New Identities in Europe*, London: Gower.

Weinreich, P. (1992) 'Socio-psychological maintenance of ethnicity in Northern Ireland: A commentary', *The Psychologist*, 5, 345–6.

Weinreich, P. (1996) 'Variations in the expression of ethnic identity', paper presented at the meeting of the British Psychological Society Annual Conference, Brighton, UK.

Weinreich, P., Luk, C. L. and Bond, M. H. (1996) 'Ethnic stereotyping and identification in a multicultural context: "Acculturation", self-esteem and identity diffusion in Hong Kong Chinese university students', *Psychology and Developing Societies*, 8, 107–69.

Weinstein, N. D. (1980) 'Unrealistic optimism about future life events', *Journal of Personality and Social Psychology*, 39, 806–20.

Weldon, E., Jehn, K. A., Doucet, L. *et al.* (1996) 'Conflict management in US–Chinese joint ventures', unpublished manuscript, Indiana University.

Weller, L., Amitsour, E. and Pazzi, R. (1976) 'Reactions to absurd humor by Jews of Eastern and Western descent', *Journal of Social Psychology*, 98, 159–63.

Westwood, M. J. and Lawrance, W. S. (1988) 'Reentry for international students', in G. MacDonald (ed.), *International Student Advisors' Handbook*, Ottawa: Canadian Bureau of International Education.

Wetherell, M. (1982) 'Cross-cultural studies of minimal groups: Implications for the social identity theory of intergroup relations', in H. Tajfel (ed.), *Social Identity and Intergroup Relations*, Cambridge: Cambridge University Press.

Wetherell, M. and Potter, J. (1992). *Mapping the Language of Racism: Discourse and the legitimization of exploitation*, Hemel Hempstead: Harvester Wheatsheaf.

Wheeler, L. and Kim, Y. (1997) 'What is beautiful is culturally good: The physical attractiveness stereotype has different content in collectivistic cultures', *Personality and Social Psychology Bulletin*, 23, 795–800.

Wheeler, L., Reis, H. T. and Bond, M. H. (1989) 'Collectivism–Individualism in every-day social life: The Middle Kingdom and the melting pot', *Journal of Personality and Social Psychology*, 57, 79–86.

White, M. and Trevor, M. (1983) *Under Japanese Management: The experience of British workers*, London: Heinemann.

Whiting, B. B. (ed.) (1963) *Six Cultures: Studies in child-rearing*, New York: Wiley.

Whiting, B. B. (1976) 'The problem of the packaged variable', in K. F. Reigel and J. A. Meacham (eds.), *The Developing Individual in a Changing World*, The Hague: Mouton.

Whiting, B. B. and Edwards, C. P. (1973) 'A cross-cultural analysis of sex differences in the behavior of children aged three through 11', *Journal of Social Psychology*, 91, 171–88.

Whorf, B. L. (1956) *Language, Thought and Reality*, New York: Wiley.

Wible, D. S. and Hui, C. H. (1985) 'Perceived language proficiency and person perception', *Journal of Cross-Cultural Psychology*, 16, 206–22.

Wiemann, J., Chen, V. and Giles, H. (1986) 'Beliefs about talk and silence in a cultural context', paper presented to the Speech Communication Association, Chicago.

Wierzbicka, A. (1993) 'A conceptual basis for cultural psychology', *Ethos*, 21, 205–31.

Wierzbicka, A. (1994) 'Cultural scripts: A semantic approach to cultural analysis and cross-cultural communication', in M. Pütz (ed.), *Language Contact, Language Conflict*, Amsterdam: John Benjamins.

Wiggins, J. S. (1979) 'A psychological taxonomy of trait-descriptive terms: The interpersonal domain', *Journal of Personality and Social Psychology*, 37, 395–412.

Wilkinson, R. G. (1996) *Unhealthy Societies: The afflictions of inequality*, London: Routledge.

Williams, J. and Best, D. (1982) *Measuring Sex Stereotypes: A thirty nation study*, Beverly Hills, CA: Sage.

Williams, J. and Best, D. (1990) *Sex and Psyche: Gender and self viewed cross-culturally*, Newbury Park, CA: Sage.

Williams, J. E., Satterwhite, R. C. and Saiz, J. L. (in press) *Cross-cultural variations in the importance of psychological traits: A 20 country study*, New York: Plenum.

Williams, R. (1961) *The Long Revolution*, London: Chatto and Windus.

Williams, T. P. and Sogon, S. (1984) 'Group composition and conforming behavior in Japanese students', *Japanese Psychological Research*, 26, 231–34.

Wilpert, B. (ed.) (1991) 'Special Issue: Latin America', *Applied Psychology: An International Review*, 40, 111–236.

Wiseman, R. L. (ed.) (1995) *Intercultural Communication Theory*, Thousand Oaks, CA: Sage.

Wish, M. (1979) 'Dimensions of dyadic communication', in S. Weitz (ed.), *Non-verbal Communication*, New York: Oxford.

Wolfgang, A. (1992) *People Watching Across Cultures Made Easy*, Toronto: Ontario Institute for Studies in Education.

Wolfson, N. (1989) 'The social dynamics of native and nonnative variation in complimenting behavior', in M. R. Eisenstein (ed.), *The Dynamic Interlanguage: Empirical studies in second language variation*, New York: Plenum.

Won-Doornink, M. (1985) 'Self-disclosure and reciprocity in conversation: A cross-national study', *Social Psychology Quarterly*, 48, 97–107.

Wood, W., Lundgren, S., Ouellette, J. A. *et al.* (1994) 'Minority influence: A meta-analysis of social influence processes', *Psychological Bulletin*, 115, 323–45.

World Commission on Environment and Development (1987) *Our Common Future*, New York: Oxford.

World Tourism Organization (1986) *Economic Review of World Tourism*, Madrid: World Tourism Organization.

Worm, V. (1996) *Vikings and Mandarins: Sino–Scandinavian business cooperation in cross-cultural settings*, Copenhagen: Copenhagen Business School.

Wright, R. (1994) *The Moral Animal: Evolutionary psychology and everyday life*, New York: Little Brown.

Xu, X. and White, M. K. (1990) 'Love matches and arranged marriages: A Chinese replication', *Journal of Marriage and the Family*, 52, 709–22.

Yamagishi, T. (1988) 'Exit from the group as an individualistic solution to free rider problem in the United States and Japan', *Journal of Experimental Social Psychology*, 24, 530–42.

Yamagishi, T. and Sato, K. (1986) 'Motivational basis of the public goods problem', *Journal of Personality and Social Psychology*, 50, 67–73.

Yamaguchi, S. (1994) 'Collectivism among the Japanese: A view from the self', in U. Kim, H. C. Triandis, Ç. Kagitçibasi, S. C. Choi and G. Yoon (eds.), *Individualism and Collectivism: Theory, Method and Applications*, Thousand Oaks, CA: Sage.

Yamaguchi, S., Kuhlman, D. M. and Sugimori, S. (1995) 'Personality correlates of allocentric tendencies in individualist and collectivist cultures', *Journal of Cross-Cultural Psychology*, 26, 658–72.

Yang, K. S. (1986) 'Chinese personality and its change', in M. H. Bond (ed.), *The Psychology of the Chinese People*, Hong Kong: Oxford University Press.

Yang, K. S. (1988) 'Will societal modernization eventually eliminate cross-cultural psychological differences?', in M. H. Bond (ed.), *The Cross-Cultural Challenge to Social Psychology*, Newbury Park, CA: Sage.

Yang, K. S. (1996) 'Psychological transformation of the Chinese people as a result of societal modernization', in M. H. Bond (ed.), *The Handbook of Chinese Psychology*, Hong Kong: Oxford University Press.

Yang, K. S. and Bond, M. H. (1990) 'Exploring implicit personality theories with indigenous and imported constructs: The Chinese case', *Journal of Personality and Social Psychology*, 58, 1087–95.

Yates, J. F., Lee, J. W. and Shinotsuka, H. (1996) 'Beliefs about overconfidence, including its cross-national variation', *Organizational Behavior and Human Decision Processes*, 65, 138–47.

Yates, J. F., Zhu, Y., Ronis, D. L. *et al.* (1989) 'Probability judgment accuracy: China, Japan and the United States', *Organizational Behavior and Human Decision Processes*, 43, 147–71.

Yeung, L. N. T. (1996) 'The question of Chinese indirection: A comparison of Chinese and English participative decision-making discourse', unpublished manuscript, Lingan College, Hong Kong.

Yik, M. S. M. and Bond, M. H. (1993) 'Exploring the dimensions of Chinese person perception with indigenous and imported constructs: Creating a culturally balanced scale', *International Journal of Psychology*, 28, 75–95.

Yik, M. S. M., Bond, M. H. and Paulhus, D. L. (1997) 'Do Chinese self-enhance or self-efface?', manuscript submitted for publication.

Yoshikawa, M. J. (1988) 'Cross-cultural adaptation and perceptual development', in Y. Y. Kim and W. B. Gudykunst (eds.), *Cross-cultural Adaptation: Current approaches*, Newbury Park, CA: Sage.

Yoshiyama, N. (1988) 'A time series analysis of minority influence on majority in a group', *Japanese Journal of Experimental Social Psychology*, 28, 27–54 (English abstract).

Young, T. R. (1995) 'Chaos theory and social dynamics: Foundations of postmodern social science', in R. Robertson and A. Combs (eds.), *Chaos Theory in Psychology and the Life Sciences*, Manwah, NJ: Erlbaum.

Yousif, Y. and Korte, C. (1995) 'Urbanization, culture, and helpfulness: Cross-cultural studies in England and the Sudan', *Journal of Cross-Cultural Psychology*, 26, 474–89.

Yu, A. B. (1996) 'Ultimate life concerns, self and Chinese achievement motivation', in M. H. Bond (ed.) *The Handbook of Chinese Psychology*, Hong Kong: Oxford University Press.

Yuen, S. (1991) 'The concern for "face": A cross-cultural examination between subjects from Hong Kong and England', unpublished manuscript, University of Oxford.

Yukl, G. (1994) *Leadership in Organizations*, 3rd edn, Englewood Cliffs, NJ: Prentice Hall.

Zak, I. (1976) 'Structure of ethnic identity of Arab–Israeli students', *Psychological Reports*, 38, 239–46.

Zarate, M. A. and Smith, E. R. (1990) 'Person categorization and stereotyping', *Social Cognition*, 8, 161–85.

Zebrowitz, L. A., Montepare, J. and Lee, H. K. (1993) 'Differentiating same versus other race individuals', *Journal of Personality and Social Psychology*, 65, 85–101.

Zebrowitz, L. A. and Collins, M. A. (1996) 'Accurate social perception at zero acquaintance: the affordances of a Gibsonian approach', unpublished manuscript, Brandeis University.

Zebrowitz-McArthur, L. A. (1988) 'Person perception in cross-cultural perspective', in M. H. Bond (ed.), *The Cross-cultural Challenge to Social Psychology*, Newbury Park,CA: Sage.

Zhang, J. and Bond, M. H. (1996) 'Personality and filial piety among college students in two Chinese societies: The added value of indigenous constructs', unpublished manuscript, Chinese University of Hong Kong.

Zhurvalev, A. L. (1990) 'The tasks of social psychology in light of perestroika', *Soviet Psychology*, 28, 28–32.

Zhurvalev, A. L. and Shorokhova, E. V. (1984) 'Social psychological problems of managing the collective', in L. H. Strickland (ed.), *Directions in Soviet Social Psychology*, New York: Springer.

Zimbardo, P. G. (1970) 'The human choice: Individuation, reason and order versus deindividuation, impulse and chaos', in W. J. Arnold and D. Levine (eds.), *Nebraska Symposium on Motivation, 1969*, 17, 237–307.

Author index

Subject index